PENGUIN BOOKS

CULT OF GLORY

Doug J. Swanson is the author most recently of *Blood Aces: The Wild Ride of Benny Binion, the Texas Gangster Who Created Vegas Poker*. He was for many years an investigative reporter and editor at *The Dallas Morning News*, and is a member of the Texas Institute of Letters. He was a finalist for the Pulitzer Prize in feature writing and spent a year as a John S. Knight Journalism Fellow at Stanford University. Swanson currently teaches writing at the University of Pittsburgh.

* * *

Praise for *Cult of Glory*

"Scorches the reputations of such legendary Rangers as Ben McCulloch and William 'Bigfoot' Wallace for massacring Native Americans and Mexican Americans willy-nilly. . . . Swanson has done a crucial public service by exposing the barbarous side of the Rangers."　　　　　—*The New York Times Book Review*

"*Cult of Glory* is a masterpiece of American history. Period. Doug Swanson has taken on the Texas Ranger legend in all of its terrifying magnificence, disassembled it, and created in its place a real, true, and shockingly new history."
　　　　　—S. C. Gwynne, author of *Empire of the Summer Moon*

"Swanson punctures the myth of the Texas Rangers as 'quiet, deliberate, gentle' men, describing them instead as 'the violent instruments of repression.' . . . *Cult of Glory* will thus surely discomfit some of those who pick it up, even as it confirms for others their sense that the Rangers frequently served as anything but impartial arbiters of justice."　　　　　—*The Wall Street Journal*

"Utterly absorbing and sweeping in scope. Doug J. Swanson has stripped away the clichés and mythology of the Texas Rangers and written a meticulous and propulsive narrative that's a delight to read."
　　　　　—Gilbert King, Pulitzer Prize–winning author of *Beneath a Ruthless Sun*

"[*Cult of Glory*] rigorously chronicles two centuries of Ranger misadventures and atrocities, as well as commendable operations undertaken by the Rangers in recent decades . . . [and] strives to be as panoramic as possible, telling a big story on a big canvas. . . . It also strives to supplant the Ranger narratives of yore by synthesizing decades of others' research as well as Swanson's own findings."

—John Phillip Santos, *Texas Monthly*

"For any student of Texas history, [*Cult of Glory*] is a treasure, on several levels. . . . A fascinating historical narrative, packed with colorful episodes and outsize characters . . . In setting the record straight about the Texas Rangers, Swanson clarifies and enriches the remarkable story of Texas for everyone."

—*Houston Chronicle*

"A harrowing deep dive into the Rangers' darkest moments . . . What Swanson found in his thousands of documents is that the history of the Rangers is hardly a pretty picture when it comes to documenting their treatment of people of color."

—*The Dallas Morning News*

"The conquest of the American West was a ruthless, sanguinary affair. At long last, Doug J. Swanson's *Cult of Glory* resurrects the truth about the Texas Rangers and their complicated history, and it's a far stranger, more fascinating tale than any you've ever read about the storied lawmen. A revelatory masterpiece."

—Melissa del Bosque, author of *Bloodlines: The True Story of a Drug Cartel, the FBI, and the Battle for a Horse-Racing Dynasty*

"*Cult of Glory* is a remarkable feat of reporting, conjuring the crimes and courage of the Texas Rangers while dismantling toxic American myths—from the romanticized antihero to American exceptionalism. Swanson refuses to reduce the Texas Rangers to a monolith, instead breathing cinematic life into their diverse makeup of white supremacists, cold-blooded murderers, and heroes. In gripping prose, he reveals the contradictions that forged America and fueled the earliest border wars. It's a wild and timely ride you need to go on—adrenaline-packed and enlightening."

—Jean Guerrero, Emmy Award–winning journalist and author of *Crux: A Cross-Border Memoir* and *Hatemonger: Stephen Miller, Donald Trump, and the White Nationalist Agenda*

"In an era in which some desire a return to a perceived greatness, books like this remind us greatness is often reliant on the selective memory of storytellers."

—*Library Journal* (starred review)

"This boldly revisionist account takes no prisoners." —*Publishers Weekly*

CULT OF Glory

The BOLD *and* BRUTAL HISTORY *of* the TEXAS RANGERS

DOUG J. SWANSON

PENGUIN BOOKS

PENGUIN BOOKS
An imprint of Penguin Random House LLC
penguinrandomhouse.com

First published in the United States of America by Viking,
an imprint of Penguin Random House LLC, 2020
Published in Penguin Books 2021

Map © 2020 by David Cain

ISBN 9781101979877 (paperback)

THE LIBRARY OF CONGRESS HAS CATALOGED THE HARDCOVER EDITION AS FOLLOWS:
Names: Swanson, Doug J., 1953– author.
Title: Cult of glory : the bold and brutal history of
the Texas Rangers / Doug J. Swanson.
Description: [New York, New York] : Viking, [2020] |
Includes bibliographical references and index.
Identifiers: LCCN 2019049804 (print) | LCCN 2019049805 (ebook) |
ISBN 9781101979860 (hardcover) | ISBN 9781101979884 (ebook) |
Subjects: LCSH: Texas Rangers—History. |
Law enforcement—Texas—History. | Texas—History.
Classification: LCC F386 .S94 2020 (print) | LCC F386 (ebook) |
DDC 363.209764—dc23
LC record available at https://lccn.loc.gov/2019049804
LC ebook record available at https://lccn.loc.gov/2019049805

Printed in the United States of America
2nd Printing

Book design and illustration by Daniel Lagin

To Katie, Sam, and Susan, with all my love

The conquest of the earth, which mostly means the taking it away from those who have a different complexion or slightly flatter noses than ourselves, is not a pretty thing when you look into it too much. What redeems it is the idea only. An idea at the back of it; not a sentimental pretense but an idea; and an unselfish belief in the idea—something you can set up, and bow down before, and offer a sacrifice to.

—MARLOW IN *HEART OF DARKNESS*

The country is most barbarously large and final.

—BILLY LEE BRAMMER

Contents

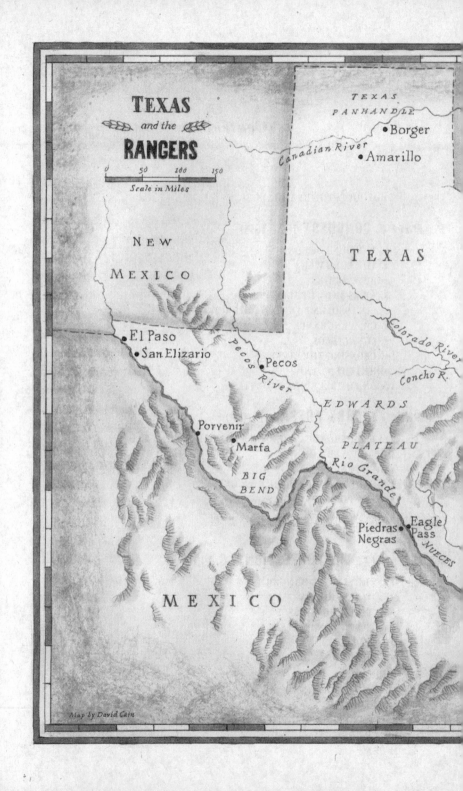

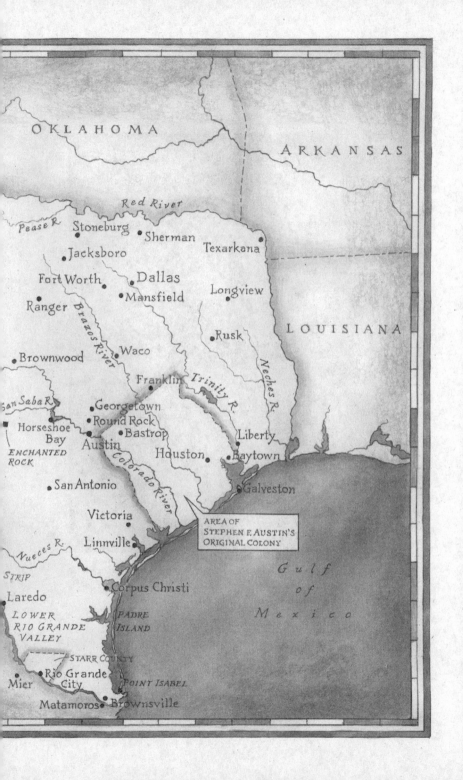

OKLAHOMA

ARKANSAS

Red River

Pease R.

Stoneburg

Sherman

Texarkana

Jacksboro

Fort Worth

Dallas

Longview

Ranger

Brazos River

Mansfield

LOUISIANA

Rusk

Brownwood

Waco

San Saba R.

Franklin

Trinity R.

Neches R.

Georgetown

Round Rock

Bastrop

Liberty

Horseshoe
Bay

Austin

Houston

Baytown

*ENCHANTED
ROCK*

Colorado River

San Antonio

Galveston

Victoria

AREA OF
STEPHEN F. AUSTIN'S
ORIGINAL COLONY

Linnville

Gulf

Nueces R.

of

STRIP

Corpus Christi

Mexico

Laredo

*LOWER
RIO GRANDE
VALLEY*

*PADRE
ISLAND*

STARR COUNTY

Rio Grande
City

POINT ISABEL

Mier

Matamoros

Brownsville

Manuel T. "Lone Wolf" Gonzaullas combined his Ranger exploits with a gift for image crafting. "The most dangerous place in Texas," a colleague once said, "is between Gonzaullas and a camera."

Prologue

THE REAL RANGER

There is not, nor has there ever been, a group quite like the Texas Rangers. For almost two hundred years the Rangers have created, maintained, and promoted an image of bold knights in cowboy hats who brought peace, law, and civilization to a violent, lawless, and uncivilized land. They have inspired hundreds of tales that relate their extraordinary toughness, skill, bravery, and heroism. Some of these are true.

The Rangers trace their origins to 1823, when Texas was still part of Mexico. As an irregular militia, they had no uniform, no flag, and—for decades—no badge. They were volunteers who arrived young, adventurous, and practically immune to danger. The early Rangers fought Indians, Mexicans, and many unfortunate others. A newspaper headline of the era called them "The Fightingest Men on Earth." Later they chased rustlers, smugglers, and roving gangs of marauders. As Texas changed in the mid-twentieth century, so did the Rangers, who were transformed into a force of professional state police pursuing gangsters, kidnappers, and lawbreakers of all stripes. The roles may have been altered, but the myth remained.

Nearly all societies foster creation narratives that recall their idealized selves. Because it was once an independent republic—for less than ten years, but fiercely independent nonetheless—Texas possesses a deep well of such material. The Alamo, with its mass sacrifice and valorous struggle, probably shines the brightest. If so, the Rangers run a close second.

"Nowhere," historian T. R. Fehrenbach wrote, "was the frontier violence in America so bloody, or so protracted, as on the soil of Texas." It is hard, maybe impossible, to believe the vast and wild territory that was Texas could have been tamed without the Rangers. With their eagerness to engage all manner of armed opponents under the harshest conditions, the Rangers played an essential role in Texas's development and ethos.

Yet most Texans, with the exception of those in law enforcement—and some criminals—probably have never even seen a real Ranger. As of this writing there are fewer than 160 active Rangers in a state with 254 counties and a population of twenty-nine million.

They have always been a small, elite force. It's the image that grew big.

The model Ranger has long been depicted as tall, steely-eyed, and strong-jawed. He shoots straight and brooks no challenge to the law or his personal code of honor. He can handle any situation. And he carries the role well, as journalist Richard Harding Davis observed in 1892. "There are still the Texas Rangers," Davis wrote, "and in them the man from the cities of the East will find the picturesqueness of the Wild West show and its happiest expression." Davis visited a Ranger camp in South Texas, marveled at their shooting skills, and gushed, "Some of them were remarkably handsome in a sun-burned, broad-shouldered, easy, manly way."

No law enforcement agency has been celebrated so much for so long in popular culture. Beginning in 1910, when a silent picture called *The Ranger's Bride* flickered briefly, more than three hundred movies and television series have featured a Ranger. Hollywood has, for example, given the world *The Texas Ranger* (1931), *The Texas Rangers* (1936), *The Texas Rangers* (1951), *Texas Rangers* (2001), and *The Texas Rangers Ride Again* (1940), as well as *Red Hot Rangers* (1947), *The Fighting Ranger* (1934 and 1948), *Bandit Ranger* (1942) and *The Ranger and His Horse* (1912). In 1943 alone, no fewer than seventeen feature films incorporated Ranger characters. Among them were *Hail to the Rangers*, *The Return of the Rangers*, and *Border Buckaroos*.

John Wayne played a Ranger on the big screen. So did Audie Murphy, Gene Autry, and Roy Rogers. Clint Eastwood too. In *King of the Texas Rangers*, released in 1941, legendary quarterback Sammy Baugh portrayed a Ranger thwarting enemy agents who attempt to attack Texas oil fields from a zeppelin.

Perhaps the most famous imaginary Ranger of them all—at least until Chuck Norris employed martial arts as *Walker, Texas Ranger* on television—was the Lone Ranger. Tales "from those thrilling days of yesteryear" began in radio serials and moved to television and film. The Lone Ranger owned a crime-fighting career that has spanned almost ninety years.

Dime novels and western pulp fiction presented the Rangers to generations of readers. Magazines like *Texas Rangers*, published from 1936 to 1958, delivered lively tales—"Lone Star Doom," for example, and "Pecos Poison"—monthly by mail. Larry McMurtry's 1985 novel *Lonesome Dove*, which won the Pulitzer Prize and was made into an acclaimed television series, had two ex-Rangers as its protagonists. Even bodice-ripper novels have done their part. *To Love a Texas Ranger*, published in 2016, gave readers the exquisitely named Sam Legend, who brings his exceptional skills to both a gunfight and the boudoir. He also offers rugged good looks.

The presentation of the quintessential Ranger owes much to fictional renderings, but a good portion of it came from the Rangers themselves. "For courage, patriotic devotion, instant obedience, and efficiency, the record of the Texas Rangers has been excelled by no body of constabulary ever mustered," wrote James B. Gillett, who joined the force in 1875. "For bravery, endurance and steadfast adherence to duty at all times the Ranger is in a class by himself." Scholar Américo Paredes assessed it as an extension of Anglo Texans' claims to racial superiority. "The Texan has no equal anywhere," he wrote of this attitude, "but within Texas itself there developed a special breed of men, the Texas Rangers, in whom the Texans' qualities reached their culmination."

Some writers insist this larger-than-life portrait is drawn from real life. Historian Walter Prescott Webb spent years studying the force. "The real Ranger," he wrote in 1935, "has been a very quiet, deliberate, gentle person who could gaze calmly into the eye of a murderer, divine his thoughts, and anticipate his action, a man who could ride straight up to death." Webb painted this real Ranger as a solitary and essential defender of civilization. "When we see him at his daily task of maintaining law, restoring order, and promoting peace—even though his methods be vigorous—we see him in his proper setting, a man standing alone between society and its enemies."

In such contemplations, the title alone conveys superior power. "There is no question but that a definite potency exists in the name 'Texas Ranger,'" a former commander of the force wrote. "Take two men of equal size and arm them with identical weapons. Call one of them a deputy sheriff and the other a Ranger. Send each of these officers out to stop a mob or quell a riot. The crowd will resist the deputy, but will submit to the authority of the Ranger."

Nurtured by popular culture over generations, the American West of the imagination has maintained consistent characters and situations: cowboys, Indians, cattle drives, gunfights. The real West was, of course, far more complicated. But those figures, incidents, and morality plays endure, and the Rangers were in many ways the progenitors and archetypes. Their emergence as folk heroes on horseback—initially a product of their service in the Mexican War—predated by several decades the rise of the American cowboy. Their battles with Indians came well in advance of many historic conflicts with Native Americans in the western United States. And they were shooting it out with outlaws long before Wyatt Earp drew down on the Clanton gang in Tombstone, Arizona. The unfaltering romance of the western frontier—in all its epic violence, grandeur, and oversimplifications—took root and was nurtured in Texas with the Rangers.

Joe Davis was a real Ranger. He joined in 1969 and spent twenty-four years with the force. He had wanted to be a Ranger since he was fourteen—inspired by TV shows such as *Tales of the Texas Rangers*, which melded crime fighting, civic virtue, and cowboy trappings. "The good guys wore the white hats, and the Rangers were the good guys," he said. "And the good guys always won."

After retiring from the agency, Davis worked to raise money for the Texas Ranger Heritage Center in the city of Fredericksburg. But one museum does not satiate interest in the Rangers. There's also the state-approved Texas Ranger Hall of Fame and Museum in Waco. Both tell of the dedicated and effective men who lived up to the good-guy, white-hat ideal. Many of these men risked their lives—and some lost their lives—in the line of duty. Frequently outnumbered, the Rangers depended on canniness, fortitude, and courage to win the day.

That has strong appeal, but it's the moral component that truly resonates with the public, Davis said. "The Rangers have always stood up for doing what's right, and doing the right thing. People are starving for stuff like that."

The Rangers' action-packed and unique history includes no shortage of such rectitude and heroism. But the movies, TV shows, museum exhibits, and adulatory accounts usually skip past a big part of the story. Across the centuries, the Texas Rangers did this too:

They were the violent instruments of repression. They burned peasant villages and slaughtered innocents. They committed war crimes. Their murders of Mexicans and Mexican Americans made them as feared on the border as the Ku Klux Klan in the Deep South. They hunted runaway slaves for bounty. They violated international law with impunity. They sometimes moved through Texas towns like a rampaging gang of thugs. They conspired to quash the civil rights of black citizens. They busted unions and broke strikes. They enforced racial segregation of public schools. They botched important criminal investigations. They served the interests of the moneyed and powerful while oppressing the poor and disenfranchised. They have been the army of Texas's ruling class.

And they have consistently lied about it.

Many police and military institutions in America, even those held in highest regard, pass through periods when the restraints slip and tethers snap. At one time or another, all comprise individuals who bend rules, break laws, or otherwise invite disgrace. Some of these incidents are so notorious that the mere mention of their name calls forth the terrible story: My Lai, for instance. Or Chicago in 1968, Kent State, Wounded Knee. As a rule, the institutions at fault do not trumpet their failures. In some circumstances they may confront their atrocities, apologize, and attempt to make amends. Or they may bury the facts and hope the public forgets.

Here the Rangers have set themselves apart. Not only have they covered up their wrongdoing, they and their willing accomplices have perfected the art of mythic rehabilitation and resurrection. For decades, the Rangers operated a fable factory through which many of their greatest defeats, worst embarrassments, and darkest moments were recast as grand triumphs. They didn't merely whitewash the truth. They destroyed it.

Individual Rangers whose actions were questionable, inexplicable, or scandalous have been draped in heroic vestments. With rare exception, the lawbreakers, oppressors, incompetents, and killers were not scorned, prosecuted, or banished. Rather, many of these Rangers enjoyed honored status and were, in historical accounts and agency lore, imbued with almost superhuman qualities.

The old comic stereotype of the Lone Star braggart had its basis in reality. Texas has long promoted its virtues with vigor and possesses a prideful sense of self that no other state can match. From its days as a republic, it has fostered a narrative of exceptionalism, and the Rangers are an intrinsic part of that. The story of the Rangers is the story of Texas, and of the American West: majestic in its sweep, unmatched in its violence, luminous in its glory, and monumental in its deceptions.

PART I

Conquest

1821–1870

Stephen F. Austin was the father of Anglo Texas. In this painting, he urges colonists to exterminate the Karankawa Indians, which they did.

Chapter 1

THE GUNS OF EDEN

"Rangers for the Common Defense"

I entered this country in 1821, and commenced colonizing when it was a perfect wilderness, and have passed a laborious life; immense obstacles opposed our settlement, growing out of the uninhabited state of the country, hostile Indians, and other causes, but we have surmounted them all.

—LETTER FROM STEPHEN F. AUSTIN, 1828

The land lay before him with beckoning promise. In the summer of 1821, Stephen F. Austin had come to the foreign province of Texas for the first time. He and his party of about a dozen men rode on horseback for more than two months, trekking from Louisiana in warm sunshine. The more Austin saw of Texas—here in its eastern regions, where rainfall could be gentle and generous—the more he embraced it as the perfect spot for the prosperous settlement of American colonists. The meadows shimmered thick and green, the lowland forests teemed with tall hardwoods and pines, and the creeks flowed clear and strong. Wild game, buffalo and deer especially, roamed in abundance. The soil felt rich and fertile, the weather temperate and welcoming. Austin wrote in his journal that he found this earthly paradise to be "country the most beautiful I ever saw."

Then he met the Indians.

On September 17, 1821, Austin and his explorers neared the Gulf of Mexico, close to the mouth of the languid Colorado River. A high-pitched sound arose from a thicket. To Austin it sounded like a "war whoop." About fifteen men, wearing loincloths and clutching longbows and arrows, emerged from the brush. They were tall and muscular, with dark tattoos on their chests and arms, their bodies slathered with grease. Size and markings identified them as Karankawas, which no doubt filled Austin with dread. They were reputed to be the most savage of the coastal tribes. The wildest of stories said they killed those who strayed onto their turf, cooked them, and ate them. Austin was a slender, college-educated, twenty-seven-year-old land speculator with a background in banking and politics, not a hardened Indian fighter. But he told his company to prepare for battle and rode ahead to meet the warriors.

The one who appeared to be the chief spoke to Austin in Spanish and asked where he was from and where he was going. He urged Austin to come to his camp. Fearing an ambush, Austin refused. The chief laid his weapons on the ground, and five women and children walked from the brush. "This satisfied me they believed us to be too strong for them and therefore that they [would] not attack us," Austin wrote, adding, "of their disposition I had no doubt if they thought they [could] have succeeded."

For the next few minutes, the man who would come to be known as the "Father of Texas" studied the newfound land's natives. "[Some] of the young squaws were handsome & one of them quite pretty," Austin wrote. They wore animal skins around their waist, he said, but were otherwise naked. "Their breasts were marked or tatooed in circles of black beginning with a small circle at the nipple and enlarging as the breast swelled." Austin gave the chief some tobacco and a frying pan, and the Karankawas offered advice on travel through the thick scrub. With that, Austin said, the two sides "parted apparently good friends." The Indians ghosted back into the thicket.

Though he had shown goodwill—and ogled the women—Austin knew this friendship could only be temporary. He considered the Karankawas more animal than human. "These Indians . . . may be called universal enemies to man," he wrote, because they would murder their rivals "and frequently feast on the bodies of their victims." He could not imagine American settlers coexisting with them. Nor could he envision their being allowed to live. "There will be no way of subduing them," Austin insisted, "but extermination."

In that simple statement lay the birth of modern Texas. It also contained the murky origins of the Texas Rangers.

For the first Europeans who cut erratic paths across it, Texas came to hold little value. The Spanish traversed the region in the 1500s and 1600s, followed by French explorers who didn't stay long. Spain established scattered missions there in the 1700s but considered it a backwater of high danger and low importance. The Marqués de Rubí visited Texas in 1766 for the king of Spain and found a thorny domain of hostile indigenes. "The country," he wrote, "should be given back to Nature and the Indians."

Mexico gained its independence from Spain in 1821, and Texas came with it. But Mexico did not control Texas. At a time when 120,000 people lived in New York City, Harvard was nearly two hundred years old, and St. Louis thrived as a modern river port for steamboats, Texas remained a soaring emptiness that belonged to the Indians. The great sweep of the province, from the far western deserts to the deep eastern swamps, more than eight hundred miles across, held no more than a few thousand men and women of European heritage. However, the Native American population in the early 1800s probably exceeded twenty thousand, many of whom proved willing to attack newcomers. Because of "savage warfare which has desolated the land," a Mississippi newspaper warned potential pioneers, Texas "presents almost literally a vast and noiseless desert."

To the south, the fresh Mexican government flailed in turmoil, the nation's economy barely functional. The country's unsteady and revolving cast of leaders thought the best way to handle Texas and provide a check on the Indians might be to allow Americans to immigrate in limited numbers and pacify the territory. They also reasoned, paradoxically and incorrectly, that it might stall U.S. expansionism.

A failed lead-mine operator named Moses Austin initially had persuaded Spanish authorities to permit the settling of families in Texas. After Moses Austin's death, Stephen F. Austin—his son—worked with Mexican officials to allow the entry of American colonists, as many as three hundred families initially. Each settler had to pledge to follow the Catholic faith and abide by Mexican law. Male colonists over twenty-one could purchase acreage at a price far less than that of property in the United States. A sum that would buy eighty acres of arable land in the South would purchase more than four thousand acres in Texas.

This modest beginning set in motion events that, within a few decades, would radically alter American territory and help forge the nation's history. From Mexico's standpoint, it proved to be a catastrophic blunder.

The settlers began to trickle in not long after Austin made his first visit to Texas and had his encounter with the Karankawas. Most hailed from Alabama, Arkansas, Missouri, Louisiana, or Tennessee. The first ones came to be called the "Old Three Hundred" families, while Austin held the grand title of their *empresario*. They and their successors homesteaded the river bottomlands of verdant south-central Texas.

Some historians have portrayed them as brave pioneers seeking the freedom and the room to pursue their expansive dreams. They were certainly brave, and they indeed sought freedom for themselves. But many of them dreamt of great tracts of rich land on which to grow cotton and of bringing their slaves to pick it. They envisioned nothing less than an unfettered extension of the Deep South's plantation economy, a Mississippi of the West. Jared Groce came from Alabama with fifty wagons and ninety slaves, who cleared land for a cotton plantation on the Brazos River. "The primary product that will elevate us from poverty is Cotton," Austin wrote, "and we cannot do this without the help of slaves."

Texas already had a significant history with slavery. For years slavers used Galveston Island as a port of entry for their human cargo from Africa, often by way of Cuba. Many were smuggled into Galveston by the pirate Jean Lafitte, whose marauders seized them from Spanish ships. Lafitte operated such a thriving practice in selling slaves that he built a large barracks for them—holding more than six hundred captives—on the west bank of the Sabine River. Jim Bowie, destined to become a Texas martyr at the Alamo, made a handsome living in the trade. From 1818 to 1820, he and his brothers purchased slaves from Lafitte—for one dollar a pound, Bowie once said—and marched them in irons through the forests of East Texas, or floated them up the bayous into Louisiana. There the brothers resold them at a handsome profit. Altogether, the Bowie family figured, they made $65,000. That's about $1.4 million in today's money.

Lafitte abandoned Galveston in 1820, but a real Texas slave empire was about to take hold. By late 1825, the Austin colony recorded a total population of 1,790. Of those, 443 were slaves.

Not all the colonists enjoyed life as moneyed planters. Some were mere yeoman farmers who traveled by schooner from New Orleans to the mouth of the Colorado or the Lavaca River, where they were deposited at the edge of the wilderness with only the personal property they could carry. They proceeded inland by foot or in wagons, and built crude, mud-chinked log cabins that had dirt floors and no windows. These early settlements did not have schools, stores, or mills. Books were scarce, and entertainments homegrown. The pioneers lived off the game they could kill, including the flesh of wild horses when deer or turkey could not be found. With space on transit ships at a premium, many brought no plows with them, so they dug their crop rows with sticks.

Medical treatment could be medieval, as was customary across the frontier. Jesse Burnam, an odd-jobber who came to Texas from Tennessee in search of a warmer climate, recalled a man named Parker with a "terribly diseased" leg. "He begged us to cut it off," Burnam said. After weeks of the man's beseeching, Burnam said, he and three others "undertook the job with a dull saw and shoe knife, the only tools we had." Using a horsehair rope as a tourniquet, they sawed off the limb. Complications set in, and eleven agonal days later the man was dead. But the patient had anticipated such an outcome, and the amputation had therefore been a comfort of sorts. "If I die," he said before they removed his leg, "I don't want to take it with me."

Like many pioneers in the West, the new Texans found their new life to be a blend of spectacular tedium and abject terror. They had dropped themselves into a virgin, bountiful land of boundless opportunity, as seen in Austin's pastoral visions. A "new country," one early settler wrote, "rich in primeval beauty."

It was also given to floods (or drought), pestilence, and terrible heat. The marshy river bottoms near the Gulf Coast were home to relentless swarms of disease-carrying mosquitoes, several varieties of poisonous snakes, and— something new to immigrants from the Appalachians and the Ozarks— alligators. Pioneers told and retold campfire tales of alligators on the prowl at night for humans. It was said the beasts would steal into settlements, clamp their powerful jaws onto sleeping children, and drag them screaming back to the river. In these stories the creatures were reported to have a special preference for the flesh of young girls.

Alarming as such threats might be, the presence of Indians caused the colonists much more concern. A number of tribes considered this part of Texas their homeland: Cherokees, Tawakonis, Wacos, Tonkawas, Delawares, and Caddos among them. According to official state history, the Caddos even gave the place its name: Tejas, their word for "friends." It was the tribe's most significant and ironic legacy, given that its members were forced off their land and onto reservations in Oklahoma.

Some Indians and settlers engaged in peaceful if wary cooperation, but conflict was the most common outcome. To a tribe in need of horses, white families' stables made for easy pickings. For them it was as natural as capturing wild mustangs—and far easier. In much the same way, some Indians did not distinguish between settlers' stockpiled belongings and salvage that washed ashore from the Gulf. To them it was all bounty for the taking. The white families of course regarded this as theft.

It soon became an article of faith among many newly arrived Texians, as they called themselves, that all Indians were thieves. Mere suspicioned intent could be punishable by death. Pioneer Abraham Alley, a French Huguenot from Missouri, recalled sixteen Wacos and Tawakonis approaching a Colorado River settlement in 1826 "professing friendship." Because they were on foot, he said, "it was believed they had come down to steal our horses," though no such theft had been attempted. That night, as the Indians slept nearby, Alley and a party of white men crept to the edge of their camp and opened fire. The Indians leapt to their feet and began to run. "Nearly all the Indians fell, either on the spot or within a few hundred yards," Alley said. "The Indians were so completely surprised that it is believed they did not shoot an arrow at us."

Any notion that the two cultures would share Texas was rarely held—and, at any rate, was doomed. "Our people were troubled by a continual sense of insecurity arising from their proximity to a race who had been the enemy of the white man for three centuries," wrote John S. Ford, later a Ranger captain. Ford spoke the truth, but a more important factor than insecurity loomed: territory. The settlers wanted the dirt these Indians lived on.

The Karankawas felt the full effects of this first. These wandering bands, traveling by foot or in dugout canoes, subsisted on deer, bison, fish, shellfish, and turtles. They had lived on or near the low, sandy barrier islands of the Gulf Coast for at least several thousand years, probably more. The first recorded instance of Karankawas setting eyes on Europeans occurred in 1528. That was when lost Spanish explorers who were trying to float from Florida to Mexico on pine rafts washed ashore in Texas, naked and starving. Álvar Núñez Cabeza de Vaca, one of the survivors, lived with the Indians for a few years—some as a slave—before making a long, tortured walk to Mexico.

A French expeditionary force arrived in the late 1600s and built a fort in the heart of Karankawa country. The Indians attacked it around 1687 and killed everyone except five children, who were taken captive. In the mid-1700s and early 1800s, the Spanish made numerous attempts, via their Texas missions, to convert the tribe to Christianity. The Karankawas proved resistant to catechism and scripture. In 1819 the Indians fought and lost—at least according to legend—an engagement with pirates from Jean Lafitte's headquarters on Galveston Island. The pirates had kidnapped some Karankawa women. All such encounters took their toll, through either deaths in battle or disease, but the tribe managed at least to survive. Then the Americans showed up.

Texas settlers had seen Indians before, but not like these. They stood larger than most—"magnificently formed," one nineteenth-century ethnologist recorded, "and approaching perfection in their bodily proportions." To protect against mosquitoes, they smeared themselves with alligator fat and shark oil, which gave off a strong odor of musk. Many displayed the ornate tattoos that had captured Stephen F. Austin's gaze. They wore loincloths of fur or buckskin if they wore anything at all. Rattlesnake tails decorated their plaited hair. Though the Karankawas had a distinct and complex culture, most colonists saw them as primitive brutes. "Their words, or rather grunts, seemed to issue from some region low down," reported one early writer, "and were uttered in spasmodic jerks, apparently without any assistance from the tongue or lips."

And, as Austin had observed, they were said to be man-eaters. This was no doubt an exaggeration. Like many tribes, they may have engaged in ceremonial cannibalism of their defeated enemies, but the stories related by settlers—however apocryphal—evoked atavistic horror. One told of a Karankawa raid on a colony in which warriors abducted a small girl. "After proceeding some distance," went the account of pioneer John R. Fenn, "they camped, killed the child, and proceeded to eat her, first splitting open the body, then quartering it, and placing the parts on sharp sticks and cooking them." Settlers attacked the Indian camp during the "diabolical and hellish orgie," Fenn said, and killed all the Karankawa except "a squaw and her two small children," who escaped. Several white men found them sitting beneath a tree. "They consulted a little while," Fenn's report continued, "and then decided it was best to exterminate such a race." The men killed all three and left the bodies where they lay.

If true, these were but piecemeal efforts at extermination. Some Texians believed that to deal decisively with such enemies they would need a special force.

The first American settlers in Texas had no courts and no police. Resolution of civil disputes often fell to a community's *alcalde*, who functioned as a sort of mayor and justice of the peace, though some cases were decided by mob rule. One Texian immigrant circulated poetry critical of Stephen F. Austin, referring to the *empresario* as a villain. Dwellers of Austin's colony tarred and feathered the man, after which they banished him from the region. More serious criminal matters might be handled with backcountry justice. Robert Kuykendall, an Arkansas fur trader who had come to Texas in 1821, helped capture two Mexicans suspected of murdering two men and stealing their horses. Kuykendall and his party executed the Mexicans, decapitated them, and stuck their heads on poles. This warning to other thieves worked, said his nephew: "The 'border ruffians' ceased their depredations within the bounds of Austin's colony."

When it came to Indians, the Mexican government provided little in the way of troops, but instead made each male colonist subject to militia duty. Securing the settlements and "chastising" Indians thus fell to a mixed bag of civilians who were part citizen soldier, part home guard, part corps of minutemen. "It was a comical sight," a German visitor said as he watched colonists assemble. "They were more like a gang of robbers about to undertake a raid than disciplined soldiers who risked time, money and life to protect their fellow citizens from future invasions of redskins." But they grabbed their rifles when needed, responded to threats, and retaliated for attacks.

The goal was protection, but they also brought about through force the colonists' expansion into what had been Indian territory. These engagements did not unfold like the battles of classic Hollywood cinema and pulp westerns' purple prose, with men on horseback thundering across sweeping vistas. In East Texas, the first encounters with Indians took place on brushy riverbanks, over foggy lowland marshes, and along hidden creeks that ran in slow dark currents. These looked more like the savage wars of rival clans in old-country bogs.

From the first days of Austin's colony, the Texians and the Karankawas had failed to mix well. The scattered tribe of perhaps two thousand constituted no small threat to the settlers, and the settlers to them. Deadly encounters were generally isolated and small, but continual. In 1822 two white men were ambushed and killed while bringing corn up the Colorado River by raft. A company of colonists led by Robert Kuykendall, intent on retaliation, gathered near a Karankawa settlement on Skull Creek, a lowland tributary of the Colorado.

Young volunteer John H. Moore crept close to the camp and heard "the beating of bamboo root" used to make a sort of bread. Then came the sound of a child crying.

Moore returned to the company of twenty-two men and told them what he had found. "We made our way to the bottom, got between the creek and the Indians, and surprised them, driving them out into the prairie," he said. The Texians fired their long rifles, mowing down the men, women, and children who ran into the clearing. "Twenty-three were left dead, without the loss of any of the whites," Moore said. The Texians, who had no provisions, scalped the Indians and ate their food. "We all felt it was an act of justice and self-preservation," Moore said. It may also have been monumental. "This was," Moore said, "the first [major] fight with the Indians in Austin's colony."

Despite such a resounding victory, Kuykendall and John Jackson Tumlinson, *alcalde* of the Colorado District, thought settlers needed more help. In early 1823 they wrote the Mexican provincial governor seeking permission to raise a volunteer company for the "protection that we so much need." With the governor's approval, they formed a ten-man squad commanded by a U.S. Army veteran named Moses Morrisson—"a young man of worth and bravery," Tumlinson wrote. Later in 1823, Stephen F. Austin proposed the hiring of men to "act as rangers for the common defense," augmenting the militia. Many therefore consider Morrisson's men the first Texas Rangers.

They were by no means aristocrats, but neither were they blackhearted gunslingers or the sort of grifting flotsam that tended to drift into the West and disappear. Young to middle-aged and possessed of roving ambition, they were second- and third-generation Americans attracted to Texas by the lure of property and the chance for a fresh start. Morrisson, thirty, had lived in Missouri. John Smith was a twenty-eight-year-old farmer with one horse. Pumpry Burnett, in his late twenties, had journeyed to Texas from Tennessee. Samuel Sims, in his early thirties, was a land surveyor who had been born in Tennessee. William Kingston, one of twelve children, came from Illinois. Caleb Bostwick had been a carpenter in New York. John McCrosky, thirty, was a farmer, as was Jessie Robinson, twenty-three. Others in the company were John Frazer, listed in district records as a forty-one-year-old farmer and schoolmaster, and Aron Linville, a forty-one-year-old farmer. The men, who wore no uniforms, furnished their own horses and muzzle-loaded long rifles. They apparently received no special training.

However historic, their venture as proto-Rangers was less than auspicious.

Though assigned to build blockhouses—small forts made of logs—at the mouth of the Colorado River, they spent much of their time hunting for something to eat. Two months into their mission the blockhouses remained unbuilt. "We are obliged continually to keep a party out Hunting as we cannot procure provisions from the settlement," Morrisson reported. The men had nearly exhausted their meager stocks of ammunition, so they could neither defend themselves nor kill more game for food. They were ordered to return to their settlements, and there is no record that they were ever paid for their service.

Worse, the two pioneers instrumental in the formation of these early Rangers soon met with misfortune. Tumlinson, the *alcalde*, was en route to San Antonio to secure aid and ammunition when Waco Indians ambushed and killed him. Kuykendall, whom some consider the captain of these first Rangers, suffered blindness and paralysis after he was struck in the head—perhaps by a tomahawk—during a subsequent fight with Karankawas. A frontier doctor treated him by drilling a hole in his skull, a technique known as a trepan that dates to prehistoric times. It worked about as well for him as it worked for the cave people. Kuykendall died at age forty.

Over the next few years, companies similar to Morrisson's formed and disbanded erratically. Skirmishes with the Karankawas occurred so frequently that settlers took to shooting the Indians on sight. The beleaguered tribe, with the help of a Catholic priest, reached a peace agreement with the colonists. The Indians agreed to abandon their original territory along the lower Brazos, Lavaca, and Colorado Rivers—land the whites wanted—and stay west of the Guadalupe River. But the arrangement did not work, and the Indians began drifting back onto their old turf. Responding to settlers' complaints, Austin wrote to a Mexican official in 1825, claiming that the Karankawas had broken the peace agreement. "I have been compelled in view of the security of our people," Austin wrote, "to give positive orders to the Lieutenant of the Militia . . . to pursue and kill all those Indians wherever they are found."

Austin's instructions were fulfilled in a climactic 1830 battle near the mouth of the Colorado. Karankawas had raided the farm of Charles Cavinagh, an original settler in Austin's colony. They killed his wife and three daughters, as well as a young girl who was visiting. A force of about sixty Texians, men who could be seen as another slice of Ranger ancestry, trailed the Indians to their camp on the river's low, wooded banks.

The commander of the original band of Rangers, Moses Morrisson, crawled to a small plateau overlooking the unaware Karankawas—a strategic vantage until the ground gave way and he tumbled into the Indian camp. J. W. Wilbarger, in his 1889 collection *Indian Depredations in Texas*, gave this account of the ensuing battle: Morrison "clung to his gun . . . and crawled into a hole in the bank, where he fought and killed five of the Indians." Hearing the gunfire, the rest of the Texians charged the camp. "The Indians had their squaws and papooses with them, and some of them were killed by the promiscuous firing that ensued," Wilbarger wrote. Those Karankawas who were not hit plunged in panic into the river and swam to the other side. The Texians reloaded and fired again at the fleeing Indians. "Even after they had succeeded in reaching the opposite shore many were shot and fell back into the stream," Wilbarger said. "An eyewitness of the scene says that the river was literally red with blood." The Texians had killed about fifty Karankawa men, women, and children.

Wilbarger's rendition may have been inflated—a common complaint against him—but there is no doubt the tribe now had entered its death spiral. About thirty-five or forty who weren't slain were forced to work as field slaves for the settlers. Some colonists, it was said, took women home as sex prisoners—though the Texas men referred to them as "housekeepers." Other members of the tribe succumbed to alcohol or disease. And, according to Texian lore, a few surviving warriors murdered their women and children, then retreated to a hidden island. There they wailed in grief and starved themselves to death.

Before long, the Karankawas were all but extinct, fulfilling Stephen F. Austin's prophecy: the extermination within decades of a people who had lived there for millennia.

The Anglo empire of Texas now began to assume its natal shape. But from the settlers' perspective, many other tribes needed elimination before the nascent empire could expand and thrive. The Texas Rangers would be built for that.

Comanche Feats of Horsemanship, 1834–1835, by George Catlin. The artist, who observed the Comanches in the field, called them "the most extraordinary horsemen I have seen."

Chapter 2

THE LONG WAR

"The Very Jaws of Death"

Texas Indians were of a different mold, and it was mainly because of
Mexico's inability to hold the territory against them that it was thrown
open to the Anglo-American. It was he who beat back the savage and
converted the wilderness into civilized homes. Why then should he not
control its destiny?

—TEXAS RANGER NOAH SMITHWICK

Sometime in 1829, probably in the bounteous warm spring, a family's creak-
ing, overloaded wagon rocked along a rutted and well-worn trail. They had
come from Alabama to settle in Texas, and they crossed the broad, lush
prairie near the town of Mina, now known as Bastrop. From the wagon, a wide-
eyed six-year-old boy named John Holland Jenkins—a future Texas Ranger—
peered at something abandoned and scattered on the ground below: human
skeletons. They lay, as he remembered, "grim and ghastly in the green grass." He
was looking at the bones of Indians who had been killed by original pioneers.
This killing would not abate for decades. The Karankawas may have been wiped
out, but many other warring tribes faced certain—if extended—doom.

By the early 1830s, nearly thirty thousand Anglo settlers had made their way into Texas. Hundreds more arrived every month. They were part of the great westward migration of Americans pushing past the Mississippi River, but these migrants were crossing into another country. Some, like the first wave of white Texans, were stockmen and farmers. Others were speculators, fortune hunters, mischief-makers, and fugitives. Years later, Theodore Roosevelt described these pioneers:

> The conquest of Texas should be properly classed with conquests like those of the Norse sea-rovers. The virtues and faults alike of the Texans were those of a barbaric age. They were restless, brave, and eager for adventure, excitement and plunder; they were warlike, resolute, and enterprising; they had all the marks of a young and hardy race, flushed with the pride of strength and self-confidence. On the other hand they showed again and again the barbaric vices of boastfulness, ignorance and cruelty; and they were utterly careless of the rights of others, looking upon the possessions of all weaker races as simply their natural prey.

Roosevelt captured their essence. The new Texans had a great desire for Indian land and little appetite for compromise. Many if not most of them considered themselves agents of God's plan for taming the wilderness, a preordained destiny in which the indigenous dwellers constituted nothing more than murderous vermin.

Against such foes the settlers enjoyed a distinct advantage in weaponry, though not all the killing was done with guns. Jenkins recalled Colonel James Neill of the Texas militia using "a singular, if not barbarous, method of sending destruction upon the Indians." Neill infected a captive Indian with the smallpox virus, Jenkins said, "and then released him to carry the infection into his tribe."

To deal with Indians whom disease did not take, the acting governor had urged a "speedy organization of the ranging corps." In 1835, the provisional government established a "corps of Texas Rangers" with three companies of fifty-six men. Each man would be paid $1.25 a day and would provide his own guns and horse. This attracted a rootless force from the settlements: hunters, trappers, adventurers, and frontiersmen comfortable in an adventurous, mobile life nearly devoid of home comforts. "Unencumbered by baggage, wagons or pack trains," one chronicler of the era wrote, "[they] moved lightly over the prairie as the Indians did, and lived as they did, without tents, with a saddle for a pillow at night." They wore buckskin clothing and coonskin hats or sombreros, and each carried a knife, a pistol, and a long rifle. Military discipline and regimental training were rare, but Rangers had to ride and shoot with skill.

They made for colorful characters at the outset. "Alligator" Davis won his moniker when he wrestled one of the reptiles—said to be more than six feet in length—out of a river. The first Ranger major was lawyer Robert Williamson. A childhood illness had left his right leg permanently drawn back at the knee, which required the use of a wooden prosthetic. This impairment did not prevent Williamson from a lifetime of gunplay with Mexicans, scoundrels, and the stray romantic rival. It did, however, provide a nickname: Three-Legged Willie.

The formation of the corps of Rangers only inflamed Mexican authorities, who already harbored deep concerns about Texas. Talk of independence from Mexico had been spreading across the unruly province, turning Austin's agricultural paradise into a breeding ground of rebellion. Several years earlier, alarmed Mexican officials had sent General Manuel de Mier y Terán to explore conditions in Texas and document colonists' frustrations. A graduate of the Mexican College of Mines, Terán was trained in mathematics, engineering, and the finer points of artillery. He traveled in regal splendor—his custom-made coach featured flourishes of silver inlay—and entered Texas in early 1828, accompanied by a cartographer, a mineralogist, and a French botanist.

Terán found the locals admirably ambitious and successful, but also haughty, restless, and resentful. They considered the Mexican government cumbersome and intrusive and its laws irrelevant. To little surprise, they wished to be left alone. Terán understood this meant nothing but trouble for the parent state. "If it is bad for a nation to have vacant lands and wilderness, it is worse without a doubt to have settlers who cannot abide by some of its laws," Terán wrote to Mexican president Guadalupe Victoria. "They soon become discontented and thus prone to rebellion."

Americans in Texas also bridled at the Mexican prohibition of slavery, a ban they had so far ignored. "Most of them hold slaves who, now having perceived the favorable intent of Mexican law with regard to their tragic state, are becoming restless to throw off their yoke, while their masters believe they can keep them by making [it] heavier," the general wrote. "They commit the barbarities on their slaves . . . They pull their teeth, they set their dogs upon them to tear them apart, and the mildest of them will whip the slaves until they are flayed."

Terán may have overestimated the proportion of Texans who owned slaves, but he had a keen sense of the colonists' prevailing grievances, which only worsened in the years after his mission.

Texas declared itself independent from Mexico in March 1836. Leading six thousand Mexican soldiers, General Antonio López de Santa Anna had already crossed the Rio Grande with plans to crush the insurrection. Santa Anna, who fancied himself the Napoleon of the West, marched his army to San Antonio. There he laid siege to the Alamo, where two hundred or so Texan defenders waited. Though victorious at the old mission—all the Texan fighters, including Davy Crockett and Jim Bowie, were killed—Santa Anna had committed a colossal strategic error. He compounded the mistake at the town of Goliad when he ordered the execution of more than 340 prisoners of war. He now had created instant martyrs of the revolution and a hunger for vengeance among Texans. Led by Sam Houston, the Texas Army routed Santa Anna's forces at San Jacinto in April 1836. The Republic of Texas, an independent nation, was born.

The new republic held almost no money but was rich in enemies, principally Mexicans to the south and Indians throughout. With only a few exceptions, Indians cared little for which government might control Texas. Raids and skirmishes kept coming no matter who wrote the laws. The Rangers as a whole had played no significant role in the revolution's key events, but they now assumed a singular duty: protecting against, and retaliating for, Indian attacks. They would come to fight other parties in their early decades, most notably Mexicans. But their formative identity—the essential, enduring idea of what made a Texas Ranger—was forged by their many armed encounters with Native Americans.

These Rangers did not act as conciliators or mediators in this role. In service to Anglo civilization's slow march, they functioned as executioners. Their job was to seize and hold Texas for the white man. The annihilation of the Cherokees provided an early example.

On a summer afternoon in 1839, the chief of the Texas Cherokee tribe—a man known to his own people as Duwali and to whites as Billy Bowles—held a solemn meeting beside a shady spring near the Neches River. A delegation from the Republic of Texas had come to him for an answer: Would he go to war, or would he surrender?

Though the chief was well past eighty, he still appeared vigorous and strong. "He impressed one with the idea that he possessed force of character and great firmness," a Texan said later. But the dilemma before him clouded his face and caused his broad shoulders to sag. By order of the president of the republic, the tribe must abandon its land—must, in fact, leave Texas altogether. Should they stay, they would be attacked. Both options were catastrophic for the chief. If he chose to fight, he said, the whites would kill him. And if he chose not to fight, his own people would kill him. As the commander of the Texas Army described it, the chief found himself "between two fires."

Sitting on a log next to the bubbling spring, Chief Bowles seemed to deliberate for a few minutes before delivering his decision. "He said he had led his people a long time," recalled a member of the Texas delegation, "and that he felt it to be his duty to stand by them, whatever fate might befall him."

The befalling wouldn't take long. Within a matter of days, Rangers would shoot the chief in the back.

The Cherokees, who called themselves the "principal people," had lived for hundreds—perhaps thousands—of years across the Appalachian South. A small branch of them migrated into East Texas in 1820, when Bowles led about sixty families from Arkansas. Like the Americans who would arrive in a few years, the Cherokees came to Texas in search of freedom and opportunity, which they briefly found.

In contrast to the primordial Karankawas, the Cherokees were considered by whites to be a civilized tribe. They grew crops, built log cabins, educated their youth, and had a written language. Some intermarried with whites. Chief Bowles was believed to be the son of a Scottish father and a Cherokee mother. It was not uncommon for members of the tribe to wear American-style clothes and speak English. "Many of the Indian tribes have acquired only the vices with which a savage people usually become tainted by their intercourse with those who are civilized," the U.S. secretary of war wrote to Congress. "Others appear to be making gradual advance in industry and civilization. Among them may be placed the Cherokees." Some Anglos admired this assimilation, but in the end the Cherokees were treated like almost every other tribe.

After Mexico gained its independence from Spain in 1821, the East Texas Cherokees sought to obtain title to the land they occupied. They had constructed settlements and cultivated farms, and their population grew to about eight hundred, three fourths of whom were women and children. Richard Fields, a one-eighth Cherokee who acted as the tribe's diplomat, wrote to the Mexican governor of Texas, "What is to be done with us poor Indians?" The answer: not much. The Mexicans never granted the tribe's request.

The Cherokees had better luck, or so it seemed, when Texas fought for its independence. Hoping to keep them neutral in the conflict, the Texas provisional government offered the tribe an incentive. With the stated goal of "a firm and lasting peace forever," a treaty between Texas and the Cherokees granted the tribe possession of the territory they had settled. In a ceremony beneath a tree on tribal land, General Sam Houston signed the document for Texas. Chief Bowles marked the signatory page with an X. Houston, who had spent time in Tennessee living, drinking, and mating with Cherokees, presented the chief with a sword, a silk vest, a sash, and a military hat. "Your land is secured to you," Houston wrote to Bowles afterward. He promised to send the chief the official documents that would "make you happy and all your people contented as long as you live."

The subsequent election of Houston as president of the Republic of Texas was therefore good news for the Cherokees, but the Texas Senate never ratified the treaty. In late 1837, the Senate's Standing Committee on Indian Affairs studied the agreement and found that "the *Promises* expressed in that declaration are *false.*" The Cherokees "have been the most savage and ruthless of our frontier enemies," the committee said, and the pact "was based on promises that did not exist."

The republic's land office issued white settlers several hundred titles to territory claimed by the Cherokees. Houston lamented his own citizens' actions in an address to the Senate: "The Indian lands are the forbidden fruit in the midst of the garden; their blooming peach trees, their snug cabins, their well cultivated fields, and their lowing herds excite the speculators . . . [who] are willing to hazard everything that is connected to the safety, prosperity, and honor of the country." Houston's concerns—and his accommodating approach toward Indians—became irrelevant in 1838 with the election of Mirabeau Buonaparte Lamar as president of the republic.

An accomplished artist and published poet—one of his best-known works was "At Evening on the Banks of the Chattahoochee"—Lamar had served with distinction as a commanding officer in the Texas Revolution. He enjoyed an easy path to the presidency after his two opponents died during the campaign. One committed suicide in a fit of lovelorn despondence; the other climaxed a week of drunkenness by falling or jumping off a boat into Galveston Bay. It might have been natural, then, for Lamar to think of himself as a man of destiny. He envisioned Texas as a formidable and expanding nation—perhaps stretching to the Pacific Ocean—that might rival the United States in influence and power.

As president he instantly instituted an Indian policy in direct contrast to Houston's. There would be no attempts at peaceful cooperation and no reservation land set aside for compliant tribes. "The white man and the red man cannot dwell in harmony together," Lamar said in his inaugural address. "Nature forbids it." He declared "a rigorous war" against Indians, which involved "pursuing them to their hiding places without mitigation or compassion." The Indians were to be expelled from Texas. Or killed.

The Cherokees sat at or near the top of Lamar's list for eradication. In the summer of 1838, Texans uncovered a plot led by a Nacogdoches businessman, Vicente Córdova, to overthrow the republic and move it back under Mexican control. The Texas militia crushed the rebellion, but a letter recovered from one of the insurgents showed that he had talked with the Cherokees about joining the revolt. There was no evidence that the tribe had agreed to participate. Merely listening to the would-be rebels, however, was enough to arouse suspicions.

It got worse for the tribe. That year, Indians raided a farm belonging to the Killough family, who had come to Texas from Alabama and had settled along a creek inside the Cherokee claim. The raiders killed eighteen men, women, and small children—the worst slaughter of whites in East Texas. Settlers blamed the Cherokees. Chief Bowles protested that members of his tribe were innocent, that "wild Indians" had done the killing, but few whites believed him.

On May 26, 1839, President Lamar sent a letter to Bowles, reaffirming the view that the treaty the chief had signed with Houston was worthless. "You and your people have been deceived by evil counselors," Lamar said. "The forked tongue of the Mexicans has beguiled you; and you are running into dangerous paths, contrived by the enemies of Texas." Because the Cherokees had "no legitimate rights of soil or sovereignty in this country," the tribe would be forced to move across the Red River, into Indian Territory. And if they didn't leave, they would be attacked. The president signed the letter, "Your Friend Mirabeau B. Lamar."

The Cherokees faced a wrenching decision: destroy themselves or be destroyed by others. Chief Bowles met with the republic's delegation on land the Cherokees claimed and asked if the expulsion could be postponed until the tribe could gather its crops. The answer was no.

War was now inevitable, and the Indians never stood a chance. The Cherokees could claim perhaps two hundred warriors. Lamar had nine hundred soldiers and several companies of Rangers nearby, ready to attack. After an initial skirmish, the main engagement took place on July 16, 1839, near the Neches River. The Cherokees repulsed two charges, but then retreated. The Texans, who shot many of the Indians as they ran, killed about one hundred. Only a handful of Texans died.

Chief Bowles was the last of the Cherokees to leave the battlefield. He rode a sorrel horse, and wore the military hat, sash, and vest given to him by Sam Houston. In one hand he gripped the sword Houston had presented to him. "His horse had been wounded many times . . . and could go no further," wrote Texas historian and politician John H. Reagan. Shot through the thigh, Bowles dismounted and tried to walk away. Henry Conner, a Ranger from Nacogdoches County, fired his rifle, striking the chief in the back. A former Ranger captain, William Sadler, fired as well, and the chief fell to the ground.

He "rose to a sitting position facing us, and immediately in front of the company to which I belonged," Reagan wrote. "I had witnessed his dignity and manliness in council, his devotion to his tribe . . . and his courage in battle, and wishing to save his life, ran towards him, and as I approached him from one direction, my captain, Robert Smith, approached him from another, with his pistol drawn. As we got to him, I said, 'Captain, don't shoot him.'"

But Smith put his pistol to the chief's head and fired, killing him instantly. Someone took Houston's sword from the chief's dead hand and presented it to Smith. One of the Texans scalped Bowles, while another cut away strips of his skin to be used as bridle reins.

Cherokees who had survived the fight made their way to safety in Oklahoma or Mexico. When they were gone, white families took over the Indians' land and began to plant cotton. As for Chief Bowles, his body was left to rot in the field where it fell, his bones to bleach for decades in the East Texas sun.

For most tribes, it was not a good time to be an Indian in Texas. In addition to removing the Cherokees, the Rangers and the militia banished several other Texas bands to reservations north of the Red River, or eliminated them where they stood. The forces of the republic accomplished this with negligible harm to themselves. They used their superior weaponry and manpower to overwhelm their opponents without mercy or accommodation.

Even at their zenith, those tribes were relatively small and weak. The Comanches presented a much larger and more deadly problem.

As more settlers poured into Texas, sodbusters and ranchers pushed ever westward in pursuit of new land, moving into the Edwards Plateau and the Texas Hill Country. Here they found a temperate region of spring-fed creeks and live oak groves. In April and May, when the rains came, a lush carpet of wildflowers covered the grasslands. The newcomers soon learned, however, that this was not the fertile crescent the original pioneers had discovered in coastal Texas. Past the north-south fault line known as the Balcones Escarpment, a thin blanket of top-soil lay on a deep bed of limestone. This country was far better suited for grazing livestock than raising cotton. With every mile west the settlers trekked, the less rain they saw. Summers stretched dry and hot. The trees grew shorter here, the cactus thicker. And with each step toward the setting sun, these Texans plunged deeper into a territory of peril and dread: the broad swath—roughly 250,000 square miles—known as Comancheria.

No whites who encountered the Comanches ever referred to them as civilized. Unlike the Cherokees, they did not raise crops, start schools, or try to live among the Anglos. They were instead a bellicose people of legendary ferocity. Before they were feared, though, they were ignored.

The Comanches had lived for centuries as an indolent, sedentary, disregarded tribe, eking out an existence among the eastern Rocky Mountains, in what is now Wyoming. They picked wild berries, killed rodents and small game, and endured bitter winters. The men hunted buffalo, but on foot; they chased the bison over cliffs and forced them to fall to their deaths. The early Comanches' only beasts of burden were dogs that dragged crude sleds made of poles. Though they fought other tribes, in their state of primitive privation they posed no serious threat to anyone.

All that ended when Spanish horses came to North America.

The Spaniards brought them in the sixteenth century, as part of the crown's lust for gold and conquest. At haciendas in Mexico, horses were bred and raised. As the settlements of New Spain spread northward, the horses came with them. Some escaped and turned feral. Eventually the horses and the Plains Indians found each other.

The Spanish mustang was perfect for these Indians: small but tough, capable of quick bursts of speed but endowed with great endurance. Like the Indians themselves, the mustang seemed built to survive harsh environments. The little horse could go a long way with almost no water. And if a mustang could not find grass to eat, it could live on bark and twigs.

For many Plains and desert tribes, historians have observed, the use of horses altered life as profoundly as the Industrial Revolution changed the course of Western civilization. No more did they chase buffalo on foot. They expanded their range by hundreds of miles. They conducted warfare in a new dimension.

This great leap forward may have affected the Comanches more than any other tribe. Their culture and behavior underwent a complete and immediate transformation—a conversion that altered the history of the continent. No longer a weak, marginal band of berry eaters, the Comanches emerged almost instantly as a conquering force. For the next hundred years they were the dominant power of the Southwest. As such, they spread a wave of death. This was their glory and, ultimately, their doom.

In the early and mid-1700s they swept south from the Rocky Mountains, over the Great Plains and into New Mexico and Texas, not unlike the Huns thundering across the Roman Empire. On the ground a typical Comanche brave looked relatively small, squat, and ungainly. On horseback, though, he metamorphosed into something close to a centaur—"half horse, half man," one contemporary historian wrote with admiration, "so closely joined and so dexterously maintained that it appears but one animal, fleet and furious." Western artist George Catlin, who visited and sketched a Comanche camp, found them to be "on their feet one of the most unattractive and slovenly looking races of Indians that I have ever seen." But he had never witnessed such skilled ridership. "I am ready, without hesitation, to pronounce [them] the most extraordinary horsemen I have seen yet in all my travels," Catlin wrote, "and I doubt very much whether any people in the world can surpass them."

The Comanches typically captured their mustangs at watering holes or by chasing them into box canyons. They found it much easier, however, to steal horses already broken and ready to ride. Raiding parties swooped into Mexico and New Mexico, seized hundreds of horses from ranches, and returned north with their bounty. They burned the grasslands behind them as they went, to discourage pursuers. Billowing clouds of smoke and wheeling buzzards marked the Comanches' receding presence. The only reason the Comanches allowed Spaniards to stay in the region, the tribe was known to boast, was to raise horses for them to steal.

Horses became the tribe's most important source and signifier of wealth. One Comanche brave might have dozens, even hundreds, of horses, while a chief might own more than a thousand. A warrior was utterly devoted to his favorite horse, and some were said to love them more than their wives or children. Among Comanches, the killing of one's favorite horse could be considered murder to be avenged with human blood.

Other tribes had horses, of course, but none could match the Comanches as mounted fighters. Hanging by a loop of rope, a warrior could lean down and shoot a stream of arrows from under his horse's neck while at a full gallop. One Ranger who came to fight many Comanches made an almost scientific analysis based on battlefield observation:

> The bow is placed horizontally in shooting; a number of arrows are held in the left hand; the bow operates as a rest to the arrows. The distance—the curve the missile has to describe in reaching the object—is determined by the eye without taking aim. Arrows are sped after each other in rapid succession. At the distance of 60 yards and over, arrows can be dodged, if but one Indian shoots at you at one time. Under forty yards the [pistol] has little advantage over the bow.

In combat, the Comanches showed their foes no mercy. "They are a warlike and brave race," western explorer Thomas J. Farnham warned in the 1830s. "Many are the scalps and death-dances among these Indians, which testify of wars and tomahawks which have dug tombs." Moving south, the Comanches overran everyone they faced—the Apaches and the Mexicans in particular. Their reign now stretched over hundreds of miles, from the Arkansas River nearly to the Rio Grande, and covered most of the western half of Texas. "They have been so long accustomed to give a loose rein to their evil propensities that they resemble convicts," declared a writer in the *Telegraph and Texas Register*. "[They] can only be kept under control by discipline similar to that which is applied to restrain men who are known to be . . . robbers, thieves and murderers. They are like Arabs, their hands are against every man, and we fear they can only be kept in check when every man's hand is against them." Buffalo hunter Billy Dixon, who fought at least one battle with Comanches, regarded them with a terrified wonder. "There was never a more splendidly barbaric sight," he recalled. "Hundreds of warriors, the flower of the fighting men of the southwestern Plains tribes, mounted upon their finest horses . . . were coming like the wind. . . . Scalps dangled from bridles, gorgeous war-bonnets fluttered their plumes, bright feathers dangled from the tails and manes of the horses, and the bronzed, half-naked bodies of the riders glittered with ornaments of silver and brass."

The Comanches launched deadly lightning raids on ranches and farms, often at night, under a full moon. White settlers came to regard the summer "Comanche moon" with dread. Before they were done, the Comanches would steal more horses and kill more whites than any other Indians in the West. Reinforcing their reputation, these Indians routinely tortured their foes—disemboweling a still-breathing captive, for example, and pouring hot coals into the cavity—and abducted women and children for sale, slavery, or abuse. "They are exceedingly fond of stealing the objects of their enemies' affection," Farnham wrote. "Female children are sought with the greatest avidity."

It's impossible to say which Ranger was the first to shoot a Comanche, but a good argument can be made for a young itinerant blacksmith named Noah Smithwick.

Smithwick left Kentucky and headed for Texas in 1827 at age nineteen. "I was but a boy . . . and in for adventure," he wrote. "I started out . . . with all my worldly possessions, consisting of a few dollars in money, a change of clothes, and a gun." More observant than most, he did not itch for a fight, but he did not shrink from one either. Once, in a dispute over money, a drunken woodcutter with an ax came at Smithwick while he hammered horseshoes. "I was working at the anvil with a heavy hammer," Smithwick said, "and, being quicker than my assailant, planted it between his eyes, felling him senseless to the ground." The woodcutter lived, "though he was laid up for some time." It presented a clear case of self-defense, but Smithwick—perhaps more prone to remorse than the average frontiersman—regretted his actions. "I began to feel very miserable over it," he said. "I paid all his bills and was glad to do it."

After bouncing around Texas and Louisiana for some years, Smithwick joined the Ranger company of John J. Tumlinson. Captain Tumlinson was the son of the *alcalde* who had helped to establish Moses Morrisson's incipient Ranger company and who had been ambushed and slain by Wacos. The Ranger captain showed himself as one quick to vengeance: he retaliated for his father's death by assembling a posse that tracked and killed twelve of the thirteen Indians believed to be responsible.

Now, in January 1836, Tumlinson's Ranger company had been assigned to build a blockhouse along Brushy Creek in Central Texas. At the end of the day's work, they pitched camp on the Colorado River, about ten miles downstream from what is now the city of Austin. It was a cold and clear night, a routine evening in the woods, when a spectral, nearly naked figure stumbled from the bushes into the flickering firelight. "Just as we were preparing for our supper," Smithwick recalled, "a young white woman, an entire stranger, her clothes hanging in shrouds about her torn and bleeding body, dragged herself into camp and sank exhausted on the ground." Traumatized and spent, she could barely talk at first, but the Rangers finally coaxed her story from her.

Her name was Sarah Hibbins. She, her husband, her brother, and her two small children had been traveling by oxcart to their home on the Guadalupe River when Comanches descended upon them. The Indians killed the two men and abducted Mrs. Hibbins and her children. They traveled north for two days with Mrs. Hibbins lashed to a horse. When the younger child would not stop crying, one of the Comanches snatched the infant from the mother's arms and— Smithwick's words—"dashed its brains out against a tree." Because of the cold, the Comanches took shelter in a copse of cedar trees. Mrs. Hibbins slipped from the camp as her captors slept, leaving her six-year-old son with the Comanches. She walked for twenty-four hours over creek beds and through brush and briars, hiding from the Indians as they searched for her, until she lucked upon Tumlinson's Rangers. "She implored us to save her child," Smithwick said.

That was all the urging Tumlinson needed. His Rangers rode through the night and found the Comanches the next morning as they prepared to break camp. "The Indians discovered us just as we discovered them," Tumlinson recalled, "but had not time to get their horses, so they commenced running on foot." Eighteen Rangers chased thirteen Comanches, with Smithwick chasing faster than most. "I was riding a fleet horse," he said, "which becoming excited, carried me right in among the fleeing savages, one of whom jumped behind a tree and fired on me with a musket, fortunately missing his aim." Smithwick leapt from his horse and pursued the Indian on foot. "I fired on him and had the satisfaction of seeing him fall."

But the brave whom Smithwick shot was not dead. Lying on the ground, he loaded his gun, stood, and aimed at Captain Tumlinson. "I sprang from my horse quick as lightning," the Ranger captain said. The Indian fired. "The ball passed through the bosom of my shirt and struck my horse in the neck, killing him immediately," Tumlinson recalled. "I aimed deliberately and fired. The Indian sprang a few feet into the air, gave one whoop, and fell dead within twenty-five feet of me."

In the gunfire, smoke, shouts, and chaos of the fight, one of the Rangers found the Hibbins boy. The Comanches had wrapped him in a buffalo robe and tied him to the back of a mule. Ranger Conrad Rohrer believed the child to be an Indian. A Pennsylvania Dutchman, Rohrer "was as brave a soul as ever drew the breath of life," Smithwick said, "but his excitable temperament rendered him as dangerous to friend as foe."

That became immediately apparent. Rohrer put the barrel of his gun against the boy's back and pulled the trigger. The weapon misfired. He reloaded and tried again—another misfire. "The third time his finger was on the trigger," Smithwick said, "when one of the other [Rangers], perceiving with horror the tragedy about to be enacted, knocked the gun up." This time it fired, but the ball went "whistling over the head of the rescued child."

All the Indians but the dead one vanished into the brush, and the Rangers let them go. The cedar brake was so thick, Tumlinson said, "that it would have been madness to have attempted to penetrate it." Rohrer pulled his knife and scalped the dead Comanche. The Rangers took a vote and awarded the pelt to Smithwick, who accepted the honor with some reluctance. They tied the "loathsome trophy" to his saddle, he said, "where I permitted it to remain, thinking it might afford the poor woman, whose family its owner had helped to murder, some satisfaction to see that gory evidence that one of the wretches had paid the penalty of his crime."

The Rangers took the boy back to the encampment where Mrs. Hibbins waited.

"The scene which here ensued beggars description," Tumlinson said. "A mother meeting with her child released from Indian captivity, recovered as it were from the very jaws of death! Not an eye was dry. She called us brothers, and every other endearing name, and would have fallen on her knees to worship us."

Despite this joyous reunion, Sarah Hibbins's life was exceptionally tragic. Indians had killed her first husband, John McSherry, at the couple's farm in 1829. Next came the death of her child and her second husband, John Hibbins, at the hands of the Comanches. She married again in 1837, to Claiborne Stinnett, the sheriff of Gonzalez County. A few months after their wedding, Stinnett was returning from a trip to buy supplies when he blundered into the camp of two fugitive slaves. They murdered him; his body was not found until five years later.

For Smithwick's company, the incident in which they recovered the surviving Hibbins child was historic. They had killed only four Indians, but the engagement counted as the Rangers' first battle with the Comanches. The war would be waged for the next forty years.

But for a case of the measles, Ben McCulloch might have died at the Alamo. Instead, he forged a storied career as a Ranger.

Chapter 3

BUTCHERIES

"What a Day of Horrors!"

Oh, pray for the Ranger, you kind-hearted stranger.
He has roamed the prairie for many a year;
He has kept the Comanches from off your ranches,
And guarded your homes o'er the far frontier.

—FROM A SONG SUNG BY TEXAS SETTLERS

Frontier life by definition was one of extreme hardships. But in nineteenth-century Texas—a time and place of perpetual armed struggle, in which each side fought for its very survival—the gruesome and the horrific entered the realm of dreadful but familiar misfortunes, like sickness or bad weather. Some pioneers could not stand the ever-hovering danger of Comanche raids and fled to the protections of the towns. Others managed to endure in a frayed state of constant alert. Some went insane.

Then there were those who deliberately hunted and fought the Indians—men like the Rangers. They plunged into peril, carnage, and savagery without pause. By one reckoning, about half of the early Rangers were killed every year. That estimate is no doubt high, but a Ranger's life in those days was one of delivering and receiving violence.

No grand designs or bureaucratic schemes had formed the Rangers. They developed organically: a mounted, roving paramilitary force whose small companies operated with independence and instinct. Because they were invariably outnumbered—there were far more Comanche warriors at this time than Rangers—they used wiliness and audacious aggression to compensate. Unlike the Spanish and Mexicans who came before them, they took the fight to their enemy. And they did so with unbounded gusto for combat, domination, and destruction.

Like all wars, this one brought forth extraordinary individuals—some heroic, some sadistic, and some who simply did their jobs with preternatural doggedness, resilience, and a tolerance for punishment. A small number won everlasting veneration, while most slipped away with no more commemoration than a marker in a country churchyard, if that.

Cicero Rufus "Rufe" Perry, an Alabaman who became a Ranger at age fourteen, experienced more than his share of serious injuries and near misses. When he was seventy-five, Perry produced a brief memoir that conveyed the excitement and travails of Ranger service with an unblinking gaze. Though lacking grammar skills, he offered vivid renditions of Ranger heart and resilience. He also portrayed rape, cannibalism, and scalping with a candor missing from similar diaries.

After an 1836 skirmish with Indians on Yegua Creek, the teenaged Perry watched one of his fellow Rangers go berserk and plunge his knife repeatedly into a fresh corpse. "The first dead Indian that hee come to hee jumpt on him and commence Stabing him." Another member of the Ranger company, Dave Lawrence, sliced the thigh from one of the fallen. He tied it to his saddle, Perry wrote, "and Said hee was a going to eat it if wee did not [get] eney thing the next day as wee had not eat eney thing for too days."

In another battle, Perry himself attempted to scalp a Comanche—apparently a gift for a young woman. "I promest Miss Elisor Haynee to bring hur a Skelp," he recalled. Perry pulled his knife on a prone Indian who, he was surprised to learn, was not dead. "When I went to raze his top not," Perry wrote, "hee razed with me." A ferocious struggle followed, but only Perry held a weapon. "I . . . had a lively time for a while," Perry remembered, "untill oald butch got the best of him."

The next day, the Rangers won a fight with these same Indians near the Nueces River in South Texas, killing two men and capturing one woman. Lipan Apaches who rode with the Rangers as scouts seized the woman as a sex slave.

They would "Sleap with hur each one evry night as thair time come," Perry said. The woman was offered to Perry and his captain as well, but they wouldn't accept this favor. "Wee did not," Perry wrote, "but let them have hur to them selves."

In August 1844, Perry and three other Rangers went to an isolated site on the Nueces where Mexican horse thieves had been reported. After some general scouting along the river, they pitched camp in a low, brushy spot—against the advice of Perry, who said they should be on a bluff, because he believed Indians were nearby. He climbed a small rise and peered across the green hills and limestone outcroppings. "I . . . Saw nothing [but] I had a prsentment that their was Something rong." Near dusk about twenty-five Comanches ambushed the Rangers, descending on the camp with war whoops. An arrow buried itself in Perry's left shoulder. "The next Shot I got was through the belley," Perry wrote, and "the third was in the temple."

He passed out briefly. When he regained consciousness, he stood and lurched toward the river. There two of the Rangers were bathing. As the Comanches mounted another charge, the Rangers fled across the clear, shallow Nueces on horseback. Perry made it to the other side by clinging to the tail of one of the horses but fainted again.

His fellow Rangers may have believed he was dead, or they may have been determined only to save themselves. Still naked from their river bath, they took Perry's gun and escaped on their horses, leaving Perry behind. When he surfaced from his blackout, Perry crept to a thicket where he hid, pushing his head against dirt and small sticks to stanch the bleeding from the arrow wound. He could hear the Indians talking and moving all around him.

Perry waited until nightfall, after he was sure the Comanches had gone. Unable to stand but desperately thirsty, he crawled back to the river, about two hundred yards distant. "It tuc mee from dark until day light to get to the wattor," he said. He filled his boot with river water and concealed himself in a hole left by an uprooted tree, where he stayed all day. After sundown he began an unsteady walk eastward toward the main Ranger camp. It was more than a hundred miles away.

He staggered in the merciless summer heat, unarmed and without provisions, across arid scrublands. Perry ate prickly pear and mesquite beans and drank what little water he could find. After seven days, dehydrated and near death, he reached San Antonio. "I was like one risen from the dead," he remembered. He spent the next three months in bed, and at one point a surgeon cut an arrow spike from his head. When Perry was well enough to ride a horse, a friend accompanied him home to Bastrop. "I lokt moar like a goast than a man," Perry said. "My one mother did not know mee."

His full recovery took two years. But Perry at last found the vigor to engage in many more hostile Indian encounters and, some years later, was named a company captain. By the end of his Ranger career, which extended over four decades, he could point to twenty old wounds from Indian arrows, bullets, and spears. He was scarred, twisted, stooped, and lame, and his left eye drooped and drifted to the side. His longtime friend John Holland Jenkins remarked upon the damage all the battles had wrought in the veteran Indian fighter, who was then in his sixties:

> I would, if possible, place before your eye two pictures or pen portraits of one man. One represents a young man—tall, muscular, erect—a perfect specimen of the strong and brave in young manhood. Dark eyes, bright with the fires of intelligence and enthusiasm gleam forth underneath the black brows and lashes, while the waving masses of black hair fall in careless grace upon a smooth, broad forehead. This was young Rufus Perry. Now, after the lapse of forty years, we behold his handsome face all drawn and scarred, his eye distorted, and twitching while he walks with the aid of a cane—all the result of Comanche arrows.

Despite long and arduous service, Rufe Perry never entered the pantheon of celebrated Rangers, but he served alongside some of those forever revered. This roster included three of the most lionized: Jack Hays, Samuel Walker, and Ben McCulloch.

Ben McCulloch was twenty-four when he followed Davy Crockett, a family friend, from Tennessee to Texas in 1835. Within twenty-five years—even before his storied career reached its sudden end—his admirers would be singing about him: *Huzza for McCulloch, the brave rifle Ranger / The friend of truth, to vice a stranger.* And: *Oh dear, oh 'tis truth what I tell / 'Mid fire and powder he loves to dwell.*

He owned a pedigree of sorts. McCulloch's mother was the daughter of a prominent Virginia planter, and his father was a military officer who had graduated from Yale. But the family had squandered much of its wealth, and young Ben had little formal schooling. He spent much of his youth rafting and hunting.

Though he loved the outdoors, Dyersburg, Tennessee, was "a slow country and slow people live in it," McCulloch wrote.

Faraway Texas offered both opportunity and excitement. McCulloch's plan had been to meet Crockett there, but a fortunate case of measles prevented him from reaching the Alamo before Santa Anna's army overran it. He fought with Sam Houston at the Battle of San Jacinto, securing a commission as a first lieutenant. He ran for and won a seat in the Texas House of Representatives. And he turned his battlefield talents to life as a Ranger, enlisting in the company assembled by Captain Mathew "Old Paint" Caldwell, a signer of the Texas Declaration of Independence. This proved to be as dangerous as expected, but in a completely unexpected way.

In 1839, near the town of Gonzales, McCulloch exchanged angry words with Ranger Alonzo Sweitzer, who had lost to McCulloch in their race for the Texas Congress. A drunken Sweitzer, who was a doctor, challenged McCulloch to a duel. When Sweitzer sobered up, he retracted his words and refused to fight. Given the era's duel protocol, known as the "code duello," McCulloch could fire only with character assassination. He felled Sweitzer's reputation with the charge that he was a "black-hearted cowardly villain."

Sweitzer might turn the other cheek, but it was too much for Ranger captain Reuben Ross, a friend who offered to take Sweitzer's place. A veteran of several tough battles along the border, Ross had also received training in the dueling arts. A Galveston newspaper described him as a "gallant but rash man," while McCulloch also embraced conflict. Thus, a duel: from forty paces, the two men pointing rifles at each other. Ross's ball struck McCulloch in the right wrist and shredded his arm up to the elbow, causing McCulloch's shot to go wild. With the face-off now consummated, Ross offered McCulloch the services of his personal surgeon, but the doctor couldn't do much. The wound had caused serious nerve damage to McCulloch's forearm. In the chastening aftermath, McCulloch and Ross declared themselves to be friends.

Nonetheless, two months after the duel McCulloch's brother Henry, also a Ranger, happened upon the chance for vengeance. Captain Ross had turned up drunk and uninvited at a Christmas party in Gonzales, where he insulted several young women. When Ross refused to leave and brandished two guns, Henry McCulloch pulled a pistol and shot him dead.

Such was life, however brutish and short, in Texas. Sweitzer was killed two years later in a quarrel with a Texas Army officer. Ben McCulloch, however, blazed a path to glory. Though he never recovered fully from the dueling injury, it did not keep him from any number of Ranger exploits. He played a crucial role, for instance, in one of the new republic's biggest engagements.

It had its origins in San Antonio, where the Texas government had invited the Penateka band of Comanches to talk peace. On March 19, 1840, some thirty-five warriors rode into the old mission town with about thirty women, children, and old men. This was something new, as these Comanches seemed eager for a treaty. Smallpox had taken a toll on the tribe, as had skirmishes with the Rangers. In a peaceful conversation with Ranger Smithwick, Chief Muguara expressed their greatest lament: "We have set up our lodges in these groves and swung our children from these boughs from time immemorial. . . . But the white man comes and cuts down the trees, building houses and fences, and the buffalos get frightened and leave and never come back, and the Indians are left to starve."

The Comanches hoped for the establishment of a line beyond which the Texans would not cross. For their part, the Texans desired the release of more than a dozen people, most of them women and children, abducted by Indians. Neither ambition stood a chance of success.

At first, however, the San Antonio gathering seemed almost festive. The Indians had brought furs and horses to trade, and the chiefs had painted themselves for a ceremonial occasion. In a courtyard, young Comanches entertained the locals by shooting arrows at coins tossed in the air by Texans. But the mood spoiled quickly. The Comanches had been ordered to bring all their white captives with them for exchange. Instead, they offered only one, fifteen-year-old Matilda Lockhart.

Matilda, the niece of a Ranger captain, had been abducted along with four other children about eighteen months before, and she suffered monstrously in her captivity. "Her head, arms and face were full of bruises, and sores, and her nose actually burnt off to the bone—all the fleshy end gone, and a great scab formed on the end of the bone," said Mary Maverick, a diarist and the wife of San Antonio's mayor. "Both nostrils were wide open and denuded of flesh."

The Comanches, Maverick wrote, had beaten and "utterly degraded" the girl—the era's euphemism for rape. Matilda told "how they would wake her from sleep by sticking a chunk of fire to her flesh," Maverick said, "and how they would shout and laugh like fiends when she cried."

The peace conference took place in San Antonio's courthouse, a one-story limestone building with a flat roof and a packed-dirt floor. Matilda Lockhart's condition shocked and infuriated the Texas Army officers who ran the meeting. They demanded that Chief Muguara, also known as Spirit Talker, produce the other captives. The chief said those were held in camps he did not control. "We have brought in the only one we had," he said, but allowed that the freedom of others might be purchased with blankets and ammunition. Then he asked the officers, "How do you like that answer?"

They did not. The Texas officers told the Comanche chiefs they would be held prisoner until the other Anglo captives were brought to town and freed. When they understood at last what was happening, the Comanches issued a "terrific war whoop"—as overheard by Mrs. Maverick, who stood outside—and rushed for the doors. One stabbed a soldier who blocked the way. Soldiers opened fire, and lead balls and arrows flew through the room. Ranger captain Caldwell joined the chaos. "When the fight began he wrenched a gun from an Indian and killed him with it, and beat another to death with the butt end of the gun," Maverick recalled. The tiny room reeked of smoke and blood.

Twelve chiefs, including Muguara, now lay dead, and the fight spread into San Antonio's public square. Caldwell, who had been shot in the leg, hobbled from the courthouse and fought off a warrior by pelting him with rocks. Comanches and Anglos engaged in hand-to-hand combat with knives and lances. One Indian shot a judge through the heart. Another killed the sheriff.

Some Comanches tried to escape via the narrow San Antonio River, where soldiers shot them as they swam. Two warriors ran into a house and bolted the door. Townspeople soaked a large ball of yarn in turpentine, set it aflame, and dropped it through a hole in the roof. The warriors stumbled outside. A Texan split the head of one with an ax, while the other was shot as he ran. By the end of the melee, thirty-three Indians were dead, including three of the women and children. The rest of the women and children were taken prisoner and thrown into the city jail. Seven whites had been killed. "What a day of horrors!" Mary Maverick wrote.

The horrors were only beginning. The incident came to be known as the Council House fight, and historians have judged it as perhaps the greatest strategic blunder by Anglo Texans in the Indian wars. When the distant Comanches learned what had happened in San Antonio, they reacted with predictable fury. They gathered their remaining white captives—thirteen in all, including children—staked them to the ground, mutilated them, and roasted them alive. After that they plotted a much grander revenge.

With so many chiefs killed, the confused and mourning Comanches needed time to regroup. Their plans took shape over the days and nights of summer. Less than five months after the Council House fight, in early August 1840, a raiding party with more than four hundred warriors lumbered out of the Hill Country and toward the great coastal plain. Led by the war chief Buffalo Hump, it was the largest Comanche force ever mounted against Texas settlers. The massive, slow-moving train included pack animals as well as women, who were brought along for logistical support. In all, the party may have totaled one thousand. It passed undetected over hundreds of miles of mostly unpopulated land, tracing the southward course of the Guadalupe River, penetrating deep into what had been considered safe territory for Anglos.

One of the first encounters with whites came near the small town of Hallettsville, less than a day's ride from the Gulf. The Indians happened upon Joel Ponton and Tucker Foley, the son of a wealthy planter, who were en route to Gonzales. Foley and Ponton—whose father had been killed by Indians five years before—spurred their horses to escape. An arrow knocked Ponton from his horse. He survived by lying on the ground and pretending to be dead. Foley dismounted and tried to hide in a creek. The Comanches roped him and dragged him from the water, sliced off the soles of his feet, and made him walk across the rough ground before they shot and scalped him.

A rural mail carrier who had spotted the Comanches' trail hastened with alarm to the town of Gonzales. In response, Ben McCulloch—his arm still in a sling from his ill-fated duel—set out with twenty-four Rangers and volunteers. More men would have joined McCulloch, volunteer W. D. Miller later said, but another group of Indians had stolen the best horses in town. One day after leaving Gonzales, McCulloch's men came upon the trail of the Indian caravan. It appeared "large and well-trodden," Miller said, big enough to indicate the presence of at least several hundred Comanches.

Thirty-six more men caught up with McCulloch's company, and they followed the Indians. They soon encountered another company, this one led by Captain John J. Tumlinson, and all 125 men—an assortment of Rangers, militiamen, and volunteers—stayed on the trail, pushing ahead in a brisk trot.

It wasn't brisk enough. As the Comanches moved south, they reached small isolated settlements, where they began cutting their swath of destruction. They burned houses, stole horses, and killed Texans as they went. Nearing the town of Victoria, they killed slaves working in fields and seized hundreds of horses. They attacked Victoria, but the inhabitants fought back. The Comanches killed a few of them, took some more horses, and kept riding toward the Gulf.

At a settlement called Nine Mile Point, they abducted a woman named Nancy Crosby—the daughter of a Ranger and believed to be the granddaughter of Daniel Boone—and her two small children. When one, an infant, cried too long and loud, a warrior killed him by bashing his head against a tree. The second child also cried. The same warrior ran his lance through him and pinned him to the ground as his mother watched and screamed.

The Rangers and volunteers still had not overtaken the Comanches. On August 8, 1840, the war party swept in a massive crescent across the prairie toward the port settlement of Linnville. Though home to only about two hundred people, it was a key shipping point for goods in and out of southeast Texas. Some of the townspeople saw the Indians coming but mistook them for friendly Mexicans with horses to sell. When they realized their mistake, they had only one way to flee: onto small boats and a schooner floating in shallow Lavaca Bay, about a hundred yards offshore. Some didn't reach their refuge. Major H. O. Watts, the collector of customs, and his wife of only twenty-one days, Juliet, tried to salvage valuables. But as they waded toward a sailboat, the Indians grabbed them. They killed and scalped Watts and took his wife captive, tying her to a pony.

From the water, the townspeople gaped in horror as the Comanches slaughtered their cattle and looted their businesses. The pillage took most of the day. The Indians pulled mattresses from homes and slit them open—they kept the ticking—and set the houses afire. White mattress feathers floated in the black smoke. By late afternoon every building in town but one had been burned.

The Rangers and volunteers were twenty miles away in Victoria.

Now began the Indians' retreat and—haltingly—the Texans' pursuit.

The Comanches had killed about two dozen men, women, and children over the course of the raid, and they had stolen perhaps three thousand horses. This new herd and the heavy load of plundered goods made their caravan even larger and slower than before. As they headed northwest toward their homeland, they made for an easy target, at least in the Texans' initial schemes. It proved to be harder than it looked.

First, Texas officers used scouts to track the Indians, but with poor results.

One scout was killed, one escaped death only by virtue of a fast horse, and one—John S. Menefee—was hit by seven arrows. He pulled each one from his body and crawled to safety.

On August 9, Captain Tumlinson's forces neared the Comanche train on a broad prairie near Linnville. A war party rode out to meet them. Here the Texans found a spectacle none had seen before, a sight both ludicrous and chilling. With loot from their raids, the Indians were—in W. D. Miller's appalled description—"hideously bedaubed after their own savage taste." One mounted warrior wore a stovepipe hat and carried an umbrella. Another donned a long-tailed coat, worn backward and buttoned from behind. The Comanches tied long red and blue ribbons to their horses' tails and inserted silver spoons into their feathered headdresses. "They seemed to have a talent for finding and blending the strangest, most unheard-of ornaments," Ranger John H. Jenkins wrote. "It was a strange spectacle never to be forgotten, the wild, fantastic band as they stood in battle array." Some had fastened racks of antlers to their heads. "One headdress struck me particularly," Jenkins recalled. "It consisted of a large crane with red eyes."

Preparing to fight, the Texans dismounted and assumed a "hollow square" formation but soon discovered that this old-school tactic wouldn't work against the mounted Comanches. "They whirl[ed] about us and around us," volunteer Miller recalled, "exhibiting the most admirable feats of horsemanship; and, being continually in motion, they were the less liable to be struck by our balls." Ben McCulloch urged Tumlinson to allow him and his men to break rank and charge the Indians, but the captain refused. After a brief skirmish, the Comanches moved on and the Texans withdrew to rest.

Through either inattention or overconfidence, the Comanches had chosen to head home along the same route they had taken when they launched their raid. If the Texans were to have any hope of stopping them, they would have to cut off the Indians before the caravan reached the wooded hills that would provide ample cover. The Texans devised a plan to mount an attack at Plum Creek, a flatland tributary near the present city of Lockhart. Some two hundred Rangers and volunteers rode about seventy-five miles northwest, a grueling trek in mid-August. It was "intensely hot," wrote John Henry Brown, one of the pursuers. "Our ride was chiefly over a burnt prairie, the flying ashes blinding the eyes."

Reaching Plum Creek, they rested and waited. The next day, they spotted the caravan's great dust cloud and soon the Comanches themselves in a column that looked to be seven miles long. The Indians showed no signs of worry as they approached the ambush. "They were singing and gyrating in divers[e] grotesque ways," Brown observed, "evidencing their great triumph, and utterly oblivious of danger."

When it came time to attack, General Felix Huston, commander of the Texas force, made the same mistake Tumlinson had committed days before: he ordered his men to dismount and form a hollow square battle line. As before, the mounted warriors thundered and swarmed around them on the brown prairie grass, thrusting and withdrawing, with little damage to themselves.

Ben McCulloch once more vented his frustration. This was his best chance to "kill and take Indians," he said, if he were to "live 100 years." As it was, he said, a flanking guard of Comanches held the Texans at bay while the caravan plodded on, unmolested. And warriors with rifles had hidden themselves in a nearby tree line, from which they fired upon the Texans with ease. Chroniclers of the battle later wrote that McCulloch vehemently pressed his case with the commander. "In the name of God, General Huston, order a charge through the timber and front rank," McCulloch is said to have demanded. "The Indians are shooting my men."

After similar entreaties from Old Paint Caldwell, who had recovered from his Council House leg wound, Huston approved a mounted charge against the Indians. Whooping and firing, McCulloch, his Rangers, and other Texans crashed into the Comanche lines. The Indians retreated, and the Texans pursued them in a running fight that lasted for at least ten miles. Many of the Indians' horses and mules became stuck in muddy creek beds. "They bogged down so close together that a man could have walked along on their bodies *dry*," Jenkins wrote. One Comanche warrior's head was "nearly blown off," Ranger Robert Hall said. "Though dead and stiff, he remained on his war horse." The horse galloped over the battlefield, the headless body still on it, before vanishing into the woods.

The Texans killed men and women alike during the battle. Their own casualties were minimal. Not until their horses were exhausted did the Rangers and volunteers stop their pursuit.

Next came the postcombat spasms. The Texans' estimates of Indian dead ranged from twenty-five to more than a hundred. Comanche corpses were strewn over the miles of prairie, and many had sunk into the creek. Rangers also discovered some of the Comanches' abandoned captives, including the young

Mrs. Watts. An "old Indian squaw" had shot the woman with an arrow, Ranger Jim Nichols said. The Indian woman then "ran for her horse, but received the contents of my holster before she could mount."

Mrs. Watts lay on the ground with an arrow in her chest. Her whalebone corset had saved her life by acting as a shield; the arrowhead had not penetrated much beyond her breastbone. Ranger Hall said he and another man used a pocketknife to dig the arrow from her chest. Mrs. Watts "possessed great fortitude," Hall said, "for she never flinched, though we could hear the breastbone crack when the arrow came out."

Nancy Crosby, the Daniel Boone descendant who had been abducted days earlier, was not so lucky. By some versions, the Comanches shot her as she tried to run away. In other accounts, they tied her to a tree and pumped her full of arrows. Either way, she was dead.

The Comanches left behind many of their own who were still alive. The Texans took some thirty women and children prisoners. They were turned over to their bitter enemies, the Tonkawas, who had provided vital help to the Rangers and volunteers in the battle. The Tonkawas "retired with the prisnrs about a mile above us," Ranger Nichols wrote ominously, "and had a big sc[a]lp dance that night." Among its highlights: much vocal celebration of victory and ritual consumption of the vanquished foe. "Our allies were cooking [a] Comanche warrior," Ranger Hall recalled. "They cut him into slices and broiled him on sticks.... They danced, raved, howled and sang, and invited me to get up and eat a slice of Comanche. They said it would make me brave. I was very hungry, but not sufficiently so to become a cannibal."

The Tonkawas held no monopoly on after-battle abomination. Nichols watched as Ranger Ezekiel Smith approached an Indian woman who had been shot through her thighs, breaking both legs. "He drew his long hack knife as he strode toward her," Nichols wrote in his diary, "taken her by the long hair, pulled her head back and she gave him one imploreing look and jabbered something in her own language and raised both hands as though she would consign her soul to the great sperit." Smith cut her throat from ear to ear. "He then plunged the knife to the hilt in her breast and twisted it round and round like he was grinding coffee," Nichols remembered. With the woman writhing on the ground, Smith put his bloody knife back in its sheath. Someone asked the Texan how he could have done that to a human being. "That ain't a human," Smith said. "That's an injun and I come to kill injuns." The incident left Nichols with an epiphany: "The American race is not wholy exemp from acts of cruelty and barberism."

Many Rangers and volunteers were too busy collecting loot to engage in bloody vengeance. The Indians had been forced to leave behind a great deal of it—a windfall for the Texans. "We captured the Indian pack train," Ranger Hall wrote. "The mules were loaded with household furniture, wearing apparel and general merchandise. There were five hundred of these pack mules." As often happened, the Rangers and volunteers regarded the goods as spoils of war. "We hardly knew what to do with all this stuff," Hall said, "and we finally concluded to divide it among ourselves."

Plum Creek represented a breakthrough for the Rangers. For the first time in a major battle, they had used Indian tactics—a moving attack on horseback—to fight Indians. In their own charitable assessment, they also prevented raids on other settlements. "But for our early interventions," volunteer Miller wrote, "it is not improbable that the sad fate of Linnville would have been the doom of her sister towns." John Henry Brown called it a "complete and crushing" defeat for the Comanches, but Plum Creek was far from a smashing victory. Most of the Indians, along with hundreds of their stolen horses, were able to escape and return to their distant homes.

Five days later, a citizens' group in LaGrange urged the Texas government to complete the chastisement with a three hundred-man armed foray into Comanche country. Newspapers agitated for a punitive expedition. Though the republic was broke, agreement came from President Lamar, who still pushed for the expulsion or extermination of all Indians. He picked Ranger colonel John H. Moore to collect volunteers and command the force.

Moore, forty, was one of white Texas's original settlers and had fought in the first big battle against the Karankawas in 1822. It was he who had crept close to the Karankawa camp and heard a baby crying and helped mount the assault that wiped out the village. A deeply religious man with a passionate hatred of Indians, Moore had built a reputation as a commander always pushing for combat. Sometimes his enthusiasm—and lack of frontier military skills—overtook him. In 1839 he led a raid against a Comanche village near the San Saba River. The attack might have been considered a success, as the Comanches scattered, but the Indians managed to sneak behind Moore's lines and steal his horses. Rufe Perry recorded the disaster: "Thay got a way with evry thing wee had." Moore's men, bearing their wounded on litters, faced a 150-mile walk home in freezing winter weather.

This time would be different, Moore vowed. He passed out circulars to recruit a company. "The first who go will surely get a fight," they promised. Moore found some men on street corners and others in local saloons. Ben McCulloch helped him assemble the willing, but they came nowhere close to signing up three hundred. Moore announced he was abandoning the mission, then reconsidered. He agreed to proceed with only about ninety volunteers.

Moore's company could be considered Rangers under the imprecise definition of the era. These were not farmers defending their homes, or minutemen taking their muskets off the wall as an imminent threat loomed. These counted as veteran fighters, some of whom had defeated the Mexican army at San Jacinto. They had been drawn into this campaign by the lure of combat, a thirst for revenge, and the chance to divide any goods they might seize.

They gathered near Austin in October 1840. Seventeen Lipan Apaches, led by Chief Castro, joined them to act as scouts and spies. The expedition rode northwest into the wooded hills along the Colorado River. It was unusually cold for October, with a howling wind from the north. One member of the company, Garrett Harrell, developed a sore throat and suffered a fatal choking spell. It may have been diphtheria. Moore's men paused to bury him on the riverbank before moving on. Despite the cold, Moore was struck by the appeal and the potential of the land—once the Indians could be removed. It was "a beautiful, fertile country," he wrote in his report, "presenting a most lovely appearance to the eye and offering many inducements for settlement."

Within three weeks, they had ventured farther into Comanche territory, some 250 miles northwest of Austin, than any such company had gone before. On October 23 they saw their first sign of Comanches: a pecan grove, where branches had been cut to harvest the nuts. Lipan scouts rode ahead and returned to report they had found the Indian camp. Lipan spies counted about 60 families and 125 warriors. Moore's men strained at the bit. "Every countenance beamed with feelings of pride and anticipation of a general engagement," he wrote in his official report.

The Comanche camp sat in a crescent of the Colorado, below a steep limestone bluff. The Texans approached in silence at dawn. Smoke from buffalo-hide tipis curled into the cold air. No Indians stirred. Moore ordered a charge, and the Texans rode in with guns blazing. Comanche men and women bolted from their tipis and were cut down in an instant. "A general and effective fire was opened upon the enemy," Moore wrote, "who soon commenced falling upon the right and left."

Dogs barked, women screamed, and gunfire echoed off the limestone wall. Many of the Comanches ran to the cold river, waded to the far bank, and began climbing a cliff to escape. Texans with their rifles picked them off. "My troops displayed their skill in rifle shooting," Moore said. "Every man was deliberate, and at the crack of his piece, it was apparent that good aim had been taken."

In about twenty minutes, the shooting stopped. "The river and its banks now presented every evidence of a total defeat of our savage foes," Moore wrote. "The bodies of men, women, and children were to be seen on every hand, wounded, dying, and dead." The Texans counted the Indian dead: forty-eight on the ground, Moore reported, and eighty in the river. Only two Texans were wounded. Moore's men seized about five hundred horses and burned the village. About thirty-five Comanche women and children who survived were taken to white settlements, where they were sold into slavery.

For the Comanches it was the worst defeat to date, and it had occurred deep in territory they considered safe from Ranger raids. In Austin the citizens exulted and "gave a splendid ball in honor of the returning soldiers, nearly all of whom attended," wrote John H. Jenkins. But while the Rangers danced, some Indians sneaked into a nearby corral and stole forty of their horses. "Once again quite a number were compelled to walk home."

Still, the Moore raid was regarded as a triumph, and it inspired similar Ranger assaults on Indian villages in the coming months. As often was the case, J. W. Wilbarger neatly stated the prevailing viewpoint of Texan settlers in his collection, *Indian Depredations in Texas*: "Little did these blood thirsty monsters think they could or would be sought out in their distant home," he wrote. "The butcheries of Victoria and Linnville were avenged."

Such revenge was important and cathartic, but overall domination of the Comanches remained elusive. One great breakthrough for Anglo Texas would come with the invention and production of a revolutionary weapon, and with the Rangers' use of it.

Many consider John Coffee "Jack" Hays the greatest Ranger of all time. A revolutionary handgun from Samuel Colt helped solidify that reputation.

Chapter 4

ARMS AND THE MAN

"The Most Perfect Weapon in the World"

The Pocket and Short Barrel Belt Pistol can be fired without powder, loaded with balls and caps only, with great accuracy, at 10 to 12 paces, and with great force, they can be loaded and fired five times in less than half a minute.

—ADVERTISEMENT FOR COLT'S REPEATING PISTOLS, 1844

He called himself "The Celebrated Dr. Coult of New York, London and Calcutta," and in 1832 he set out to make his fortune. Though still a teenager, he claimed to be a trained chemist, a lecturer in philosophy, and an expert in certain areas of the medical arts. He pushed a handcart up and down the East Coast of the United States, through small towns and big cities, a one-man show.

At each stop he enticed customers to inhale what he called "Exhilarating Gas," or nitrous oxide. For a fee of twenty-five to fifty cents—children were half price and ladies free—anyone could partake. His promotional handbills promised the gas would produce "the most astonishing effects upon the nervous system" with no hangover. Those who were intoxicated would sing or dance, or be moved to deliver inspired speeches. "In short," Dr. Coult promised, "the sensations produced by it are highly pleasurable."

Except when they weren't. At a show in downtown Pittsburgh a few audience members danced and jumped under the happy influence of the laughing gas, but some wanted to fight. One man turned "as furious as an enraged lion," a newspaper reported, and "drove every soul out of the room and into the street, beating two or three very severely."

Such small disasters aside, the celebrated doctor made steady progress toward a larger goal. His real name was Samuel Colt, and each time a bliss-seeking rube dropped two bits into his palm, the wheel of history moved a tick or two. In time—and with money saved from his traveling show—Colt would develop the weapon that helped shape the fate of the American West.

Not long after Colt began to make his way in the world, a young man named Jack Hays embarked on his own path. Within a dozen years, Hays emerged as the Texas Ranger of imagination, model, and exaggeration, the leader against whom others would forever be measured. Samuel Colt played a large role in that too.

Jack Hays was born in Tennessee in 1817, and he had soldiering in his blood. His father, Harmon Hays, had fought under General Andrew Jackson in wars against the Creek Indians and the British. When Harmon's second child was born, he named him John Coffee Hays, in honor of one of Jackson's commanders, General John Coffee. One of Jack Hays's biographers would write that he appeared exceptional even as a newborn: "a handsome baby, not red like most newcomers to this planet."

Young Jack was raised in the shadow of the Hermitage, Jackson's Nashville plantation home, which Hays's grandfather had sold to Jackson. At age fifteen, after yellow fever killed his parents, Hays went to live with relatives in Mississippi. There he learned to be a land surveyor. He came to Texas at age nineteen, arriving soon after the new republic gained its independence. Hays sought adventure and may have found it when a local tough pulled a gun on him at a Nacogdoches saloon. "With a movement as quick as lightning," one writer said, Hays drew his own weapon and fired. "The desperado was a corpse when his body touched the ground."

Quick-draw Hays worked as a surveyor, a job in high demand on the frontier, and one that entailed constant danger. The Texas government gave aspiring settlers a land title known as a head grant, but the plot had to be surveyed. This required surveyors to drag their equipment into remote territory, where they toiled alone and unprotected. It didn't take Indians long to understand that the presence of a survey crew meant the hated land-grabbing farmers and ranchers would soon follow. They attacked with ferocity and frequency.

Supervising and guarding the surveyors, Hays came to regard the Indians with both wariness and fascination. He delighted in creeping close to the tribes and, while hidden in the brush, observing them and their command structure. Hays came under fire during one such foray; he shot back and hit a chief. One biographer described the young man's elation: "He jumped up and hallooed, 'I've killed an Indian! I've killed an Indian!'" It was the first of many.

Hays was by 1840, at age twenty-three, the captain of a Ranger company based in San Antonio. He didn't really look the part of a commanding officer. In a collection of battle-hardened but still young men, Hays "was the most boyish looking of them all," Ranger confederate C. W. Webber wrote. Webber might have stopped there but didn't:

> His figure, though scarce the average height, was stout, and moulded with remarkable symmetry—his hands and feet were womanishly delicate, while his Grecian features were almost severely beautiful in their classic chiseling. The rich brunette complexion and sharp black eye, indicative of Italian blood, would have made the fortune of a city belle. The softness of his voice, and his caressing manner, increased the attraction of his appearance; and, but for a certain cold flash from those brilliant eyes, I should have been entirely in love with him at once.

Others noted Hays's reticent manner and piercing gaze but didn't swoon quite so much. To them he seemed to radiate a quiet but intense authority. "When Jack Hays's eyes begin to darken with a flash in them like lightning out of a black southwest cloud," Indian fighter Edward Burleson Sr. said, "it's a good time to let him alone."

The cash-strapped Texas Republic had disbanded its army, so far-flung settlers depended for protection on volunteers—those farmers and ranchers who functioned as unofficial, unpaid militia when danger loomed—and Rangers. Hays's companies, which sometimes included Ben McCulloch as lieutenant, were chartered by law as "Mounted Gunmen to act as Rangers on the Western and South Western Frontier." Like other Rangers, these men furnished their own horses and guns. When the impecunious republic's treasury could find the money, Hays was paid $75 a month while company privates received $30.

These Rangers spent much of their time and effort patrolling the border in search of highwaymen. In some beleaguered regions, gangs of mounted gunmen who infested the dirt roads and desert trails had brought commerce to a near halt. A Texas newspaper noted that a "a large quantity of goods" had been shipped to San Antonio for sale in Mexico, "but so many parties of robbers are now roving west of the city that few traders dare to come in." The story added that Hays and McCulloch "are collecting troops to disperse these marauding bands."

The Rangers sometimes couldn't tell robbers from soldiers. Texans believed that the Mexican government, which still refused to accept the Lone Star republic's independence, encouraged both outlaws and cavalrymen to cross the Rio Grande for larceny and mischief. When Mexican marauders—or perhaps military—occupied the border town of Laredo in 1841, Hays approached with a force of twenty-five. Though outnumbered, he rejected advice to retreat. "We made a charge," Hays wrote, "and the enemy gave way." The Rangers killed several Mexicans and took twenty-five of them prisoner. The rest fled.

President Sam Houston had declared martial law in the Nueces Strip in 1843, giving Hays and his men virtually unlimited power to chase and punish Mexican outlaws. They did not hesitate to use it, as when they seized a trio of Mexicans acting as lookouts for itinerant bands of thieves. Such suspects required no trials. "Capt. Hays arrested three of these spies . . . and shot them," one newspaper reported. "He is enforcing the martial law agreeably." Hays may have decided to act because the court system in San Antonio would not. The chief justice of the district was reputed to be dead drunk each morning by nine.

Hays's reputation soared, and press accounts routinely referred to him as the "gallant" Ranger captain. "That man eminently deserves the gratitude of his country," wrote the *La Grange Intelligencer*. "With a handful of brave men, [he] is constantly scouring our extensive frontier, and enabling the whole country to enjoy the blessings of peace."

The Rangers devoted far less time and effort to chasing the many Anglo bandits who raided and pillaged the villages of Tejanos—Texans of Mexican descent—all across the borderland. One of the most feared was a gang led by Mabry "Mustang" Gray. A Texas military veteran who fought in the Battle of San Jacinto, Gray vowed to kill nearly every Mexican he encountered in the Nueces Strip. John J. Linn, a Texas pioneer and member of the Republic's Congress, called

Gray a "moral monstrosity" as well as a "cold-blooded assassin" who committed any number of "fiendish atrocities." According to Linn, a party of seven Mexican traders was returning home from South Texas in 1842 when Gray's gang, known as the Men-Slayers, accosted them in their camp. The Texans tied the Mexicans together, told them to pray for their souls, and shot them, then stole their dry goods and tobacco. All were killed except for one man, who was saved when a corpse fell on him. He managed to untie himself and make his way to the town of Victoria, where he told his story of the murders. "Good people were horror-stricken at the outrage," Linn said, "but no attempt was made to bring the criminals to justice."

Not only did Gray escape prosecution for such crimes, but within a few years he became a captain in the Texas Rangers.

When Hays and his Rangers weren't hunting Mexican robbers, they rode west and north of San Antonio in a quest for Comanche raiders who made stealth assaults on farms and ranches. Their mission was to intercept and kill the marauders before they could strike. These encounters gave life to the early versions of the Ranger myth, with its hard-won celebrations and self-serving hyperbole.

Hays brought to his command a character suited to the demands of the warring Texas hinterlands. He stayed cool in planning, it was said, but turned explosive in action, and he had learned the ways of Indian war from his Lipan Apache scouts. In battle he mimicked the Comanche tactic of charging the enemy, feinting a retreat, and flanking them, pincerlike, as they moved into the trap. Other times, he was reputed to lead at the point of assault with an approach both audacious and calculated. "Though a lamb in peace, he was a lion in war," one man who served under Hays wrote, "and few indeed, were the settlers, from the coast to the mountains of the north, or from the Sabine to the Rio Grande, who had not listened in wonder to his daring, and gloried in his exploits."

It was said that he once spotted two hundred Comanches herding stolen horses, turned to his company of twenty men, and said, "Yonder are the Indians, boys, and yonder are our horses. The Indians are pretty strong, but we can whip them, and recapture the horses, what do you say?" His Rangers supposedly replied, "Go ahead, we'll follow if there's a thousand of them." The Rangers charged the Indians on horseback, with Hays leading the way. They routed the superior force and seized the stolen horses.

Was the story true? With Hays and the Rangers of this era, it's sometimes impossible to know. Hays filed relatively few official reports, like many Ranger captains, and historians devoted to his early years have labored with a shortage of original sources. Many accounts of his exploits have come from writers repeating hand-me-down anecdotes supplemented with imagination. If such an incident actually occurred, the numbers were no doubt inflated. That would not be unusual. Numerous Ranger anecdotes described small collections of Texans conquering superior numbers of Indians—and later Mexicans and rioters—with relative ease.

One of the most stirring tales of a Ranger's skill and bravery, one that has endured for 175 years, tells of a day Hays became separated from his company. Hays continued his solitary scout until he encountered a band of Comanches. Greatly outnumbered, he spurred his horse for safety. Arrows flew past him as the whooping Indians gave chase. When his horse began to tire, the Ranger captain dismounted and scrambled to safety high atop a Central Texas landmark known as Enchanted Rock.

This massive bald dome of pink granite rises out of the flat earth like the crown of a buried moon. It is 425 feet tall and can be seen from miles away. On summer nights, it creaks and groans as the hot granite cools and contracts, and it was said to be haunted. A Spanish priest claimed to have been swallowed by the rock and spat out two days after. Some Indians considered it a holy site. At this moment, Hays simply needed it for protection.

He reached the summit of the dome. As the Indians clambered after him, Hays assembled some loose rocks into a rampart. He was determined—in the words of a contemporary—"to sell his life dearly, for he had scarcely a gleam of hope left to escape." Meaning he would kill as many as he could before they killed him.

The Indians charged his position, "howling around him all the while," by one retelling, "like so many wolves." Hays used his rifle and his pistol to pick them off, one by one. "He would come out of his retreat, fire on them, and drive them back, and then return to it again," a friend, Major John Caperton, wrote. This lasted for three hours, maybe four. "He had driven them back several times in this way," Caperton said, "until about a hundred of them had collected at the base of the rock, and surrounded it on all sides." Hays now believed he would surely be overtaken. "Just then, however . . . his men appeared in sight, having heard the firing and the yelling of the Indians," Caperton wrote. "They fought their way through [the Comanches] and compelled them to fall back, and thus rescued their commander."

His courageous combat and narrow escape cemented Hays's status, even among the enemy. "The Indians who had believed for a long time that he bore a charmed life," one admirer claimed, "were then more than ever convinced of the fact."

This heroic yarn has been related many times by Hays's numerous biographers and assorted Ranger historians, beginning with the publication of a book in 1847. His one-man stand eventually entered the realm of official history and celebration. In 1936 the State of Texas commemorated the encounter with a granite marker that still stands. Its engraved legend relates the story in brief: "Hays, while surrounded by Comanche Indians who cut him off from his ranging company, repulsed the whole band and inflicted upon them such heavy losses that they fled."

However, no actual evidence, from agency records to contemporary diaries, documents that the standoff ever took place. If Hays told anyone about it at the time, those accounts have vanished. The newspapers of the day said nothing of it. Independent corroboration does not appear to exist.

In addition, the details ring false. Enchanted Rock is a peak of gentle slope, and its summit can be easily reached from many directions. The dome became a state park in 1978; preschoolers and grandmothers walk to the top with moderate effort. It strains credulity to envision Comanches allowing themselves to be shot to pieces by scaling only one path. That dozens of these wily and experienced warriors would attack only a few at a time, letting their prey fire and reload for hours, seems absurd. So does the notion that Hays could, with only a few rocks, hastily assemble an impregnable fortress. Finally, the many accounts of this skirmish fail to explain how twenty Rangers managed to disperse five times their number of armed and ready Comanches—without suffering a single casualty—to rescue their captain.

The Enchanted Rock narrative may well belong in the catalog of Wild West fables alongside Pecos Bill using a rattlesnake for a lariat. But it stars a gun-toting, dead-aim superman who, against overwhelming odds and everyday logic, used backbone and grit to fashion a thunderous, epic, and righteous victory. It may therefore be the perfect Texas Rangers story.

Despite the unreliability of some accounts, there is no doubt that many of Hays's contemporaries looked upon him with awe. A European nobleman, Prince Carl of Solms-Braunfels, had come to Central Texas in 1844 with plans to establish a

German colony. The prince regarded much of the new republic with a cultured skeptic's eye. He lamented its searing summer heat, stinging insects, and poor food, with extra scorn directed toward its dependence on slavery to bring in the cotton crop. Americans in Texas loved money more than anything, the prince said, and were "self-opinionated and boastful, unpleasing in their social dealings, and very dirty in their manners and habits." His time as an Austrian military officer left him with little respect for the haphazard Texas militia. "A more undisciplined soldier cannot be found than . . . a bunch of American volunteers, nor are crueler deeds than theirs imaginable," he said. "Farmers as well as townfolk recall with horror the cruelty of the volunteers . . . with friend and foe alike."

Yet of Hays's Rangers, Prince Carl offered only praise. "Whenever this troop of forty men fought, it always came out victorious," he wrote. "They displayed great bravery, and their leader . . . was in his day known as the greatest Indian fighter." By working as a surveyor and patrolling as a Ranger, the prince said, Hays had gained an intimate knowledge of the region. When Prince Carl went to Hays with questions of topography, the Ranger would unroll a large map on his floor and proceed to point out its errors. "I assumed the course of the rivers and the boundaries were correct," the prince said. "But [Hays] took a pencil and made insertions that greatly differed from the original."

Hays's insistence on fielding well-trained companies set them apart from the normal run of Rangers. Already competent horsemen, his men honed their riding skills to match those of the masterly Comanches. Ranger Jim Nichols recalled the regimen in his journal: "After practisng for three or four months we became so purfect that we would run our horses half or full speede and pick up a hat, a coat, a blanket, or rope, or even a silver dollar, stand up in the saddle, throw ourselves on the side of our horses with only a foot and a hand to be seen, and shoot our pistols under our horses neck." They also practiced shooting for weeks. Two posts "about the size of a common man" were stationed forty yards apart. "We would run our horses full speed and discharge our rifles at the first post," Nichols recalled, then "draw our pistles and fire at the second."

The drills made Hays's Rangers into expert marksmen. "At first thare was some wild shooting," Nichols said, "but we had not practiced two months until thare was not many men that would not put his balls in the center of the posts." Hays urged his men to keep training, Nichols said, telling them "it beat the Indians at their own game."

These exercises, along with Hays's weeding out men not up to his standards, may have made them the best group of riders and shooters the Rangers had ever assembled.

"The men are all well-armed, and are probably the most happy, jovial and hearty set of men in all Texas," the *Telegraph and Texas Register* said. "They have several full-blooded racehorses, remarkable for their fleetness, and with them they can attack, pursue or escape from Indian or Mexican enemies at their pleasure."

Sometimes dividing themselves into two or three squads of about ten men each, the Rangers traveled light on their patrols, with no mule trains hauling supplies. Each man carried his own provisions in satchels that held salt, parched corn, and tobacco. They lived on game they killed and often rode at night, making their way by stars and moonlight. When they did stop to rest, one Ranger recalled, it was "in the most secluded situation we could discover." If they thought Indians were near, they made cold camps, without fires that might give away their whereabouts.

Common afflictions of the trail received treatment from the saddlebag and the ground. Should a snake bite one of them, the others cut deep incisions into the fang marks and packed them with salt. For infections and fever they applied mud or prickly pear poultices. Drinking bad water from stagnant pools caused diarrhea. The Rangers countered it with tea brewed from snakeroot weed or the bark of a cottonwood tree. And for men who spent hours on horseback, hemorrhoids presented an occupational hazard. A suppository of salt and applications of buffalo tallow brought relief.

Hays seemed to enjoy this Spartan life. He possessed an "iron constitution," wrote J. W. Wilbarger: "I have frequently seen him sitting by his camp fire at night in some exposed locality, when the rain was falling in torrents, or a cold norther with sleet or snow was whistling about his ears." Wilbarger said the Ranger captain acted "as if he had been seated in some cosy room of a first class city hotel."

The most noteworthy encounter involving Hays, his Rangers, and the Comanches—and one that enjoys historical corroboration—took place on what had been a quiet afternoon. It was in many ways a routine convulsion of frontier violence, one that might have passed with little notice outside Austin, San Antonio, and isolated Anglo settlements scattered across the Texas Hill Country. But the

Battle of Walker's Creek, as it was later christened, changed the course of American history.

Texas president Sam Houston, who had been elected a second time, was pursuing peace treaties with some of the tribes, but the largest band of Comanches had not agreed to anything. Their raids continued, so in early June 1844, Hays and fifteen Rangers patrolled north of San Antonio. They crisscrossed the rocky, scrub-patch land between the Pedernales and Llano Rivers, in the heart of Comanche country. Yet they had found no Indians for days and prepared to return to their home base.

One of Hays's newer Rangers was a singular private, Samuel Hamilton Walker. He was born in Maryland in 1817, and at nineteen he joined the army to fight the Seminoles in Florida. Among the grizzled men of the battlefield, Walker seemed almost delicate in appearance. He was clean-shaven and thin with patrician features, and his presence failed to fill a room. One historian described him as "unassuming to the point of girlish modesty." Neither tobacco nor liquor held any attraction for him; war was his drug. Walker pronounced himself "naturally fond of military glory" with a "love of chivalric immortal fame."

An unhappy stint in railroad construction provided neither glory nor fame, so Walker traveled to Texas. By 1844 he had joined Hays's Rangers, and with them he found the excitement he sought. In one engagement, according to a Ranger's account, Walker faced off with an Indian who was wanted for arrest. The Ranger's description: "Several shots at close quarters were interchanged, the Indian's horse was killed, Walker's spirited mustang was wounded, became unmanageable and threw him, and as he was rising from his fall he was shot by the Indian with an arrow through the shoulder, then fired . . . his pistol and dispatched his troublesome antagonist."

Now, on this June afternoon, Walker, Hays, and the rest of the Ranger company rode their horses across low, rolling hills of cedar and live oak, and through creeks running shallow over limestone beds. The early summer sun had parched the grass and turned the men's skin a leathery brown. The Rangers wore wide-brimmed hats and carried pistols and knives on their belts. As always, they ate what they could find. When two of Hays's men climbed a tree to retrieve honey from a beehive, a rear guard of Rangers spotted a party of mounted Comanches headed their way. "I could have no doubt but their intentions were hostile," Hays later said.

Hays told his men to saddle up and prepare for another fight. He did so with some confidence, for they held a decided—if untried—advantage in firepower: the Paterson Colt five-shot revolver.

Samuel Colt was not the first to conceive of a revolving pistol, but he was the first to deliver a workable one.

Colt was born near Hartford, Connecticut, in 1814. From an early age he loved to tinker with gunpowder and electricity. He was only sixteen when one of his fireworks experiments set a building ablaze at the school he was attending, Amherst Academy. This caused authorities to expel young Colt. His father, a textile manufacturer, put the wayward wunderkind on a sailing ship bound for London and Calcutta. While on board, Colt carved a rudimentary wooden prototype of a firearm with a rotating cylinder. From this vision arose a transformation. No longer would single-shot firearms prevail as battlefield standard. With the Colt, a combatant would be able to fire multiple balls without reloading.

Working with experienced gunsmiths and using his "Dr. Coult" proceeds as seed capital, he built a prototype. In 1836, at age twenty-two, Colt patented his revolving chamber pistol in the United States. He began that same year to manufacture the gun at a factory in Paterson, New Jersey. Problems plagued the early versions. They had been "got up in a hurry," Colt admitted, and were "very imperfect." The first prototype exploded on discharge. Despite subsequent improvements, the gun sometimes caught fire when the trigger was pulled. And it tended to go off accidentally if bumped or dropped.

Colt personally pursued government and military contracts but found almost no customers for the new weapon. The guns performed poorly in army tests, and at more than $25 apiece, the weapons were expensive. A national financial panic compounded by disputes among Colt's investors—most of them family members who had lost money—made matters worse. The factory closed in 1842, leaving Colt broke. "I hardly knew where the dinner of tomorrow would come from," he recalled. He turned his attention to other inventions, such as a bank of underwater explosives he called "Colt's Submarine Battery," to be used for harbor defense against large warships.

An unexpected customer helped put Colt back in the business of pistols. For reasons never fully explained, the ill-fated Texas Navy had ordered 180 of the new Colts in 1839. It represented an odd purchase for a force that was, on the whole, poorly funded and miserably equipped. The Texas Republic's seamen had fought heroically in several encounters with Mexican warships, but the navy faced continual hardships.

Drunken sailors aboard one of its schooners, the *San Antonio*, mutinied in 1842. They shot the duty officer—with a Colt revolver—and hacked him to death with their cutlasses. Three of the rebellious sailors received a hundred lashes each, while four were hanged from the yardarm of the Texas schooner *Austin*. Seven months after the mutiny, however, the *San Antonio* disappeared in a storm off the coast of Mexico. Another schooner, the *Zavala*, was in such poor repair that the crew ran it aground in Galveston to prevent it from sinking. Inspectors discovered that the ship's hull was, according to one report, "considerably worm-eaten."

In 1843, Texas president Sam Houston climaxed a dispute with the navy's commander—a "bloated maggot," in Houston's description—by declaring Texas Navy sailors to be, in essence, pirates. The Texas Congress disbanded the navy at his urging. As a result, sailors never used the Colts for much beyond their insurrection. In a transfer whose details are lost to history, some of the guns wound up with Hays's company of Rangers.

Before Colt, the standard weapons of the field were a single-shot handgun, which an unreliable weapon good only at close range, and a muzzle-loaded flintlock long rifle. Generally known as Kentucky rifles, they were sturdy, deadly, and accurate to two hundred yards or more. They might have been perfect for hunting game, but they proved disastrous when fighting Indians on horseback. Preparing to fire one—pouring a charge, ramrodding a ball down the barrel, placing powder in the pan—could take as much as half a minute. In that time a warrior could send a dozen arrows flying. Comanches had learned on the battlefield to send out a few braves to draw fire, then attack en masse as the Texans were reloading.

The Paterson Colt handgun used a recent innovation, the percussion cap, which was a far more reliable system than the old flintlock for igniting powder. And—the real departure—it employed a revolving cylinder with five rounds. But it came with some drawbacks. It was fragile, and fired a much smaller ball than long rifles. It was heavier than conventional pistols; some called it a "hand cannon." Accuracy was suspect, with a useful range of about fifty yards. Reloading required replacement of the entire cylinder, a difficult operation in the smoke and fury of combat. Still, the weapon had two enormous advantages: it could be used from the saddle, and it could be fired five times in fairly rapid succession.

Each Ranger carried two of the guns, which meant up to ten shots in perhaps forty seconds.

Hays's Rangers readied their weapons as a few Comanches moved within sight. The Indians wore bright war paint and carried lances and shields. They shouted insults in Spanish, and Hays shouted some back. The Comanches disappeared into some woods, which Hays recognized as an old ruse—an attempt to draw Rangers into an ambush. When that failed, the Comanches gathered on horseback on the crest of a rocky hill. Hays ordered his men to circle the base of the hill and charge the Indians' flank.

Ranger diarist Rufe Perry once again found himself in the heart of the action. He described what happened next: "Aboute Sixty of the read devels come oute of the brush." Close, furious fighting erupted, with the Rangers in a tight circle and the mounted, howling Indians darting all around them. Flying arrows hit three Rangers. One of the Comanches pinned Walker to the ground with a lance, but the Rangers fired their Paterson Colts and Indians fell. Perry again: "Thay woold charg three in a line the first expecting to bee Shot while the other too used thair lances but when wee cept on Shooting thay commenced runing."

As the Comanches fled, the Rangers rode after them, and a moving two-mile fight ended only when Hays's men ran low on firepower. One Ranger had a single shot left. Hays ordered him to kill the Comanche chief who was urging his braves to mount one more assault. The Ranger fired. "At a distance of 30 steps the ball did its office," a newspaper correspondent wrote. "Madly dashing a few yards, the gallant Indian fell to rise no more, and in wild affright at the loss of their leader, the others scattered in every direction in the brushwood." The battle was over, with more than twenty Comanches killed. One Ranger was dead.

"We were right glad they fled," Hays told San Antonio resident Mary Maverick a few days later, "for we were nearly used up with the fatigue of a long day's march . . . and we were almost out of ammunition." The Ranger captain said the Comanches had, as usual, battled with ferocity. "The Indians made a magnificent fight under the circumstances," he said. "They seemed to be a band of selected braves in full war-paint." The braves probably planned to raid settlements, Hays said, "and great would have been the mischief done by such a number of savages."

Given the superior numbers of the Comanches, the Colt revolvers probably saved the Rangers from slaughter. "I cannot recommend these arms too highly,"

Hays wrote in his report of the battle. "Had it not been for them, I doubt what the consequences would have been."

Sam Walker was badly wounded by the Comanche lance but recovered. In his honor, Hays named the stream along which the engagement occurred Walker's Creek. Two years after the battle, Walker penned a thank-you note of sorts to Colt. "Up to this time these daring Indians had always supposed themselves superior to us, man to man, on horse," Walker wrote. "Without your Pistols we would not have had the confidence to have undertaken such daring adventures." The Rangers now believed the Colts would give them a distinct edge on the battlefield. "Their confidence in them is unbounded," Walker said, "so much so that they are willing to engage four times their number."

More engagements followed, and the repeaters cut the Comanches down as they had done at Walker's Creek. "Several other Skirmishes have been equally satisfactory, and I can safely say that you deserve a large share of the credit for our success," Walker told Colt. "With improvements I think [the revolver] can be rendered the most perfect weapon in the World for light mounted troops[,] which is the only efficient troops that can be placed upon our extensive Frontier to keep the various warlike tribes of Indians & marauding Mexicans in subjection."

In Texas, the balance had now shifted, though no one quite understood the broad portent at the time. Much more blood had yet to flow from both sides, but the end was in place. The Colt revolver—along with the Rangers—would be instrumental in the ultimate destruction of the Comanches.

Many of the other epic Indian wars of the American West were decades away. Colorado's Sand Creek massacre, in which volunteer cavalrymen slaughtered more than a hundred Cheyennes and Arapahos—most of them women, children, and old men—took place in 1864. The Sioux annihilation of George Armstrong Custer and his men at Little Bighorn would not occur until 1876.

The battles between Rangers and Comanches of the 1840s unfolded as prologue. Walker Creek served as a proving ground for the Colt repeating pistol. In further iterations and campaigns, the Colt came to be called "the gun that won the West." It started in Texas with the Rangers.

William "Big-Foot" Wallace was a towering Ranger who fought hard and told his tales well. Before killing Mexicans, he claimed, he first gave them a running start.

Chapter 5

"AN INSOLENT AND SAVAGE RACE"

Rage, Revenge, Statehood, and War

Half the Nation are thieves in Prison and the other half are thieves un-caught.

—A TEXAN'S VIEW OF MEXICO, 1844

During those difficult days of the early 1840s, the citizens of the Republic of Texas might have struggled to say which hostile force posed a bigger threat—Indians or Mexicans. They feared the Comanches, but they loathed the Mexicans. As always, there were exceptions. But a great many Anglo Texans believed the natives of rural Mexico—and the Tejanos, those of the bloodline who lived in South Texas—to be indolent and filthy imbeciles. They belonged to a class, a white Methodist minister wrote, "inferior to common nigers [*sic*]."

Mixed Spanish and Indian ancestries made them "mongrels." Dark skin and dark hair earned the label "greasers." (That was for males. Females were called "greaser women.") It was axiomatic that they could never be trusted. A Mexican "will feed you on his best, 'senor' you, and 'muchas gracias' you, and bow to you like a French dancing-master, and wind it all up by slipping a knife under your left shoulder blade," said Ranger captain William "Big-Foot" Wallace. "And that's one reason I hate them so."

The war the two sides had fought in 1836, resulting in Texas's independence, no doubt deepened this racial animosity. And two monumental encounters during that conflict set Texans' hatred afire. There had been the Alamo, of course. On top of that, General Santa Anna had ordered the massacre of several hundred prisoners at Goliad.

Since then, Anglo Texans believed, additional Mexican atrocities demanded payback. One of them was the slaughter of defeated fighters who had attempted to surrender. Another was a mass execution by lottery. And a third was the imprisonment of Texans who were chained, beaten, starved, and driven into forced labor.

These more recent entries in the catalog of outrages did not rise to the level of the Alamo or Goliad. Strictly on their own terms—and judged by traditional military standards—they constituted minor clashes and backyard tragedies. The death tolls stayed relatively low, and no large or vital territory changed hands for more than a few days. But their repercussions were momentous. These events played a key role in bringing Texas into the Union, and they served as crucial preludes to the war between Mexico and the United States. Without them, it could be argued, America would look nothing like it does now.

The six-year-old Texas Republic faced many problems and perils. Its government remained broke and barely functional. Mexico refused to recognize Texas's independence and threatened to retake the land it considered its own. But Mexico was itself roiled by financial woes and political instability and did not have the military wherewithal to mount a full-scale takeover. General Santa Anna, who had ascended to the presidency, ordered his generals instead to wage a campaign of harassment in Texas.

The Mexican army mounted a couple of small invasions followed by swift retreats. These initial incursions caused little damage, other than rattling Texans' fragile sense of security. But in the late summer of 1842, General Adrián Woll crossed the river with fifteen hundred infantry and cavalry. A French soldier of fortune, Woll had served in Napoleon's army and fled to Mexico after the emperor's fall. Now, on a foggy September morning, he and his troops moved into San Antonio. This time the Mexicans took the Alamo simply by showing up.

In response, about two hundred Texan volunteers and Rangers, under the command of Old Paint Caldwell, gathered at Salado Creek, northeast of San

Antonio. Though badly outnumbered, Caldwell and Jack Hays hoped to win by outsmarting Woll. One idea: lure some of the Mexican soldiers into an open prairie and shoot them down. It worked even better than expected.

Early on a Sunday morning, Hays and thirty-eight others rode the six miles to San Antonio on the best horses they could find. The Reverend Z. N. Morrell, a Baptist minister known as Wildcat, went with them, observing along the way that he was more accustomed to sermons than combat at this hour of the Sabbath. While most of the party paused a mile from town, Hays—"our intrepid leader," Morrell said, "his black eyes flashing decision of character"—took seven men to the main plaza.

"They went down close to the Alamo," Morrell said, where they shouted insults at the Mexican soldiers. Hays and his crew hoped this ploy would cause perhaps fifty cavalrymen to pour from behind the walls of the Alamo and chase them, and be led into a trap. "Contrary to this expectation," Morrell said, "four or five hundred cavalry turned out in hot pursuit. Hays soon approached with the command, 'Mount!' We moved off briskly through the timber."

As the Texans envisioned, the Mexicans chased them to Salado Creek. There the rest of the Rangers and volunteers had hidden themselves in thick woods, protected by an eight-foot creek bank. They "skirmished with the enemy at long range," Morrell said, "killing a number of Mexicans." Woll's army fired muskets and cannons at them, wounding only three. More Mexicans arrived, bringing the force to about one thousand. The "motley mongrels," as one Texan called them, mounted a full charge over open ground as their band played marching songs. "The Mexicans now advanced upon us," Morrell recalled, "under a splendid puff of music, the ornaments, guns, spears and swords glistening in plain view."

The Texans waited until their gaudy opponents were within thirty feet and opened fire. One volunteer likened the results of the fusillade to a slaughter of cattle: "Here, there and everywhere we see the wretches tumble down like beeves."

They kept coming, and the Texans kept firing as the piles of bodies began to impede the Mexicans' charge. "Thare was so many of them kild," Ranger Jim Nichols wrote, "that the dead and wounded obstructed their way." This continued for most of the afternoon, until Woll's bloodied infantry could take no more. Their bugle sounded retreat, and the Mexican army turned and fled.

Only one Texan had been killed and twelve wounded. "The Mexican army had scedadled and left us masters [of the] situation," Nichols explained. It would have been a glorious triumph but for what happened next.

Captain Nicholas Dawson and more than fifty Texan volunteers had ridden from LaGrange to help in the fight against Woll. However, they arrived late and ran headlong into the retreating Mexicans. Dawson wanted to withdraw, but his officers insisted they stand their ground. They had confidence, one Texan said, that "they could whip 200 Mexicans under any circumstances." From a mesquite grove they took shots at Woll's forces. At one point Dawson—a veteran of the Battle of San Jacinto—gunned down a Mexican officer, turned to his men, and said with a smile, "That is the way I used to do."

The smile fell away as Woll's soldiers regrouped and fired their cannons with devastating effect. This "made an awful havoc among our men," one of the Texans said, as "death in every shape stalked through our thinned ranks." Dawson was shot in the hip. Seeing his men outgunned and surrounded, he tied a white blanket to his rifle and waved it as he limped toward the Mexicans. This did not even slow the fighting, much less stop it. "The enemy showed no respect but continued their murderous and galling fire," said Henry G. Woods, a member of Dawson's company. Dawson delivered his dying words to his men: "Sell your lives as dearly as possible. Let victory be purchased with blood."

Woods, who was once a Ranger, had seen his father and brother shot down in the battle already. He had been wounded in the shoulder. Now he watched as a wave of Mexican infantrymen closed for the kill. "Near sundown the enemy charged," he said. "Then began the work of death in its most horrible forms." The Mexicans overran the Texans' position, and savage hand-to-hand combat ensued. The Texans used their Bowie knives and swung their rifle butts. The Mexicans hacked and slashed with their swords. Woods said the wounded who lay on the ground "were massacred like brutes" by the Mexicans.

He was able to escape by killing a Mexican and taking his horse. One other Texan managed to slip away as well. But thirty-five of Dawson's men were killed and fifteen taken prisoner. When the guns were finally silent, General Woll delivered a rousing congratulatory speech to his soldiers, who cheered loudly and resumed their retreat.

The next morning, four men from Hays's company rode to the scene of Dawson's defeat and, in the stillness, found the carnage. Even Rufe Perry, no stranger to gory battles, was sickened. "That was the moast horrowble Sight I ever saw," he wrote.

The Reverend Morrell walked among mutilated corpses. "Thirty-five dead bodies of friends lay scattered and terribly mangled among the little clusters of bushes on the broad prairie," he recalled. "The place was so horrible that two of the men with me rode away."

Morrell took a pencil from his pocket and went from body to body, writing the names of the dead on a piece of paper. His mission now was to take the names back to his town of LaGrange, where he would inform and comfort the bereaved. "I recognized the body of nearly every one. Here were twelve men, heads of families, their wives widows, and their children orphans; and here, too, lay the dead bodies of promising sons of my neighbors. . . . One or two of my neighbors' sons were so badly mangled that I could not recognize them at all."

General Woll gathered his own dead, abandoned San Antonio, and escorted what was left of his army back to Mexico. His expedition had been a waste of money and lives, with its only real effect the acceleration of Texans' rage.

The disastrous defeat of Dawson's company could have been avoided via the Texans' withdrawal. But the Anglo citizenry did not see it as a tactical blunder. It had now become—as Ranger John H. Jenkins said—"one of the most cruel and murderous massacres in all the annals of history." With the desire for revenge burning white hot, Texans clamored for a retaliatory strike across the Rio Grande.

President Sam Houston knew the government couldn't raise the money or the military for such an effort. Strong agreement came from Joseph Eve, the U.S. chargé d'affaires to Texas. The Lone Star republic, he wrote, was "a young nation just emerging from its cradle with a population of less than 100,000 souls without a dollar in its Treasury, not a regular soldier belonging to it, without credit sufficient to borrow a dollar at home or abroad, constantly at war with numerous tribes of canibal [sic] Indians, and at the same time making offensive war upon a nation containing a population of eight millions, strange as it may seem."

At the same time, Houston recognized he could not fight the people's passion. He hit upon a brilliant strategy: incompetence at the top. Houston announced his decision from the little town of Washington, later known as Washington-on-the-Brazos, which served as the capital-in-exile of the republic. It was a fitting symbol for the struggling nation. Houston had moved the seat of government there because Austin, only seventy-five miles from San Antonio, stood a good chance of being overtaken by Mexican forces. In this provisional capital, the Texas Senate met on the second floor of a small general store. The House convened above a saloon run by Basil Hatfield, a riverboat captain. The president's office was a one-room cabin on Ferry Street. From there, Houston named General Alexander Somervell to lead the campaign into Mexico.

To the men he would command, the short and stubby Somervell seemed an odd and ill-informed choice. He was a former secretary of war for the republic who had compiled a less than distinguished record as a military leader. Men serving under him complained, or would come to complain, that he was plodding, weak-willed, and unsupportive of the troops—"no more fit to command an army of men," one soldier wrote, "than a ten year old boy." Another said his particular company "loathed General Somervell from their hearts." Still another claimed the general had a "weak heart, and old woman's Soul."

Somervell therefore emerged as the perfect fit for Houston's scheme: possessing the credentials to launch the mission, yet sufficiently inept to ensure that it would not succeed. One of his soldiers scoffed that he was "a man designed by Houston to ruin the expedition and well calculated in every respect for that purpose." It's doubtful Houston could have imagined, however, how catastrophically it would fail. Nor could he have foreseen the deep and lasting bitterness this failure would engender.

Volunteers for the invasion began to gather near San Antonio in early October 1842, only days after the Dawson massacre and Woll's retreat. Rangers Jack Hays, Ben McCulloch, and Sam Walker joined the gathering. A religious warrior and Ranger captain named Samuel Bogart also rode in, bringing his company of sixty men with him.

At forty-five, Bogart was older than most Rangers. He had fought with the U.S. Army at the Battle of New Orleans in 1815, after which he was court-martialed for stealing and discharged for "inability." He moved to Missouri. There he served as a militia captain in the blood-soaked "Mormon War" of 1838, in which members of the faith were expelled from the state. Bogart and his men arrested Mormons, burned their houses, and shot their livestock. His "zeal in the cause of oppression and injustice was unequaled," Mormon founder Joseph Smith said. "[His] delight has been to rob, murder, and spread devastation among the Saints." Riding his newfound fame, Bogart was elected to a county judgeship in Missouri. But during a postelection argument, he gunned down a nephew of his opponent. Like many before him, Bogart sought refuge from prosecution in Texas. Within a few years he became a Ranger captain.

Some of the volunteers in San Antonio had distinguished pasts and promising futures. There were former cabinet members and congressmen among them. General Somervell's aide-de-camp, Peter H. Bell, would be elected the third governor of Texas before the decade was done. Even Bogart would fashion a successful political career in Texas.

But others had slipped in from the criminal shadows and joined the force for the chance to steal with official approval. "Dare-devils they were all, and afraid of nothing under the sun (except a due-bill or a bailiff)," said Big-Foot Wallace, who was with the volunteers. "A motley, mixed-up crowd we were . . . broken-down politicians from the 'old States,' that somehow had got on the wrong side of the fence, and been left out in the cold; renegades and refugees from justice, that had 'left their country for their country's good,' and adventurers of all sorts, ready for anything or any enterprise that afforded a reasonable prospect of excitement and plunder."

The situation in San Antonio began to unravel right away. The old mission town of limestone buildings and adobe houses had already been ravaged by years of fighting and occupation. Harvey Adams, a member of Captain Bogart's company, found a corral behind the Alamo "where the insatiate Mexicans had burnt the bodies of their slaughtered victims, after subjecting them to mutilation and satanic indignity." The ground was still black, Adams said, covered with "ashes, charcoal and remnants of bones." Most of the Anglos had evacuated San Antonio after the Woll invasion, leaving about fifteen hundred Tejanos.

General Somervell was late in taking command—he had paused en route for an extended session of drinking and dancing—which left volunteers to scavenge for food and sleep unsheltered in the cold rain. "I stood by the fire all night," one volunteer said, "and got as wet as a drowned rat." A few picked pecans along the river, sold them in town, and bought provisions with the proceeds. Others simply stole the supplies they needed. Two of them broke into the house of the aged Mexican widow of Deaf Smith, a hero of the Texas Revolution and a Ranger, and made off with three blankets.

More enterprising thieves looted the sacramental artwork of local churches. Some roved the countryside looking for cattle to rustle from Tejano settlements. Once there, Harvey Adams said, "in order to gratify their beastly lusts [they] compelled the women and girls to yield to their hellish desires, which their victims did under fear of punishment and death."

The lack of food, shelter, and discipline took an early toll. About five hundred of the twelve hundred men who had originally assembled left in disgust, disillusionment, or impatience.

The Southwest Army of Operations, as it came to be called, finally departed for the border—a march of more than 150 miles—in late November 1842. "There

were 700 men, 200 pack mules and 300 beeves for the use of the troops," a Ranger
wrote. The procession also included several preachers for those in need of spiri-
tual sustenance.

As the long line of mounted adventurers, statesmen, rapists, and misfits
made its way south into brush country, Ranger captains Hays and Bogart jock-
eyed for status. President Houston had instructed Somervell to "rely upon the
gallant Hays and his companions," so the general appointed him to act as lead
scout. That meant Hays and his men rode well in advance of the main body of
volunteers, which Bogart resented. He also worried that he and his men would
not be able to share equally in any captured spoils. Bogart and his officers visited
Hays's camp one night to express their displeasure, and came close to fisticuffs—
if not a gunfight. "A number of Captain Hays' men crowded around," recalled
Sterling Hendricks, one of Bogart's officers. They "interrupted the course of conversation, and repeatedly and rudely insulted Captain Bogart."

The rain of insults left Bogart smarting the next day. He had, Hendricks
explained, "been made subject to every rude assault that a ruffian set could offer."
As the army resumed its march, Bogart mounted his horse and, with his company, charged ahead of Hays and his men. Hays's company struggled to retake
the lead. "It was indeed a beautiful and inspiring sight to see some sixty men on
either side," Hendricks said, "all noble, fine looking fellows, well mounted and
thus marshaled, trying to outstrip each other for the highest post of honor." On
the wide prairie, he said, they looked, "like two gloomy clouds . . . frowning
darkly at each other."

They stayed this way for about four miles, until Somervell overtook them.
Unlike Hendricks, the general did not appreciate the poetry and grandeur of the
race. He "rode up besmeared with sweat and almost foaming with rage," Hendricks said. Somervell ordered Bogart to back off his challenge to Hays's primacy. The general vowed to court-martial Bogart, though he didn't follow
through on the threat.

As the volunteers rode on, the weather turned miserable, with bitter north
winds and incessant cold rain. Soon they marched unwittingly into a deep bog.
"The mud was in many instances belly deep to our horses," Hendricks recalled.
A number of horses that sank into the muck could go no farther, Adams said, so
the men shot them and "left . . . their bones to bleach in that desolate country."

The hardships mounted from there. Some of the volunteers cooked and ate
a plant that reminded them of a turnip. Before long, a member of the expedition
said, they were "punished by a few hours of torturing sickness, some even with

thoughts of death." The rain kept falling. A thunderstorm caused horses and mules to stampede.

On December 3, the army crossed the Nueces River and moved into the "profound and cheerless desolation," as one soldier called it, stretching toward Mexico. It took five hard days to reach the forsaken border town of Laredo.

Perched along the Rio Grande on a treeless plain that was sun-blasted in summer and windswept in winter, Laredo had long been poor and squalid. Conditions had only worsened in recent years. Floods had wiped out some of the primitive homes, followed by drought that shriveled the thin crops. Hunger, disease, and Indian attacks had cut the population to fewer than two thousand. A Mexican official who visited a few years earlier judged it to be an impoverished Gomorrah. Its residents were "all care-free people who are fond of dancing and little inclined to work," he wrote. He found the women, however, to be quite lovely with "rather loose ideas of morality, which cause the greater part of them to have shameful relations openly."

Though Laredo was on the Texas side of the river, most if not all of its inhabitants considered themselves citizens of Mexico. The approaching Texans believed that some eighty Mexican soldiers were garrisoned there, so this would be their first battle. But the Mexican soldiers had departed, as had most of the other men. The Texans—expecting to participate in the glorious "Siege of Laredo"—found mostly women, children, and a few old men waiting for them. Somervell's army took the town not to the sound of gunfire but the barking of stray dogs. The left-behind residents greeted the conquerors with cake.

After the Texas flag was raised over the main plaza, the general ordered his army to camp a few miles out of town. As many as two hundred of Somervell's men decided to add pillaging to Laredo's dismal mix. They looted stores and homes. They broke down doors and carried away food, baby clothes, and women's underwear. They stole cows and mules. They put a rope around the neck of the town's *alcalde* and threatened to hang him if he didn't lead them to some hidden silver. At the city jail, they chased away the guards and demanded that the twenty prisoners give three cheers for Texas. "This," a newspaper reported, the inmates "did with high glee." The prisoners were set free. That night the rampaging volunteers got drunk on mescal they had seized.

A mortified Somervell ordered his men to return some of the stolen goods, and they were instructed to stack the loot in one spot. "The plunder when deposited," a soldier observed, "made a pile the size of good large house." Said another: "It was a mountain of no inconsiderable size. . . . There were saddle blankets,

soap, candles, flour, sugar . . . books, baby clothing, bedding, pillows and cush-
ions nicely embroidered . . . ad infinitum." This chastisement angered the thieves,
who believed they had merely taken the spoils of war. A great many of them quit
the force on the spot.

Somervell's army had now dwindled to about five hundred, yet he decided
to push into Mexico. He crossed the Rio Grande fifty miles south of Laredo. Rain
began falling again, drenching the volunteers in their ragged clothes. They drew
near to Guerrero, another dirt-poor village of small adobe houses and wood
shacks.

Hays, Bogart, and about fifty of their men rode into town. At the main plaza
they met the *alcalde* and delivered Somervell's demand: the village must furnish
them with a hundred fresh horses or pay the equivalent of $5,000 in Mexican
money. If neither was forthcoming, they said, Somervell's army would sack the
place. The Rangers waited for two hours while the *alcalde* scavenged for cash.
The women of Guerrero brought them tortillas and breadsticks for lunch, Adams
said, as the men of the village "looked daggers at us." Finally the *alcalde* stacked
the currency he had collected on a marble table in the front room of his house
and invited some of the Rangers in. The tribute totaled only $381, so the Rangers
placed him under arrest.

When Somervell heard the news, by one account, he flew into a rage. He did
not, however, launch the promised attack on the village. Instead, he released the
alcalde and abruptly ordered his troops to return to Texas. The general may have
concluded at last that he couldn't control his men well enough to continue. He
also may have been acting upon reports of a large Mexican force advancing toward Guerrero.

Somervell proved as ineffective at aborting the great invasion as he had been
at starting it. His decision "caused almost a mutiny in camp," Adams said. "The
men became perfectly wild and called the general a perfect old Grannie." They
also began to suspect they had been snookered, that Somervell "had secret orders
from [President] Houston to drag the men round till they would be glad to get
home again."

About two hundred of the volunteers acceded to the call for withdrawal.
Hays and McCulloch stayed to do some scouting, then departed as well. But
about three hundred Texans, Sam Walker among them, decided to continue the
incursion under the command of Colonel William S. Fisher. A former secretary
of war for the republic, Fisher was intelligent, articulate, and, in the words of a
battlefield contemporary, "one of the tallest men in the country." In addition, he

had long harbored ambitions—with many other Texans—to seize control of northern Mexico. Prior efforts had collapsed. This ragtag army gave him another chance.

They approached Mier, a small town of goats and adobe on the Mexican side of the Rio Grande, on Christmas afternoon, 1842. McCulloch had already scouted the region for the invaders, learned that hundreds of Mexican troops were in the vicinity, and returned to give warning. "You have had a trap laid for you," he was reported to have said. Fisher chose to ignore the advisory. The presence of the troops, Big-Foot Wallace said, only made the Texans more eager for a fight. Though outnumbered by more than three to one, they boasted that no Mexicans could beat them.

The Rangers and volunteers advanced as Mexicans fired their *escopetas*—loud, inaccurate muskets. "They are good for nothing," Wallace said, "except to make a noise." The Texans moved toward the town, forcing the Mexicans to retreat, and spent a fairly quiet night believing that victory lay at hand. The next morning the two sides fought street by street in a light rain. A Mexican attack from the rear pushed the undrilled Texans into chaos. Defections mounted as the Rangers and volunteers ran short on food, water, and ammunition. Fisher surrendered, and his men—with great reluctance and hesitation—threw down their arms.

The Texans were "bound hand and foot, and delivered over to the tender mercies of these pumpkin-colored Philistines," Wallace recalled. "Never shall I forget the humiliation of my feelings, when we were stripped of all our arms and equipments, and led off ignominiously by a numerous guard of swarthy, bandy-legged, contemptible 'greasers.'"

Now came the terrible consequence. The Texans expected the Mexicans to confine them as prisoners of war. Fisher said as much in a letter to Mexican officials, insisting his men be held under the "principles of civilized warfare." They were treated instead like common criminals. The Mexicans marched their captives deeper into the interior, parading the stumbling and hungry prisoners through small towns en route. The men of these villages were "cursing and stoning them as they moved through the streets," one historian—deeply sympathetic to Texans—wrote a few years later, "and the women [were] spitting on them with all the malice of she-wolves."

It got worse. In the tattered settlement of Salado, Sam Walker and others overpowered hapless guards and led a mass escape. But after days of wandering in the desert, a contemporary wrote, "the weak began to perish of hunger and thirst." The stronger ones soldiered on with cracked lips and swollen, blackened tongues. "Some became insane and rushed wildly about scratching into the earth for water." Others sliced open the veins of their horses and "sucked the blood . . . of the poor staggering beasts."

The Mexicans recaptured them. Once more, Santa Anna had a chance to punish Texans, and he took it, ordering the execution of all 176 of the surviving escapees. When Mexican general Francisco Mejía objected to mass murder, the decree was modified: every tenth man would be put to death.

Mexican soldiers filled an earthen pitcher with dried beans, seventeen of them black, and held a drawing at gunpoint. Each Texan took a bean from the jar; a black one marked that man for death. The lottery unfolded with eerie calm. One of the Texans, it was said, was a noted gambler from Austin. When his time to draw came he said, "Boys, this is the largest stake I ever played for." He reached in and withdrew his hand with a black bean between his thumb and forefinger. "Just my luck," he said with a smile.

The gambler and other unfortunates were culled from the pack of prisoners. "They were marched off in two squads, and shortly afterward repeated volleys of musketry were heard," Wallace said, "and we knew that their cares and trouble were forever ended in this world." Another Texan recalled it more directly: "Well, they just took them out and shot them—just mangled them, and stripped them and let them lay outside in the street there, like so many hogs."

The Mexicans dug a long ditch and dumped sixteen bodies into it. One Texan had been wounded—half his face shot away—and left for dead. He crept away in the night, before the burial, but was recaptured and killed. On orders from Santa Anna, the Mexicans also executed Ewen Cameron, who had been elected captain of the captives. "When the Mexican Government saw that he did not draw the 'Black bean,' it then had him taken out and shot like a *dog*," wrote one of the prisoners, Joseph D. McCutchan. "The murder of Cameron was an act which should have called fourth the vengance [sic] of the world on an insolent and savage race!"

Many of the surviving Texans were cast into the prison at Perote, a dank castle-fortress complete with a moat and a drawbridge. "I am now . . . in the confines of the most miserable prison upon earth," William S. Wilson wrote to his family in 1844. Mexican jailers forced the prisoners into hard labor, which included the hauling and disposal of bodily waste. Some prisoners were made to carry bags of sand on their backs while chained at the ankles. If they did not work, they were beaten. "We perform all this in a naked condition, not half fed, guarded by the most vile of human species," Wilson wrote. McCutchan told in his diary of rice "spoiled by a rat being cooked in it." He also described the heavy shackles that were never removed: "Locked up as usual. 8 men have about 30 pounds each of iron, and are in a dark dungeon called the Caliboose. [A] man who was so severely beaten on the 7th is in the hospital with double irons on him."

Dysentery and typhoid killed some of the men. A few escaped. In September 1844 Mexico released the remaining Texan prisoners, including Big-Foot Wallace.

The miseries of Perote now formed—along with the Dawson massacre and the black bean episode—a retributive holy trinity. Those who had lived through such atrocities, or their survivors, vowed that Mexico would pay for its base cruelties.

However, the narrative that depicted Mexicans as irredeemable sadists had some holes. The invading force of Texans did not carry the imprimatur of an official army engaged in what Colonel Fisher had called "honorable combat." To the extent that such status existed in the first place, it vanished when Somervell ordered the retreat from Mexico. Those who remained and continued the incursion were considered by Mexicans to be nothing more than a gang of rampaging freebooters. The treatment they received as prisoners, however punitive, was in many cases better than that of Mexican raiders caught on the other side of the border. Texans summarily executed those highwaymen.

Another: After General Santa Anna ordered the killing of Ewen Cameron, the captain of the prisoners, many Anglos eulogized him as a martyr. The State of Texas named Cameron County for him. But Cameron, a barely literate Scottish stonemason, had been one of Mustang Gray's "Men-Slayers," the gang that robbed, killed, and terrorized Tejano ranchers and farmers in the same territory that would bear his name. And like William Fisher, he had taken up arms against the central Mexican government in 1839 to establish the breakaway Republic of the Rio Grande, an effort that included the sacking of numerous Mexican towns. Cameron may have been a hero to Texans, but to many Mexicans he was a killer of innocents and a seditionist.

In addition, there's the story of John Christopher Columbus Hill. He was only fourteen when he joined the Mier expedition. As the climactic battle ended and the Texans were surrendering, Hill refused to lay his gun down. He had, it was said, killed at least twelve Mexicans. His audacity drew the attention of Mexican general Pedro Ampudia, who befriended him. Within a day or so, according to a newspaper account, "the small boy who fought so bravely" was "running about town as gay as a lark." Ampudia sent the boy by special military escort to Santa Anna. Either the president or the Mexican minister of war adopted him; accounts vary. Hill later attended the Colegio de Minería, took the name Juan Cristóbal Gil, and became a successful civil engineer in Mexico as well as a practicing physician.

Santa Anna also took mercy on at least one other prisoner. In 1836, after his defeat at San Jacinto, Santa Anna had been imprisoned in Texas. Despondent and in shackles, he attempted suicide with an overdose of laudanum. Dr. James Phelps pumped his stomach, saving Santa Anna's life. Now the president learned that Orlando Phelps, the son of James Phelps, was being held at Perote. Santa Anna ordered that he be released and given a room in the presidential palace.

These and other mitigating factors did not fade the Texan captives' passion. "Oh! that I, or that *Texas* could but for one day hold the avenging power of supernatural beings and that she might with one stroke hurl this debased Nation into the vortex of Oblivion," Perote prisoner Joseph McCutchan wrote. "*My blood boils* within me as if *heated by the demons* from the *infernal pitt of Hell!* Would to heaven! that I had power to avenge the sufferings of this band and the death of my fallen countrymen . . . Long—*long* should Mexico remember the name of her bloody butcherer."

On a cold, windy dawn in November 1844, the steamship *New York* came in sight of Galveston Island. McCutchan and seventy-five other former prisoners from Perote were on board. Many of them stood shivering on the deck, gazing upon Texas for the first time in almost two years. "You could see happiness in every face," McCutchan wrote in his diary. "*We would soon be on the soil of that country for which we suffered, many bled, and many died!*"

The *New York* docked at a Galveston wharf on November 10. On that same day, James K. Polk was well on his way to being elected the eleventh president of the United States. (The 1844 election was held on different days in different states.) Polk's victory and the prisoners' return seemed at the time to be largely unrelated. But they ultimately would join as vital components in the American rush to war with Mexico.

Few people came away from a handshake with new President Polk thinking they had encountered a giant of statesmanship. At forty-nine, he was the nation's youngest chief executive yet, but one whose youth projected more callowness than vigor. He was short, thin, and often sickly. An excruciating surgical procedure to remove urinary stones, performed when he was seventeen, had probably left him impotent. His fairly undistinguished personal history included time as a Tennessee country lawyer, a marginal politician, and an unapologetic slaveholder. A protégé of former president Andrew Jackson—Polk wore the sobriquet "Young Hickory"—he struck his detractors as narrow-minded, sanctimonious, suspicious, and perhaps a tad dim. They dismissed him as "Little Jimmy Polk of Duck River."

Polk, however, possessed determination and drive with a taste for action, and he believed himself to be a man of destiny. One modern historian called him a "smaller-than-life figure with larger-than-life ambitions." Little Jimmy harbored a grand and overarching goal: the extension of U.S. territory to the Pacific Coast. He wanted California, which was part of Mexico. To get California, he probably would have to go to war, and to do that, he required Texas.

For its part, Texas needed Polk and the United States. The republic had an empty treasury and non-existent army, and—as General Woll's 1842 incursion had shown—still faced the continuing threat of invasion from Mexico. Texas agreed to join the Union and became the twenty-eighth state in December 1845. Thus ended its relatively brief but never-to-be-forgotten reign as an independent nation.

The annexation process did not unfold smoothly, for many in the northern United States opposed the addition of another slave state. It also put the United States on a straight path to international conflict. "Annexation and war with Mexico are identical," wrote Henry Clay, Polk's Whig Party rival for the presidency. Mexico considered Texas's statehood a hostile act and viewed the seizure of the Nueces Strip, the territory between the Nueces River and the Rio Grande, as nothing short of theft. "Indelible is the stain that will forever darken the counterfeit virtues of the North American people," Mexican general Francisco Mejía said in an official proclamation. He called the annexation a "most degrading robbery."

Whether it was robbery or manifest destiny—the American doctrine of the era, which posited that expansion had been ordained by providence—Polk had no intention of backing off. He ordered nearly four thousand U.S. troops to the border, where they and the Mexican army stared at each other for weeks. Washington and Mexico City launched some halfhearted diplomatic efforts, but those predictably failed. The powder keg blew on April 26, 1846, after some sixteen hundred Mexican cavalrymen crossed the Rio Grande. Sixty-three American dragoons went on a reconnaissance patrol to find them. Badly underestimating the Mexican manpower, the Americans blundered into an attack. Mexican soldiers wounded or killed seventeen of them, and the rest surrendered and were taken prisoner.

It was a complete failure as an American military maneuver, but the political timing could not have been better. The dead and captured soldiers gave Polk his casus belli. "Mexico has passed the boundary of the United States," the president said in a proclamation, "has invaded our territory and shed American blood upon the American soil." On May 13, 1846, after heated and rancorous debate, Congress agreed to the war, though the lawmakers' approval arrived a bit late. By the time they acted, serious fighting had already broken out along the border.

The conflict was not popular in much of the United States—opponents of "Mr. Polk's War" included philosopher-woodsman Henry David Thoreau and an obscure freshman congressman from Illinois named Abraham Lincoln—nor one that posterity has honored on the scale of others. But the war would give Polk the western expansion he so badly desired, making the United States a continental empire.

As for Texans, the war granted them something they craved: the chance for retribution. Many Rangers garnered generous praise for their heroism and bravery on the battlefield. At the same time, they served as the tip of the retaliatory spear. They became the collectors for those who believed Texas was owed a great debt for abominable treatment, and they made sure the debt was paid with blood.

THE DEATH OF CAPT. WALKER. AT HUAMANTLA IN MEXICO.

As he fell he exclaimed, "Boys, forward, and don't flinch a foot; I know I am dying but don't give up."

Sam Walker died in the Mexican War, at the Battle of Huamantla. This 1847 illustration provided Americans with a dramatic depiction of his death, though it probably didn't happen this way.

Chapter 6

CRY VENGEANCE

The War's First Hero

Then mount and away! give the fleet steed the rein—
The Ranger's at home on the prairies again;
Spur! spur in the chase, dash on to the fight;
Cry Vengeance for Texas! and God speed the right.

—"THE RANGER'S SONG," BY JAMES T. LYTLE, C. 1846

Sam Walker never seemed to stop fighting. He escaped execution in the black bean lottery and was imprisoned at Molino del Rey, in a powder mill and foundry converted to a penal colony near Mexico City. One account of his time there, from a fellow prisoner, said a guard whipped Walker "in a spirit of wanton levity" as he worked on a road crew. "Instantly [Walker] dropped the burden he was carrying up the hill, and sprang upon the offender with the fury and strength of a tiger." The other guards clubbed Walker with their muskets. "He was sent to the hospital nearly lifeless," the prisoner said, "and remained there for two months."

When he recovered, Walker escaped from Molino del Rey by scaling a wall and lowering himself with torn blankets. He and two other fugitives were recaptured the next day and locked up in a village jail. They pried the cell door off its hinges and headed into the mountains, where they passed themselves off as English mineworkers. For about ten days they walked back roads and remote paths until they reached Tampico on the Gulf Coast. There, with the help of the U.S. consul, they managed to secure passage on an American ship out of Mexico. Walker made his way back to Texas, where—eager as always for armed combat—he joined Jack Hays's Ranger company to shoot Comanches.

The abuse Walker endured at the hands of the Mexicans left him with a deep desire for retribution, one that the Indian wars did not diminish. He expressed this wish with such frequency and passion that his friends took to calling him "Mad" Walker. Writing to his sister-in-law, he invoked the black bean massacre. "My experience thus far has only increased my anxiety and ambition to fight the mexicans," he said. "I have witnessed the murder of 18 of my comrades in cold blood and I am determined to revenge their death if I have the opportunity."

His chance came as General Zachary Taylor's U.S. troops massed on the Texas-Mexico border.

Taylor was a paunchy, unschooled, career military man with a face like lumpy mashed potatoes. Raised on a Kentucky plantation, he joined the army in his early twenties. He learned his craft in the War of 1812 and in numerous Indian conflicts, including the Seminole War. As a field commander, Taylor wore civilian clothes and a large straw hat, and he had not enjoyed a wide reputation as a gifted military tactician. He was "a plain old farmer-looking man," one soldier recalled, with "no particular indications of smartness or intellect," and he sometimes rode his horse like a woman—sidesaddle. But the rank and file adored the brusque general's willingness to get into the mud with them. His nickname was "Old Rough and Ready."

With war looming in late 1845, Taylor marched his men from Louisiana into Texas. They spent several months in Corpus Christi, which was then a ragged bayside smuggler's village where they fought only boredom and dysentery. "This is the dirtiest place, I believe, I was ever in," an army officer from New England wrote to his wife." In February 1846, Taylor was ordered to move his force 150 miles south, to the edge of Mexico on the northeast bank of the Rio Grande.

Two of their biggest problems as they crossed the dry South Texas wastelands—"not fit for a hog to live in," by one soldier's assessment—were heat and rattlesnakes. Rangers and other Texans had long learned to cope with such hazards, but American soldiers—many of whom were European immigrants by way of northern cities—found conditions beyond arduous. "The sun streamed upon us like living fire," an American captain wrote after a day's march, even though it was not yet summer. Several nights before, the captain said, "I killed with my sword, immediately in the rear of my tent, a huge rattler nearly six feet in length." So thick were the snakes in places that an advance line of dragoons fronted the main column, killing or scattering the serpents as the soldiers approached. Blood-sucking insects tormented them too. "We are completely overrun with wood ticks," an officer wrote. "I pull out of my flesh on an average fifty per day."

Reaching the Rio Grande, Taylor settled his men across the river from the Mexican town of Matamoros and pointed his artillery toward it. Next they constructed an earthen breastwork and christened the outpost Fort Texas. An army band played "The Star-Spangled Banner" and "Yankee Doodle" as soldiers raised the American flag over the newest state in the Union. From Matamoros, where Mexican forces had gathered, bands responded with their own songs and flags.

Agents for Mexican general Pedro Ampudia smuggled handbills into the U.S. camp promising to pay Americans for defecting. As many as fifty U.S. soldiers jumped into the Rio Grande and swam to the other side. Taylor posted guards on the riverbank with orders to shoot to kill any others who bolted. It was "probable," a newspaper report said, "that two or three of the deserters were reached by musket-balls, wounded and perhaps, in consequence, drowned."

With soldiers like that, Taylor could use a man such as Sam Walker, who was begging for action. Walker was now twenty-nine, and his wounds from Indian battles had healed. In the spring of 1846 he rode for the Rio Grande to volunteer. Taylor had initially resisted enlisting Texans, but he relented and put Walker in charge of a company of "Texas Mounted Rangers." Walker volunteered himself and his men for dangerous scouting expeditions in the surrounding hard country, which was crawling with Mexican patrols.

The army had received reports that a large Mexican force was moving toward an American garrison at Point Isabel, thirty miles east of Fort Texas on the Gulf of Mexico. Walker was sent on reconaissance. If Mexicans took Point Isabel, the main port for schooners bringing weapons and food, they could cut off American supply lines. Walker and about two dozen mounted Rangers rode fifteen miles into the flat, sandy landscape and set up a base camp. However, these were not Jack Hays's well-trained, battle-tested frontier troopers. Many of them had never faced military combat before.

While Walker and several others went away to scout, fifteen of the men settled into a small clearing next to a shallow lagoon. Night fell, and they failed to post a proper guard, which allowed a patrol of Mexican soldiers to approach undetected and attack. "We were all asleep," one of the Texans, George Washington Trahern, recalled. Some of the men panicked, broke ranks, and fled. One tried to get away on his horse. A Mexican soldier tossed a lariat around his neck. He "was probably choked to death before he was pulled off his horse," an American officer wrote.

Trahern said he and several others fought for a while but soon gave up and ran for their lives into the heavy scrub. "They were so heavy and strong against us we just broke through this laguna, a little lake . . . and went on the other side into the brush there," he said. "There was only seven or eight of us—just deserted everything and scattered. They killed two of the boys and the balance of us laid around in the brush." Trahern's count might have been off. Other versions put the tally at six dead and four captured.

The imbroglio did little damage to Walker's reputation. In a report to the army adjutant general, General Taylor placed full blame on Walker's inept company. "Had the men who were left obeyed the injunctions of the captain, a tried frontier soldier, they would never have met such a disaster," Taylor wrote. "Our men and officers have spirit enough, but lack prudence, which a little active service will soon teach them."

Taylor had moved most of his force to Point Isabel, leaving what amounted to a skeleton crew at Fort Texas on the river. On May 3, Mexican cannons in Matamoros opened fire on the fort. In response, U.S. artillerymen sent their own cannonballs arcing over the river and into the city. "The four gun battery in our camp was immediately opened" on Matamoros, an American correspondent wrote. "The Mexican battery was silenced in thirty minutes."

Someone needed to get word to Taylor that Fort Texas had held. Walker and fourteen others left at night, riding into the pitch-dark chaparral. With hatchets and Bowie knives, they hacked their way through the brush and cactus—"six miles of the worst thicket it has ever been my lot to encounter," one of his men, William Oury, recalled. "Add to the thorns, a night so dark that the nearest object was invisible, with not a star to guide our course, and the difficulty of the undertaking may be imagined."

At sunrise they emerged from the brush into a vast prairie. An enemy force of some five hundred lancers spotted Walker and his Rangers as they spurred their mounts toward Point Isabel. Now it became a horse race. "It was a thrilling chase on that early still morning," Oury said, "for the handful of men hotly pursued by some five hundred hostile cavalry over the plain, where the slightest accident, the misstep of a horse, would doom its rider to certain death."

The chase lasted for miles, until the Rangers and their flagging horses reached the Point Isabel garrison. After outrunning the Mexicans, the Texans barely missed destruction by American soldiers, who initially mistook them for attackers. "The artillery were seen standing to their guns ready to fire upon us and our pursuers," Oury said. "But Gen. Taylor was upon the parapet with a glass to his eye, and recognized Capt. Walker. . . . Our pursuers fled back to their army."

Walker delivered his news that Fort Texas had withstood Mexican cannon fire.

An army officer on the scene praised his bravery. "Walker ran a great many risks making his way to the fort," Captain W. S. Henry wrote, "and deserves great credit for the fearless manner in which he effected communication."

The first major engagement of the war came less than a week later, May 8, 1846, on a broad stretch of low-lying coastal prairie between Fort Texas and Point Isabel. The Battle of Palo Alto—named for small rises of trees surrounding a flat open field—began when Taylor's force met Mexican general Mariano Arista's army along the old road from Matamoros to Point Isabel. Arista had thirty-two hundred men to Taylor's twenty-three hundred, but Taylor owned the advantage in artillery. In addition to some smaller howitzers, the U.S. forces employed two eighteen-pound siege cannons drawn by oxen. These weapons launched a deadly array of projectiles: solid cast-iron cannonballs, "grape"—a mass of iron balls that sprayed like large shotgun pellets—and spherical case shot, which contained an explosive charge fused to detonate in flight.

Rather than charge the Mexicans, Taylor held his soldiers in a defensive posture and rolled his cannons forward. The Americans fired 3,000 rounds during the battle to the Mexicans' 650. The U.S. cannon shot tore into the lines of Mexican infantry, killing or wounding more than two hundred, while the Mexican cannonballs often fell short.

The Mexican cavalry charged the American flanks. "They rode upon us eight hundred strong," wrote Captain Ephraim Kirby Smith. "When about a hundred feet from us they delivered their fire. . . . A few of our men fell wounded but not a man wavered." Walker's twenty-five-member company stood among the soldiers returning fire. They wielded two types of Colt guns: revolving pistols and revolving rifles. "Walker's rangers, about twenty of whom were on our right, gave them their rifle balls with their usual coolness and deadly aim," Smith said.

After four hours of battle, as night fell, the Mexicans began to withdraw. "The prairie was burning brilliantly between the two armies and some twenty pieces of artillery thundering," Smith wrote, "while through the lurid scene was heard the trampling of horses and the wild cheering of the men."

The next day the fight resumed several miles away at Resaca de la Palma, an old and dry channel of the Rio Grande. Taylor charged the Mexican army before it could regroup from the previous day's combat. Unlike the first battle, Mexicans and Americans now fired their guns at close range in the thick chaparral and slashed at each other with swords and knives. "Repeatedly were bayonets crossed," Captain Henry wrote, "the enemy giving way slowly, and fighting for every inch of the ground." The ferocity of the Mexicans may have surprised some of the Americans. "The enemy here fought like devils," Captain Smith said.

But as their lines collapsed, the Mexicans retreated in chaos and fled across the border, which meant swimming the river. "We have heard that three hundred were drowned in crossing," Smith wrote, "including their priest and several officers." They paused only briefly in Matamoros and moved south, leaving behind several hundred wounded and dying soldiers.

Nine days later, on May 18, 1846, Taylor's army crossed the river and captured Matamoros with no resistance. The Stars and Stripes now flew over the Mexican state of Tamaulipas, and Taylor penned his official reports from the "Head Quarters of the Army of Occupation." Army captain R. A. Stewart, a minister, delivered a Sunday sermon to the U.S. troops in Matamoros and reminded them why they had fought their way there. The American victory, he said, "showed most plainly and beautifully that it was the order of providence that the Anglo-Saxon race was not only to take possession of the whole North American continent, but to influence and modify the character of the world."

Anglo-Saxon primacy notwithstanding, these first encounters between the two armies shoved the horrors of war into full view. On the night after the Battle of Palo Alto, Captain Henry wrote, many wounded American soldiers required amputation of their arms and legs. "The surgeon's saw was going the livelong night," Henry said, "and the groans of the poor sufferers were heart-rending." In a letter to his wife, Captain Smith described the reeking mounds of Mexican dead in the field after the Resaca de la Palma rout. "I saw eighty-three in one pile already partially decomposed by the side of the pit into which they were to be thrown," he wrote. "Many hundreds were lying about and the vultures were already at their widespread feast, the wolves howling and fighting over their dreadful meal. Before morning the scent of the carnage became almost insupportable."

During the Palo Alto battle, a cannonball struck U.S. captain John B. Page in the face. It tore away his jaw and upper teeth. "The under jaw is gone to the wind pipe and the tongue hangs down upon the throat," wrote Ulysses S. Grant, the future president who fought at Palo Alto. "He will never be able to speak or to eat." In the hands of American newspaper writers, Page's terrible wound became a source of both national mourning and patriotic inspiration. "POOR CAPTAIN PAGE!!!" read a headline in the *Philadelphia Sun*. The reading public was kept current on the efforts of Page's wife to travel from the northeast to Texas and reach her husband. "Her spirit was disturbed by the reflection that her bleeding husband might need her help, and like a dove that seeketh its mother's nest, she would not be stayed," one correspondent wrote. "The wings of love were not easily wearied." She made it, and stayed at Page's side for two months until he died. Page was "a gallant soldier in whose bosom dwelt the soul of honor," a newspaper obituary noted. "His mission was ended, and he died when all the better feelings of the human heart were concentrated upon him, as a flower that perisheth at mid-day."

If Page could be considered the war's initial martyr, Sam Walker emerged as its first hero. General Taylor, of course, was hailed on the home front as a strategic genius who won the hearts of his men by sharing the dangers of the battlefield. Some domestic journals were already mentioning Old Rough and Ready as a prime candidate for president. But when it came to field soldiers, Walker moved to the fore. His coolness and competence under fire had impressed Taylor, who singled out Walker in his official battle report: "Capt. Walker's company of volunteers effectively repulsed the enemy."

Newspapers throughout the country lavished praise upon him. Walker's "services upon the Rio Grande have endeared his name to all who honor gallant men," the *New Orleans Daily Picayune* proclaimed. The intrepid former Ranger fought Mexicans "by instinct," a Connecticut newspaper said. "As a scout, or skirmisher, he has not a superior." Another publication said the "gallant Ranger" had volunteered for a mission "so desperate as to be thought fool hardy" but had "fully succeeded."

The *New Orleans Tropic* proposed a grand, if fanciful, position for him. "We nominate Walker, the brave Texan soldier, as the first American Governor of the [Mexican] State of Tamaulipas," the newspaper said. Though that didn't happen, Walker was promoted to army captain. He was now so famous and revered that he even spawned an impostor. "A thief calling himself Capt. Walker of the Texan [*sic*] Rangers cut quite a swell in New Orleans one day last week," a newspaper reported. He purchased swords, epaulettes, and spurs on credit, and directed the bills to be sent to the U.S. government. The faux Walker was at last "set upon by police," the story said, "and locked up very much to the dismay of the swells who had been associating with and lionizing him."

Not everyone found Walker's conduct heroic. A writer for the *New York Daily Tribune* called the war a "disastrous conflict," and said Walker distinguished himself only by fleeing to the safety of the Point Isabel garrison with extraordinary speed. "He came in ahead of the remnant of his flying corps," the *Tribune* said, "and there can be little doubt that his 'time' was about the best on record."

But that represented a minority view, and soon the stories of Walker's exploits began to grow. One newspaper claimed that Walker and only twelve Rangers had battled and subdued a force of fifteen hundred Mexicans. Another said Walker's horse was shot from under him by a cannonball. As Mexican lancers closed in, Walker played dead. But one lancer came too close. "The moment the Mexican's horse was within his reach," a correspondent wrote, "[Walker] jumped up, seized the reins, dropped the lancer from his saddle with his unerring five shooter, then jumped into the saddle himself."

That these accounts had the hallmarks of hyperbole and propaganda seemed not to matter. Some wealthy patrons in New Orleans bought Walker a handsome new steed, named Tornado, and shipped it to the front. The *New Orleans Delta* was so excited that it combined its storm metaphors: "The gallant Captain, when mounted on Tornado, will sweep through the Mexican host with the . . . devastating ravages of the hurricane."

So elevated was Walker's stature that in the fall of 1846 he was sent back to Washington, D.C., to recruit enlistees for service in Mexico. His reputation preceded him. Between five hundred and one thousand men and women—the published estimates varied—thronged to the Odd Fellows Hall in Washington to catch a glimpse of him. Walker gave a short speech and invoked the men serving in Mexico. "He said not a word too much, nor one too little," a report in the

Baltimore Sun related, "and left on the minds of all present the impression that his modesty is no less remarkable than his military skill and success."

During the same trip, Walker called on none other than President Polk, who received him warmly. Walker also traveled to New York City, where he met for the first time one of his heroes—Sam Colt. They got along famously, touring New York gun shops, drinking brandy, and discussing weaponry. Walker presented Colt with a list of suggested modifications to his revolving pistol. Among them: a larger and heavier gun (so it could be used as a club), a longer grip, and the capacity for a six-shot chamber.

Colt's Paterson factory had long ago closed, but he remained eager to reenter the business. He listened intently to Walker's suggestions and agreed to incorporate them. He also persuaded Walker to lobby the U.S. military to buy the new and improved weapons. It worked. On December 7, 1846, the War Department's chief of ordnance wrote to Colt: "At the instance of Capt Walker, the Secretary of War desires you to furnish one thousand revolving pistols. . . ."

With that, Colt's gun-making career had been raised from the dead. The new revolver would be called the Walker pistol. The army soon ordered more of the firearms, and Colt opened a large factory in Hartford, Connecticut. Advances in design and production led to the manufacture of the Colt "Peacemaker" six-shooter. The weapon's reliability, accuracy, and power—it was at the time the most powerful handgun in the world—made it the revolver of choice for cavalrymen, Indian fighters, lawmen, outlaws, everyday cowpokes, and cinematic gunslingers. Billy the Kid carried a Colt. So did Wyatt Earp, Jesse James, Bat Masterson, and Butch Cassidy.

Long after Sam Walker and Sam Colt were gone, the gun they launched became the emblematic weapon of the American West.

Walker's stateside respite from the Mexican War culminated in a glorious spring afternoon, April 1, 1847, on the Ohio River waterfront. He had completed a bountiful recruiting mission, enlisting nearly two hundred volunteers to take up arms in the distant desert. The men had first been sent to the army garrison in Newport, Kentucky, for training. Now they stood aboard the steamer *Albatross* in their new uniforms. Politicians gave speeches, a band played, and the American stars and stripes flew from the stern. Young women lined the Newport wharf and waved their handkerchiefs at the freshly minted soldiers, and they kept waving as the *Albatross* slipped from the harbor and chugged out of sight.

Paddlewheels churning, the steamship headed downstream toward the Mississippi River. From there it would travel to New Orleans. There the recruits would board another ship loaded with horses and weapons and sail to Veracruz. The night they left Kentucky, Walker sat in his cabin and put pen to paper in a letter to his new friend Colt. "We are now on our way to the seat of War," he wrote. "I have a fine set of men that will give a good account of themselves as soon as they have an opportunity."

They certainly looked the part. On May 25, 1847, Walker and his two companies of riflemen rode into Perote, which had been captured the night before. This was the site of the prison where many members of the Mier expedition had been held and abused. Now, as Walker's companies entered, they caught the admiring eye of Pennsylvania volunteer J. Jacob Oswandel. "They are all fine, strong, healthy and good looking men," Oswandel wrote in his diary. "Nearly every one measured over six feet."

Their job was to keep the National Road open between Perote and the city of Jalapa. "So guerrillas . . . take warning," Oswandel wrote, "for the renowned Capt. Samuel H. Walker takes no prisoners." It was common knowledge in Mexico that the adversaries who encountered Walker and his riflemen either retreated or were killed on the spot. Walker was propelled by both his continuing quest for vengeance and—as he revealed—a remarkable assent from the very top.

In mid-1847 Walker wrote to his brother and told of his capture of Mexicans "who have been guilty of many acts of barbarity towards every unfortunate man who fell into their hands." His men did not, however, seize these Mexicans as prisoners. They were instead executed. "I of course took summary measures with them," Walker acknowledged. President Polk himself apparently had signed off on such acts, and with enthusiasm. "The course I pursued . . . was approved and applauded by the commander in chief," Walker wrote. "I have been left here for the purpose [of] freeing this part of the country from the bands of maurauders [sic] that infest it."

Other soldiers admired his aggression in the face of fire. "Who, I ask, has not seen or heard of the gallant Walker's bravery?" one officer wrote from Perote. "He is one of the few who retain their courage and composure under all circumstances. In perils the most appalling he has the courage of one born to command." They saw this on June 20 in the town of Las Vegas. Walker, riding point, ordered his men to prepare to charge a force of Mexicans. As Walker's company assembled, their horses bucked and bridled. "They could hardly be managed, panting and snorting all the time," Oswandel wrote in his journal. "When the order was given, 'Ready! Charge!' off they went with about fifty men with the awfulest rattling and crackling of horses' feet, and jangling of swords and scabbards, and yelling."

As the Mexicans fired on them, Walker's horse was shot. It stumbled and fell. Walker righted himself and joined the assault on foot—"running after his company," Oswandel said, "until the charge was accomplished."

Walker's last battle came in the Central Highlands east of Mexico City. On a cool, sunny day in October 1847, a U.S. Army column approached the town of Huamantla. Its narrow streets and small, whitewashed adobe buildings appeared serene and oddly inviting. Franciscan monks had settled the village in the early 1500s, and it had until now been spared the ravages of war with the Americans. The central plaza, like many in Mexico, featured a fountain and was lined with poplar trees. A "beautiful town," said Lieutenant William D. Wilkins of the U.S. Army's 15th Infantry, "charmingly situated."

For months the war had been staggering toward its conclusion and was by now all but over. U.S. troops had seized Mexico City, forcing General Santa Anna's army to flee the capital. But the Mexican president devised one last-gasp plan: to cut off American supply caravans from the coast. A spy informed General Joseph Lane that Santa Anna's forces were hiding in Huamantla. Lane sent a mounted advance party of about two hundred men, led by Captain Walker.

As the Americans entered Huamantla, about five hundred Mexican lancers—uniformed troops—met them. Walker's response was characteristic: he charged. "Suddenly a small body of a horse broke from our ranks, headed by a tall cavalier, and dashed like a thunderbolt into the midst of the glittering Mexicans," Lieutenant Wilkins recalled. "It was Walker with his Rangers who performed this gallant feat."

A ferocious battle was joined. "Here rose a wild yell," remembered George W. Myers, a sergeant in the U.S. Mounted Rifles, "and such a charge—the flashing of the sabres, the thundering of the horses' feet over the paved streets, were enough to strike terror into the hearts of the enemy." The Mexicans retreated, and Walker's men held the town square. Soon, however, Santa Anna counterattacked with some two thousand lancers. "We were now completely hemmed in, for every street was blocked up with them," Sergeant Myers said.

Walker gathered his men in a walled churchyard to make their defense against overwhelming numbers. "The battle raged for some time, our men doing considerable execution among the enemy, and suffering some loss," Sergeant Myers said. Walker shouted orders to fire a cannon, then crumpled, mortally wounded.

A widely circulated illustration showed him on horseback as a Mexican lancer stabbed him through the abdomen. More reliable accounts say he was shot. A "cowardly Mexican greaser, from the window or housetop, fired and shot him through the head," said Oswandel of the Pennsylvania volunteers. "Another one shot him through the breast from behind the corner." Walker "sank down upon his knees, striking his forehead upon the ground," Sergeant Myers wrote in his diary.

His men carried him to the churchyard and laid him in the doorway. Walker gave his Colt revolving pistols to one of them, Sergeant Myers said, and told them, "Boys, fight to the last. . . . Never surrender this place as long as one of you is living!" He lasted about fifteen minutes more. The men wrapped his body in white linen and concealed it. Myers said Rangers and soldiers were "bursting into tears as the cry spread among them: 'Captain Walker is killed!'"

The Americans kept the Mexicans at bay until General Lane arrived with his full complement of troops, who overtook the lancers. "The carnage was awful," wrote Oswandel. Lane's men were "cutting the enemy down right and left, just like a mower cutting grass or grain." Santa Anna's forces again retreated, badly beaten, but Walker's death crushed any American elation. "He was a father to us in his care, and one of the very best I have met with in my walks through life," Sergeant Myers wrote. "Capt. Walker was a man universally beloved." Colonel Francis Wynkoop also was moved to tears. "I would give six years of my existence to have spoken with Capt. Walker before he died," the colonel said. He was, Oswandel wrote in his memoir, "without a doubt, one of the bravest officers in our army."

The Americans wanted vengeance. "Our men looked upon Capt. Walker's death as murder," Oswandel said. General Lane told his men "to avenge the death of the gallant Walker." The townspeople bore the brunt of this retribution.

Soldiers broke open bars and guzzled alcohol. Now "maddened with liquor," Lieutenant Wilkins said, they committed "every species of outrage," a range that included rape and murder. "Old women and girls were stripped of their clothing," he remembered, "and many suffered still greater outrages." Mexican civilians tried to protect their families, stores, houses, and churches. Drunken Americans shot them where they stood, and plundered the buildings. "Dead horses and men lay about pretty thick," Wilkins said. "Such a scene I never hope to see again. It gave me a lamentable view of human nature . . . and made [me] for the first time ashamed of my country."

Army captain Samuel Peter Heintzelman rode into Huamantla and found Walker shot "above the eye & in the right breast." The soldiers' frenzied sacking of the town was already under way. "I could do nothing with them," Heintzelman wrote in his journal. The Americans "killed every Mexican they saw," he said, and "dead Mexicans [lay] about in every direction." He added, "We are a strange people."

That evening the soldiers were marched back to quarters. "Half our men were drunk," Wilkins said. "When we arrived in camp, near 200 men were missing, who lay along the road, unable from intoxication to move."

The rape of Huamantla, as it came to be called in some circles, survived as little more than a historical footnote. Walker's memory, however, generated lush praise as he was mourned as a martyr to courage. "Walker's splendid record attracted to him public attention, not only in the army, but throughout the country," said Captain Edmund L. Dana of the Pennsylvania volunteers. A politician in Walker's home state of Maryland delivered a public eulogy. "There is, perhaps, no man whose history, the past twelve years, is so deeply fraught with scenes of deeds of noble daring, hardship and peril," intoned alderman John T. Towers of Baltimore.

A play that ran in Philadelphia and New York after the war, *The Campaign on the Rio Grande, or, Triumphs in Mexico*, had a main character named Sam Walker. Composers penned patriotic songs about him, and a Philadelphia magazine published a tribute in verse:

> *For a braver, or a better, or a more chivalrous knight*
> *Never put his lance in rest in the days when might was right;*
> *And he had the fox's cunning, and the eagle's restless eye,*
> *With his courage, to see danger, and that danger to defy.*

He was of course no hero to the other side. One Mexican officer called him "the terrible Texan Walker" who had "strewed death and desolation." Writing after the war, Ramón Alcaraz described how Walker's men swept ruthlessly down the Veracruz Road and attacked ranchers. They "committed the greatest cruelties, perchance on innocent rancheros, who formed no part of the Mexican guerrillas," Alcaraz wrote. "The cottages [were] burned, the ranchos deserted, and the dead bodies of men and the carcasses of mules lay unburied along with broken and plundered wagons."

In the United States, this only enhanced his status. Walker showed himself over the course of the war to be "one of the best . . . rangers on the continent," a newspaper correspondent wrote. "Endowed with great activity and skill in the use of arms, whether the deadly rifle, the sure revolver, or the irresistible bowie knife; capable of great endurance against all the dangers, sufferings and trials of the battle, of captivity, chains, want, and starvation—he was a terror to the Mexicans."

On that last part both sides could agree.

Walker wasn't the only one. Well before the serious shooting started, eager Rangers had readied themselves to fight in Mexico. Jack Hays, Ben McCulloch, and others went to towns such as Austin, San Antonio, and Goliad to enlist volunteers for the war. Recruiting proved to be no great challenge. In the spring of 1846, about five hundred Rangers—the title being loosely applied—rode for the border. "The rangers are all well mounted and have long been wishing for a brush with the Mexicans," the *Telegraph and Texas Register* said. "We doubt not that they will give a good account of themselves, if they can get within gunshot of their old enemies."

Walker also was not alone in his use of rage and racial animus to fuel valor and spread terror, as these Rangers would show. "Some of us," Ranger Buck Barry said, "had traveled six hundred miles to kill a Mexican." A few weeks after General Taylor's troops occupied Matamoros, the *New Orleans Picayune* gave a taste of things to come: "A Mexican was shot by a Texan Ranger in a billiard room up town yesterday. The fellow is not dead yet. The Texan accused him of having been instrumental in adding to the distress of the Mier prisoners some years ago." The correspondent added a warning to other Rangers contemplating similar acts. "Whether the charge was just or not, the assassin will find that he cannot with impunity act as an avenger of blood."

This prediction turned out to be woefully wrong, as demonstrated by any number of assaults, attacks, and slaughters of the innocents. To their advocates, the Rangers were colorful, patriotic warriors. To their targets, they rampaged across Mexico as a bloodthirsty horde. Other Americans committed atrocities—as did the Mexicans—but the Texans seemed to excel at it.

Young lieutenant U. S. Grant, not a man who shrank from the barbarities of combat, was struck by the Rangers' fury. "About all of the Texans seem to think it perfectly right to impose upon the people of a conquered City to any extent, and even to murder them where the act can be covered by the dark," Grant wrote to his fiancée. "And how much they seem to enjoy acts of violence too!"

The terrified Mexicans gave the Rangers a name: *Los Diablos Tejanos*—the Texas Devils. The Mexicans raised it as a cry of alarm, or they spat it as a curse. The Rangers wore it as a crown.

No Ranger could match John S. "Rip" Ford's wide range of talents and experiences. He fought Mexicans and Indians, and devoutly promoted the idea that slavery was ordained by God.

Chapter 7

LOS DIABLOS

From the Halls of Montezuma

The Rangers were the Scouts of our Army and a more reckless, devil-may-care looking set, it would be impossible to find this side of the Infernal Regions.

—SAMUEL CHAMBERLAIN

American generals in Mexico did not, on the whole, consider the opposing military a well-trained, highly prepared force. The Mexicans doubted themselves too. "Strictly speaking, the army does not exist," one Mexican politician admitted. "What today bears that name is only a mass of men without training and without weapons." Much of the weaponry they did possess was of poor quality; the government had purchased used muskets—thirty-year-old surplus weapons—from the British at clearance-sale prices.

Some of the Mexican soldiers did wear striking uniforms, and their swords flashed brilliantly in the bright sunlight. Many of them fought with courage. But a great number of the Mexican infantry were drunks, layabouts, and prisoners pressed into service. Most had never fired a gun before they put on a uniform, if they even had a uniform. A considerable number of them went into combat wearing plain cotton garments and sandals. Indians were captured and brought in chains to barracks, where they were conscripted into the army. Large collections of officers sprang from political hackdom with faint military knowledge or competence. Desertion among the ranks was epidemic.

Still, the U.S. Army faced a daunting task in the invasion of a foreign country. It needed more men, including those of the sort that Texas could uniquely provide. Before the war was officially under way, General Taylor asked the new governor of Texas, James Pinckney Henderson, for four regiments. The governor himself volunteered.

Rangers who enlisted to fight in Mexico no longer held a spot on the state muster rolls, for they now had joined U.S. forces, which meant they served as official Texas Rangers no more. But no one could mistake them for riflemen from, say, New York. If anything, their Ranger-ness was magnified in the new surroundings. They served in their own discrete units, and they were still referred to as Rangers.

Regular U.S. soldiers wore standard uniforms: dark blue jackets with brass buttons, sky blue pants, and belts with buckles that bore the letters *US*. The Rangers dressed in whatever fashion pleased them, and they honored few of the usual military protocols. Their uniform, it was said with mordant humor, was "a dirty shirt and a five-shooter." The normal run of troops regarded them with a combination of awe, resentment, and disbelief. "The best of them," wrote Lieutenant Napoleon Dana, "looked as if they could steal sheep."

Samuel Chamberlain, an army cavalryman from Boston, had never seen such characters. "Some wore buckskin shirts, black with grease and blood," he recalled. "Some wore red shirts, their trousers thrust into their high boots." All of them, Chamberlain said, armed themselves with Bowie knives. Steel blades up to twelve inches long made these knives useful as tools, and they could be deadly weapons in close combat. In addition, the Rangers' Colt revolvers gave them a decided battlefield advantage over opponents who carried single-shot pistols. Some Mexican soldiers ascribed magical powers to the Texans' guns. The "untutored greaser," Ranger Ephraim Daggett said, regarded the Colt revolvers "with holy awe and superstition." Many of them believed "the ball would revolve in all directions after its victim, run around trees and turn corners, go into houses and climb up stairs, and hunt up folks generally."

Thus outfitted, the Rangers affected a menacing strut. "With their uncouth costumes, bearded faces, lean and brawny forms, fierce wild eyes and swaggering manners," Chamberlain said, "they were fit representations of the outlaws which made up the population of the Lone Star State." To enhance this package, the

Rangers employed a bloodcurdling yell on the battlefield, not unlike the one later used by Rebels in the Civil War. "Such yells exploded on the air," a Texas governor, Oran Roberts, wrote. "[They] have been heard distinctly three miles off across a prairie, above the din of musketry and artillery."

The Rangers also possessed crucial skills that set them apart from army regulars. "As a mounted soldier [the Ranger] has had no counterpart in any age of country," wrote Captain Luther Giddings of the Ohio volunteers. "Chivalrous, bold and impetuous in action, he is yet wary and calculating, always impatient of restraint, and sometimes unscrupulous and unmerciful. He is ununiformed, and undrilled and performs his active duties thoroughly, but with little regard to order or system. He is an excellent rider and a *dead shot.*"

General Joseph Lane of Indiana was impressed with their fire and their grit. The Rangers, he said, "love to fight better, can stand hunger longer and endure more fatigue" than regular soldiers. Major Roswell Ripley acknowledged they would "not easily submit to discipline." But the Rangers' hard-won knowledge from the Indian wars, he said, would allow them to "take the field in rough, uncouth habiliments, and, following some leader chosen for his talent and bravery, perform partisan duties in a manner hardly to be surpassed."

Field conditions in Mexico could range from punishing to deadly, especially in summer, when it was—in one Ranger's description—"too hot for a lizard to live." On an infantry march near Reynosa, soldiers felt "the sun pouring its hottest rays directly upon their backs," one newspaper correspondent wrote. "Several fell to the ground exhausted by the heat." John Duff Brown, a physician who volunteered for war duty, recalled "Camp Maggot" on the Rio Grande. It sat downstream from the army's slaughter pens, from which rendering waste was dumped into the river. "We used the river water," Brown said, "and some days we were forced to wade out fifty or sixty yards to get clear of maggots." Sickness was constant among the troops.

The Rangers already knew how to survive a sun-scorched, hostile landscape. In the desert, they searched for low ground that might contain stagnant watering holes for them and their horses. "Sometimes we traveled for miles, without a single sign to guide us over the untrodden hills, but the position of the sun in the heavens," wrote one Ranger. "Sometimes we followed the trail of innumerable droves of wild horses that roamed in freedom over this immense range of waste country."

Even Texans accustomed to harsh surroundings found Mexico extraordinarily tough. "In all my life I was never as hot. . . . It is so hot that there is danger in exposing our muskets to the sun for fear [of] firing them off," Ranger James K. Holland wrote in his diary. "The water that we have is not fit for a hog to waller in."

Other problems arose from waging war in a strange and distant land. Supply lines could be unreliable, owing to hard terrain and attacks by guerrillas. And the Americans were marching across territory unknown and largely uncharted. Again the Rangers brought their unmatched skills and their unbridled embrace of peril.

In mid-May 1846, McCulloch and his men prepared to depart the town of Gonzales for a three hundred-mile ride to the border. They went first to Corpus Christi, then—avoiding the troublesome Nueces Strip—rode toward Padre Island.

This low, sandy barrier isle was only a few hundred yards wide at some spots, but it extended southward for more than a hundred miles, separating the mainland from the Gulf of Mexico. It had once been the hunting grounds of the fierce Karankawas, who lingered now on the cusp of Ranger-assisted extinction. Nearly treeless with waves of dunes, Padre seemed to the sunburned and wind-chapped riders like an endless slice of the Sahara. "Never were a set of men or horses more heartily tired of any one portion of this earth's surface," recalled Samuel Reid, a member of the company. "It is one of the most gloomy and desolate looking places which it has ever been our bad fortune to visit."

Five days later they reached the Palo Alto battlefield, where they camped but did not sleep well, tormented by mosquitoes. The next day they crossed the Resaca de la Palma battlefield into clouds of flies and the stench of dead horses and mules, the carcasses left behind after the battle less than two weeks before. They rode on, and Matamoros finally rose into splendid view—the white adobe walls and turrets catching the light of day's end, with the American flag flying above it. The site summoned "beautiful dreams of Moorish palaces and Oriental gardens, orange groves and shady avenues," Reid said.

His exotic visions did not survive close inspection. Reaching the Rio Grande, Reid said, they found "rude mud-built houses . . . windows without glass, hot dusty streets and a dirty, lazy, and most unpoetical looking set of inhabitants." The Rangers' makeshift camp was even worse. Because they had not been issued tents, they slept in shelters of sticks and brush. Reid said the bivouac resembled "a collection of huts in a Hottentot hamlet."

They wouldn't stay long. Zachary Taylor's planned next move was an assault on Monterrey, the city to which the Mexican forces had retreated. It lay two hundred miles west of Matamoros—a hard march—and Taylor needed McCulloch to scout the region for the best way to go. McCulloch's company surveyed possible routes for the presence of Mexican guerrillas and the availability of water.

A correspondent for the *New Orleans Picayune*, George Wilkins Kendall, accompanied McCulloch's company of forty men on some of these missions. He wrote of the Rangers enduring fatigue and hunger as they tracked enemy infantry and guerrillas across northern Mexico. Newspapers across America reprinted Kendall's dispatches as he turned McCulloch and his Rangers into stars of war. "There was not a minute at any time when any man's pistol or rifle would have missed fire, or he would not have been up and ready for an attack," Kendall wrote. "I have seen a goodly number of volunteers in my time, but Capt. Ben McCulloch's men are choice specimens."

Taylor moved on Monterrey in September 1846. As they marched toward the city, set in a verdant valley, many American soldiers—who before now had seen only searing deserts and ragged villages—were struck by its temperate loveliness. Green fields of corn lined the roads, and in the distance fleecy clouds skimmed the Sierra Madre foothills. "A river, clear as crystal, flows on one side of the city," wrote Captain Giddings, "on whose borders there are romantic rural cottages, and gardens with thick foliage." Taylor encamped at a spring-fed grove, which had served as a picnic grounds for Mexicans. So pleasant were the surroundings that many soldiers took to sightseeing strolls along the outskirts of the city, unarmed, as if in a park. Taylor had to put up perimeter guards, and officially forbade his men from straying from camp.

When it came to leisure, the Rangers had other ideas. On September 19 a heavy fog cloaked the valley. The mist began to lift around noon and the "Black Fort," a citadel outside Monterrey, loomed into view. As their tricolored flag waved above them, Mexicans fired their cannons at the Americans, but they missed high, low, and wide. The artillery's only effect was to entice the mounted Rangers, who were in a taunting mood.

Against Taylor's orders the Texans with their trademark yell spurred their horses toward the fort. The Mexicans tried to shoot them, which only added to the Rangers' excitement. "Every fire was met with a hearty response of 3 cheers and such waving of hats," Ranger Holland wrote. "The Texans proved their spunk by the utter carelessness with which the[y] [received] the Enemy's shot."

Captain Giddings watched the Rangers employ mounted maneuvers that came straight from the Comanches. "Like boys at play . . . those fearless horsemen, in a spirit of boastful rivalry, vied with each other in approaching the very edge of danger," Giddings wrote. "Riding singly and rapidly, they swept around the plain under the walls, each one in a wider and more perilous circle than his predecessor." The Mexicans kept firing at them, Giddings said, but "might as well have attempted to bring down skimming swallows as those racing dare-devils."

The 250 Rangers at Monterrey were under the command of none other than Jack Hays. He answered to General William J. Worth, a New Yorker for whom the city of Fort Worth later was named. Worth reported to Taylor, who decided the Rangers would be at the forefront of an imminent attack. "Now that danger is expected," Ranger Holland wrote in his diary, "old Taylor has put us in front." They were among those sent to seize the Saltillo Road as part of the American advance into the city. From this arose another story of Hays's guile and daring, as related by Ranger sergeant James "Buck" Barry in his memoir.

Two days after the riding display at the fort, the Rangers found themselves on this road, confronted by a regiment of Mexican lancers. Badly outnumbered and not yet ready for battle, the Rangers needed to buy some time. That, Barry said, is when Hays rode ahead, his saber in his hand, and challenged Lieutenant Colonel Juan Najera, the commander of the Mexicans, to a swordfight. Smart money was not on the Ranger leader. "Hays knew no more about saber fighting than I did," Barry said.

When the two men were about forty yards apart, the Mexican officer charged. All pretensions to chivalry vanished at that point. "Within a few feet of the Mexican," Barry said, "Hays pulled a pistol and shot him dead from his horse."

Though quite a tale, it probably isn't true. Two accounts written by men present—one a Ranger in Hays's company and the other newspaper correspondent Kendall—make no mention of such an encounter. Nor does Hays's report. Several histories of the war, including one by General Cadmus Wilcox, who was at Monterrey, cast serious doubt on the story. Wilcox and others say Najera was mortally wounded in the subsequent battle between the two forces.

"The clash was great," wrote Sam Reid, from McCulloch's company. "We saw their lieutenant colonel fall, while in the thickest of the fight." Reid was a lawyer who had only recently arrived in Texas and thus harbored few of the prevailing grudges against Mexicans. That might explain his admiring portrait of Najera as the "brave" and "dashing" commander lay dying: "He was a tall, splendid-looking fellow, with a fierce moustache and beautiful teeth, which were set hard as he lay on the ground with his face partly turned up, his eyes yet glassy in the struggle of death, and his features depicting the most marked determination."

After overcoming the Mexicans on the Saltillo Road, the Rangers and other volunteers conquered two fortified hills on the edge of town. "The dreaded Texans, who had unnumbered wrongs to avenge, were picking off each his victim at every shot," Kendall wrote. "From every cover [they] issued a leaden messenger of death." The assault was accompanied by the Texas yell. "Onward, still onward, pressed the stormers," Kendall said, "louder and louder grew their shouts as the front ranks of the enemy recoiled." They took the Bishop's Palace, which bristled with artillery—the Rangers "brave as lions" in Lieutenant Dana's view—and pushed into the city itself on the third day of the battle.

"[It] was done in quick time under the heaviest firing of grape Canister and musketry—we faced it like men," Ranger Holland wrote. "[We] went running in to Town to the astonishment of Genl Taylor—to the great confusion of the Enemy—they did not understand such bold movement." The Rangers fought from house to house, Holland said, with "bullets whizzing by us on all sides."

Here every house had a flat roof, with two-foot walls around the roof perimeters. "Which made every house a fortress," wrote Buck Barry, "and every street a plain road to death." Walls also lined the streets, so the Rangers used sledgehammers, axes, and crowbars to punch holes in them. "It was nothing strange for the muzzles of the Texans' and Mexicans' guns to clash together, both intending to shoot through the hole at the same time," Barry said.

The next day Taylor ordered the Texans to withdraw so American shelling of Monterrey could commence. This enraged the Rangers. "We had the city almost completely under our command," Holland said. "If he had let us alone we would soon have had it in such a condition there would have been no need" of bombardment. On September 24 both sides signed a truce. The Rangers were in no mood to celebrate an end to the fight for Monterrey. In fact, Reid wrote, they "were maddened with disappointment."

Though the Rangers believed their mission was cut short, their reputation as fearless, unbeatable, and merciless combatants had taken root. "Their tiger-like ferocity at Monterrey is but a foretaste of what the Mexicans may expect," the *New York Herald* said. "God have mercy on them if the Rangers in an open field pounce down upon them with the war cry of 'The Alamo.' Very few prisoners will be taken, you may rest assured."

The enlistment terms of many of the Texans who volunteered at the start of the war expired after the battle for Monterrey. The army, however, still needed Rangers. After Monterrey, Hays sailed to New Orleans with Walker. "They were warmly greeted by thousands," a local newspaper said. "The arrival of these gentlemen . . . created a sensation throughout the city." While Walker went east to recruit, Hays returned to Texas to sign up more volunteers. McCulloch also went to Texas to find more willing combatants. All three soon returned to the front lines in Mexico.

McCulloch and his scouts may have saved hundreds, if not thousands, of American lives. The Rangers slipped behind enemy lines near Agua Nueva in February 1847 and discovered twenty thousand of Santa Anna's men in position to ambush advancing Americans. Taylor withdrew to a more defensible position and defeated the Mexicans at what came to be known as the Battle of Buena Vista. "The services rendered by Major McCulloch and his men," Taylor wrote, "were of the highest importance."

Hays's new group of Rangers enjoyed a run of successes. Commanders often employed them as a rapid-strike team—a quick reaction force, in modern military terms. In December 1847, Colonel Francis Wynkoop learned that guerrillas had attacked the tail end of a long army march. The soldiers, who had fallen behind and stopped to sleep, were under siege. Wynkoop sent Hays's Rangers in the dark of night to rescue them. After a few hours—having quickly and efficiently ended the matter—they returned to camp. Two dead American soldiers, whose throats had been slit by the guerrillas, were tied to the back of a mule. The Rangers had shot and killed two Mexicans, but they also turned over two prisoners to Wynkoop. "This is one of the seven wonders, that the Texan rangers brought the guerillas in as prisoners," Pennsylvania volunteer J. Jacob Oswandel remarked in his journal, "for they generally shoot them on the spot where captured."

In a November 1847 battle near Puebla, according to an army report, Hays commanded an advance guard of thirty-five men against about two hundred Mexican lancers. They charged the lancers and forced them to retreat into nearby mountains. The Mexicans regrouped and charged the Texans, who were running out of ammunition. Hays ordered his Rangers to retreat. He stayed at the rear of the retreat. As the Mexicans drew closer, Hays stopped, aimed, and shot two of them dead.

"Never did any officer act with more gallantry than did Col. Hays in this affair," reported General Lane of Indiana. He had led the front of the assault, Lane said, and was "the last man to quit the field" when the battle was done.

Hays had of course gained notice in his battles with the Comanches. His feats in Mexico, said Ranger John "Rip" Ford, only added to his renown. "He was almost idolized by many. . . . He was cool, self-possessed, brave, and a good shot," Ford wrote. "At Veracruz all the distinguished personages of our army and navy sought his acquaintance and prized his friendship. In passing by the troops of other States of the Union, they would rush from their tents and 'Hurrah for Colonel Hays!'"

The fighting in Mexico lasted less than two years. More than thirteen thousand U.S. troops died, most of them felled by infection or disease. Mexican deaths were estimated at twenty-five thousand. The war officially ended with the signing of the Treaty of Guadalupe Hidalgo on February 2, 1848. The treaty ceded California and much of the American Southwest to the United States. Most important to Texas, it set the Rio Grande as the boundary between Texas and Mexico.

American officials sought to portray the Mexican War as one fought with chivalry, decorum, and a humane concern for those caught in the crossfire. Early on the War Department issued a mollifying proclamation that was printed and distributed to Mexicans. "We come to make no war upon the people of Mexico," it said. "We come among the people of Mexico as friends and republican brethren."

It was, of course, an absurd declaration. Long after the war's conclusion, Ulysses S. Grant wrote: "I do not think there was ever a more wicked war. . . . I thought so at the time, when I was a youngster, only I had not moral courage enough to resign." Thousands of civilians died, and U.S. troops burned a swath of villages across northeastern Mexico. "They make a wasteland and call it peace," one disgusted American officer said.

One of the worst examples of the wickedness cited by Grant came at the hands of Arkansas volunteers, known as Rackensackers. On Christmas Day 1846 some of the Rackensackers raided a ranch at Agua Nueva, where they raped a number of the women. They were "fighting over their poor victims like dogs," a witness recalled.

Mexicans retaliated by capturing an Arkansas cavalryman and subjecting him to their most favored form of torturous death: dragging him behind a horse with a rope around his neck. In February 1847, the Rackensackers took their own revenge. They rounded up civilians—none of whom were known to have been involved in the death of the Arkansas soldier—and forced them into a cave near Saltillo.

Samuel Chamberlain of the U.S. Army was among those who happened upon the scene after hearing the shouts and cries of women and children. He recalled the sight: "The cave was full of our volunteers yelling like fiends, while on the rocky floor lay over twenty Mexicans, dead and dying in pools of blood." The Arkansans had scalped the Mexican men as the women and children shrieked for mercy, Chamberlain said. "A rough crucifix was fastened to a rock," he added, "and some irreverent wretch had crowned the image with a bloody scalp."

Though the Rackensackers were arrested, a court of inquiry failed to identify the individuals responsible for the massacre. And General Taylor couldn't send all the Arkansans home because he needed these troops for battle. Therefore, Chamberlain said, "no one was punished for this outrage."

The Arkansas volunteers' actions constituted some of the worst on record. But when it came to the overall wreaking of vengeance in Mexico, Texans seemed to occupy a special tier.

Zachary Taylor both required and rejected the Rangers. "On the day of battle I am glad to have Texas soldiers with me for they are brave and gallant," he was reported to have said, "but I never want to see them before or afterwards, for they are too hard to control." Though they performed with valor, a number of them had "disgrace[d] their colors and their country" by committing "extensive depredations and outrages upon peaceful inhabitants," Taylor wrote.

He didn't provide specifics, but the general pulled no punches. "There is scarcely a form of crime that has not been reported to me as committed by them," he said in letter to the army's adjutant general. "The mounted men from Texas have scarcely made one expedition without unwarrantably killing a Mexican." Taylor decided he had seen enough, and many of the Texans were sent home. "The constant recurrence of such atrocities . . . is my motive for requesting that no more troops may be sent to this column from the State of Texas."

Captain Giddings echoed Taylor's ambivalence toward the Rangers. "They were excellent light troops," he said, but possessed of a "lawless and vindictive spirit." Taylor thanked them for their service, Giddings said, "and we saw them turn their faces toward the blood-bought State they represented, with many good wishes and the hope that all honest Mexicans were at a safe distance from their path."

Among the regular troops, the Rangers owned a deeply rooted reputation as arrant killers. "Most of these rangers are men who have been either prisoners in Mexico, or, in some way, injured by Mexicans," wrote Frank S. Edwards, a Missouri volunteer. "They . . . spare none, but shoot down every one they meet. It is said that the bushes, skirting the road from Monterrey southward, are strewed with skeletons of Mexicans sacrificed by these desperadoes."

Edwards recalled the Rangers' execution of a Mexican they accused— without evidence—of being part of a band of marauders. "The Texians pretended to consider him as such," he said, "but there was no doubt this was only used as a cloak to cover their insatiable desire to destroy those they so bitterly hate." They led the man into a public plaza, let him light a small cigar, and shot him. The man "fell a corpse," Edwards recalled, "with the still smoking cigarito yet between his lips."

It was no accident that many of those Texans accused of the worst atrocities came under the command of Ranger captain Mustang Gray. Before the war he had led the "Men-Slayers" in the Nueces Strip. Now he was in charge of "Gray's Company, Texas Mounted Volunteers," out of Corpus Christi.

The twenty-nine-year-old Gray loved to dance, drink, and kill. Some nights during the war, it was said, he would leave his post, ride his horse miles to town, and dance for four or five hours with Mexican women. The irony of this was not lost on Gray's biographer of sorts, Jeremiah Clemens: "The loveliest of the mingled blood of the Spaniard and the Aztec learned to forget, in the voluptuous contact of the mazy dance, that the strong arms which held them, and the pleading tones which charmed their willing ears, belonged to their country's foes."

When the music stopped, Gray would jump on his horse and be back at camp by daybreak. His various exploits inspired a ballad: *There was a noble Ranger / They called him Mustang Gray / He left his home when but a youth / Went ranging far away.* Some frontier mothers were known to sing it as a soothing lullaby.

The song left out any references to his heavy drinking. Even an admiring chronicler had to admit that Gray consumed stunning amounts of liquor. Clemens, a Mexican War veteran and U.S. senator from Alabama, wrote in his 1858 book *Mustang Gray; A Romance* that Gray always traveled with a packhorse bearing casks of alcohol. "It mattered little to him what it was—whiskey, m[e]scal, brandy—anything, as he expressed it, that would make the blood flow more freely," Clemens wrote. "Or, in the rude, though expressive phraseology of one of his comrades, 'Anything that would make the drunk come.'"

Clemens praised Gray for bravery in Mexico but acknowledged that he never lost his desire to shoot defenseless Mexicans. "The long habit of retaliation was too firmly fixed to be easily shaken off," Clemens said. "He could not learn to forget the bloody feuds of years." After the landmark Battle of Buena Vista, Gray and his men were ordered to escort a number of prisoners from Monterrey to Camargo, Clemens wrote, but the prisoners "never reached their destination." Gray reported to his superiors the Mexicans had escaped en route, which no one swallowed. "The 'Mustangers' (as Gray's company were called) had established a reputation that threw many doubts on the truth of the story," Clemens observed. "The General himself utterly disbelieved it."

Though little noted back in the United States, Gray's infamy spread throughout the U.S. Army in Mexico. Dr. S. Compton Smith, a field surgeon under General Taylor, admired most Rangers. But Gray's men composed a "gang of miscreants," Smith said. "This party, in cold blood, murdered almost the entire male population of the old rancho of Guadalupe—where not a single weapon, offensive or defensive, could be found! Their only object being plunder."

This incident had its origins in February 1847, when Mexican guerrillas attacked an American wagon train, torturing and killing the teamsters who drove it. By one report, more than forty American teamsters were slain, their bodies mutilated—eyes gouged, hearts cut from their bodies—and left for buzzards and wolves. Some were burned alive. "After being smeared with tar, [they] had been burnt to a crisp upon the wagons," wrote Captain Giddings, who came upon the scene days later. "I saw the half of a human head, which had been cleft from the crown downward, lying on the road at a great distance from any corpse. The face was upturned to the sun, and the shrunken and ghastly features caused some stanch old horses . . . to snort and tremble with fright."

Samuel Chamberlain penned a vivid picture of instant retaliation: U.S. commanders "let loose on the country packs of human blood-hounds called Texas Rangers," he wrote. Mustang Gray and his men rode to a ranch near Agua Fria, Chamberlain reported, and dragged "all the males capable of bearing arms"

from the houses. All were tied to posts, and a gun was placed in the hands of a
Ranger who had, under unspecified circumstances, "been castrated by Mexicans
in Chihuahua." His name was said to be Greasy Rube.

"The grim old Ranger would coolly fire his rifle from the distance of one
hundred yards and send the ball crashing through the poor devil's brain, keeping tally by cutting a notch on the stock of his fatal Rifle," Chamberlain wrote.
"Thirty-six Mexicans were shot at this place, a half hour given for the horrified
survivors, women and children, to remove their little household goods, then the
torch was applied to the houses, and by the light of the conflagration the ferocious [Texans] rode off to fresh scenes of blood."

In a letter to the U.S. Army adjutant general, General Taylor wrote that he
believed Rangers and others had committed an "atrocious massacre" at the
ranch. But he said he was unable to identify those responsible because terrified
survivors would not talk—"doubtless afraid that they might incur a similar fate."
Gray's Corpus Christi Rangers were mustered out of federal service in 1847. Gray
returned to the Nueces Strip and died the next year of cholera.

After the Americans took Mexico City in 1847, Hays and the Rangers arrived in
the capital as sensations, parading through the streets with their unique flair.
Some rode backward on their horses, while others made their way standing on
the saddle. "Here they came, rag-tag and bob-tail, pell-mell and helter-skelter,"
reported Lieutenant Colonel Ebenezer Dumont of Indiana. "The head of one
[was] covered with a slouched hat, that of another with a towering cocked hat . . .
whilst twenty others had caps made of the skins of every variety of wild and tame
beasts."

Many Mexicans strained for a glimpse of them. "They . . . excited as much
lively interest as if President Polk and the American Congress had suddenly set
themselves down . . . to organize and regulate a government and laws for the
people of this benighted land," a New Orleans correspondent wrote. But other
Mexicans fled to safety. "Women, affrighted, rushed from the balconies into
houses," he wrote. "The Mexicans believed them to be a sort of semi-civilized,
half-man, half-devil, with a slight mixture of the lion and snapping turtle, and
have a more holy horror of them than they have of the old saint himself."

However fascinated they might have been, sensible locals kept their distance. "The greasers must not interfere with them, as was illustrated this evening,"

the correspondent wrote. As the Rangers were passing down a street, a crowd of *leperos*—derogatory slang for young toughs—gathered around them and began throwing stones. "Never," Colonel Dumont observed, "was a guilty act more instantly punished."

The Rangers pulled their guns and fired away. "In a very few minutes there were ten dead Mexicans lying in the street," the New Orleans reporter wrote, "and two men, badly wounded, taken to the guard house."

General Winfield Scott heard of the Rangers' actions and pronounced himself deeply troubled. "Having exerted himself to suppress all disorder and prevent all outrages, the commanding general was extremely wrathy, and despatched an order for Col. Hays to appear instantly before him," Dumont said. Scott demanded to know if the accounts were true. Hays responded that the information was correct, Dumont said, and told the general the Rangers were "not in the habit of being insulted without resenting it." The general's anger soon abated. "The two men talked pleasantly over coffee," Dumont said, "then the Texas Ranger returned to his command to tell his boys that they must watch their step from now on."

They didn't. Early in 1848 a Ranger named Adam Allsens—also identified as Alsans and Alsence—wandered alone into a part of Mexico City known as Cutthroat, where a mob attacked him. "He was assailed by a murderous crowd and almost literally cut to pieces," wrote Ranger Rip Ford. "Those who saw him said his heart was visible, and its pulsations were plainly perceptible." After eight hours he died, and the Rangers buried him with full military honors. "He was a good and a brave man," Ford said, "and had the esteem and the confidence of the whole command."

His fellow Rangers brooded in silence, Ford said, until that night, when fifteen or twenty Texans made their way to the dark streets of Cutthroat. From their headquarters, American officers heard multiple gunshots. The firing continued for more than an hour. Hays dismissed it as a company of "horse marines" conducting drills. When it was over, more than eighty Mexicans lay dead—"a fearful outburst of revenge," Ford said. Though the incident was reported in American newspapers, the U.S. Army apparently did not investigate.

Early in the war a New York newspaper correspondent wrote that the Rangers had one overriding goal in Mexico: to kill General Santa Anna. "He may capitulate—he may surrender—he may be under the shelter of . . . Gen. Taylor, but if the Rangers come within reach of him, they will slay him," the writer predicted, "even if it be at the table of the American commander."

They had their chance in the spring of 1848. With the fighting finally at an end, Santa Anna found himself at such a table—not of the commander, but of a U.S. Army officer. Deposed and defeated, he was by now a morose, portly has-been with a peg leg, dependent on the Americans for dispensation until he could transit to exile in Jamaica.

On this afternoon he took his dinner with his wife and daughter at an estate near Jalapa. A crowd had formed outside the door to the dining room. Major John R. Kenly of Maryland, who was with the general, noticed Hays among the onlookers. The famous Ranger wore a sombrero, a jacket, and, around his waist, a silk sash. Kenly knew Hays, and he had heard of Rangers' threats to kill Santa Anna. A lawyer by training, the major sought to defuse the situation. He went to Hays and said, "Suppose you let me present you to General Santa Anna."

Santa Anna was eating fruit as the two men approached the table. He started to rise, and Kenly introduced Hays. "When I pronounced this name, [Santa Anna's] whole appearance and demeanor changed," Kenly recalled, "and if a loaded bombshell, with fuse burning and sputtering, had fallen on that dinner-table, a greater sensation would not have been caused."

Mexican officers rose in alarm, Kenly said, and the general's wife turned pale. Santa Anna abruptly sat down and resumed eating his fruit, his gaze on the table. "Colonel Hays, gentleman as he was, bowed politely and withdrew from the room," Kenly said. The matter of Santa Anna's future safety, Kenly thought, had now been defused.

That wasn't exactly true. About the same time Hays was showing courtesy to the general, others were plotting his death. Hearing of these plans, adjutant Rip Ford rode to the nearby Ranger camp. "We discovered everything at a white heat," Ford wrote. "Revenge was the ruling passion of the hour."

The Rangers once more presented their litany of Santa Anna's offenses: the Alamo, Goliad, the black bean incident—all part of an "inhuman and un-Christian war upon the people of Texas," Ford acknowledged. They said they planned to line the road on which Santa Anna would soon travel and kill him as he rolled past in his gilded carriage.

Ford believed he had to head this off. Instead of vowing to punish the men, he said, he appealed to reason and honor. "Santa Anna dishonored himself by murdering prisoners of war," Ford said he told them. If the Rangers responded by assassinating him, Ford said, "you would dishonor Texas."

The appointed hour arrived. After his postprandial cigar, Santa Anna prepared to depart with his wife and daughter. They boarded their carriage, pulled by eight mules, and left the estate. A line of Rangers formed on each side of the road. They sat silently on a stone wall as Santa Anna, flanked by a badly outmanned honor guard, rolled toward them. "There were several hundred of them," Major Kenly said of the Rangers, "as quiet as if at a camp-meeting listening to a sermon."

The carriage passed into the Texans' gauntlet. Now would have been the time to show their fury, but the Rangers stayed silent, as did Santa Anna. "The old warrior's face blanched a little at the sight of his enemies of long standing," Ford said. "He might have thought of the bitter recollections these bronze and fearless men had garnered up from the past, and how easy it would be for them to strike for vengeance and for retribution."

None of the Rangers moved. They watched their sworn enemy fade untouched into the distance, and returned to a subdued camp. "The memories of the bloody past were buried," Ford said, "and no one cared to disturb their repose."

They had passed on the chance to kill their most hated foe, but the Rangers' thirst for revenge did not abate. "Some seventy-five or eighty of the Texas Rangers, officers as well as men, discharged from our service a few weeks since . . . have banded together for the purpose of robbing the defenceless Mexicans this side [of] the mountains," the New York Tribune reported in late 1848. The newspaper said the Rangers had descended on the town of Los Sabinos, near Mexico City, "and after various murders and other outrages . . . demanded a contribution of a large sum of money, threatening in the alternative the total destruction of the town." Once the "imbecile inhabitants" paid them, the newspaper said, the Rangers moved to another village and employed the same scheme. The correspondent had nothing but contempt for Mexicans, who were "treacherous and heartless." Yet the Rangers were worse, he said. "The Texan stock of Americans . . . so far surpass in brutality and universal scoundrelism all Mexican examples as to set at defiance any attempts at comparison."

Hays, McCulloch, and many others returned to Texas to great and deserved acclaim. But some Rangers kept the rampages going well after their service in Mexico. "The Rangers . . . are the very dregs of society, and the most degraded of human creatures," said Emmanuel Domenech, a Catholic priest from France who found himself on the border at war's end. He described an attack by the Rangers on a Lipan Apache camp—a purportedly peaceful village—west of San Antonio. "They slew all, neither woman nor child was spared," Domenech said. "These blood-thirsty men . . . have neither faith nor moral feeling."

The Mexican War turned the United States into a continental empire, though it never quite captured the national imagination as either a grand victory or a just cause. However, Zachary Taylor, fresh from success in Mexico, was elected president in 1848. And the Rangers, despite some coverage of their worst moments, emerged from the war with an aura of honorable swashbuckling that resonated with the American public—an image that preceded by several decades, and set the tone for, the national infatuation with the cowboy West.

As soon as the shooting stopped, a novel hit print: *The Texan Ranger; or, The Maid of Matamoras, a Tale of the Mexican War.* Sam Walker makes an appearance in the book as a Mexican officer laments, "Nothing born south of the Rio Grande can withstand Walker and his Rangers." In another scene a Ranger comes upon a wounded Mexican soldier. The surrendering Mexicans expect to have their throats cut "as they would have cut the throats of their conquerers had the battle gone the other way." But the fictional Ranger declares, "Texians kill men only in fair combat, not murder them when they are beaten. . . . Do you think I am a butcher?" He gives the wounded man water. "In this manner," the author explains, "did the brave Rangers temper their war-like courage with the sweet virtues of humanity."

So went the American dehorning of the Texas Devils. The Rangers' excesses in Mexico, should they merit a mention, were generally passed off as more than justified. "Was it a wonder that it was sometimes difficult to restrain these men . . . who were standing face to face with the people whose troops had committed these bloody deeds?" wrote Rip Ford.

Samuel Reid, after riding with McCulloch, published in 1847 a well-received account of the war that depicted the Rangers as valorous and essential. As Reid noted, many of the Rangers encountered Mexicans who had killed other Texans. "Yes! some of the incarnate fiends . . . boldly walked the streets," he said. But Reid described the Rangers' response obliquely and raised the novel theory that Mexicans had committed suicide out of guilt. "If some of the most notorious of these villains were found shot or hung up in the chaparral . . . the government was charitably bound to suppose, that during some fit of remorse and desperation, tortured by conscience for the many evil deeds they had committed, they had recklessly laid *violent hands upon their own lives!*"

Big-Foot Wallace, who fought with Hays, explained the Rangers' actions with his own winking approach. "Is it any wonder," he said, "with the recollection of such treatment still fresh in their memory, that in the war . . . the Texans should have sent many a 'greaser' 'up the spout,' without the formality of a court-martial to decide upon his guilt or innocence." Wallace, whose brother died in the Goliad massacre, said he never killed any Mexicans in cold blood. However: "I always turned them loose first and gave them a chance for their life; nevertheless, very few of them ever were heard of again, as in those days I was hard to beat in a 'foot-race.'"

Thus did the Rangers gain a reputation they have held since. Even a military man well aware of their excesses in Mexico draped them in virtue, patriotism, and wide-open-spaces individualism. "A nobler set of fellows than these . . . never unsheathed a sword in their country's cause," Lieutenant Colonel Dumont of Indiana wrote. "Young and vigorous, kind, generous and brave . . . they are neither regulars nor volunteers common, but Texas Rangers—as free and unrestrained as the air they breathe."

The war between Mexico and the United States was over. The war between Mexicans and these free and unrestrained Rangers had many more years to run. The fighting would be, in many cases, just as fierce.

YOUNG TEXAS IN REPOSE.

An abolitionist cartoon, published in New York around 1845, shows a representative of the nation's newest state atop a manacled black man. The markings on the Texan's arm say "Murder," "Incest," "Rape," "Fraud," and "Slavery."

Chapter 8

CROSSING THE RIVER

"Men of the Frontier! Come, Then, and Help Us"

> It is hard to convince the Texans that retaliation on the innocent is not
> the way to correct the evil.
>
> —BREVET MAJOR GENERAL PERSIFOR SMITH, U.S. ARMY

The Mexican army had been soundly defeated, but the home front—those great and lonely expanses of South and West Texas—remained a field of war. The Indian attacks kept coming.

Westward expansion brought whites into conflict with Native Americans elsewhere in the United States during the early 1850s. The Yuma War took place in Southern California and Arizona. And Anglo gold seekers rushing into the mountains of Northern California killed thousands of Indians or enslaved them in the mines. Much of the era's worst fighting, however, occurred in Texas. "Some of the fiercest and most insolent of the tribes" in North America roamed the state, the U.S. secretary of war, C. M. Conrad, reported in 1851. A newspaper correspondent described the constant fear: "At this moment there is not a father of a family in Western Texas who may not find, on his return home after an hour's absence, his wife and children weltering in their blood, or carried into a captivity a thousand times worse than death itself."

Comanches were feared the most. But others, such as some bands of Lipan Apaches, also instilled terror and dread in farmers and ranchers. Weakened by war and disease, many of the Lipans had retreated to the northern Mexican state of Coahuila. From there, they recuperated enough to launch forays over the Rio Grande to take Texans' horses and kill their cattle.

Bands of Seminoles, who found refuge in Coahuila after they were driven from Florida by the U.S. government, also forded the river to plunder. Some were under the sway of Wild Cat, also known as Coacoochee, a tall, charismatic chief who had led the flight to Mexico. Wild Cat embodied the white man's idea of the Noble Savage. He made the occasional visit to Texas towns, speaking English and bowing to ladies. "His whole attire had the rather un-Indian merit of neatness," wrote Cora Montgomery—the pen name for Jane Cazneau, a former mistress of Aaron Burr's who now found herself on the border. "A row of crescent-shaped silver medals, arranged in something like a breast-plate, glittered on his breast, and he had good arms," she wrote. "Perhaps he reads Bryon."

When not inspiring Romantic delusions, the Seminole chief practiced war and banditry with skills that gained him great notice. A newspaper described his escapades: "Seminole Indians are committing depredations on the frontier, headed by the famous Wild Cat. . . . About sixty head of horses and mules were driven across the Rio Grande in broad daylight, and Wild Cat himself led the marauding party."

The government of Mexico showed little interest in stopping Indians from poaching across the border. Some Americans suspected the Mexicans even encouraged it. The U.S. Army had the job of controlling Indians but performed erratically at best. The soldiers, many of whom were muttonchopped European immigrants, weren't particularly good at frontier fighting, having been trained in the regimented formations of old-style infantry. The Indians, however, fought as guerrillas. And the territory the army patrolled loomed big and empty, so the task of tracking and capturing stealth bands of wily horsemen was like chasing smoke.

These army regulars, stationed in a land of miserable heat and bad water, also faced poor health and a lack of supplies. "There is a great deal of sickness among the troops," Brevet Major General Persifor Smith, commander of federal forces in the state, wrote in the summer of 1854. "Many suffer from the scurvy, for want of lime-juice." Others were afflicted with fever and dysentery. At one Texas post, the soldiers had no horses because Congress failed to appropriate the necessary funds.

News of Indian attacks made for a frightened and agitated public. Indian agent Robert Neighbors wrote Texas governor Elisha M. Pease in April 1854 to tell him of "one of the most horrible and cold-blooded massacres that it has ever been my painful duty to record." At a settlement northwest of San Antonio, Neighbors said, Indians of the Wichita tribe killed a man and his three young daughters and abducted his eight-year-old son. "INDIAN OUTRAGES!!!" read the headline from the *San Antonio Ledger.* "ONE MAN MURDERED!!! PROBABLE MUR-DER OF FOUR CHILDREN!!!"

Like many governors before and since, Governor Pease summoned the Rangers.

The Mexican War had made them heroes, but the Rangers still lacked perma-nent financing and institutional structure. Essentially leaderless, they operated with a rotating cast of irregulars, many of whom had had their own prior run-ins with the law. As had been the case in Mexico, rigidly trained military men dis-paraged them as well-armed louts.

"Rangers are rowdies," wrote General Albert J. Myer, a surgeon and founder of the U.S. Army Signal Corps, "rowdies in dress, manner and feeling." Myer, a New Yorker assigned to the frontier, dismissed the popular depiction of the Tex-ans. "Now, don't picture to yourself the Ranger, as you have read of him in the newspapers," he wrote, "the personification of the brave and reckless—wild, per-haps but with a redeeming trait of lofty chivalry." Instead, Myer advised in an 1855 letter to a friend:

> Take one of the lowest canal drivers, dress him in ragged clothes . . .
> put a rifle in his hand, a revolver and big Bowie knife at his belt—
> utterly eradicate any little trace of civilization or refinement that may
> have by chance been acquired—then turn him loose, a lazy ruffianly
> scoundrel in a country where little is known of, less cared for, the laws
> of God or man, and you have the material for a Texan Mounted Ranger,
> an animal—perhaps I should say brute.

Despite these qualities, or more likely because of them, the Rangers re-mained the state's best anti-Indian force, though many of their campaigns were desultory and inconsequential—a product of poor funding and inept command. (Jack Hays and Ben McCulloch had departed Texas for California.) Higher ambitions prevailed on July 5, 1855, when Governor Pease authorized Ranger captain James H. Callahan to "raise a company of mounted men" to "pursue any marauding parties of Indians" and "chastise them wherever they may be found." The state government was in such poor shape that it couldn't buy food, ammunition, or other supplies for Callahan's company, much less pay salaries. Pease hoped the Texas Legislature would reimburse the Rangers.

The governor had turned to a proven warrior when he chose the forty-year-old Callahan. A native of Georgia, Callahan had served as a soldier in the Texas Revolution, during which he was taken prisoner by Mexicans and escaped. Later, when not farming or operating a store, he joined other Rangers in turning back Mexican forces that made ill-fated excursions over the border. They fought Indians too. Callahan was, by all accounts, fearless in the exercise of his duties.

As a Ranger, he did not shy from the harsh application of justice—making horse thieves, for instance, dig their own graves before their summary execution by firing squad. Sometimes he didn't even grant them those few minutes. A. J. Sowell, a fellow Ranger, recalled the discovery of a Mexican who was suspected of stealing horses near the settlement of Seguin. The man, who had been shot in the leg, signaled that he wished to surrender. "Come then," Callahan said from his horse, "and get behind me." Sowell described the rest: "The Mexican then took a large silk handkerchief, and binding it around his wounded leg, hopped to Callahan's horse to get up, but was instantly shot dead with a pistol by the ranger captain."

With the governor's edict, Callahan had a mission. He might make some money as well, as the governor's commission to chase and chastise Indians provided cover for potential riches. Historical evidence strongly points to a secret plan by Callahan for the pursuit, capture, and sale of runaway slaves.

Stephen F. Austin's original settlers envisioned a cotton empire in Texas, and their dream had come true. By 1850, Texas was producing about thirty million pounds of cotton a year. Most grew in the rich river valleys of the eastern half of the state, where slaves picked much of it. The population of Texas numbered about 154,000 free whites and 58,000 black slaves, with more chattel on the way. Ships from New Orleans, with slaves shackled in their cargo holds, arrived weekly in the port of Galveston, where the mayor personally supervised auctions.

At the same time, the abolitionist movement was growing as a political force in northern and border states. Yet few Texans dared publicly question the morality or propriety of slavery. The planter class was relatively small but of elite status in the years before the Civil War. Slave owners held many of the state's political offices, and abolitionists, if they existed at all, stayed hidden. A white man who openly declared his opposition to slavery often found himself run out of town, if he was fortunate. In Fort Worth a vigilante mob seized abolitionist Methodist minister Anthony Bewley and lynched him. Bewley was buried in a shallow grave—so shallow his knees protruded from the ground. Weeks later his bones were disinterred and scattered on the roof of a storehouse belonging to Ephraim Daggett, who had been a member of Jack Hays's Mexican War company. There children played with them.

Cotton planters in Texas, and across the South, believed that the expansion of their production was limited only by a shortage of forced labor. An 1808 federal law forbade the importation of slaves from other countries. The planters reasoned that if the law could not be repealed, it could at least be circumvented. One scheme targeted the small Central American country of Nicaragua, which lay about twelve hundred miles by ship from the port of Galveston.

Under this plan, the Mosquito Coast could be used as a way station in the smuggling of captured Africans. It would require, however, the takeover of a foreign nation, an endeavor for which Texas Ranger mercenaries would provide muscle and firepower. Though it violated federal neutrality laws, this mission received the hearty endorsement of the editor of the *Galveston News*: "Those who are not for us must be against us. Those who deny slavery and the slave-trade are enemies of the South."

William Walker of Nashville led the initiative, proclaiming Nicaragua an independent republic with himself as president. Walker's supporters urged Texans to immigrate to the isthmus nation to supplant the "imbecile race" who had controlled it. Among those raising money and men for the effort were Mirabeau Lamar and David Burnet, both former presidents of the Texas Republic, and Hardin Runnels and Francis Lubbock, both of whom were future governors of the state.

Responding to a call for volunteers, several hundred men who described themselves as Texas Rangers departed Galveston by steamer for the Nicaraguan jungle. They were not officially sanctioned by the State of Texas, but they included a number of actual Rangers, past and present. A group of one hundred from San Antonio bore the name "Alamo Rangers" and carried a banner—presented to them by women of the city—that said ALAMO RANGERS, REMEMBER YOU ARE TEXANS.

Some of these Texans were good fighters who had been trained well. Others seemed intent on pillaging in Central America and broke away from Walker's freelance army—with catastrophic results. "It appears that the company reported as having deserted in a body consisted of thirty men, calling themselves 'Texas Rangers,' who, having been mounted and equipped with carbines at the expense of the state, forthwith abandoned the service and started off on a predatory expedition among the mountains," the *New York Journal of Commerce* reported. "They are said to have met the fate they deserved from natives exasperated by their atrocities."

The Rangers who came to fight rather than steal did not fare well, either. Native rebels defeated many of them in battle, while tropical diseases felled others. Walker's scheme ultimately collapsed, which led to his execution by firing squad.

Texans who owned slaves complained of another problem: here the Underground Railroad ran south. Mexico had outlawed slavery in 1829, which meant freedom was just across the Rio Grande. "There wasn't no reason to run up North," said Felix Haywood, who had been a slave in Texas. "All we had to do was to walk, but walk South. . . . In Mexico you could be free. They didn't care what color you was."

Crossing the border put runaways outside the reach of the federal Fugitive Slave Act, which required the capture of escapees within the United States and a return to their masters. The passage to Mexico, however, was treacherous. Runaways had to traverse hundreds of miles of arid brush-and-cactus country on foot, without maps or guides. They faced starvation, thirst, and rattlesnakes. Slave hunters tracked them with bloodhounds. An 1854 public notice in the *Texas Planter* newspaper offered the services of a "celebrated pack of negro dogs" for $5 a day.

Newspapers routinely ran advertisements setting a handsome price for fugitives. "One Hundred Dollars' Reward!" proclaimed a typical 1850 posting, "for the apprehension and delivery of my Boy, Toney." Toney had escaped from North Texas fields with his brother, Sam. The public notice continued: "Toney is about 26 years old, very black, perhaps a little over 6 feet high, slow-spoken, has a scar about 2 inches in length on his forehead, was shot, with a rifle-ball, through the top part of the right thigh, has a good many whip-marks on his back and breast."

Professional slave hunters roamed the border in search of fugitives. If the hunters did not catch the runaways, Indians might. In 1850, army captain Randolph B. Marcy came upon two slave girls purchased from Comanches in Texas. The pair had been with a group of fugitives heading for the Rio Grande when the Indians intercepted them. All were killed, Marcy said, except the girls, who were "taken to the camp, where the most inhuman barbarities were perpetrated upon them." The Comanches scraped away layers of the girls' skin to see how deep their blackness went and burned them with live coals to see if they felt pain the same as others. By the time the army captain saw them, "the poor girls were shockingly scarred and mutilated."

To abolitionist sympathizers like Frederick Law Olmsted, who traveled through Texas in the early 1850s, the flight to Mexico revealed great courage. "Brave negro! say I," Olmsted wrote. "He faces all that is terrible to man for the chance of liberty." Folklore had it that at least one fugitive floated across the Rio Grande on a bale of cotton, gaining freedom on the very material that spawned his enslavement.

Despite the risks and hardships of the journey, by the mid-1850s an estimated four thousand runaways had found refuge south of the border. Some of them even lived with Wild Cat and the Seminoles. Angry Texas planters pressed the federal government for an extradition agreement with Mexico, to no success. At towns across the eastern and central parts of the state, the masters met to devise ways to thwart escapes and capture fugitives.

One of their most vocal champions was Rip Ford, Ranger veteran of the Mexican War. Ford's Austin newspaper, the *Texas State Times*, gave him a forum for strong opinions, including his fervent belief that runaways should be caught in Mexico and repatriated to Lone Star cotton fields. These fugitives, Ford reminded his readers, were individuals who were "owned by men living in Texas," and their Mexican freedom came at great cost to these owners. "The average value of each negro may be set down at $800," Ford wrote, so the "aggregate loss" exceeded $3 million.

Like many of his fellow Rangers, including Callahan, Ford belonged to a secret group known as the Knights of the Golden Circle. The Knights entertained visions of infiltrating or invading Mexico, where they would set up an independent slaveholding nation with its capital in Havana, Cuba. It would, the leader of the Knights predicted, "vie in grandeur with the old Roman Empire."

Plans for this domain, however, still reposed in the hallucinatory stage. In the meantime, slaves belonging to Texans had to be seized and returned. "The evil is augmenting daily," Ford warned. Because the U.S. government had proved hapless in this enterprise, he said, alternative initiatives must prevail: "Let men, goaded by frequent losses, once shoulder their rifles and make a forward movement in direction of the Rio Grande, and nothing short of success will satisfy them."

Into this breach stepped Captain Callahan, who by some reports had personally lost some slaves to Mexico. He began assembling his men for an expedition to the border and beyond. Ford foresaw a divine hand in such action. "Heaven," he wrote, "would bless this enterprise with success." More earthly blessings were pending as well: Texas slaveholders had assembled a bounty pool to pay for the return of the runaways. By the summer of 1855 it had reached $20,000.

Rangers had been tracking down runaways on the Texas side of the border for years. Sometimes they acted within the law, and sometimes they did not. Charles W. Webber, a writer and confederate of Jack Hays's vaunted company, told of an escaped slave who reached San Antonio, where "he was arrested by the vigilant Rangers [and] thrown into chains." (Webber later joined one of William Walker's invading forces in Nicaragua and was killed in a skirmish.) A. J. Sowell recounted an 1838 battle near Austin between Rangers and a ragtag force of Cherokees, Mexicans, and runaway East Texas slaves. The Rangers shot one runaway three times. "But seeing that his shot did not kill him, [a] ranger dismounted, and drawing his Bowie knife, gave him some ugly cuts," Sowell wrote. Still the slave did not die. "A doctor who accompanied the rangers dressed his wounds, sewing up the knife cuts," Sowell said. The Rangers sold the man for $800 and divided the proceeds.

Another runaway, captured unhurt by the Rangers, was transported to the nearby town of Seguin. Along the way, he claimed he had "killed women and children enough to swim in their blood," Sowell said. When the Rangers arrived at Seguin, Sowell reported, "he was taken out and shot."

Those were isolated events involving individuals or small groups of men. Callahan's endeavor, by contrast, was envisioned as one of the biggest and most ambitious of slave hunts. One of his first actions was to meet in San Antonio with Bennett Riddells, a slaveholders' representative who had spoken with officials in northern Mexico. "He told me that there would be no difficulty to my crossing," Callahan said. Riddells supplied Callahan with a written agreement from Mexican authorities that promised the Ranger force could proceed unmolested.

Assurances in hand, Callahan planned his expedition from a camp near Enchanted Rock, the massive granite dome west of Austin. In a letter written to his quartermaster, the captain made clear his plans for plunder: "If any property is taken," he wrote, "I want it to be understood that it belongs to those that go and will be divided accordingly." But he wished to conceal the true nature of his mission from his men until they crossed into Mexico. "I believe some of the boys have found out the arrangement," he wrote, but it would be best to "keep the matter as much of a secret as possible." That might be difficult, as even Major General Smith, the army commander, had heard reports "that a party was organizing to go into Mexico, and take negroes that had run away from Texas."

Callahan's company of eighty-eight men ranged in age from sixteen to forty-four, a mix of battle-hardened veterans and raw farm boys. Soon they were joined by those under the command of another Ranger captain, William R. "Big" Henry. The grandson of founding father Patrick Henry ("Give me liberty or give me death"), he was known in polite circles as an adventurer. Those less charitable considered him a border pirate. Henry had previously fought alongside Mexican revolutionaries to establish, without success, the Republic of the Sierra Madre in northern Mexico. And he had launched a number of so-called filibusters—illegal fortune-seeking raids—south of the Rio Grande, including at least one attempt to capture fugitive slaves.

Most recently Henry had led a company of Rangers commissioned to work with the U.S. Army's Indian-fighting efforts. They found few Apaches but plenty of liquor. Some of Henry's men broke into the D'Hanis, Texas, post office and shot up the small town west of San Antonio, breaking windows and killing pigs. "I have now charges on hand against the captain for misconduct while drunk," Major General Smith wrote to the U.S. secretary of war.

In mid-September 1855, the Callahan expedition—which eventually numbered about 130 men—commenced its 175-mile ride to the border. A seemingly endless scrubland of low ridges and shallow ravines sprawled before them. There were no paved roads and few settlements. The railroad had yet to reach this far. No one controlled it, and no law ruled it.

Heavy rains made for a difficult trek over muddy trails and swollen creeks. The men finally reached the Rio Grande on September 29, near the remote town of Eagle Pass, where, on a modest bluff, the U.S. Army had established Fort Duncan. The commander of the fort, an army captain and West Point graduate named Sidney Burbank, would not allow Callahan's company to cross there because they had "no business" in Mexico. Callahan moved his company a few miles downriver, where they could make their passage without federal interference.

The Rio Grande under usual conditions ran placid and narrow here. At some points, less than twenty-five yards of sluggish green water normally separated Texas from Mexico. But the rains had turned the river wide and fast. Any man who tried to wade or swim it now would likely drown. The Rangers improvised: they seized some private ferry boats at gunpoint, and about 110 men made the crossing, their horses swimming alongside. The rest of the men stayed behind to guard the pack train.

Now in Mexico, the mounted company marched through sand hills and mesquite thickets toward the isolated village of San Fernando de Rosas. Seminoles had settled near there, along with fugitive slaves. About eight miles in, the Rangers were warned of an ambush. "We met a Mexican, who said they were waiting for us," recalled J. S. McDowell, who was part of Callahan's company. "We did not believe him. . . . We rode on, cracking jokes."

The first sign of trouble was a cloud of dust from a stand of small trees 250 yards away. "Then," McDowell said, "the movement of men and the glistening of arms were seen in the timber." From the woods, three horsemen emerged, "two of which were apparently Indian chiefs, gaudily dressed." One of them let fly an arrow over the head of the Rangers—either a warning shot or a ceremonial gesture. The Rangers weren't in the mood for either. Two of them took aim with rifles and fired back; they missed the Indians but wounded one of their horses.

Next, a force of about five hundred men, a mix of Mexicans and Indians, filtered from the trees and formed a line facing the Rangers. The Seminole chief Wild Cat was believed to be among them. "Callahan now rode down his line and gave the men a short talk, telling them their only chance was to make a desperate fight," A. J. Sowell wrote. The captain ordered his men to charge. They did so, and the battle was joined with "the yell of the Texans, the warwhoop of the Indians," as Sowell described it.

The Rangers broke through the lines of the Mexicans and Indians and took cover. After hours of their firing at each other, the skirmish ended when the Rangers' adversaries withdrew—"their excuse, as I afterward learned, being a lack of ammunition," McDowell said. Four members of Callahan's company were killed and seven wounded. The Rangers claimed to have killed ninety on the other side, though the Mexicans reported only four dead.

Callahan had enjoyed relative success in this battle, but he clearly had miscalculated. He believed now that the Mexicans who had made promises of safe passage had tricked him. Their real plan, he concluded, was to "induce me to march . . . into the interior, and then overwhelm us with numbers and massacre the whole command."

Any further engagement would probably be disastrous. Callahan ordered his men to retreat to the Mexican town of Piedras Negras, directly across the Rio Grande from Fort Duncan. The village, with three dirt streets, was home to about five hundred peasants. Many were yard farmers who might own a cow or a pig. Some lived in shelters that weren't much more than mud burrows. "Their houses were chiefly *jacales*, or Mexican huts, and many of them consisted of holes or cellars dug in the bank of the river, covered with thatch, without door, window or sides," a U.S. government lawyer noted. "The people were wretchedly poor." Most of them fled in a panic as the Rangers advanced on the town.

Callahan rode to the house of the *alcalde* of Piedras Negras. "Whereupon the alcalde, a short, fleshy man, waddled out, nervously waving a hastily improvised flag on a short stick," McDowell said. He relinquished authority to the Texans and promised to surrender all arms in the town. The Rangers lined up some oxcarts as a perimeter defense and proceeded to loot the village. There wasn't much to grab—corn and flour, a few chickens, some blankets. One Ranger got a custom-made saddle. Others stole some cheap rings and necklaces. "Which," wrote one witness, "they seemed to take delight in displaying."

Wounded Rangers were ferried across the Rio Grande to Fort Duncan. Captain Burbank, the fort's commander, offered Callahan protection if the rest of his men would leave Mexico. Burbank had ordered the turning of several cannons toward Piedras Negras "in such a position as to command the ferry and crossing." But Callahan refused to bring his men back to Texas now; he preferred to finish the fight.

The Ranger captain called for help. "We are in hourly expectation of an attack from a thousand Mexicans and Indians, but we can whip them," he wrote. "We fought all these tribes yesterday, and, as we learn, the celebrated Seminole chieftain, Wild Cat." Callahan warned that the Indians—"whose demonic hands are still wet with the blood of Texan women and children"—must be killed. "If they are not exterminated," he said, "any hour may ring the death-knell of some of your kindred and friends." He closed with an impassioned plea: "Men of the frontier! Come, then, and help us. Let none come but those who will and can fight. If you come, come quickly, and come well-prepared."

However stirring his plea, there was no chance it would be answered. Major General Smith, the army commander, ordered his men to arrest anyone who tried to cross the Rio Grande to help Callahan's raiders. Smith wasn't buying the business about demonic Indian hands wet with blood. The illegal expedition, he wrote, "was originally intended as an inroad into Mexico in search of negroes." Worse for the Texans, the force of one thousand Mexicans and Indians had almost reached Piedras Negras, and their commander vowed to kill every one of the "American dogs." Callahan's men began to desert by the dozens.

Only about seventy Texan fighters were left in the Mexican village now. Callahan at last accepted that he must retreat across the river, but he needed to keep the Mexicans and Indians at bay while the Texans fled. He ordered his men to set fire to Piedras Negras. Rangers on horseback galloped through the dirt streets, touching torches to straw roofs. It was like putting a match to dry prairie grass.

Captain Burbank watched from Fort Duncan, incredulous, as the wind-whipped blaze lit the night. "To my astonishment, the Texans commenced firing the town," he reported, "and in a few minutes nearly every house in the place was in flames." Most of the village burned to the ground. Hundreds of innocent and desperately poor Mexicans lost all their meager possessions. From the Texans' point of view, though, the tactic served its purpose. It provided, as Callahan said, "a wall of fire now preventing any attack upon us." The Rangers had no choice, he insisted. "Nothing saved us but the firing of the town."

The remaining members of his company used skiffs and rafts to flee to Fort Duncan. They left thirty horses behind in Mexico and "about thirty pistols, guns, or rifles," Captain Burbank reported, "which were picked up by the Indians."

What began as a simple raid had now become an international incident. Mexicans were outraged by Callahan's actions. "A multitude of innocent families are without shelter—homeless and ruined," wrote Emilio Langberg, the Danish-born military commander of the state of Coahuila. "But the shame of this barbarous and unjustifiable act shall be as lasting as the remembrance of the occurrence."

Mexico's minister to the United States, Juan M. Almonte, demanded that the "wicked men" who had invaded his country be held responsible for the damages. That was unlikely, for most Texans saw the episode in a different light. "The Mexicans have themselves alone to blame for the burning of their town," the *San Antonio Herald* proclaimed. And the U.S. secretary of state, William Marcy, defended Callahan, insisting that the border crossing was "justifiable by the law of nations."

Major General Smith predicted that Callahan's raid would provoke more Indian attacks. "The Indians will be led to retaliate," he wrote in a report to the U.S. secretary of war. "We may look for an inroad from the Seminoles to murder and scalp, not merely to steal." Though disgusted by Callahan's actions, Smith believed that reigning public sentiment would allow the Ranger captain to go unpunished. "A criminal prosecution of the offenders would be futile anywhere in Texas," he said. He noted that Callahan and his allies "represent the whole affair as a brilliant and successful exploit."

Callahan and remnants of his company decamped to San Antonio. Over the next few days, they tried to mount one more expedition to Mexico, again in the guise of chasing Indians. No new company formed, however. Less than two weeks after the Piedras Negras incident, the governor relieved Callahan of his Ranger command. "Your encounter with and defeat of such a large body of Indians reflects great credit upon yourself and the brave men under your command," Governor Pease wrote to Callahan. But, he added, "you had not the right to take possession of or to occupy Piedras Negras."

The Texas public may have supported him, yet by every reasonable standard, Callahan's mission had failed. He recovered no stolen horses and killed few if any Indians. And he had no fugitive slaves to sell. What's more, his three-year-old son, William, had died in early September. Perhaps seeking an interlude, the Ranger captain repaired with his family to a Central Texas farm, in Blanco County.

He did not find a quiet respite from violence. Callahan soon shot and killed a neighbor's slave who had, he felt, threatened him. "He plumped him in the back with his six-shooter, and that was the last of 'Poor Old Edward,'" the *Seguin Mercury* related with admiration. "The Captain's experience with the 'Injins' doubtless assisted him in this affair."

In April 1856, more shooting spilled more blood, as reported by a Texas correspondent for the *New Orleans Daily Picayune*: "Capt. Callahan, the gallant ranger, the quiet but fearless gentleman, has been dastardly murdered."

A neighbor named Blassengame had been making unflattering comments around town. Some accounts say they involved Callahan's burning of Piedras Negras. Others say they were directed at Callahan's wife. Regardless, Callahan rode to the Blassengame homestead to confront the man. As he waited, someone from inside the house shot the captain off his horse. He was dead at forty-three.

"By this cowardly and fiendish act," the *Picayune* writer said, "we lose one of our most efficient citizens." The correspondent also warned, "His host of warm personal friends will be apt to take vengeance into their own hands." Those were prophetic words. News of Callahan's slaying reached Seguin, the town fifty miles to the south where he had once lived, spinning his friends and relatives into fury. About a hundred of them rode to the Blassengame house, where the mob dragged two of the men outside, beat them, and shot them both to death.

For all his adventures, Callahan did not compile a sterling record as a Ranger. Yet only a year after his death, a member of the Texas Legislature, John Henry Brown, sought to assign immortality.

Brown, a former newspaper editor, had urged that abolitionists be hanged. As a legislator, he pushed for the resumption of the African slave trade. He warned a state House committee hearing that a "free negro population is a curse to any people." He also had been a Ranger captain. Now a new county was being formed in West Texas, and it needed a name. Brown successfully pushed a measure through the legislature to christen it in honor of a fallen Ranger whose actions backed Brown's own beliefs. To this day it is known as Callahan County.

The peasants of Piedras Negras who lost their homes to the Texans' arson sought reparations. It took seventeen years, but in 1872 the Joint Commission of the United States and Mexico decided that 150 claimants would be paid $50,000. This represented a setback in the molding of the Callahan-as-paragon narrative, *Indian Wars and Pioneers of Texas* gave this summary of the Mexico expedition: Callahan "displayed such admirable tact and courage as to not only preserve the utmost coolness among his followers but to repulse the frequent attacks of his pursuers."

Ranger Rip Ford also published an account of the raid about the same time, from the writings of participant McDowell. The "brave and daring Callahan," this version said, had a singular purpose in crossing the Rio Grande: "to chastise the Indians and leave harmless the persons and property of the Mexicans." It mentioned slavery—by now legally abolished in the United States—not at all. Callahan's motive was "pure and patriotic," it said, and his raid had only one goal: "to give peace and security to the suffering frontier of Texas."

The molding of history continued apace. In 1911, John W. Sansom, a Ranger who had taken part in the Callahan raid, wrote his own laudatory remembrance,

Chapter 9

HEATHEN LAND

"The Crack of Texas Rifles"

The sight of an American makes me feel like eating little kids.

—STATEMENT ATTRIBUTED TO JUAN CORTINA

O f all the striking characters who passed through the Ranger ranks in the nineteenth century, none could match John Salmon Ford's breadth of ambition, bravado, action, and rhetoric. Old Rip, as he came to be known, was a Sunday school teacher who read the Bible every night, as his mother had instructed. At the same time, he seemed always to be looking for the next new excitement.

He didn't have to look far in the Texas of his day. "Ours has been a wild life," he said with understatement. A frontier polymath in buckskin, Ford felt at home in a literary salon, in a political debate, or on the field of war. He wrote for newspapers and he held public office. Ford also led men in many hard battles against Indians, Mexicans, and—during the Civil War—the U.S. Army. He blazed a trail across the uncharted desert. He ran the state Deaf and Dumb Asylum, where the in-house newspaper was titled the *Texas Mute Ranger*.

Through his acts and his writing, he evinced a love of adventure and a sense of duty undergirded with Old Testament absolutism. "If savagery is right," Ford once wrote, "civilization is wrong. There can be no middle ground." One of Ford's most active periods, among many, spanned 1858 and 1859. These were by some reckonings the bloodiest years in Texas—and just across its borders—since the revolution. Then in his mid-forties, Ford had moved well past the age when many battling frontiersmen retired to the farm, ranch, or parlor. Yet he assumed a commander's role in two of the greatest fights of that period.

Born in South Carolina in 1815 and raised on a small plantation in Tennessee, Ford trained as a young man in the medical arts. He migrated to East Texas soon after the birth of the republic and hung his shingle: John Salmon Ford, Doctor. Tall, lean, clear-eyed, and jug-eared, he also dabbled in land survey. He studied law at night. He was elected to the Texas Congress. By 1845 he had bought his way into the newspaper business in Austin.

Journalism gave Ford a platform to agitate for one of his favored causes, the capture of runaway slaves. In addition, the *Texas Democrat* rarely missed a chance to praise the Rangers. "There is a devil-may-care, confident, contented look about one of this class, which indicates a prompt readiness to meet any emergency," read a passage that, over time, gained a measure of fame. It continued:

> [A Ranger] is at home everywhere. In the prairie, or the timbered bottom, in the fastnesses of the mountains, the wigwam, the parlor, the boudoir, he is at ease. Hungry or full, clothed genteely or in rags, with a full pocket or an empty one, is the same brave generous fellow. He can ride like a Mexican, trail like an Indian, shoot like a Tennessean, and fight like a very devil—strictly in subordination where there is danger, but hard to keep within bounds when nothing is to do. The Ranger is a kind of anomalous creature, an uncouth but active soldier, always on the alert.

An uncouth but active man at ease in the wigwam and the boudoir could craft an audacious life on the Texas frontier. Ford seemed determined to prove this personally.

He enlisted with the Texas volunteers in the Mexican War and joined Jack Hays's corps of Rangers. Ford emerged from the war with malaria and a nickname. The fevers and fatigue of the disease would dog him for years. The moniker Rip was said to have come from his many reports of men killed in action, as he signed each one with the valediction *RIP*.

Ford's service in the war seemed to make him even more restless. In 1849, at the urging of some locals, he and Robert Neighbors, the supervising agent for Texas Indians, set out to blaze a trail from San Antonio to El Paso. Prospectors and others headed for the California gold rush would use this "road." Merchants hoped to sell them goods as they departed on their journey through the barrens of West Texas.

Hays had already tried to find a suitable route but ended up in Mexico, the apparent fault of a wayward guide. Ford and Neighbors recruited Comanches—with whom they were enjoying a rare moment of peace—to show the way. They faced many hardships: bad water, snow, hunger, sickness, a hazardous river crossing, a mule stampede, and—this being the Lone Star hinterlands—rattlesnakes. It took them fifty-five days to reach El Paso and make the return trip, a voyage of nearly twelve hundred miles in all. The route became known as the Ford and Neighbors Trail.

At trail's end Ford made the acquaintance of a large and famous woman known as the Great Western. Her real name was Sarah Bowman—at least for a while, because she married several times. Over some years she nourished a reputation as an entrepreneur and for being, as one of her contemporaries called her, "the greatest whore in the west." Standing six feet, two inches, she towered over many men, including most Texas Rangers, and weighed close to two hundred pounds. "She was very tall, large and well made," Ford recalled.

Much of her background is undocumented, but she was believed to have accompanied her husband, who was a member of General Zachary Taylor's force, to the Rio Grande at the start of the Mexican War. As Mexicans bombarded Fort Texas—later christened Fort Brown—she calmly operated the officers' mess and kept going even when a shell fragment pierced her sunbonnet. When her husband died, she reportedly recruited another soldier spouse with this query: "Who wants a wife with fifteen thousand dollars and the biggest leg in Mexico? Come, my beauties, don't all speak at once. Who is the lucky man?"

After the war she operated a hotel in El Paso, which was where Ford met her. The normally prolific scribe offered few details of the encounter. "She had the reputation of being something of the roughest fighter on the Rio Grande," Ford wrote, "and was approached in a polite, if not humble, manner by all of us, the writer in particular."

As he had shown in his dealings with Ranger captain Callahan, Ford yearned to extend the Lone Star realm to the south. He forged an alliance with José María de Jesús Carbajal, who fancied himself the George Washington of northern Mexico. Carbajal plotted to seize control of the region and liberate its people from the oppressive thumb of the central Mexican government. In exchange for help from Texas, he promised to return all escaped slaves to their American owners and to close the border to further runaways.

Ford praised Carbajal for his crusade to oppose tyranny and promote the cause of free men. He also noted that Carbajal's scheme held "the hope of strengthening the institution of slavery in Texas and in the South." That, Ford observed without irony, "caused Texians to sympathize with a people struggling for liberty."

This notion prompted Ford to raise a company and join Carbajal's "Liberating Army of Northern Mexico" in 1851. Commissioned as a colonel, he led a force of Texans attacking Matamoros, on the Mexican side of the Rio Grande. But when Ford craned his neck through a doorway, a musket ball creased his scalp, causing a concussion. This created, Ford said, "a temporary forgetfulness of words." He was removed for medical treatment, but the battle kept going without him. Some of the remaining Americans set fire to the town and shot Mexicans who tried to salvage their burning homes. When it was clear he could not win, Carbajal withdrew from Matamoros and suffered defeat in two more attacks on other towns. The Texans had fought with "indomitable courage," Ford concluded, but "the revolution was virtually at an end."

Still, he held hope for a slave empire. In addition to the economic arguments, Ford put forth a religious imperative for such dreams and schemes. "The South has the Bible on their side," he wrote. "If there is any one institution by the Word of God, it is that of slavery. From Genesis to Revelations there is not one word against it, and thousands in favor of it." He added that Jesus rebuked "every species of sin" but "never raised his voice against the legitimacy" of involuntary servitude. "If slavery is wrong," he thundered, "the Bible is wrong."

Ford joined and became a leader of a group known as the Order of the Lone Star of the West. It was a clandestine club, with special handshakes, elaborate rituals, and secret passwords that Ford described as "cabalistic." Like the Knights of the Golden Circle, the order envisioned control of a vast slaveholding territory with Havana, Cuba, as its capital. Ford traveled to New Orleans and met with General John A. Quitman, a former governor of Mississippi and hero of the Mexican War who was planning a Cuba invasion. But the project did not look feasible to Ford, who was brave but not foolhardy, and he declined to participate. He no doubt recalled an earlier failed takeover of Cuba, launched from the

United States in 1851, which ended with the execution of many privateers. Ford wrote of his hesitance: "The risk of landing in Cuba, of being left without the means of withdrawing, and of being garroted might have had an influence."

Ford was elected to the Texas Senate in 1852 and continued his career as a newspaper publisher. But he still itched to fight again. Sam Walker was dead. Hays and Ben McCulloch had departed Texas for California. That left Ford at the forefront of Ranger glory. He cemented his position with a major campaign against an old enemy.

By the late 1850s, U.S. Army units were being withdrawn from Texas, which the Comanches exploited. Mounted raiding parties departed the forbidding Llano Estacado—the high western plains, where few white men dared go—and followed the Colorado and Brazos Rivers to farms, ranches, and lonely cabins. "Within a few months after the [cavalry] patrolling ceased," historian T. R. Fehrenbach wrote, "a hundred Texas farm houses had gone up in flames and more than a hundred sun-bloated corpses were buried in the bitter frontier soil." In 1857, "the fall and winter saw them entering . . . in greater force," said Ranger Buck Barry, "killing, scalping, kidnapping and plundering."

Sam Houston, then a U.S. senator, told his congressional colleagues that the regular army wasn't fit for Indian fighting anyway, so it might as well leave Texas. Dressed in his customary deerskin leggings, moccasins, and a Mexican serape, Houston appeared on the Senate floor in early 1858 and requested federal money to pay for Texas Rangers, not U.S. soldiers. "I ask you to give us one regiment of a thousand men of Rangers, and you may withdraw your regular troops and dispose of them accordingly," Houston said. "Give us one thousand Rangers, and we will be accountable for the defense of our frontier."

Houston, it should be noted, had long supported plans to turn Mexico and parts of Central America into an American protectorate. In his more expansive moments, he envisioned himself as a Lone Star Caesar, crossing the Rio Grande to conquer "our poor, distracted, adjoining neighbor" with a massive Ranger force—perhaps a thousand of them—at his command. Not surprisingly, Congress refused to fund the Rangers for Indian wars, a new invasion of Mexico, or anything else. "Thus Texas . . . is left by the Federal Government to protect herself from the savage foe," the Austin *State Gazette* concluded with disgust, "or to heedlessly stand by and witness the daily and brutal murder of our people."

Newly elected governor Hardin Runnels signed into law a bill that authorized

$70,000 to equip and pay one hundred Rangers for frontier defense. Runnels named Ford senior captain one day later. Though effective and ferocious, many of the Rangers' prior actions had been more tactical than strategic as they fought any number of small battles. The army had done the same; the aim of these skirmishes had been to intercept Comanche raiding parties and push them back.

Now, however, the governor called for a major punitive expedition into the Comanches' territory, the likes of which had not been mounted since the days of Hays and John S. Moore. "I impress upon you the necessity of action and energy," Runnels told Ford. "Follow any trail and all trails of hostile or suspected hostile Indians you may discover, and if possible, overtake and chastise them." Ford believed he had license to hit them where they lived, to "let their families hear the crack of Texas rifles and feel the disagreeable effects of hostile operations in their own camps." It would be, he warned, "war to the knife."

The Rangers still did not enjoy the status of a permanent, standing force, so Ford had to recruit and enlist. He assembled an army of hard riders, experienced Indian fighters, and some "old Texas Rangers" with the skills and fortitude for a long and arduous campaign. The team left Austin in February 1858 and rode north, trailed by sixteen pack mules with supplies. They paused at the Brazos Reserve, a reservation of about two thousand Indians in the hilly brush where North Texas meets West Texas, to recruit reinforcements. Indians who hated and feared the Comanches were urged to join the expedition.

Before they could assent, the Indians required a war dance—a "grand, gloomy and peculiar" affair, according to Ford, with brilliant face paint and lurid theater in the flickering firelight. "Every participant had his own way in the matter," Ford wrote. "Some sounded the fear-inspiring warwhoop; others crept along, cat-like, to pounce upon their astonished and demoralized foes. . . . Many sang in a style which would have crazed an old maiden music teacher." In the end, the veteran Ranger captain seemed a bit overwhelmed: "Hell has taken an emetic, and cast up devils upon the earth, and here they are."

Perhaps, but these devils were willing to fight alongside the Rangers. More than a hundred agreed to join Ford's company and take up arms against the Comanches. They came from at least half a dozen tribes, including the Caddo-Anadarko group and the Tonkawas. This enhanced force, now more than two hundred strong, departed the reservation in April 1858. Ford's target was a Co-manche village near the Antelope Hills, along the Canadian River in what is now

Oklahoma. That it was federal Indian Territory, where Ford's Rangers had no jurisdiction, seemed not to matter.

His scouts found a large Comanche camp on May 11. The next day, as Ford's men prepared to attack, Comanche warriors in war paint and bison headdresses came to meet them on the rolling plains. The Comanches outnumbered the Texans and their Indian allies by a hundred. As they howled, gestured, and capered on their horses, the warriors seemed primed for an epic battle. The chief known to the whites as Iron Jacket rode to the front of his army.

"He was a great medicine man," Ford said, and was reputed to "blow arrows aside." The chief won his name and reputation by wearing a vest fashioned from a shingled coat of mail—armor probably taken from the bleached skeleton of a Spanish conquistador. Now he gestured with his lance and "expel[led] his breath from his mouth with great force," Ford said. Iron Jacket appeared "confident of being invulnerable."

The Texans had placed their Indian allies at the tip of their advance. Iron Jacket might therefore have thought he faced only arrows and spears, which his Iberian vest would repel. The Rangers, however, carried powerful Sharps rifles. As Iron Jacket blustered, these whiskered, sunburned men moved to the fore and raised their guns. "About six rifle shots rang on the air," Ford said. "The chief's horse jumped about six feet straight up and fell. Another barrage followed, and the Comanche medicine man was no more."

Fierce, rolling combat now ensued, in several villages across six miles, with each side charging the other throughout. The mounted clash of two forces on an open plain, Ford said in his report to the governor, seemed almost medieval at times: "It reminded me of the rude and chivalrous days of knight-errantry." The fighters rode "prancing steeds" and brandished lances and shields. "And when the combatants rushed at each other with defiant shouts, nothing save the piercing report of the rifle varied the affair from a battle field of the middle ages."

Though they fought hard, the Comanches couldn't match the firepower of Ford's men. "The din of the battle had rolled back from the river," he recalled. "The groans of the dying and the cries of the frightened women and children mingled with the reports of firearms and the shouts of the men as they rose from hill top, from thicket, and from ravine." After seven hours the Comanches were beaten.

When it was done, and the surviving villagers had fled, the Rangers and their allies counted seventy-six killed while losing only two dead. Beyond routing the Comanches, the Rangers had sent a message: the Indians could not be safe from attack anywhere. The encounter became known as the Battle of Antelope Hills. The *Dallas Morning News*, in a 1907 retrospective account, called it "one of the greatest scenic and dramatic incidents . . . in the history of Indian warfare in Texas." The newspaper did not mention that Ford's incursion into Indian Territory violated federal laws.

The victory could not have been accomplished without significant assistance from the Brazos Reserve Indians. They had fought side by side with the Rangers, and without their help, the battle might well have turned out differently. But if they expected a display of gratitude from Ford, they would be disappointed.

In 1858, two days after Christmas, two dozen or so members of the peaceful Caddo and Anadarko tribes left the Brazos Reserve on a week-long hunting trip sanctioned by their agent. Seven of them were men, the rest women and children. They camped that night along Keechi Creek. As they slept, armed men stole into their camp, opened their tents, and began firing. Seven of the Indians were killed, three of them women. Children, including two infants, suffered serious wounds.

Initially, no one could understand why they had been attacked, for these Indians were not known to have engaged in any raids against white settlers. Brazos agency agriculturalist J. J. Sturm went to the scene the next day. "There, on their beds, lay the bodies of seven of the best and most inoffensive Indians on the reserve," he reported, "their bodies pierced by buck shot and rifle balls." If they truly were innocent, the *Dallas Daily Herald* declared, "the annals of Texas furnish no darker record of blood—no baser murder."

Soon a posse of white vigilantes from Erath County admitted the attack. They said they did it because Indians from the reserve had committed depredations in the region. "We have no apology to offer for what we have done," they wrote in a letter. Those they had killed "claimed to be friends and good Indians," the men said, but "our people could not distinguish one tribe from another." They dismissed Texans who condemned them as "sickly sentimentalists."

Pressure from Indian agent Neighbors, who warned of reprisals by reservation Indians, moved the government to action. A judge issued a warrant for the arrest of eighteen of the vigilantes. He ordered Ford and his Ranger company to capture them and bring them to Waco "to be dealt with as the law directs." In addition, Governor Runnels instructed Ford to assist civil authorities in executing the warrant.

The Rangers' duty was clear. They had made these sorts of arrests on many occasions, had in fact touted their talent for rounding up outlaws—the tougher the fugitive, the more gratifying the capture. Ford's own newspaper had said of the Rangers, "There is probably no set of men on earth readier for a fight, a chase, a fandango or anything else which may come up."

But this time Ford refused to act, and he offered an argument that seemed to cast the Rangers as newly converted Quakers. "Now, how did [the judge] expect an organized body of men to be arrested except by force? Was this warrant anything more or less than a command to me to take my company and attack a body of American citizens?" Ford wrote. "My duty was to disobey it." In so doing, he said, he "saved the State of Texas from being the theatre of scenes of violence and homicide."

Texas was of course already that and more, but Ford had his finger to the political winds. With the exception of agent Neighbors—Ford's fellow trailblazer—few Anglos in the region would support the arrest of whites for killing Indians. (Three white men in Indiana were hanged in 1825 for murdering nine Indian men, women, and children, but such punishments were exceedingly rare.) It mattered not at all that Brazos Reserve Indians had been critical to Ford's success at Antelope Hills. The murders went unprosecuted, and in the following summer, all the remaining Native Americans were removed from the reservation and marched north of the Red River, to present-day Oklahoma. Agent Neighbors, who feared for the Indians' continued safety in Texas, persuaded them to move with the promise of more and better land.

For whites, the expulsion had two distinct advantages. It opened even more of Texas to them. And with the reservations closed, all Indians in the state could be considered enemies. Now, said Ranger Buck Barry, "when we saw an Indian we knew how to treat him."

A disconsolate Neighbors, who had accompanied the tribes on their exodus north of the Red River, wrote to his wife like a forlorn Moses: "I have this day crossed all the Indians out of the heathen land of Texas."

Neighbors soon returned to Texas and was slain the next day in Belknap—shot in the back of the head by a white man whose motive was unclear. It was said that when the Indians who once lived on the Brazos Reserve heard of his death, they wept and keened for days. Neighbors may have been an "Indian lover," an epithet hurled at him by embittered Texans, but he was white, and his murder could not stand. A party of vigilantes—possibly including some Rangers—took his killer into the country far from town and imposed the death penalty for his crime.

As for Ford, he soon regained his appetite for armed combat. His next big fight began quietly, with a budding revolutionary's cup of coffee.

The knife and the gun still ruled the Nueces Strip, that desolate and disputed land between the Nueces River and the Rio Grande. The Treaty of Guadalupe Hidalgo, which ended the Mexican War, formally established the Rio Grande as the U.S.-Mexico boundary. But the treaty did nothing to civilize the Strip. In its more remote stretches—which is to say nearly all of it—the region remained the province of rustlers, ruffians, freebooters, and a collection of highwaymen known as prairie pirates. These robbers were known for "seizing any property that comes in their way, murdering travelers, and making descents upon trains and border villages," Frederick Law Olmsted wrote. "Their operations of this sort are carried on under the guise of savages, and at the scene of a murder, some 'Indian signs,' as an arrow-head or a moccasin, is left to mislead justice."

A few towns were settled, most notably Brownsville, which had risen at the site of Zachary Taylor's fort on the Rio Grande. Brownsville became the seat of Cameron County and a center of Texas-Mexico trade—and smuggling. Other vices found a home as well. "The city is infected with lewd and abandoned women," one newspaper correspondent wrote, "and it is impossible for any respectable lady to walk out in the evening, without being made an eye-witness to the most disgraceful and disgusting scenes."

By January 1849 it had a population of about one thousand, but a cholera epidemic that spring killed nearly half its people. "The Destroying Angel is among us," wrote Helen Chapman, the wife of an army officer stationed at Fort Brown. "In Brownsville, the mortality has been dreadful." The disease was caused by fecal contamination of drinking water, and Brownsville drew its water from the dirty Rio Grande. Only one medical doctor practiced in the region. Infected people were dying so fast that the casket makers could not keep pace. Bodies were stacked in the street before they were hauled away by mule-drawn carts and dumped into trench graves outside town.

Another serious outbreak occurred ten years later. This was a "land of pestilence and cutthroats," lamented one traveler, who in April 1859 stopped near Brownsville en route to California. In a letter to his father, he described a cascade of horrific events. It began when cholera felled twenty members of the thirty-person party. One of those not stricken, a Mr. Rowan, went to town to purchase a span of mules. Then, the traveler reported:

> He reached Brownsville after a toilsome journey, and finding that he, himself, was seized with cholera, went and placed himself in the Hospital. But melancholy to relate that he lived but eight hours . . . I loaned my horse to a Mr. Glover to go down town to find his uncle, who was confined by an attack of cholera. When he arrived he was told [the uncle] had died that day; and it being too late for his return that night, he [asked] Curtis to bring my horse. On his journey back the poor fellow was attacked by a party of Indian robbers, and shot; being first lassoed, and when he was dead, his body was thrown into the river near the Brownsville ferry.

Writer and army officer Randolph B. Marcy, who spent years on the border, saw a society that was "eminently impulsive, unsettled and lawless." Courts had been established and law enforcement put in place, Marcy said, but "authorities were, as a general rule, almost entirely disregarded, and virtually set at defiance by the lawless desperadoes along the borders, and crimes of the greatest turpitude were perpetuated almost daily." In such a climate, Marcy wrote, "the most foul and premeditated murders were allowed to pass by unnoticed."

Abner Doubleday, a captain in the U.S. Army—and the purported inventor of the game of baseball—regarded the Nueces Strip with a sort of horrified bemusement: "One of our officers remarked to me one day, 'Isn't it strange that every gentleman to whom I have been introduced here has murdered somebody?'" When official justice prevailed, it tended toward the crude and vindictive. Catholic priest Emmanuel Domenech, a Frenchman, happened upon the administration of punishment. "I saw at Brownsville Mexicans whom the sheriff was flogging to death with his ox-hide lash," he said. "They were bound, half-naked, their arms extended across the prison door, and then scourged on the sides and loins with the most brutal violence." After the whipping, Domenech said, the corpses were sent back to Mexico, "their frames lacerated with stripes."

One of the most notorious desperados making his way through the Strip was John Joel Glanton, a former Ranger. Samuel Chamberlain of Boston wrote of watching Glanton—a man "with eyes deeply sunken and bloodshot, and coarse black hair hanging in snakelike locks down his back"—argue with another Ranger over a card game in a San Antonio saloon. Glanton's opponent pulled a gun, Chamberlain said, but it misfired. "Glanton sprang up, a huge Bowie knife flashed in the candlelight, and the tall powerful young Ranger fell with a sickening thud to the floor a corpse, his neck cut half through."

After fighting in the Mexican War under Ford, Glanton went into the Indian-scalp-hunting business, which paid well for a while. Officials of Chihuahua, Mexico, whose citizens suffered under Apache raids, offered an official bounty. (Paying for Indian scalps was nothing new. In 1755, the lieutenant governor of the province of Massachusetts Bay in New England offered hard cash for the scalps of Penobscot Indians, including women and children.) Glanton and his gang, some of whom were also ex-Rangers, killed dozens—perhaps hundreds—of Apaches and sold their scalps to the Chihuahuan government. They eventually ran out of Apaches to kill, so Glanton's men began shooting and scalping Mexicans, including women and children. To claim the reward, they said the scalps came from Indians. "In the carnival of blood," a contemporary wrote, "Glanton and his Rangers made an easy campaign and a brilliant success."

Another Ranger scalp hunter was Michael Chevallie, who had served valiantly under Hays in Mexico. The New York Herald reported in 1849 that Chevallie was being paid $200 for each Apache scalp. "Whatever the morality of this contract," the newspaper said, "the Major, with his twenty-five men and their six-shooters, will soon realize a rich reward from their bloody bargain." Another newspaper said of Chevallie: "By the latest accounts he had with him nine scalps and four prisoners."

As the criminals and bounty hunters ran rampant, so did the land grabbers. Throughout South Texas, Anglos took possession of vast tracts that had been claimed by Mexicans or Tejanos for generations. Many of the white newcomers who assembled large farms and ranches bought their property fair and square. Others underpaid, however, or swindled it outright. Some challenged old Spanish land grants, Mexican deeds, and titles from the Republic of Texas in American courts, where Tejanos rarely prevailed over Anglos. An untold number simply took the land by force, casting aside peasant farmers and penniless goat ranchers.

Though Tejanos had fought for Texas's independence from Mexico, a substantial portion now found themselves dispossessed. "The Mexicans were treated for a while after annexation like a conquered people," wrote Olmsted. "Ignorant of their rights, and of the new language, they allowed themselves to be imposed upon by the new comers, who seized their lands and property without shadow of claim, and drove hundreds of them homeless across the Rio Grande."

The setting was therefore ripe for an avenger of the aggrieved, one who could light the fuse of their bitterness and hatred—and here emerged the improbable figure of Juan Nepomuceno Cortina. He rose from obscurity to a pedestal from which he could grandly pronounce, "I saw myself compelled in Texas to defend the Mexican name." Or to steal the property of Anglos, depending on one's viewpoint.

Rip Ford took the demonization even further: "He was the enemy of the United States."

Cheno Cortina had spent his entire life on the Rio Grande. He was the unaccomplished son from a Mexican family of some wealth and position. Their holdings included property in Texas before statehood, which made him an American citizen. Young Cheno had neglected school and probably could not read or write. He liked parties and women, but he also fought to defend Matamoros against the so-called liberating army of Ford and Carbajal. At present, locals knew Cortina as the armed escort for teamsters who hauled supplies across the perilous scrublands, and as a suspected cattle thief. Those outside the region knew of him not at all.

That began to change on the morning of July 13, 1859, another border day of terrible heat. Cortina rode the dirt streets of Brownsville with a pistol on his hip. He hitched his horse at Market Plaza and walked into Gabriel Catsel's cantina for some coffee.

As he enjoyed his cup, the thirty-five-year-old Cortina looked through the cantina window and saw city marshal Robert Shears on the street, making an arrest in characteristic fashion.

A squinty-eyed former Ranger, Shears was known to manhandle suspects, especially Mexicans and Tejanos. On this day he apprehended Tomás Cabrera, an old vaquero who had worked on the ranch belonging to Cortina's mother. Shears said later he possessed a warrant "to arrest a disorderly Mexican." It's not clear if Cabrera resisted, nor is it known what he might have said to the marshal. But at some point Shears began pistol-whipping the old man.

Cortina left the café, mounted his horse, and dashed to where Shears was beating his prisoner. After he and the marshal exchanged angry words, Shears fired a shot at Cortina, striking his saddle. Cortina pulled his gun from its holster and fired two times. Shears claimed Cortina shot him first in the back. A second shot, Shears said in an affidavit, "took effect in my left shoulder, the ball coming out in the back." As the badly wounded marshal lay stunned and bleeding in the street, Cortina hoisted Cabrera onto the back of his horse and galloped out of town in a dramatic display of heroic triumph.

For several months afterward, Shears said, Cortina seemed remorseful, and sent him several messages from Matamoros "offering money to reconcile & compromise the shooting affair, and the damages and pains I sustained." Cortina apparently had a change of heart, and the war began.

Hours before dawn on September 28, 1859, Cortina and about seventy armed men on horseback swept into Brownsville. As he entered the city, Cortina carried a list of enemies marked for death. Some of his gang stormed the jail, released all prisoners—freeing murderers and thieves, county officials said—and killed the jailer on duty. They dragged another jailer into the street, shot him, and mutilated him with knives in front of his wife. The Cortinistas galloped to the house of Shears, the marshal, with plans to kill him too. "Fortunately I had absented myself a few moments previous," he said.

Cortina and his posse raised the Mexican flag over Brownsville and, after the sun rose, rode out of town. They had put to death five men in all. In the immediate aftermath, the *Dallas Daily Herald* reported, someone identified only as Mrs. Woodhouse also died—"of nervous excitement."

Two days after the attack Cortina issued a pronouncement. "Ordinary people and honest citizens" had nothing to fear from him, he said. He and his followers only wished to punish the "criminal, wicked men" who had stolen land from Mexicans and spread terror among them.

His words and actions made Cortina an instant hero to many Tejanos and Mexicans, who saw him as a Robin Hood of the Rio Grande. Hundreds grabbed their guns and joined his movement. "He was fearless, self-possessed and cunning," Ford said in a series of somewhat backhanded compliments. "In native intellect Cortina ranked high. No uneducated man could have played the part he did otherwise. . . . He was extremely popular among his countrymen, especially the lower classes. . . . To the poor who heard of him, Cortina was a sign of hope in a land where hope had no meaning."

As Tejanos enjoyed possible vindication, Anglo Brownsville panicked. The city's population exceeded three thousand, and most were of Mexican heritage. Most of them lived in poverty. Anglos held nearly all the positions of wealth and power, and these terrified city officials now issued urgent pleas for help. They organized around-the-clock citizen sentries and erected barricades on town streets.

In late October 1859, a Brownsville resident named W. J. Miller fled the city by swimming his horse across the river to Matamoros and boarding a ferry to South Padre Island. From there he made his way to Corpus Christi, where he began telling all who would listen that Cortina's forces had overrun Brownsville. With cries of "Death to all Americans," Miller said, the Mexicans slew every man they had taken prisoner after "five hours [of] hand-to-hand fighting."

Miller gave this declaration as a sworn and notarized statement, but it wasn't remotely true. However, telegraph lines did not extend to Brownsville. The mail could take days or weeks to arrive, if it arrived at all. Cortina's men had intercepted postal riders and stolen their horses. News therefore traveled by word of mouth, along with fear and exaggeration. As a result, many Texans now suspected that the Cortinistas held a sacred goal of recapturing the Nueces Strip for Mexico, or more. Some envisioned this legion of marauders galloping 350 miles north to Austin, raping and killing as they went, like Mongols in sombreros.

While Miller and others were trafficking in false tales, Brownsville believed itself to be under siege. The mayor of the city, Stephen Powers, wrote an open plea for help to the residents of New Orleans, some six hundred miles across the Gulf of Mexico. Powers asked that one hundred "well-armed men" board a steamship bound for Brownsville, which was "in great danger of destruction by the large force of the enemy." The mayor added that with Brownsville "being utterly impoverished," perhaps the citizens of New Orleans could pay for the volunteer force.

About the same time, the *New Orleans Crescent* published a letter from "a highly respectable gentleman in Brownsville," who could be "fully depended upon as stating nothing but the simple truth." This gentleman depicted Cortina's forces as a swarthy horde frothing at the gates of the city. "Cortina cannot now stop in his career and disband his men, if he were inclined to do so," the gentleman wrote. "His men live on meat alone; some have expended all their means, and they are clamorous for vengeance, and plunder, and they will make one desperate effort before they will disperse."

One of the town's newspapers, the *Brownsville Flag*, fanned the flames. "Mexicans are against us," it said. "The horrible and disgusting mutilation of the bodies of those murdered by Cortina and his co-operators warn us that instead of a revolution we are being warred upon by atrocious savages, who would as soon beat out the brains of an infant as shoot an undoubted spy." This conflict, the *Flag* said, "is a war upon the American race."

Such warnings were fueled in part by recent events in Harpers Ferry, West Virginia. There, less than three weeks after Cortina's assault on Brownsville, radical abolitionist John Brown had tried to spark an armed slave uprising. Texans speculated that like Brown, Cortina plotted to exploit the volatile rage of the repressed, who would rise up en masse and slit the throats of their oppressors. Cortina was in these fevers the Nat Turner of the borderland, and unfounded reports circulated that New England abolitionists secretly funded his rebellion.

A report by a Brownsville grand jury framed the matter in stark racial terms. "Most of the Mexican inhabitants within the State of Texas, and near the Rio Grande, are united with those upon the other side of that river in a secret body . . . with the intent to expel all Americans," the report said. Tejanos who had lived north of the Rio Grande for generations were now U.S. citizens, but that didn't make them—in the grand jury's eyes—Americans. Their sympathies, the grand jury said, were "with the marauders," which made them "alien enemies of Texas and the United States." To the grand jury, the only true Americans were white Texans like them.

Cortina did little to dispel this notion of a race war, though he flipped the dynamic. The white Texans who had come to the border and seized the land of Mexicans were "flocks of vampires in the guise of men," Cortina declared in a pronouncement to his supporters. "Many of you have been robbed of your property, incarcerated, chased, murdered, and hunted like wild beasts." He warned that Tejanos who sought their rights would fight to the death.

Many of Cortina's raiders, however, seemed more intent on seizing livestock and cash than sparking revolt. The marauders targeted Peter Champion, an Italian immigrant who operated a ranch near Port Isabel. Champion said Cortina's men came to his home and demanded $100. "They insisted that I should give this amount or that something else would happen to me. I saw that their intention was wicked," he said in an affidavit. "I went to my bureau and emptied in their presence a little purse which in change contained $13.25." The men put a noose around Champion's neck and demanded more. His wife ran to a neighbor's house "and begged for all the money she had to save my life." It was apparently enough.

Throughout the fall of 1859, the wildfires of rumor swept across South Texas: That Cortina had assembled a force of a thousand men. That he had many cannons. That he had two thousand men, or three thousand. In many towns, Anglos formed minute companies and waited for the hordes to descend. The Knights of the Golden Circle resurfaced and once more made unconsummated plans to invade northern Mexico and declare a Republic of the Sierra Madre. Some officials in Austin heard reports—erroneous, as it turned out—that Cortina had invaded Corpus Christi and burned it to the ground.

It was time, Governor Runnels decided, for the Rangers.

Within days about one hundred Rangers came together under Captain William Tobin, a San Antonio businessman. Tobin had no border-fighting experience and wore no Mexican War medals, but he ascended to command leadership in a time-honored way: he married the daughter of San Antonio's mayor. In mid-November 1859 he and his Rangers arrived at the edge of Brownsville, though residents mistook them for Cortinistas and began firing at them. No one was hurt, and the Rangers moved into the town, where they quickly dashed expectations.

"We had looked to [Tobin's] arrival here as the end of our immediate troubles, but we are disappointed," a Brownsville resident wrote. The company seemed callow and undisciplined at best, the citizen complained. "Scarcely any of his men are of the old Texas Rangers, of whom so much has been said." These new Rangers weren't much interested in maintaining order, as they showed the night after they arrived. Exhausted and surly from crossing the Nueces Strip, they poured into Brownsville's saloons. From there they made their way to the jail, where Tomás Cabrera—the old man whose confrontation with a city marshal had provoked Cortina in the first place—was behind bars. He had been re-arrested days earlier by a Brownsville sheriff's posse. The mob of Rangers and others hauled Cabrera out of the jail and lynched him from a tree in Market Plaza.

To say the Rangers had no competent leaders would not be true. They had one, but they lost him when he fell from a carriage and the wheel crushed his neck. "We are now at a great loss in regard to having a good officer," the company's surgeon, Powhatan Jordan, wrote from Brownsville. He added: "Tobin does well but has not the confidence of the men as Jack [Hays] had." The Rangers suffered another blow when Cortina's men ambushed one of their patrols. Four Rangers died; one had been taken prisoner and tortured to death. The Texans found the bodies the next day, stripped and mutilated. The enraged Rangers exacted their revenge by riding to the nearby town of Santa Rita, a cluster of shacks and huts occupied by hardscrabble Tejanos, and burning it.

After pleas from Texas officials, federal troops were also dispatched to the Rio Grande, under the command of Major Samuel Peter Heintzelman. A cultured West Point graduate and a veteran of the Mexican War, Heintzelman reached Brownsville in early December. His first reaction was bafflement. "This is quite a good sized town & how they could fear the outlaws is more than I can see," he wrote in his journal on December 6. It was believed Cortina and his army had camped upriver, Heintzelman said, but "the Rangers don't care to attack him." His discomfiture with the Rangers did not abate over the next few days. A week later the soldiers were preparing to attack Cortina's camp, but "I cannot get the Rangers to do anything effective in the way of scouting," Heintzelman complained.

In his diary the major penned other concerns about the Texas rowdies, who could on occasion match Cortina in the wreaking of havoc. "The Rangers are shooting all the dogs & killing all the chickens, not only in town but in the neighboring ranches," he wrote. Heintzelman also found Tobin's command sorely lacking. "If he dont keep better order & do something I will write to the Governor to have the Rangers recalled. They are doing no service & only bringing disgrace upon the country." And he worried that the Rangers had alienated potential allies by setting fire to Tejanos' houses as they moved through the backcountry. "The Rangers were burning all—friends & foes." They also hanged at least one man—"a well dressed Mexican," Heintzelman said, whose only offense was to be on the range, looking for his cattle. "It will have a very bad effect," the major predicted. "Tobin says he knew nothing about it."

On the cusp of battle, Tobin himself showed little confidence in his Rangers. "The fight will commence tonight or in the morning," he wrote in a letter to his wife. "The force of Cortina is more than three times our own, and we have no advantage in arms. . . . God only knows who will be victorious but we trust in a just cause and the superiority of men."

Proving further that he was no Jack Hays, Tobin fretted over the hostile landscape. In a letter to the governor, he noted thickets of prickly pear cactus and "the chapparal of this region whose thorny impenetrability extends from the sea to the limits of our settlements." Cortina took full advantage of this. "It is not his policy to stand and receive an open attack but to draw his opponents into ambuscades . . . and when overpowered to slide away unnoticed into his thorny fortresses," Tobin wrote. "Not only are they all well acquainted with the various paths in the woods, but they are also prepared with leather clothing which enables them to traverse the woods without a scratch while we in following bleed at every pore."

In late November Tobin's men made a couple of tentative strikes on Cortina, encountered return fire, and retreated to Brownsville. "It was a wise decision," Heintzelman wrote. "In their disorganized condition an attack would have brought about certain defeat." A subsequent skirmish ended in disappointment, Heintzelman said, when Tobin's men failed to seize one of Cortina's cannons. "Here the Rangers had an admirable opportunity for capturing the gun," the major said, but they pulled up short. "We would undoubtedly have done better without the Rangers."

The situation was about to change, for Old Rip had been sent to the border. "It is reported that Col. Ford and 120 picked men are within three days' march— so look for stirring times," a correspondent for *The Delta* of New Orleans wrote from Brownsville. "They are the Old Rangers."

Ford had little or no intention of going to Brownsville, but that changed when he talked with state senator Forbes Britton. They met on Congress Avenue, the main thoroughfare in Austin, near the state capitol building. Britton, from Corpus Christi, had heard the rumors that Cortina had sacked and burned his coastal city. Now his eyes "danced wildly in their sockets," Ford said, "his chin trembled, and his voice quivered with emotion." Governor Runnels happened to be walking past and joined the conversation. The governor was "deeply moved," Ford recalled, and he exclaimed, "Ford you must go; you must start tonight, and move swiftly."

The next day Ford and a company of eight Rangers—not one hundred twenty, as the New Orleans correspondent had figured—rode south. Ever the prolific writer, he gathered intelligence as they went and sent it to Austin. "I arrived here yesterday," Ford wrote to the governor from Goliad. "On the road I conversed with every person I met who could throw any light upon the condition of affairs on the Rio Grande." Ford said one trail driver, whom he identified as a "gentleman of known truth and responsibility," told him Cortina controlled about seven hundred men in his camp as well as a force of two hundred men marauding along the road from Rio Grande City to Brownsville. "The object is to . . . rob and kill all passing Americans," Ford reported. He added that the "whole Mexican population on both sides of the river are in favor of him."

Cortina said he would leave Texas in return for $100,000 cash, Ford told the governor. Also, Cortina demanded that Texans he had marked for death be surrendered to him for execution. "His terms presuppose deep humiliation on our part," Ford said. The conversations persuaded Ford that the Cortinistas posed a dire threat to Anglos in South Texas: "The contest is in fact for supremacy. If Cortina is not arrested and punished the Americans will be expelled from the Rio Grande."

Ford picked up more volunteers as he went, and his company arrived in Brownsville in early December 1859. Major Heintzelman saw right away that Ford's leadership skills exceeded Tobin's. "He is by all odds the better man," the major wrote in his journal. "I would rather have Ford with 50 than Tobin with all his men."

Cortina had worked his way up the Rio Grande, raiding along the way. "He burnt the ranches of the brothers Turner," said William D. Thomas, a scout and interpreter for Ford. "Cortina next robbed the store of one Reist and burned his houses and fencing. He likewise robbed the house of William Neale and burnt it. . . . The house of Charles Stillman . . . was robbed by him and burned. So were the houses of Thaddeus Rhodes and others. . . . My house at Tio Cana was robbed and burned, and my horses, cattle and sheep driven in to Mexico." This list of pillages ran on, a catalog of destruction.

By late December 1859, Cortina and his army had taken possession of Rio Grande City, an isolated town of several hundred residents about a hundred miles upriver from Brownsville. The forces of Heintzelman and Ford rode to confront them. On a morning of thick fog, Ford charged with eighty Rangers straight into the face of Cortina's cannons, which were discharging buckshot. "The fire of the enemy was terrific for a while," Ford said. "Every time they discharged a piece of artillery those near by . . . felt as if struck by handfuls of gravel." Ford said almost a hundred tiny pieces of shrapnel hit him alone.

The Cortinistas also tried to repel the Rangers with small arms. "The opposing forces were within a few yards of each other," Ford said. "The very heavy fog rendered it difficult to distinguish a Mexican from an American at the distance of twenty yards. Our men fought with gallantry."

Cortina's buglers sounded a charge, Ford said, but the Texans held. "Many a charger galloped off, carrying an empty saddle; Cortina's bold riders were left on the ground." Soon the Cortinistas broke rank and scattered to the river, where they swam for Mexico on the other side. Rangers stood on the bank and shot them in the water. "None of them proposed to surrender," Ford said of the swimmers. He later heard the story of "one Mexican who crossed the river, jumped in the air in glee, and fell dead, pierced by a rifle ball." Among those who safely made it across the Rio Grande was Cortina.

There would be in the ensuing weeks more battles, some quite deadly, but Cortina now spiraled toward inexorable defeat. On December 28, 1859, the day after the engagement at Rio Grande City, Ford wrote to Mifflin Kenedy, a prominent South Texas rancher and steamboat operator. Cortina "has been beaten well," Ford said in the letter, written in his distinctive upright hand. "His whole force was scattered to every quarter, his cannons have been taken, and he has left the country."

Ford knew, however, that the defeat of one self-proclaimed revolutionary would not solve the deep political, cultural, and economic divides along the border. "The moral effect will be great and beneficial to our cause," he wrote to Kenedy, "yet it might be hoping for too much to believe the end of the troubles has come, or is even near."

Others regarded the "Cortina War" with similar prescience, including General William T. Sherman. "Cortina is simply a creation," Sherman said. "If you kill Cortina, another like creature will come in his place."

One of those who came in Cortina's place was Cortina himself, and the Rangers would once again be summoned to the border. But that lay some years away. In the meantime the Rangers had more Indians to fight.

Cynthia Ann Parker and her daughter, Prairie Flower, were captured in a Ranger raid on a Comanche village. Neither of them enjoyed a good or long life in the white man's world.

Chapter 10

ON THE BLEEDING FRONTIER

Two Battles and the Making of a Political Career

Kindness to Indians is cruelty to ourselves.

—TEXAS FRONTIER MAXIM

Three weeks before Christmas, in the terrible year of 1860, a man named W. W. O. Stanfield mailed a desperate plea for help to the governor of Texas. "The Indians are again amongst us," Stanfield wrote. A new and terrifying round of raids on farms and ranches had begun, which meant more fresh graves in the prairie earth. Only a few days before, he said, "we buried five that was killed in the most savage like manner that I have ever herd of." Children were stabbed with spears and beaten with rocks, and "there was an old lady 65 years of age shot through with an arrow."

Stanfield posted his letter from the North Texas town of Jacksboro, a thrown-together settlement on the north-south line that marked what came to be called the bleeding frontier. White citizens on the eastern side of this shifting boundary passed their days in relative safety. But those who lived along and beyond this arc—the pioneers who pressed relentlessly westward with their plows, cattle, and Calvinist determination—dwelled in a world of constant danger. Huddled in their mud-chinked wood cabins with dirt floors and the family

Bible, they deemed themselves the agents of God's will, but they had invaded and taken land the Indians considered their own. The consequence—a collision of two aggressive, violent societies—was a war for sheer survival. "They had to fight the red man at every step," Ranger A. J. Sowell wrote, "and many a lonely grave can be seen . . . that marks the footsteps of the pioneer."

Countless skirmishes and battles took place along this raw and ragged divide, and the Rangers fought in many of them. The story of two of these encounters—one exalted and one mostly forgotten—shows how truths were buried and false legends were born.

Stanfield's letter to the governor described a series of attacks that had begun in late November 1860, when a band of fifty or so mounted Comanches left their camp some hundred miles west of the frontier line. Though weakened by actions such as Rip Ford's assault at Antelope Hills, the Comanches remained fearsome. They were also hungry and desperate. Drought, overhunting, and Anglo incursions had depleted the buffalo herds. With starvation looming, their recourse was plunder.

Peta Nocona, an imposing, muscular warrior, may have led this party of raiders. With painted faces, they rode eastward through driving rain. Their path took them across rolling grassland, past live-oak groves and limestone outcroppings, and over rocky creek beds and low mesas. On November 26, 1860, the raiders descended upon the farm of James Landman, about five miles north of Jacksboro. Landman was away from his cabin, cutting wood with his son. The Comanches killed Mrs. Landman and grabbed two girls, Jane and Katherine Masterson, who were visiting. They threw Katherine, fifteen, across a horse, while twelve-year-old Jane was roped and dragged behind.

The raiders rode about a mile west to Calvin Gage's cabin on the banks of Lost Creek. There they cut the twelve-year-old girl loose. She was battered and bloody but alive, until they shot her. At the Gage cabin the Comanches killed Katy Sanders; she was the "old lady . . . shot through with an arrow" to whom Stanfield referred. The Indians also took a two-year-old girl, threw her into the air, and let her hit the ground. This was done again and again until the child was dead. They abducted Matilda Gage, fourteen, and raped her, along with Katherine Masterson, and released them.

That was the first day. On the next they attacked the farm of John Brown in Parker County, about twenty-five miles to the south. They stabbed him with lances, scalped him, cut off his nose, and left his body to be found and buried by his family. The raiders moved west, through the Cross Timbers region, to Palo Pinto County. At Staggs Prairie, near the present town of Mineral Wells, seventeen of them approached the farm cabin of Ezra and Martha Sherman. The Shermans were newcomers to the frontier, and so great was their faith, or their naiveté, that they did not own a gun. The family was sitting down to dinner when the Indians burst into their cabin. The intruders appeared at first to be friendly, and indicated they were hungry. They even shook hands with the Shermans. One told them, in broken English and Spanish, "Vamoose, no hurt, vamoose."

The Shermans and two of their children left the cabin and hurried in the cold, stumbling across their fields toward a neighbor's farm. They were half a mile from home when the braves reappeared on their horses. One grabbed Martha, who was nine months pregnant, by the hair and wrenched her away. Ezra ran to the neighbor's house to get a gun. The Indians stripped Martha, stabbed her with arrows, and raped her. One sank his knife blade into the skin below her ears. He cut a circle around her head and tore away her scalp. "The agonizing screams of the victim seemed to delight the heartless monsters," an imaginative recorder of Indian attacks wrote.

The warriors beat her with a stick, rode their horses over her, and left her for dead. Next they ransacked the Shermans' cabin, stealing food and Martha's Bible. (Comanches often took books from settlers. They stuffed the pages between the stretched buffalo hides of their shields, which made them thick enough to stop bullets.)

When they were gone, Martha crawled across the rocky ground to her cabin. Ezra returned with a gun, too late. His wife told him—as much as she could—what had happened. She lingered for four days, delivered a stillborn child, and died.

In all, the Comanche raiders killed twenty-three people over the span of two days.

The attacks terrified and enraged the communities—in no small part because Martha Sherman's mutilated body was displayed in an open-casket funeral. Some settlers abandoned their homesteads and fled eastward, toward Fort Worth. If this continued, newspapers warned, frontier counties faced complete depopulation.

Charles Goodnight, a twenty-four-year-old scout, went ranch-to-ranch to recruit a posse for hunting Comanche marauders. "The rain was falling in torrents," said Goodnight, who would become a famous cattleman. "I rode all night." At daybreak he reached the dog-run cabin of Isaac Lynn, whose daughter and son-in-law had been killed by Kiowas two years before. Since then, consumed by grief and hatred, Lynn had asked Indian hunters to bring him death trophies.

Goodnight found Lynn sitting at his fireplace, cooking a lump of skin and hair on a forked stick. "As he turned it carefully over the fire, the grease oozed out of it," Goodnight remembered. "He looked back over his shoulder, bade me good morning, and then turned to his work of roasting the scalp. I do not think I ever looked upon so sad a face. . . . I asked him what he was trying to do with that infernal scalp. He replied: 'The weather's so damp and bad I was a-feared the damn thing would spoil.'"

The Rangers still carried the reputation, won in the Mexican War, of crusaders on horseback. As always, they wore no uniform, carried no flag, and displayed no badges. Most of them were young, late teens to early twenties, with an uncommon attraction to adventure. Many had a hardness about them that—even in a harsh land of steely, ornery resilience—gave them special standing. A Ranger could ride and fight for days in the open country despite poor food, bad water, and no shelter. "A norther last night, little rain," one wrote in his diary in 1860. "Lay out on this open prairie, wet, and slept like a wet dog." He was observing, not complaining.

The story is told of a Ranger named Jim Tackitt, who in the winter of 1860 fought a Comanche raiding party intent on stealing cattle. A Comanche shot an arrow that struck Tackitt in the forehead. The iron-spike arrowhead lodged in his skull "between an eye and the brain pan," as one account described it. Tackitt tried to pull the arrow free but it broke at the shaft. After the shootout—in which the Indians were defeated—one of his brothers held his head steady while another brother attempted to extract the spike with a pair of shoemaker's pincers. The arrowhead would not budge. A doctor tried as well, but soon gave up. "The surgeon then announced," a frontier correspondent wrote, "the skull would burst before the spike would give way." Tackitt went about his daily business with several inches of rusting iron protruding from his head. "He was a hero," the correspondent wrote, "and quietly submitted to the inevitable." This lasted for five months and eight days, until flesh and bone unexpectedly loosened enough that the arrowhead could be removed.

They were, then, exceptionally tough. But more to the point, the Rangers operated as professional and merciless executioners. The Texas Indian conflict, with its special depravities, seemed to require this sort of combatant. Ineffable cruelty and the killing of women and children with impunity were common tactics. "True, the Indian mode of indiscriminate warfare was barbarous," Ranger Noah Smithwick wrote, "but there were not wanting white men to follow their example. Extermination was the motto on both sides."

Many Ranger companies performed as disciplined outfits. But, as might be expected from a force with few enlistment standards and scant regimen, some proved less than exemplary. Earlier in 1860, Governor Sam Houston—back in the statehouse after losing his U.S. Senate seat—authorized a Fort Worth political crony, Middleton T. Johnson, to raise a force of mounted Rangers. Their job: kill the Indians who were raiding settlements. Johnson's Rangers were headquartered at Fort Belknap, a remote army post on the Brazos River, where they didn't kill much of anything except bottles of whiskey.

"Some of the boys got drunk," Ranger lieutenant Willis Lang wrote at the time. "Dick Harris shot Frank Dunklin in a drunken spree through the thigh." Colonel Johnson spent a good part of his tenure, and significant state funds, romancing and marrying a young widow in Galveston. While he was gone, the Rangers held a dance among themselves—"some [Rangers] without boots, some minus pants," Lang said. "This is a strange scene for the wilderness."

Their attempts to locate Indians were futile. An expedition into the backcountry encountered no hostiles, so the Rangers abandoned the search. On their way back to Fort Belknap, they made camp and settled in for the night, at which point Comanches stampeded their horses. "Most of the men [were] compelled to reach the settlements on foot, under great suffering, and exposure," J. W. Wilbarger wrote in *Indian Depredations in Texas*. The Rangers made another foray, only to be turned back when Indians set fire to the prairie—a blaze that scorched hundreds of thousands of acres.

For all these reasons, Houston disbanded the Johnson regiment in August 1860. John R. Baylor, a former Indian agent who harbored a deep and abiding animosity toward these same Indians, lambasted Johnson in his Weatherford newspaper named, tellingly, the *White Man*. Johnson's stillborn campaign was a "miserable and ridiculous failure," Baylor wrote. And the Rangers, he said, were among its victims. "They were under the control of the Col., and upon him rests the responsibility of an inglorious failure and one that has brought reproach on the name of Texas Rangers, and emboldened our enemies by demonstrating to them that *Rangers are perfectly harmless*."

Baylor preferred swift and decisive action. In the summer of 1860, Comanches killed Josephus Browning, the twenty-one-year-old son of a settler. The young man's family laid his body on a table in their log cabin. A "large piece of his scalp" had been ripped away, a family friend said. "His throat was cut, his breast was full of stabs . . . and his hands were cut to pieces, showing that he had used them to ward off the knife." Baylor led a posse to track down the Comanches; they caught and killed thirteen. Afterward, Baylor returned Browning's scalp to his father.

A celebration followed in the Parker County courthouse, with several hundred people dancing through the night, beneath a rope from which hung the scalps of the dead Indians. It was a joyous "war dance among the white folks," said a letter writer to the *Fort Worth Daily Gazette*, and Baylor—or more likely his brother George—even "played the fiddle for us."

The job of righting Colonel Johnson's mishaps now fell to Captain Lawrence Sullivan Ross, and here the fable began to take shape.

At age twenty-two, Sul Ross was already battle-tested. He had fought with the army against Indians and, in 1858, suffered a serious gunshot wound to the shoulder, from which he had now recovered. Wiry and pugnacious, he possessed a college degree and boiling ambition. When Sam Houston commissioned him a Ranger captain, Ross brought discipline to the force and a pressing need to show results. He immediately set out to find and kill those Indians responsible for the latest settler attacks, among them the gruesome death of the pregnant Mrs. Sherman. As Ross later explained in a fit of grandiloquence: "I determined to attempt to curb the insolence of those implacable hereditary enemies of Texas . . . and to accomplish this by following them into their fastnesses and carrying the war into their own homes."

In December 1860, Ross left Fort Belknap with some forty Rangers, twenty army soldiers, and about ninety volunteers. They rode northwest on tired horses, fighting sideways rain and a winter wind, over mesquite prairies and through caliche ravines. "We took our time," Ranger Ben Dragoo said. "We knew we would tree our game, somewhere." After several days, advance scouts found fresh signs of Indians. They also discovered Martha Sherman's Bible, discarded on the ground.

The scouts followed the trail, topped a ridge, and saw an Indian camp below. It lay along the banks of Mule Creek, which fed into the Pease River. Thin gray smoke rose from cooking fires. "We could see the Indian children playing about the tepees and the bucks and squaws moving about," said Peter Robertson, one of the scouts. "There were just seven big tents or tepees, and along the creek above where the tents stood was a big herd of horses."

That night the Rangers and soldiers rested. "It was bitter cold," Dragoo recalled. Because of their closeness to the Indian camp, they did not make a fire. To sleep, he said, "the boys would collect in groups of three, four or five and huddle together on the ground, forming the center of a circle around which their horses stood." The next morning Ross climbed a hill overlooking the creek and inspected the camp through field glasses. There were "eight or nine grass huts," Ross said, "which the Indians, fifteen in number, were just deserting." Though they were preparing to depart, the Indians appeared to be in no hurry. It was clear they did not know the posse was near.

Ross ordered his men to charge, and Rangers and soldiers advanced within two hundred yards before the Comanches saw them. They thundered into the camp on horseback as the Indians scrambled and panicked. "Some were trying to rally their braves," Dragoo said. "Others were mounted, women and children were screaming and above all this pandemonium rang the defiant war whoop, the yells of the rangers and the crack of the six-shooter." Dragoo's account included a startling capture: "I saw several mounted Indians. . . . I rushed in among these, shooting right and left," he said. "I dashed alongside an Indian woman . . . mounted and carrying a babe in her arms. I was just in the act of shooting her when, with one arm, she held up the baby and said, 'Americano!'" The woman, though dressed as a Comanche and covered in grime and buffalo grease, appeared to be—in the parlance of the times—a "white squaw."

The attack was a rout: no Rangers or soldiers were killed, while perhaps a dozen Indians died. At least four of them, by one count, were women. Three people, including the white woman and her baby, were captured. The fighting was over in a matter of minutes. The saga would take years to manufacture.

The blue-eyed woman who cried "Americano!" was Cynthia Ann Parker, who had been abducted at age nine. She was one of the most famous of such captives. In 1836, the year Texas gained its independence from Mexico, several hundred Indians raided a settlement known as Fort Parker. Most were Comanches. They killed five men, severely wounded several women, and seized Cynthia Ann from her mother. For years, the Parkers—a prominent family in the state—searched for her, to no avail. Cynthia Ann lived as a Comanche over the next two and a half decades. Her tribal name was Nautdah.

Her plight sent at least one scribe into a strange verbal rhapsody. "As the years rolled by Cynthia Ann developed the charms of captivating womanhood," wrote General George F. Alford, a Texas politician and businessman, "and the hearts of more than one dusky warrior was pierced by the Ulyssean darts of her laughing eyes and the ripple of her silver voice." Whether or not darts and ripples were involved, she did become a wife of Comanche chief Peta Nocona and bore him three children. To most whites on the frontier, this would have been tantamount to a descent into hell.

But now, thanks to the Rangers, she and her infant daughter, Prairie Flower, were thrust back into civilization, or at least the Texas version of it. Though it would be hard, Texans believed, she could be returned to a life of Christian decency. "She has adopted all the manners and customs of the Indians," one newspaper said, but "we are told that traces of beauty and intelligence still linger in the lineaments of her sun-browned face."

The celebration greeting her return may have eluded Sul Ross. About two weeks after the engagement, Ross gave a statement to the *Dallas Daily Herald*. It was brief, noting that thirteen Comanches had been killed at Pease River. Ross mentioned a "woman prisoner" but said little else about her. On January 14, 1861, Ross filed a report of the incident with Governor Houston. He told Houston that twelve Comanches were killed, forty Indian horses were seized, and a "white woman threw up her baby and cried, 'Americano.'" He did not identify her as Cynthia Ann Parker.

Not long after Pease River the Civil War broke out, and Ross left Texas to fight for the Confederacy. He saw action at Pea Ridge and Vicksburg and was promoted to brigadier general. After the war he spent eight years farming near Waco. He entered local politics and was elected sheriff of McLennan County in 1873. Seven years later he was elected state senator.

In 1875, the account of Pease River and Cynthia Ann Parker came back to life, when the *Galveston Daily News* printed a letter, purported to be from Ross, relating the "correct history" of the battle. Ross now said that his men seized 350 horses from the Comanches. Beyond that, he told of chasing a chief named Mohee for two miles on horseback, catching him and killing him. And, perhaps most important, Ross claimed he learned right away that the woman captured during the battle was "one of the Parker children."

The story had more growing to do.

The state Democratic Party nominated Ross for governor in August 1886. Within two days, an article in the *Fort Worth Daily Gazette* gave a stirring account of Pease River. It said Ross "in a single hand-to-hand combat" killed a Comanche chief during the fight. And not just any chief: Ross's opponent was identified as Peta Nocona, Cynthia Ann Parker's husband. "The gigantic Indian, as graceful and handsome a warrior as ever rode to deadly lists, fought with superb bravery and skill," the dispatch said. "But he had met a good match in the mere stripling who daringly confronted him. Ross' courage, while not as 'loud' as the Indian's, was of finer grain, and the Comanche bit the dust." No longer was Pease River a minor encounter with negligible consequences, according to this report. "This decisive battle broke the power of the Comanches for many years and gave peace and security to the entire frontier of Texas for a long time."

Another version was made public that same year, this one presented as Ross's personal account. Ross said in this rendition that he, not his scouts, discovered the Indian camp. During the battle, according to Ross, Peta Nocona fled on a horse with a young girl. Cynthia Ann Parker and a child also were "mounted on a fleet pony." Ross and his lieutenant pursued them, which led to a face-off between Ross and Peta Nocona. "I shot the chief twice through the body," Ross said, "whereupon he deliberately walked to a small tree nearby . . . [and] began to sing a weird, wild song—the death song of the savage." When Peta Nocona refused to surrender, Ross directed his Mexican servant to "end his misery by a charge of buckshot."

Ross now portrayed the battle as a turning point in Texas's war with the Comanches. "The fruits of this important victory can never be computed in dollars and cents," he wrote. "The great Comanche confederacy was forever broken, the blow was decisive, their illustrious chief slept with his fathers and with him were most of his doughty warriors."

To little surprise, Ross won his election easily. A contemporary of his said the Pease River fight and the capture of Parker "made Sul Ross the governor of Texas." He was reelected in 1888. In the popular imagination he had become, as one headline described him, "DARING SUL ROSS, BRAVE TEXAS RANGER AND GOVERNOR [WHO] WIPED OUT THE COMANCHES."

He was the fighter who finally defeated the fiercest of Indian tribes. He was the Ranger who killed the killer, Peta Nocona. And he was the governor who had saved a flower of Lone Star girlhood from a life of paganism, primitive misery, and unthinkable humiliation. In fact he was none of those. Yet the Battle of Pease

River came to be—and is still—considered a signature event in the history of the state. To this day, streets, schools, parks, and a state university in Texas all carry the name of Sul Ross.

White Texans trumpeted Cynthia Ann Parker's salvation at the hands of Ross and his Rangers, but she didn't slide easily into the world she had been snatched from long ago. Her new life was dismal. Shortly after her removal from the Comanches, she was put on public display at a Fort Worth general store. It was such a momentous occasion that children were dismissed from school to see her. A witness described the spectacle: "She stood on a large wooden box, she was bound with rope. . . . She made a pathetic figure as she stood there, viewing the crowds that swarmed about her. The tears were streaming down her face, and she was muttering in the Indian language."

For years afterward, Parker mourned the Comanche children she wouldn't see again, and she would not speak English. Prairie Flower—her "little barbarian" in one Texas congressman's phrasing—died in 1864. Cynthia Ann sat weeping for hours, tried many times to escape, and attempted to starve herself to death. Some ten years after the Rangers captured her, Cynthia Ann died of influenza, possibly complicated by starvation.

Ross's claim that he had forever vanquished the Comanches in 1860 proved to be laughable. Texans and the U.S. Army engaged in hard battles against the Comanches for the next fourteen years. Comanche raiding parties attacked frontier settlements often, with 1864 considered the worst in history for these raids. Chief Quanah Parker, son of Peta Nocona and Cynthia Ann, led some of the bloodiest.

The idea that Ross wounded Peta Nocona and ordered his killing also was challenged—by none other than Quanah Parker. When all the fighting was done, Quanah made himself into a peaceful, successful businessman who was welcomed into white circles. He delivered speeches at the Texas state fair in 1909 and 1910, where he insisted Sul Ross had no role in Peta Nocona's death. "He no kill my father," Parker said. "I want to get that in Texas history straight." Peta Nocona was not present at the Battle of Pease River, his son said. He died several years afterward, Parker said, of illness.

Other versions of the Pease River fight surfaced over the years, including purported eyewitness accounts from men who were not there. Some claimed glorious roles in what they described as a major historic event. Others dismissed the battle as a minor skirmish, and a fairly nasty one at that. Sixty-eight years after it happened, Ranger Hiram Rogers was asked about it. "I was in the Pease River fight, but I am not very proud of it," he said. By his count, sixteen Indian women were shot down that cold morning. "That was not a battle at all," Rogers said, "but just a killing of squaws."

There are no universities in Texas named for Hiram Rogers.

While the Battle of Pease River ascended to heraldic status in Texas and Ranger lore, another encounter—the disastrous engagement known as the Battle of Dove Creek—faded into the historical mists.

Dove Creek was in some ways a by-product of the Civil War. Many current, former, and future Rangers joined the Confederate Army when the war began in 1861. Among them was Ben McCulloch, who had returned from California, and who still held his stellar reputation from the Mexican War. Unfounded rumors spread through the North that he and five hundred Rangers were poised to invade Washington and assassinate or kidnap President Lincoln. In 1862, Mc-Culloch was shot dead from his horse in the Battle of Pea Ridge, Arkansas.

Texas sent its young men by the tens of thousands to fight for the Confederacy in other states, which left its frontier even more vulnerable to raids by Kiowas, Comanches, and other tribes. "Thousands of the citizens of the frontier counties are absent from their homes in the military service," said Pendleton Murrah, a future governor. "When the ruthless savage threatens their homes, their families and all that is dear to them, they cannot rally to repel him." To deal with this, the legislature formed the Frontier Regiment in 1861.

Also known as the Texas State Troops, these units were first controlled by the state government. Beginning in 1863, when they were called the Frontier Organization, they were mustered into the Confederate forces but stayed in Texas. They became the home-front manifestation of the Rangers.

Many who joined were seasoned Indian fighters living far west of the state's plantations—men who owned no slaves and had scant enthusiasm for secession. Their mission was frontier defense, but poor equipment, untrained personnel, and faulty leadership plagued some units. Sickness swept the camps, with no medicine to be found. Substandard gunpowder wouldn't fire. Old and over-worked horses gave out.

Dove Creek would mark one of the lowest points.

In early December 1864, Ranger captain N. M. Gillentine and his company of twenty-three men made a routine scout along the headwaters of the Brazos River in the big-sky emptiness of West Texas. They marched for two days, pushing beyond the stone ruins of a forsaken army outpost, Fort Phantom Hill, before they came to an abandoned Indian village. The willow framework of nearly a hundred wigwams stood along a riverbank. Their buffalo-hide coverings had been removed.

The village was immense, almost half a mile long. By the looks of the camp—the decomposing bear heads and buffalo feet left behind, dog feces on the ground—its inhabitants had abandoned it two days before. "I sopose them to be 500 . . . or more Indians," Gillentine wrote in his report. These types of wigwams were not like those of the Comanches or Kiowas—the Indians who were doing most of the deadly raiding—but the scouting party made no attempt to identify the tribe.

The men did find a fresh grave, which they unearthed. "In the grave [was] a female Just Buried," Gillentine reported. Some of the men pulled beads, trinkets, and pieces of the clothing from the grave as souvenirs. Gillentine took a moccasin from the corpse. It would be a gift for his commanding officer and—if some superstitious militiamen were to be believed—Gillentine's death sentence.

Gillentine and his men returned to Erath County to sound the alarm over this sizable assembly of Indians. A state militia group was assembled, led by Captain Silas Totten, a former Confederate officer who had been wounded in the Civil War. As a Ranger captain, Totten showed great enthusiasm for tracking down war deserters. He was "unpopular with certain classes" of his freewheeling Rangers, one assessment found, because of his heavy-handed discipline. While Totten gathered his troops and procured replacement ammunition—thousands of percussion caps provided by the state were faulty—a group of Confederate soldiers, led by Captain Henry Fossett, headed west to find the Indians.

A hard cold wind blew from the north as they rode. "It was a wild and uninhabited country without roads," said I. D. Ferguson, one of Fossett's men. They found and followed a trail more than fifty yards wide, an indication that they were tailing hundreds of Indians. The next day the Confederates reached the north fork of the Concho River, a clear, tree-lined stream with water bubbling over rocks. They discovered another abandoned Indian village and counted five hundred wigwam frames. "Our best estimate was that there must be at least 5,000 Indians in the party we were following," Ferguson said. "We also found where they had blazed a tree with an axe and made a target, and had been at target practice with their guns. This proved that they were armed with firearms and were splendid shots."

Fossett sent eight scouts ahead. They located the camp about fifty miles away, in a timber grove along a small tributary of the Concho known as Dove Creek. "From the information brought us by the scouts," Ferguson said, "we believed we could whip the redskins and capture all their horses." Their plan was to approach the Indian camp at night and attack at dawn. The Texans would "make easy work of it by taking them by surprise," Ferguson said. Reinforcements arrived in the form of Totten's militia, bringing the total force to about 380. However, Totten's men were exhausted from their long march, and their haphazard collection of weapons did not impress the Confederates. "The 'flop-eared militia,' as we called them, were armed with all kinds of firearms, shotguns, squirrel rifles, some muskets and pistols," Ferguson said.

Texan officers held "a council of war," but not much of one. Brigadier General J. D. McAdoo of the state troops later listed its deficiencies: "Without any distribution of orders, without any formation of a line of battle, without any preparation, without any inspection of the camp, without any communication with the Indians or inquiry as to what tribe or party they belonged to, without any knowledge of their strength and position, the command 'forward' was given." Totten admitted that his Rangers didn't know what awaited them, because the Indian warriors had hidden themselves well. "Their position was such," Totten said, "that it was impossible to ascertain its strength until the attack was made."

Not only was it an ill-conceived attack, it was unnecessary. These Indians were—at least at this time and place—peaceful. They had made no raids on settlements, ambushed no travelers. These were Kickapoos migrating from their reservation in Kansas to a settlement in Mexico. They had undertaken a slow, laborious, frigid trek of a thousand miles, with women, children, old folks, dogs, and horses. In early January 1865, when they had reached Dove Creek, about fifty of the Kickapoos approached the nearby ranch of Richard F. Tankersley, one of the region's white pioneers. An Indian waved a white flag and called, "Me no fight." The Kickapoos told Tankersley they had camped there to rest and replenish their food supply. "They were very friendly," Tankersley's daughter recalled, "and in scouting some days later, found some of our horses which had strayed off and brought them home."

Though the Texan forces knew none of this, they still had a chance to avoid bloodshed. At some point, an Indian named Aski approached the militia to say that the Kickapoos came in peace. One of the frontier captains ordered his execution on the spot. "Aski tried to shake hands and make peace with the Texans," Kickapoo chief No-ko-aht said, "but they shot him." By one account Totten told his men, "Shoot them all, boys, big, little, old and young, and don't leave one of them to tell the tale."

On the morning of January 8, 1865, the militia charged the Indians, plunging into the cold water of the creek. Chaos was instant. "Such screaming and yelling of Indians and barking of dogs as occurred there cannot be described," recalled I. D. Ferguson, who watched from a hillside. The Indians were ready for the attackers. They had positioned themselves perfectly, along the creek bank, hidden by weeds, and they were armed with Enfield rifles. They fired, and Rangers fell. "To get at the Indians, it was necessary to wade Dove Creek which was from knee to waist deep," wrote Lieutenant Colonel Buck Barry, a frontier regiment commander. That "afforded the Indians a fine opportunity to inflict severe losses."

Some of the fighting was hand-to-hand, knife-to-knife. Captain Gillentine was shot; he turned to a Texan next to him and spoke his last words: "John, I am a dead man." Totten ordered a retreat. "The militia was thrown into a panic," Ferguson said, "and fled like stampeded cattle out of the camp with about one hundred Indians pursuing them, and drove them clear off the field of battle."

For their part, Captain Fossett's Confederates captured some of the Indians' horse herd. Fossett ordered others in his unit to attack the Indians' flank, but they were driven back. More fighting followed, as the Indians advanced. The Confederates retreated. "All in all, it was the worst managed fight that ever was," Ranger W. R. Strong recalled. Fossett "was a good old man but no more fit for such a place than a ten-year-old child. He would stand off and cry, 'Come here my men, come here my men,' but they did not pay any attention to him." He was only a part of a complete leadership void. "Nobody being in command," Strong said, "was what caused so many to be killed.'"

A crude field hospital was set up in a grove of live oaks. "I counted thirty-five wounded lying in the shade of the trees," Ferguson said. About three that afternoon the militia captured an Indian boy. Only then did the officers learn they were fighting Kickapoos. "The only thing now to be done," Ferguson said, "was to hold our own and fight until we could get darkness to cover our retreat." The Indians fired on the men as they fled. "A stream of singing bullets clipping my clothing, the air seemed to be alive with flying lead . . . I became resigned to my fate," Ferguson said. "I imagined that after death the wolves would sneak up and gnaw my bones."

He and others stopped on a prairie ridge and vowed to make one last stand. "We held up our hands," Ferguson said, "and all took an oath that we would stay there as long as a man was alive." Though surrounded, they managed to hold off the Indians. When night fell at last the shooting stopped and the Kickapoos withdrew. If they had kept coming, they could have wiped out the troops. The final casualty count for the Texans was twenty-six dead and twenty-three wounded. It was the biggest Indian battle in Texas during the Civil War, and the worst.

The Texans left their dead where they had fallen. Those who survived huddled around campfires as snow began to fall. "The cry of the wounded men and the groans of the wounded horses, with the white snowflakes falling through the firelight furnished a weird picture of distress rarely seen in Texas," Ferguson said. They used tree branches and blankets to make litters for the wounded. The weather worsened; conditions were punishing. Militia member Lowry Scrutchfield wrote in his diary, "Made the attack. Got whipped . . . January 9: Stayed in camp; snow fifteen inches deep. January 10: Marched down the Concho carrying the wounded on litters—snow deep—starvation in the camp." As their injured mounts collapsed and died, the men cut off hunks of horseflesh and cooked it. "It smelled all right to a starving man," Ferguson said.

Captain Fossett filed a report with his commander, Lieutenant Colonel Barry, about three weeks after the battle, and rarely has a complete defeat been described in such glowing terms. "All the officers in the fight acquitted themselves honorably," Fossett wrote, "and many of the soldiers fought with courage." The Kickapoos had much better firepower, he said. "They fought us with the best of guns and ammunition (much superior to ours.)" Though the Texans had been forced to leave their dead behind, Totten and some of his Rangers reclaimed them after the Indians had departed for Mexico. "Captain Totten has returned and reports that our men killed were not scalped," Fossett said. "He found only 17 of the dead, and of these one of them had his head cut off and stuck upon a pole. He could not find any dead Indians. . . . They carried off their dead." In the last line of his report, Fossett noted that his men had—even as they were turned back by the Kickapoos—exacted some punishment: "We got 16 scalps."

Well after receiving Fossett's report, Barry found some rationale for the Dove Creek calamity. "It was not a victory for the whites but was courageously enough fought by the contestants," he wrote. "It may have been that they [the Kickapoos] were merely migrating across Texas with no intention of raiding at this time . . . but the emigrants selected a poor time . . . for their crossing."

In an acidic aside, Barry invoked the looting of the Indian grave before the attack, when Captain Gillentine took a moccasin and others stole keepsakes. Some in the militia had warned them, Barry said, "that their trinkets might prove to be 'bad medicine.'" The grave robbers had dismissed these augurs with laughter, but Barry recorded the thieves' fate: "The men encountered no visible results of their ghoulish act until the battle . . . when every possessor of a trinket met death."

Deadly consequences mounted long after the battle was silenced. The Kick-apoos in Mexico—who now considered Texans their mortal enemies—conducted raids across the border for the next twenty years. These incursions were, by one historical assessment, "unmatched for calculated viciousness, vindictiveness, and destruction of life an property." An 1874 newspaper story bore witness: "In the last raid of the Mexican Kickapoos into Texas, they are reported to have captured two families and to have killed the men and carried the families away into slavery. One of the young women, having made repeated attempts to escape, was exposed to the licentiousness of the camp and then burnt at the stake."

For some Texans who fought at Dove Creek, the memories remained raw for years. I. D. Ferguson, who lived to enjoy a long career as a lawyer and judge in Denton County, recalled the battle from the vantage of nearly five decades. "It has been a long time ago," he said. "I was a boy then, but still the scenes are fresh in my memory. I seem to hear the neigh of the horses, and see the glimmering camp fires and the flying snowflakes, and hear the moans of our starving wounded as we traveled down the banks of that beautiful river, the Concho."

Overshadowed by the Civil War and unobserved by dint of calamity, the battle hid for decades in memory's back rooms. More than eighty years after Dove Creek, a writer for the *Frontier Times*, a Texas periodical venerating all things rootin'-tootin', reconsidered the incident. "Fifty [sic] brave frontiersmen lost their lives in the Battle of Dove Creek and about the same number of Indians were killed," he wrote. "The attack was undoubtedly a mistake, but those [white men] who participated in it are not to be blamed. . . . Each mind was fresh with the memory of some horrible deed the savages had perpetrated along the frontier and all red men looked alike to them."

The author claimed to have gone to a Kickapoo settlement in Mexico and found some "withered old warriors" who had fought against the heroic Texans. They would be well into their nineties by this time, and seemed to have stepped freshly from a cartoon. "These Indians harbor no ill will towards the paleface. . . . They have thrown away their tomahawks and live in peace," the writer concluded. "Whenever the subject of this fight is mentioned to one of these warriors he will take a deep puff at his pipe, blow rings of smoke up toward the sky and with a sad, far away look on his face, will say: 'Heap big mistake of the Tehanas (Texans).'"

With the end of the Civil War, the Rangers had been in existence—in various forms and numbers—for close to half a century. They had acted, despite their struggles and excesses, as a courageous and vital force in the creation of the State of Texas. For better and worse, the Rangers had come to symbolize the place that produced them.

The next sixty years brought new challenges as the state grew and changed. The Rangers were called upon to pacify crime-ridden boomtowns, control race riots, and settle violent rangeland disputes. In this tumultuous era, they spent much of their time and energy on the U.S.–Mexico border, where old tensions flared anew. As before, they mixed bravery and heroism with oppression and atrocity.

Their fame spread nonetheless, and many chroniclers of the new period regarded them with adulation. At the same time, their baser actions—up to and including cold-blooded mass murder—would threaten the very survival of the Texas Rangers as an institution.

PART II

Dark Ages

1871–1930

Leander McNelly, portrayed in this modern painting as a figure of vibrancy, was in reality racked by tuberculosis and other ailments. Despite questionable actions and motives, his legend grew over the years.

Chapter 11

THE STRANGE CAREER
OF LEANDER McNELLY

A Coney Island Fabulist Tells the Tale

The Texas Rangers, so called, have been a source of danger to the United
States, rather than assistance, in the matter of frontier defense.

—GENERAL WILLIAM TECUMSEH SHERMAN, 1877

Ninety-five years after his death, Captain L. H. McNelly appeared at the
White House in the form of an oil painting. The portrait belongs to the
school of western heroic romance: a strapping McNelly, the literal picture
of lanky power, has dismounted from his gray horse. With a Winchester rifle in
his right hand and a pistol on his hip, he casts an intense, steely gaze across a
broad desert gorge. No sane badman of the badlands would dare tangle with
such a force.

Never mind that the real McNelly was short, gaunt, thin of voice, and racked
by tuberculosis. To a newspaper correspondent of his day, he appeared as "the
very reverse of robust." One of his own men—an ardent admirer—described
him as "sick and puny . . . a little runt of a feller." At the peak of his career, he was
sometimes so weak he could barely stand.

Despite his infirmities, McNelly persevered and prevailed as captain in the
Special State Troops of Texas. In 1875 his force of several dozen men did some

hard charging on the Texas-Mexico border, and he led them with courage. He "didn't have a man in his company but what would of stepped in between him and death," one of his men recalled. "For we all loved him like a father as well as a captain. . . . He never sent us where he wouldn't go himself."

McNelly also committed major mistakes. He plotted to start an armed conflict, if not a full-blown war, between the United States and Mexico. His border campaign was notable, even by the loose code of the day, for its summary executions. He invaded another country illegally. And his chief triumph, when the shooting finally stopped, was the recovery of livestock.

Yet this brief and checkered career brought him posthumous fame and an enduring accord approaching reverence, not to mention a painting for the president. Some have called him one of the greatest Texas Ranger commanders, and he holds a coveted spot in the official Rangers Hall of Fame. "McNelly is an appealing composite of warlord and Christ figure," *Texas Monthly* magazine declared several decades back. "Courageous and gentlemanly, utterly devoted to his men and his mission, a remorseless killer, and dead himself by the holy age of thirty-three. From McNelly flows the rich blood of Ranger lore."

Part of his stature derives from McNelly's bravery and guile. There were others, however, of equal valor and greater success who never achieved his stardom, much less his status as an exemplar of Ranger-ness. McNelly had something many of them didn't have. He had a writer. This writer—who was also a Ranger—compiled a lengthy record of serious literary offenses. But when it came to birthing a Texas giant in the mind of the public, few performed better.

Leander McNelly arrived in Texas as a child in the 1850s, when his well-to-do farming family—wealthy enough, at least, to own a few slaves—migrated from what is now West Virginia to the Brazos River valley. As a youth McNelly contracted tuberculosis. Still, when the Civil War broke out in 1861, he joined the Fifth Texas Cavalry of the Confederacy. He was sixteen or seventeen. McNelly fought with distinction, rising from private to the rank of captain. As the South neared its defeat, he returned to Texas to hunt Confederate deserters.

After the war, McNelly married and worked his Washington County farm in south-central Texas. Soon he joined the Reconstruction-era Texas State Police. The state police were widely reviled by white Texans, because many of them were black. They were disbanded in 1873, when Democrats—a number of whom were unrepentant Confederates—regained control of state government from Republicans. It is perhaps a testament to McNelly's qualities that he emerged from the organization with his reputation intact.

The Rangers had passed through the war in a much-weakened and ineffective position, and in the postwar turmoil they barely existed at all. But in 1870 the sclerotic and destitute Texas Legislature authorized Ranger companies of twenty-five to seventy-five men for each county "infested . . . with marauding or thieving parties." These initial efforts to reestablish the force were ragged at best. Any number of unsavory characters—many of them detritus of the war—signed on.

John "Red" Dunn of Corpus Christi joined a Ranger company in 1870 and found himself among "the worst mixed lot of men that ever came together in one organization . . . the most dilapidated, diseased, moth-eaten specimens of humanity I have ever seen." And that was only part of the crew. "The rest of the company," Dunn said, "were fished out of the slums of San Antonio." They managed a single accomplishment: to be the only company in Ranger history to mutiny in the field, the final act of a dispute over drinking in camp. After that, "we were marched to the old Capitol and disbanded," Dunn said. "Some of the boys were so drunk that it took two sober ones to hold each of them up while waiting for their discharge."

In 1874, the Texas Legislature voted to form the Frontier Battalion. The law created six Ranger companies of seventy-five men each. The salary for privates was $40 a month, and each man was required to furnish his own six-shooter and "suitable horse." The battalion was put under the overall command of Major John B. Jones, who had been an officer in the Confederate Army. At the end of the Civil War, Jones went to Mexico to find a possible site for a Confederate colony but returned to Texas disappointed. Now forty, Jones did not fit the wild and woolly Ranger stereotype that had emerged from the Mexican War. "By birth and education a gentleman, and by profession a lawyer," the *Houston Telegram* said, "this daring chief . . . is a small man scarcely of medium height and stature, whose conventional dress of black broadcloth, spotless linen and dainty boot on a small foot would not distinguish him from any other citizen." Nonetheless, the newspaper said, Jones was "the hero of many a daring assault and wild melee . . . and the terror of frontier forayers."

As true as that may have been, the commander of the new Ranger force encountered a familiar frustration: the state couldn't pay many of the Rangers on time.

"I find much dissatisfaction," Jones wrote in a September 1874 report. "I fear serious trouble with many of the men." Some had debts coming due. "Others have mothers, sisters and brothers dependent upon them to whom they expected to send money."

A few companies were disbanded, and with reduced manpower the battalion swung into operation. Many of the Rangers went to North and West Texas to fight Indians. "During the first six months of service there were more than forty parties of Indians on our frontier," Jones said. "We had fourteen engagements with them besides giving chase to many that we could not overtake." Two years later, Jones reported, only six bands of Comanches and Kiowas were known to be roaming the region. He noted that many of the counties that Anglos had deserted during the Civil War because of Indian attacks were open safely for settlement again. "The appropriation for frontier defense has proven a good investment," Jones wrote. A letter to the *Galveston Daily News*, signed only "Ranger," argued that the battalion's success could be easily measured: "Though we have not exterminated the Comanches, we are willing to count scalps with the . . . Indians killed while raiding in Texas, and bet that we have ten to their one."

As those Rangers fought Indians, others headed for the border. The results weren't so praiseworthy.

Red Dunn enlisted with the Rangers a second time, riding with a company commanded by Captain Warren Wallace that roamed the lower Rio Grande Valley. "The country was over-run with Mexican cattle- and horse-thieves as well as cutthroats," Dunn said. These Rangers were known to execute suspected lawbreakers on the spot without regard to possible innocence. "We transferred that part of the matter to the Deity," Dunn explained, "and left them to settle it with Him." As Adjutant General William Steele noted, "There is a considerable element in the country bordering on the Nueces and west that think the killing of a Mexican no crime." Many Rangers were part of that element.

Wallace compiled a "registration" of more than eighteen hundred "irresponsible and most generally worthless" Tejano men in the region, and his Rangers set out to eliminate many of them. The Mexican consulate filed protests, and the company was disbanded. "Captain Wallace appears to have exercised no control over the bloodthirsty instincts of many of his company," Adjutant General Steele concluded. Dunn and several other Rangers were charged with murder but were acquitted. "We had been indicted," Dunn said, "for the disappearance of every Mexican who did not respond when his mama called."

Anglos on the border, especially those with property and political power, begged for more protection. "Men have been murdered in cold blood in almost every conceivable way," said a written declaration by Rip Ford and others in Brownsville. They referred to white Texans murdered by Mexicans, not the reverse. "They have been shot, stabbed, burned alive, and strangled, and their bodies have been indecently mutilated; women have been captured, their person violated; captive children have been held and sold as slaves. . . . It is a contest between civilization and savagery."

Many blamed their old nemesis, Juan Cortina, who they believed controlled a vast network of bloodthirsty thieves from the office of the mayor—a title held by Cortina himself—across the river in Matamoros. A U.S. government report, assembled by special commissioners friendly with ranchers, cited such desperados. "These thieves have, with astonishing boldness, penetrated at times 100 miles and even farther into Texas," the report said, "and by day and night have carried on this wholesale plundering."

By way of response, a Mexican government commission issued its own report, describing Texas as a refuge of evil and depravity. The thieves who took stolen cattle into Mexico, the commission said, were actually Texans. "They are quite capable of any crime in the calendar."

In reality, the lines were blurred and the loyalties mixed. As Ranger Dunn described it, "Most of the depredations were incited by renegade white men who were living among the Mexicans and were profiting by their crimes."

In Austin, Governor Richard Coke heard the pleas of the Anglo ranchers. He turned to a proven commodity, a man who could knife through the uncertainties, ambivalence, and danger to deliver the goods: Leander McNelly. Coke named McNelly to the captaincy of Company A of the Washington County Volunteer Militia.

McNelly's company was not, strictly speaking, a part of the Rangers. It functioned separately from the Frontier Battalion and didn't report along the usual chain of command, though it did answer to the adjutant general. However, McNelly's men considered themselves Rangers and called themselves as such. They were young and raw; some had arrived straight off the farm. But they looked like Rangers, with Bowie knives, broad-brimmed hats, and a cast of eye that suggested a yearning for action. "Somehow you wouldn't pick a one of them to push around," company member George Durham said. The pay was

$32 a month, and—in the Ranger way—each man furnished his own horse and gun.

Their captain had long, silky brown hair and a beard that reached his chest. McNelly dressed neatly in duck pants and calfskin leggings and commanded with quiet authority. "Here was a man who could tell you what to do and you'd do it and never have any suspicion that he might be wrong," George Durham recalled. "When he spoke we hardly breathed. . . . Even the horses seemed to quit swishing and stomping."

He demanded toughness; his men would sometimes ride night and day with only brief pause, or go thirty-six hours without rations. They would be so hungry they ate the bitter beans from mesquite trees. McNelly engendered loyalty by enduring the hardships with them.

He also was the sort of man, his company would soon see, who could shoot an opponent in the teeth and read Scripture to him as he expired. They came to understand that he did not hold prisoners. McNelly's company, like many Ranger forces on the border before him and after, employed *la ley de fuga*: the law of the fugitive. It meant prisoners were routinely executed, and the Rangers would claim they had been killed while trying to escape.

Now, in the spring of 1875, McNelly and his forty-two men rode toward the border. They crossed the broad, empty coastal plain, a sweep of mesquite, grassland, and the occasional grove of stunted oaks that ran to the flat horizon. Two hundred miles to the south the Rio Grande flowed green and slow, its low banks lined with heavy brush and canebrakes, and emptied into the Gulf of Mexico.

As in years before, savagery reigned in the open country here, where solitary citizens traveled at great peril. "Billy McMahan, a very popular inoffensive American school teacher . . . was waylaid by desperadoes," a contemporary historian wrote of an 1874 incident. "These men tortured McMahan by cutting off his fingers, toes, wrists and ears. They finally severed his legs from his body and left him lifeless."

McNelly's men first pointed their mounts toward the bayside town of Corpus Christi and discovered it battened down in alarm. A few weeks earlier about thirty-five raiders—believed to be Cortinistas—had attacked the nearby hamlet of Nuecestown. They killed a man, burned a store, and took prisoners whom they whipped and tortured before releasing. With that attack the banditti, as they were sometimes called, had ventured far deeper into the interior than ever before.

In reprisal, white vigilante "minute companies" ignited a wave of vengeance across the county, hunting people who had lived there for generations and whose only crime was their ethnicity. The posses hanged farmers and stockmen and burned their houses and ranches. Tejano-owned stores were set afire.

"The acts committed by Americans in this section are horrible to relate," McNelly wrote to the adjutant general. "Many ranches have been plundered and burned, and the people murdered or driven away; one of these parties confessed to me in Corpus Christi as having killed eleven . . . men on their last raid. Mexican citizens have no security for life or property in this section whatever." Unlike Ranger captain Wallace, McNelly did not believe Tejanos constituted a broad class of thieves. "I do not know of any Mexican who owns a ranch on this side of the river and who lives in Texas whom I do not consider to be a good citizen," he said.

McNelly ordered vigilante companies to disband, though he made no move to arrest them. He and his company headed southwest, toward a region known as the Wild Horse Desert. The sun shone bright and hot in the clear April sky as they passed through villages turned to smoking ash by vigilantes. Farther on, they came upon two dead Mexicans, their necks in nooses, dangling from a trestle. The Rangers kept going, to the Santa Gertrudis Ranch and the man with the money, Richard King.

A former Rio Grande steamboat captain, King possessed vision, energy, and a ruthless drive to acquire and dominate. He had begun procuring land in the region in 1853. Much of the property sacked and burned by the Nuecestown vigilantes eventually became his as well; he gained possession after those who lived there were killed or fled. Ultimately his King Ranch would become one of the world's great cattle empires, covering nearly thirteen hundred square miles, an area bigger than Rhode Island.

As a Texas cattle baron—and by common reckoning the richest man in the state—King enjoyed considerable influence with Governor Coke, so it was no surprise that McNelly's Rangers came to him. King greeted them warmly and furnished McNelly's company with shelter, food, fresh horses, saddles, and cash. McNelly himself was given one of King's most prized horses. And they got new guns to replace their Sharps carbines. "Those old smoke poles were 50 caliber, single-shot weapons, entirely unsuited for combat," wrote W. W. Sterling, who later served as adjutant general. "Captain King . . . furnished the entire company with the Model 1873, 44-40 caliber Winchesters. These repeating rifles increased McNelly's firepower nearly tenfold."

Soon the Rangers were on their way again, this time to the border in search of cattle—a great deal of which had been stolen from King.

By June 1875, McNelly's company had reached Brownsville and made camp at an old hacienda. "It was only about ten miles back from the Rio Grande," Durham said, "and seemed to belong to anybody who was man enough to hold it." At Fort Brown, the army post near the river, officers told McNelly that stolen cattle had been driven across the river by the hundreds. His response: "I think you will hear from us soon."

McNelly had learned during the Civil War the importance of gathering intelligence on his enemy, and he continued this strategy on the border. First, he established a network of informants within the rustlers' gangs. "I am *well* posted in all that the thieves are doing by spies (Mexican cattle thieves) on the other side," he wrote to Mifflin Kenedy, a former business partner of Richard King's. "I have kept in constant employment four men at the rate of sixty dollars per month each." McNelly obtained about half that from the state by listing the men on his company roll. The rest came from ranchers. "I need some money at *once*," McNelly wrote to Kenedy from Brownsville. "I would like to get some help from you and Capt. King."

McNelly's second mode of intelligence gathering was interrogation. He sent his Rangers on scouting expeditions with orders to arrest anyone they encountered. The captives were brought back to camp, where they were questioned by Jesus Sandoval, who went by the moniker Casoose.

Casoose had long red hair, a scraggly beard, and blue eyes that, to Durham, "seemed to throw off sparks." He had been a South Texas rancher, and he claimed that Mexican raiders had raped his wife and killed his daughter. Though lacking in evidence, this tale was widely believed—in part, Durham said, because he "looked like a crazy man." Casoose spoke little English, Ranger Bill Callicott recalled, "but he could say, 'Son-of-a-bitch, kill 'em.'"

To interrogate someone, Casoose stood the man on the back of the horse. A noose was fastened around the captive's neck, with the other end over a tree limb. The rope would be tightened when persuasion was required. "As far as we knew," Callicott said, "this treatment always brought out the truth." Once the Rangers believed they had gained all possible information, Casoose would slap the horse's hindquarters, and the animal would bolt, leaving the captive kicking the air as he died. Fellow Rangers admired Casoose's professionally meticulous approach and honored it with mordant humor. "Their own mothers could not be more tender," one said, "their own children no more respectful. . . . He is so kind and considerate that it is almost a pleasure to be hanged by such a nice gentleman."

McNelly learned from spies and at least one man questioned by Casoose that some Cortinistas were heading for the Rio Grande with stolen cattle. The Rangers chased and found the raiders on the plain of Palo Alto, the site of the first major battle, in 1846, of the Mexican War. With McNelly in front, the Rangers charged the rustlers, firing their rifles. One Ranger, L. B. "Sonny" Smith, was killed in the gunfight. He was believed to be seventeen. "Dear Madam, he is gone," a member of the company wrote Smith's mother, "and while we (his companions in arms) deeply sympathise with a mother who has lost a son, we almost envy him his Glorious death. Who would not be wiling to die fighting for the liberty and the rights of mankind?"

Post-battle, McNelly acknowledged some respect for the enemy. "I have never seen men fight with such desperation," he said of the Cortinistas. "Many of them after being shot from their horses, and severely wounded three or four times would rise on their elbows and fire at my men as they passed." Despite the Ranger's death, McNelly's men had scored a clear victory. "Had a fight with raiders," the captain said in a triumphant telegram to the adjutant general, "killed twelve and captured two hundred and sixty-five beeves. Wish you were here." The *Galveston Daily News* told of the battle in a story topped with this headline: "Captain McNelly and His Rangers Heard From. They Give the Greasers a Taste of Old Times."

An ebullient Governor Coke sent a letter of congratulations to McNelly. "The skill and gallantry displayed by all in the signal blow struck [against] the freebooters . . . merit and receive the highest praise from the authorities and the people of the State," the governor wrote. "The pride of true Texans in the historic fame of the Texas ranger is fully gratified in the record your command is making."

The dead rustlers' bodies were collected and put on bloated display, in the heat and the flies, at the Brownsville plaza. Private Smith, whose father also was a member of the Ranger company, received a full military-style funeral— McNelly's orders. Neither action proved popular with some of the townspeople.

"The Mexican residents of Brownsville . . . are public and violent in the denunciation of the killing," McNelly said in a report, "and the attention given my dead soldier seems to have exasperated them beyond measure."

The Rangers did not try to placate them, George Durham said. "They claimed that Palo Alto was a butcher job, that some fine, decent citizens were shot down and their bodies were stacked like cordwood on the plaza. Captain could have . . . proved the talkers wrong, but he wasn't one to jaw and palaver."

McNelly had no time for that. Soon he was busy planning his next move: to make a strike, he wrote, "that will forever stop our border troubles."

International plunderers and big ranchers from Texas had long pined to seize a great swath of northern Mexico. Though their vision of a slavery-based empire there was now obsolete, many still dreamt of pushing the border well below the Rio Grande. But that would take more than the Rangers. The U.S. military would have to be drawn into the fight.

McNelly now placed himself and his men in service to this stratagem. "You may feel sure that I am going to have the U.S. authorities onto it as much as I am," he wrote to Kenedy, "as that is the only effectual way of getting into a 'row' that cannot be compromised." In late 1875, McNelly learned that a band of rustlers was herding stolen cattle toward a large ranch—believed to be a refuge for Cortina's forces—in Las Cuevas, Mexico. This would provide him with the opportunity he had sought. He hatched a plan with, of all people, a U.S. Navy officer.

President U. S. Grant had received numerous entreaties for assistance on the border, so he ordered the navy to help. In response, the USS *Rio Bravo*, a twenty-year-old sidewheeling gunboat armed with four cannons, steamed up the shallow Rio Grande. It was intended as a show of force and a means to interdict river-crossing rustlers. But McNelly and the captain of the *Rio Bravo*, Lieutenant Commander DeWitt Clinton Kells, had other ideas.

In late October or early November 1875, Kells and McNelly met with army colonel Joseph Potter from Brownsville. "The meeting was held by order of Gen. [E. O. C.] Ord," McNelly wrote. Ord was commander of federal troops in Texas. At this conference, McNelly said, "Capt. Kells says to me that Gen. Ord told him to do anything I advised." Therefore, McNelly predicted, "something can be done & done *at once*."

He and Kells hoped to provoke Mexicans to fire on the *Rio Bravo*. If that didn't work, they proposed sending Rangers across the river and having them pretend to be Mexicans firing shots at the gunboat. And when that happened, McNelly promised rancher Kenedy, the U.S. Cavalry "will cross the river anytime that I will lead the way." The intent was clear: to start an armed conflict between the United States and Mexico.

Thomas Wilson, the American consul in Matamoros, learned of the plan. Wilson suspected it was part of a larger design by "men of means" in South Texas—men like Kenedy and King—who could "expect to reap large profits" by selling supplies and services to the army if such a conflict should occur. He alerted Washington, and officials ordered Kells to stop any maneuvers with the *Rio Bravo*. Kells was removed from his command and court-martialed.

The great scheme for invasion and war had fallen apart. McNelly prepared to cross the river anyway.

On the night of November 18, 1875, McNelly assembled his company, now numbering twenty-five to thirty, on the muddy banks of the Rio Grande. "He said, 'It is like going into the jaws of death . . . in a foreign country where we have no right according to law,'" Callicott wrote. "He said, 'Some of us might get back, or part of us, or maybe all of us, or maybe none of us will get back.'" McNelly offered to let any of the Rangers having second thoughts to "step aside." When none did, Callicott recalled, "He said, 'All right, boys, that's the way to talk it. We will learn them a lesson that they have forgotten since the old Mexican War.'"

The Rangers crossed the river, three at a time—not in a U.S. Navy vessel but in a small, leaky dugout canoe. In a thick fog, they followed a narrow cow trail through the brush. At dawn they reached a ranch and prepared to attack. "I want you to kill all you see," McNelly told the Rangers, "except old men, women and children."

Casoose led the charge with a "Comanche Indian yell," Callicott said, and the Mexicans never knew what hit them. "If the angels of heaven had flown down amongst them they would not have been any more surprised, as we were the first Rangers or soldiers that had been in Mexico since the old Mexican War," Callicott said. "Lots of the men were on their woodpiles cutting wood while their wives were cooking breakfast outdoors. Not one of them moved a muscle. We shot them down on their woodpiles and wherever we saw one. We killed till we killed all we saw at the ranch." George Durham added: "I heard later it was twelve."

There was a good reason for the Mexicans' surprise, and for their complete lack of resistance: the Rangers had raided the wrong ranch.

McNelly and his company did not pause to consider their mistake or aid the wounded. "The Captain said, 'Come on, boys,'" Callicott wrote. Their real target lay about half a mile up the trail. There they found several hundred hostile Mexicans waiting for them. After a brief gunfight, McNelly ordered his men to retreat. The Rangers ran back through the first ranch they had attacked, "and there was nothing there except the dead," Callicott said, "and they lay like they fell, on the woodpiles and in the streets or roads." Reaching the river, the Rangers gathered with their backs to the Rio Grande, ready to make a last stand. "If they charge us," McNelly said, "they will have to come across that open field for a hundred and fifty yards and we can stand here and mow them down with but little danger of even getting hit with a bullet unless it is in the head. And if you do, the pain won't last long."

The Mexicans did charge, several times, and the Rangers repulsed them. On the Texas side of the river, army captain James Randlett watched, and heard McNelly yell. "He now cried out, 'Randlett, for God's sake, come over and help us,'" the army captain said. "I believed his command was in danger of annihilation." Against orders, Randlett sent forty of his soldiers across the river to assist. More Mexican attacks followed. The Rangers and the soldiers fired back, killing General Juan Flores Salinas, the *alcalde* of Las Cuevas.

On the next day, November 20, the Rangers dug a trench into the riverbank. It would be a second Alamo, some said. But eventually a white flag came out on the Mexican side and talks began. The final result: McNelly bluffed the Mexicans into turning over sixty-five head of cattle.

Though that was but a small portion of the livestock at Las Cuevas, Texans hailed a victory engineered by McNelly. "Instead of being surrounded by Mexicans and treating for surrender," the *Galveston Daily News* said, "he actually dictated the terms of his withdrawal from Mexico, which were that Mexican authorities promised to return the stolen cattle and surrender the thieves."

In truth, no thieves were surrendered, but—good news for the Rangers— about thirty of the cattle were found to have belonged to Richard King. Four of McNelly's men were selected to drive the livestock back to his ranch. "Captain King sent Captain McNelly a check on the Brownsville Bank for one thousand dollars," Callicott said, "to divide with the twenty-six of us that were there with him in Mexico."

For Mexico, a different set of heroes emerged from the clash. The townspeople of Las Cuevas saw the battle as the resounding defeat of an invading force. They erected a monument to General Juan Flores Salinas, the slain *alcalde*. Its inscription memorialized him as a man who died fighting for his country.

McNelly's Ranger company moved on to less spectacular missions. However, it did make at least one noteworthy arrest—that of outlaw King Fisher in June 1876. The flamboyant Fisher, who carried two ivory-handled pistols, led a South Texas gang of robbers and rustlers and was rumored to have killed more than a few men. But two days after his arrest by the Rangers, Fisher was released on bond and managed to avoid trial. "It is useless to bring prisoners here," McNelly complained, speaking of Eagle Pass, "[because] the authorities are much too alarmed to try them."

The captain still harbored plans for a takeover of northern Mexico—hoping to assemble an invasion force of five hundred—but worsening tuberculosis kept him in bed much of the time. An odd *New York Herald* story in December 1875, written from Brownsville, had praised McNelly as a paragon of elegance, vigor, and herculean strength. "He can lift two bales of cotton at a time, one with each hand," the *Herald* said, "or better, lift 1,200 pounds with both." That would constitute a world record then and now. In October 1876, McNelly wrote the adjutant general that his doctor had ordered him to stay indoors, because "exposure just now would doubtless result fatally." Another doctor found that he had "fever, tape-worm and pulmonary disease." He was not, a medical report said, "fit for active service" in his current state.

In early 1877, Adjutant General Steele unceremoniously removed McNelly from the Rangers. Steele said he took the action because the captain's medical bills were mounting, and a successor captain "in the full vigor of early manhood and health" waited in the wings. Complicating matters, McNelly had been "extremely negligent in making his reports," Steele said, which made accurate bookkeeping impossible.

Soon the state's newspapers started a death watch. "The dashing frontier soldier is gradually sinking," the *San Antonio Herald* reported in August 1877. "Even as we write, the dread summons may have come and this truly brave man be numbered with the historic dead." McNelly lasted a few more weeks in an opiate-instilled delirium. He died on September 4, 1877, at age thirty-three, and was buried in Washington County. His soaring granite tombstone—a "very handsome monument," the local newspaper reported—cost $3,000. Rancher Richard King paid for it.

A flurry of obituaries followed. But in the twenty or so years after his death, McNelly was seldom mentioned in public print. True, he had acted with cold-blooded effectiveness, but not in pursuit of liberty or freedom. He had, in the starkest analysis, killed some people and caught some cows. Like many other lawmen of his time and place, McNelly seemed fated to obscurity, remembered if at all in remote monographs, yellowing records, and small-town monuments.

But that was about to change, thanks to an ex-Ranger growing long of tooth and light in bank accounts, toiling in the outer reaches of working-class Brooklyn, New York.

Napoleon Augustus Jennings was born in 1856, the son of a successful Philadelphia businessman. He received a prep school education in New England and could have eased himself into a life of merchant-class gentility. But stirred by "a spirit of unrest," he decided at nineteen that he would seek his fortune in a wild and dangerous place he had only read about in magazines. "I made up my mind that life would not be worth living outside of Texas," he said. "I should be a cattle-king, the owner of countless herds of beeves and unlimited acres of land."

Young Jennings made his way to Austin by train and to San Antonio by stagecoach. Abandoning his plans to purchase a ranch, he worked as a cowhand and, a bit later, managed to join McNelly's company as a clerk. Jennings spent about eight months with the Rangers before mustering out. After that he turned to journalism, writing for several New York newspapers. He took to calling himself "Colonel" Jennings, and managed the European career of his wife, an aspiring opera singer.

By the 1890s, he had returned to Texas, this time in the company of R. G. Dyrenforth, a professional rainmaker. Or as Jennings called him, "General Jupiter Pluvius Dyrenforth," a man of science who could "turn on the heavenly faucet whenever and wherever he pleases." Dyrenforth was, in the parlance of the times, a "concussionist." He—and many others—propounded the theory that airborne explosions would bring rain to thirsty lands. By the firing of cannons and raising dynamite on balloons and kites, Dyrenforth believed, a low-pressure vortex would form and attract "moisture-laden" air.

Jennings, sporting a thick mustache and a pith helmet, functioned as Dyrenforth's rainmaking assistant and chief propagandist on a swing through bone-dry West Texas in the summer of 1891. On a cattle ranch near Midland, Dyrenforth filled the sky with explosives, and Jennings crafted dispatches that proclaimed the general's monsoonlike triumph to two dozen newspapers across the country. "Great is the name of Dyrenforth" in West Texas, Jennings declared. When the general "did literally pull cold water down upon this parched country," Jennings reported, cowboys wore slickers to their "festive roundups" and jackrabbits were forced to "use their ears as umbrellas."

It took a correspondent from the *Farm Implement News* to expose them. The Texas experiments, he wrote, were in truth a ridiculous failure. A writer for the *New York Times* examined one of Jennings's newspaper reports on Dyrenforth. "This article," the *Times* found, "is a tissue of falsehoods from beginning to end and describes thunder storms that never occurred." The newspaper had to acknowledge, however, that Jennings depicted the bogus storms "in a most realistic manner." Additional press reports ridiculed Dyrenforth as the "Rain Fraud" and "General Dryhenceforth." Funding for his experiments, some of which had been provided by the federal Department of Agriculture, evaporated.

Undaunted, Jennings returned to the East Coast and put his hand to poetry and patriotic songwriting. He also pursued a new subject in promotional newspapering: the Texas Rangers. In 1895 he penned an article for numerous big-city papers that portrayed them as fearless crusaders of the plains. "There is, I will venture to say, not a member of the Texas Rangers today who would not go merrily to certain death to uphold the ancient glory of the name that he bears," Jennings wrote. "They live the hardest, roughest lives and danger is their delight."

From a modest cottage on Surf Avenue in Coney Island, Jennings regaled visitors with tales of his Ranger days. He displayed Bowie knives on the walls and said nicks on the blades were from the bones of men those knives had killed. Among the talents he perfected with the Rangers, Jennings boasted, was the mimicking of a diamondback's rattle, which he employed to clear western saloons of riffraff.

And now he was working on a book. "I am a writing man," he explained. "I needed money. I had a story to tell. I told it." In 1899, Scribner published *A Texas Ranger,* Jennings's tale of Captain McNelly—years dead and generally forgotten—and his company of volunteers. It was an action-packed, heroic first-person account.

Jennings's colorful description of McNelly's Rangers may be unrivaled in west-of-the-Mississippi literature: "Their broad-brimmed, picturesque cowboy hats, flannel shirts open at the throat, high boots, well-filled cartridge belts with dangling pistol holsters and bowie-knife scabbards, their carbines slung at the side of the saddles, their easy and perfect manner of riding, their sun-tanned faces, their general air of wild, happy, devil-may-care freedom and supreme confidence in themselves, showed that the Captain indeed chose wisely when he picked out the men for his dangerous mission."

As for McNelly, Jennings said the captain "was greatly loved by all the men" and "a more cool and collected individual under fire it would be impossible to imagine." Here was a Ranger captain who sacrificed his health—who drove himself to death, really—for the sake of decency and justice.

In a postpublication letter to McNelly's widow, Jennings said he strove to give readers "a true idea of the life of the old Rangers" and of her late husband. "I must have succeeded, if I may judge by the hundreds of splendid notices the book has received," he wrote. "*Without a single exception* they have been of a highly complimentary nature. From Maine to California the papers and reviews have treated the work most kindly and my publishers report big sales, not only in the West, but in the New England states!"

Jennings noted that the *San Francisco Chronicle* said the book would prove to be "the Rangers' most enduring monument." The *Detroit Free Press* cited the book's accuracy and liveliness in its depiction of "that famous body of frontier fighters." Other publications echoed the praise. "So, you see," Jennings assured Mrs. McNelly, "after all these years the world will know of the work your brave husband and his men did for civilization in Texas, and it is well that such deeds be made a matter of record."

There was but one problem. As with the West Texas rainmaker, Jennings had fabricated much of the story. Or, as George Durham put it, "The boy took it mostly out of his head."

Jennings told, for example, of joining McNelly in his courageous charge against the rustlers at Palo Alto. "Captain put spurs to his horse and we followed him with a yell," Jennings wrote. "The next instant we were upon them, shooting and yelling like demons. They stood their ground for a moment only; then turned and fled." He added this vivid eyewitness account of the death of Ranger Sonny Smith: "We all saw him fall and the sight roused a fury in our hearts that boded ill for the men in front of us." Jennings, McNelly, and the Rangers responded. "Crack! bang! bang! went our revolvers, and at nearly every shot one of the raiders went tumbling from his saddle. . . . We flew over the prairie at a killing pace, intent only on avenging our comrade's death."

This fight took place months before Jennings became a Ranger. The entire volume is similarly filled with dramatic descriptions of events the author—who often gave himself a starring role—could not possibly have witnessed. And it contains numerous factual errors.

"You probably noticed in the book," Jennings wrote to McNelly's widow, "that I made myself a member of the company a year before I actually joined." He had his reasons. "I did that to add interest," Jennings said. "Told in the first person, adventures hold the attention of the reader much more closely than at second hand."

With that, the McNelly saga took flight.

In 1914, Zane Grey, the dentist turned famous western pulp novelist, published *The Lone Star Ranger*, a fictional treatment. Gunslinger Buck Duane joins Mc-Nelly's company in this tale and finds the captain to be "shrewd, stern, strong, yet not wanting in kindness." Just before a shootout, McNelly offers Buck timely advice for his courtship of a fetching lass: "You can win her, Duane! Oh, you can't fool me. I was wise in a minute. Fight with us from cover—then go back to her. . . . That girl loves you! I saw it in her eyes."

Grey's novel was made into movies in 1919, 1923 (starring Tom Mix), and 1930. Also in 1930, Jennings's McNelly book was reissued, and J. Frank Dobie, one of Texas's leading men of letters, wrote an enthusiastic introduction for that edition. "I defy anyone to read it without being engaged by its brightness and ranger-swift directness," Dobie said. Jennings may have "telescoped some events," Dobie acknowledged, and distorted others. But the book was, he said, "a brave, clean-cut narrative, simply and honestly told, about those brave and clean-cut frontiersmen, the Texas rangers."

C. L. Douglas's 1934 book *The Gentlemen in the White Hats* was purported to be nonfiction. It devoted three chapters to McNelly, "one of the greatest of the bold captains who rode the wild border." About that same time, a San Antonio newspaper writer tracked down former McNelly Ranger Durham, who was working on the King Ranch. The two collaborated on an autobiography published first in serial form in 1937 and later as a book. Though Durham stuck to the facts as he knew them, he was recalling his story after more than five decades.

"The farther the years moved us away from the man," Durham said of McNelly, "the bigger he and his time looked."

In 1942 one more remake of Grey's *Lone Star Ranger* hit the screens. A year after that, a Liberty ship—a World War II freighter—was named for the captain. The SS *L. H. McNelly* sailed from the port of Houston as an Associated Press story about the christening termed Jennings's book "perhaps the best account of the Ranger chieftain's exploits."

During another war, the Ranger captain became a favorite character in tales told by President Lyndon Johnson. "One of the stories . . . I have repeated most often through the years," Johnson wrote in 1965, was that of McNelly's determination. "Captain McNelly repeatedly told his men that 'courage is a man who keeps on coming on.'" When, under LBJ's administration, the country found itself mired in Vietnam, the president was said to have invoked that aphorism—however apocryphal it might be—with regularity. "As if, literally, such men were bulletproof," writer Larry L. King lamented. "He took the Texas Ranger myth . . . too much to heart; it made him say foolish things."

The man who succeeded Johnson in the Oval Office, Richard Nixon, didn't do much Ranger quoting, as far as was known, but he was the recipient of the portrait rendering the vibrant McNelly. Painted by Texan Joe Grandee, it was presented at the White House in 1972 to celebrate the coming 150th anniversary of the Rangers' creation. The portrait subsequently joined the holdings of the Nixon Presidential Library in Yorba Linda, California, where it remains.

One of the more recent McNelly tributes is the 2001 feature film *Texas Rangers*, which tells the story of his company of volunteers. Bringing the matter full circle, the original screenplay was based on N. A. Jennings's book.

The film stars Dylan McDermott, who plays McNelly as a brooding leader with traces of a Yonkers accent. As with most such movies, reality takes a back seat to dramatic necessities, and in this case the liberties far exceed any of Jennings's. A few among many: Here McNelly is driven not by a need to recover stolen cattle but by personal tragedy; bandits have abducted his wife and three sons. King Fisher reigns as the film's chief villain, the leader of a band of sombrero-wearing thieves, rapists, and murderers who open the film by gunning down dozens of innocent townspeople. In a climactic scene, Fisher is shot dead by a character based on none other than N. A. Jennings. (The real Fisher lived to become the sheriff of Uvalde County.) And in a reversal of geography and gravity, the river that is supposed to be the Rio Grande flows away from the Gulf of Mexico.

Throughout the film, McNelly's methods are depicted as harsh, but in service to a far greater good—the elimination of a roving gang of killers. McNelly's death scene rounds the story to a close, as he whispers some final words for the Jennings-based character to record for posterity: "Let them not remember us as men of vengeance, but as men of law and justice." The real captain didn't glide toward his exit like that. But as a newspaperman in a more famous western movie, *The Man Who Shot Liberty Valance*, once said: "This is the West, sir. When the legend becomes fact, print the legend."

A typical Ranger company toward the end of the nineteenth century—heavily armed and backed by the Texas flag.

Chapter 12

SALT WAR

"All Was Silent as Death"

I have been attacked by the mob and had to surrender.

—RANGER LIEUTENANT JOHN B. TAYS

The Trans-Pecos region, at the far southwestern tip of Texas, is a remote expanse of basin and range, where the last gasp of the Rocky Mountains meets the unforgiving reach of the Chihuahuan Desert. New Mexico lies to the north, and to the west and south the Rio Grande's erratic channel has carved the international boundary with Mexico.

In the 1870s only a few thousand people lived and struggled here, most of them Tejanos. Mexican culture prevailed and generational ties ran deep in the hardscrabble villages, meager farms, and sunbaked settlements along the river. These Spanish speakers dwelled at a far remove from *norteamericano* customs and rules.

Anglos accounted for only about 2 percent of the population, but they controlled the money and the political power, much of it from the flyspecked towns of El Paso and Ysleta. They ran the county as they pleased, and it was scandalous even by the loose standards of the Texas outback. The district attorney had resigned. The county commissioners had been accused of pilfering public funds.

The county judge was a drunk. The justices of the peace knew almost nothing of the law. "In any other country than this they would be regarded as ignorant men," Sheriff Charles Kerber said of the justices. "In this community, they are a little above the average in intelligence."

The sheriff added that few criminal trials could be held because there weren't enough English speakers to fill a jury. In addition, the county had no jail, because the government did not have the money to build one. The state's laws, a U.S. Army colonel observed, were "very loosely administered." He was being generous in his assessment.

This collection of woes—poverty, a racial chasm, lawlessness, ignorance, arrogance, and vast distance—gave rise to the San Elizario Salt War of 1877. This war did not enter the register of Ranger triumphs or contribute to its roll of heroes. Its participants did not vault into the Ranger Hall of Fame or inspire worshipful pulp westerns and flattering movies. This was a war they lost, after which they ran wild.

At the foot of the mountains, one hundred miles east of El Paso, lay enormous dry salt lakes. For years these had been common property, open to all. The poor and ragged on both sides of the border crossed the heat-shimmer flats to fill their oxcarts with salt, for which they paid nothing. Salt was used in cooking and in curing meat, and miners employed it in large quantities to extract silver from ore. For the Tejanos and Mexicans who gathered and bartered it for food and supplies, salt meant survival.

In 1877 lawyer Charles Howard of El Paso and Austin banker George Zimpelman, his father-in-law, revived an old plan to lay claim to the salt lakes and charge a fee for the collection of minerals. "These lakes are very valuable," said Howard, who encountered immediate and predictable resistance to his scheme. "The people, and by this I mean the Mexican population of El Paso County . . . said that they had been advised by Louis Cardis that the lakes belonged to them."

Cardis was an Italian immigrant and fluent Spanish speaker who represented the region in the state legislature. Several years earlier, he and others had tried without success to seize control of the salt lakes. Now, however, he championed the cause of the wretched Tejanos, who needed salt more than ever after a crushing drought destroyed their crops. Cardis's current position was motivated in no small part by his hatred of Howard, a pugnacious and obnoxious Confederate veteran with whom he had conducted a lengthy political feud. Howard dealt with his archenemy as so many other Texans had handled theirs. On

October 10, 1877, he walked into an El Paso general store with a double-barreled shotgun and blew Cardis away.

The cold-blooded murder of a state official in front of multiple witnesses might have, within other precincts, resulted in incarceration and a speedy trial. But Howard was allowed to flee across the state line to New Mexico. The sheriff in El Paso, a friend and an admirer of Howard's, believed his killing of Cardis deserved a statue. "If it was in any other county but this," Charles Kerber wrote, "a monument would be erected to his memory for delivering us from a tyrannical, unscrupulous scoundrel."

In reaction to the salt fees and the killing of Cardis, an armed collection of Tejanos and Mexicans took to the dirt streets, seizing government officials and private property and threatening to kill anyone who opposed them. They considered themselves morally justified insurrectionists, a natural rising of the oppressed. Anglos saw them as violent rabble and sought help from Austin. "There is neither law nor order in the county," merchants and others wrote to the governor. "The lives and property of the Americans and their few friends in this county are in imminent danger. . . . They hang upon the caprice of an ignorant, prejudiced and blood-thirsty Mexican mob."

Working his own political connections, Howard asked the governor for protection in the form of Rangers. Howard's plea contained a basic flaw: "At that time," said Ranger Jim Gillett, "not a company of the Frontier Battalion was within five hundred miles of the town." The governor hastily dispatched Major John B. Jones, commander of the battalion.

The major traveled from Austin to El Paso by train and stagecoach. (The railroad did not yet extend that far.) After a circuitous journey of two weeks, Jones found himself dropped into a foreign land. It was "pretty wild," he said of the region. "It is some 700 miles from the settlement of Texas . . . and just back of the town of El Paso rise the Guadalupe Mountains, whose lofty eminences loom up in the blue distance like grim sentinels guarding the dim gates of the West."

When not waxing poetic about the landscape, Jones noted the ethnic makeup of the towns on the Texas side of the river. "All these places are inhabited chiefly by Mexicans, for that whole region is nothing but a Mexican country whose people, with the exception of a few Americans, are one and in unison with the dwellers south of the Rio Grande," he said. "They are related and intermarried together and . . . indeed, a considerable proportion of the Mexicans in El Paso County were born in Mexico."

And now they had coalesced in fury. Jones surveyed the scene and reported by telegram to the adjutant general, "Serious trouble here." He tried to quiet the insurrectionists by meeting with their leaders, which prompted Sheriff Kerber to issue a warning, one Anglo to another. "Be on the lookout, Major," the sheriff said. "These greasers are very treacherous."

Jones also began to recruit a company of about twenty new Rangers to keep the peace. His curious pick for commander was John Tays, a thirty-five-year-old expatriate Canadian. Tays had done some farming, smuggled cattle from Mexico, and invested in El Paso property but boasted no experience in law enforcement. Jones said he selected Tays "for his courage and coolness," and did not elaborate except to say it was "difficult to get Americans at all" in El Paso County.

Howard remained nervous. "John Tays is a good man," he wrote to Jones, "but he is very slow." Howard urged Jones to add twenty men of Mexican heritage to the company. Such a move would not only bulk up the force but might ease racial acrimony. There was precedent for it: Tejanos served in earlier versions of an El Paso Ranger company, fighting Indians. Some of them had now joined the insurgents.

The major rejected Howard's idea outright. "I determined not to enlist Mexicans," Jones said, "as I could not trust them." However, he said, he "had to accept" two Tejanos and "a half-breed." Ranging in age from nineteen to over sixty, the new company made for a mixed bag of veteran fighters and grifting incompetents. One was a doctor, another a rustler and gunslinger. And one of them, John McBride, was known to Tejanos as Howard's enforcer in the salt trade.

The next step for Jones was to equip his men. On November 14, 1877, he wired the adjutant general in Austin, urging the delivery of weapons: "Send by stage to Lieut Tays . . . ten Winchesters, twelve pistols, belts and scabbards also cartridges for both."

With the El Paso Rangers armed and in place, Jones returned to Austin. The situation fell apart from there.

By December 1877, Howard had left New Mexico and come back to Texas. The Rangers gave him safe passage to San Elizario, a town of squat adobe buildings that broke the desert bleakness about fifteen miles southeast of El Paso. There the portly and combative Howard swaggered through the plaza, threatening the arrest and prosecution of anyone who had stolen salt from his lakes. He also "incensed the Mexicans by calling them 'greasers' and other opprobrious epithets," said customs inspector Sherman Slade, "and by inviting them to come and take him now."

When he had finished baiting the locals, Howard joined the Rangers at a house and corral they used as a barracks. Armed insurgents began to gather as word spread that Howard had been seen. On the night of December 12, the insurgents met in a nearby house to plan their next move. "We could hear them yelling and giving orders," Tays said. Charles Ellis, an El Paso merchant and former sheriff, volunteered to investigate. He put a revolver in his boot and stepped outside, a singular mistake.

By one account, as Ellis questioned some insurgents, a man approached on horseback and lassoed him around the neck. The horseman dragged the ex-sheriff through San Elizario's dirt streets and left him dead in the dunes outside town. "His body was found in the sand hills," Lieutenant Tays wrote, "his scalp, eye brows, and beard taken, his throat cut from ear to ear, and stabbed twice in the heart."

About four hundred insurgents now surrounded the barracks and an adjacent building, vowing to kill everyone inside unless the Rangers delivered Howard to them. The Rangers barricaded the doors and windows and cut portholes for their guns in the walls, but they still held out hope that federal troops would ride to the rescue. And that looked as if it would happen. When he received their plea for assistance—which the Rangers had sent before the insurgents had sealed the perimeter—U.S. Army captain Thomas Blair and eighteen mounted men hurried on a moonlit night to San Elizario.

Insurgents met Blair at the edge of town and told him they would fire on his soldiers if they went farther. Here the army's will buckled. "We were surrounded by not less than from 120 to 150 men, all well armed," Blair said. "Under the circumstances, I did not consider it my duty to try to force an entrance. It would have been worse than useless had I done so." Blair and his men turned their horses and withdrew, leaving the Rangers to fend for themselves.

Hours after the soldiers left, not long after the sun rose, the first shot was fired. It came from the window of a house, and it cut down Ranger sergeant C. E. Mortimer. "He cried out, 'I am shot,'" Tays said. "The ball entered his back and came out below the right nipple." He lingered for a while, Tays said, and died at sundown.

Sporadic fighting ensued with the insurgents attacking the barracks and the Rangers—though outmanned and outgunned—driving them back each time. This lasted for four days. Ammunition ran low. The Rangers needed sleep, and they believed the insurgents might be digging a tunnel to place explosives under the barracks. In a telegram from El Paso, Sheriff Kerber alerted Governor R. B. Hubbard to the Rangers' desperate plight. Hubbard in turn sent a telegram on December 14 to U.S. president Rutherford B. Hayes. The United States, Hubbard said, had suffered an "invasion" of its territory by a "Mexican force." Because this force was "too strong to be repelled by Texas troops," Hubbard asked the president to send the U.S. Army.

The thought of federal reinforcements found little sympathy in some distant quarters, such as the *New York Herald.* "Hubbard is an imbecile," the newspaper said, neglecting to note that he was a Harvard graduate. "It is no invasion, but a mere local disturbance in Texas, which the government of that state ought to be ashamed to ask the United States to suppress." Nonetheless, the president agreed to send help. On December 16, Governor Hubbard wired Sheriff Kerber: "President Hayes telegraphs he has ordered United States forces from New Mexico to San Elizario to preserve peace."

Kerber responded to the governor with a message of his own: "Your telegram received . . . The first help is expected in forty-eight hours. I fear it will be too late."

On the sixth day of the siege, Howard volunteered to give himself up. "He said, 'I will go, as it is the only chance to save your lives,'" Tays reported, "'but they will kill me.'" Tays then committed a colossal mistake: under a white flag, he walked with Howard to the insurgents' makeshift headquarters. A local merchant, John Atkinson, came as an interpreter. Atkinson earlier had brought a trunk containing $11,000 to the barracks. Now the insurgents put Atkinson in another room. There, it is believed, he agreed to hand over the money to them if they would release Howard, the Rangers, and everyone else in the barracks.

The insurgents made the deal. Chico Barela, their leader, "swore by the holy cross that he would faithfully keep his part of the agreement," said Juan N. García, who claimed to have witnessed some of the events. After that pledge came a cascade of misunderstandings, deceptions, humiliations, and murder.

Atkinson returned to the barracks and—without the knowledge or approval of Tays—coaxed the Rangers outside. "He . . . told the boys that I had ordered them to come down with their arms as everything was peaceably arranged," Tays said. "When my men arrived they were disarmed and imprisoned. . . . My men had surrendered." Tays didn't blame the Rangers. "Atkinson, to save his own life, had betrayed them."

If so, Atkinson badly misplayed his hand. The insurgents first led Howard into the street and put him against a wall. "Howard instantly stopped and . . . faced the mob," García said. "They were drawn out in a line. All was silent as death." As García recounted it, Howard faced a firing squad and—belligerent to the end—told them, "You are now about to execute three hundred men." This was apparently a prediction of coming reprisals. With that, Howard ripped open his shirt, baring his chest, and shouted, "Fire!"

They did. Howard fell to the ground, where he kicked and squirmed. An insurgent named Jesus Telles stood over him with a machete and swung the blade toward the writhing figure. Telles missed his target and cut off two of his own toes. Others stepped in with their own blades, mutilating and finally killing Howard. They dragged the body to an old well and threw it in.

The insurgents next brought out Atkinson and Ranger John McBride, Howard's enforcer, and stood them on the same spot where Howard met his end. Atkinson said in Spanish, "Let me die in honor." He removed his coat and vest and opened his shirt. He "looked at the party of eight men who stood with their guns ready to fire," García said, "and said in a cool manner, 'When I give the word, fire at my heart. Fire!'"

A volley struck him "in the belly," García said. Atkinson staggered and said, "Más arriba, cabrones." Translation: "Higher up, bastards." "Two shots were then fired, and he fell, but still was not dead," García said. "He motioned toward his head, and . . . the commander of the firing party put a pistol to his head and finished him."

McBride, the Ranger, said nothing and taunted no one. Looking baffled and mournful, McBride was "instantly killed," García said.

The insurgents now called for the blood of the remaining Rangers, but their leader, Barela, forbade them. "He told them if they killed one more man he would turn his command on them," Tays said. The Rangers were freed, though they had to leave their weapons behind. The insurgents took from them thirteen rifles, four shotguns, and twenty-four pistols.

With few martyrs and no glory, San Elizario did not stand as a second rendition of the Alamo. Most of the Rangers had survived, but by any measure the engagement counted as a disaster. They had lost the man they were to protect, they had given up while still able to fight, and they endured humiliation as newspapers across the country ran stories about their capitulation to Mexicans and Tejanos. It was, then and now, the only mass surrender by Rangers.

Federal forces had finally arrived from New Mexico, far too late to head off the original siege. But U.S. Army colonel Edward Hatch and his men stayed in the region to help maintain a fragile peace. That did not require clamping down on the insurgents. A new wave of unrest arose from a different, if predictable, source: the Rangers.

Texas governor Hubbard had ordered Sheriff Kerber to "raise 100 men" to put down the insurrection. Kerber was able to find only about thirty, most of whom he imported from Silver City, New Mexico. A Santa Fe newspaper described one of the recruits, John Kinney, as the top rustler in the state. "He is a braggart," the story said, "talks loud, drinks hard, lacks prudence, has killed two men, brags of killing others." Others possessed similar credentials. Now, under Kerber's command, they—the Rangers and the New Mexicans—swept with a vengeance through Tejano settlements, hunting for those who had mounted the San Elizario attack.

On the morning of December 23, 1877, Colonel Hatch approached Socorro, another forsaken village on the Rio Grande. "I heard sharp, desultory firing," he said, and rode into town with an orderly. Hatch found a justice of the peace and asked him what had happened. "[I] learned from him that the Texas Rangers were killing residents of the village."

Kerber's posse galloped through the streets, robbing and shooting at will. They killed dogs and people, and stole chickens, guns, and what money they could find. No one could stop them. Many of the armed insurgents had already melted into Mexico. Now women and children fled to the other side of the river, where they huddled in the winter cold without food or shelter. Those who remained in Texas did so at their peril.

A team of Rangers, along with a deputy sheriff, tracked and killed Jesus Telles, the insurgent who had hacked Charles Howard with his machete. "They reported that Telles had resisted arrest," Lieutenant Tays said, "and that they had shot and killed him."

The posse also caught two men who they believed had led the insurgents. They bound their hands with rope and put them on a wagon. Near Socorro, Rangers shot both of them and claimed they had killed the men as they tried to run away.

Colonel Hatch found the bodies in the road. "One had some five or six bullet-holes in his head," he said. "The other was shot in the forehead and in the side." Both had been drilled at close range. Hatch also saw bloodstains in the wagon that had transported them. The Rangers' story, the colonel concluded, was a blatant and murderous ruse. "I then denounced this inhumanity in no measured terms," Hatch said, "and informed the sheriff it was his duty to arrest the murderers immediately [and] that atrocities of this nature would not be for a moment tolerated."

Kerber ignored Hatch's order and made no arrests.

There were more incidents. A woman named Mariana Nunez said Kerber and about a dozen Rangers came to her house in Socorro and forced their way in. She and her husband hid in the kitchen, behind a closed door. "The Rangers then commenced firing through the door," she said in a sworn statement. One shot struck her husband in the forehead, and another "in the pit of his stomach." A third shot hit her in the side, she said. The Rangers pushed the door open, Nunez said, and shot her husband twice more as he lay on the floor. Then they ransacked the house.

On that same day in Socorro, Kerber and Rangers confronted a man named Cruz Chavez. They demanded that Chavez give them any guns he was carrying. When he refused, Chavez said, a Ranger shot him in the chest. Noverto Pais claimed that Rangers pistol-whipped him—"I have the marks yet," he said months later—and stole a rifle from his home.

Salome Telles of Ysleta said two Rangers forced their way into the house where she was staying. They ransacked the place, she said, and pocketed the few dollars they found. Then, "one of the Rangers went out and stood guard on the outside, while the other . . . pointed the pistol at my breast and forced me to give up my person to him."

When army major James F. Wade and his men rode into Ysleta that day, they were received with grateful relief. "All people . . . came out to meet us," he reported to Hatch, "and say they fear nothing but the Rangers."

Sometimes the Rangers had cause to fear themselves. In late January 1878, Rangers John C. Ford (not to be confused with the more famous John S. "Rip" Ford) and Sam Frazer rode toward their quarters in Ysleta. The two men disliked and distrusted each other. Frazer had bragged of working as a hired killer and had threatened in the past to shoot Ford. Now, in the Rangers' corral, Ford leveled a double-barreled shotgun at Frazer. He said, "Sam." Frazer turned and raised his hands when he saw the gun. He screamed.

Ford fired, hitting Frazer in the right side, and fired again, but missed. Frazer staggered and fell to a sitting position. He pleaded with Ford, "Don't shoot any more." A witness, El Paso lawyer John W. Hughes, said Ford pulled his revolver, walked to Frazer's side, "and emptied the six chambers . . . five shots taking effect in the head."

Ford was tried for Frazer's death. A jury found the homicide justifiable, and he rejoined the Rangers.

The army conducted an investigation into the Salt War and sent officers to Texas to collect sworn testimony. The final report, titled "El Paso Troubles in Texas," cited post-siege "atrocities" committed by the Kerber-Ranger posse. "The force of rangers thus suddenly called together contained within its ranks an adventurous and lawless element," the investigation found. "Though not predominant, [it] was yet strong enough to make its evil influence felt in deeds of violence and outrage matched only by the mob itself. . . . These are regarded by the Board as wanton outrages."

The Rangers claimed the gang from New Mexico committed these outrages, but much of the evidence presented to the army showed otherwise. "I know Lieutenant Tays by sight," said Antonio Cadena. He testified that Rangers broke into his house, threatened to kill him, and stole his gun, his saddle, and two horses. Tays "was with the party which came to my house that day," Cadena said.

The investigators also attempted to explain the genesis of the uprising and the anger of the insurgents. When Howard killed Cardis, the report said, "it was but natural that when their favorite was slain by one whom they distrusted and hated, they should feel the blow thus aimed at them." After all, the report said, the insurgents were "of an ignorant and hot-blooded race." And they traveled with a bad crowd: "The avengers of blood brought in their train a mongrel following of thieves and robbers, birds of prey scenting the quarry from afar."

The investigators recommended establishing a permanent military force at Fort Bliss, near El Paso, to ensure a rapid response to any further uprisings. "This done," the board concluded, "the salt war is probably ended."

That proved to be true. Some smaller disturbances flared from time to time. But banker Zimpelman—with some new associates—kept charging fees for salt as if the war had never happened.

Despite the lengthy investigation, one question was left unanswered: Could the San Elizario surrender and ensuing orgy of revenge have been avoided if someone more savvy and battle-tested than Lieutenant Tays had been in command? His Ranger career was brief—less than twenty weeks—and included nothing beyond the Salt War, so he chalked up no compensating heroics. Those who revere the force have over the years dismissed Tays as not a "real" Ranger. He was, of course, as real as Jack Hays, Sam Walker, and the rest. He simply presided over a catastrophe that no historical papering-over could conceal.

Tays's life and adventures extended beyond his Ranger days. He resigned his commission in March 1878 and spent some time as the postmaster of El Paso. In 1883, he moved to Southern California, where he amassed considerable wealth as a farmer and landowner. He also developed a strong interest in South American gold mining, especially in the wild and distant colony of British Guiana.

In the late spring of 1900, a river steamer named *Mabel* departed a dock on the Potaro River in the Guianese jungle. It towed three smaller boats and carried about 120 passengers. The captain of the *Mabel* intended to dock at the village of Tumatumari, but a strong current carried the steamer past the landing. A line thrown to shore fell short. A passenger jumped in and tried to swim with the rope to the dock, but he too was caught in the flow. He saved himself by grasping a hanging tree limb.

Swift water bore the unmoored steamer toward the churning Tumatumari Falls. Passengers began to scream, and some leapt overboard. Then, disaster. "The steamer, as soon as she got in the rapids, blew up and went under," said an Associated Press report. "The cries of the passengers at this time were most awful. The angry waters carried many of them to their doom, their bodies dashed with great violence against the sharp coral rocks."

At least half of those onboard were killed. Among the dead, the story said, was Tays, forty-eight, identified only as "an American gold miner who had been prospecting on the Potaro and Minniehaha rivers."

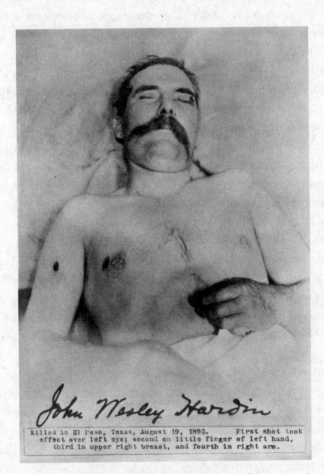

John Wesley Hardin

Killed in El Paso, Texas, August 19, 1895.   First shot took
effect over left eye; second on little finger of left hand,
third in upper right breast, and fourth in right arm.

The Rangers put notorious gunslinger John Wesley Hardin in prison. A
lovers' triangle may have sent him to his grave.

Chapter 13

THE FADING FRONTIER

Buffalo Soldiers, Gunslingers, and the Last Indian Fight

Soon the name of Texas Rangers will be an echo of the past.

—CAPTAIN GEORGE WYTHE BAYLOR

The Gilded Age dawned over much of America in the late 1870s, a time of great advances in industry and technology. In 1877 alone, Thomas Edison demonstrated the first phonograph, and an astronomer at the Naval Observatory discovered the two moons of Mars. The Brooklyn Bridge neared completion in New York. A telephone was installed for the first time at the White House.

At the same time in Texas, a backcountry version of progress began its slow crawl across the state's vastness. Railroad tracks were laid through pine forests and over the prairie. Dallas, Fort Worth, San Antonio, and Houston grew into small cities. The state's population nearly doubled between 1870 and 1880, reaching almost 1.6 million. Most immigrants, however, were white Southern agrarians, and more than 93 percent of Texans made their homes in rural areas. Many of them, small-stakes farmers and stockmen, lived much like the original settlers: building their own cabins, cutting wood for fuel, killing game for food, and making their own household utensils and furniture.

Even as the population increased, great portions of the Lone Star State remained dangerous and difficult. "Ever since the [Civil] War, Texas, to some extent, has been almost helpless in the hands of lawlessness and crime," a Dallas newspaper declared in 1877. "Whole districts of country have been terrorized, the laws suspended, the courts insulted, jails ravished [and] good people murdered."

The Rangers of this period therefore pursued yesterday's adversaries: Indian raiders, stagecoach robbers, cattle rustlers, and maniacal gunfighters, to name a few. They never wanted for engagements, and they extended their record of triumph and death.

The Civil War ended in 1865, but Texas suffered its unceasing and self-inflicted ravages long after the South's surrender at Appomattox. Though not so wretched as other regions of the Confederacy—relatively few battles had been waged in Texas, and no protégé of General Sherman had burned a path to the Gulf—the state confronted a Reconstruction economy in shambles. Its plantation agriculture no longer enjoyed the forced labor of slaves (though some slavery persisted in altered forms), and many of its institutions lay in ruins.

As in other former Confederate states, white gangs in Texas hunted and killed emancipated slaves who were guilty of imagined offenses. The era produced a "frightful story of blood," according to a special committee on lawlessness and violence established by the 1868 Texas constitutional convention. The committee found that from 1865 to 1868, Texas recorded 939 murders. Of those, 373 were murders of blacks committed by whites, but only 10 were of whites by blacks. "'The war of races,'" the committee concluded, "is all on the part of the whites against the blacks." A study by the Texas Freedmen's Bureau over the same period found 1,524 acts of violence by whites against blacks, and 42 by blacks against whites.

Children were not immune from the attacks. In January 1867, the Freedmen's Bureau in Texas received this report from an officer: "I have arrested two citizens of Bosque and McLennan counties for committing one of the most atrocious deeds in the annals of barbarity, that is Castrating a Freedman and he a mere boy." One month later, in Leon County, white night riders torched four farmhouses occupied by black families. They killed two people, one a twelve-year-old boy who was trapped in his burning house. The freedmen's offense, according to state reports: their farms were more prosperous than those of some white farmers.

On a February Sunday in 1875, armed men in Houston attacked black churchgoers in Freedmen's Town, killing twenty-five. It was a "slaughter of the innocents," the *Panola Watchman* reported. "Stripping them of their coverings amid horrible jokes and unfeeling laughter," the newspaper said, the killers "disemboweled and quartered the poor victims, hanging them up by the legs like hogs."

The Rangers' Frontier Battalion had its own encounters. In the early spring of 1878, a black woman named Ida Miller sent a letter to Fritz Tegener, a justice of the peace in Travis County. "Dear Sir," it said in an even hand on lined paper, "I have had my husband and one of my little girls killed the other day by the Rangers."

The woman wrote of an incident from three months earlier, when five Rangers on a scouting expedition rode into Menard County, 150 miles northwest of Austin. Menard County was home to Fort McKavett, where several hundred U.S. Army "buffalo soldiers," black members of the 10th Cavalry, were stationed. The 10th Cavalry had fought well in campaigns against the Plains Indians and had performed valuable and comprehensive scouting missions in West Texas.

However, the black soldiers and white locals often did not mix well. In 1869 a white rancher, John M. "Humpy" Jackson, shot and killed a black cavalryman from McKavett for sending a love note to his daughter. Jackson was arrested and jailed by military authorities. He killed his two guards—also black soldiers—and escaped. Though he was recaptured, he was later released and never stood trial.

The Rangers also had several prior run-ins with the 10th Cavalry. In the fall of 1877, near Fort Concho in West Texas, some Rangers were drinking at a saloon when black soldiers began dancing with Mexican senoritas. This displeased the Rangers, who pulled their guns and shot up the establishment. The soldiers retrieved their weapons, and in the subsequent firefight a bystander was killed. "In the place of keeping the peace," a local citizen complained in a letter to Austin, the Rangers "broke it."

Now, on New Year's Eve, 1877, the five Rangers set up camp near Fort McKavett. With tidy buildings of native limestone, the fort had been called the prettiest in Texas. But across the narrow, rocky San Saba River lay Scabtown, a collection of unpainted shacks along dirt streets. Scabtown's smoky and raucous saloons, dice rooms, brothels, and dance halls drew current and former soldiers from the fort. This, as some Rangers saw it, upset the natural balance of race relations. "These blacks had associated with white gamblers and lewd women until they thought themselves the equals of white men," wrote Ranger James B. Gillett, "and became mean and overbearing."

The five Rangers were tired and bedded down. But their cook—"our negro, George," Gillett called him—wished to attend a dance in Scabtown. "He was a light mulatto, almost white, but well thought of by all the boys in the company," Gillett said. "He obtained Lieutenant [N. O.] Reynolds' permission to attend the dance, and borrowed Tim McCarty's pistol to carry to it."

At the dance, held in the house of an ex–buffalo soldier named Charles Miller, the husband of Ida Miller, the locals fingered the cook as an interloper. "They jumped on George, took his pistol, and kicked him out of the place," Gillett said.

When they learned of the incident, the five Rangers went to the house to retrieve their gun. "The negroes refused to deliver the pistol," the county sheriff wrote. Ida Miller tried to end the standoff. She took the gun and was about to hand it over, the sheriff said, when her husband snatched it from her and told the Rangers, "Here, take your damned old pistol."

The sheriff's account continued: "Tim McCarty stepped up to receive it, and when within four feet of the door [Charles] Miller fired at him but missed. McCarty and Miller fired about the same time. [McCarty] fell, saying, 'Lieutenant, I am killed . . .' Several shots were fired and Miller fell. The others were then ordered to surrender. . . . They answered, 'No, we'll die first.'"

The Rangers opened fire as the "negroes emptied their six-shooters," Ranger Henry McGhee recounted. "It was right lively for a little while. I got in ten shots with my Winchester rifle, and I would not be surprised if I did some damage." Even the cook took part. "Negro George fought like a tiger," Gillett said. Once the guns fell silent, the Rangers charged into the house. "When the smoke of battle cleared," Gillett said, "they found four dead men and a little girl who had been killed by accident."

Ida Miller put it wrenchingly in her letter: "My little child's head was shot to pieces." The girl was four years old. Mrs. Miller's husband was dead as well.

The Rangers believed their actions to be justified and appreciated. "The Citizens are Jubilent over the Killing of the Negroes," Lieutenant Reynolds wrote to the adjutant general, "and I think this Place will be quiet for Some time to Come." A subsequent letter from Ranger McGhee was published in a Waco newspaper. Fort McKavett was "a pretty rough place," McGhee said, "and the negroes here need killing." A white coroner's jury in Menard County seemed to agree. The jury ruled that the ex-soldiers "came to their death while resisting officers in the discharge of their duty."

About three months after the incident, Mrs. Miller wrote her woeful letter to Tegener, the justice of the peace. "Since they killed my people . . . they have robbed me of my property in Menard County and left me helpless with one arm broken into pieces," she said. "They threatened my life if I should go back to McKavett to look after my effects or to make complaints, as the Lieutenant of the Rangers fears the consequences of his bloody work should I appear at District Court." Mrs. Miller asked Tegener, for whom she once worked as a laundress, to use his influence "to bring the murderers of my husband and child to summary justice." The justice of the peace referred the letter to the governor's office, where it had no apparent effect.

The dead child was forgotten. The capture of John Wesley Hardin, however, became an eternal part of the Ranger legend.

The diminutive son of a Methodist minister, Hardin committed his first murder at age fifteen, pumping five bullets into a freed slave who had beaten him in a wrestling match. About six weeks later, in East Texas, he claimed to have shot and killed three soldiers who were searching for him.

The skein of slayings grew longer over the next few years: a rival gambler, a pimp, an Indian, a Mexican, a cowboy, a member of a traveling circus troupe, and more. It is said that in Abilene, Kansas, he backed down Wild Bill Hickok. In a famous and perhaps apocryphal story, Hardin shot a man for snoring. "He did not like to be disturbed in his sleep," a newspaper story explained, "and so he arose in the silent night and slew the snorer."

In October 1871, two members of the Reconstruction-era Texas State Police, both of them black, came to the Central Texas town of Smiley Lake to look for Hardin. They found him in a local store, eating cheese and crackers. One of the officers, Green Paramore, drew on him. In his memoirs, Hardin described Paramore as "a big black negro with his pistol cocked." When Paramore demanded that he surrender his weapon, Hardin extended his Colt .45 revolvers with the butts outward. It was an old trick of his. "One of the pistols turned a somerset in my hand and went off," Hardin said. "Down came the negro, with his pistol cocked." Paramore was dying on the floor "with a bullet through his head, quivering in blood." From the store, Hardin shot through a window and wounded the other officer, who escaped on a mule.

Hardin claimed—without corroboration—that a revenge-minded "posse of negroes from Austin" next came to capture him. "I met them prepared and killed three of them," he wrote. "They returned sadder and wiser."

On his twenty-first birthday, Hardin enhanced his notoriety by shooting to death a deputy sheriff outside a West Texas saloon. "He kills men just to see them kick," wrote a Ranger who used the pen name Pidge. "He can take two six-shooters and turn them like wheels in his hands and fire a shot from each at every revolution. . . . He is said to have killed thirty men and is a dead shot."

With a $4,000 reward hanging over him, and pursued by Rangers, Hardin fled Texas. A special Ranger named Jack Duncan—a Pinkerton detective appointed by the governor—trailed him to Alabama. Duncan wired Ranger lieutenant John B. Armstrong, who had served with Leander McNelly's Special Forces on the border, and who was now chasing Hardin. Armstrong met Duncan in Alabama, and they followed Hardin to Florida. Outside Pensacola, Armstrong recruited a local sheriff to assist. On August 23, 1877, the Ranger, the Pinkerton man, the sheriff, and a deputy boarded a train where Hardin and three accomplices relaxed in a passenger car.

The story of what happened next varies with the storyteller. This is Hardin's version, recounted in a letter to his wife: "4 men grabed me one by each arm and one by each Leg." Hardin struggled for his gun but could not free himself. At one point he yelled, "Texas, by God!" Armstrong raised his Colt revolver and brought it down hard on Hardin's head, knocking him unconscious. During the melee one of Hardin's men pulled a gun, but someone—by some accounts Armstrong—shot him dead. Passengers panicked. "Everybody in the car stampeded," Duncan said, "and went out of the windows and doors."

Later that day, Ranger Armstrong sent a victorious telegram to the adjutant general: "Arrested John Wesley Hardin, Pensacola, Florida this afternoon. He had four men with him, and we had some lively shooting. . . . Hardin fought desperately." Hardin softened by the time he was back in Texas. From the Travis County jail he told a reporter, "The officers treated me kindly, and they deserve the greatest praise for capturing me alive."

Hardin stood trial for the murder of the deputy sheriff; he was found guilty and sentenced to twenty-five years in prison. Armstrong and Duncan apparently pocketed the $4,000 reward. And the Rangers won plaudits as an effective force for law and order, as chronicled in the *Austin Statesman*. "The arrest of this notorious character with two of his men, and the killing of the fourth, not only adds new laurels to the achieved honors of the State troops," the capital's newspaper said. "The event will be the means of causing consternation and demoralization among the desperate characters and thieving bands that curse some localities." The *Dallas Daily Herald* agreed. "No police organization has ever rendered better service than this force has," the newspaper said of the Rangers. "Hardin's arrest . . . is its crowning glory."

Hardin's capture marked a high point for the Rangers, but the humiliation of the Salt War—which happened a few months later—faded some of the acclaim. The Rangers needed another outlaw to restore their luster. Sam Bass gave them that.

Bass was an illiterate, orphaned Indiana farm boy who arrived in Texas as a nineteen-year-old. He indulged an early interest in horse racing and herded longhorn cattle from Texas to Dodge City, Kansas. From there he wandered to Deadwood, South Dakota, the legendary gold-mining town of gambling dens and bordellos. Deadwood proved to be a good place to recruit criminals, and by 1877, Bass had assembled a gang to rob stagecoaches. Their big score was the holdup of a Union Pacific passenger train in Nebraska. Bass and his bandits took $60,000 in newly minted twenty-dollar gold pieces.

Returning to Texas, Bass—by now an outlaw folk hero—robbed more stagecoaches and trains and plotted to hit banks. The Rangers mounted a company in pursuit, but their incompetence and Bass's caginess caused them to be outwitted at every turn. "Bass and his gang . . . played with it as a child plays with toys," Ranger Jim Gillett wrote. Many suspected that citizens and authorities in Bass's adopted hometown of Denton, north of Dallas, protected him. "His friends watch and even question every stranger that visits Denton, reporting every move to Bass, who pays liberally," one newspaper wrote. "It is said he has six men, regularly employed, who receive $60 gold each, per month, besides their drinking free."

With his frustration building, Major Jones, commander of the Frontier Battalion, persuaded a low-level bandit named Jim Murphy to infiltrate the Bass gang. Murphy managed to pull it off and told the Rangers that Bass would be in the town of Round Rock, north of Austin, to case a bank.

Jones and three other Rangers took the train to Round Rock. On the morning of July 19, 1878, lawmen spotted Bass and his accomplices in a general store. A broad-daylight shootout followed, and Bass was hit in the hand and back. He fled on horseback. The Rangers found him the next day, mortally wounded beneath a tree. They took Bass to a small house, where a correspondent for the

Galveston Daily News interviewed him as he lay on a cot dying. Among his last words, the writer said, were: "I am Sam Bass, shot to pieces, and no use to deny." He died forty-eight hours after the gunfight, at age twenty-seven.

The story of the infamous robber's demise hit newspapers across the country. "The name of Sam Bass, the dead robber chieftain, is on every lip in Texas," wrote a florid correspondent for the *St. Louis Globe-Democrat*, "and all other topics have been for the last few days sunk in the blaze of romance in which the ill-fated sun of this modern Robin Hood has descended to its last and final rest."

Bass's capture thus enhanced the Rangers' image of tireless man-hunters. That didn't do much, however, to ease the lingering Salt War rancor in far West Texas. The adjutant general said he required a new commander there "of some established character," an officer who would "avoid further trouble." He sent forty-six-year-old George W. Baylor, a man of letters who played the violin and had twice been acquitted of murder. "I want you to remember," Governor Oran Roberts told Baylor, "that out in the far, wild country, you represent the honor and dignity of the great state of Texas."

A tall, teetotaling Episcopalian, Baylor came from a Texas family both prominent and infamous. An uncle, R. E. B. Baylor, had cofounded Baylor University. After completing his education at that institution, George Baylor sought his fortune in the California goldfields. He amassed no riches, but he did join a group of vigilantes and killed a "dangerous character"—as the locals described him—in a shootout. Baylor, who was wounded in the gunfight, stood trial in the man's death. A jury found him not guilty. "It did not take them long," he wrote, "to bring in a verdict in substance, 'served 'em right.'"

Returning to Texas in 1859, he reunited with his brother, John R. Baylor, the zealous Indian scourge who published the *White Man* newspaper. George Baylor accompanied his brother's missions to slay Comanches and apparently notched his share. One press account, George Baylor noted with some pride, said he had "killed and scalped six Indians one morning before breakfast." In the 1860 census he listed his occupation as "Indian Killer."

With the outbreak of the Civil War, Baylor joined the Confederate Army as a lieutenant. He fought in the Battle of Shiloh, was promoted to colonel, and saw more fighting in Louisiana. Near the end of the war, he settled a personal dispute with a Rebel general by drawing his Colt revolver and shooting the unarmed man dead in a Houston hotel. Though he was acquitted of murder charges, Baylor said the incident lingered for years as a "matter of sorrow and regret." Nonetheless, he said, "I would do the same thing again."

Now, in August 1879, he was riding into history as a newly commissioned Ranger. Baylor, his wife, two daughters, and a sister-in-law departed San Antonio for the trip west. Six Rangers, including James Gillett, accompanied them on horseback. One wagon carried household goods, including a piano and Baylor's beloved violin. At the rear of the wagon was a coop full of game hens. The women and children clustered in a hack drawn by a pair of mules.

The six hundred-mile trek took them through some of the most barren and dangerous land in the Southwest. "Not a drop of rain fell," Gillett recalled. Near the Pecos River they passed the charred remains of a wagon train attacked by Indians only months before. "All the mules had been captured, the teamsters killed, and the train of sixteen big wagons burned," Gillett said. "Had the same Indians encountered our little party . . . we would all have been massacred."

After forty-two days they reached Ysleta, the scene of numerous Ranger assaults on the populace after the Salt War. Baylor, who spoke fluent Spanish—"the sweet Castilian tongue," he called it—commenced mending fences. "His open, friendly personality endeared him to the Mexicans," Gillett said. "Always they showed him every courtesy in their power."

The quality of his new Ranger company, however, often fell short, as Baylor proved to be a poor judge of character. "He was as tender-hearted as a child and would listen to any tale of woe," Gillett said. "All men looked alike to him, and he would enlist anyone when there was a vacancy in the company. The result was that some of the worst . . . rustlers got into the command and gave us no end of trouble, nearly causing one or two killings in our camp." They behaved poorly in town too. The marshal of El Paso, Dallas Stoudenmire, complained to the state attorney general that Rangers were "more ready to aggravate" than serve, and they rode "shooting through the streets."

The criminality of his men may not have mattered much to Baylor. He showed little interest in the pursuit of robbers, killers, rustlers, and the ordinary run of lawbreakers. "Sometimes we would have as many as six or eight criminals chained up in camp at one time," Gillett said, "but [he] would never come to see them, for he could not bear to see anyone in trouble." The Ranger leader chose instead to go after Indians. He was, after all, a Baylor.

Although the Rangers fought the Comanches hard for years—and struck some crippling blows—it was the U.S. Army that finally pushed them out of Texas. In 1874 the cavalry began a campaign against the Comanches and the Kiowas that became known as the Red River War. The army engaged the weakened Indians over the course of a few months and pushed them back into the Oklahoma Indian Territory. Never again did Comanches significantly threaten Anglo settlers in Texas. The guns of the white man had reduced them, like the buffalo, from overwhelming presence to vestigial oblivion.

Like the Comanches, bands of Apaches had been forced onto a reservation—this one in Arizona. Conditions were miserable: bad water, poor rations, disease, and no game to hunt. Several hundred tribesmen left with Victorio, a legendary if aging chief of the Eastern Chiricahua and Mescalero Apaches. In the 1850s Victorio had ridden with Geronimo on raids into Texas. American military commanders considered him to be a skilled battlefield tactician. Though he was now at least fifty-five, Victorio and his band of warriors began marauding again.

Many of the raids took place in Mexico, but Texans around El Paso believed he would hit them too. "Victorio knew every foot of the country and where to find wood, water, grass and abundance of game," Baylor said. "I knew it was only a question of time before old Victorio would be on our side again murdering and robbing."

In the summer of 1880, Baylor and his Rangers rode in pursuit, though with little success. A few months later Mexican soldiers managed to trap the chief and his warriors, along with women and children, in the Tres Castillos Mountains. Victorio was killed, as were most of the others. Only a dozen or so warriors, along with a handful of women and children, managed to escape to Texas. "At once this band began a series of pillages and murders that has no parallel," Gillett said, "considering the small size of the party."

Their last attack came in early January 1881, as the Overland Mail stage bumped through rocky, desolate Quitman Canyon, southeast of El Paso. The driver, whose name was Morgan, had worked the San Antonio to El Paso route dozens of times. He carried one passenger this day, a gambler named Crenshaw. Pulled by mules, the stage clattered through a narrow passage known as the Apache Post Office, so named because of pictographs on the rock walls. It was there that Victorio's remnant band ambushed them.

When the stage failed to make its next stop at Fort Quitman, ranchmen and

Overland employees mounted a search. Leading them was none other than Rip Ford, the former Ranger, now living nearby. The searchers found the abandoned stagecoach. One mule was dead. Mailbags had been cut open, the mail scattered on the ground. Morgan and Crenshaw, dead or alive, were nowhere to be seen. Ford sent a letter to Baylor describing the scene. There were some initial suspicions, Baylor said, that the driver and passenger of the stage might have faked the robbery. "I deemed it best to go down & see for myself," he wrote.

On January 16, 1881, Baylor—who had been promoted to captain—and twelve of his men from Company A left the town of Ysleta to investigate. Three Pueblo Indians rode with them. They loaded ten days' worth of rations on two pack mules and headed into the rough country of desert foothills. Within several days, the Rangers found the trail and followed it into Mexico. Along the way, a dead horse—butchered for food—and a pair of old moccasins told them they were following Indians. "Next morning the trail crossed back to Texas," Baylor said, and "we all felt in some degree the pleasure of being again on our own soil."

They rode into the Eagle Mountains and discovered a hastily abandoned camp. Blankets and baskets had been left behind. A mule tongue stewed over a fire. Some postcards from the stagecoach mailbag lay nearby. But because "the night had been bitterly cold," Baylor wrote, and the ground was frozen "hard as flint rock," the Rangers had lost the trail. They had the good fortune to encounter another Ranger search party as they turned back toward Mexico. From them, Baylor learned of a fresh trail. Though rations had run low, the pursuit continued into the sere and forbidding Sierra Diablo Mountains.

The Rangers spent the night on some cliffs overlooking Rattlesnake Springs. The next day they found another abandoned camp. The Indians couldn't have gone far; their fires were still burning. "The chase was getting to be exciting," Baylor wrote. On the morning of January 29, almost two weeks since the Rangers had begun their quest, one of the Pueblo scouts pointed and whispered, "*Están los Indios.*" Baylor gazed across the valley and saw their campfires.

On foot, the Rangers crept undetected within two hundred yards of the camp. The Apaches "were huddled up around their fires cooking breakfast," Baylor said, "and not conscious of a Ranger being within a hundred miles." Baylor knelt and motioned his men to form a line. With the signal of a gunshot, "we charged them with a Texas yell."

The staggering Indians could not mount a defense. "The Apaches ran like a herd of deer," Baylor said. "Unlike our Comanches . . . these cowardly rascals ran like sheep." With the warriors in retreat, "of course the women were the sufferers." The women stumbled from their tipis, wrapped in blankets, and the Rangers cut them down. "Few could tell men from women," Baylor said. Not that it mattered. "In fact the law under which the [Frontier Battalion] was organized don't require it."

Two women were killed, and one was mortally wounded. Baylor listed others: "2 children killed & 1 squaw captured [with] the latter wounded having 3 bullets in her hand and 2 children captured, one of them shot through the foot." Baylor considered taking the injured child home as a souvenir for one of his daughters. "My little girl had always asked me to bring her ferns, flowers, pretty rocks or something every time I went on a scout." For this last mission, he said, she issued a special request. "As we rode off she said: 'Papa, please bring me a little Indian.'" The captain thought better of it when the Indian child came upon the bodies of those the Rangers had killed. "Her eyes flashed fire and she looked like some wild animal."

After the last shot was fired, Baylor's men combed the camp. They found six saddles, Baylor said, that had belonged to a U.S. Army patrol ambushed several months before. They also recovered some guns and the harness reins from the stagecoach attacked at Quitman Canyon. This proved, he believed, that they had found the remnants of Victorio's band.

The Rangers now were hungry, having eaten nothing since the night before. They roasted the Apaches' venison and ate it on the spot. "We took our breakfast on the ground occupied by the Indians," Baylor wrote, "which we all enjoyed." As the Rangers ate, they marveled at the spectacular vista of the surrounding mountains and canyons, and tried not to look at the bullet-riddled bodies of women and children a few feet away. "We had almost a boundless view from our breakfast table. . . . The beauty of the scenery [was] only marred by man's inhumanity to man," Baylor said, noting "the ghostly forms of the dead lying around."

The captain admitted to one regret: his men didn't carry breech-loading shotguns. If they did, he said, they could have unleashed quicker and more lethal rounds, and "I don't believe a single Indian would have escaped." Still, he regarded the engagement with satisfaction. Never again, Baylor said, would the Indians "sit down to eat breakfast without looking around to see if the Rangers are in sight."

The boast was obsolete even as he made it. All the epic clashes, the bloodsoaked but forgotten skirmishes, the scalpings, the tortures, the bravery, and the depravities had now run their course. This small, obscure massacre would come to assume monumental proportions. With Company A's purge of these few Apaches on a cold morning, the Rangers had fought their last battle with Indians.

The Frontier Battalion was witnessing the end of the frontier. With most of the Indians dead, pacified, or on distant reservations, the Texas range opened. Cattle raisers pushed into regions of the state where, only a few years before, encroachment would have been tantamount to suicide. At the same time, the era of the great and legendary cattle trail drives was drawing to a close, replaced by the spread of ranches. This tectonic shift, combined with a new type of fence, brought the Rangers into a different sort of conflict.

Modern barbed wire, developed by an Illinois famer, was patented in 1874. The product initially found little use in Texas. Reasons varied, but many Texans simply believed the thin strands would not hold cattle. In 1876, while taking his dinner in a San Antonio chili parlor, an enterprising salesman had a vision. John Warne Gates, a twenty-one-year-old drummer for a fencing company, decided to build a small corral of barbed wire in San Antonio's central Military Plaza. He filled it with 25 to 135—the reports differ—longhorn steers.

The new fencing was, he crowed, "light as air, stronger than whiskey and cheaper than dirt." And as he demonstrated to the large crowd that had gathered, it would keep cattle from stampeding or wandering away. Angry longhorns charged the fence, only to be repulsed by the barbs. By the end of the day Gates had sold hundreds of miles of the wire at eighteen cents a pound, and a revolution had begun. Soon mile upon mile of barbed wire, nailed to mesquite and cedar posts, stretched across what had been Texas open range. Standing Deer, a Pueblo Indian chief, described the confounding scene to Ranger and rancher Charles Goodnight: "Wire, wire, wire! Everywhere!"

Landowners fenced their property with it, and they fenced government land they perhaps intended to buy. They fenced roads and rivers. They sometimes fenced entire towns. Nomadic grazing practices that had prevailed since the Spaniards claimed Texas became obsolete almost overnight. Cattle owners who had grown accustomed to free access to pastures and watering holes now found themselves cut off by endless stretches of the devil's rope. Naturally, the backlash hit hard. As fast as some fences went up, fence cutters armed with wire snips took them down. An unconfirmed story has it that the first fence cutting in Texas was done by the old Ranger Big-Foot Wallace, who was said to declare that the men "who whipped the Indians out of the country should have first choice of the range."

However noble Wallace's sentiment might have been, it couldn't beat money. Over more than three years, the cash-starved state government had sold vast tracts of public land for fifty cents an acre. This allowed men of foresight and capital to assemble some of the great, sprawling cattle ranches that became a part of Texas lore. The land for the world's largest ranch, the XIT Ranch in the Texas Panhandle, was deeded to a Chicago syndicate in return for building the new capitol. Much of the XIT's three million acres of arid grazing land came to be protected by wire fence, which ultimately stretched for six thousand miles.

In many if not most cases, the fence-cutting disputes pitted the big ranchers—a number of whom had international financial backing—against small, struggling stockmen. "Down with monopolies," read a handbill posted on the streets of the West Texas town of Coleman in 1883. "Away with your foreign capitalists; the range and soil of Texas belong to the heroes of the South."

The severe drought of 1883 made matters worse, as farmers found themselves cut off from dwindling sources of water by endless stretches of barbed wire. A letter writer to the *Galveston Daily News* urged the state to act. "I do not believe," he wrote, "that eternal Providence created land for cattle to live fat and people to starve."

Brown County, a patch of rolling grassland near the geographic center of the state, had been for decades the domain of the Comanches. Later John Wesley Hardin and his gang ran rampant there. Now fence cutting was reported to be widespread and the opposing sides on hair trigger. One estimate placed the losses from destroyed fences at $1 million. Others put the cost even higher. Landowners said the fence cutters not only did their usual destructive work but delivered dire threats and damaged other property as well. Coffins were placed on doorsteps as not-so-subtle intimidation. Houses went up in flames. Shots were fired into homes at night, and some ranchers were told to leave the area or be killed.

Panic seized the county seat in December 1883, as the *Austin Statesman* reported a looming peasant revolt: "Yesterday was a very awful day in Brownwood. About three o'clock in the morning it was announced that over two hundred fence cutters were in arms, and determined to lay Brownwood in ashes and kill some of its citizens. All the citizens were immediately notified and flew to arms, and the opera house was at once converted into an arsenal." The attack did not occur, but the fear remained.

As the problem spread, Governor John Ireland threw his support to the cattle kings with a rousing 1884 speech to the Texas Live Stock Association. "I believe the man who can educate himself to think that it is not wrong to maliciously tear down and destroy persons' fences," the governor said, "is also capable of educating himself into the belief that it is not wrong to set fire to our houses or to hurl dynamite into our public buildings." The audience responded with hearty applause.

Ireland called a special session of the Texas Legislature, in part to "provide a remedy for wanton destruction of fences." Lawmakers made fence cutting a felony, punishable by one to five years in prison. With the statute on the books, it was time to send in the enforcers.

At first the state hired private eyes, including some from the famed Pinkerton agency. But detectives out of Chicago—even those who were sworn as Rangers— somehow couldn't crack cases on the Texas range. One Pinkerton operative, for instance, spent several days hanging around a saloon in the town of Taylor, but reported that "fence cutting was not discussed with much feeling."

Adjutant General Wilburn King decided that actual Rangers should perform some detective work, though most had little experience in undercover operations. One of those assigned was Ira Aten, a garrulous and energetic twenty-four-year-old. Aten claimed to have witnessed the shooting of Sam Bass, which made him want to be a Ranger. Now, in pursuit of fence cutters, he knew his superiors had inserted him where others had failed. "Detectives has been sent into that country many times but to no avail," Aten wrote. "Several of them barely escaped with their lives."

Some of the fence cutters were rustlers or common outlaws. Ranger captain Baylor believed a few of them "may have been drawn into fence cutting under communistic teachings." Other cutters merely wanted water and grass for their cattle. Whatever their motives, the "knights of the nippers" were hard to catch. To solve the crime, a Ranger or sheriff had to penetrate a family or a gang of night riders who admitted no outsiders. "They are the best organized band that I ever worked after," lamented Ranger John R. Hughes, who became a captain. "They keep spies out all the time."

It didn't help the Rangers that many in the rural precincts saw the cutters as heroes. "The big pasture men live in town and people in the country are almost all in sympathy with the wire cutters," Hughes said. When authorities managed to make arrests, local juries often refused to convict their neighbors for destroy-ing the fences of absentee owners. A law enforcement operative in Erath County complained that a member of the grand jury, which had refused to indict any fence cutters despite ample evidence, was "one of the chief advocates of wire-cutting." And the Erath County sheriff, the operative said in a report to the ad-jutant general, enjoyed "strong support among the fence-cutters."

In the town of Sweetwater, Ranger private Ben Warren gathered evidence on a fence-cutting gang and was prepared to testify against them at trial. Warren stood in the office of the Central Hotel one winter's night, tending a stove, when someone fired a shot through a window. The bullet struck Warren in the face, and—blood spurting from the hole in his cheek—he collapsed in a chair, where he died. The primary suspects were two of the accused fence cutters. "The fence cutting element in the interior," the *Austin Statesman* said in the murder's after-math, "are much elated."

Facing such obstacles, a Ranger could not simply ride into town, eyeball the suspects, and toss them in the county jail. Ranger Aten, sent to Brown County, adopted infiltration as his initial tactic. "I posed as a poor orphan boy with no home, who was just being kicked about from pillar to post," he said. He had a secret list of suspected fence cutters. "I hung around a store in the neighborhood where these men lived, sleeping in hay stacks or wherever I could get shelter for several days."

One of the suspects hired Aten to do odd jobs. "I milked the cow, fed the chickens and pigs, chopped the wood, and was just a handy boy around the ranch," Aten said. Still, he provoked suspicion. "Some of this man's friends said I was no good and should be killed or run out of the country."

He stayed, though, and "at last the opportunity I sought arrived." He was offered the chance to sell some stolen horses, which he pretended to do. This gained him more credence with the cutters, and "I was ready to spring the trap I was laying." He positioned a company of Rangers to ambush midnight nippers. Shots were fired—the Rangers may or may not have pulled their triggers first—and two of the cutters lay dying on the fence line. In the parlance of the day, it was a "Ranger conviction." And that "stopped the fence cutting in Brown County," Aten said.

He moved on to Navarro County, about fifty miles south of Dallas. Aten and another Ranger posed as itinerants—"wagon hoboes," Aten said, "out hunting cotton to pick." A few weeks in the cotton fields, however, left him restless and bored, so "I got a scheme in my head." He decided to booby-trap some of the fences. "They sent me here to stop fence-cutting any way I could," he reasoned. "And that is what I am doing."

Using old shotguns and some dynamite he bought in Dallas, Aten fashioned an underground device that would explode when the barbed wire was cut and the supporting post fell. "Well," he wrote, "if that don't kill the parties that cuts the fence, it will scare them so bad they will never cut another."

Aten called his invention the "dynamite boom" and the "boom rocket." He assured his supervisors in Austin that he was taking precautions to set the traps safely, though accidents could happen. "Keep your ears pricked, you may hear my boom clear down there," Aten said. "However, if I get blowed up, you will know I was doing a good cause."

To Aten's surprise, officials in the state capital did not share his enthusiasm. He was ordered to meet with Governor Sul Ross, the ex-Ranger who had succeeded Ireland. Aten tried to explain to the governor how the boom rocket would work, which only seemed to infuriate Ross. "That bald head of his got redder and redder, and when I finished my story it was on fire," Aten said. "I thought he was going to have me court-martialed and then shot."

He promised the governor he would remove the dynamite. "Instead, I exploded the bombs and they were heard for miles around," he said. "Next day people gathered about the little store to see what it all meant, and the word was passed through the crowd there were bombs planted on all the fences, and these people were ready to believe it. That settled the fence cutting activities in Navarro County."

Afterward, he and Governor Ross "became fast friends," Aten said. And his dynamite boom put him in the Texas Ranger Hall of Fame, one of only thirty-one men to be so honored.

As the nineteenth century drew to an end, a story in a Pennsylvania newspaper asked if the Rangers were destined now to fade away, victims of their own success. "With the disappearance of the bad men and the gradual extinction of the wild tribes of Indians infesting Texas and the Southwestern frontier, another hardly less important and far more picturesque and necessary type of men are becoming memories of the past as the days of their usefulness are drawing to a close," the *Philadelphia Times* said. "The pride of the Lone Star State, the Texas Ranger . . . is gradually shrinking away to mere nothingness before the march of civilization, law and order."

Only a writer some fifteen hundred miles away on the East Coast could think enlightenment had waltzed across Texas, or that most of the state's "bad men" had been contained. It was true that the Rangers' duties were shifting, making them less a paramilitary group and more a statewide police force. Some Rangers now rode trains instead of horses. Others had never even killed an Indian.

The state disbanded the Frontier Battalion and replaced it with a Ranger Force in 1901. (Officials had discovered well after the fact that under the original law creating the battalion, Ranger privates did not have the power of arrest. Thus the Rangers had been policing illegally for a quarter century.) The new statute empowered the governor to assemble four companies of one captain, one sergeant and twenty privates each. Captains were to make $100 a month, privates $40, and they would "always be under the command of the Governor." The law strictly prescribed daily rations for every Ranger, from beef and bacon down to the amount of pickles: "one sixth gill," or less than an ounce.

As always, the force was underfunded, but the Rangers remained quite alive. Abundant wildness persisted in Texas yet. There was, for example, that perpetual cauldron, the Texas-Mexico border, where much trouble awaited.

No Ranger was more adept at self-promotion or had more talent for crafting aphorisms than Captain Bill McDonald. Those gifts brought him lasting fame.

Chapter 14

CAPTAIN BILL TO THE RESCUE

"I Think I'm a Dead Rabbit"

Indeed, they have been from the beginning not unlike the knights of old who rode without fear and without reproach to destroy evil and redress wrong.

—ALBERT BIGELOW PAINE, DESCRIBING THE TEXAS RANGERS

News out of Brownsville, Texas, in August 1906 made the headlines scream: "DASTARDLY OUTRAGE BY NEGRO SOLDIERS" and "REIGN OF TERROR." The papers reported that drunken black army troops had "gone on the warpath" and gunned down innocent white folks. As Captain William J. McDonald saw it, this called for the presence of a courageous Texas Ranger, namely himself, so he caught a train for the old border town.

McDonald was already famous, perhaps the most celebrated Ranger of his time. Many knew him as Captain Bill, a slim gent with a flowing mustache, impeccable penmanship—he had taught handwriting as a young man—and a penchant for informing others of his ample virtues. The very mention of his name, his authorized biographer would write, "makes the pulse of a good citizen, and the feet of an outlaw, move quicker." Among the bad men of Texas, of whom there were many, "there grew up a superstition that he was bullet-proof."

And now he headed south at locomotive speed to handle what he came to call the "Brownsville Outrage."

With a population of about eight thousand, Brownsville was at the beginning of the twentieth century what it had been for decades before: a poor, steamy, verminous place, with recurrent cholera epidemics and outbreaks of yellow fever. The city had yet to install an electrical grid or provide running water. Hewing to its Mexican War origin as a military outpost, Brownsville provided temporary and unhappy quarters to 167 black soldiers from the army's 25th Infantry—"colored troops," as they were known.

On the night of August 13, 1906, about a dozen men took to the narrow dirt streets of the town, firing rifles. One citizen, a white man, was killed. Two others were wounded, including a policeman. Suspicion fell immediately on the black soldiers. Residents of Brownsville, already uneasy about the presence of the infantrymen, feared more killing to come.

McDonald was more than five hundred miles away, working as the sergeant-at-arms for the state Democratic convention in Dallas, when he heard about the incident. He insisted he should "go down and settle that Brownsville business." The man in charge of the Rangers, Adjutant General John A. Hulen, ordered McDonald to stay out of it, because state police had no authority to investigate or arrest federal troops.

That might have stopped lesser men, but McDonald had his reasons: "Why, them hellions have violated the laws of the state." His talent for such inspired phrasing was notable. One of his aphorisms in particular gained a hallowed place in Ranger lore: "No man in the wrong can stand up against a fellow that's in the right and keeps on a-comin'."

This notion—justice fortified with persistence invariably wins out—may have propelled McDonald toward the border. Or it may have been that he spotted the chance for abundant press coverage. Like any number of Rangers, McDonald did not fear a plunge into perilous situations. Many of them did so with a reluctance to call attention to their actions. Captain Bill suffered from no such reticence.

Born in Mississippi in 1852, McDonald spent his early youth on his family's cotton plantation, an enterprise with half a dozen slaves. His father, a Confederate major, died in 1862 at the Battle of Corinth, and McDonald's widowed mother moved the family to Texas.

When McDonald was sixteen, at the height of Reconstruction, a distant relative named Peter Green was murdered in Rusk County in East Texas. Five suspects—all black men—were arrested, after which a white mob pulled them from the county jail and lynched them. There is little doubt McDonald was part of the mob. "If he did not help pull a rope that night," his sympathetic biographer wrote, "it was only because the rope was fully occupied with other willing hands." Young McDonald "was hot-blooded in 'sixty-eight," the biographer explained, while "the situation was not one to develop moral principles." And he seethed with anger at the death of his "hero father, shot dead while leading his regiment against [the] men in blue."

Federal troops marched into the county after the lynching and garrisoned themselves in the courthouse. With another relative, McDonald fired random shots at the courthouse windows. He was arrested and prosecuted "for aiding in the crime of treason," according to his biographer, but was acquitted at trial.

Some time after that, McDonald settled down and seemed destined for the relatively placid life of a small-town merchant. He graduated from Soule's Commercial College in New Orleans and opened a grocery store back in East Texas. But he went broke in 1877, after which he worked as a deputy sheriff. He tried ranching in West Texas but kept his connection to law enforcement as a deputy in Hardeman County. In 1891 an old friend, Governor James Hogg, appointed the thirty-eight-year-old McDonald a Ranger captain.

His duties included the pursuit of bank robbers, attempts to settle deadly feuds, and the prevention of prizefights. Boxing matches were illegal in Texas. When a promoter tried to arrange an El Paso bout in 1896, McDonald and at least eighteen Rangers—a "manly looking set of men," the local newspaper observed—moved in to stop it. The boxers were Bob "Ruby Robert" Fitzsimmons, middleweight champion from New Zealand, and Peter Maher, an Irish brawler and heavyweight champ. Fitzsimmons, also known as the "Fighting Blacksmith" and the "Freckled Wonder," brought his pet lion, Nero, with him. The lion caused a stir one morning in Juarez when it slipped its collar and killed a Mexican's goat.

McDonald and the Rangers made it clear that no fight could take place on Texas soil. The promoter then had his workers set up the ring in the Mexican state of Coahuila, on a sandy flat along the Rio Grande. After all that, the match itself wasn't much. Fitzsimmons knocked out Maher less than two minutes into the first round. The Rangers watched from the Texas side of the river.

Before the Brownsville affair, perhaps McDonald's most noteworthy incident as a Ranger occurred in 1893, when he engaged in a duel with a county sheriff on a West Texas street. Shot twice, McDonald suffered a broken collarbone and a punctured lung. "Well," he said as he sank to the ground, "I think I'm a dead rabbit." But he recovered and, after a long convalescence, went back to work. The sheriff had committed the capital crime of cursing McDonald and had accused the Rangers of rustling. He was shot at least three times and died of an infection.

This had not been a classic, cinematic Wild West showdown, with one flinty-eyed gunfighter facing another at high noon. An examination found the sheriff was shot in the back, quite possibly by some of McDonald's Rangers. No matter. The fatal encounter made news as far away as California, where the *Los Angeles Times* ran a story saying Captain Bill, "one of the bravest officers of Texas," had single-handedly shot it out against four armed adversaries. For the rest of his life McDonald would tell admirers he had so much lead in him that if he tried to swim, he would sink.

Even before the guns went off, racial tension was already at a boil in Brownsville. White residents had expressed deep unhappiness and anxiety about having black troops in the city. "To hell with the colored soldiers," one white army lieutenant recalled townspeople saying. Nor did the soldiers, many of whom had served in Cuba and the Philippines, want to be stationed where Jim Crow laws of segregation still held. One black soldier walked into a Brownsville saloon called the White Elephant and asked for a drink, the lieutenant said. A deputy marshal—and former Ranger—named W. B. Bates "turned to the solder and said no nigger could drink at the same bar with him." When the soldier responded he was "as good as any white man," the lieutenant said, the deputy marshal "drew his revolver and hit the soldier over the head."

At saloons where they were served, infantrymen said, bartenders broke the glasses from which they had sipped, so that no white man's lips would touch them. Soldiers said they had been jostled or cursed by whites on the streets, while citizens complained that a black man in uniform had grabbed a white woman by the hair and thrown her to the ground.

Around midnight on August 13, under a near moonless sky, a dozen or so shadowy figures—maybe dressed like soldiers, maybe not—stalked the narrow streets near Fort Brown. With rifles, they began shooting at stores, houses, and a hotel. A mounted police lieutenant was hit, his arm shattered. It had to be amputated. The men fired into the Ruby Saloon and killed a bartender. Another person was wounded. After ten minutes, the shooters melted into the night.

Circumstantial evidence pointed to the soldiers. The area of the shootings was close to their barracks. Empty shells found on the sidewalk appeared to come from army rifles. And eight townspeople claimed they recognized the men as soldiers. However, their commander, Major Charles Penrose, insisted they had been confined to barracks that night. Brigadier General William S. McCaskey, who oversaw the army's Southwestern Division, warned of a rush to judgment. "Citizens of Brownsville entertain race hatred to an extreme degree," he advised in a telegram to the War Department.

On a sweltering evening one week later, McDonald stepped off the train at Brownsville. Four Rangers from his Company B joined him. The captain launched his investigation by meeting with local officials. They informed him that Major Penrose had vowed to solve the case if it took ten years. McDonald erupted. "I told them he could do it in ten minutes if he tried," he said.

Next he went to Fort Brown, where the soldiers were garrisoned, to see Penrose. McDonald wore a holster with two pearl-handled .45-caliber revolvers and cradled a shotgun. "The guns he carried were almost half his size," a Brownsville resident observed, "and helped him, proportionately, to the publicity he craved."

Armed guards blocked his entrance. According to his authorized biography, McDonald began dispensing orders: "You niggers, hold up there! You've already got into trouble with them old guns of yours. I'm Captain McDonald of the State Rangers, and I'm down here to investigate a foul murder you scoundrels have committed. I'll show you niggers something you've never been used to. Put up them guns!"

As the episode suggests, he did not shy from confrontation. "If McDonald started hellwards," an admiring correspondent once wrote, "he would come back with the devil handcuffed and tied across the pommel of his saddle." And he was, like many of his day, an unreconstructed and unapologetic racist. "A white man who has committed a crime is, to him always a 'scoundrel,' or worse," his biographer wrote. "A black offender, to him, is not a negro, or a colored man, but a 'nigger,' usually with pictorial adjectives."

So it went in the confrontation with the black soldiers. The *Houston Post* gave this fawning account, based on an interview with McDonald: "There was a ring in the captain's voice that they did not mistake. That ring carried time backward in its flight more than forty years. It was not United States soldiers standing menacingly over a civilian. It was negroes—the old-time plantation negroes—in the presence of a Southern gentleman. 'Yas, sir, cap'n; yas, sir. Majah Penrose he ovah dar in his house.' 'One of you black scoundrels show me to him.' They all bent their bodies in a bow." Then, "a darkey led the way."

The Rangers learned that a bar frequented by the soldiers had closed early the night of the riot, which McDonald believed was proof an assault had been planned. He interrogated soldiers rapid-fire and considered their silence an admission of guilt. "We didn't say anything because there was nothing to say," Private Dorsie Willis recalled. "We didn't do it."

McDonald also discovered that a cap bearing the initials of one of the soldiers had been found along the route of the riot on the morning after. This made the man, Captain Bill said, "one of the guilty parties." When Major Penrose did not leap to agree with his conclusions, McDonald reminded him that "people who tried to shield criminals were accessories to the crime."

A Brownsville citizens committee conducted its own investigation, which foundered. No one who witnessed the shootings could identify a single soldier, and a check of the soldiers' rifles showed that they had not been recently fired. But an undeterred McDonald secured from a local judge arrest warrants for twelve soldiers and one ex-soldier. "I hereby demand the delivery to me of the men of your command that I yesterday gave you warrants for," McDonald wrote to Major Penrose. The major's written response: "After a most careful investigation, I am unable to find any one or party in any way connected with the crime of which you speak."

The army planned to ship the men elsewhere, while McDonald wanted them to stay in town and face prosecution. The Ranger captain launched a counteroffensive. He telegrammed a report to Governor Samuel W. T. Lanham: "The [army] officers are trying to cover up the diabolical crime I am about to uncover and it will be a shame to allow this to be done," he wrote. "Please send assistance." He wired U.S. senator Joseph W. Bailey of Texas. "Am about to uncover the whole thing," McDonald said, "and some of the officers seem to be trying hard to shield the guilty parties." He also made sure that newsmen on the scene had access to the correspondence—"wishing to explain fully," he said, "all that I have done."

Those charged with keeping the peace locally worried that the Ranger captain was headed for an armed confrontation with the army. Jim Wells Jr., Brownsville's most powerful political figure, told McDonald to stop. "He said, 'McDonald, I am a friend of yours, but you are only a Ranger captain, and if you keep going along the way you are doing you are going to precipitate us into trouble,'" recalled Mayor Frederick Combe. Officials also feared a race riot. "You think you are doing right," Wells said to McDonald, "but if you attempt to interfere with those soldiers down there, this matter will break out anew, and we will lose a great many lives here. You must remember our wives and children."

The judge who had issued the arrest warrants demanded that McDonald return them. With several dozen armed men, he confronted the Ranger—also armed—in the lobby of the Miller Hotel. McDonald regarded them with a sneer. "You all look like 15 cents in Mexican money," he said, and refused to surrender the warrants. Another gunfight seemed to be brewing. But McDonald had to back down when he received a wire from the governor, instructing him to take his orders from the judge and the sheriff.

Captain Bill now found himself at a dead end. "Of course I could do no more," he reported, "so I quietly left town the next day with my four rangers while champagne corks were popping and old McDonald was being denounced and compared to a sausage and the murderers went on their way rejoicing."

The army put the soldiers on a train for Oklahoma. The *Brownsville Herald* was glad to see them go. Otherwise, the newspaper said, "if those black beasts had been left here in our jail it is more than likely that the people would have taken the law into their own hands."

In late 1906, once passions had cooled a bit, a Brownsville grand jury considered the case against the soldiers and indicted no one.

The decision on the soldiers' fate now lay with President Theodore Roosevelt. McDonald knew the president from a 1905 wolf-hunting trip they had taken in Oklahoma, and had served as a bodyguard for Roosevelt during a swing through Texas. Shortly after his Brownsville case fell apart, McDonald wrote the president personally and complained of army officers "trying to cover this outrageous murder up." It's impossible to know if Roosevelt was influenced by McDonald, but he certainly agreed with the captain. In November 1906 the president ordered that all 167 of the men who had been garrisoned at Fort Brown be discharged without honor. Not one of them stood trial.

"The townspeople were completely surprised by the unprovoked and murderous savagery of the attack," Roosevelt wrote. He said he based his decision on findings by Major Augustus Blocksom, whose brief investigation determined that between nine and fifteen unidentified soldiers fired the shots. "The soldiers were aggressors from start to finish," Roosevelt said, while "their comrades privy to the deed have combined to shelter the criminals from justice." It was a "conspiracy of silence," the president said. "They perverted the power put into their hands to sustain the law into the most deadly violation of the law."

The president's action notwithstanding, McDonald emerged from the affray with his image in tatters, at least in some quarters. The *Brownsville Herald* accused him of using the incident simply to promote himself: "He seeks by means of the press, or such members of it as will lend themselves to his rather apparent purpose, to aggrandize himself and add to the lustre of his reputation at the expense of an outraged, insulted, and misunderstood people." In an unrelated matter, Judge Welch—the jurist who issued and repossessed the arrest warrants—was murdered in a nearby town two months after the Brownsville affair. Jim Wells wired the governor, beseeching him to send Rangers to investigate. But he asked for captains other than McDonald, who, apparently, had worn out his welcome in that part of the Rio Grande Valley.

William Kelly, chairman of the citizens committee that investigated the shootings, said at a 1907 congressional hearing he had urged local authorities to throw McDonald in the Brownsville jail. The Ranger captain's tactics and overheated accusations could have started a bloody fight between townspeople and soldiers, he said. And seven months after the Brownsville incident, Fort Brown commander Penrose said of McDonald: "He is a thorough coward."

Some years after the shootings, Brownsville lawyer and historian Harbert Davenport reflected on the Ranger. "To be accurate, the old-timers of Southwest Texas did not consider Bill McDonald a Ranger Captain at all," Davenport said in a letter. "I have never found a Border man who had the slightest respect for Bill McDonald. He was, to them, a troublemaker, an advertiser, a dealer in false tales of which he was usually the hero, inclined to act—and act violently—on false information, vain and selfish."

They were harsh words. But, as with Rangers past and future, they could not blunt the inevitable propaganda to come. The remaking of McDonald's image started early and spanned decades. It began when Albert Bigelow Paine, one of the preeminent chroniclers of his era, published *Captain Bill McDonald, Texas Ranger*, a 396-page biography, in 1909. The publication was arranged by Edward M. House, a wealthy Texan with deep political connections.

Paine depicted Captain Bill as a lawman-superman who "faced death almost daily" and who had single-handedly transformed wild and woolly Texas into "a condition of such proper behavior that nowhere in this country is life and property safer." The biographer admired many of McDonald's qualities but especially his nose. It was "of that stately Roman architecture which goes with conquest, because it signifies courage, resolution and the peerless gift of command." Captain Bill did encounter a setback in Brownsville, Paine acknowledged, but that only enhanced his stature. "After all, it requires defeat to reveal true greatness."

In 1914, McDonald recounted his Brownsville tale to a correspondent for the *Brooklyn Daily Eagle* who had ventured to Austin. This version featured an enhanced retelling of McDonald's initial entrance into Fort Brown: "He walked into the very muzzles of their rifles and took command by no other authority than that which exists through a recognition of courage and natural dominance." And the mission was no failure, the *Eagle* concluded, as Captain Bill "overrode all the authority of the army and its red tape and got results as usual."

McDonald died in 1918, but the hagiography continued. Walter Prescott Webb, in his landmark 1935 history of the Rangers, said McDonald conducted a "courageous investigation" of black soldiers in Brownsville who had begun to "drink and conduct themselves in an obnoxious manner." Webb used the Paine biography as his primary source material. He did quote Harbert Davenport's letters, but with judicious editing omitted any of his criticism of McDonald.

Another book, *Riding for Texas: The True Adventures of Captain Bill McDonald*, was published in 1936. This, too, was done under the auspices of Edward House. It told of Brownsville residents joyously exclaiming, "Here's Captain Bill!" when McDonald arrived. "The cry soared from a hundred throats," the narrative continued. "Women who had scarcely dared to walk out, crowded after the ranger; men began to take on again their pre-raid swagger. Brownsville laid off its stupor of fear." The book also described how McDonald held the black troops at gunpoint to keep them from leaving town and escaping punishment—a complete fabrication.

In 1959, a former Texas adjutant general declared McDonald "the most spectacular Ranger commander of his era" and Brownsville his signature case. "Captain McDonald could see but one point in the whole matter," W. W. Sterling wrote. "A breach of the peace, which included murder, had been committed on Texas soil." Sterling, who spent two years as commander of the Rangers, added this justification for McDonald's zealous pursuit of the black soldiers: "The personnel of the Twenty-fifth Infantry was made up of the most ignorant class of Negroes from the old Southern states, most of them signing their enlistment papers with an 'X.' These illiterates were easily agitated into violence, and when plied with busthead whiskey, they could be led into any sort of deviltry."

Sixty-six years after the Brownsville incident, at the urging of Congress, the Pentagon reinvestigated the case. As a result, the secretary of the army determined a gross injustice had occurred and awarded all the soldiers honorable discharges. Only one of the 167 black infantrymen, Dorsie Willis, eighty-six, was known to be alive. "We didn't do those people any harm," he said of Brownsville. "And this thing has hung over my head my entire life."

Rare is the account of McDonald in Brownsville that doesn't feature the words of army major Blocksom, who said Captain Bill was "so brave he would charge hell with a bucket of water." It's a stirring encomium, a colorful vision that typifies the institutional ideal. No wonder it's been repeated hundreds of times and cited as a Ranger touchstone. It's even part of McDonald's Texas Ranger Hall of Fame credentials.

But when Blocksom said it, he wasn't speaking out of admiration. "It is possible," the major said in prefacing the remark, "McDonald might have fought the entire battalion with his four or five rangers were their obedience as blind as his obstinacy." This was not a pure tribute to the Ranger captain's indomitable valor. Blocksom was describing McDonald's arrogance, monomania, and blatant disregard for legal procedure. The Hall of Fame citation doesn't mention that part. Nor does it note the congressional exoneration of the Brownsville infantrymen—those soldiers memorably described by Captain Bill in his official report to the governor as "the coons who were committing murder."

Dead Mexican Bandits.

Postcards like this one that showed Rangers posing above dead Mexicans, killed in a shootout, set the tone for bad relations on the border.

Chapter 15

THE POLITICS OF MASSACRE

"A Lousy, Rotten, Ghoulish Business"

A Texas Ranger never wounds a man; he shoots to KILL! Texas Rangers never fear a superior force. Outnumbered ten to one, they merely think the sport interesting. They've been brought up to that game!

—*THE DAY BOOK,* CHICAGO, MARCH 17, 1914

Jim Wells Jr., the powerful Democratic politician known as the "boss of South Texas," had for several days ridden in a car along the old Brownsville Road. This was, by Wells's reckoning, some time in 1915 or 1916. The narrow route ran straight as a rifle shot through lonely flatlands thick with mesquite and prickly pear. Wells, a lawyer, was on his way with others to court in the town of Edinburg. Each time the car chugged past a railroad depot known as Ebenezer, Wells noticed a wake of buzzards and a sickening smell. "I knew what that meant," he said—probably an animal carcass bloating and rotting in the hot sun.

The car had mechanical problems one morning, and the owner stopped to fix it near the depot. Someone from the traveling party walked into the brush to investigate the stench. He returned looking "rather excited and perturbed," Wells recalled, "saying there was a lot of dead men."

Wells and others went to see for themselves. They found eleven bodies on the sandy ground, aligned in the formation of execution. "Mexicans," Wells said, "lying there side by side with their clothes on and everything, and the buzzards had picked their eyes and faces." Each man had a bullet hole "right above the eyes," Wells said. "Great big holes you could stick your finger in. . . . It was a very gruesome sight." Gruesome, certainly, but not all that unusual, for this was the time and place of the border troubles.

No one could prove that Texas Rangers had killed the Mexicans in the brush, but they were the most likely suspects. The Rangers of this era shot or lynched hundreds of Tejanos and Mexicans, and they did so without pause, deliberation, or explanation. Some of the dead were criminals who had preyed upon, and killed, Anglo farmers and ranchers. And some died solely because they had brown skin.

A journalist for a New York magazine who ventured along the border in 1916 depicted the Rangers as roving assassins. "Twenty-five or thirty years ago they were a fine body of men," George Marvin wrote. "But in recent years the rangers have degenerated into common man-killers." They performed their work, he said, with impunity. "There is no penalty for killing, for no jury along the border would ever convict a white man for shooting a Mexican."

The terms "death squads" and "ethnic cleansing" would not enter common usage for another sixty years or so, but that was what the Rangers were and what they did. Their actions along the Rio Grande, however, were not those of lawless mercenaries or agitating rebels. With their summary executions and other measures—burning the houses, for example, of Tejanos who refused to vacate land the Anglos wanted—the Rangers did the bidding of powerful interests. They carried out government mandates, and they operated with unsparing effectiveness. The Rangers once more endeavored to make the land safe for the white man.

The lower Rio Grande Valley could not be considered a valley in the conventional topographic or aesthetic sense. Spare of natural splendor, it stretched one hundred featureless miles upriver from the Gulf of Mexico: a subtropical alluvial plain with a cover of inhospitable brush and cactus. At the beginning of the twentieth century, the overwhelming majority of the region's residents were of Mexican heritage.

Though lightly populated and remote from any cities, the valley of this era saw continual tumult. It is hard to conjure any other time in American history when so many overwhelming political, racial, economic, and murderous forces converged in one relatively small place. Between 1910 and 1920, this ragged and riven swath of Texas seethed with war, espionage, pestilence, political intrigue, and random slaughter.

The Mexican Revolution was but one cause. It erupted in 1910, when young upstart Francisco Madero challenged Porfirio Díaz, who had begun his iron-fisted presidency of Mexico in 1876. Díaz thwarted Madero by having him arrested, but Díaz's government soon collapsed. Madero was elected, then assassinated. General Victoriano Huerta seized power. His presidency, which was more properly described as a dictatorship, drew the opposition of the U.S. government. A rebellion by U.S.-backed Venustiano Carranza, the governor of Coahuila, drove Huerta from power in 1914. Instability reigned.

At about the same time, the Rangers' fortunes hit a low point. The penny-pinching state legislature had, as usual, left the force underfunded. At one point it shrank to only thirteen men. Citizens from various Texas towns complained of drunken boorishness and unnecessary gunplay. A 1901 law had placed the Rangers under direct control of the governor; their opponents portrayed them as political tools for the chief executive. Running a successful campaign for governor in 1910, Oscar Colquitt wondered if the famous lawmen had rampaged too wildly or had outlived their purpose. "It was not intended when the Rangers were created," he said, "that they should become the personal agents of the governor to be sent to different points to harass and shoot down inoffensive citizens."

Colquitt's view, and that of many others, changed when Mexico's political and economic turmoil spilled across the narrow, shallow river and into Texas. The Rangers hastened to the border, and the state began a beefing up of the agency. Soon more than fifty of them would be in the region, as anachronistic malefactors became sought-after protectors. To call them bloodthirsty might be an overstatement. But low pay, relaxed standards, and harsh conditions attracted Rangers who confused derring-do with a license to lay waste. Many of them had killed men in the past, which in some circles was required for appointment to the border corps. It didn't help that two respected Ranger captains of the period, John Rogers and John Brooks, had left the force. Another, John Hughes, would soon depart. Their replacements did not in general rise to their caliber.

Nonetheless, Anglo residents welcomed the new enforcers. "We look upon the Rangers as more or less a godsend to our Valley," said William Morrison, a San Benito lawyer. The U.S. Army already patrolled the region, but many white

Texans believed the Rangers possessed special qualities. "They are courageous," San Benito resident Alba Heywood said. "They will fight buzzsaws."

Of immediate concern was a manifesto known as the Plan of San Diego. The plan was not written in San Diego, a South Texas farm town, but it may have been signed there in January 1915. It called for a "Liberating Army for Races and Peoples" that would take the states of Texas, New Mexico, Arizona, Colorado, and California from U.S. control. Land that had belonged to the Indians would be returned to them, with the rest becoming an independent republic that could be annexed by Mexico. And every Anglo male over age sixteen was to be executed. The *Waco Morning News* summarized it with a front-page headline: "Plan of San Diego Calls for Wholesale Massacres."

Local officials went on the alert for the infiltrators from the liberating army. District Attorney John A. Valls of Laredo wrote Ranger headquarters to report that he had "kept a vigilant watch" for suspicious activity and had sent spies to restaurants, saloons, and other establishments frequented by "mischief makers." He found nothing, yet vowed not to falter. "I have no doubt there is a disturbing element in Laredo that is holding secret meetings," the DA wrote. "Many automobiles from San Antonio loaded with strange Mexicans have arrived here." The Rangers stood guard too, as Captain J. J. Sanders reported from San Benito: "The San Diego Revolutionists still continue to hold their meetings and are causing considerable uneasiness among the White people."

Despite the watchfulness, raids kept coming. In 1915 alone, gunmen believed to be from Mexico killed more than twenty Anglos in the valley and wounded many more. Some Anglos fled their farms and ranches, while others huddled in fright. In the river town of Santa Maria, where an attack was rumored to be imminent, women and children barricaded themselves in a local hotel while men took up arms and patrolled the streets. Residents of Lyford, forty miles north of Brownsville, directed a plea to the governor. "For God's sake," they wrote, "do something!"

Suspected *sediciocos* burned railroad trestles, looted stores, cut telephone wires, and fired into passing cars. A young woman in Harlingen reported that some men attempted to kidnap her, but she drove them away with a pistol. The night watchman at a cotton gin was gunned down as he made his rounds. "Marauding Mexicans," as one Texas newspaper described them, descended on the village of Sebastian, where they confronted a father and son operating a corn-shelling station. They executed A. L. Austin, who was president of the local Law and Order League, a pro-Anglo vigilante group. Austin had a reputation for harsh treatment of Tejano employees. Nellie Francis Austin discovered her husband with four bullet holes in his back. Her son, Charles, lay dead nearby.

Walter Noble Burns, a noted western historian of the day, announced he had discovered the cause of the attacks: "the hatred for gringos that burns undyingly in the Mexican people." Such animus, he declared, was "bred to the bone" in "almost every man, woman, and child in Mexico." This was demonstrably absurd, but these thoughts reflected the runaway fear and mistrust. Some Valley Anglos proposed putting Tejanos in camps or deporting them to Mexico. Those who remained were to be killed. The death scheme was never adopted, though the Rangers acted at times as its ex officio agents.

On the sweltering evening of August 8, 1915, some sixty armed and mounted men rode onto the southern end of the great King Ranch. Some were Mexicans, some Tejanos. Luis de la Rosa, a Tejano supporter of the Plan of San Diego, led them. At a two-story ranch house, the headquarters of ranch foreman Caesar Kleberg, they opened fire. Kleberg was not there but had foreseen the attack. Army cavalrymen and a deputy sheriff awaited the raiders. A gunfight of nearly three hours left five of the attackers dead.

The Rangers missed it all, having been miles away in a search for these same raiders. But they arrived for the aftermath, and three of them lassoed four raiders' corpses. A photo of this scene—the Rangers on horseback, the bodies on the ground, the lariats taut between them—appeared on postcards with the caption "Mexican Bandits Killed at Norias." The cards were sold in drugstores and tobacco shops across South Texas and came to symbolize, for both sides, the essence of the Rangers in the border war.

As in the days of Leander McNelly, the Rangers maintained a close and mutually beneficial relationship with the King Ranch. Kleberg, manager of the Norias section, supplied the Rangers with horses and equipment in exchange for their protection. The four dead men at the end of the ropes were only the start. "Immediately following the Las Norias Raid," Brownsville businessman Frank Pierce wrote, "the Rangers began a systematic manhunt, and killed, according to a verified list, 102 Mexicans." That count was probably low. "It is claimed by citizens and Army officers who saw many of the bodies," Pierce said, "that at least 300 Mexicans were so killed."

The marauders struck again about two and a half months after the Norias shootout. Below a gibbous moon, they removed the railway spikes on a dark stretch of tracks north of Brownsville, then hid in the brush. As a southbound passenger train barreled toward them, they used a heavy wire to pull the rail away. The steam locomotive hit the gap, shot into the darkness, and overturned. Several other cars jumped the track. Masked men barged into the derailed cars, where they robbed and shot Anglo passengers. They left three dead and three wounded. It was, a newspaper said, "the most spectacular and bloodiest train robbery of many years in the Southwest."

Captain Henry L. Ransom of the Rangers arrived on the scene the next day. Ransom, forty-one, had been appointed a Ranger captain only a few months before. He was short—an un-Rangerish five feet, eight inches—and had the gray hair of an old man but was not to be dismissed by those who opposed him. In 1910, as a special officer for the Houston police chief, he shot to death a prominent lawyer who was defending an accused cop killer. Ransom plugged the lawyer five times as the counselor stood on a Houston corner, awaiting a streetcar. A jury acquitted Ransom of murder. Before that he had served with the U.S. Army in the Philippines, fighting insurgents. W. W. Sterling, who would go on to become Texas adjutant general, recalled hearing Ransom's stories of torture and murder. "The tales [he and others] told about executing Filipinos," Sterling wrote, "made the Bandit War look like a minor purge."

Now four Tejano men had been arrested on suspicion of derailing and robbing the Brownsville-bound train. Ransom had them in custody, said Cameron County sheriff W. T. Vann, and did not need a hearing to decide their fate. "Captain Ransom . . . walked over to me and says, 'I am going out to kill these fellows. Are you going with me?'" Vann recalled. "I says, 'No, and I don't believe you are going [to].' He says, 'If you haven't got the guts enough to do it, I will go myself.' I says, 'That takes a whole lot of guts, four fellows with their hands tied behind them.'" After he left, Vann said, Ransom and his Rangers took the four men into the brush and executed them.

The Rangers widened their sweep of the countryside in pursuit of bandits, or suspected bandits, or men who might possibly become bandits if allowed to keep breathing. One Tejano woman described an early-morning Ranger raid. "Three of them entered our home, yanked us out of bed and threw us on the floor," she said. They seized her twenty-one-year-old cousin, whom they believed had joined some raiding parties. "They took him to a cemetery about a block away, placed him in front of a cross and shot him dead," the woman said. "We were afraid to challenge them because they were like animals and had guns."

R. B. Creager, a Brownsville lawyer and unsuccessful Republican candidate for governor, said the Rangers compiled a "black list" of Tejanos and Mexicans, and they "evaporated" as many as two hundred of them. "In my judgment 90 of those killed were as innocent as you or I of complicity in those bandit outrages," Creager testified at a legislative hearing. He described Rangers on the border as "hot-blooded young fellows without much education" who roamed unchecked. "We would be infinitely better off without the Ranger force," he said, "unless you have some restraint thrown around them that will protect the citizens of the state."

The killing became almost casual at times. "Yesterday we caught a Mexican by name Tomas Aguilar, one of the 3 that robed the Depot at Combs and set the R.R. Bridge on fire," Captain J. Monroe Fox reported to the adjutant general. "Of course he tried to make his Escape but we killed him."

Roland Warnock, a South Texas cowboy, recalled the fate of two Tejano men who had treated the wounds of Mexican bandits. The Mexicans had been shot in a raid on a Valley ranch. If the Tejanos did not aid the Mexicans, Warnock said, "the bandits would have killed them."

It was a death warrant either way. The next day, the two Tejanos rode near the Rangers' encampment and were spotted by Captain Ransom. One was Jesús Bazán, sixty-seven. The other was Bazán's son-in-law, Antonio Longoria, forty-nine. Both held U.S. citizenship. "The captain of the Rangers recognized them . . . and began to follow them," Warnock said. "These two [Tejanos] pulled over to the side of the road to let them pass, and when they did, the Rangers just shot them off their horses, turned around and went back to the ranch and went back to sleep."

Two days later, Warnock said, he retrieved the bodies and buried them. "It was some mighty dirty work going on then," he said. "A man's life just wasn't worth much at all." In many instances, he said, a Tejano or a Mexican simply seen with a herd of cattle could be marked for execution on the spot. "I knew of one time when they hung 18 men in a grove of trees. . . . There were so many innocent people killed in that mess that it just made you sick to your heart to see it happening."

But many Anglos—especially ranchers—did not share in the heartsickness. They believed the Rangers were all that stood between them and obliteration. "I want to say this for the Rangers," wrote Sam Householder, a state legislator from the valley. "I never yet saw one with a pair of wings . . . but when it came to putting the fear of God and respect for the law in the hearts of the cunning, reckless and murderous outlaws, they were in a class by themselves." Householder acknowledged the Rangers often executed suspects without a trial, but "there seemed to be no possible way under the conditions prevailing of bringing those desperados to justice through the ordinary processes of the law." C. B. Hudspeth, a congressman from West Texas, agreed that due process didn't apply. "A Ranger cannot wait until a Mexican bandit behind a rock on the other side shoots at him three or four times, and put down this lawlessness," said the man for whom Hudspeth County was named. "You have got to kill these Mexicans when you find them, or they will kill you."

Ultimately, though, the Rangers' excesses could not go unaddressed. In November 1915 Governor James Ferguson—responding to complaints not from Mexico but from a general in the U.S. Army—officially ordered the Rangers to cease the "summary execution of Mexicans."

Adjutant General Henry Hutchings also admitted to a problem with the homicidal character of his men. "Considerable adverse criticism of the Ranger Force has recently reached the Governor and much of it from sources worthy of most serious consideration," he wrote in a memo to commanding officers. Perhaps, Hutchings ventured, the answer could be found in recruiting. "Some of our friends believe that in enlisting Rangers too much stress is laid upon the record of the applicant as a man killer, and that such record is taken as proof of bravery." Henceforth, he directed, "men will not be enlisted . . . who have been unfortunate enough to have had to kill their fellow men." The rule was generally ignored.

Back on the border, the Rangers and their supporters scoffed at such administrative queasiness. To them this was war, and an especially nasty one at that. All they had to do was point to the treatment of army private Richard Johnson. In September 1915 guerrillas from Mexico attacked the river town of Progreso. They captured Johnson, a twenty-one-year-old New Yorker, and took him into Mexico. There they killed him, cut off his ears for keepsakes, and displayed his severed head on a pole as a trophy.

There was more. In January 1916, the Cusi Mining Company gathered American employees for transit to its silver mine in the Mexican town of Cusihuiriachi. The employees, who included top management and engineers, had fled the mine weeks before and crossed into Texas. Now, however, the Carranza government promised to protect them if they returned. Carranza had gained the recognition of U.S. president Woodrow Wilson, but he also faced a troublesome rival—Francisco "Pancho" Villa.

The Americans boarded a Mexico North-Western Railroad train in Ciudad Chihuahua for a trip of some hundred miles across the desert. About halfway through the journey, near the village of Santa Ysabel, the train entered a canyon. Wreckage on the track ahead forced it to stop. Men armed with Mauser rifles burst into a Pullman car where the twenty or so Americans sat. The raiders were led by Pablo López, an officer in Villa's rebel force.

López cursed the Americans—and President Wilson—and ordered them to remove their clothing and leave the train. They did so and gathered barefoot, in their underwear, alongside the tracks. Some ran toward a river.

"They started to run, and then our soldiers began to shoot," López said afterward. "The smell of powder makes our blood hot." Others were executed where they stood. Eighteen Americans in all were killed.

As they searched for suspected raiders in the valley, the Rangers also used pressure, vandalism, and beatings to crack down on critics. When the *Brownsville Sentinel* published an essay accusing the Rangers of a "campaign of extermination," Captain Charles Stevens paid a personal visit to the editor. Stevens expressed his belief that such writings were the work of German propagandists—the Great War having commenced in Europe—and he threatened the arrest of those involved. The editor "then seemed to be very sorry that he had published this article," Stevens reported to Ranger headquarters.

The small Laredo newspaper *El Progreso* published a story critical of American forces on the border in 1914, so the Rangers went to Laredo to shut down the paper. One of its writers, a slender twenty-nine-year-old woman named Jovita Idar, stood in the doorway to block them. As a crowd formed, the Rangers backed away. The idea of a free press prevailed until the next day, when the Rangers returned. With Idar absent this time, they forced their way into the office and smashed the printing press. They also tracked down the writer of the offending story, beat him severely, and arrested him. Only the actions of a local judge compelled his release from jail for medical treatment.

Thomas W. Hook, a crusading Kingsville lawyer, wrote to President Wilson in 1916 and enclosed a petition that protested the treatment of Tejanos and Mexicans by the Rangers. He specifically mentioned two men who were suspected of planning raids, and who had been turned over to Ranger Captain J. J. Sanders. As with many other suspects in the custody of Rangers, the two men then disappeared without explanation.

Sanders later saw Hook in a Falfurrias courtroom and asked, "Are you the son of a bitch that wrote that petition?" When Hook said yes, Sanders pulled his handgun and tried to club the lawyer. "I warded the pistol off with my left [hand] and he recovered himself and came down again," Hook said, "and again I caught his pistol and warded it off." Four times Sanders struck and four times Hook— who was not carrying a weapon—deflected the blows until a deputy sheriff intervened.

"I struck at him with my six-shooter," Sanders said, and he acknowledged a breach of pistol-whip protocol. "I apologized about hitting him without first asking him whether he was armed or not. . . . A man can be worked up to doing a heap of things he ought not to do."

Mexico had never really recovered from its mid-1800s war with the United States—at least in regard to the rural poor—and the turmoil of the revolution only made bad problems worse. Desperate refugees, in filth and rags, massed at the Texas border. Ranger captain K. F. Cunningham reported "bands of beggars" crossing the river at Eagle Pass, driven by hunger. "Those caught swimming . . . do not care what is done with them for they would rather be imprisoned than starve," he wrote to headquarters in Austin. Disease spread through the shanty-towns along the Rio Grande. "Smallpox is quite prevalent on the both sides of the River now."

Though Mexico suffered, the Texas side of the Rio Grande Valley enjoyed a protracted economic boom. The St. Louis, Brownsville and Mexico Railway had connected the region to Houston in 1904. Developers and farmers dug irrigation canals that spread water from the Rio Grande over thousands of acres. Stingy ranchland turned into fertile farmland.

Values soared. The taxable property in Cameron County alone increased from $3.2 million in 1903 to $10 million in 1909. "Lands which fifteen years ago were selling at from one to two dollars an acre are now selling, with an excess of buyers, at from $100 to $500 per acre," businessman Pierce wrote at the time. "Thousands of home-seekers desiring a milder climate than that of the frozen north have settled within the territory."

Locals derided the home-seekers as "home-suckers." Real estate salesmen brought these potential buyers to the valley in special trains and enticed them with cornucopian visions of citrus and cantaloupes. In these spiels, the Rio Grande was poised to become the American Nile. "The home suckers succumb by the hundred," journalist George Marvin wrote. "They have come down well heeled and, wanting to escape the rigors of a hard climate, expect onions and oranges with Mexican labor to make the paper profits dazzlingly brandished before them."

Much if not most of the land the newcomers bought had been held by generations of Mexicans and Tejanos. When the original owners fled the "evaporations" of the Rangers and other lawmen, Anglo developers seized their property or bought it on the cheap. If they didn't vacate their holdings, they were often forced off, said Emilio Forto, a former mayor and sheriff in Brownsville.

The typical "border Mexican," Forto wrote, "is a peace loving, law abiding and pleasure seeking individual" who "seeks no one's injury as a rule," but Anglo newcomers to the region regarded Tejanos as "filthy, unsanitary and sickly makeshift." The Anglos sometimes used the Rangers, Forto said, to banish or kill the occupants of the land they wanted. "A campaign of extermination seemed to have begun . . . when the cry was often heard, 'We want to make this a white man's country,'" he wrote. "Many well to do native Texans of Mexican origin were driven away by Rangers who in some cases told them, 'If you are here within the next 5 days, you will be dead.'" The Rangers burned their homes, and the Tejanos—taking only what they could carry in their oxcarts—escaped across the river.

In the eyes of many, the Rangers had been crucial to bringing peace to the Valley. "There are only a few men around Brownsville who are against these Rangers," Captain Stevens said about some of his men accused of murder, "and they are men who stand for nothing that is good for the interest of the country."

But there were those—respected figures and law enforcement officers among them—who believed that the Rangers had ridden into a terrible situation and made it worse. From the vantage of several years, Sheriff Vann of Cameron County was so disgusted that he proposed abolition of the agency. "We do not need the Rangers anymore," he wrote to a colleague. They weren't merely unnecessary, he said; they were destructive. "The Rangers make more trouble than peace," Vann said, "and they do it at the expense of the state."

Brownsville lawyer Creager said the Rangers' tactics—and those of other Anglo lawmen—transformed placid Mexican-Texans into ferocious enemies. The Rangers and others "would go out and hang them to trees until practically dead, or would shoot and leave dead on the ground some Mexican who was as innocent as you," Creager said. "The result of that was you would make that man's brothers and relatives for two or three generations bandits or potential bandits." And on it rolled.

No one could say when the cycle of vengeance would end. All they knew was that blood demanded blood. On a bitter winter night in 1918, eight Ranger horsemen, accompanied by army cavalry, rode across the West Texas desert. Their destination: the tiny, poor doomed settlement of Porvenir. Weeks before, Mexican raiders had crossed the river and attacked a Texan's ranch, murdering three innocent men. Now someone had to pay, so the riders spurred their mounts toward the dark village. Rangers carried Winchesters and had liquor on their breath. Some wore masks. Soon the killing would start—a cold-blooded slaughter—and the cover-up could begin.

This occurred along the Rio Grande but far from the lower valley—some seven hundred miles upriver. Here was a place of stark beauty and hard settlement: the Big Bend region of the Texas borderland, in the far southwestern corner of the state. The name derived from the great sinuous loop, southeast to northeast, of the upper Rio Grande. The river ran placid in stretches and in others rushed through deep canyons. Early Spanish explorers called the region *el despoblado*—the uninhabited.

The Chihuahuan Desert sprawled for hundreds of miles, across two nations, broken by rugged mountains. Hot springs boiled into rocky pools, and ragged arroyos cut the flats. Much of the vegetation was stunted, spare, and menacing. "Each plant in this land is a porcupine," one nineteenth-century traveler wrote. "It is nature armed to the teeth." In the 1800s, some U.S. Army units found the Big Bend to be best traversed on camels. Robert Keil was only fifteen when he ran away from his father's Pennsylvania farm and—lying about his age—joined the U.S. Cavalry. In 1913, the army posted him in the Big Bend. "The land is dry and barren, wild and spooky," he wrote. "It is a wild, strange country."

Though it was territory of mean bounty, men had been fighting over it for hundreds of years. The Apaches and Comanches warred with each other, with the Spaniards, and later with the Texan settlers. The Indians were driven out in the late nineteenth century, but the region still had its perils. Outlaws, banished from other Texas criminal Edens, found refuge and opportunity there. Robert T. Hill of the U.S. Geological Survey explored the Big Bend in 1899 and noted that some called it the "Bloody Bend," where "civilization finds it difficult to gain a foothold."

That may have been an exaggeration; railroad towns such as Marfa and Alpine were well established by then. But in the early twentieth century the general situation along the border in the Big Bend might best be described—like the lower Rio Grande—as a state of shifting, amorphous, and undeclared war. In May 1916, for instance, Mexican raiders overran the town of Glenn Springs, Texas, killing three American soldiers and a seven-year-old boy before burning the place down.

In such a climate, a Mexican crossing the Rio Grande on horseback, especially a man who was armed, was assumed to have malicious intent. Rangers and others hid in the riverbank brush and, armed with high-powered rifles, shot such men with impunity. An untold number of Mexican and Tejanos fell victim to ambushes. The Rangers' twist on an old cowboy folk song expressed their outlook:

> O bury me not on the lone praire-ee
> where the wild coyotes will howl o'er me!
> In a narrow grave just six by three
> where all the Mexkins ought to be-ee!

It wasn't only the Rangers who felt this way. "They are killing and plundering," an editorial in the *El Paso Herald* said of Mexicans. "There is some satisfaction in killing them afterward, but death of half a hundred of the worthless brutes does not compensate for the murder of a single American."

Ranger Company B patrolled the Big Bend, with its fifteen or so men under the command of Captain J. Monroe Fox, who had worn out his welcome in the valley. A former county constable given to self-promotion, the fifty-one-year-old Fox did not own a sterling reputation among some peers. Captain Sanders, for instance, objected when his son, also a Ranger, was assigned to Fox. In a letter to the adjutant general, Sanders cited the "lack of discipline and unpleasantness with men" under Fox. Fox's company also failed to impress General Frederick "Fighting Fred" Funston, who commanded army forces along the border. The number of Rangers in the Big Bend was "entirely inadequate," the general said. What's more: "These men are stationed at Marfa, and as far as can be ascertained they visit the border only when they hear of some impending trouble and by the time they reach the district where the trouble occurs, the outlaws have disappeared."

Fox wrote periodic reports to Austin headquarters that either sugarcoated his company's actions or offered little detail. He routinely concluded his brief messages with "Everything quite." Fox meant quiet, though a Ranger's life in the Big Bend was rarely that. In January 1916, the governor's office received a letter from Ysleta, an old mission town near El Paso. Three dozen citizens asked for a detachment of Rangers "for our protection against Horse and Cattle Thieves." Several Rangers were sent in response.

Nine months later another letter from Ysleta hit the governor's desk. "Please," wrote Mrs. A. Alderete, the proprietor of an ice cream parlor, "have the Ranger camp entirely removed." She penned a roster of complaints: "Thuggery and murder is a past time with them. . . . They are in the street most of time appearrantly doing nothing but going from one dance hall to another, and loud and boisterous and occasionaly beating some one on the head with their guns." One Ranger in particular drew Mrs. Alderete's ire: John Dudley White. He was, she wrote, "a deliberate fiend and bloodthirsty villain." Mrs. Alderete believed that Ranger White itched to shoot her husband, who was active in local political circles. "Nightly White with a gang lurks outside of my place cursing and threatening, waiting for Mr. Alderete to come out to say a word so he can pick a fight with him, or kill him."

Captain Fox went to Ysleta, asked around, and crafted a response to Mrs. Alderete's accusations. As usual, he found no problems. "I have been here all day and have went to all the business end of the town," he reported to the adjutant general, "and all of the citizens say that her statement is faulse and without foundation." Nonetheless, the Ysleta detachment was reassigned.

The Big Bend Rangers had bigger concerns than one woman with an ice cream parlor. Perhaps their most persistent nemesis was a complicated figure named Chico Cano, a Mexican revolutionary of shifting allegiances. Long, lean, and mustachioed, Cano was a crack shot and a canny opportunist. Some saw him as a rapacious bandit, while others envisioned a champion of the poor. Few doubted that he worked both sides of the border with consummate skill. A Federal Bureau of Investigation memorandum claimed that Cano was selling cattle to Texas ranchers—cattle that was in all likelihood stolen from other Texas ranchers—and using the proceeds to buy ammunition "with which Cano and his gang seem to be always plentifully supplied." The bureau also believed that many in Cano's band of guerrillas were Tejanos who had left the United States to avoid the draft.

Cano had a long-standing feud with Joe Sitter, a customs inspector and former Ranger. Sitter arrested Cano in 1913 for livestock smuggling, but Cano's gang freed him in a gunfight that wounded Sitter. In 1915, Sitter—after the punitive interrogation of a prisoner—learned that Cano might be hiding near Pilares, a Big Bend river town. With three Rangers, two of whom had scant experience, Sitter walked into an ambush. He died, as did Ranger Eugene Hulen, who had been on the force less than two months. Sitter "had been shot about ten times and his head beaten with rocks," Captain Fox said in a report that, for once, included details. Hulen was found about ten feet way. "He had been shot about eight times and his head beaten in a pulp with rocks." Cano and his band were suspected of killing the two men, but this was never proved.

Mistrust and dread prevailed, as shown by Sam Neill, sixty, whose career in the Texas borderland included stints as a customs inspector and a Ranger. "We knew what we were up against when we seen a bunch of Comanches. There were two things to do, fight or run," he said. "You meet a bunch of Mexicans and you don't know what you are going up against, whether they are civilized or not. That's the way I look at it."

On Christmas Day 1917, Neill was staying at the headquarters of the Brite Ranch, at the foot of Capote Peak in Presidio County, some twenty-five miles from the border. The 125,000-acre spread, one of the largest in the region, had a well-stocked general store and a post office. At dawn, Neill peered from the window of a ranch house and saw men—apparently Mexicans—approaching on horseback. Neill grabbed his guns. The men may have been supporters of Pancho Villa, or of Mexican president Carranza, or simply bandits. Whoever they were, Neill did not have to guess their intentions, because one of them "hollered at his men to kill all the Americans," Neill recalled. "And as he said it, I shot, and he didn't, of course, holler no more."

Neill was wounded in the ensuing gunfight; one bullet grazed his nose and a second struck his leg. The raiders ransacked and looted the general store and seized about twenty horses. When a mail coach approached, they shot and killed two passengers who were, as it turned out, Mexicans. They hanged the Anglo coach driver, Mickey Welch, from the ranch store's rafters and slit his throat. The body fell to the floor, and they left him dead in a pool of his own blood.

News of the raid reached the army cavalry, who gave chase—this being the dawn of the modern era—in borrowed automobiles. They gained ground as the raiders' horses began to flag. Among those in the pursuit was Robert Keil, the Pennsylvanian who had headed west for adventure and joined the army. "I have never seen such whipping and spurring," he said of the fleeing men, who were making for the Rio Grande. The soldiers fired their rifles at the raiders, and there were "thirteen bandits killed down in the Rim Rock foothills," Keil said. Cavalrymen on horseback pursued those who escaped into more rugged country. The American troops killed ten more raiders and recovered some of the stolen goods.

Despite the lure of plunder, one mortally wounded Mexican told army officers the Brite Ranch raid had primarily been intended as revenge. The raiders, he said, were atoning for Texans' ambushes of Mexicans along the river. As Keil wrote: "They were only the words of a bandit, but from one who was dying, and whatever the case, it added up to the pattern that followed: kill, kill, ambush, ambush, then more raids. . . . Oh, it was a lousy, rotten, ghoulish business."

No one expected the chain of retributions to break. The only questions were when and how the killings would begin anew. "After the Brite raid, a deathly quiet settled over the Big Bend," Keil said. "No one had a name for it, but it was like the stillness that precedes a cyclone."

Ranger captain Fox also had the sense that something big was about to take place, though his forecast contained more cheer than Keil's. Four days after the Brite raid, Fox wrote his quartermaster in Austin with a request for additional rifles and ammunition because "it looks like business is going to pick up." And he invited the quartermaster to "come out and see the circus show when we do get started."

So it happened that in late January 1918, about a month after the Brite raid, a handful of Rangers and four ranchmen rode their horses into the army's Camp Evetts, a lonely, Spartan outpost near the border. This group of Rangers was not, on the whole, a seasoned crew. One was Bud Weaver, a forty-three-year-old widower who had been a Ranger for only a few months. Allen Cole, thirty-eight, previously a clerk in Wisconsin, had been a Ranger for less than five months. W. K. Duncan, twenty, was a cowboy with four months as a Ranger. Max Newman, thirty-one, had been on the force a few months. Howell McCampbell, twenty-two, had joined the Rangers only three weeks before. The three veterans were Clint Holden, thirty-eight, a former druggist; Andy Barker, twenty-six, a farmer before signing on; and Boone Oliphant, twenty-nine, who had almost two years' experience.

The army did not readily welcome them to the camp. Cavalry rank and file distrusted them, in part because Rangers sometimes extorted money from off-duty soldiers in Marfa. They would arrest the army men for offenses such as drinking or whoring and offer to set them free for a fine of $20, which the Rangers would pocket. On this day the Rangers presented a letter from Colonel George Langhorne, army commander in the Big Bend, to the troop's captain. It ordered army assistance for a night mission to Porvenir. The Rangers said they believed that Chico Cano might be hiding in the village. This puzzled Keil, who had been to Porvenir with other cavalrymen that afternoon to buy eggs. "Not once had any of them caused us any trouble whatever," he said of the men and women there. "They were all good Mexicans. . . . These people were our friends."

The sky was clear, the night cold. Some of the Rangers at Camp Evetts gathered close to a campfire and passed around a bottle. "I suppose they were drinking to give themselves courage," Keil said, "because each one acted like the very Devil was chasing him." Soon the Rangers, the ranchers, and about forty cavalrymen mounted their horses and rode across the desert. A full moon, a local man wrote, "was shining nearly as bright as day." They reached Porvenir around midnight.

The village, on the Texas side less than a mile from the Rio Grande, was home to poor Mexican American farmers and laborers. They lived in *jacales* of mud and sticks, with no running water or electricity. The nearest store was a day's horseback ride away. Each family had a garden and some raised goats or cows. At this hour no one was awake.

"We surrounded the small village before a single dog barked," Keil said. Soldiers or masked Rangers—accounts vary—rousted several dozen men, women, and children from their homes. The families huddled around a fire, shivering. "We told them they should not be alarmed," Keil wrote. "It was only a check by some Rangers who were after a bandit." Though the words were meant to comfort, they didn't. "The word 'Rangers' inspired terror," Keil said.

A search of the *jacales* produced only a single-barreled shotgun with no shells and a few knives. But the Rangers, Keil said, insisted on questioning some of the villagers without cavalrymen present. Fifteen men and boys, ages sixteen to seventy-two, were marched from the village along the river road, out of sight. Near a rocky bluff, perhaps a quarter mile away, they were bound together with rope.

"Then we heard shots, rapid shots," Keil said, "echoing and blending in the dark."

The Rangers took to their horses and, with whoops and yells, vanished into the dark. Children cried as women wailed and keened. Some pointed toward the bluff. "We had a few flashlights, so we threw beams toward the place they were pointing," Keil said. "At the foot of the bluff we could see a mass of bodies, but not a single movement. . . . As soon as we were close, we smelled the nauseating sweetish smell of blood, and when we could see, we saw the most hellish sight that any of us had ever witnessed. It reminded me of a slaughterhouse." All fifteen villagers, still bound by rope, were dead. "The professionals," Keil said, "had done their work well."

The terrified women and children fled across the river to Mexico. There, hours after the shootings, a woman gave birth to the daughter of one of the dead men. The next morning, an old woman returned to Porvenir with a horse-drawn wagon. The remaining soldiers loaded the fifteen corpses onto the wagon, and she took the bodies back across the river, where they were buried. Among the dead: Román Nieves, who had seven children; Manuel Morales, who had seven, including the one born the night of his death; and Eutímio Gonzáles, who had nine. All told, forty-two children were left fatherless.

When the bodies were gone, a detail of soldiers burned the huts of Porvenir to the ground.

Now it was time for the Rangers to cover their tracks. Two days after the massacre, Fox sent a handwritten message from Marfa to Adjutant General James A. Harley in Austin. "I beg to make a report of a fight with Mexicans on the night of the 28th," Fox wrote. He said eight Rangers and four ranchmen were "scouting on the River and found several Mexicans." The Rangers "gathered several of them together," Fox said, and "were fired upon by other Mexicans." A gunfight followed, and "next morning 15 dead Mexicans were found." Fox added accusations of the Mexicans' complicity in the Brite Ranch raid. "Several artakles were found in there posesion belonging to Mr. Bright taken when Raid was made Dec 25th."

None of this was true, of course, except the part about fifteen dead. The captain either was badly misinformed about his men's actions or was lying to protect them. A gruesome side note: killing that many people apparently depleted stocks of ammunition. Three days after Porvenir, Fox wrote to the Ranger quartermaster, seeking additional Winchester cartridges. His men, Fox reported, "have ben using a good many lately" and "might run out."

The Rangers weren't the only government agency filing false reports. In a memo, army colonel Langhorne, relaying information from his men, said Porvenir had served as a point of rendezvous for "bandits and generally bad characters." On the night in question, the colonel said, "the Rangers had been fired on while making some arrests" and "a fight had occurred in which several Mexicans had been killed."

John Pool, one of the ranchers with the Rangers at Porvenir, backed these accounts in a sworn statement. Tejanos along the Rio Grande may have lived on the American side, Pool said, but their loyalties lay elsewhere. "It is a well known fact they act as spies and informers for the thieves and bandits from the Mexico side of the river," he said, and "they furnish the information to the desperate characters along the river in Mexico and lead them to our ranches." At Porvenir, Pool said, he and the Rangers were "fired upon by unknown parties" while searching the men of the village. "We returned the fire and when the firing ceased we retired to safety. . . . I don't know whether we killed anyone or not, but it was reported that there were about fifteen dead Mexicans the next morning."

The truth was being buried, and it might have stayed that way but for a man named Harry Warren. Born in Mississippi, Warren earned a bachelor's degree in philosophy before coming to Texas. In 1918 he was Porvenir's schoolmaster and lived about a mile from the village. The day after the massacre, Warren went to Porvenir and walked the killing field in grief and horror. "There was not a single bandit in the 15 men slain," he wrote. "These men were all farmers—2 of them were boys about 16 or 17 years old." All had been shot in the head, and the faces of some had been mutilated with knives. One of them was Warren's father-in-law. Warren wrote of what he found to Governor William P. Hobby. "The object of this appeal," he said to Hobby, "is to call to your attention this unprovoked and wholesale murder by Texas Rangers."

Army colonel Langhorne, for one, dismissed Warren as a desert-rat crank. "He married a Mexican woman and divorced her, took another woman, and then employed the divorced wife as a nurse for the child," Langhorne wrote in a memorandum. "What I have heard of this man is that he was well educated but lost his position of trust through drink. . . . He is one of three white men in this county that has failed to work with the others for preservation of order." The colonel added, disapprovingly, that Warren "lived like the Mexicans."

The true story began to emerge, in pieces, from other sources. A Mexican court of inquiry in Ojinaga brought forth sworn statements from survivors. In early February the Mexican ambassador in Washington filed a formal protest with the U.S. State Department, which ordered an investigation. The news hit the papers right away. Some of the coverage, in a departure from previous patterns, did not cast the Rangers as heroes. An Associated Press account called the incident a "wholesale killing" and added, "Every effort apparently was made in the Big Bend district to suppress the story."

The Rangers' first response, from their top officer, was one of denial. Adjutant General Harley told Texas newspapers that the Rangers at Porvenir "were fired upon in the dark and returned the fire in self defence." However, he felt pressure from Washington to commission an investigation. It was a sham from the start, for Harley sent Captain W. M. Hanson to the Big Bend.

Hanson's previous life had been that of a gringo *jefe*, operating large citrus farms over the border, making money in the oil business there, and immersing himself in Mexican political affairs. He was forced from the country under suspicion of operating a spy ring during the revolution. Back in Texas, holding the title of "special investigator" for the Rangers, Hanson spent time searching for Germans. Other Rangers did the same. With the U.S. entry into World War I in 1917, Americans suspected that Germany used Mexico as a base for propaganda and espionage. The Texas Legislature created a new branch known as Loyalty Rangers, whose job was to work secretly to find domestic traitors.

Hanson was put in charge. At one point he mailed to Austin a long list of suspected German sympathizers in the Mexican government, information he said he received from a "disgruntled secret service man" in Mexico City. Hanson also said he was watching in Texas a "German Professor . . . who need[s] working over." The Ranger agent proposed locking the professor away. "I think the Professor should be interned on general principals [*sic*]," Hanson said. "He is a dangerous man just now and smart as a whip." Hanson also proposed that all telephone connections between the United States and Mexico be severed because Mexican phone operators "at heart are Anti-Americans."

When he wasn't hunting Germans, Hanson functioned primarily as a political operative. His mission: make sure the Rangers did all they could to ensure the election of Governor William P. Hobby. A former lieutenant governor, Hobby had ascended to the state's highest office with the 1917 impeachment of Governor Jim Ferguson. Now Hobby was facing Ferguson in the coming Democratic primary.

Via his dispatches to Adjutant General Harley—who had been appointed by Hobby—Hanson destroyed any illusion that the Rangers operated independent of state politics. He reported his visit to a saloon in St. Hedwig, a small town of German and Polish immigrants near San Antonio. The establishment's owner had made public his dislike of the Rangers and the governor. "I suggested to him that the saloons of St. Hedwig should be closed as a public nuisance," Hanson reported, "and from that moment he was strictly for the Rangers and Hobby."

Hanson also worked the network of Special Rangers, whose ranks swelled under Hobby. In the original intent, such a title—and badge—would go to cattle inspectors and the like whose roles could complement the regular Rangers, especially as it involved catching rustlers. But in acts of political patronage, special commissions also were granted to bankers, lawyers, doctors, merchants, and others who could sway votes. Hanson proposed that Hobby's campaign headquarters receive a list of names of all Special Rangers. "I will further suggest that each one," Hanson said, "be given a bunch of Hobby literature for distribution." With the election approaching, Hanson told the adjutant general, "There is nothing like keeping these men actively in the harness for the next thirty days."

The Porvenir affair loomed as a potential liability to the governor's election. Hanson took the Southern Pacific train to Marfa in early February 1918. After talking to Captain Fox and some local businessmen, including one of the ranchers who had been with the Rangers at Porvenir, Hanson had nothing but scorn for those who claimed a massacre of innocents. The Big Bend crawled with Mexican thieves and killers, he noted in a report to the adjutant general. "Every time a bunch of these same bandits get over here on a marauding tour, and our boys has to deal with them," Hanson said, "they are no doubt reported as being a bunch of the leading citizens of Mexico, and murdered in cold blood by our officers and Citizens."

That settled, Hanson turned to frontier-style ward heeling. "I finally suggested to Capt Fox that I was of the opinion that it would be very much appreciated if Marfa had a strong 'Hobby Club,' but of course he could not have anything to do with it," Hanson wrote. Fox "caught the cue," Hanson said, and offered to find a friend to handle it. "Within two hours, his friend showed up with a list of fifteen signatures of the best men in Presidio County, who are now forming the club." Hanson added: "I believe Capt Fox is loyal to the core and that he is doing his full duty."

Political matters seemed to be progressing smoothly in the Big Bend. For broader concerns, though, those on the border might have consulted schoolmaster Warren's letter to the governor. "This unlawful deed," Warren said of

Porvenir, "has enraged the Mexicans on the other side to such an extent that we may hear soon of their retaliating on the whites on this side. It will be productive of the most evil consequences." He was proved right within two months.

Ed Nevill's cattle ranch, a relatively modest operation, stretched for eighteen miles along the Rio Grande. His cabin of cottonwood and adobe stood six miles upriver from Porvenir, and he had no close neighbors. Through the years, Nevill had enjoyed a good relationship with Mexicans and Tejanos, some of whom worked for him, and he had never lost any cattle to raiders. But on March 25, 1918, Nevill was in Van Horn, about thirty-five miles north, to pay bills. He talked to some soldiers there who warned him of rumors about an impending raid from Mexico. Nevill rode his horse back to his ranch, where all was quiet. With his son, Glenn, he ate supper prepared by his maid, Rosa Castillo. At dusk Nevill heard "the tramp of feet" outside. He opened his front door and saw men who appeared to be Mexicans approaching on horseback. "There was something like 50 of them," he said.

They dismounted, and some "went to shooting at the house," Nevill said, while others stood with their guns in their hands. "They were waiting for us to come out [the] door so they could kill us." As soon as he could make his way to it, "I picked up my Winchester," Nevill said, and "my boy picked up his."

The men outside kept firing. "Those bullets came in through the walls just like paper," Nevill said. His best hope, he believed, was to hide in a ditch about three hundred yards from the house. "I called to my son to come on." As the two ran for cover, the raiders fired away. "They shot my hat off, and shot my rifle out of my hand three times."

He lost track of his son—"I supposed he got away and ran down in the hills"—but made it to the ditch. There, Nevill hid in the dark while the raiders ransacked his house. When they were gone, he found Glenn near the front door. "[He] had been shot all to pieces," Nevill said. "You could drop a hen egg through this hole in his forehead. . . . He had been beat with rifles and a stick, and he was black and blue all over." Glenn Nevill died a few hours later. In the kitchen, Rosa Castillo lay dead. The maid had been raped with a stick of firewood, mutilated— her breasts severed and left on the floor beside her—and shot in the head.

The next day, U.S. Army cavalrymen trailed the raiders across the river into Mexico and found them in Pilares. In a gunfight the soldiers—armed with Browning automatic rifles—killed more than thirty of the Mexicans. Only one cavalryman died. The American soldiers found horses and guns from the Nevill Ranch, and one dead Mexican wore Glenn Nevill's cowboy boots. The cavalrymen burned Pilares.

Several of the raiders who were killed, the army determined, had been residents of Porvenir or had family who had been executed there. Again, Keil said, reprisal had run its course. "We learned later," he wrote, "that the raid on Nevill's ranch was planned in revenge during the burials at Porvenir."

As pressure built, the Porvenir cover-up began to unravel, and officials in Austin conspired to control the damage. Among them was special investigator Hanson, who realized that a special army investigation, then under way, could be catastrophic. "I think some action must be taken to keep our Department from getting the worst of it from the U.S. Government," Hanson wrote to the assistant adjutant general in May. "If this was possible it would ruin the Ranger force and the [Adjutant] General if he does not take action. Call his attention to it." About the same time, a Hobby ally in Marfa, lawyer C. E. Mead, wrote the governor's campaign manager to advise that Captain Fox "was a snake in the grass" who "had been secretly working for Ferguson all the time."

The election was less than two months away. In early June, Governor Hobby disbanded Company B and fired five of the Rangers who had been at Porvenir. Three others had already quit. Fox resigned too, but he didn't go quietly. "I don't feel that I am getting a fair deal," he said.

On June 11, 1918, Fox penned an angry letter of resignation to Hobby. The captain insisted that his men should not have been discharged. They were following orders, he said, and "unfortunately had to kill any number of Mexican bandits." He directly impugned the governor's motives. "There is no use in trying to have me believe that this action was brought about by anything other than your political reasons," Fox said. "Why do you not come clean and say that this is purely politics just to gain some Mexican votes?" Fox added a personal parting shot at Hobby, a big-city newspaper publisher not known as a rugged outdoorsman: "We have stood guard to prevent Mexican bandits from murdering the ranchmen, the women and children along this border while you slept on your feather bed of ease."

Adjutant General Harley drafted a heated response. The "trouble maker and lawless Ranger has no place on the border," he told Fox. "Every man whether he be white or black, yellow or brown has the Constitutional right to a trial by Jury."

Fox's resignation, Harley said, "came in the interest of humanity, decency, law and order." Harley circulated his letter to Texas newspapers. Few if any Rangers had ever been condemned in such a public manner.

The sheriff of Pecos County, D. S. Barker, leapt to the defense of Fox and his Rangers, who, after all, had killed only Mexicans. "For those sort of greasers you have seen fit to fire the rangers," the sheriff wrote. "I do not deem it a crime to kill those kind of sneaking thieves, especially when they are resisting an arrest."

If there had been any doubt that Rangers top command had reversed itself on Porvenir, Harley's reply to the sheriff dispelled it. After a "thorough investigation," he said, "the fact is established that these Mexicans were killed without any authority in law, civilization or reason." The adjutant general laid the problem at the feet of "incompetent and disobedient Rangers." And, of course, Fox: "While he did not admit the facts in the beginning, [he] now says that he ordered the wholesale slaughter of these men."

Hobby's response to Porvenir, however belated, may have been deft. He defeated Ferguson with ease in the Democratic primary. In Presidio County, the heart of the Big Bend, Hobby outpolled his opponent by a 3–1 margin.

One year—almost to the day—after the Porvenir massacre, the Rangers were compelled to, in essence, stand trial.

State Representative J. T. Canales, scion of a Rio Grande Valley ranching family, introduced a bill aimed at reforming the force. "There are now, and there have been for some time, in the state Ranger force men of desperate character, notoriously known as gunmen, their only qualification being that they can kill a man first and then investigate him afterward," Canales said. By appointing such men, Canales charged, the adjutant general was "either negligent . . . or else it is his policy to have such characters in the Ranger force to terrorize and intimidate the citizens of this state."

Canales lodged a number of specific charges against the Rangers. They had unjustly killed Tejanos and Mexicans in the Rio Grande Valley, he said, and had covered up their crimes. Of Porvenir, Canales wrote: "I charge on or about January 28, 1918, fifteen Mexicans, after they had been arrested and disarmed by State Rangers under Captain J. M. Fox's command . . . were murdered by said Rangers without any justification or excuse and without giving said Mexicans an opportunity to prove themselves innocent of the offenses charged against them."

The purpose of his bill was not to abolish the Rangers, he said, but to cultivate a better class of lawmen. The current force "was honeycombed with undesirable characters," including "cut-throats and murderers," Canales said. He proposed raising the Rangers' pay and putting each Ranger under bond.

A Senate-House committee then was formed for "the investigation of the Texas State Ranger Force." On January 31, 1919, it convened on the second floor of the capitol building and held twelve days of hearings. Eighty witnesses testified, and the official transcript exceeded sixteen hundred pages.

Many of the witnesses expressed support for the Rangers, but many others testified to the bloody search-and-destroy border missions. Front-page headlines told the story to the nation. "Texas Rangers Called Menace," said one. And "Texas Rangers Murdered More People Than Outlaws." A United Press report cast a hard eye on the scene: "Stripped of the mantle of romance which for half a century has made the picturesque 'border police' legendary heroes of epic and song, the Rangers today were being grilled . . . in a probe of charges of murder, lawlessness and cruelty."

Complicating matters, during the hearings one Ranger shot and killed another only a few miles from the capitol. The two had argued after an all-day whiskey binge.

In the end, though, the Rangers generally prevailed. Anglo legislators weren't about to side with a Mexican American colleague, no matter how distinguished, against a storied group of lawmen, no matter how troubled. The committee report faulted some "unnecessary taking of life" and other lawlessness but spared top agency officials from censure. Special investigator Hanson exulted in the findings. "Committee report all we could ask for," he said in a telegram to allies. "Vindication complete."

The bill to reform the Rangers was rewritten and gutted. New legislation raised the Rangers' pay and scaled back the agency's size, but it introduced no significant strictures or reforms. "I do not recognize my own child," Canales lamented on the House floor.

Though the Rangers' actions at Porvenir had broken nastily into public view, no Ranger was prosecuted for his role. The ground may as well have been salted at the village itself. Surviving residents never returned, and the gardens and fields were given back to the desert.

For his part, Ed Nevill could not keep living on the ranch where his son had been killed. "We had to abandon it," he said. He sold the land and moved to Marfa, where he ran a café for many years. It wasn't long before Nevill received an appointment as a Special Ranger, and that was about the time he began to seek his own form of recompense.

As his daughter, Kelley, told it, every night when he came home from his restaurant, Nevill would put away the bag containing the day's proceeds. Then, she said, he "picked up his cartridge belt, buckled it up, examined his gun, stuck it back into its holster, put on his jacket and went out into the night."

Sometimes he went alone. Other times, his daughter said, he was accompanied by a friend, Texas Ranger Jefferson Eagle Vaughan. Nevill kept a black book in which he had written about sixty names. They were some of the men he believed had made the raid on his ranch, and he was out to kill them all, night by night, one by one. "Without let-up for years each night he went into each Mexican house in Marfa searching each for the bandits," she said. Ranger Vaughan "once got his throat cut when he stepped into a Mexican hut on one of those nightly searches."

When Nevill met with success, he marked through the man's name in the book. "From time to time," his daughter said, "I would find it and see more names crossed through." Once, when Nevill believed the local sheriff was concealing one of the raiders, "I remember Mama arguing Papa out of killing [the sheriff] for hiding the bandit." The quest ended only when Nevill died in 1952—thirty-four years after the raid.

Nevill wasn't the only one intent on retribution. Ranger Bud Weaver, one of those fired after Porvenir, forged a long career in law enforcement as a mounted customs inspector. In his seventies, retired from Big Bend duties, he sat under the oak trees outside his Kimble County home and told a nephew the story of the Nevill Ranch raid. The sight of the dead and dismembered maid, Rosa Castillo, had enraged him, Weaver said. "I just couldn't take that." Eventually, "I found out who did it." The man was hiding in Mexico, so the Ranger crossed the river. "I found him," Weaver said, "and I hung that son-of-a-bitch."

Even the defrocked Monroe Fox found a path to vindication. In 1925, with Porvenir forgotten and Hobby out of office, he rejoined the Rangers as a senior captain. He remained on the force for two more years. Less than ten years after that, Fox had a chance to recast history on his own terms. Wearing a Stetson and drinking beer in an Austin café, he talked with journalist C. L. Douglas for the book *The Gentlemen in the White Hats: Dramatic Episodes in the History of the Texas Rangers*. Fox's account of "Parvenier," as Douglas called it, placed himself at the scene and upped the death toll by one. He, his men, and some ranchers encountered a "raiding party" there, Fox said. "We got them where they couldn't get away, and then we just lay behind a few little knolls and played a waiting game. We'd wait for a bandit to reveal his position and then we'd let him have it. Only a few of the gang escaped . . . for when the scrap was over we found sixteen bodies in the brush."

It was, in Douglas's 1934 rendition, a story of "Ranger justice, swift and sure," though he did acknowledge the international political consequences. "Over the killing of those sixteen a great cry went up from the Mexican population," Douglas wrote, an apparent reference to the Canales hearings. As Fox recalled it, "there was an investigation, but it ended in justification for the Rangers and the ranchers."

Some forty years after Porvenir, an aging Robert Keil—still haunted by what he had seen as a farm boy turned army cavalryman—began to put his memories to paper. "I have waited all these years for the story to be told," he wrote, "and now I will tell it myself. I am going to do my damnedest." Night after night in his Tucson home, Keil pecked with two fingers on an old manual typewriter. His daughter, Linda Davis, said her father would cry as he recalled the Porvenir victims. "He loved all those people," she said. "He couldn't stand what happened down there. He told me it was the biggest atrocity in the world. He witnessed it, and he felt so horrible about it."

Keil completed his writing sometime around 1963 and put the manuscript in a cardboard box. He died in 1972 with his story still packed away. "It was his last wish that maybe someday he could get the story out," Davis said. She brought it to Sul Ross State University in Alpine, Texas, which published Keil's *Bosque Bonito* in 2002.

This version of events—the Rangers executing villagers while the unknowing cavalry stood at a distance—might have served as the final word on Porvenir. But in 2015 a group led by historian Glenn Justice, former Texas Land Commissioner Jerry Patterson, and an archaeologist went to the ruins of the village. At the site of the massacre, they collected cartridge casings and bullet fragments that, ninety-seven years later, still lay in the desert sand. Some of the slugs were embedded with tiny pieces of shattered bone.

A forensic ballistics analysis led to a stunning conclusion. While some slugs came from .45-caliber Colt revolvers, which the Rangers used, many of the other bullets had been fired from .30-06-caliber rifles. In 1918, that weapon was commonly carried by cavalrymen.

That meant the Rangers did some killing that terrible night at Porvenir, but the U.S. Army—with its own thirst for vengeance—did too.

Up and down the river, perhaps the only fact that has never been disputed is that many people died unjustly. The last word may rightly belong to J. J. Kilpatrick, a Big Bend justice of the peace and contemporary chronicler of the bloody era. "The waters of the Rio Grande . . . as they flow to the sea, are ever murmuring the funeral dirge of innocent human beings cruelly slain," he wrote. "Oh God of mercy, how they groaned and writhed while dying, their staring eyes fixed on those who were killing them."

Richard "Two-Gun Dick" Herwig and his dogs ruled the raucous oil boom-town of Borger, Texas, until the Rangers sent him packing.

Chapter 16

BOOGER TOWN

"I'm Frank Hamer"

There is the mighty Frank Hamer, senior captain at Austin, the hero of many a hot exchange of lead and perhaps the best shot in Texas. He is a living embodiment of Pinkerton and Kit Carson, a relentless, cunning, straight-shooting officer with the mind of a sleuth and the physical courage of a tiger.

—ERIC G. SCHROEDER

The far upper reaches of the Texas Panhandle had been the site of some of Texas's most fierce Indian battles through the 1870s. At the opening of the twentieth century, much of the land remained empty, though the Comanches and Kiowas had been vanquished long ago. Distant Lone Star cities such as Dallas and Houston enjoyed population increases and development. The completion of the transcontinental railroads brought rapid growth to parts of the American West and along the Pacific Coast. But places like Hutchinson County, in the dry and windswept northern Panhandle, seemed fated to exist, now and forever, as miserly ranchland. Census takers in 1910 counted 303 people scattered across 809 square miles. There were one hundred head of cattle for every human. No railroad crossed the county, and its roads were dirt.

All that began to change in the early 1920s as wildcatters drilling for oil made promising strikes. More gushers followed, and it soon became clear that Hutchinson County sat on top of—in the words of a state official—"one of the greatest oil and natural gas fields ever discovered in the history of the world."

Such an oil patch would need an oil town. In 1926 a speculator named A. P. "Ace" Borger and some partners bought 240 acres on a bleak, treeless reach of short hills cut by raw ravines. They subdivided the tract, sold lots, and named it after its principal founder. "Your Opportunity Lies in Borger," crowed the newspaper ads they bought, "The New Town of the Plains." Borger began to fill almost immediately, and within a few months the area's population had grown to more than forty thousand. An estimated two thousand of them were prostitutes.

Oilfield workers flocked to Borger, of course, drawn by the opportunity for honest, well-paying work. Preachers, teachers, and shopkeepers came too. So did gamblers, bootleggers, and other aspiring felons. "Thousands of human parasites," an official's report noted, "crooks of every kind, including the murderer[s]." Many of the newcomers lived in tent cities and thrown-up shacks and drove their cars on a dusty, unpaved main street that became a sinking bog in the occasional heavy rain. Like other oil boomtowns, Borger sprang to life as a bedlam of stench, noise, and unrestrained commerce. "It is not a community," the *Dallas Morning News* sniffed in an editorial. "It is just a collection of strangers who come together and even collide in the pursuit of riches."

Oil derricks surrounded the settlement. Great dark clouds of smoke rose from quickly constructed carbon black plants. A by-product of natural gas production, carbon black was used in the manufacture of automobile tires. The plants brought jobs and money and rained soot on the shanties. A "world of smoke and grease," one contemporary writer called Borger. "Oil seems to have corroded this little settlement, left it overcast with a gangrenous pallor."

The artist Thomas Hart Benton visited Borger soon after its founding and was both repulsed and captivated by the "exploitive whoopee party" he saw. "It was a town then of rough shacks, oil rigs, pungent stinks from gas pockets, and broad-faced, big-boned Texas oil speculators, cowmen, wheatmen, etc.," he wrote. "The single street of the town was about a mile long, its buildings thrown together in a haphazard sort of way."

Benton painted a portrait of Borger he called *Boomtown*. It shows a ramshackle collection of buildings—hotels, a movie theater, and some stores—along a couple of crowded dirt streets. Oil derricks sprout in the distance, and a monstrous plume of black smoke looms. The townspeople he depicts walk to the movie house, shake hands over a business deal, or engage in a bloody fistfight on the corner, apparently over a woman.

"Every imaginable human trickery for skinning money out of people was there," Benton wrote of Borger. "Devious-looking real-estate brokers were set up on corners next to peep shows. Slot machines banged in drug-stores which were hung with all the gaudy signs of medicinal chicanery and cosmetic tomfoolery. Shoddy preachers yowled and passed the hat in the street. Buxom, wide-faced, brightly painted Texas whores brought you plates of tough steak in the restaurants."

Corruption in Borger was present at the creation and radiated from the top. Ace Borger's business partner, John R. Miller, served as the town's first mayor. He hired an old friend to be city marshal, Richard Emerald "Two-Gun Dick" Herwig, who carried a couple of revolvers, one on each hip. Though he usually employed the weapons to pistol-whip his hapless victims, he fired them when necessary. As a deputy sheriff in Oklahoma he had unjustly shot a man, which resulted in a conviction for manslaughter. Herwig won parole and rolled into Texas with a couple of snarling German shepherds.

The mayor and Two-Gun Dick established a criminal scheme that came to be called "the ring." In exchange for bribes, they countenanced prostitution, gambling, and—with Prohibition still the law of the land—bootlegging. Herwig walked the town's dirty streets to collect payoffs, his pants cuffs stuffed into his boot tops and his German shepherds on a leash. Depending on his mood, lawbreakers reluctant to pay bribes might get a beating or a dog bite. "He was symbolical of the gang in action," a state law enforcement account said. "He was cruel to the weak, and commanded tribute from the strong in the underworld."

The women who toiled in the brothels each paid Herwig $18 a week in tribute, which meant great stacks of cash for racketeering officials. "On Dixon Street over a thousand of these women lived," wrote John H. White, who represented Hutchinson County in the state legislature. "Many of these women supported their husbands by their sinful occupation, who did not seem to mind in the least, just as long as they did not need to work." Business was brisk for the young women who, in another writer's description, presented faces "decorated with livid rouge" and had "experienced painted lips [that] emitted endless rings of cigarette smoke." Venereal disease was said to be epidemic among oilfield workers.

So it went for about a year in Texas's Sodom, as many called it. Locals preferred the sobriquet Booger Town. The bars, whorehouses, and gambling dens openly operated around the clock. Dozens of murders occurred without investigation or prosecution—in part because the district attorney got so drunk during business hours he had to be put to bed, according to a local justice of the peace. In some cases the victims were worth more dead than alive. Crooked undertakers—cronies of Two-Gun Dick—were believed to kill intoxicated vagrants so they could collect a $100 fee for burying paupers.

The criminals occasionally went too far, even for Borger. In one incident robbers shot to death a fifteen-year-old girl identified in news stories as "pretty schoolgirl" Mildred Poothman. Outrage stirred at last, which prompted Texas governor Miriam Ferguson to send four Rangers to town. They stayed only a few weeks and were withdrawn after a request from the mayor. Local police, including Two-Gun Dick, assured the governor and the public they had criminal matters in the region well under control.

Less than a month later, the night police chief was killed in a shootout with a suspect. Three months after that, a Borger policeman was shot and killed while making an arrest. Then, after less than two weeks of relative peace, two Hutchinson County deputy sheriffs were slain late at night alongside an empty road. Both had been shot in the head at close range. The suspects were well-known desperados who had just robbed a bank.

A new governor, Dan Moody, dispatched ten Rangers—or, as one reporter called them, those "picturesque detectives of the plains." Picturesque they were in their white cowboy hats with suits and ties. But they came to Borger as enforcers, not sleuths. "The gentlemen of the press asked me what tactics would be employed by the Rangers," Captain W. W. Sterling said. "I replied that we were simply going to reverse the customary Borger procedure. Where the criminals had been killing officers, we were going to kill off some of the crooks."

They hit Booger Town in early April 1927 and checked into the Marland Hotel. Among them was Captain Frank A. Hamer.

At six feet, three inches and 230 pounds, Francis Augustus Hamer towered over mortals and carried himself like a cowboy out of a pulp western. A "giant of a man," in one reporter's description, "moon-faced . . . and as talkative as an oyster." Hamer named his favorite pistol, a Colt .45 revolver, "Old Lucky." Before his career was over, he would say he had been shot at fifty-two times and "wounded by bullets 23 times." And he added, "Several of those bullets are in me yet."

Given such material, many writers of Hamer's era portrayed him with ado-
ration, even if some of their efforts couldn't withstand close scrutiny. A "fearless
man-hunter," one called him. Hamer was tough but fair, a Dallas newspaper
said: "Bullets of bandits and other law violators scar his body, but it is his record
that he has never shot a man who had not fired first at him." He was a crack shot,
the Associated Press observed, but not cruel. "This big man who has worn a six-
shooter almost since he discarded his swaddling clothes and who can puncture
a bull's eye without half trying is tender-hearted in spite of the many frigid
hearts he has dealt with."

And above all, he was not to be denied: "If all the criminals in Texas were
asked to name the man they would most dread to have on their trail, they would
probably name . . . Frank Hamer without hesitation," Ranger historian Walter
Prescott Webb speculated. "There is not a criminal in Texas who does not fear
and respect him." Webb did not provide the evidence that led him to this conclusion, but Hamer himself did little to dispel such notions. When it came to law
enforcement, he often said, "nothing was as effective as a .45 slug in the gut."

Hamer was born in the Texas Hill Country in 1884, the son of a hard-
drinking blacksmith. According to family lore, by age sixteen young Frank had
already killed a man—a rancher who had shot him first. Afterward, the story
goes, he went home, put his hand on the family Bible, and swore to God to "pursue outlaws relentlessly and bring them to justice." Though it has been repeated
many times, the tale is not factual, according to a recent biography of Hamer.
The man he was said to have killed died years later of natural causes.

Hamer signed on with the Rangers in 1906, listing his occupation as "cowboy." His early years with the agency, which he left and rejoined several times,
were spent on the border. In 1917, Hamer—now in West Texas—married Gladys
Sims, a pretty, petite woman who packed a pistol and had, while still a young
woman, shot at least three men. She was at the time of their betrothal under
indictment for murdering her ex-husband while her two daughters watched in
horror. The charges were dismissed, but the man's death accelerated an inter-
family feud. Hamer was working as a Special Ranger, which meant he chased
rustlers for the Texas cattle raisers. Along with his brother, Harrison, he also
served as Gladys Sims's personal armed escort.

The Hamer brothers cut intimidating figures in the ranching town of Snyder. "These men . . . ride around . . . in their automobiles with big cartridge belts
and guns, making rather a display of their arms," the local sheriff and county
attorney wrote to Governor James Ferguson. "These extra guards and gun

displays are only agitating trouble, rather than keeping it down. These men, the Hamers, are antagonistic to the local officials."

The county attorney and others in Snyder, including the sheriff, asked the governor for help. Ferguson ordered the adjutant general to "rush" two Rangers to Snyder to keep the peace. The adjutant general canceled Hamer's commission as a Special Ranger, after which Hamer became a full-time bodyguard for his wife's family. As often happened with Hamer, serious action followed.

Hamer, his wife, his brother, and his brother-in-law were driving home on October 1, 1917, when a tire on their Cadillac went flat. They pulled into a garage in Sweetwater, a railroad and ranching town on the West Texas plains. Two armed men approached. One of them was Gee McMeans, a former Ranger who was the brother-in-law of Gladys's dead ex-husband. "The shooting began immediately," one press account said, though it wasn't clear who fired first. Hamer was hit twice, in the shoulder and the thigh. Gladys blazed away with her pistol from the car but missed the assailants. Staggered by his wounds and bleeding heavily, Hamer managed to kill McMeans and send the other gunman running for his life. He would have killed that man too, Hamer said, but "I couldn't shoot the damned coward in the back."

Hamer claimed self-defense, and a grand jury no-billed him. He recovered from his wounds and in 1921 worked as a federal prohibition agent. Hamer was stationed in El Paso, a chaotic and violent port of entry for black-market opium and liquor from Mexico. Smugglers routinely shot at those who tried to stop them, and American law enforcement officials returned fire, with many deaths on both sides. The legal niceties of arrest and trial rarely applied. On a spring night, for instance, Hamer and his posse hid along the river until they spotted six men they believed to be smuggling liquor. They opened fire on Hamer's orders and killed the six on the spot.

By 1921 he was back with the Rangers as a captain. His fellow Rangers considered Hamer a man of prodigious and varied talents, especially when it came to tracking criminals. He also had a Tarzan-like ability to call owls. "Driving through the woods in the daytime," Ranger captain W. W. Sterling recalled, Hamer "often stopped his car and gave what must have been their distress cry. All sleeping owls within the sound of his voice would wake up and fly to the spot."

When not luring birds, Hamer was known to disable adversaries with a kick—stronger than a mule's, many said—or a swat to the side of the head. "Captain Hamer's open palm always took the fight out of the hardiest ruffian," Sterling wrote.

Hardy ruffians weren't the only targets of his wrath. In 1918, Hamer confronted Texas state representative J. T. Canales on a Brownsville street. Hamer had heard that Canales was collecting allegations of Ranger atrocities against Mexican Americans for his legislative inquiry. "If you don't stop that," Hamer told him, "you're going to get hurt." The local sheriff, no admirer of the Rangers' tactics, had some advice for Canales: grab a double-barreled shotgun and "kill that man." The sheriff added, "No jury would ever convict you."

Canales declined, though he did complain about the incident. The Rangers' top brass wasn't particularly troubled by Hamer's threatening the life of a state legislator who had the agency in his investigative sights, though Adjutant General Harley did send a mildly admonishing telegram. "Under Governor's orders," the adjutant general told Hamer, "you are instructed not to make any threats against the lives of any citizen, especially J. T. Canales. . . . Undertake to adjust differences as best you can without causing any trouble."

Hamer preferred action over threats anyway. He once dealt with a newspaper reporter who had misquoted him—or so Hamer believed—by pistol-whipping the man on a Houston street. When the reporter struggled to his feet and ran away, Hamer fired his gun. "I did not shoot to hit him," Hamer said, explaining why the bullet from Old Lucky did not strike the hapless newsman. "I wanted to scare him." Hamer pleaded guilty to aggravated assault and paid a fine of $25.

The moral of the stories: No one who had a bit of sense messed with Frank Hamer. Here stood a man, it was said by fawning scribes, whose mere presence could stop criminals in their tracks. There was, for instance, his 1922 appearance in Corpus Christi.

Hamer and several other Rangers had traveled to the bayside city after the Nueces County sheriff shot to death Fred Roberts, a prominent local landowner who was also a Ku Klux Klan leader. Roberts's demise climaxed a volatile dispute over county politics. A Hamer biography, written after his death with the cooperation of his family, described the tense scene the Ranger captain faced when he arrived in Corpus Christi: no one had been arrested, and the sheriff and his accomplices had barricaded themselves inside the county courthouse, guarded by forty or so henchmen "armed with shotguns and rifles." Undaunted, Hamer kicked in the courthouse doors and strode fearlessly alone into this den of snakes. Then, the biography said, he seized instant control:

> "I'm Frank Hamer, Texas Ranger," he said, with an icy stare. "I have a warrant for the arrest of the men involved in the murder. . . . The rest of you put up those guns and get the hell out of here." He walked up to the accused men and began to read the warrants. As he did so, the others—overpowered by the strength of Hamer's personality alone— slowly began to file out of the courtroom. Hamer, his handcuffed prisoners, and the other Rangers departed for the county jailhouse.

However thrilling, this account was not fully supported by most contemporaneous press coverage. Multiple newspapers reported that Corpus Christi police chief Monroe Fox—the same Monroe Fox who as a Ranger had tried to cover up the Porvenir massacre—arrested the sheriff and three others long before Hamer got there. According to the Associated Press, the men were "being held in custody at the courthouse." Hamer merely "ordered them placed within cells in the jail."

Hamer took over the investigation because he believed Fox had shirked his official duties. The police chief "hasn't been of the slightest assistance to us in securing evidence against the men who killed Mr. Roberts," Hamer said, and "seems to be spending his time looking for an excuse for them."

The Ranger captain succeeded in securing murder indictments against the sheriff and three other men. But testimony at trial showed the Klansman may have reached for his weapon before the sheriff shot him. The sheriff and his alleged accomplices were acquitted.

As Texas became the nation's leading oil producer, black-gold boomtowns sprouted in such places as Wink, Electra, and Mexia. Before oil, the tiny settlement of Desdemona—orginally known as Hogtown—was home to a collection of contented socialists. But in 1918 a big well came in, and raw capitalism took over. Soon Desdemona had bordellos, tent cities, and water poisoned by crude.

Every boomtown faced similar problems to varying degrees, all related to a sudden mixture of people, money, and anarchy. When crime and chaos threatened to overwhelm these places, the governor might send the Rangers to make arrests and clean up. The locals did not always welcome such efforts.

Some of the strongest opposition arose, ironically, in Ranger, a town named in honor of the agency. Located between Fort Worth and Abilene, Ranger was a poor, struggling rural village until 1917, when the ground began to shake and a well on John McClesky's farm blew. Less than two years later, twenty-two wells were producing in the area, eight refineries were open or under construction, and the city's four banks recorded $5 million in deposits.

With such instant wealth came the usual scourges. Torrential rains turned Ranger's Main Street into such a bog that a mule drowned in the mud. Typhoid swept the town—and killed newly rich John McClesky. Brothels and gambling halls operated with impunity. This brought the Rangers to town, and they wasted no time. "The boys had to kill a fellow last night," Ranger sergeant Sam McKenzie reported to headquarters in December 1918. "They raided a gambling den and this man made fight and the boys shot him. . . . He resisted arrest so everything is all right."

But it wasn't. A citizens group complained to the governor that the Rangers had murdered one of the town's "most honorable, peaceful, law-abiding citizens" in "his own place of business," a store. "Texas civilization," they added, "has reached that high plane which requires real peace officers and not criminals to protect the dignity of the state." The two Rangers were convicted of murder and sentenced to prison, but the convictions were overturned on appeal.

Through it all, the town continued its wide-open ways. In 1921 Texas adjutant general Thomas D. Barton said he had received complaints that conditions in Ranger "would be a disgrace to be permitted in old Mexico, Spain or any other semi-civilized country." In response, a team of five Rangers shut down a large gambling operation at the Commercial Hotel. Some small fines were paid, and one of the proprietors stood trial, but a jury of his peers found him not guilty. The raid had accomplished little except to inflame the locals.

The town's state representative, Joe Burkett, officially protested "the needless stationing of Rangers . . . especially as long as they do not conduct themselves within the pale of the law." Though some were "excellent officers," Burkett said, "there have been too many . . . who are too handy with their guns and have abused the power vested in them." Some of them, Burkett said, opened fire on a carload of deputy sheriffs. Four Rangers were accused of sideswiping two pedestrians with a car and beating them with revolvers. Burkett also alleged that the Rangers made numerous arrests and house raids without warrants. (This was hardly a new charge. One year earlier, Rangers pursuing bootleggers had been withdrawn from El Paso after public outcry. Officials there said the Rangers searched the cars of motorists without warrants and assaulted and cursed those who protested.)

Burkett's allegations prompted Adjutant General Barton to hold an angry press conference. Citing his own "moral, political and physical courage," Barton threatened to place fifty of his officers in the town. That would teach them not to disparage the Rangers. But Barton soon backed down, and within two months all Rangers were out of Ranger.

As bad as the town of Ranger and others were, when it came to governmental corruption and officially sanctioned sin, Borger may have led the pack.

The governor sent the Rangers to Borger in early April 1927 with instructions to "stay there until peace is declared between the law and the lawless." Hamer and a Ranger force went on the offensive as soon as they arrived. They confiscated dozens of slot machines and took axes to stills. They shut down drug dens. They even banished Mattie Castlebury, who owned the White Way Dance Hall and the Tokio Club. She exited the scene in her yellow Cadillac.

"Practically all women [were] ordered to leave Borger," the Associated Press reported. Merchants peddling the pleasures of liquor and wagering also found themselves cast out of the vice garden. Caravans of black Model T Fords—the cars packed with gamblers, bootleggers, petty thieves, and whores—streamed from town along the narrow roads that led to Amarillo and Fort Worth. The less moneyed fled on foot. One newspaper story told of "more than a dozen girls, with bundles on their backs, walking along the highway."

Men who didn't leave were subject to arrest based on the toughness of their fingers and palms. Captain Sterling said Rangers with a police wagon stopped men on the street and demanded to see their hands. "If an examination . . . showed callouses or other evidence of honest toil, he was free to go about his business," Sterling said. "But if he had the soft, white hands of a gambler or other parasite, the hoodlum wagon gained another passenger." They were taken to the town jail, which had no bars on its windows, only boards. Prisoners were shackled to a central post known as the "snortin' pole."

Mayor Miller was indicted on charges of accepting a bribe to protect a gambling house. Though he insisted he had been framed, Miller resigned from office. The Rangers also ran Two-Gun Dick out of Borger, but he didn't go far. Herwig settled in Jal, New Mexico, another boomtown just across the Texas line. There he was named deputy sheriff, and he opened a roadhouse that served forbidden liquor. Apparently possessed of a sense of mockery, Herwig posted a large sign on the front that said EIGHT MILES FROM TEXAS RANGERS.

The Rangers of course had no jurisdiction outside the state. But Captain Will Wright, a highly regarded veteran of the Mexican border smuggling wars, arranged to have himself and his company temporarily commissioned as federal officers. Armed with machine guns, they crossed into New Mexico and shut down Herwig's establishment. As the *El Paso Herald* described it, Captain Wright personally took Herwig's guns from him. Herwig protested, "I'm deputy sheriff here." Wright answered, "You ain't nothing." Herwig subsequently returned to Oklahoma, a place more forgiving of his illegal quirks, and joined the state highway patrol.

In late April 1927, less than three weeks after their arrival, Hamer announced the Rangers had pacified Booger Town. "We have broken the backbone of the lawlessness, and it will stay broken," he said. Borger was "now as quiet as any Sunday school town." He added: "And we did it without firing a shot." The captain pegged the success to the Rangers' banishment of shady characters. "When we told the crooks they would have to get out, they moved and none of them has attempted to return," he said.

The Texas papers lapped it up. "BORGER IS NO LONGER LAWLESS," said a headline in the *Dallas Morning News*. "RANGERS TAME BORGER," trumpeted the *Austin American-Statesman*. It was an inspiring story, but it wasn't true.

Three months after Hamer's declaration, Borger's former city secretary wrote a letter to the governor that claimed that the Rangers had been hoodwinked. "In the main the Borger mess is a worse mess now than it was when the State took action," Sam J. Little said. "The Rangers . . . went only half way. They evidently did not have sufficient evidence, or were misled by petty self-serving politicians." The new cast of local officials, Little said, was just as crooked as the old one. A Borger grocer named O. C. Goodwin wrote the governor with similar concerns and said other honest businessmen had stayed silent "for fear that . . . thugs will shoot them in the back some dark night."

Despite these missives, Governor Moody pulled all but a few Rangers out of Borger. They had worn out their welcome, as indicated by several petitions sent to Moody by Borger businessmen urging the Rangers' withdrawal. This sentiment may have been due in part to some spirited gunplay. Ranger Jack Degraftenreid had been arguing with a deputy sheriff about the custody of a prisoner.

The Ranger beat the deputy with his pistol and fired a shot. The bullet tore through the deputy's pants but didn't hit him—"missing a fatal shot, and doubtless a killing," the *Hutchinson County Herald* tautologized. A grand jury indicted Degraftenreid for assault with intent to murder. He was tried and found not guilty.

Several months later, State District Judge Newton P. Willis, a jurist with a spotless reputation, raised far more serious concerns than one trigger-happy Ranger. In a letter to Governor Moody, Willis said citizens complained that Rangers who were supposed to clean up Borger had instead engaged in widespread shakedowns and theft. "They claim that the rangers are dishonest," the judge wrote. The Rangers were accused of collecting fines from those they arrested and pocketing the money "without any legal proceedings." And, the judge said, citizens alleged that Rangers would "sell intoxicating liquors that they confiscate." Willis told Moody he had "not been satisfied that these things are true." However, the judge said, the people of Hutchinson County "are practically unanimous . . . in their opinion that the rangers should be removed."

Within a few months, the Rangers were out of Borger, which was welcome news in Austin. The agency had spent much of its surplus budget to keep them in the Panhandle. Though the legislature had authorized a force of thirty-eight Rangers overall, the manpower level stayed at thirty to save money.

The town itself went on to make many improvements: adding churches and schools, paving streets, and building a sewage plant. Railroad lines and highways now ran through the county. In the summer of 1927, Borger merchants conducted a "rat war," which ended with 1,245 carcasses collected, and they were king-sized vermin. "It was estimated," the Associated Press reported, "that the dead rats weighed 2,409 pounds."

Rodents were one thing, criminals another. Borger still contained strong elements of the old Booger Town, as the new district attorney discovered. John Holmes, a thin man with a wide-eyed gaze that always seemed on the verge of alarm, had been in office only a year. He was forty-three, a Mississippian who had attended law school at the University of Texas. He moved to Borger in 1927 and set up a private practice. When the county's former district attorney was forced from office, Holmes was appointed to succeed him.

Some suspected Holmes to be yet another tool of the Borger mob, but the new prosecutor presented himself as a crusading reformer. However, he needed backup. In March 1929 he wrote Governor Moody and asked him to send two

Rangers to Borger. "I can clean up conditions in this county if only you will help me," Holmes said.

The governor promised that help was on the way. The Rangers came back to Borger long enough to make at least one high-profile bust. Dressed as hayseeds, in faded overalls and ragged straw hats, they infiltrated a band of liquor-guzzling wheat harvesters and made thirty-six arrests. But the Rangers did not stay long, and Holmes once more wrote to the governor. "Just as soon as the Rangers leave town," he lamented, "all the joints open up again." At the same time he was seeking aid from the state, the district attorney was working with federal authorities in Amarillo to bring charges against city and county officials. A federal grand jury was scheduled to convene on September 16, 1929, to probe the Borger "ring." Holmes was to appear before the panel to present findings.

On the night of September 13, Holmes pulled his car into the driveway of his small stucco house in Borger and stopped near his garage in the backyard. His wife, Velma, and his mother-in-law emerged from the car. They walked to the house as Holmes drove into the garage. He stepped out of the car and was closing its door when someone hiding behind a bush fired five shots from a .38-caliber handgun. Three of them hit Holmes, one of them a fatal shot to the back of his neck. As Velma Holmes ran screaming from the house toward her husband, the gunman fled into the dark.

Texas had a history of outrageous murders that few states could match, but with the assassination of a district attorney, a line had been crossed. Headlines blared and politicians blustered. A federal judge in nearby Amarillo called it the worst crime in Texas in thirty years, which covered a lot of bloody ground. It wasn't simply that a prosecutor had been murdered but that members of the local government were believed to be culpable. "The hand that fired the gun," Judge James C. Wilson said, "was the hand of an official or had official sanction."

Once again the governor directed the Rangers to Borger, with Hamer in charge. "They sent one of those clear-eyed, calm-spoken, straight-shooting westerners," said a story in the *Pittsburgh Press*. "He is Frank Hamer—six feet tall and 250 pounds of law and order. Governor Dan Moody picked this Ranger captain to 'tame' Borger and his record indicates he is the man who can."

Hamer and Ranger Tom Hickman went to work investigating Holmes's death and quickly announced they had cracked the case: a cabal of city and county officials were responsible. The slaying grew from the illegal liquor trade, Hamer said, and he had affidavits to prove the conspiracy. The Ranger captain predicted arrests within one day. But these arrests did not occur the next day, or the day after that, or the day after that. Hamer took his allegations of a deep conspiracy to Governor Moody, calling Borger's setup the "worst organized crime ring" he had seen in twenty-three years of law enforcement.

Many locals disagreed. "It's a lie," said Sheriff Joe Ownbey. The *Borger Daily Herald*, in a front-page editorial, challenged Hamer to prove his allegations and arrest those responsible. The governor nonetheless believed him, and called in armed reinforcements. Citing "an organized and entrenched criminal ring" and a "conspiracy between [police] officers and the law violators," Moody declared martial law in Hutchinson County on September 28, 1929. He deployed the Texas National Guard to Borger.

The guardsmen were commanded by Brigadier General Jacob Wolters, who applauded the Rangers. "It is a proud boast of the Texas Rangers, running back to the time of the Texas Republic in 1836, that they have always accomplished their mission," he wrote, but followed that with some deflating words. In Borger, the general said, the Rangers were badly overmatched. "For once in the ninety-three years operations of the Texas Rangers, they found themselves baffled," Wolters said. "Those persons who might be in possession of any leads or facts were afraid to talk; witnesses were told by members of the police and the constable department to leave, and leave they did."

As a result, "the Rangers were helpless." Even with Hamer and others in town, Wolters said, the "entire community was in a grip of frozen terror" and "people were in terror of their lives."

About one hundred national guardsmen traveled by train from Fort Worth to the Panhandle. They took possession of the Borger city hall and disarmed the police department. "Occupation of the town was accomplished quietly and quickly," the local newspaper reported.

Wolters convened a court of inquiry but had trouble extracting much useful information from residents. "It soon became evident that persons good, bad or indifferent were still afraid to talk," he wrote. The reason: "The principal law violators, well-known characters in the town, were still walking the streets." He ordered the detention of all persons believed to be part of the entrenched criminal ring cited by the governor.

Though Rangers were accustomed to working independently and answering to no one but themselves, those in Borger now took orders from Wolters and his officers. The Rangers were instructed to raid stills, shut down pool halls, throw prostitutes in jail, and arrest drunks. "On the third day, after a diligent search," Wolters said, "not a drunk could be found by the Rangers and soldiers in Borger."

Many of those merely suspected of crimes were charged with vagrancy and given the choice of jail or leaving town by sundown. "They left," Wolters said, "by the next bus or train out." Not all of them went like sheep, said Ranger sergeant Manuel T. "Lone Wolf" Gonzaullas. "Some of them tried to get smart with us," Gonzaullas said, "but we just smacked 'em around and hitched a few to the snortin' pole at the jail. That took the wind out of 'em and they didn't give us any more trouble."

Under pressure, the old city and county officials resigned. Wolters and his associates handpicked their replacements. The former sheriff was replaced by a Ranger, and an ex-Ranger took over as police chief. "The entrenched criminal ring . . . had been destroyed," Wolters said. "We had taken the city government out of the hands of the ring and restored it to the law respecting people." After nineteen days, the national guardsmen departed.

The Holmes assassination case still loomed. About six weeks after his death, the sheriff's office filed murder charges against two men: Sam Jones, a former deputy constable, and Jim Hodges, manager of a local boiler works. No motive was publicly announced, and despite the early assertions by Hamer, evidence against the men was weak. Both were freed on bond, and neither went to trial. The state eventually dropped all charges, and no one was ever convicted in Holmes's death.

In the early 1930s, Borger finally calmed down, thanks in part to the aftereffects of martial law. The Great Depression had a lot to do with that too, as did a decline in oil and gas prices. At the same time, the efforts of clergy and citizens who promoted responsible government helped Borger begin to resemble more sedate small cities. No one called it Booger Town now.

Hamer moved on to other assignments. One of them—a most shameful moment in the state's history—would go to the heart of the Rangers' image.

George Hughes was charged with assaulting a white woman. Escorted to the courthouse in chains, he would fall victim that same day to a lynch mob.

Chapter 17

ONE RIOT

The Rangers Make a Phone Call

Get this, boy, when the black man or the yellow man lay their hands upon the white woman to do her physical violence, then it is that all the hell of the jungle days are unloosed, men go wild, like the incoming tide of the ocean, like an avalanche tearing down the mountain side, sweeping everything before it, destruction in its wake. . . . The mad mob—Vengeance. It has ever been thus.

—*ALBANY (TEXAS) NEWS*

The statue of an unidentified Texas Ranger stands in the main terminal of Love Field, the City of Dallas airport. Made of bronze, the Ranger rises twelve majestic feet atop a granite pedestal. He wears a Stetson, of course, and his pants are tucked into his cowboy boots. Two pistols are packed in twin holsters. He extends one hand as if to calm any fears, while the other is poised for a quick draw should a preflight fracas erupt at the Dunkin' Donuts on the mezzanine. More than 1.3 million airline passengers walk past this sculpture each month. Those who glance at the pedestal can see the inscription: ONE RIOT - ONE RANGER.

This declaration serves as an unofficial slogan of the Rangers. According to numerous written accounts, it was born long ago when a single lawman—perhaps Captain Bill McDonald—showed up to quell a mob. An incredulous local asked why he was alone, and the Ranger responded, "You only have one riot, don't you?"

Many historians agree that no Ranger ever seriously uttered such a thing. Yet it has endured as a pithy expression of the agency's ethos, because "One Riot, One Ranger" conveys a necessary, defiant confidence. Frequently outnumbered by the opposition, the Rangers had to employ individual strength, guile, courage, and integrity to win the day. In that realm, the words become the true distillation of a Ranger ideal.

The Texas Ranger Hall of Fame and Museum, the official repository of agency history, used "One Riot, One Ranger" in big, bold letters on many billboards for years, a come-on for tourists along Interstate 35. As late as 2018, one could scarcely make it through the city of Waco, home of the museum, without seeing the phrase half a dozen times.

But the facts don't always match the advertising, even if that advertising is etched in stone beneath a statue. Nearly a century ago, Frank Hamer waded into one of the worst race riots in the state's history. One Ranger was not nearly enough.

In many ways, particularly the worst ones, the racial climate in Texas during the first third of the twentieth century mirrored that of the Deep South. Jim Crow segregation prevailed. Members of the Ku Klux Klan exercised political power by day and spread terror by night. A black man accused of a serious crime against a white person often met death at the hands of a mob, though in some cases the accusations need not involve criminal activity. In the North Texas town of Farmersville, a black man was hanged after a white telephone operator said he had spoken rudely to her.

There were more than 450 lynchings in Texas between 1885 and 1930, and nearly three fourths of the victims were black. These actions provoked, on the whole, little in the way of community outrage or shame. Government officials in Texas, almost all of whom were white, tended to look the other way. White citizens in many cases treated them as public entertainments—spontaneous and gruesome versions of the county fair. Vendors circulated through the mobs with refreshments. Photographs of corpses hanging from nooses were sold, and mailed, as picture postcards.

In the six decades from the end of Reconstruction through the Great Depression, Texas trailed only Mississippi and Georgia in the number of lynchings. They were common enough that most attracted scant outside notice. Occasionally, though, the excess of brutality and spectacle compelled attention, such as the 1893 torture and death of Henry Smith.

Smith, who was black, confessed to the kidnapping, rape, strangulation, and dismemberment of a three-year-old white girl, the daughter of a police officer, in the northeast Texas city of Paris. A mob seized him without a trial. As ten thousand or more spectators cheered, the father and brother of the dead girl tortured Smith with red-hot irons. They started with his feet, worked their way up to his face, and plunged the irons into his eyes, after which they tossed him onto a pile of burning wood for a live cremation. Smith writhed and screamed in the initial moments on the pyre. From the crowd came jeers and laughter. The *Dallas Morning News* described it as "the most horrible death ever inflicted on a human being."

The Texas Legislature passed an anti-lynching law in 1897, in part a reaction to national condemnation of Henry Smith's public execution. But prosecutions of lynch mob leaders were uncommon, and convictions virtually nonexistent. .

Though they were the only statewide law enforcement agency, the Rangers did not frequently prevent or investigate lynchings during this period. They—and the politicians who directed them—had more pressing concerns, such as catching cattle rustlers, stopping illegal prizefights, and patrolling the Mexican border.

There were exceptions. In 1908, Hamer was sent to Beaumont, where "the excited citizenship," according to a Ranger report, wished to lynch two black men suspected of rape. Hamer hid in a barn with the prisoners, the report said, "without being detected by the mob, who seemed to be hunting vigorously everywhere . . . shooting and hallowing." Hamer's captain praised his "presence of mind, coolness and courage." And in 1922 Hamer and four other Rangers rushed from Austin to Waco to confront a mob that threatened to pull black murder suspects from the county jail. Hamer stood on the courthouse steps with a Thompson submachine gun, and the mob dispersed.

Because the force was small and the state big, the Rangers often could only deal with the tail end of a racial bloodbath. They were deployed to the 1910

Slocum Massacre in East Texas after white men had shot and killed at least eight unarmed black men—and probably many more. "These negroes have done no wrong that I could discover," said the local sheriff, W. H. Black. "There was just a hot-headed gang hunting them down and killing them."

In 1919 the Rangers protected a black man on trial in Hillsboro, south of Dallas. After Bragg Williams was convicted of murdering a white woman and her child and sentenced to death, the local district attorney told the Rangers they were no longer needed. They departed for Austin. Then a mob pulled the man from the county jail and burned him at the stake. Dozens of women and children were among those watching, a Dallas newspaper observed. "The crowd was orderly and there was little excitement."

That year, 1919, is generally considered the worst year of racial strife in the United States, with a succession of lynchings and riots. One of those riots took place in the East Texas city of Longview. The trouble began when a group of white men beat and shot to death a black man in the nearby town of Kilgore. His offense: a consensual relationship with a white woman. A month later, a black teacher in Longview published an article in the *Chicago Defender* in which the white woman claimed she had been in love with the black man and had hoped to marry him.

For his crime of writing, a group of white men beat the black teacher severely on a downtown street. A mob set fire to his house and to the house of the black physician who had treated him for his injuries. This time, however, blacks fired back on white attackers, and a full-scale race war seemed about to erupt. Governor William P. Hobby ordered Rangers and one hundred National Guardsmen to the scene.

The guardsmen calmed the town as the Rangers arrested twenty-six white men and twenty-two blacks. The white men were released on bail, while the black men stayed behind bars. Ultimately, local officials worried that juries would convict the black men and acquit the whites, which could lead to another riot. The charges against all, black and white, were dropped.

The Longview disturbance alarmed the Rangers enough that they finally began to investigate racial problems in Texas. That didn't mean an official campaign against the the Ku Klux Klan. It was an open secret that an untold number of Rangers held Klan sympathies, if not memberships. Instead, Rangers spread across the state to dispense warnings—backed by vague rumors—of an armed black uprising against whites. They launched probes of black groups, including chapters of the National Association for the Advancement of Colored People.

The NAACP advocated racial equality, a ranking Rangers official explained, which could cause public disorder. And the Rangers, he said, had a duty to suppress disorder.

To accomplish this, the Rangers set out to ensure that several constitutional freedoms did not extend to black people. A 1919 memo to the adjutant general from Ranger Frank W. Matthews, for example, was titled "Investigating Negroes' Organizing." From the East Texas town of Marshall, Matthews conferred with the local "white vigilance committee," the members of which pressured local merchants not to sell guns or ammunition to blacks. (Whites remained free to buy as much as they pleased.)

Matthews also reported to his boss that the county sheriff had stopped local black residents from "selling radical Negro papers on the streets." Some of the newspapers arrived by mail, however, so the Marshall postmaster was "watching for them and would not let them be delivered." The Ranger added that "negroes have been holding secret meetings," but the sheriff planned to place a spy in their midst to "see just what they are doing." A day later, Ranger Matthews reported from Dallas that the NAACP chapter held weekly gatherings. "I find that a negro Atty. Wells of Dallas is President of the organization here and a negro woman, by the name of Shaw is the secretary," he wrote, "and the Sunday meetings are held in a negro lodge hall on East Elm." He passed this information to Dallas authorities.

In August 1919, two high-ranking Rangers, W. M. Hanson—now a senior captain—and Major Walter Woodul, met with thirteen county sheriffs at the Rice Hotel in Houston. Again, the Rangers were not focused on the prevention of lynchings or the arrest of those who committed these crimes. Their concern, as one participant described it, was black citizens "saying they were going to get their rights." A typical entry in the official minutes was this advisory from the sheriff of Brazoria County, on the Gulf Coast: "Negroes are holding meetings in his county. There has been a yeller nigger woman organizer in his county." Another sheriff, this one from Waller County, reported that he had heard "negroes were going to demand social equality." He pledged to make a "thorough investigation."

This Houston conference did not occur as part of a rogue operation. The minutes of the meeting stated that it was held on the orders of Governor Hobby.

Such actions and attitudes brought the NAACP's chief executive, John R. Shillady, from New York to Austin in 1919 to confer with state officials. The governor would not meet with him. Instead, Shillady spoke with Assistant Adjutant General W. D. Cope, number-two commander of the Rangers. Cope told him that the Rangers' investigations of black groups would continue. Shillady, no doubt sensing hostility to his presence in Austin, asked Cope for protection by the Rangers. The assistant adjutant general refused.

That afternoon, Shillady was seized and hauled before a secret impromptu "court of inquiry" convened by Austin's county judge, Dave J. Pickle. During the proceedings, the county's attorney had a number of questions for Shillady, who was white. Among them: "If you're such a nigger lover, why don't you go and stay in a nigger hotel?"

The judge released Shillady, who spent the night at the Driskill Hotel, Austin's best. The next day, Judge Pickle, accompanied by a constable and several other men, accosted Shillady on the sidewalk in front of the Driskill. They asked again why he was inciting blacks in Texas and "stirring up trouble." Shillady responded: "You don't see my point of view."

The constable—who would later serve as a Texas Ranger—said, "I'll fix you so you can't see." He punched Shillady in the eye, and the others joined in the beating. They left Shillady crumpled on the sidewalk, bleeding badly. The NAACP chief was not the only one hurt in the attack. "Judge Pickle's right hand was badly sprained," a newspaper reported, "as a result of blows rained by him upon Shillady's face." Shillady left town that day on a train for St. Louis. He never recovered physically or mentally from the beating and resigned his NAACP post soon thereafter.

About a week after the attack, Governor Hobby addressed Shillady's treatment at the hands of public officials. "I believe in Texas for Texans only," the governor said in a speech. "I believe in sending any narrow-brained, double-chinned reformer who comes here with the end in view of stirring up racial discontent back to the North where he came from, with a broken jaw if necessary."

The attackers were never prosecuted or disciplined, and Hobby suffered only mild rebuke for his comments. The *Dallas Morning News*, for example, called his language "plug-ugly" and said he did not speak for the people of Texas, a dubious assertion.

By 1922, however, the state had a new governor, Pat Neff, and perhaps a new outlook toward mob rule. The year before, across the Red River in Oklahoma, white rioters looted, burned, and murdered their way through the African American Greenwood district in Tulsa. As many as three hundred people, almost all of them black, may have died in the rampage. One year later, back in

Texas, several hundred white men marched through the oil town of Brecken-
ridge, demanding that all blacks and Mexican Americans be forced to leave the
county. Neff sent Hamer and three other Rangers to keep the peace. "I will positively handle the situation, protecting every citizen, regardless of race or color,"
Hamer announced. And this time it worked. Tempers cooled within a few days,
and the Rangers were able to withdraw.

The number of lynchings in Texas dropped in the ensuing years, which gave
hope that the darkest days had passed. Then a black man was accused of assaulting a white woman in the North Texas city of Sherman. Again Hamer arrived to
handle it.

Named for a hero of the Texas Revolution, Sherman was a farm and railroad
town on the rolling prairie south of the Red River. About fifteen thousand people
lived there. It was the seat of Grayson County and liked to call itself the "Athens
of Texas" because it had three small colleges and a city library.

The city faced the usual array of racial problems endemic to the time and
place. Klan meetings in the area sometimes drew as many as four thousand
participants. However, Sherman also boasted a small but thriving black merchant and professional class. Whites and blacks lived separately but, in general,
peacefully.

All that changed on a spring day in 1930 when a forty-one-year-old farmworker named George Hughes was arrested. The news of it flashed through town
as the Sherman newspaper ran a banner headline on the front page: "NEGRO
HELD FOR ASSAULT NEAR LUELLA." The victim, as the newspaper informed, was
a white woman.

Hughes had gone to his employer's house, five miles east of Sherman, seeking his pay. The man wasn't home, but his wife was. She said Hughes bound her
wrists with electrical cord and sexually assaulted her. When deputies tried to
arrest him, Hughes fired a shotgun in their direction. They eventually disarmed
and jailed him. Authorities said he confessed to the crime.

On a Monday, two days after his arrest, Hughes was indicted for assault and
attempted murder. The trial was set for the following Friday, May 9—the earliest
possible date under Texas law. It had all the hallmarks of an open-and-shut case.
Few doubted that Hughes would be convicted and sentenced to prison.

But the community was growing restive. On Tuesday, a group of white teenagers appeared at the jail and demanded to see Hughes. Someone broke a

window. A few of them dragged an old telephone pole to the street with threats to use it as a battering ram. Around one in the morning, the sheriff escorted five of the teens through the jail to show that Hughes was not in the building. He was being held in an adjacent county.

This defused the situation for a few hours, but another crowd of young men came to the jail on Wednesday, again demanding the appearance of Hughes. No violence had occurred—unless one counted the trampling of the sheriff's wife's flowers outside the jail—but local officials worried that bigger trouble could erupt when the trial began. They asked for help, and Governor Dan Moody responded. On the afternoon of Wednesday, May 7, Hamer and three other Rangers left Austin on a train for Sherman. The next day, Hughes was escorted to the courthouse and arraigned without incident.

Trial day, Friday, brought the big crowds. The two-lane farm roads leading to Sherman were bumper-to-bumper with old Model T Fords. Hundreds of people, many of them men in faded bib overalls and sweat-stained hats, gathered outside the courthouse.

As with other county seats in Texas, the Sherman courthouse had been built on a square block at the center of town. Four streets named for the greatest heroes of early Texas, including Davy Crockett and Sam Houston, defined the square. A small lawn, with oak and pecan trees, surrounded the two-story stone building. Early that morning, in the mild spring sunshine, two Rangers and the sheriff walked Hughes, his hands and feet in chains, the two blocks from the jail to the courthouse. The Rangers carried shotguns.

Court convened at 9:30 a.m., and by noon a jury had been chosen. Men and women pressed into the hallways and stairwells leading to the second-floor courtroom. The mood of the crowd loomed angry and tense. Yet officials were not overly worried, for—as United Press put it—"the negro was guarded by the redoubtable Captain Frank Hamer, two-fisted, two gun Texas Ranger who is known as the official 'mob buster' of the state."

The first of the prosecution witnesses took the stand about 12:30 p.m. Defendant Hughes seemed uninterested in the proceedings, staring vacantly at the floor with his elbows on his knees. The crowd outside the courthouse stayed calm until an ambulance rolled up. The ambulance's back doors swung, and the woman who had accused Hughes of assaulting her was brought out, lying on a stretcher. The sight of her excited the spectators, and some hurled rocks at the courthouse windows. A few women onlookers began to taunt men in the vicinity, accusing them of cowardice.

The mass of people surged forward. "It was while the first State witness was on the stand testifying," Hamer wrote, "that the crowd made a rush on the District Court room to get the prisoner." They broke down a set of double doors leading to a hallway outside the courtroom.

The judge recessed the court. Hughes was taken to a steel-and-concrete walk-in vault on the second floor, used for storing county records, and locked inside for his protection. The mob, one reporter wrote, "was clamoring for the negro." The Rangers hurled tear gas canisters. Gas filled the stairwell, and the agitators, as Hamer called them, retreated. "The crowd made two other attempts to rush the court room," Hamer said, "and was beaten back each time."

Hamer told his men that if the mob assailed the courtroom again, he would fire on them. "In a few minutes the mob attempted to rush the court room again, coming up the stairways," Hamer said, "and I fired a shotgun loaded with buckshot, wounding two men. . . . This stopped the mob."

Now a rumor swept the crowd that Governor Moody had instructed the Rangers not to harm anyone further. That proved to be untrue, but the report emboldened the mob. One of the men walked to the foot of the stairway and demanded that the Rangers give up the prisoner. Hamer refused. "Well, we are coming up and get him," the man said. Hamer replied: "Any time you feel lucky, come on. But when you start up the stairway once more, there is going to be many funerals in Sherman."

For about half an hour, the crowd turned quiet. Hamer was confident the budding riot had been contained. "When I fired on the crowd in their last attempt to rush the courtroom," he wrote, "we had them Whipped off and they could not have taken the prisoner from us in any way."

Unless they burned the place down.

It was about 2:30 in the afternoon that a woman threw a rock through the window of the tax collector's office on the first floor, breaking the glass. Two young men hoisted a five-gallon can and poured gasoline into the office. Someone tossed in a lighted match, and there was a flash of flame. A cheer went up.

The fire department arrived within minutes, but vandals rendered them instantly useless: "One large man," a reporter observed, "walked around with a long-bladed knife in his hand and cut hose after hose." The firemen watched helplessly as the courthouse burned.

The blaze raged across the first floor. "Then all at once," Hamer said, "the flames from the lower story of the courthouse swept up the stairways and on up to the ceilings." The judge and court clerks escaped from second-floor windows via fire department ladders. The Rangers followed them down, having "barely escaped the burning building," Hamer said.

Only one person was left in the courthouse now: Hughes, who remained locked in the vault. Nearly the entire building was in flames. The heat drove the crowd on the courthouse lawn backward but seemed only to increase its fervor. Hamer and his men faced a mass of rage. Civil order had collapsed.

It was one riot, four Rangers.

"We stood around a few minutes," Hamer said. Then—to the bafflement of some onlookers and the delight of others—Hamer and the other Rangers got into a borrowed car and drove away. "Bidding good-bye to the mob," one newspaper reported, they "left the city, going toward Dallas."

Hamer later explained that the Rangers departed Sherman because he needed to speak with Governor Moody. "I thought it necessary for me to communicate with you, as I heard the troops were on the their way," Hamer wrote in a letter to the governor. "Not caring to discuss this with you from Sherman, we were talking to a man and I asked him if he had a car."

The man with the car drove the Rangers to the small farming town of Howe, about ten miles south of Sherman. There, Hamer phoned the governor's office. But while waiting for the connection, he said, "I heard the operator say to someone over the phone, 'I am glad they burned the courthouse.'"

Hamer decided he and the governor should not talk with this particular operator listening in. The Rangers went for another drive, this time to the town of McKinney, an additional twenty miles south. That is where, Hamer said, they "waited for further communication."

As Hamer and his crew stood down, Governor Moody was scrambling to find other Rangers. He finally located Sergeant Manuel "Lone Wolf" Gonzaullas in Dallas. The governor ordered Gonzaullas to drive to Sherman and keep the rioters from seizing any other prisoners now held in the county jail. By Gonzaullas's account, he set up a one-man guard post outside the jail, wearing a white hat while armed with two pistols, a sawed-off shotgun, and a Thompson submachine gun. When some of the mob approached him, he said, he fired buckshot over their heads. Soon, several more Rangers arrived to help.

The governor also dispatched units of the Texas National Guard, who arrived in Sherman by late afternoon. They marched through the downtown streets with fixed bayonets. Young boys followed the guardsmen, tripping them. Some in the crowd threw rocks and bottles. Several of the guardsmen were seriously hurt.

After sundown, the situation seemed to calm. But another rumor took hold, that Hughes had escaped, or the guardsmen had rescued him. Around midnight, more than one thousand people crowded onto the town square. The courthouse fire had finally burned itself out, with the building a deserted, smoking ruin.

Some of the mob climbed the charred stairs to the vault that had held Hughes. The steel door to it was locked. A man carried in an acetylene torch and used it to cut away part of the outer shell of the vault. A stick of dynamite, placed there and detonated, blew a hole into the chamber.

Two blocks away, Rangers still guarded the county jail. None of them went to the courthouse in response to the explosions.

When the smoke from the blast cleared, someone with a flashlight crawled into the vault and shouted, "Here he is." They found Hughes unconscious, probably dead. He may have suffocated. He also had suffered a massive head wound, most likely from the explosion's shrapnel.

Men dragged his body to a second-floor window and pushed it out. It rolled down a ladder and hit the ground with a thud, near the county's soaring Confederate monument. "Women screamed and clapped their hands," the Associated Press reported, "and a great cheer went up from the mob."

Hughes's body was chained to a car. Local police directed traffic while the mob marched along with the body as it bumped over rough pavement at the end of the chain. The car dragged Hughes several blocks down Crockett Street to the black section of town. "There were two pregnant ladies, so big you'd have thought they were about to have those babies right then," a witness said. "They were right behind where they were dragging him. They were hopping up and down and squealing and laughing. The whole street was full of people."

The body was strung from a cottonwood tree. One man with a knife severed Hughes's penis and stuffed it in the dead man's mouth. Some from the crowd piled boxes beneath the body and started a bonfire. The body of Hughes was roasted. "A brilliant Texas moon," the Associated Press said, "added its rays to the gruesome sight."

Mulberry Street, where this scene occurred, was the center of black commerce in Sherman. It had a movie house, a funeral home, a barbershop, a drugstore, and a hotel. A dressmaker's shop was next to a tailor's. A grocery store stood near a doctor's office and a restaurant. Now men with axes and guns broke into them and looted them, and most were set on fire. The mob destroyed or heavily damaged them all.

Once the crowd had tired of lynching and pillaging and had gone home, guardsmen cut Hughes's body from its chain. The black funeral homes had been destroyed, so a white undertaker was persuaded to take the body. It was placed in a cheap wood coffin and buried in an unmarked grave at the county farm.

By late Saturday the town was quiet. Nearly all the black people who lived and worked there had fled. Some hid in thickets, some in sewers, while others found refuge in darkened hog pens. Sympathetic whites gave shelter to a number of them. Those families who owned cars were able to escape the county.

Now their neighborhood was silent. "There was not a Negro in sight Saturday," a Dallas newspaperman wrote. "They have gone from Sherman."

By Sunday, Hamer and his original company of Rangers were themselves back in town. Some officials wondered aloud if they had done all they could have to prevent the riot. "I asked Adjutant General Robertson why he had not sent more men, as these situations are always full of dynamite," Ranger captain Sterling said. "He replied, 'They only asked for four.'"

Hamer placed the blame on three factors: the number of women and children in the crowd, which made enforcement difficult; the false rumor that the governor had ordered that no rioter be harmed; and the fire itself. "We never dreamed of the gang doing that until the building was enveloped in flames," he wrote.

The Rangers began jailing men who had led the riot. Ultimately, forty-three people were arrested and fourteen indicted. Governor Moody vowed that "every power of the state" would be employed to "punish the persons responsible." But only one of them, J. B. "Screw" McCasland, was convicted. He got two years in prison for arson and 180 days for a separate charge of chicken theft. None of the others even came to trial.

On the whole, the Rangers' performance in Sherman did little to dim their aura in the state itself. Many editorials in Texas newspapers said that Hamer and his crew had performed their best under difficult circumstances. Some even blamed the lynched man for inciting the riot. "He doubly deserved every pain he endured, every twinge of torture that convulsed his beastly frame," said the *Saint Jo Tribune*. "Even Dante's Inferno does not suggest an adequate punishment for such a beast." A writer for the *Albany News*, a West Texas journal, said the cause of riot was easily understood: "A brute in human form laid his black hands upon white flesh," causing otherwise fine citizens to go "on a rampage with torch and gun and club."

Only a few public voices were impolitic enough to mention the sudden departure of Hamer and his crew, though the *Wichita Falls Times* used it to pronounce the death of the one-riot, one-Ranger canard: "Not just one ranger, but several, constituted the force at Sherman and proved all but helpless against the mob. The stock of the rangers has taken a terrific tumble, as a result." The Rangers' national reputation, the newspaper concluded, "has been badly fractured, if not shattered."

Many non-Texans saw the riot as a terrible display of savagery. The London *Evening Standard* claimed to have interviewed Governor Moody by "Ocean Phone" and offered this quotation from the governor on race relations in the state: "Waal, it's our law here in Texas that if a black man even leads a lil' white girl by the hand, he's lynched—if the Guard don't get there in time to stop it." As to why the Rangers and National Guardsmen did not use their guns to prevent the lynching, the governor, according to the *Standard*, said, "I ain't allowin' them . . . boys to start pullin' their guns on a mob of men and women just on account of a nigger."

This registered high on the galoot scale, even in Texas. To counter criticism, Moody directed one Ranger, Captain Tom Hickman, to England. Hickman sailed on the steamship *Leviathan*, accompanied by the Simmons University Cowboy Band, from Abilene, Texas. Hickman's mission: to "set Londoners right on the lynching at Sherman." British papers had printed some salacious details, such as allegations that some flowers of Texas womanhood had tossed fuel onto the fire that burned Hughes's corpse. "Capt. Hickman will assure London that nothing of that sort happened," an Associated Press story said, overlooking the fact that such reports were true.

Neither the riot nor the resultant fallout seemed to chasten Governor Moody, who paradoxically had made his early reputation as a KKK-busting prosecutor. In a strange and ill-timed outburst only six months after Sherman, he announced his personal remedy for a string of gangland slayings making headlines in Chicago: send the Texas Rangers to Illinois.

"In Texas we respect the law and authority," Moody said without a trace of irony. "If we had Chicago in Texas . . . the crime wave would have been broken and the gangsters prosecuted." Moody did not, of course, make any reference to Sherman. The governor also failed to note that gangsters controlled gambling and bootlegging establishments in many Texas cities, and the Rangers had been unable to slow them, let alone stop them.

While the governor displayed his arrogance, the Rangers drew some lessons from Sherman. "You learn every time you get kicked," Ranger Gonzaullas said. Several months later they used a combination of subterfuge and a display of weaponry to keep a black defendant from being lynched in the West Texas town of Shamrock. "The Rangers brought with them," one press account noted, "two machine guns, 10,000 rounds of ammunition, 100 gas hand grenades . . . rifles, shotguns and pistols. The machine guns will shoot 800 bullets per minute."

In early 1931, about ten months after the Sherman riot, newly elected Governor Ross Sterling announced a new goal: a year without a lynching in Texas. The state did not record another one until April 1932, when four white men in Crockett seized a black tenant farmer accused of entering a white woman's bedroom uninvited. They hanged him from an oak tree.

Hamer soon turned to other matters. Monitoring a 1931 parade by Communists in Austin, he spotted marchers carrying signs that said *Equality for the Negro Masses*. He confiscated the signs on the spot. That same year, he warned of a Marxist plot to destroy oil facilities in Texas. "I have been receiving information that there is a movement on foot among Communists, or Reds, to dynamite all tank farms and pipelines throughout this state," he wrote in a letter to thirty-eight oil companies. The plot never materialized.

In 1934, after resigning from the Rangers, Hamer signed on as a "special escape investigator" for the Texas prison system. His assignment: stop Bonnie and Clyde, the notorious bank-robbing duo. Hamer led the ambush that killed them in Arcadia, Louisiana, which brought him worldwide fame.

The acclaim didn't change Hamer much. A few months later, he learned that a promoter who operated a traveling lecture on Bonnie and Clyde had included some erroneous information. Hamer decided to interrupt the show. "I slapped that guy clear across the room," he said, "and told him that if he ever showed those pictures again I would crawl on my knees to South America to kill him."

The ex-Ranger soon found another job, this one helping to break a 1935 longshoremen's strike in Houston. According to his family-authorized biography, Hamer single-handedly settled the matter by confronting an angry gang of "tough stevedores" who had formed a mob. "Hamer strode up to the largest man in the front ranks," the account said, "and with his open hand, knocked him senseless to the ground. 'I'm Frank Hamer,' he said. 'This strike is over!'"

In reality, Hamer supervised a private police force—often referred to as a "protection agency"—hired by steamship operators. He and his men made sure non-union workers could cross picket lines. The strike lasted two months and ended only after lengthy negotiations between the parties.

Hamer found other jobs preventing, controlling, and suppressing union activities on the waterfront. In 1939 he was charged with aggravated assault for beating and kicking a member of the Maritime Union on strike in Houston. He justified the attack by claiming without evidence that squads of Chicago gangsters had come to Texas to kill him. Hamer added, "There is not a man in Texas who has as much blood in his body as I have lost in trying to protect the public."

That same year, Hamer and forty-nine other retired Rangers offered their services to the king of England. They said they would defend the country against any invasion by Nazi Germany. This was before the U.S. entry into World War II, and the State Department quietly nixed the proposal.

The Sherman riot, in the years after its occurrence, received the usual historical whitewash. Walter Prescott Webb's massive 1935 history of the Rangers, for example, devoted a twenty-nine-page chapter to Hamer's exploits but made no mention of Sherman. A 1935 *San Antonio Light* story said Hamer and his Rangers "held a mob of 5,000 at bay nearly all day." As he had done with other Rangers, C. L. Douglas gave Hamer a hero's role in his 1934 book, *The Gentlemen in the White Hats*. "He stood on the steps of the courthouse and defied a mob of howling citizens who threatened to enter and take a negro prisoner," the author wrote of Hamer in Sherman. "The mob didn't try." More than two decades later, an Associated Press story repeated that version of events almost word for word.

When Hamer died in 1955, of a heart attack at age seventy-one, newspapers from coast to coast published his obituary. Most described Hamer as the Ranger captain who had killed Bonnie and Clyde—though he had not been a Ranger at the time—and few recalled Sherman. In 2003 the *Texas Ranger Dispatch*, the publication of the Ranger Museum, said Hamer "is the man that many believe to be the greatest Texas Ranger of the first half of the twentieth century." He was named a member of the Rangers Hall of Fame. His display in the Rangers museum in Waco highlights Bonnie and Clyde but says nothing of Sherman.

Today's visitors to the museum can find his biography, *I'm Frank Hamer*, on sale in the gift shop. It proclaims Hamer the "greatest Texas Ranger of all time." Museum visitors can purchase other commemorative items as well, including a special kitchen cutting board. This could be the perfect accessory, a museum catalog suggests, for a chef using *The Authorized Texas Ranger Cookbook*.

Four words are etched prominently into the cutting board's surface: ONE RIOT, ONE RANGER.

PART III

The Professionals

1931–

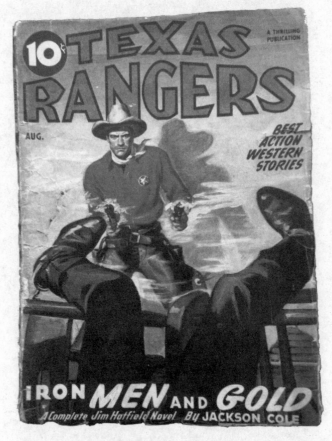

Pulp magazines like this depicted the Rangers as upright, honorable western men of action. But by the mid-1930s, the Rangers as an institution were near collapse.

Chapter 18

THE SINGING RANGER

A Badge for the Pea Curer

And so it is with the Ranger. When we see him at his daily task of maintaining law, restoring order, and promoting peace—even though his methods be vigorous—we see him in his proper setting, a man standing alone between a society and its enemies. . . . It has been his duty to meet the outlaw breed of three races, the Indian warrior, Mexican bandit, and American desperado, on the enemy's ground and deliver each safely within the jail door or the cemetery gate. It is here recorded that he has sent many patrons to both places.

—WALTER PRESCOTT WEBB

The blockbuster musical *Rio Rita* premiered in New York City on October 6, 1929, with the customary hoopla for a big-budget release. "The Earl Carroll Theater was the scene of one of those glittering movie openings last night," the *Brooklyn Daily Eagle* reported. The *Eagle* praised the film as a lavishly produced romance "whose dazzling costumes, resplendent settings and huge cast would invite the envy of an impresario less extravagant than the great Ziegfeld himself."

What's more, it featured a dashing, handsome Texas Ranger named Captain

Stewart. He wasn't a real Ranger, of course, but he was played by an actual Texan with a fine tenor, John Boles. This role had him chasing a Mexican bandit known as the Kinkajou and, en route, falling hard for Senorita Rita. The comeliness of Rita caused Captain Stewart to burst into song: *Down by the river Rio Grande, / On silver sand, that's where I found you, / And now my heart's at your command.*

A number of other fictional Rangers had graced the screen before the lovestruck captain came crooning. The legendary Tom Mix, for instance, appeared as a Ranger pursuing a kidnapper in the 1925 silent film *Riders of the Purple Sage*. But *Rio Rita* seemed to presage a great wave: over the next ten years, studios released at least fifty-nine films that featured the Rangers. They included *The Kid Ranger, The Unknown Ranger, The Dude Ranger,* and *The Gun Ranger.* During this time Hollywood also birthed *Whistling Bullets, Fast Bullets,* and *Galloping Dynamite,* all with fictional Rangers. Johnny Mack Brown played a Ranger in the 1931 cowboy love story *Lasca of the Rio Grande.* (Lasca was apparently as lovely as Rita.) Hoot Gibson had his turn in *Trigger Tricks.* And there was *The Sagebrush Troubador,* from Republic Pictures in 1935, starring Gene Autry as a singing Ranger named Gene Autry.

One of the greatest storybook Rangers, the Lone Ranger, made his radio debut in 1933 on WXYZ in Detroit. The Masked Man owned a compelling backstory and a natural nom de guerre: he was the sole survivor of a criminal ambush that killed five others. His faithful Indian companion, Tonto, explained it as only Tonto could: "Other Texas Rangers all dead. You only Ranger left. You lone Ranger now."

As the country fell into the Great Depression, audiences seemed especially eager for adventurous stories that pitted criminals against police and federal agents. In the case of hugely popular westerns, Indians and black-hatted gunslingers served as antagonists. To defeat them, hundreds of white-hatted, crime-busting cowboys stampeded the nation's movie houses and vacuum tube radios.

Like cinematic G-men gunning down gangsters, the Rangers of the Bijou offered both escapism and reassurance. Depictions of catastrophic race riots or the sanctioned massacres of unarmed villagers did not spoil the view. The public found delight in tales of Rangers who fought tirelessly for right, who never wavered from their duty, and who prevailed with honor—and perhaps a catchy tune. Almost none was based on actual Rangers or real events, or drew from the messy lessons of history. In general, the tales were uncomplicated, the characters flat, the motives pure, the Rangers heroic.

The great irony was that after enduring some of their most difficult decades, the Rangers had fallen into turmoil. Their ranks seethed with corruption and political patronage, and their foundation rotted toward collapse. As their popularity soared, the Rangers faced a hard choice: change or die.

Only a few years earlier, a Texas judge went so far as to declare the Rangers unconstitutional. Prohibition remained the law of the land then, and the Rangers spent much of their time and energy chasing the merchants of vice. This did not endear them to the state's more libertine pockets, in cities such as San Antonio. There the Rangers' efforts—aimed at arresting "the thief, the gambler, the bootlegger, the drug addict, and the street woman"—had been aggressive. A state district judge in San Antonio found in 1925 that Ranger activities violated the Texas constitution and ordered them to cease at once.

An appeals court set aside the lower court's injunction and dismissed the case. But in the process, Chief Justice W. S. Fly of the state's Fourth Court of Civil Appeals castigated the Rangers for their "tyrannous" pursuit of petty offenders. They had, he said in a ruling, descended upon "unoffending communities to establish a system of espionage on . . . citizens and spend their time in arresting crap throwers [and] chicken fighters."

There were subsequent challenges to the Rangers, but none so dire as the governors Ferguson. Known throughout Texas as Ma and Pa, James and Miriam Ferguson were a married couple for whom the oft-used journalistic adjective *colorful* never quite sufficed. James, the son of a farmer, became a lawyer after little or no formal study. The chairman of the bar exam committee was a friend of his father's. He was elected governor in 1914 and reelected in 1916 but was impeached and removed from office for misapplication of public funds. With Pa's political career in ruins, Ma ran for governor in 1924 and won. The first female chief executive of Texas, she had never held office before. Her two-year term was marked by repeated allegations of corruption—she was accused of, among other offenses, selling convict pardons—and she lost her race for reelection.

She ran again in 1932, against Governor Ross Sterling. Many, if not most, of the Rangers openly supported Sterling, an oilman and banker. Mrs. Ferguson "was simply a figurehead . . . and a rubber stamp for her husband," said then Adjutant General W. W. Sterling (no relation to the governor). "His leaning was always toward the criminal element." Yet Ma won, in part by cranking up her

base—rural voters whom the adjutant general dismissed as snuff-dipping yokels—
with revelations that the incumbent owned a mansion with thirty bathrooms.
(In truth, it had only fifteen.)

Once elected, Mrs. Ferguson wasted no time in exacting revenge. She dismissed the entire force of forty-four Rangers, effective on her inauguration day,
and replaced them with an abundance of cronies and hacks. The state legislature
piled on: it reduced the force to thirty-two men and cut pay, slashing the Ranger
budget by 45 percent.

This gutting of the Rangers came at an unfortunate time. As the Depression
wore on, name-brand criminals landed starring roles in the nation's headlines
and newsreels: Pretty Boy Floyd, John Dillinger, Ma Barker, Baby Face Nelson.
Texas had its own lawbreakers who inspired perverse wonderment, most notably
Bonnie and Clyde and their occasional confederate, a young gunsel named Ray-
mond Hamilton. Like many Texas criminals, Hamilton had crawled from the
typhoidal slums of West Dallas. He was serving a combined sentence of 263
years for murder and bank robbery when he broke out of a Texas prison in 1934.
During the escape a guard was killed. Adjutant General Henry Hutchings ordered two Ranger companies to join the statewide fugitive search.

The Rangers of the nineteenth century had tracked their human prey on
horseback and on foot with relentlessness and skill. The agency failed to adapt,
however, to some of the modern world's technologies. Rangers now drove their
personal cars, which tended to be cheap and slow, while nouveau riche bank
robbers favored swift V8s.

This was on raw display when, a few weeks after Hamilton's prison escape,
two Rangers thought they spotted him near Blanco in the Texas Hill Country.
They chased his Ford sedan and forced it to the side of the road in front of a café.
As diners watched, the Rangers approached the escapee with six-shooters drawn
and acclaim in the offing: Hamilton's arrest would be a rare triumph for Ma
Ferguson's men. But Hamilton drove away in a spray of gravel and bullets. "They
emptied their pistols at his [car] as it sped off, but without effect," an Associated
Press story said. "Hamilton answered with a burst of machine gun fire." The
Rangers gave chase again but couldn't keep up with the lead-foot desperado.

Highway roadblocks erected by local law enforcement also failed to net the
fugitive. He probably evaded them on one of the many dirt roads that wound
through the region's lightly populated, cedar-choked hills—territory where,
ninety years earlier, Jack Hays had fought the Comanches. Aircraft might have

helped in the search, but the Rangers had access to none. They did manage to nab two other bank robbers, a man and his wife, the next day. The couple carried a German Luger and had stuffed more than $8,000 in hot cash under their clothes. The additional arrest of a suspicious-looking woman driving a new car appeared promising at first, but she turned out to be a mentalist and palm reader en route to an Austin radio station, and the Rangers set her free. Hamilton, alas, had disappeared. He was next seen about three weeks later, 470 miles to the north, robbing a bank in the Panhandle town of Pampa.

Occasional Wild West shootouts on the highway captured the public imagination, but the real crime problem was low-voltage vice that pervaded the state. Dozens of gambling dens in Dallas and Fort Worth operated as open secrets in the early 1930s, so long as the racketeers paid off the local authorities. On Galveston Island, historically a haven for pirates and slavers, a couple of Italian immigrants ruled a kingdom of speakeasies. Salvatore and Rosario Maceo—otherwise known as Sam and Rose—were barbers who peddled bootleg liquor. They got into the nightclub business in 1926. Soon their syndicate controlled the town with dinner clubs, gambling joints, and a company called Gulf Vending, which placed slot machines in almost every bar, café, barbershop, and betting parlor. The island became known as the "Free State of Galveston," and the Rangers of the 1930s wouldn't and couldn't touch it. Other than gambling and bootlegging, Galveston was generally safe and clean. A squad of Maceo vigilantes known as Rose's Night Riders saw to that.

A Texas Senate committee sent its investigators across the state to look for lawbreaking, and they encountered no shortage. "There has existed for some time in Texas a great wave of lawlessness," a Senate resolution said, "such as kidnapping, bank robberies, hi-jacking, gang murders and . . . all forms of gambling, sale and transportation of intoxicating liquors, vice, and various and sundry forms of other crimes."

Over the course of five years, the committee determined, more than four thousand indictments had been returned for murder in Texas. But about half of those charged were either acquitted or given suspended sentences, or had their cases dismissed. "We have in this state too many killings and too few convictions," the 1935 Senate report said. "Human life is cheap. Men are slain in this alleged Christian land for less silver than led Judas to betray his Christ."

While the committee praised the Rangers in principle, it found serious corruption within the agency. A law enforcement officer "of unquestioned integrity," as the committee report described him, told the senators that a Ranger offered him $5,000 to allow a gambling house to operate. Another committee witness testified, "Our Rangers are selling liquor personally and openly."

The report said a Ranger captain "permitted the operation of gambling houses, saloons, houses of prostitution, and other illegal activities." He also took bribes from the proprietors and a percentage of their revenue. Though the Senate committee did not name him, the captain was James Robbins, who led Company D in the South Texas town of Falfurrias. Ma Ferguson had appointed Robbins to his captaincy after a recommendation by a state senator to whom Robbins paid a $3,200 bribe. At one point Robbins and his Rangers raided two gambling clubs and forced the owner to leave town. Robbins then operated the clubs himself. When a local rancher asked for help in catching rustlers, Robbins refused because he didn't have a Ranger who could ride a horse. Robbins was convicted of embezzlement and sent to prison for eight years.

As bad as some Rangers might be, the men commissioned as Special Rangers often were worse. They were not paid as Rangers, but they carried a badge—and a gun if they wished—and had the power of arrest. These commissions were originally intended for investigators who chased rustlers for cattle raisers. But Ma Ferguson used them to repay political debts, reward supporters, and curry favor with big shots. Her Special Rangers included Elliott Roosevelt, the son of the sitting president, and singer Kate Smith, the "first lady of radio." Tom Mix got a badge too, as did Frank and Leon Weaver, who appeared on vaudeville as musical Ozark hillbillies. Needless to say, none played the slightest role in fighting Texas crime.

The Senate committee compiled a list of 1,620 Special Rangers appointed by Mrs. Ferguson. "For what purpose all these commissions were issued is not apparent from the record," its report said. Among Special Rangers' actual occupations were undertaker, painter, oil mill operator, cook, dentist, barber, X-ray technician, and locomotive engineer. Also, retail liquor dealer, professional wrestler, and "curer of peas."

The report added that Special Rangers were working "as bouncers in night clubs, as officers in gambling houses, as traffic officers and guards at horse and dog tracks." One was a bag man for bribes. Some set up speed traps with "roadside courts" that would extort cash from out-of-state motorists. Still another took it upon himself to destroy illegal slot machines—but only those operated by the rivals to his employer, who ran his own gambling den. In general, the committee concluded, Ma Ferguson had created "a class of gun-toters who may become a menace to law-abiding citizens."

The storied agency had hit bottom, and its demise was widely predicted. It began to recover when James Allred, a crusading attorney general, was elected governor in 1934. Allred vowed to reform and rebuild the Rangers. He decommissioned the Special Rangers and discharged most of the force appointed by Ferguson. Allred also pushed through sweeping legislation that created the Texas Department of Public Safety (DPS), which absorbed the Rangers.

The Rangers had enjoyed a century of independence, but now the state's bureaucracy had them in its grip. No longer would they be the governor's private police force, although the chief executive could still dispatch them to trouble spots. But they would officially answer to a three-member public safety commission appointed by the governor.

For the first time, new Rangers had to meet strict qualifications. They had to be between thirty and forty-five when appointed, stand at least five feet, eight inches, and be possessed of mental and physical soundness. They also received training in criminal investigation and evidence analysis—a first. "Work of the Rangers is not what it was in the old days," said Homer Garrison Jr., assistant director of the department. "Then the Rangers caught criminals and stamped out bad men generally because they had the best horses and were the best shots. Now they must be scientific. That's why they are going to school."

In 1938, Garrison was named director of the public safety department, a position he held for the next thirty years. Garrison, who had been a deputy sheriff and an inspector for the state highway department, protected the Rangers' independence and insisted on enhanced training and better equipment. "Every patrolman and Ranger I knew worshiped Homer Garrison," wrote Ranger Joaquin Jackson. He was "the man most responsible for modernizing the department and salvaging the Texas Rangers."

While the governor and the legislature were remaking the agency, the Rangers enjoyed a public relations boost. Historian Walter Prescott Webb's book of nearly 600 pages, *The Texas Rangers: A Century of Frontier Defense*, was published in 1935. A professor at the University of Texas at Austin, Webb had labored over the book for seventeen years. It was the first comprehensive history of the agency, and the Rangers could not have asked for a more favorable treatment.

A Texan, journalist Stanley Walker, reviewed the book for the *New York Times*. It was "a bit on the patriotic side, perhaps," Walker wrote, "but far and away the best work of its sort ever to come out of Texas." Texas's resident man of letters, J. Frank Dobie, called it "the beginning, middle, and end of the subject."

Webb did write about Rangers' misdeeds in the Rio Grande border war. "Some of the Rangers were good and efficient," he concluded, "but some were totally unfitted for the service." But with few other exceptions, his Rangers were valorous, intelligent, skilled, and absolutely dedicated to duty. Webb's research was both wide and deep, but his depiction of the Rangers over the course of a century was broadly heroic. He sugarcoated the massacre at Porvenir, for instance, and papered over the atrocities of the Mexican War. The professor did not obscure his racial views. White Texas pioneers were "intelligent, cool [and] calculating." The typical Mexican, however, was cruel, superstitious, ignorant, and dishonest. "For making promises—and breaking them—he had no peer," Webb wrote.

Next came the movie. Webb sold the film rights for his Rangers history to Paramount Productions for $11,000. Directed by King Vidor, who was born and reared in Texas, *The Texas Rangers* was—despite being the nominal offspring of Webb's book—a work of pure fiction. It was also filmed mostly in New Mexico. The picture starred Fred MacMurray and Jack Oakie as two outlaws who reform themselves and join the force. They then fight Indians, save an orphan, and do their part for honest government.

The film premiered in Dallas on August 21, 1936, during the state's centennial celebration, when Texas marked the hundredth anniversary of its independence from Mexico. The *Dallas Morning News* found it fitting that the Rangers should be so honored during the centennial, despite their recent problems. "Their record has brought glory not only to the Rangers themselves but to all of Texas," the newspaper said in an editorial. "If they have faltered a few times, it has been because they are human."

After the Texas premier, *The Texas Rangers* went into nationwide release, giving the country yet another taste of celluloid Ranger heroism. "It stopped just short," film historian Don Graham later observed, "of declaring their sainthood." A review in the *Boston Globe* said the movie was one of the most "thoroughly spine-chilling adventure films ever brought out." The Beantown rave continued: "There certainly was never a more breathless moment than that in which Fred MacMurray single-handed quells the three savages who are hurling enormous rocks down the mountainside to bounce upon the heads of the beleaguered Rangers." Other critics, writing from cities that had never seen a Ranger, praised it as well. The New York *Daily News* called it a "vivid, virile" movie that showed how the real Rangers had freed Texas from "hostile Indians, cattle rustlers and civic corruption." And the reviewer for the Appleton, Wisconsin, newspaper pronounced it a "historically accurate" production that "outlines the work of the band of fearless men who brought order to the Lone Star State."

For all his praise of the Rangers, historian Webb believed the force would not survive its absorption into DPS. Their role, he lamented, would "gradually slip away" in a "practical abolition of the force."

Webb was not alone. With modernization—by the late 1930s, for instance, the Rangers were patrolling the Mexican border in airplanes—many others worried that they would disappear. But Dallas newspaperman Felix McKnight foresaw a qualified immortality. "The Texas Rangers, perhaps the best known peace officers in the world, will never die," he wrote in 1941. "Not while there's a Texas."

McKnight was right. The idea held—part truth and part purest fantasy, with a vaporous line between them. Hollywood seemed to agree and kept pumping out Ranger-related movies well into the next decade. One was a 1942 remake of *Rio Rita*. It starred the comic duo Bud Abbott and Lou Costello and involved their efforts to thwart evil Nazi spies in Mexico. Chaos and hilarity ensued. In the end, naturally, the Rangers rode to the rescue.

Ranger Jay Banks saw no need to remove the effigy of a black student hanging from the entrance to a high school. "They were just salt-of-the-earth citizens who had been stirred up by agitators," Banks said of white citizens who opposed integration.

Chapter 19

"WHAT GOD HAS MADE"

Upholding the Will of the Mob

I don't think it would be safe for any colored person to go near that school.

—NAACP LAWYER L. CLIFFORD DAVIS, MANSFIELD, TEXAS, 1956

It's a classic cowboy pose: the Texas Ranger leaning against an oak tree, one leg cocked, with a polished western boot on display. He has pushed his Stetson back at an angle suggesting relaxation, and he has casually hooked his thumbs in his belt, but his holstered pistol stands at the ready. In a photograph of this moment, he looks calm yet vigilant.

To the Ranger's left, the Mansfield, Texas, high school looms. Nine or ten students have gathered near the main entrance of the building. They are white. Above them, someone has suspended a figure—a dummy, made of straw. It depicts a black person hanging by a noose. Both the Ranger and the effigy serve the same purpose on this hot, sunny day. They are there as a warning.

The placid farm and ranch town of Mansfield found itself convulsed by racial matters in the late summer of 1956. Black residents, led by the NAACP and backed by federal courts, attempted to integrate its high school. White mobs formed to stop them. As threats of violence rose, the governor of Texas ordered the Rangers to Mansfield.

Similar confrontations erupted elsewhere in America about the same time. State police in a Kentucky town had to escort black students into a white school. In Tennessee, National Guardsmen kept enraged white protesters at bay while black students enrolled. Later, federal marshals did the same—at the risk of serious injury and death—at the University of Mississippi.

Unlike them, the Texas Rangers did not part a sea of angry white supremacists so black pupils could go to school. They did not shield frightened teenagers who carried their books past howling, spitting men. Nor did they confront gun-toting rioters to ensure racial justice.

The Rangers had a different mission in 1956. Their job was to keep black children out.

The civil rights struggle in Texas of the 1950s ran a course of fear, heartbreak, tragedy, and injustice. The old ways of the Old South did not die easily. The story of the Rangers in this period may best be told through two of their most esteemed lawmen, Sergeant E. J. "Jay" Banks and Captain Bob Crowder.

Banks grew up on a small West Texas cotton farm. Crowder was a tall, laconic former Marine who had spent time as a motorcycle cop. Both were white. (No black man wore a Ranger badge until 1988.)

Crowder became known for his ability to obtain confessions. His tactic: keep the suspect awake and isolated from lawyers. "Then you go to work on him—talk, talk, talk," Crowder said. "Hell, I've sat up three days and nights talking [until] I'd get the best of him." In the mid-1950s, Crowder held the rank of Ranger captain and commanded Company B out of Dallas. Banks was his sergeant. Though neither had much affection for the other, both shared a sense that, as Rangers, they had climbed a great peak. "I wouldn't swap the job for the Presidency of the United States," Crowder said.

Company B's territory extended into East Texas, an insular red-dirt region of tenebrous forests, Southern temperament, and troubled race relations. It was there, near the city of Longview, that a white man named Perry Dean Ross, twenty-one, was drinking beer on October 22, 1955. He was so drunk that he was thrown out of Tatum's Tavern, one of his regular spots. Around midnight he grabbed his .22-caliber semiautomatic rifle and told a friend, Joe Simpson, "Let's go on a raid." Which, as he later explained, "was the name we used for shooting at Negroes." They had done it many times before.

With his friend, Ross drove an old Ford on dark, two-lane State Highway 149 toward the community of Mayflower, a place of sagging frame houses and tenant farmers' shacks set deep in the pines. Soon they reached the Hughes Café, a "colored" joint just off the highway. "I told Joe Simpson to hand me the rifle," Ross said. "He asked me what I was going to do and I said I was going to shoot the gun myself."

Inside the small tin-roofed café, music poured from the jukebox. A sixteen-year-old black boy was drinking soda and dancing. His name was John Earl Reese, and he had returned home after three weeks of picking cotton near Dallas. Some of his earnings had bought the new clothes now folded on his bed at his grandmother's house. He was in the tenth grade at Mayflower's colored school. The girl with whom he danced was his thirteen-year-old cousin, Joyce Fae Nelson. "We were children," she recalled, "doing nothing wrong."

From his car, Ross blazed away. "I held the steering wheel with my left hand and laid the gun across the left door," he said. "I was going 85 miles per hour at the time, and I fired nine shots in the front of the Hughes Café." The bullets tore through the door and windows. One of them struck John Reese in the head. His cousin remembered: "John Earl Reese fell on the floor out of my arms."

Ross and Simpson sped away and drank more beer. Ross went to work the next morning at a munitions plant, came home at five o'clock, and heard that a boy had been killed at Hughes Café. He felt no remorse, but he did have the presence of mind to tell his friend to get rid of the rifle. His friend threw it in the Sabine River.

The local sheriff, who showed little interest in pursuing a serious murder investigation, conjured a wide range of possible suspects. "It could be whites just as well as could be niggers," he said, adding that some locals believed that a Communist might have pulled the trigger. Because of the sheriff's reluctance and some jurisdictional questions, Rangers Crowder and Banks took over the case. They and others questioned more than three hundred people, and the Rangers succeeded in prying a detailed confession from Ross.

His subsequent indictment for murder was an anomaly in East Texas, where whites rarely faced prison time for killing blacks. The Rangers' performance delighted the state office of the NAACP. "A feeling of security has been re-established in the hearts of many Texans," the group's executive secretary wrote to the Texas Department of Public Safety. "People, rich and poor, great and small, feel reassured that they can live freely and without fear."

This cause for elation didn't last. At trial, Ross's father claimed that the Rangers had cut a deal to secure the confession. "They told me that . . . if [Ross] would tell everything he knew, they would do their best to help him get a suspended sentence," the father testified. "I thought they could do right smart." If true, the Rangers had committed a critical blunder, because a confession given after such a promise was inadmissible in court. Banks, questioned on the stand, said he did not remember making an agreement with Ross's family. Crowder testified no arrangement had been made in his presence. The judge admitted most of the confession, but the issue of leniency now stood before the court.

In his closing argument, Ross's lawyer had this advice for the all-white jury: "Call it a bad day and let the boy get on with his life." The panel apparently agreed. Ross was convicted of murder but sentenced to five years in prison, suspended. He walked from the courthouse a free man.

The daily newspapers in the region gave it scant attention, and the merchants of Ranger romance ignored it. The Reese murder faded into quick obscurity. Not so the incident that marked Crowder's career and set the tone for events to come: a bloody riot at the Rusk State Hospital.

The brick and steel hospital compound, in the dense woods of East Texas, was originally built as a prison. It had been converted by the state into an overcrowded, antiquated mental institution. In its maximum-security unit for the criminally insane, with barred cells and an electric fence, conditions ranged from primitive to punitive. Some patient-inmates slept on concrete floors. The miserly budget allowed for little in the way of therapy. Authorities controlled inmates with strong antipsychotic drugs, serial electroshock treatments, and the occasional frontal lobotomy. Numbed men spent their empty days on wooden benches lining the corridors. They would "just sit," one investigator observed, "like cigar-store Indians."

As was customary in Texas, the maximum-security unit had been officially, and rigidly, segregated by race. The white side may have been bleak, but the other side was worse. It was, by common description, a hellhole, a snake pit for the triple-cursed: black, felonious, and deranged. Sweltering in summer and freezing in winter, it stank of sweat and sewage, and had rancid food, few toilets, and no place for recreation. White attendants routinely addressed the inmates with racial slurs. Trustees known as floor bouncers clubbed misbehaving inmates with rubber hoses.

On April 16, 1955, some eighty inmates—described by one reporter as "crazed Negroes"—seized control of the unit. They were led by a towering, muscular inmate named Ben Riley, a paranoid schizophrenic who had, as a juvenile, killed a man in a dispute over money. The rioters overpowered two attendants and used ice picks and mop handles to attack the bouncers who had victimized them, critically injuring one. "His head was beaten to a pulp with a baseball bat," one account said. They also took the unit's physician and an assistant supervisor hostage. Some of the inmates—intent on direct revenge—tried to hook the physician up to the electroshock machine, but they couldn't make it work. Riley forced the doctor to phone the hospital's chief officer and lure him to the unit. He became a hostage as well.

Local police arrived, followed by state troopers. Though some of the hostages had been released, three remained. A standoff was now under way. Homer Garrison sent Captain Crowder from Dallas. Riley, the riot leader, had demanded to negotiate with a ranking government official, but he agreed that Crowder could act as a surrogate. Crowder was, after all, a Texas Ranger.

They spoke first by hospital phone. "I don't want no foolishness," Crowder said. He warned Riley that he would enter the unit with a .45 pistol on each hip. "I'm not coming in unarmed," he said, "because you've already got three people over there as hostages and I don't want to be the fourth one—and I'm not going to be. . . . I just want to tell you this. If something goes amiss, I know who's going to fall first."

Crowder strode into the maximum-security yard and met Riley on the steps of Ward 6. It made for an irresistible image—a singular brave lawman confronting violent lunatics who were, in the popular imagination, little better than rabid dogs. The newspapers couldn't resist it: "Captain Crowder, a big, impressive man . . . walked through the fence gate and up to the building held by the rioters." The notion of the lone heroic Ranger wasn't entirely accurate, though. From fifty yards away, highway patrolman and future Ranger Jim Ray watched it all through his rifle scope, keeping Riley in his crosshairs. "I had a sniper rifle trained on this person," Ray said decades later, "in case he tried to do anything."

Crowder and the shirtless Riley, who was armed with an ice pick and a knife, talked for about twenty minutes. The Ranger did not threaten Riley or try to cow him. Instead, he offered reasoning and the promise of help. If the rioters surrendered, Crowder told Riley, "I'll see that you get a hearing." He added: "I think you will get more consideration from [state officials] if you'll throw down your weapons and act like men."

The word of the Ranger was enough. With "perspiration gleaming on his chocolate-colored skin," the Associated Press reported, Riley "threw down the ice pick and a big knife from his belt." The other inmates also laid down their weapons and freed the hostages. The riot was over.

Crowder was hailed as a hero, a paragon of cool toughness under extreme duress. He had defused a potential disaster simply by promising the inmates they would receive a fair airing of their grievances. That, however, didn't happen. The executive director of the state hospital board hurried to Rusk, spent a few hours, and announced he found no basis for the inmates' complaints. Few changes were ordered, other than increased security. The maximum-security units remained segregated by race. For his role in leading the riot, Riley was thrown into twenty-four-hour solitary confinement, where hospital staff gave him extra doses of the powerful antipsychotic Thorazine and additional rounds of electroshock.

Any trust Riley and the others had put in Crowder's assurances proved to be misplaced. Crowder was not to blame, of course. He had merely served as a tool for higher authorities. He and the Rangers would play much the same role a year later, when the school integration movement bubbled up in Texas.

The landmark 1954 U.S. Supreme Court decision *Brown v. Board of Education* held that racial segregation in public schools, which had prevailed for decades under the spurious doctrine of separate but equal, violated the Constitution. In 1955 the Court ordered states to remedy this by integrating schools with all deliberate speed. Lawyers from the NAACP used *Brown* to bring lawsuits across the South on behalf of black schoolchildren. They filed one of them against the Mansfield, Texas, school district.

Mansfield had persevered as a nondescript prairie town of some 1,500 people, about 350 of them black. Age-old rules of race separation prevailed. A 1956 editorial in the *Mansfield News* explained the dominant white attitude of the day: "We are not against the Negro, but we are against social equality." White-owned farms grew cotton, and black sharecroppers worked the fields. At downtown cafés, blacks were required to enter at the rear and dine in separate rooms. Elementary students who were not white attended the Mansfield Colored School, which until 1954 did not have electricity or running water. As for secondary students, Mansfield did not even rise to the level of separate but equal. The town had built no high school for black students. They were bused twenty miles to a segregated high school in Fort Worth.

The Mansfield school case came at a time of great racial upheaval and transformation across the Deep South. In August 1955, white men in Money, Mississippi, tortured and murdered black teenager Emmett Till because they believed he flirted with a white woman. His mother insisted that the fourteen-year-old's mutilated body be displayed at an open-casket funeral to show the world the horror of his death. In December 1955, Rosa Parks refused to surrender her seat on a Montgomery, Alabama, city bus to a white man. The resulting bus boycott marked the emergence of Dr. Martin Luther King Jr. as a national figure.

In Texas, business and political leaders, including Governor Allan Shivers, voiced strong public opposition to the *Brown* decision. Many of them promoted the canard that blacks' struggle for civil rights was part of a Communist plot to weaken America. Shivers, a conservative Democrat, had established a relatively progressive record as governor, pushing for improved aid for the elderly and higher teacher salaries. He drew the line, however, at integration. A lawyer and decorated World War II army officer, Shivers did not embody the strutting, race-baiting demagogue of Dixie statehouse caricature. But he vowed that integration of Texas schools would never occur while he held office. Separation of blacks and whites, at least in the classroom, had been brought forth by divine genesis, he declared. "No court can hand down an edict," Shivers said, and "no group can pass a law to change what God has made."

The governor was mistaken, at least as it regarded the courts. A federal judge in Dallas initially dismissed as "premature" an NAACP suit seeking admission of three black students to Mansfield High School. But in August 1956 the Fifth U.S. Circuit Court of Appeals ruled the students had the right to enroll. This was the first time a federal court had ordered a Texas school to desegregate.

It soon became clear the locals would resist. About four hundred men, most of them angry and all of them white, assembled outside Mansfield High School. They vowed to block the passage of any black student who tried to enter, and they carried hand-painted signs that said THIS IS A WHITE SCHOOL and DEAD COONS ARE THE BEST COONS.

When an assistant district attorney waded into the swarm of protesters and advised them against causing trouble, he was cursed and pushed to the ground. "Anyone with a silk shirt and fancy pants who comes down here and tells a man in overalls what to do," a man in overalls explained, "he is looking for trouble." Some in the crowd threatened reporters and smashed photographers' cameras.

White vigilantes stopped and searched cars coming into town. One participant was asked if he was leading the segregationists. "There ain't nobody leading this," he said. "This is just a mob."

The first effigy was raised on Mansfield's Main Street. Hanging from a strand of barbed wire, its face was painted black and its clothes were splattered with red paint. A hand-lettered sign on one leg said THIS WOULD BE A HORRIBLE WAY TO DIE. A placard on the other leg said THIS NEGRO TRIED TO ENTER A WHITE SCHOOL. Two more effigies went up at the school itself. One hung by its neck above the main entrance, while the other swung from the flagpole. The school principal, a man named Willie Pigg, refused to cut them down because he didn't put them up. "They might stay up there until Christmas," he said.

As was their intent, such actions alarmed L. Clifford Davis, the Fort Worth lawyer for the NAACP. Davis warned in a telegram to Governor Shivers that "violence is almost certain to occur when these students attempt to enroll on Friday." He asked the governor to send more law enforcement to Mansfield "to assure that law and order will be maintained." Davis added, "These Negro students are exercising a constitutional right and the full strength of law enforcement agencies of the state should protect them."

The governor wasted no time. He responded to the request that same day with an order of protection—but not for the NAACP or the black students. Shivers was looking out for the white folks.

At about the same time, a mob formed in the coal-mining town of Sturgis, Kentucky, to keep blacks from integrating schools there. But Governor A. B. "Happy" Chandler believed the black students had a right to attend. "If anybody shows up to go to school," Chandler said, "we are not going to let anybody keep them from doing it." Chandler deployed the National Guard—with tanks—and the Kentucky State Police to enforce his order.

In Texas the governor didn't need the National Guard, and he didn't need tanks. He had the Rangers. Shivers ordered them to Mansfield. From Dallas, Captain Crowder dispatched Sergeant Banks and several others.

Banks was brawny and good-looking and did not mind displaying these qualities for the cameras. "He was always on the cover of a magazine or newspaper," one Ranger recalled without fondness. In early 1956, he was selected for the first-flight entourage when Braniff Airways inaugurated nonstop service from Dallas to Newark. "I was part of all these festivities because I was a 'famous Texas

Ranger,'" he wrote, "with the Rangers being the real symbol of Texas at the time." When they arrived in New Jersey, Banks walked off the plane right behind Miss Texas. He made the celebrity rounds in New York, including an appearance on NBC's *Today* show with his Stetson on his head and his pistol on his hip. "It seemed natural," he said, "that a big event like this would need the famous Ranger in order to make for more jubilation."

Jubilation was in short supply and Miss Texas nowhere in sight when the famous Ranger arrived in Mansfield on August 30, 1956. Banks wrote in his official report that he faced a "large crowd of angry white people gathered at school declaring their intention of resisting, by force if necessary, any effort by Negroes to register."

Those angry white people, however, didn't constitute his major concern, because Banks, with his rural upbringing, believed he understood them. "The people gathered did not have the appearance of rough types," he recalled. "They were just salt-of-the-earth citizens who had been stirred up by agitators. They were concerned because they were convinced that someone was trying to interfere with their way of life."

Second, and more important, the governor of Texas—unlike his counterpart in Kentucky—didn't want the Rangers interfering with these protesters. "It is not my intention," Shivers said, "to permit the use of state officers or troops to shoot down or intimidate Texas citizens who are making orderly protest against a situation instigated and agitated by the National Association for the Advancement of Colored People."

The Rangers in Mansfield were therefore forbidden from escorting any black students past the mob and into class. The governor directed that any blacks who tried to enroll at Mansfield High School would be immediately transferred out of the district. And he ordered the Rangers to arrest any of them who attempted to enter the school.

With those instructions, Banks—wearing Rangers khaki and a black necktie—took up position outside the high school. The crowd of protesters milled nearby. Much more dangerous than the mob, to Banks, was a man distributing pro-integration flyers. This "inflammatory literature," in the Ranger's judgment, merited quick action. "I seized the literature and escorted him out of the area," Banks said. "He was somewhat reluctant until assisted by the toe of a Ranger's boot."

Banks also expelled—though without having to kick him—an Episcopal priest. In full clerical garb, the Reverend D. W. Clark arrived from Fort Worth and delivered a sidewalk sermon to the mob, with a call for peace and under-standing that included a plea to love one's neighbor. "Negroes aren't our neigh-bors," a man in the crowd responded. More Bible talk from Clark only fueled the protesters' outrage. "The swarm of angry faces grew tighter around the slight clergyman," one reporter wrote. "Shouts became louder. Fists were shaken."

As Banks saw it, Clark was "inciting the anger of the crowd when he at-tempted to preach to them, criticizing their actions." He did not arrest—or even warn—anyone who had threatened the priest. Instead, the Ranger took Clark by the arm and led him away. "I suggested he go home and leave the disturbance for the experts to handle."

At one point Captain Crowder also came to Mansfield and met with the school superintendent. "The tall Ranger captain went about his work quietly," a local newspaper reported with reverence. "He let it be known that the Rangers were there to prevent violence and protect human lives and property. . . . That done, he planted a booted foot on a post and methodically began to whittle." Crowder stayed only long enough for photographers to capture him in the pose that had become his trademark. "When he puts his booted foot up on a stump and starts to whittle," an admiring writer observed, "law and order has arrived."

Another photo drew even more attention. Newspapers across the country published the shot of Banks leaning against the tree with the effigy hanging from the high school. The caption, as written by United Press, reported that Banks was "on guard" and keeping "a watchful eye." Neither he nor Crowder made any at-tempt to remove the effigy.

For the most part, this was easy duty for the Rangers. That was because, as Banks observed in his official report, "no Negro students showed up" to enroll. As a result of their actions, Banks recalled, the Rangers "seemed to have gained the respect and support of the local white citizens." And the black citizens "felt intimidated by the show of force."

It was, in truth, the lack of force by the Rangers that intimidated black resi-dents. They believed that Banks and the other Rangers would not protect them. Left undefended—President Dwight Eisenhower had declined to provide any federal assistance—the black students stayed away. After several days, the NAACP announced it was suspending its efforts, at least temporarily, in Mans-field. "We could not take them in there while that mob is standing there ready to do violence," said Davis, the NAACP lawyer.

From a black perspective Mansfield had been an ugly defeat. It would be even worse in a few days, when the scene shifted to another Texas town. There, as an NAACP lawyer complained, the governor used Banks and other Rangers explicitly "to protect the will of the mob."

One of the last recorded lynchings in Texas occurred in Texarkana, a city in the far northeastern corner of the state. In 1942 a black man accused of assaulting a white woman was pulled by a group of men from his hospital bed, where he was being treated for a gunshot wound. They dragged him behind a speeding car to the edge of town and hanged him from a cotton gin winch.

Fourteen years later, in September 1956, racial strife burst forth once more in Texarkana. No black men were accused this time of assaulting white women. Instead, two black students committed the offense of seeking to attend the whites-only Texarkana Junior College, a publicly funded institution.

When the news of this spread, a cross was burned outside the entrance to the college. Shots were fired at a black church while a choir practiced, and shotgun pellets shattered the window of a gas station owned by a black advocate of integrated schools. The president of the college did little to calm the situation. In a public speech on integration he told his white listeners, "It is not only your right but your duty to resist it." Angry white men gathered in front of the Texarkana campus, and a lawyer for the NAACP once more asked the governor of Texas for help. Without it, the lawyer said in a telegram, "a state of anarchy will exist as to the Negro students and they will be at the mercy of a maddened mob."

Governor Shivers again ordered the Rangers to the scene, and Captain Crowder sent Banks with several others. Upon his arrival in Texarkana, Banks surveyed the protesters and determined "there was plenty of evidence that a large segment of the crowd had plans to keep the black students from registering." Some chalk marks outside the college provided a clue. A line had been drawn on the sidewalk, and next to it was scrawled this caution: "The nigger who crosses this line will die."

Like their counterparts in many Southern cities, some of Texarkana's more influential residents had formed a White Citizens Council. Such groups shared the basic goal of the Ku Klux Klan—opposing integration—but citizens councils wished to separate themselves from the dirt farmers and rubes of the KKK. These were businessmen and powerful civic figures who did not wear hoods or conduct secret meetings at night with crosses aflame. They operated more like civil-rights-quashing Rotarians. They gained the informal title of the "uptown Klan."

Banks learned that some in the crowd outside the college were citizens council members. He arranged for a meeting with their president, J. F. Williamson. "I told him exactly what his group could do without crossing us," Banks said. "We got along fine. We were soon good friends."

On the morning of Monday, September 10, 1956, two black students arrived outside the college in a Red Top cab. One was Jessalyn Gray, eighteen, who had already passed an admissions exam. She had pinned her hair back neatly and wore a long floral-print skirt. The other was Steve Posten, seventeen, who had taken the exam and was now returning to see if he passed. He wore thick-framed glasses and carried a briefcase.

"We were expecting to start school," Gray said. They were both aware that no black students had been allowed to attend the college. "We didn't see any reason why things couldn't change," she said.

The mob had gathered at the side of the road, some in overalls and some in business suits. "They were yelling and screaming," Gray recalled more than sixty years later. "That can be pretty scary." Banks and several other Rangers had come too. "There were signs all through the crowd that read, 'No NAACP Coons,' . . . 'No NAACP Communism,' and similar slogans," Banks said. A noose had been tied to the limb of a tree.

Two newsmen tried to question the students, but Banks intervened. "They were obviously out of town reporters trying to start trouble," he said. "We told them if they wanted to stay in the area they would have to mind their own business, otherwise they would be removed or arrested." Another reporter and photographer approached. "I immediately took hold of them and informed them they were aiming for trouble," Banks said. "I instructed the two of them to leave the area or face arrest."

While Banks was threatening journalists with jail, the two students walked toward the school, holding hands, but they didn't get far. The mob blocked them. They tried to go around, and the crowd moved with them. Protesters with jutting jaws stood only inches from the students. One man shouted, "Go home, nigger!" They surrounded Posten; some kicked him. Others threw gravel. The Rangers watched it happen and did nothing.

Banks later offered a bloodless description. "The two black students found that they couldn't get around the human barrier formed by the crowd," he said. "So they retraced their steps, got back in the taxi and left."

The crowd cheered. After about forty-five minutes, Jessalyn Gray returned by cab, determined once more to enroll. Again the jeering mob blocked her way.

But she saw one person among them she thought might help her, a man who represented her government: a Ranger. She approached Banks, who stood grim-faced at the forefront of the hundreds who opposed her. Behind him, a man raised a sign that said NIGGERS STAY OUT!!!

Jessalyn Gray pleaded with Banks for protection. He refused.

"We were under no obligation to escort any person in or out of the school," he explained afterward. Not only did Banks—the ranking law enforcement officer on the scene—decline to assist the young woman, he threatened to arrest her if she tried to enroll. "The Rangers were there to keep order," Banks recalled. "If it could be preserved only by not permitting the student entry, that was their job."

Despite Banks's efforts to restrain journalists, *Life* magazine photographer Joe Scherschel was able to work close to the crowd. "I've never seen a meaner mob in my life than the one that surrounded" the two students, he recalled. "These kids were literally run off by the mob. . . . There were at least three Texas Rangers in the crowd, and not one of them lifted a finger."

Jessalyn Gray returned to the taxi and did not try again to enter Texarkana Junior College. She enrolled instead at North Texas State College in Denton.

With a significant assist from the Rangers, the Texarkana mob had won. It was a great victory for the White Citizens Council as well. Council president Williamson sent a telegram to Governor Shivers praising the way Banks and his men "controlled the situation . . . where the Communist NAACP has attempted to force Negroes into a white school over opposition of the community."

Banks and the other Rangers departed Texarkana in the warm glow of segregationists' appreciation. But before they left, the citizens council "gave us a big chicken dinner," Banks said, "and we all parted friends." The Rangers' high command apparently was pleased too. Sergeant Banks was soon promoted to captain.

Many in Texas, including some of the most powerful state officials, believed the best solution to the school integration question would be to destroy the NAACP. State Representative Joe Pool of Dallas—described by one writer as someone "who forever looks like an angry toad in search of a subversive fly"—pledged to introduce legislation to ban the NAACP from Texas and "protect our public institutions from its insidious influence." While he was at it, Pool promised, he would strengthen state laws that prohibited interracial marriage. The governor himself said "agitators"—meaning NAACP lawyers—"ought to be put in jail."

The Rangers, who had in previous years operated secret anti-NAACP campaigns, started a new one. In late September 1956, Thurgood Marshall—the group's chief counsel and future Supreme Court justice—complained to the U.S. Justice Department that Rangers in Dallas had harassed and intimidated his clients. Marshall said unnamed Rangers went to the homes and workplaces of people who had sued the Dallas school district over segregation. The Rangers threatened some with jail, Marshall said, while others were told they would lose their jobs if they persisted in bringing legal action. FBI director J. Edgar Hoover ordered an investigation, but only after informing Garrison, director of the Texas Department of Public Safety, that G-men would be sniffing around his agency. The FBI's Dallas office determined that the Rangers had indeed warned litigants of job loss or imprisonment, but agents found no civil rights violations.

Marshall and the NAACP soon faced much bigger problems than any such attempts at individual suppression. Texas attorney general John Ben Shepperd charged that the group had violated state law by inciting black citizens, including those in Mansfield, to file suit against school districts. Defending the NAACP, Marshall argued that the group had done nothing illegal and had merely pursued its clients' rights as determined by the U.S. Supreme Court. "We have done nothing worse," he said, "than getting Texas people to obey the law of the land."

Like the Rangers of the early twentieth century, the attorney general's staff crisscrossed the state to investigate the NAACP, raiding the group's offices and seizing its records. To travel to eight cities in three days, an assistant attorney general leading the investigation flew on a state airplane piloted by a Ranger. Shepperd presented the findings to a state district court judge in the East Texas city of Tyler. The judge declared, "I ain't got nothing against the nigger people," but granted Shepperd's motion for a permanent injunction against the NAACP. This in essence shut it down in Texas for years, until a federal court ruled the order unconstitutional. The attorney general's success wasn't quite enough for the Texas Legislature, which in 1957 passed segregation laws aimed at blocking the Supreme Court's *Brown* decision.

The resistance to integration would take generations to wither and would never truly die, but the coming decade brought some reckoning and recompense. Texarkana Junior College admitted its first black students in 1963. And in 1965 the Mansfield school district, facing the loss of federal funding, quietly integrated its high school. Willie Pigg, who had risen from principal to district superintendent, gave the new black students a tour of the campus from which they had been banned only nine years before. "Times have changed," he said.

Few Americans—save the dwellers of the darkest ideological corners—now openly honor those in various public positions who tolerated or promoted racial injustice. They are generally viewed as, at best, benighted products of their time and place. As for the Rangers, a charitable modern assessment of their actions would perhaps find them captives of circumstance. Crowder and Banks were not to blame, despite possible investigative missteps, if white jurors spared the white killer of a black child. At Mansfield and Texarkana, their manner and tactics might be questioned, but they could not be faulted for following the governor's orders. The most ardent of their admirers might treat this period with a discreetly averted gaze. That, however, would not be the Ranger way.

Cantankerous essayist J. Frank Dobie was one of the few Texans who directly criticized the use of the Rangers at Mansfield. "This was probably the first time in the history of the state," Dobie wrote, "that the chief executive dispatched armed forces not to quell a mob but uphold it." Some years later, Garland Smith, a member of the Texas Civil Rights Advisory Committee, wrote that the Rangers' behavior "told every bigot in Texas . . . , 'If you will only assemble a mob, or threaten to do so, the power of the Texas Rangers will be on your side to deny civil rights to school children.'"

Such views did not carry the day. As so often happened, the Ranger-friendly propaganda machinery fabricated a new and more glorious truth: it wasn't the black children facing mobs who showed courage in Texas of 1956. It was the Rangers. Only a few weeks after Mansfield and Texarkana, a Dallas newspaper insisted that violence had been averted in both places "thanks in good measure to the Rangers' presence." An Associated Press story said their actions at Mansfield "represented all the respect—and almost reverence—that Texans hold for one of the most distinctive law enforcement agencies in the world." One year later, the Associated Press was reporting that Banks's "latest exploits" included "helping break up anti-integration crowds at Mansfield and Texarkana."

Mainstream newspapers of the day—owned, written, and edited by white men—were naturally inclined to applaud such larger-than-life characters, even if they had to create them. These refurbished Rangers were not complicit with white supremacists; they had instead been transformed into champions of justice. In 1960, a *Dallas Morning News* editorial marked Banks's "dashing career" with this hallucinatory recounting of the Mansfield protest: "The big Ranger—six-shooters strapped to his side—walked up to the mob. In a mild drawl, Banks ordered: 'Now you all go back to your homes.' The mob quietly disbanded." Less than two weeks later, *Newsweek* used nearly identical language in praise of Banks, which the magazine called a "steel-nerved . . . personification of the Ranger legend."

Banks served as the live model for the famed Texas Ranger statue bearing the legend ONE RIOT - ONE RANGER that was unveiled at Dallas's Love Field in 1961. When he retired from law enforcement in 1982, he received a letter from Shivers. The governor who had ordered the Rangers to block integration wrote that Banks deserved the respect of "all Texans who believe in law enforcement with dignity and recognition of all human rights."

The *Texas Ranger Dispatch*, the official purveyor of Ranger lore, continued the song of praise for Banks. In 2004 it said this of Mansfield: "Sergeant Banks and his fellow Rangers kept things quiet and peaceful. . . . With their evenhanded display of impartiality, Jay and the Rangers gained not only the respect of the locals, but also the public gratitude of state and federal authorities." The *Dispatch* said nothing of the effect on black citizens and failed to discuss Texarkana.

Crowder also enjoyed a soaring reputation, much of it based on his handling of the Rusk State Hospital takeover. A year after the episode, dozens of newspapers printed an Associated Press account insisting that Crowder had "walked unarmed into the midst of a violent riot." Subsequent stories echoed the notion of Crowder's fearless victory. The "surly and belligerent rioters," a newspaper recalled years afterward, "threw down their arms . . . when the rawhide-tough Ranger faced them." An editorial in the Paris, Texas, newspaper also recalled the tale of Crowder and the rioters "who meekly laid down their arms" at his command. "That's the Rangers," the *Paris News* proclaimed, "bigger and better than the script writers would dare make them."

Crowder went on to be named to the Texas Ranger Hall of Fame. His had been a stellar career, it was noted, but his greatest achievement had come at Rusk. Not only had he single-handedly disarmed the rioters, Crowder's Hall of Fame plaque declared, but he had done it by assuring them that "their grievances would get a fair hearing."

The plaque didn't mention that a fair hearing never took place. Nor did it add the obvious conclusion: like so many others, the Rusk inmates fell for the Ranger myth.

Henry Marshall, a federal agricultural official, had been dead for about a year when his body was exhumed. A Ranger captain and a West Texas con man tried to pin Marshall's death on a conspiracy that would reach the White House.

Chapter 20

"BILLIE SOL WHO?"

The Captain and the Con Man

Remember, even liars sometimes tell the truth.

—PAM ESTES PADGET

The dawn of the television age broadened the Rangers' appeal beyond movies and radio. Top officials in Austin welcomed TV series that would—if properly controlled and monitored—portray the Rangers as handsome, honorable, and courageous crime fighters. At the same time, some individual Rangers also chased the bright lights. Money and fame were there for the taking, which might explain the otherwise inexplicable: the relationship between Clint Peoples and Billie Sol Estes. Together, they tried to pin a murder on a former president of the United States. Now *that* would make a good television show.

Peoples, a decorated Ranger captain, wore the aura like a tailored western suit. On horseback, he cut a figure of towering authority and galloping vanity. Estes greased through life as a fast-talking, Scripture-quoting promoter from the cotton patch. He proved that with keen ambition and hard work, a young man could rise above humble beginnings to become a swindler of epic proportions.

A suicide brought them together. At least that was what the local sheriff called it, but Peoples knew better. So did Estes. Across decades, the Ranger pursued the case while the con man milked it, and along the way they forged an arrangement: they would solve the forgotten death of a minor government official. They would show that he had been killed as part of an elaborate political scheme involving a shadowy hit man with a sordid past. It would be, Peoples vowed, "one of the most jarring international scandals that's ever been."

The seeds of this relationship were planted in May 1962, when the head of the Rangers, Homer Garrison, telephoned Captain Peoples at his Waco home. "What do you know about this Henry Marshall case down there?'" Garrison asked.

The name meant nothing to Peoples. "Not a thing in the world," he said.

"Well, you better get your teeth in it," Garrison said. The Ranger boss had been stirred to action by a U.S. Senate investigations subcommittee whose members had taken a keen interest in Marshall. He was a federal agriculture department official who, before he died, had probed the financial shenanigans of Billie Sol Estes.

Estes owned political connections that appeared to reach the White House. His portrait graced the cover of *Time* magazine one week, a spot normally reserved for somber heads of state and the occasional movie star. The "Billie Sol Estes Scandal," as *Time* christened it, was "the hottest thing around." As a result, the magazine said, Washington politicians were "shaking in their boots," and unanswered questions had "set off investigations galore."

The FBI put its own agents on the case. And now, with Peoples en route, so had Rangers. The two mistrusted each other from the start.

The son of an itinerant East Texas farmer, Peoples became a deputy sheriff at age twenty. He went on to serve in the Texas Highway Patrol and joined the Rangers in 1946. Early in his Ranger career, he specialized in undercover work, busting gambling dens and whorehouses, and he objected with vigor to any doubts about his tactics or honesty. During a South Texas trial, a Latino defense lawyer asked Peoples if he had cavorted with any of the prostitutes he arrested. Peoples answered no. The lawyer asked once more. Peoples gave another denial and warned him not to ask again. The lawyer persisted. Peoples requested a recess and waited for the attorney in a courthouse corridor. "I hemmed him up against the wall and I told him, 'You Mexican son-of-a-bitch you, I told you never to say anything like that to me again,'" Peoples recalled. "And I bumped his head against that wall. And when we went back in court . . . he never asked me another question."

Within seven years Peoples had attained the rank of captain, an unusually rapid rise. Few doubted his courage and skill, but some found him too chummy with the state's most powerful politicians. And he seemed to cultivate, if not crave, public attention. When Peoples cracked a case, he made sure reporters knew who had done the cracking. Better yet, for writers, was his mastery of the lively quote, as in the story he often told about an escaped murderer hidden in a crawl space. "I stuck my sawed-off .12-gauge under the house and visited with him for a second," Peoples said. "He was dead and full of buckshot when we pulled him out." Peoples did indeed shoot the man. But an inquest showed that a deputy sheriff fired the fatal shot, a detail the anecdote lacked.

One of his most famous acts as a Ranger came in 1955. Peoples was driving north toward Oklahoma to attend a law enforcement conference when a radio call reported that the sheriff of Limestone County, in Central Texas, had been killed. Though he was about a hundred miles away, Peoples sped to the scene.

A psychotic farmer named N. J. Tynes had shot the sheriff between the eyes and barricaded himself in a rickety wooden house. Peoples, wearing pleated pants and two-tone wingtips, commandeered an armored car from a nearby military base. As an army sergeant maneuvered the vehicle close to the house, Peoples sent tear-gas canisters crashing through the windows. One of the un-fired canisters exploded next to him, and Peoples poked his head through the vehicle's hatch for air. Tynes fired his rifle. The bullet knocked off the Ranger's hat and clipped a lock of hair. Peoples shot another tear-gas canister into the house. It struck Tynes in the wrist and nearly severed his hand.

Tynes was captured and taken to a hospital, where he died a few hours later. Peoples gave interviews to newsmen, quipping that his near miss was "the closest shave I've had in a long time." With regal aplomb, he posed beside the armored car for photographers, his .45 pistol jammed into his belt. After washing off blood and tear gas, he drove to the conference in Oklahoma and delivered his talk on "understanding the criminal mind."

He was, in other words, not a man given to hesitation, self-doubt, or retreat. In May 1962, when Peoples hit Franklin, Texas, he began to probe the death of Henry Marshall right away. And right away he saw a problem: Marshall had supposedly committed suicide by shooting himself five times. And he had done it

with a rifle. In customary fashion, Peoples later brandished the weapon and offered reporters quotable gold.

"If he can kill himself with this gun," the Ranger said, "I'll ride a jackass to
the moon."

Henry Marshall also grew up on a farm. He was valedictorian of his high school
class and worked for a while as a teacher. In 1934 he took a clerk's job with the
federal Agricultural Adjustment Administration, and he turned it into a career
with the U.S. Department of Agriculture.

Friends and neighbors regarded Marshall as reserved, even standoffish, but
no one doubted his dedication to his job or his reputation for honesty. He engaged in minor disagreements but collected no known enemies. Nor did he face
financial problems, and his marriage seemed stable. Though he had had a heart
attack several years before, his health appeared to be relatively good for a fifty-
one-year-old man of regular habits.

On Saturday morning, June 3, 1961, he left his home in Bryan for the thirty-
mile drive to his fifteen-hundred-acre farm near Franklin, where he planned to
do some fieldwork. When he did not return by late afternoon, his wife asked her
brother to check. The brother and a neighbor drove to the farm. They found
Marshall lying in pasture grass, near his pickup truck, dead. His .22-caliber rifle
lay next to him. Blood was spattered on both sides of the truck. Marshall's wallet,
watch, and eyeglasses and a half-empty box of raisins sat in a neat array on the
truck's seat.

The sheriff was called, and he investigated the scene as if late for supper. The
county coroner, who had no formal training in forensic science, assisted. They
took no photos of the body or the blood on the truck. They checked nothing for
prints, including the rifle. They did not take samples of the blood on the truck's
exterior. The sheriff seemed to have decided on the spot what happened: "The son
of a bitch shot himself."

If so, Marshall had been possessed of mighty determination, for he was shot
five times in the chest and abdomen. And it was done with a bolt-action rifle,
meaning that after each shot he would have to eject the spent shell and recham-
ber a live bullet.

But the death certificate said suicide, and Marshall was buried—without an
autopsy—at the Franklin city cemetery. He did not, however, rest in peace. Estes
and Peoples saw to that.

Billie Sol Estes had been raised on a farm near Clyde, Texas, one of six children in a struggling family. To make ends meet, his mother sold home-churned butter door to door. His father paid the doctor who delivered him by selling some of his hounds. "There is nowhere to go but up," Estes liked to say, "when you are traded for dogs."

As a young man he showed little interest in sports or girls or cars. His youthful passion was agribusiness, and when he was twelve he traded a barn full of oats for a tractor. The adult Estes was jug-eared, fleshy, and bull-necked, with a thick sweep of jet-black hair and horn-rimmed glasses. His cotton farming proved so successful that the U.S. Junior Chamber of Commerce named him one of their outstanding young men of 1953. This was quite an achievement for someone living in Pecos, on the flat emptiness of West Texas.

His gifts as a cotton farmer notwithstanding, Estes found his real talent in salesmanship. "Making a deal," he said later in life, "is better than getting high." Not that Estes would know much about getting high. A devout member of the fundamentalist Church of Christ, he neither drank nor smoked, and—like others in that denomination—considered dancing a sin. When he supervised church pool parties, Estes insisted that "mixed bathing" not be allowed. Girls got an hour in the water, and then the boys had their turn to swim. He taught Sunday school. At Christmas he dressed as "Santa Sol" and drove around Pecos giving toys to poor children.

His companies dug wells and sold farm implements and fertilizer. He even owned a funeral parlor, but it never seemed to turn a profit. Many thought it was too fancy for humble Pecos. That represented a rare failure, for by age thirty-five Estes pegged his personal fortune at more than $400 million.

He had now ascended to the ranks of the bumpkin-riche, a status he secured by conducting high-level business at the local Dairy Queen. "Let those big shots from Dallas do the steaks at fancy restaurants," he said. "I have made million-dollar deals over a hamburger." Estes sported a diamond stick pin in the lapels of rumpled suits that looked to have been bought off the bargain rack in Mule-shoe. A chauffeur-driven limousine bore him across Pecos—a city of thirteen thousand people that was less than two miles wide—to the grocery store. The front yard of his pink stucco house featured palm trees imported from the Rio Grande Valley, and its grass was dyed a shade of green found only in Easter baskets. Visitors to his living room gazed wondrously upon an electrically powered waterfall. Across from the fake Niagara stood a cage that held Cheeta, the children's pet spider monkey. Such was Estes's local celebrity that Cheeta's fatal bout with pneumonia made the society page of the Pecos newspaper. The family employed a butler named Homer.

After business and church, Estes's passion was politics. In 1956 he supported Adlai Stevenson for president, though he apparently found the Democrat's campaign tactics deficient. Estes offered to pay for a flock of parakeets that would be trained to fly over American cities in formation, spelling out I LOVE ADLAI. He was disappointed to learn that parakeets would not take to the air in unison. Estes claimed to have given hundreds of thousands of dollars to Democratic candidates, including John F. Kennedy and fellow Texan Lyndon Johnson.

Politicians were, of course, happy to cleave to Estes as a dear friend, at least until he got himself into serious trouble. And that was bound to happen sooner or later, because devout, canny, and generous Billie Sol had another side: scam artist. "He'd lie about anything," said a journalist who knew him well. "He'd lie about his name if he thought it would make him some money."

Estes had constructed any number of shady enterprises. Perhaps his most blatant was the mortgaging and leasing of fertilizer tanks—an honorable operation, except that most of these tanks did not actually exist. At the same time, he was taking high-level U.S. Department of Agriculture officials on shopping sprees at Neiman Marcus in Dallas. In early 1962, Estes was charged with fraud. Federal investigators began knocking on doors and serving papers all over Pecos, and Washington too.

That was when he hit the cover of *Time*. So big was the scandal that even President Kennedy felt the need to address the matter. "The government is staying right on Mr. Estes's tail," he declared in a news conference. In private, Kennedy had his own concerns about unseemly connections. An assistant attorney general phoned FBI director J. Edgar Hoover in May 1962 to say JFK had seen a newspaper photo of Estes in his office. Framed on Estes's wall was an autographed portrait of Kennedy. "The President would like to know," an FBI memo noted, "whether the photograph of himself . . . was signed personally." To the White House's apparent relief, an agent in the bureau's El Paso office determined that the signature "looked 'canned.'"

Officeholders who had accepted money from Estes now affected amnesia. "Billie Sol who?" became a rueful laugh line on Capitol Hill. Folk singer Phil Ochs took note of politicians' sudden case of nerves with "The Ballad of Billie Sol." Those who had to "face elections in the fall" and couldn't "handle an agricultural scandal," Ochs sang, had removed all photos of Estes from their office walls and were claiming never to have met the man.

As the indictments rolled in and his loans were called, Estes's fortune collapsed. A Pecos bank president lamented the fall of a once-promising favorite son: "The sad part of it is that he could have been an honest millionaire instead of a broke crook." In addition to the fertilizer tank deals, the feds were probing other strange bits of Estes's business. One involved the arcane world of cotton allotments.

The agriculture department had imposed strict production controls on cotton. Estes, as was his wont, finagled his way around them: a complex scheme in which farmers would buy land and rent it to Estes, in essence transferring the allotments to him. This would let him grow more cotton than federal limits would ordinarily have allowed, which could mean millions in additional revenue. Some of this extra money, Estes later claimed, was paid to such powerful men as Vice President Lyndon Johnson.

Henry Marshall oversaw the granting of cotton allotments in Texas, and he did not approve of Estes's arrangements. He vowed to crack down and threatened prosecution, until they found him full of bullet holes.

In May 1962, Ranger Peoples faced a difficult task: investigating a death case that was nearly a year old, and for which little evidence had been preserved. Beyond that, the local sheriff and district attorney showed no interest in assisting him. "I couldn't get any cooperation whatsoever," Peoples said. "I ran into a brick wall." He interviewed friends and relatives, and pored over the death scene on his hands and knees, looking for spent ammo. Also, he talked to a gas station attendant who said a man had asked directions to Marshall's farm around the time of his death. Based on the description, a Ranger artist produced a sketch of the possible suspect. "The more I looked into it, the more it looked like something had gone awry," Peoples said. "The deeper I got into it, the more I knew it wasn't suicide."

Peoples needed more, though. He needed to see the body. At his urging, and that of the Marshall family's lawyer, a grand jury was convened at the county courthouse in Franklin, and an exhumation of Marshall's corpse was ordered. Twelve days short of a year from his death, three men with shovels dug him up.

Dr. Joseph A. Jachimczyk, the chief medical examiner in Houston, performed an autopsy. Dr. Joe, as he was known, found that one bullet went through the left lung, one through the liver, and one through the stomach. Marshall's aorta was severed and his right kidney was damaged. Marshall also had carbon monoxide in his lungs, had suffered a hard blow to head, and showed bruises on backs of his hands. Dr. Joe initially said Marshall's death "was not a suicide," but he stopped short of that in his official findings. Suicide was "most improbable," he determined, "but not impossible." He later added: "If, in fact, this is a suicide, it is the most unusual one I have seen during the examination of approximately 15,000 deceased persons."

From Washington, the Kennedy administration paid close attention to the grand jury. Every day it was in session, Attorney General Robert Kennedy phoned the judge overseeing the panel to inquire about developments. Vice President Johnson's office called as well.

FBI director Hoover was keeping the pressure on his agents at the same time and expressed doubt over the coroner's original findings. "I just can't understand how one can fire 5 shots at himself," Hoover wrote at the bottom of one report. His agents on the scene, however, could uncover no clear evidence of Marshall's murder. And they complained bitterly of grandstanding, in the form of frequent comments to reporters, by the Ranger captain. "Peoples has stimulated publicity as to murder theory for sake of personal publicity," said an agent's teletype to Hoover.

Then the man himself—Estes—showed up, in response to a subpoena. He breezed into Franklin in a two-car caravan of white Cadillacs with his attorney, John Cofer of Austin, a confidant of Lyndon Johnson's. This caused, a local state senator said, "the biggest stir around here since the big watermelon harvest of 1948." At least the big harvest gave them watermelons. Though Estes spent almost two hours before the grand jury, he coughed up nothing. For almost every question, he invoked his Fifth Amendment right against self-incrimination. "That was the end of the day with him," Peoples said. Billie Sol and his lawyers piled back into their Caddies and left town.

And that, soon, signaled the end of the investigation. The grand jury was dismissed. Peoples blamed the presence of Harold "Barefoot" Sanders, then the U.S. attorney for North Texas, who was also a Johnson crony. "He was sent down there by Bobby Kennedy and Lyndon Johnson to look into this thing, and to try to get this thing cooled," Peoples said. "And they flat did get it cooled because the district judge down there right away after that excused the grand jury."

The FBI finished its probe too. Despite Director Hoover's initial skepticism that a man could shoot himself five times, the bureau determined that Marshall's suicide was plausible for a host of personal reasons. "Our investigation has disclosed Marshall had a 'nagging wife,' suffered a heart attack in 1958, was a withdrawn, introverted 'lone wolf type,' and shortly before his death complained of being overtired and his wife described him as being depressed," an agent's report said. There was, he added, no "credible motive for murder."

The bureau also took another shot at Peoples. His findings of murder, an FBI memo said, "appeared to be a wild effort . . . to get publicity and keep the matter alive." Hoover himself was angered by a newspaper story in which Peoples said the Rangers and the bureau found no evidence to support an informant's story that he had been offered $5,000 to kill Marshall. At the bottom of the story Hoover scrawled, "I wish this 'blabber-mouth' would stop speaking for the FBI."

For his part, Peoples believed the FBI had botched its investigation, either by incompetence or out of political fear. "That little FBI agent down there . . . never even investigated a murder case in his life," he said years later. "Henry Marshall was killed as a result of possibly this cotton allotment program, because Henry Marshall was going everywhere blowing the whistle on Billie Sol Estes. And when he blew the whistle on Billie Sol Estes, he blew the whistle on some big politicos."

In 1963, Estes was convicted of fraud for the nonexistent fertilizer tanks and sentenced to prison. Kennedy was assassinated that same year, and Johnson was sworn in as president. Such events eclipsed the Marshall case, but the Ranger captain vowed to keep searching. "I feel like one of these days we will come up with something," Peoples said. "We will never close the book on it."

While Estes passed his days in federal custody, Peoples continued to rise in the Ranger ranks, where he prized loyalty and adherence to his interpretation of the proper agency image. For example, men under his command could not divorce their wives because it would "cast a reflection upon the integrity of the Rangers." In 1969 he was named senior captain, the capstone to a career.

Colonel Garrison, the top boss, continued to push for better training and equipment for the Rangers. Garrison also guarded their public image closely, especially when it came to popular entertainment. He demanded script approval for every TV show whose producers sought the Rangers' cooperation. The show *Trackdown* won Garrison's endorsement by billing itself as "an authentic series about a great police force of the world, the Texas Rangers." It starred Robert Culp as Hoby Gilman—a "hell of a Ranger," in the producers' description—and ran on CBS from 1957 to 1959.

Another Garrison-approved television series was *Tales of the Texas Rangers*, which CBS broadcast from 1955 to 1958. It was originally to have featured an actual retired Ranger, Manuel "Lone Wolf" Gonzaullas—a favorite of Garrison's— as a lead-in narrator.

If ever there was a Ranger made for TV, it was Gonzaullas. He served by all accounts as a competent and active lawman. He helped control the riot in Sherman—albeit after most of the damage had been done. He sought to bring order to anarchic oil boomtowns like Kilgore, in part by padlocking suspects to a long, heavy chain he called "the trotline." As the first DPS intelligence chief, he honed an expertise in ballistics and fingerprinting. His biographer marveled at his ability to question suspects. "Gonzaullas's gray-green eyes disconcerted men who had something to hide," Brownson Malsch wrote. "Some of his associates firmly believed that he was endowed with extrasensory perception. He might well have been."

Throughout his career, Gonzaullas cultivated his public image as if it were a hothouse orchid. "The most dangerous place in Texas," his former partner once said, "is between Gonzaullas and a camera." He was thin and stood well under six feet. But with a big hat, diamond rings, and an exquisitely pressed outfit, he cut a striking figure. "Neat," said Ranger Glenn Elliott. "Man, he looked like he just walked out of Neiman Marcus every time you'd see him."

He carried pistols with jeweled handles and mounted a Thompson subma-chine gun near the passenger seat of his 1932 Chrysler coupe. Gonzaullas did little to dispute the widely repeated—and ridiculous—notion that he had killed more than seventy-five men. "Just write that I found it necessary to kill several," he told a reporter. "I don't want to give you a number." He claimed to have been born in Spain to parents who were washed away by the great Galveston hurricane of 1900. "He said he served with the Mexican army during the revolution be-tween 1910 and 1916," said Robert Nieman, a Ranger historian. "Another story was that he was in China during some of the revolution over there. And he tells the story of once in 1898 he was with his father in Cuba . . . after the [USS] *Maine* blew up." Nearly all these tales eluded verification.

Newspaper reporters of the day never tired of the yarns, no matter how implausible. The *Dallas Morning News* christened Gonzaullas the "most colorful Texas Ranger" and the "last of the quick-drawing lawmen." When he shaved in the morning, one writer observed, he wore underwear, cowboy hat, and boots. "I always put my hat on first when I get up," Gonzaullas explained, "then my boots."

It therefore came as no surprise when Gonzaullas was hired as a consultant for *Tales of the Texas Rangers* and as an on-camera narrator—a famous, real Ranger introducing the imaginary kind. When his big moment came, however, he froze. "I remember the day they brought the crew down to Dallas," Lewis Rigler, a Ranger captain, recalled. "And they were going to have [Gonzaullas] setting at the desk and making an opening statement. And they had the cameras set up and everything and he tried it about ten, fifteen, twenty minutes, and he couldn't get it out. He couldn't do it. He couldn't talk. Finally he said, 'You'll have to do it some other way, I can't do it.'"

Unlike the Lone Wolf, Senior Captain Peoples did not have stage fright. The big Ranger seemed at home in green rooms and on red carpets. For years he had served as the official celebrity greeter for the Headliners Club of Austin—a loose-knit band of politicians and journalists united by gossip and liquor—and in the process collected autographed photos of himself with such stars as Lucille Ball, James Arness, Carol Burnett, and Carol Channing. In 1972 he flew to New York to appear on the TV game show *To Tell the Truth*.

Those were innocuous ventures, the sort of public relations ornamentals tacitly encouraged by Ranger brass. But in 1973, the new head of DPS, Colonel Wilson Speir, learned that Peoples had secretly negotiated with West Coast interests for a television series about the Rangers. Speir sent Jim Ray, then the chief of criminal law enforcement, to California to investigate. Ray discovered that Peoples had held several meetings with a B-list actor and a producer to discuss the show.

Peoples claimed he could offer the duo personal knowledge of Ranger ways and promised inside dope on agency cases. "He had access to the [case] files," said Donald Barry, the actor who met with Peoples. "He could get at the files for us." Barry, who was born and raised in Houston, believed that a Rangers movie or series could provide the sort of wholesome entertainment the nation lacked. "The motion picture business has been so prostituted by the Marlon Brandos and

Jane Fondas that today I cannot, along with millions of other fathers, find a movie to take my children to see," he wrote to Colonel Speir. "I hope to change that to some extent."

The need for wholesomeness aside, Peoples packed Hollywood heat like a guy with a copy of *Daily Variety* rolled in his gun belt. He demanded a fee of $500 a week plus 5 percent of production costs to serve as a technical adviser. And he told producers he was the only Ranger who could make it all happen. "He insisted that only through him," Barry said, "could we make this deal."

For the sin of going rogue and cutting the agency out of the action, Peoples faced serious discipline if not outright dismissal from the Rangers. He quickly announced his retirement from the force and, working political connections, secured an appointment as a U.S. marshal for the Northern District of Texas. Because the Rangers kept the unsavory details of his exit secret, the move was portrayed as a promotion. His authorized biographer was able to proclaim a few years later that as a marshal, "Peoples had reached the top of his profession."

Even there, he found time for Billie Sol.

Estes was paroled from prison in 1971, but within eight years he landed in trouble again, this time for tax fraud. His defense: the assets he was accused of hiding were simply products of his insatiable need to brag. "Regretfully," he testified in court, "I have become a liar."

The tactic didn't work, and he was sentenced once more to do federal time. By happy coincidence, Peoples, as a U.S. marshal, escorted Estes from Dallas to prison in El Paso. In the rear of the airplane, the two of them got to talking about Henry Marshall's death. "I asked him, 'Billie Sol, you've got some information on that case.... I think you could help clear this case up,'" Peoples recalled. "But he said, 'I cannot tell you anything. I will not tell you anything until I get out of the penitentiary.'"

By 1984 he was out of prison and ready to talk. Twenty-three years had now passed since Marshall died. Finally, Peoples thought, the mystery would be solved. He put the question directly to Estes: "There's one thing I want you to tell me. Who murdered Henry Marshall?" And at last Estes answered, "Mac Wallace."

The name would have meant nothing to almost anyone. But Peoples remembered it well, from decades back. He knew Wallace as a pervert and a friend of Lyndon Johnson's. And, most important, as a killer.

Malcolm "Mac" Wallace had been student body president at the University of Texas at Austin, where in 1947 he earned a master's degree in economics. He dabbled in Texas politics and did some work on Johnson's 1948 U.S. Senate campaign. With the help of the LBJ connection, he landed a job as an economist at the U.S. Department of Agriculture.

In the early 1950s, Wallace had an extramarital affair with Josefa Johnson, Lyndon's younger sister. Josefa was beautiful and wild, and like some others in the family she could not control her drinking. Around Austin, rumors abounded: she was a lesbian, some said, who conducted her liaisons in a public park. Others whispered that she turned tricks in Hattie Valdes's upscale brothel on the south side of town. It was beyond dispute—because they appeared together in public—that she was seeing an Austin golfer and amateur actor named John Douglas Kinser, who was said to favor bedroom sessions that included spanking. Kinser also hoped to lure LBJ into investing in a small golf course he owned. To complicate matters even further, Kinser was having an affair with someone else: Mac Wallace's wife.

So Wallace shot him.

It happened on October 22, 1951. After an argument with his wife, Wallace drove to the Pitch & Putt golf course in South Austin. He found Kinser in the clubhouse, at the cash register, and plugged him at point-blank range with a .25-caliber pistol. Wallace was arrested the same day outside Austin. Among those investigating the case was Texas Ranger Clint Peoples.

The Ranger believed he had uncovered much more than a jealous husband's revenge. "All investigations showed that Doug Kinser was a homosexual," Peoples said years afterward. "Mac Wallace's wife, I've got a statement in my files . . . showing that she was a homosexual. Mac Wallace was, and also all the evidence pointed that Lyndon Johnson's sister was a homo." What's more, Peoples said, he believed Wallace had engaged in incest. "You are not dealing with Sunday school and church people at all."

Little of that material came before the jury at Wallace's murder trial, where he was represented by Lyndon Johnson's attorney, John Cofer—the same lawyer who would appear for Estes in 1962. The jury found Wallace guilty and assessed a sentence of five years but recommended that it be suspended. Wallace was a convicted killer, and he was free.

"Five years suspended for murder with malice!" Peoples said. "Never in all my tenure in law enforcement have I heard of this happening." Though he had no hard evidence, Peoples believed that Johnson—who had been unhappy about his sister's licentious ways—had used his substantial influence to make sure

Wallace stayed out of prison. "Every indication points in that direction," Peoples said. "The smell of politics was all around there."

And now here sat Billie Sol Estes hanging the murder of Henry Marshall on this same Mac Wallace. It made sense to Peoples. Wallace had a connection to Johnson, however tenuous. He also bore a passing resemblance to the old Ranger sketch of a man who asked directions to Marshall's farm around the time of his death. Estes "laughed at me about this," Peoples said. "He said, 'I just can't figure out yet why you didn't suspect it.' He said, 'It's all put right together.' I said, 'Yeah, it is now.'"

Then the show really started.

Peoples phoned the district attorney in Robertson County and persuaded him to have yet another grand jury to look into the death of Henry Marshall. This time, they believed, Estes would tell the full story. To ensure his cooperation, he was granted immunity from prosecution. Billie Sol was on his way.

In March 1984, after a stop at Dairy Queen for a cup of coffee, Estes rolled into the Franklin town square in a black Cadillac. A small clutch of spectators and some television news trucks awaited. "I was just a broken down old farmer, but I can still draw a crowd," he wrote. "Everyone wants to see Billie Sol, the last of the wheeler-dealers."

Estes walked into the grand jury room with Peoples at his side. For the next four and a half hours, he delivered his version of events, and he had quite a story to tell. Estes claimed that in 1961 he attended a meeting with Lyndon Johnson, Mac Wallace, and Cliff Carter, a close aide to the vice president. It took place, he said, in Johnson's backyard in Washington. The topic: Henry Marshall's investigation into Estes's cotton allotments, and, by extension, the money funneled to LBJ. "He [Estes] said that they had that meeting together and they discussed the facts," Peoples said, "that there wasn't any way they could hush Henry Marshall up. Henry Marshall was blowing the whistle . . . and they were all going to the penitentiary."

Johnson suggested that Marshall be bought off with a promotion but was told Marshall wouldn't accept it. Then, Estes claimed, Johnson said of Marshall, "It looks like we'll just have to get rid of him." And because of that, Estes said, Mac Wallace went to Franklin and committed murder.

Estes offered no evidence that this conversation ever took place—no tape, no notes, no photos, no diary. At this point, Johnson was dead. So was Carter. So was Wallace, the victim of a single-car crash in 1971.

Though grand jury testimony is by law secret, leaks to reporters began before the courthouse closed for the day. Such news was, needless to say, sensational. Reporters swarmed. A television station helicopter landed on the courthouse lawn. The *Dallas Morning News* bannered its headline across the top of page one: "Billie Sol Links LBJ to Murder."

Friends and supporters of Johnson erupted. "Billie Sol Estes is a con man and a pathological liar," said Robert Hardesty, a former aide to LBJ. Wallace's family responded that he had been in California when he was alleged to be in Texas killing Marshall. The grand jury determined that Marshall's death was murder but returned no indictments; none of the alleged conspirators was alive.

That might have meant the end, but Estes wasn't finished. He directed his lawyer, Douglas Caddy, to draft a letter to an official at the U.S. Department of Justice. Estes would link Lyndon Johnson not only to Marshall's murder, the letter promised, but to the assassination of President Kennedy as well. And to the deaths of several others involved with Estes. And, for good measure, to the abrupt departure of Josefa Johnson, whose 1961 death at the LBJ Ranch had been attributed—without an autopsy—to a cerebral hemorrhage. Lyndon Johnson had ordered each hit, Estes said, and Wallace did the killing.

Before he would spill the details, Estes wanted protection. "He said, 'I need immunity from the federal government to tell what I know,'" Caddy said. The feds insisted on more information first, so Caddy set up a meeting with three FBI agents at a hotel in the West Texas city of Abilene. The agents were waiting for Estes when he walked into the lobby. "And," Caddy recalled, "the first thing he said was, 'I'm not going to say anything.'" The agents caught the next flight out of Texas, and the deal died.

Estes didn't explain his sudden silence that day, though he later claimed some "Italian friends" warned him that if he talked, "my life would end." Someone may also have reminded him that lying to federal agents was a crime. Peoples put forth his own theory, according to Caddy: "He said Billie Sol backed out because another family member might have been involved in some of this skullduggery."

At any rate, with Estes mute the big story faded fast. Peoples, however, felt he still had work to do. "A lot of people take the position, oh well, he [Marshall] is already dead.... The hell with that," Peoples said in 1984. Those who had been responsible, even if they were no longer alive, should be exposed "as a deterrent against future things like this." He railed against "the cheap politicians and these cheap people that will get in and try to cover it up in order to protect a low-life politician." Though he had long ago left the force, Peoples invoked the lofty principles of Rangerdom. "I don't like it," he said. "This is not protecting society . . . I hope and pray to God that this whole thing someday will unravel."

It was a noble pronouncement, but other factors may have motivated him. Though they have been publicly overlooked, they could shed light on why a respected lawman would—without the scantest proof in hand—cast his lot with, and bet his reputation on, a convicted felon who swore under oath that he was a liar.

Peoples still yearned for Hollywood. More than that, he sought stardom.

The proposed television series that caused his departure from the Rangers was not his only show business venture. For years after that, Peoples negotiated quietly with other producers for a TV series or a feature film that would showcase his professional exploits, including the Henry Marshall case. With his close cooperation, several screenplays were written. One was titled *Quiet Power: The Making of a Lawman*. In the script, Ranger Peoples makes a heroic entrance when he confronts a crooked deputy sheriff: A door opens, the script says, and "Clint, shirtless, stands with his gun pointed in the deputy's face. Clint is six feet tall, well-muscled, blond, blue eyes, in his late forties. The deputy instinctively backs off from the force of Clint's powerful presence."

The script depicts Peoples and his powerful presence pursuing a number of criminals, Marshall's killer among them. In a climactic scene, Estes, Mac Wallace, and Lyndon Johnson meet at LBJ's ranch. "Billie Sol," Johnson says, "you know that Marshall is going to blow the whistle on you. . . . He's got to go!"

In a nod to verisimilitude, Peoples the movie lawman does not succeed in putting LBJ behind bars. "Clint Peoples knew the truth," one character says. "But even a Ranger captain couldn't stop that kind of cover-up." As the final credits roll, according to the script, a narrator delivers a parting tribute: "The people of Texas are fortunate to have had a man of his caliber in its service for so long. . . . Peoples is indeed a legend in his own time."

There were other projects. In 1987, he worked with a writer on a treatment for a television series titled *LBJ, Accessory to Murder*. In it, Peoples—described as a tall and handsome Ranger who never made a single mistake—would reveal "how a man who became President of the United States ordered a man's death."

For a time, he and his manager also circulated a proposal for a six-hour "Clint Peoples Made for TV Movie." Another television series proposal of theirs, this one called *Men and Power*, offered the story of a "dynamic, intelligent man whose life has touched more Texas history than any other lawman." Which was to say, Peoples. The Henry Marshall case would serve as the centerpiece. "All the powerful men," the proposal promised, "come head to head with the personal power of one lawman, Clint Peoples."

In 1988, a Los Angeles producer wrote him, expressing serious interest in a TV mini-series that Peoples and his manager were shopping. She said she hoped to "proceed with great vigor" to "get your project into development with a major network." This version, too, would have Peoples on the trail of Lyndon Johnson. What he could not accomplish in real life, he would do on the screen. He would be the Ranger who brought down a president. As Peoples said in 1984, "Every dog has a chance to wag his tail some time, and I hope I do."

It didn't happen. The films and the television series never hit the screens, and Peoples died in a car crash in 1992 at age eighty-one.

In his winter years, Estes moved to Granbury, Texas, southwest of Dallas, where he operated a used-car lot. Newspaper reporters still stopped by on occasion, and he entertained them with some of his old stories, sans gusto. Billie Sol had passed from national sensation to relic of curiosity.

He published his autobiography in 2005—distributed by his felicitously named publishing company, BS Productions—in which he granted himself the honorific of "Texas legend." Estes addressed Henry Marshall's death in a few pages and claimed he had been kicking back some of his cotton allotment money to Lyndon Johnson. LBJ wanted to be sure that Marshall "would never disclose his full knowledge," he wrote, so Mac Wallace was recruited to commit the murder. Again, however, Estes offered no evidence, and the book attracted little notice.

Estes died in his sleep in 2013. He was eighty-eight and expired in his easy chair with a bag of Oreos in his lap. The *New York Times* marked his passing: "a fast-talking Texas swindler . . . a good-ol'-boy con man . . . a predator and a romantic outlaw." Scandals and dead bodies had seemed to follow Estes throughout his colorful life, the *Times* observed, but "many of his statements were self-serving and never proved."

At his funeral, Estes lay in an open casket. His hands were folded over a copy of a book resting on his chest: *Billie Sol: King of Texas Wheeler-Dealers.*

The author of that book was Pamela Estes Padget, his daughter. *Billie Sol* had hit the shelves in early 1984, and Estes and his daughter put together a statewide publicity tour. As part of it, they traveled to a shopping mall in Longview, where they autographed copies. Estes used the occasion to tell customers his life would make a great movie, and he hoped that Willie Nelson would play him. "The greatest actor in the world," Estes said. "He could play an actual portrayal of just about anybody."

Only two months earlier Estes had appeared before the grand jury in Robertson County, where he unleashed his wild, lurid, proof-free tales of Johnson and his killing crew. Now, fueled by headlines about Billie Sol, LBJ, and murder, the book-promotion caravan moved on, to Dallas and Lubbock and anywhere else suckers might part with $16.95 per copy. Like the Ranger, the con man had a story to sell.

Alfred Y. Allee, photographed as a young man, joined the Rangers in 1935. Much had changed—in the Ranger force and in the country—by the time he retired more than thirty years later.

Chapter 21

THE MELON HARVEST

"This Damn Era We Live in Now"

This civil rights, that's the doggondest business I ever heard of.

—CAPTAIN A. Y. ALLEE

Many men could lay claim to being Texas's toughest Ranger, but Captain A. Y. Allee may have secured the title when he pistol-whipped a highway patrolman who wrote his wife a traffic ticket. Or it could have been the time he pulled his gun on a small-town political boss for, among other sins, being late to court. And there was that afternoon on a public sidewalk when he kicked a district attorney in the shins with his cowboy boots. The DA, Allee explained, had "tried to belittle the Rangers."

For nearly forty years, Alfred Allee conducted himself as an old-school lawman, without apology. He began his career with the Rangers on horseback and finished it in a Plymouth Fury. Few who met him forgot him: a paunchy cigar-chewing lawman with a voice like a can full of rusty washers. Jowly and beetle-browed, he had a face—in one writer's description—"like a sunburned potato."

His men loved him. "There has never been a greater Ranger Commander than Alfred Allee," wrote Colonel Homer Garrison. "He is dedicated, fearless, honest and sincere." But those unfortunates on the receiving end of the kicks and pistol blows saw a different man. José Ángel Gutiérrez, who rose to political prominence in the Rio Grande Valley, said the Ranger captain beat him—for no apparent reason beyond adolescent insolence—when Gutiérrez was sixteen years old. "He was always trying to be meaner than a junkyard dog. It was all a show," Gutiérrez said. "I think he was sick in his head and he was a psychopath."

Viewed from a more neutral perspective, Allee operated as a traditional Ranger who settled disputes with expedience. "Sometimes we had to get a little rough," he said of those he arrested, "but they brought it on themselves." Men like Allee drew sharp lines between good and bad and granted suspected lawbreakers not the first whiff of succor or indulgence.

"He could be meaner than a barrel of rattlesnakes," Ranger Joaquin Jackson said. Jackson meant it, for the most part, as a compliment. He recalled a standoff with armed prisoners who had seized the county jail in Allee's hometown of Carrizo Springs. Allee told the inmates he would give them a chance to surrender peacefully. "Captain said, 'I'll give you SOBs 'til ten to . . . put them guns down and come out of there,'" Jackson recalled. "And he counted to three and started shooting. I said, 'Captain,' I said, 'that's not ten.' He said, 'Them SOBs can't count.'"

These tactics and strategies may have played well to certain constituencies in a passing era. But by the mid-1960s even the most insular and intransigent Americans confronted a growing sense that old attitudes, rules, and strictures no longer held. Anyone with a TV tuned to the nightly news could see the fractures. Across the nation, blacks marched for equal rights and students demonstrated against Vietnam. In California's Central Valley, farmworkers had gone on strike for a living wage.

South Texas, isolated by geography and custom, presented no one's idea of a revolutionary laboratory. Yet even there the day broke when brown people who picked the white man's vegetables said they wouldn't do backbreaking labor for pennies an hour. They had grown weary of primitive living in wooden shacks and of being treated like wretched peasants. So in 1966, and the year after that, the field workers in Starr County, Texas, did something momentous: they called a strike at the peak of the melon season.

To no one's surprise, the companies who had hired them resisted their resistance. The anxious growers, who stood to lose millions if the crops were not harvested, asked local officials to seek the help of the Texas Rangers.

This vaulted the agency into one of America's most turbulent—and, to the Rangers, surpassingly strange—decades. With the outside world looking on, they performed their duty as they saw it. Their commander on the scene was Captain Allee, and it soon became clear that while the country had changed, the man himself had not.

Starr County hugs the Mexican border about one hundred miles upriver from the Gulf. Without cultivation it was an arid thicket of cactus and mesquite—a thorn scrubland, in the botanists' apt phrasing. But a mild winter climate, good soil, and artesian wells made the region ideal for growing fruit and vegetables. And it had one more resource prized by those who owned the crops: an abundance of cheap labor.

In the mid-1960s the county existed as a modern-day feudal empire, with a small group of propertied Anglos and Hispanics holding nearly all economic and political power. It was the poorest county in Texas, as well as one of the poorest in the United States. Average per capita income barely topped $500, and nearly three fourths of families—almost all of them of Mexican origin—subsisted below the federal poverty line.

For them, schools were poor and medical care ranged from inadequate to nonexistent. Farmworkers lived in tin-roofed hovels without electricity or running water, and they picked the crops for as little as fifty cents an hour. "There is nothing but stoop labor and little enough of that," said the local school superintendent, Rodolfo de la Garza. Children worked the fields alongside their parents. The toilet was the nearest bush and in the punishing heat of a summer afternoon, a cup of clean, cold water could rarely be found. "We would drink from puddles left by the irrigation system, full of frogs and crickets," one woman remembered of her childhood.

To union organizers such a place seemed full of opportunity. The National Farm Workers Association, led by Cesar Chavez, had organized a 1965 strike against grape growers in California's Central Valley. It brought international attention to the workers' cause. In 1966, Chavez sent one of his lieutenants, Eugene Nelson, to Texas, along with others.

The FBI had closely monitored the union's California operations and noted Nelson's migration eastward. But the bureau mustered only mild and fairly absurd interest in Texas farmworkers and their confederates. Through a confidential informant, the FBI surveilled an El Paso woman. She was an Avon sales agent—and a Communist, the FBI said—who held meetings in support of the farmworkers at the local Wyatt's cafeteria. One bureau memo reported that a "sullen looking" man, believed to be a union official, had visited her residence for purposes unknown. A 1966 pro-farmworkers' rally in San Antonio didn't excite agents because, as their report said, informants "did not observe any subversives taking part."

Some residents of South Texas, however, embraced a more expansive definition of subversion. Young, bearded union organizers who appeared in small farm towns made the landed locals more than uneasy. The union reps may have considered themselves advocates for the downtrodden, but to those on the other side of the debate they were unkempt Marxist agitators. As a Starr County grand jury declared, their activities were "contrary to everything that we know in our American way of life."

The organizers' initial efforts met with paltry success; a 1966 Starr County strike failed after growers bused replacement workers in from Mexico. But that summer hundreds of farmworkers marched from Rio Grande City to Austin to call attention to "La Causa." They had been inspired in part by the 1965 Selma-to-Montgomery civil rights marches led by Martin Luther King Jr. The farmworkers' procession did nothing to improve conditions in the fields, but it did generate news coverage. "The march did not win any contracts or even passage of a $1.25 minimum wage," a farmworkers' newsletter said. "But it ended forever the myth that Mexican-Americans were 'happy, contented, satisfied' with second-class citizenship and a life of poverty." Ignored for generations, the plight of the Rio Grande Valley workers now had caught the notice of activists and, perhaps more important, some of the state's politicians.

Starr County's growers were watching too. They had seen what happened in California—including a grape boycott that spread across North America—and were not about to allow it on their turf. With another harvest approaching, they asked the local county attorney, Randall Nye, to request the presence of the Rangers. Nye, who happened to be on retainer to one of the biggest growers in the area, did not hesitate.

This was nothing new. The Rangers had waded into many labor actions over the decades, and they invariably declared themselves to be impartial peacekeepers. Yet they were almost always welcomed by management and viewed with suspicion or hostility by labor. In 1883, for instance, several hundred cowboys from three large Texas Panhandle ranches went on strike for higher wages. The ranchers brought the Rangers in to help break it. Five years later, nine Rangers broke up a West Texas coal miners' strike. The owner of the mine, near the small town of Thurber, supplemented the Rangers' pay and treated them as his own private police force.

In 1947, Governor Beauford Jester deployed the Rangers to the Gulf Coast during an oil workers' strike. The workers' union claimed in a lawsuit that the Rangers—acting as "strike breakers and goons"—harassed and beat picketers. In 1957, a bitter and violent strike lasted for more than forty days at the Lone Star Steel Company in the East Texas town of Daingerfield. At least a dozen Rangers were sent, and again they said they were not taking sides. But Lone Star Steel was secretly picking up the tab for many of the Rangers' expenses, according to former senior captain Clint Peoples. Lone Star paid "for a goodly number of the meals of the Rangers," he said, and may have paid for their motel rooms. In exchange, the Rangers were "more or less guarding the plant, Lone Star Steel, against the people that worked there," Peoples said long after he had left the force. "What you're doing there, instead of enforcing the law, you are accommodating management."

The Starr County strike brought an additional component—race. Among the workers, the Rangers' reputation on the border was forged in the troubles of the early 1900s. Tales of Ranger transgressions against Mexicans and Mexican Americans had been passed down from generation to generation. "Whether it was last year or one hundred years ago, it's still in the family's memory," José Ángel Gutiérrez said. "We feared the Rangers." They were, in other words, still *los Rinches*—the Mexican American name for the Rangers, dating from the border wars and connoting oppression and terror.

The Rangers "are the Mexican Americans' Ku Klux Klan," said a state senator from San Antonio, Joe Bernal. "All they need is a white hood with '*Rinches*' written across it." As one mordant border joke put it, "All Rangers have Mexican blood—on their boots."

Into this realm, chewing a cigar and packing a .45 automatic on his hip, strode Captain Allee, now sixty-one. He arrived untroubled by history, ambiguity, irony, or nuance. "No one fears the Rangers," he said, "if they are not violating the law." As he saw it, he and his company had been directed to Starr County to enforce the statutes on the books, nothing more and nothing less. "I've come down here as a law enforcement officer to preserve life and property," he said. "We're not damn strike breakers."

Allee had joined the Rangers in 1931. Like many young men of that time, he did not finish high school. "It is not necessary to have a doctor's degree," he once said, "to be a Texas Ranger." Early in his career, he patrolled the wild and empty

Big Bend backcountry on a horse named Quatralgo. "We rode horseback and we had pack mules, by God, chasing some doggone rum runner or smuggler, and we didn't have any two-way radios," he said. "Just, by God, our grub and bedroll, and if a fellow ever camped out he enjoyed it and the smell of that old campfire." The experience—Rangering the old way—never left him. "There are many times," he said much later, "when I am driving, and a cool breeze rises, that I seem to be back in those old rugged mountains in the Big Bend and I hear Quatralgo's hoofs on those rocky trails."

He spent most of his four decades as a Ranger along or near the Rio Grande. Allee considered this his ancestral turf; his forebears had a long and bloody history in South Texas. "My family's fought for Texas ever since there was a Texas," he said. Allee's grandfather was a rancher and deputy sheriff who shot and killed five men. The victims included a bank robber, an unarmed train porter, and a newspaper editor who had written critically of him. The grandfather was convicted in none of these shootings but was himself killed in 1896 when a city marshal stabbed him with a dagger in a Laredo bar. Captain Allee's father, Alonzo Allee, was a rancher who held a commission as a Special Ranger. He shot and killed three men over property disputes. In 1917 he was killed—shot in the back in a Crystal City drugstore—by the young son of one of the men he had gunned down.

Captain Allee was not so freewheeling with his gun, though he did kill a prisoner who grabbed the Ranger's weapon and shot him first. One of his favorite methods of punishment was an open-handed blow to the head. In 1948 a picketing oil worker didn't move aside fast enough for the captain, so he slapped the man. "A mild reprimand," Allee said. In 1953 a lawyer in Brownwood jokingly accused Allee of lying on the witness stand. Allee met the attorney in the courthouse hallway and slapped him. In 1961 another lawyer, this one in Beeville, disparaged the Rangers in court. Allee took him aside afterward, the lawyer said, and slapped him—twice.

Sometimes the hand doing the slapping held a gun, as when Allee confronted the highway patrolman who had ticketed his wife, Pearl, for not having taillights on a horse trailer. "When they got to talking about the traffic stop, he insinuated that Mrs. Allee was lying," Joaquin Jackson said of the highway patrolman. "And Captain jumped up and hit him across the head with a pistol." No one in his right mind accused Allee or his family of bending the truth, Jackson said. "You were gonna get hurt if you did."

In 1954, George Parr, a corrupt South Texas political boss, scuffled with

Allee in a courthouse corridor. Parr had irritated the captain by not showing up on time for a hearing. Allee, with gun in hand, rapped Parr on the side of the head, leaving him with a bloody ear. "I personally don't like nothing about him," the captain explained. He was indicted for assault with intent to murder, but the charges were dropped as the case was going to trial.

Allee showed fierce loyalty to the men who worked for him. He defended them against all critics, bought them lunch on the road, and went to the funerals of their loved ones. "I mean he guarded over us men like a setting hen," Jackson said. In hazardous encounters, Allee walked point. "If there was going to be a firefight or there was gonna be any trouble, he'd be out in front," Jackson said. "He always said no one is going to kill one of my men without killing me first." At the Carrizo Springs prisoners' takeover, for example, Allee led the Rangers' charge up the stairs, firing a submachine gun as they retook the jail. When the lockup was secured and the inmates in cuffs, he stood on the courthouse lawn and calmly unwrapped a cigar. "Y'all hungry?" he said to the Rangers gathered around him. It was, Jackson said, "as if we'd just walked out of an afternoon cowboy matinee."

To many Latinos in South Texas, Allee did little to dispel their fear and mistrust of the Rangers. José Ángel Gutiérrez recalled the captain's confronting— and allegedly shoving—the Hispanic mayor of Crystal City at a rowdy city council meeting. "[Allee] tells him, 'You goddamn Mexican. Tell these goddamn Mexicans to shut up,'" Gutiérrez said. "Something made Allee hate Mexicans."

When asked about such matters, Allee expressed bewilderment. "I spoke the Mexican language as much as my own, for I had been reared with Mexican kids," Allee told one writer. "Right today, I have as many friends among the Mexicans, on both sides of the Rio Grande, as I do my own people." Friends, perhaps, but not co-workers. There were no Hispanic Rangers in 1967, which perturbed Allee not at all. "I don't see any Japanese here," he said. "I don't see any Chinamen. We can't hire every doggone breed there is in the United States."

In May 1967, eight Rangers came to Rio Grande City, seat of Starr County, to handle the melon strike. They set up headquarters at the Ringgold Hotel, a time-worn establishment of frayed carpet, peeling wallpaper, and swayback beds. One contemporary writer described it as a "two-story hostelry before which one can so readily imagine stagecoaches and horses tied." The Ringgold sat at the center of a sunbaked town that endured as a generally peaceful if flyblown place. With its palm trees and old stucco buildings, the city exuded a subtropical somnolence and an air of decrepitude, and seemed to have drifted through the decades with dust unstirred. Now, however, there were reports of trouble. Growers alleged strikers had engaged in vandalism and harassment. A railroad trestle was burned, and someone put sugar into the gas tanks of farm equipment.

No one was ever charged for those offenses, but the newly arrived Ranger force could employ other laws to arrest the strikers. In Texas, a state that fostered a general loathing of organized labor, it was illegal to engage in "mass picketing." Picketers were required to be at least fifty feet apart. And state law forbade "secondary picketing," which involved picketing an affiliated party, such as—in the case of the Starr County strike—the railroad that shipped the crops. Union organizer Nelson was arrested for obstructing a public bridge. He spent the night in the Starr County Jail, a classically fetid border hoosegow. By sunrise, he said, he had killed 212 cockroaches in his cell.

The Rangers had several duties, one of which was to give the harvested inventory an armed escort out of town. "Union pickets followed a train of melons as they left . . . en route to markets," a Ranger memo noted. "Eight Texas Rangers and armed Missouri Pacific special agents rode the train 75 miles from Rio Grande City to Harlingen." When not riding the rails, they kept the picketers at bay.

The striking farmworkers primarily sought higher wages, to about $1.25 an hour. They picketed the roads lining the farms and held signs along the railroad tracks. With bullhorns, they exhorted laborers in the field to join them. Along with local law enforcement, the Rangers arrested the marchers, more than one hundred in all. An internal tally by the Rangers showed that most were charged with disturbing the peace or unlawful assembly. Some were cited for "using abusive language," while others were jailed for "preventing a person from pursuing his lawful occupation." That meant they had urged workers to strike. Charges against most of those arrested were dropped.

The Rangers had evolved, over the course of a hundred years, from fighting fierce Comanches to pinching humble fruit pickers—a transition not lost on U.S. senator Ralph Yarborough of Texas, a liberal Democrat. "It must be an unsavory duty for the Rangers," he said, "inheritors of a proud tradition, to be ordered to keep wages low in Texas." Adding to the unseemliness were accusations that strikers were manhandled or beaten. "Captain Allee and the boys moved in," said union organizer Gilbert Padilla. "They arrested people indiscriminately, even people who were not in the picket line, and shoved people, and verbally intimidated as many as they could. . . . The Rangers do anything they want."

Some journalists also complained of Ranger misbehavior. An Associated Press photographer said Allee ordered him to stop snapping photos. "If you take any more pictures," the captain was reported to have said, "I'll take your damn camera off of you." A local television cameraman said one Ranger told him, "If you want that camera busted, just use it again." The Rangers threatened another photographer with jail if he didn't stop. "They were pushing people (strikers) around," a newsman said, "and they didn't want us around."

Company D Rangers said they had not mistreated anyone, though it was hardly the first time they had been accused of such. A few years earlier, three men confessed to Rangers under the command of Allee that they had burglarized a succession of South Texas grocery stores. The men sued the Rangers in federal court, alleging the confessions had been coerced. The Rangers had taken them to a ranch, their lawyer said, stripped them, and strung them up by their ankles from a tree. Then, he said, the Rangers beat the men with ropes and used an electric cattle prod on "delicate portions of their bodies" until they confessed.

Allee, who was not named as a defendant, denied the allegations against his company. The suit never went to trial. It was dropped, the suspects' lawyer said, in exchange for a light sentence on the burglary charges. Of the Rangers accused in that case, two were called in to work the farmworkers' strike.

Two Ranger actions in Starr County drew the most publicity and sparked the most controversy in the strike of 1967. Both involved Captain Allee.

The first occurred when the Reverend Ed Krueger and his wife, Esther, went to the nearby town of Mission to assist strikers. The Kruegers had come as representatives of the Texas Council of Churches. Allee and several other Rangers were on the scene, Krueger said, and the Ranger captain confronted him. "He said, 'Krueger, you ain't a preacher,'" the minister recalled fifty years later. "He said, 'You're just a troublemaker. You're masterminding this whole thing.'" The captain arrested Krueger.

They were standing next to railroad tracks as a Missouri Pacific freight train rumbled by—transporting, fittingly enough, Starr County melons. "Allee grabbed me by the belt and collar and turned me over to another Ranger," Krueger said. That Ranger, the minister said, held Krueger's head inches from the passing boxcars. "That was a very unforgettable moment," Krueger said. "With one step I would have been right on the tracks." Krueger's wife tried to photograph the incident. She too was arrested. "One of the Rangers came after me and twisted my arm back and took my camera away," she said. A Ranger opened the camera, she said, and exposed the film.

Allee said he arrested Krueger because the minister demanded, with "loud and abusive language," to be detained. Mrs. Krueger was arrested, Allee said, because he thought she was about to hit a Ranger with her camera. Both were charged with unlawful assembly.

The second incident started when a union backer named Magdaleno Dimas went looking for dinner. "Magdaleno had gone rabbit hunting," said Alejandro "Alex" Moreno, then a college student working with strike organizers. On his return home Dimas passed by a packing shed for a company targeted by strikers. "He apparently raised his rifle and shouted at the people," Moreno said. Some witnesses said Dimas yelled, "*Viva la Huelga.*"

Dimas was a tattooed ex-con—he had a dragon on his right arm and a rose on his left—with a long rap sheet that included a murder conviction. "He was an enforcer for the union is what he was," Joaquin Jackson said. After a farm manager complained about the shouting and gun waving, Allee and another Ranger went to union offices in Rio Grande City. There, according to some witnesses, they leveled shotguns at union organizers. "Y'all have gone too far this time," Allee told them, and demanded to know the whereabouts of "that son-of-a-bitch Dimas." No one coughed up Dimas's location, but Allee and the second Ranger tailed one of his associates to the home of a union member.

Alex Moreno, who was in the house, had gone outside. "As we walked out we saw the Ranger cars out there," he said. "Captain Allee is standing by the gate, and as I pass by the gate, he grabs me by the neck with one hand. And with his other hand he has a shotgun and pokes it into my ribs."

Allee and the other Ranger, still carrying shotguns, entered the house. "The place just rocked," Moreno said. "You knew there was a terrible beating going on inside." Allee had found Dimas and another union member in a back room, sitting at a table. He ordered them to put their hands on the table. When Dimas did not move fast enough to suit him, the captain hit the man's head with the butt of his shotgun. Dimas later said he was struck and kicked multiple times by the Rangers. Allee claimed Dimas hurt himself when he tripped over furniture as he was being removed from the house. Dimas was taken to jail. A doctor who examined him there said he had a deep cut on his head and showed signs of a concussion. "He was beaten out of his wits," the physician said.

It might have been worse. "I could have killed him if I had wanted to," Allee said. The captain insisted he had arrested and jailed a dangerous man who had threatened violence. "I honestly believe," Allee said, "that our actions prevented someone from getting killed on this date." Yet the charges against Dimas made him sound more like someone who interrupted a ladies' tea. He was cited for shouting in a "manner calculated to disturb the person or persons on the premises." And he had "rudely displayed a deadly weapon in a manner calculated to disturb." Both were misdemeanors.

The union accused Allee and his fellow Ranger of being drunk when they arrested Dimas, and of using "Gestapo terror tactics." That anyone would take Dimas's side over his mystified Allee. "This damn era we live in now," he said. "A man who works to violate the law has more civil rights than good people."

Such matters generated headlines, and in early June 1967, Joe Bernal and two other state senators went to Starr County to investigate. "We found that from the first day of their arrival in Rio Grande City, the Rangers gave every appearance of being on the side of the employers," they reported. "This has severely tarnished the image of the Texas Rangers." They and five other state senators, all liberal Democrats, wrote to DPS director Garrison, requesting that he withdraw the Rangers from the strike scene. "I feel that the people of Rio Grande City are living under a police state," Bernal said.

The U.S. Commission on Civil Rights, a federal agency, also took notice. Its field representative, William B. Oliver III, wrote to Allee and invited him to a meeting in Rio Grande City "to share . . . general information concerning the problems in Starr County." Within three weeks, the DPS Intelligence Division had assembled a lengthy dossier on Oliver. The tactic was reminiscent of the Rangers' secret campaign against the NAACP in earlier years. This time, though, the findings were laughably innocuous. The file noted that Oliver subscribed to a socialist magazine and was "the first white pastor to take over an all Negro church in the history of [the] United Church of Christ." The eight-page document, complete with a mug shot of Oliver, also said that when he had been arrested at an East Texas civil rights protest march, "four prophylactics spilled out of the subject's pockets." And the dossier listed traffic citations Oliver had received over the course of ten years.

Unimpeded by any revelations of condoms and speeding tickets, the commission's state advisory committee held a hearing and concluded that the

Rangers, along with local law enforcement, had denied farmworkers their legal rights. Many Hispanics, the committee said, see the Rangers as "a symbol of oppression." The Rangers had encouraged workers to cross picket lines, the committee found, and their appearance in Starr County "only served to aggravate an already tense situation."

Despite the rain of criticism, the Rangers felt good about their performance in Starr County. So did the growers. That was because the strike had failed. The Rangers' presence, a state court injunction against the picketing, and the importation of workers from Mexico kept the harvest on schedule. Starr County's growers said it was the best melon crop they could recall.

Though the produce had been shipped, the public relations battle raged on. The Rangers called on their friends in the Texas press corps. A story in the *Dallas Morning News* portrayed Allee as one of the great humanitarians of the Rio Grande Valley. "Those who know him best insist that a heart of pure gold beats beneath the Texas Ranger badge worn by Capt. A. Y. Allee, despite his reputation as a man of steel," the first sentence said. He was, the story continued, a "former Baptist Sunday school teacher" who lent money to the down-and-out of all races and dispensed "sage advice" to "youngsters who get into trouble." More than once he was "called upon to arbitrate marital disputes, and his wise counsel is credited with having saved a great many homes."

Several hundred local residents bought a full-page advertisement in the *Carrizo Springs Javelin*, headlined as a tribute to Allee and expressing "the high regard we have for him as a man and as a Texas Ranger." The Missouri Pacific Railroad Company, whose trains the Rangers had escorted, had nothing but praise for Allee and his men. "I feel that we have indeed been fortunate to become your friends," a railroad district superintendent wrote to the captain. "I would be grateful if you would convey to each of your men our warmest thanks for a job *WELL DONE*."

Across Texas, many members of the public—Anglos at least—showed passionate support for the Rangers' actions in Starr County. "Most of these smart punks down there need their heads rapped a few times to teach them respect for the authority of the Rangers," a Corpus Christi oilman wrote to Colonel Garrison. A Dallas businessman, D. H. Byrd, wrote that he had moved his farming operations out of South Texas because of the "shameful racketeering practiced by pawns of . . . Teamsters." Byrd, whose Petroleum Club Building office bathroom featured fourteen-carat-gold fixtures, commended the Rangers and, like many others, blamed outsiders. "When rabble-rousers are allowed to go from state to state stirring up trouble to satisfy their own greed," he said, "it makes us wonder if we shouldn't bring back horsewhipping."

DPS chief Garrison admitted to no problems with the Rangers' behavior and called any fault-finding unfair and undeserved. As he wrote to a county judge in the Texas Panhandle, "You have no doubt noticed that some of the enemies of the Rangers have been having a field day in the press which is not unusual in these times."

National publications were not enemies of the Rangers, but they weren't their lapdogs, either. *Newsweek* headlined its story "Trouble in the Melon Patch" and ran a photo of "crusty" Allee chewing a cigar. "Texas' finest stood accused of even pushing little girls around," the magazine said, "and it had become clear that no matter how splendid their legend, the Rangers suddenly had a bigger-than-life image problem on their hands." The *Wall Street Journal* weighed in, calling the strike an "uproar that could threaten [the Rangers'] national reputation as elite lawmen." The *New York Times* cited critics who "charge that the elite unit has operated virtually as a private police force to protect the interest of the wealthy landholders and ranchers." The story was accompanied by a photo of Allee with a scowl and a cigar.

Next came the courts, which delivered the worst public spanking to the Rangers since the Canales hearings of 1919. In 1967 the United Farm Workers Organizing Committee filed a federal civil complaint against Allee, the Rangers, and Starr County officials. *Medrano v. Allee* was heard by a three-judge panel. The judges took five years to reach a decision, but they found for the union, and they recounted the sins of Allee and the Rangers over many pages. In one instance, the judges said, Allee ordered the arrest of striking farmworkers who were merely resting in the shade. Their offense: they were not reclining fifty feet apart from each other. The judges also determined that Allee's arrest of Magdaleno Dimas had occurred in a "violent and brutal fashion." The decision concluded: "The police authorities were openly hostile to the strike and the individual strikers, and used their law enforcement powers to suppress the farm workers' strike." The strikers' constitutional rights, the judges said, were "irreparably injured." And the court declared unconstitutional five state statutes, including those that banned mass picketing and secondary picketing. In 1974, the U.S. Supreme Court affirmed the lower court's findings against the Rangers.

It was a tardy and hollow victory for the farmworkers. A few months after the strike, Hurricane Beulah hit South Texas. The Category 3 storm devastated the local agricultural economy. That and other factors caused the influence of the union to fade. Farm laborers saw marginal improvements in the coming years—slightly higher wages and portable toilets in the fields, for example—but Starr County remained one of the poorest counties in the nation.

The political impact of the strike was perhaps more significant, as those who considered themselves the Rangers' nemeses believed their cause had been invigorated. "Political insurgency was sparked in South Texas," said Robert Hall, one of the lawyers who filed *Medrano v. Allee*. The case "proved that even the vaunted Texas Rangers could be restrained by law, thus stripping them of the most effective weapon of any oppressive power: the perception that resistance is hopeless and futile."

Less than three years after the strike, the Raza Unida Party, promoting Hispanic political influence, was formed in nearby Crystal City. One of its principal founders was José Ángel Gutiérrez, who had been beaten by Allee as a teenager. The party subsequently won a number of local elections in South Texas and helped bring about the rise of the Chicano movement—a combination of cultural celebration and political efforts by young Mexican Americans. Alex Moreno, the college student in whose ribs Allee stuck a shotgun, went on to become a lawyer and a Texas state legislator. The farmworker's strike, he said, "is considered the first actual event in the Chicano movement."

The Starr County court case had one more consequence—an official policy change that was, despite its importance, enacted with little fanfare: the Rangers would no longer be the state's first choice to police labor disputes.

Allee died in 1987 at age eighty-one. The last surviving member of his company, Joaquin Jackson, published an autobiography in 2005. In it, he praised the captain as a courageous leader but acknowledged that in matters such as the melon strike, Allee might have been the wrong man at the wrong time. "Was he a racist? I suppose that he was," Jackson wrote. "But this is a blanket indictment of his entire generation. He was perhaps the last of a long line of Texans bred to think of Mexico and her people as an enemy of the Lone Star State. . . . He adhered to a code too simplistic to guide us in modern times."

This was a startling and candid admission for a Ranger, and Jackson may have had second thoughts. Three years later he published a sequel in which he charged that accounts of the Starr County strike had been unfair to him and his colleagues. "The actual events have become shrink-wrapped into a passion play of social stereotypes, of potbellied, bullying Rangers swinging nightsticks and pistol-whipping hapless terrified Hispanic farmworkers," Jackson wrote. "We performed the role that fate placed us in. . . . I take comfort in believing that we did our job, which was to enforce the law as it was written at the time."

The Rangers were faulted by the courts, Jackson said, because they saw no use in defending themselves before judges or anyone else. "By the time the testimony was taken and the stories were written," he wrote, "Captain Allee and the other Ranger principals had become so disgusted by the circus-like quality of the proceedings that they refused to acknowledge a no-win situation, since no one was going to believe them anyway."

It is not hard, from the perspective of decades, to see Captain Allee as a grand symbol of Ranger anachronism. While the rest of the country was, for better or worse, rocketing into the future, the Rangers under his command were figuratively and literally riding a slow train on bad tracks across the Texas outback. The state itself had changed: more urban, more diverse, less parochial, more sophisticated. Yet Allee and the Rangers remained hidebound, proud, and absolutely sure of themselves. "Captain Allee was a great law enforcement officer," said Wilson Speir, who succeeded Garrison as head of the DPS. "He believed in Texas and he believed in America."

The majority in the Texas Legislature seemed untroubled by any fallout from Starr County. In 1969 a new state budget increased the size of the Ranger force from sixty-two to seventy-three. With that, DPS director Speir blasted the agency's critics. "Widespread recognition from the world at large," he said, "is almost invariably accompanied by fierce attacks on the part of [a] jealous few to suppress, depreciate or destroy."

Allee, in the last year of his Ranger career, seemed to back away from his scorched-earth image, if briefly. "Really," he said, "I'm not quite the bad character some papers have tried to make me seem." A bit later he reverted to form. "As long as my folks and my friends remember me and respect me," he said, "I don't give a damn what the rest of the people think." Allee departed the Rangers in 1970. He was sixty-five, mandatory retirement age, but looked older. He had survived two heart attacks, a broken neck, and no small amount of public condemnation, yet the fire still burned. "I don't regret anything I have done," he said at his farewell party. "I would do the whole thing all over again."

Some things didn't change, even in retirement. One year after he left the force, he walked into a Carrizo Springs grocery store to buy a five-gallon jug of water. The clerk, a young Hispanic man, rang up a tab of $1.75. Allee believed the actual price to be $1.35. The sixty-six-year-old former captain—now on the state rolls as a Special Ranger—settled the forty-cent dispute the best way he knew. He slapped the clerk and pulled a gun on him.

Henry Lee Lucas, seen here under the watchful eye of Ranger Bob Prince, confessed to killing people from coast to coast. Each time he admitted another murder, the Rangers put a pin in their map.

Chapter 22

CELEBRITY

The Killer Drives to Japan

It all seemed fun to start with.

—HENRY LEE LUCAS

In time he would be given the title of the greatest serial killer in American history, a criminal genius who could murder hundreds of people one by one and never leave a single clue. Many in law enforcement, including the Texas Rangers, would stake their reputations on his confessions of coast-to-coast slaughter. For the moment, though, Henry Lee Lucas was nothing more than a luckless itinerant, a fifth-grade dropout living in a converted chicken coop.

He had drifted into a North Texas backwater with his common-law child bride, Frieda "Becky" Powell. He was forty-five. She had just turned fifteen. They were broke, dirty, and thumbing a ride in the spring of 1982 when a roofer and part-time evangelist gave them a lift.

The preacher collected lost souls at his self-styled House of Prayer, which he had fashioned from an abandoned poultry farm outside the tiny town of Stoneburg, Texas. With minimal improvements, the coops became housing for the faithful, including Henry and Becky. Lucas began working with the preacher on roofing jobs, which provided sufficient scratch for three things he truly loved: coffee, Pall Mall cigarettes, and strawberry milk shakes.

His childhood had unspooled as hillbilly grotesque. He grew up in a filthy shack near Blacksburg, Virginia. "There are four rooms," Lucas's juvenile detention record noted, "one of which houses two goats that belong to a roomer who is a half-witted man." Henry's father, a legless illiterate, found occasional work selling moonshine. His mother, a snuff-dipping prostitute, turned tricks at home while Henry watched. "They was all the time pounding on me," Lucas recalled of his parents, "but I guess I deserved it."

The tale of hard times and bad behavior rolls on: young Henry lost an eye in a childhood accident. His string of youthful burglaries put him in a Virginia state reformatory. "He ran away from the school twice," the state record observed, "for which he received thirty whip strokes." On his sharper days, Lucas attained an IQ of eighty-seven. By the time he reached Texas, he had already done a ten-year stretch in Michigan for killing his mother. Prison doctors diagnosed him as a severe schizophrenic.

Still, Lucas had been welcomed at the House of Prayer, where he helped the cause by repairing small appliances sold in the church thrift shop. This chicken-ranch monkdom was soon interrupted, however. The sheriff of Montague County, one "Hound Dog" Conway, began asking questions about an eighty-two-year-old woman for whom Lucas had done odd jobs.

Not long after Lucas left her employ, Kate Rich had gone missing. Young Becky Powell vanished too. Lucas was arrested and thrown in the county jail. His cell was cold, and he couldn't get his coffee and smokes, much less milk shakes. He began to talk—through the feeding slot to his cell, known as the "bean hole"—to the jailer. Lucas said, "I've done some bad things."

He later talked to Texas Ranger Phil Ryan, whose territory included Montague County. Lucas told Ryan that over the course of seven years he had crisscrossed the country, murdering seventy-seven people in thirteen states. He even admitted to killing his fifth-grade teacher. Ryan, however, could not confirm that any of those seventy-seven murders had occurred. The teacher whom Lucas claimed to have slain, for example, was still alive.

As a test, the Ranger began fabricating cases and presenting them to Lucas, who kept pinning guilt on himself. "I would say I probably fed him about 15," Ryan said of the phony murders. "He probably took [confessed to] all of about six or seven." A measured and deliberate lawman, Ryan harbored no illusions about Lucas and his bloody tales: "From the beginning," he said, "it was no secret that Henry was lying."

Authorities did manage to file two cases against this one-eyed loser with blurry green tattoos and crooked yellow teeth—the murders of his common-law wife as well as the elderly woman who had disappeared. He received one sentence of seventy-five years and one of life.

As horrific as those two crimes were, they could be considered relatively routine. Lucas had merely been convicted of killing a couple of women he knew. The Texas prison system held many men like that. But Lucas got a chance to move up in slayer class with a phone call from Hound Dog Conway to Jim Boutwell, the sheriff of Williamson County in Central Texas. "Jim," the Montague lawman said, "I got an old boy up here you might want to talk to."

Sheriff Boutwell maintained a deep interest in the death of a young woman known to police only as Orange Socks. Her body had been found on Halloween afternoon in 1979, facedown in a concrete culvert along Interstate 35 in Boutwell's county, thirty miles north of Austin. Believed to be in her early twenties, she had brown hair and fingernails painted a bright red. She wore only the orange socks. The investigation into her death had been stalled for years, but as soon as Boutwell asked Lucas about "some things that happened down my way," it all fell into place.

"I've kidnapped some women from there," Lucas said. He went on to describe stabbing a woman he had picked up hitchhiking. Boutwell showed him a photo of Orange Socks. "That is the one I killed," Lucas said, "and there ain't no doubt about it." As far as the sheriff was concerned, the lingering, frustrating Orange Socks case was now closed.

Lucas began to confess to even more murders, and in so doing, he found himself on the road to criminal superstardom. No longer were his admissions the mere rants of an attention seeker. It now seemed he might be what he claimed to be: a specter from the American heart of darkness, the cold-blooded phantom who roamed from town to town, state to state, picking his victims by chance and dispatching them with gleeful ease.

He had emerged at the peak of the national obsession with, and fear of, serial killers. These monsters were "a terrible new phenomenon," the *New York Times* said then, adding that the U.S. Department of Justice believed that a minimum of thirty-five serial murderers traveled the land. By one estimate, they killed four thousand people a year. As a live specimen in captivity, Lucas attracted a great wave of attention.

This overtaxed Williamson County's small sheriff's department, which now had custody of him in its old limestone jailhouse. Boutwell, who had been a Ranger in the 1950s, sought help from Colonel Jim Adams, the DPS director. In November 1983 Adams gave him the full-time services of two Rangers to operate the Henry Lee Lucas Homicide Task Force, as it was officially named.

Bob Prince, a sergeant from Waco, was initially put in charge, and he saw right away he had inherited a criminal sensation. On the first day there were seventy out-of-state phone calls to return. As Lucas put it, "Things really skyrocketed in Georgetown."

From across the nation, police detectives wanted to know if Lucas could solve uncleared murders on their books. Each agency was instructed to send the task force information on the crime, such as offense reports, photos, and maps. Prince or the other Ranger, Clayton Smith, would question Lucas based on the material received.

Before each interrogation, Lucas was allowed to see photos of the victim or read a brief synopsis of the case—"enough to jog his memory," Smith said. Lucas was, after all, recalling a multitude of killings in dozens of states over many years. If he confessed to a murder—which happened with almost daily regularity—the out-of-state cops might come to Georgetown to interview him. When they did, the Rangers always had some advice: bring Henry a carton of Pall Malls and a couple of car magazines, and never call him a liar. Should he be accused of lying, Lucas would force the confession sessions to an abrupt halt. And nobody wanted that.

Next came the Henry Lee Lucas road show. The Rangers flew with him to California, Florida, Georgia, Louisiana, and other jurisdictions. There, as he recalled his depravities, Lucas typically descended into a spooky semitrance. "It was just like a person would go into a very deep meditation," Ranger Smith said, "and he would get plumb weird looking in the face." Then he would show the detectives where he killed and dumped his victim.

Police were struck by the way Lucas could, even years after an incident, summon minute details: the color of a victim's hair, for example, and the dress she wore, or the look on her face, and the way he killed her. He compiled a stunning list of random slayings. In 1982 alone, he said, he murdered thirty-five people.

The portrait of Henry the serial killer now emerged fully drawn. He was not only insatiable, but terribly competent as well. While committing one random homicide after another, he never left a single piece of evidence—not a hair or a fiber or a fingerprint or a drop of blood—that could be tied to him. He drove to crime scenes, often in remote wooded areas, but police never found a tire track to match. No weapon had been recovered. No witnesses had seen him leaving the sites of his savageries. He established no pattern. "He may have had a low IQ," Ranger Prince said, "but he had a high street-smart IQ."

With such a wily killer on the loose, no citizen was safe—certainly not solitary women, but even armed men didn't stand a chance. The death of a policeman in West Virginia had initially been ruled a suicide. But Lucas described shooting the officer and making it look as if he had killed himself. Lucas even possessed the cunning to force the victim to write a bogus suicide note before slaying him with his own weapon.

This was Jack the Ripper with car keys and a road atlas. Worse, there were two of these master fiends. For many of these murders, Lucas said, he had a sidekick and traveling companion, a hulking bisexual pyromaniac named Ottis Elwood Toole. The pair operated, in Lucas's telling, as homicidal Renaissance men. "We cut 'em up," he said. "We ran 'em down in cars. We stabbed 'em. We beat 'em. We drowned 'em. There's crucification. There's people we filleted like fish. There's people we burnt. We strangled 'em. We even stabbed them when we strangled them."

The pair not only killed in nearly every imaginable way, Lucas said, they defiled corpses as well. Sex with a dead woman was a favorite, followed by dismemberment. Lucas had his limits, though. Toole would sometimes barbecue and eat the victims, a feast in which Lucas declined to partake. "I don't like barbecue sauce," he explained.

Admitting to a vast catalog of unsolved murders had its advantages. Carolyn Sue Huebner, a missing-children's advocate working with the task force, watched the Rangers and Sheriff Boutwell treat Lucas like a star. "Whatever Henry wanted," she said, "Henry got." He occupied his own individual cell at the county jail with carpet on the floor. He wore civilian clothes. He watched cable shows on his private color television, complete with remote control. As a landscape artist of the primitive school, Lucas enjoyed a never-ending supply of paint and brushes.

The art supplies were furnished by "Sister" Clemmie Schroeder, a lay minister to inmates. Lucas didn't like jail food, so he dined on T-bone steaks from

Sister Clemmie. Or she brought him burgers from the Georgetown Sonic. When Lucas had trouble sleeping, a doctor prescribed Thorazine, an antipsychotic medication. The merciless killer had sinned his way into a lockup Eden. "I never had a house this nice before," he said.

It was as good or better on the road with the Rangers: fresh air, nice scenery, restaurant meals, and plenty of milk shakes, courtesy of the local police. Some of them would give him $20 for one of his paintings, which he might use to buy a gift—a modest necklace, say—for Sister Clemmie. The supply of Pall Malls never ran low. All Lucas had to do was keep the confessions coming.

The grand Lucas tours also meant celebrity status for the Rangers who traveled with him. They were welcomed as law enforcement royalty and were showered with gifts and proclamations. Here was the most crafty, dangerous, and prolific serial killer of the American twentieth century, and the legendary Texas Rangers—who else?—had him in cuffs. Not only that, they had him talking, solving cases that had baffled the local cops for years.

The Rangers even bestowed blessings on the dispossessed. Once the West Virginia policeman's cause of death was changed from suicide to murder, thanks to Lucas and the Rangers, the officer's widow received an $80,000 life insurance benefit. "Henry was made to feel really good by everyone," Sister Clemmie said, "like he did a wonderful thing."

Not since the Lone Star Steel strike of 1968 had a single initiative so consumed the Rangers. As many as forty Rangers—more than half the active field force—interviewed Lucas about murder cases. Two DPS crime analysts also were deployed.

The image-enhancement sector of the Rangers' operation stayed busy as well. At task force headquarters in Georgetown, a map of the United States hung on the wall with a pin in each place Lucas had confessed to a murder. Should news photographers wish for Prince and Lucas to pose with this map, that request would be happily granted. One reporter watched as Lucas helped tape homicide reports—murders to which he had admitted—to the office wall near the map.

"Like a teacher's pet," the writer for the *Chicago Tribune* observed, "Lucas smiled benignly with the few yellow teeth he still has and handed [a Ranger] pieces of tape. Joking calmly with the Rangers, who treat him cordially to keep him talking, the potbellied prisoner looked more like an eager prison trusty than a sexually deranged sociopath."

By June 1984, only eight months after the task force started, the Rangers announced that Lucas's confessions had solved more than 130 homicides in eighteen states. A Rangers public relations man offered a novel theory on how the cagey killer had evaded detection for so long: "If he was going to do a couple of murders in a town, he would do them differently to confuse investigators." That did not, of course, fool the Rangers.

Ultimately, with the task force's coordination, police agencies in twenty-six states closed the books on 229 murders. Almost none of them advanced to the trial stage, though the Orange Socks case did go to court. On the strength of his confession, Lucas was found guilty and sentenced to die.

As hustling writers and aspiring filmmakers descended on Georgetown, the Rangers steered Lucas toward those they trusted. Sergeant Prince had a friend from Waco named Johnie Dodd, who was said to know someone involved in the making of *Star Wars*. Prince arranged for Lucas and Dodd to take a meeting.

A part-time deputy constable, Dodd exuded rural-route savoir faire. "He has all these diamond rings and gold necklaces, and chews tobacco and spits in a cup," said Sister Clemmie, who was now acting as Lucas's agent. Within a week she had brokered an arrangement.

The *Waco Citizen* made it front-page news, with a photograph of a smiling Lucas as he signed a contract giving Dodd exclusive book, television, and film rights. The story did not elaborate on any Hollywood connections Dodd might bring to bear, but it did note that he "operates Johnie's Used Cars on S. Loop Drive."

There it was: used-car salesmen cutting film deals. Police clearing cases by the score. Lucas enjoying steady rations of free smokes and art supplies. The Texas Rangers basking in nationwide acclaim with more—once the movie was made—sure to come.

Once again the Ranger myth was manifest, floating on a sort of perverse local pride. Texas owned the worst serial killer on earth and the best law enforcement agency to crack him.

Everyone involved had crafted a beautiful arrangement. Then a newspaper reporter and a district attorney ruined it.

At age fifty-two, Hugh Aynesworth had been a journalist for decades. He covered the Kennedy assassination for the *Dallas Morning News* and had worked for several other newspapers and United Press International. Most recently, he had cowritten a book on serial killer Ted Bundy. Though handsome and highly intelligent, Bundy managed to murder only thirty or so. Yet Lucas—unsightly, malodorous, and something less than brilliant—had more than quintupled Bundy's total. "I thought, I gotta talk to this guy," Aynesworth said. He lined up a jailhouse interview with the new champ, who launched into a recitation of his murderous exploits. When Aynesworth said, "Bullshit, Henry," Lucas began to cry.

They engaged in more than forty interviews over the next year. Lucas revealed himself as someone who would admit almost anything to anyone, no matter how ridiculous, if the admission gained him privileges or attention. To a group of Japanese filmmakers, he said, "You know, I even killed some in your country." An incredulous Aynesworth asked, "Henry, how did you get to Japan?" Lucas's answer: "I drove."

When he wasn't talking with the man, Aynesworth was traveling, to establish Lucas's whereabouts over the course of a decade. But he soon ran short of money, so he signed on with the *Dallas Times Herald*. He and reporter Jim Henderson continued to trace Lucas's path. On April 14, 1985, the *Times Herald* published its first story. Lucas, it said, "may be the perpetrator of the largest hoax in law enforcement annals."

By meticulously cross-checking Lucas's confessions with his court documents, work papers, rental receipts, jail rosters, and other records, the reporters found that Lucas probably did not commit more than three murders—those of his mother, his common-law wife, and the old woman for whom he had worked.

As for the hundreds of others to which he admitted, Lucas simply could not have been where they occurred when they were committed. "To accept that Lucas could kill 210 people in an eight-year period," the *Times Herald* said, "authorities had to accept that he was not just an idle drifter but a maniacal nomad, racing at nearly impossible speeds from one side of the country to the other, careening with direction along interstate highways in dilapidated automobiles, compulsively driving for days without sleep and finding victims conveniently waiting at every junction."

Among those was the Orange Socks case. Records showed that Lucas had been in Jacksonville, Florida, more than one thousand miles distant, working as a roofer and cashing his paychecks at a small grocery store, when she was killed. The Rangers knew of the work records but accused a foreman of fabricating them. They never interviewed the grocery store owner who regularly cashed Lucas's checks.

The Rangers dismissed the stories in the *Times Herald* as a hatchet job and stuck to their public position that Lucas was a mass murderer extraordinaire.

There were, however, other serious cracks in the Lucas-as-criminal-superstar narrative.

Charles Fagan, a sheriff's detective from Lake County, Illinois, had flown to Georgetown in 1984 to speak with Lucas about the kidnapping and beating death of a twelve-year-old girl. As was his custom, Ranger Prince instructed Fagan to furnish in advance crime scene photography, a map, and a synopsis of the case. Fagan refused, opting instead to interview the suspect cold.

Lucas wasted little time in confessing, but Fagan wasn't buying it, because Lucas—deprived of his normal study aids—knew nothing about the incident. "I don't recall him being right on anything in regards to her murder," Fagan said. The detective returned to Illinois and told the girl's parents that her killing remained an open case.

Yet the Rangers, in their official Lucas tally sheet, showed that it had been cleared. With that, another pin went into Prince's task force map.

Fagan later testified about his experience with the task force. "Do you feel," he was asked, "like the Texas Rangers tried to use you?"

"Yes, sir, I do," he answered.

"To put another notch in their gun, another case-clearing on their statistics?"

"Whatever vernacular you use," the detective said, "yes, I believe so."

Bob Lemons and his wife, Joyce, lived in the West Texas city of Lubbock, where they owned a sheet metal shop. In 1975, their eighteen-year-old daughter, Deborah Sue Williamson, was murdered—stabbed seventeen times at her home. The case stymied police for nearly a decade, until they heard about Lucas. They brought him to Lubbock in 1984, and he admitted to killing the young woman. As always, no physical evidence matched Lucas to the crime, but his confession was enough for authorities to consider the murder solved.

After the years of grief and fear, Bob and Joyce Lemons finally gained some measure of peace: at least their daughter's killer no longer roamed at large. This lasted until they met with the Ranger and the Lubbock detective who had worked the case. The couple read Lucas's confession. They also listened to the recording of Lucas talking as the Ranger drove him past the crime scene. Nothing, they saw right away, was right.

Lucas got the original color of the house wrong. He said he had broken in through a side door, but a large hutch had blocked that entry. And Lucas completely botched his recounting of the killing itself. "Seems like I chased her through the house, maybe through the kitchen and into a bedroom," he said on the tape. "I stabbed her lots of times, seems like. I killed her in the bathroom and had sex with her."

In reality, the woman was killed outside the house, in a carport. There was no evidence of rape, and the inside of the home showed no signs of a struggle— and no blood, despite Lucas's claims of multiple stabbings.

"We both realized," Bob Lemons said, "that Henry Lucas knew absolutely nothing about what had transpired in Deborah's case." They told the Ranger and the Lubbock detective that Lucas did not kill their daughter. "And they tried real hard," Bob Lemons said, "to sell us on the idea that yes, he indeed did."

Neither he nor his wife had any experience in criminal investigation. But they did the sort of legwork that any detective would consider routine. They called the Michigan prison where Lucas served time and discovered he had been freed only two days before their daughter's murder. Upon his release, he had boarded a bus for Maryland, where he stayed with family members before taking another bus to neighboring Pennsylvania.

Lubbock is seventeen hundred miles from Maryland. Unless Lucas had access to a private jet—an unlikely circumstance for a penniless ex-con—it would have been impossible for him to be in West Texas when Deborah Sue was killed. A detective for the Maryland State Police, whom the Lemonses contacted, did his own interviews and confirmed these findings. But no police from Texas, including the Rangers, had asked such questions.

In late 1984 the couple took their evidence to task force headquarters in Georgetown, where Ranger Prince stopped the discussion after only a few minutes. "I kept trying to tell him, 'Look, I got the record.' And he didn't want to hear it," Bob Lemons said. "Bob Prince specifically told me that I would either get up and leave his office or he would bodily throw me out." (Prince said many years later that he asked Lemons to leave because Lemons demanded, in a "very belligerent" way, to speak with Lucas.)

The Rangers had a single, misguided mission, Lemons said at the time. "They weren't interested in the truth. They just wanted a mass murderer. . . . All we got out of there was lies."

About the same period *Dallas Times Herald* reporters were examining Lucas, Vic Feazell, the district attorney in Waco, was conducting a probe of his own. An ordained Baptist minister who had been elected DA at thirty-four, Feazell had the thick mane of a televangelist and high political ambitions. He thought he might be attorney general someday, or even governor. In 1985, the Rangers said Lucas had confessed to three murders in Feazell's county, and they wanted to bring him to town—another stop for the serial-killer touring company. "'It will be a good photo op,' they told me," Feazell recalled. "'Plead him guilty, get on TV, and we'll be on our way.'"

But the confessions failed to withstand a cursory investigation by the Waco DA's staff. Lucas couldn't have committed the crimes because he had been half-way across the country at the time. "I asked myself why the Rangers could not have discovered what we had found in just a few short weeks," Feazell said.

He secured a warrant and brought Lucas seventy-five miles north to Waco for an appearance before a grand jury, and he made no secret of his intentions: he would investigate the Lucas task force. This did not sit well with the Rangers, as the DA discovered during an encounter with Bob Prince. "He's got a hand like a ham," Feazell said. "He put his finger in my face—he was almost touching my nose—and he said, 'Mark my words, you're going to live to regret the day you ever heard the name Henry Lee Lucas.'"

As the Waco grand jury convened, the Rangers' elaborate construct was falling apart like wet cardboard. Jurors learned of the time-space impossibilities that Aynesworth exposed. They also heard some alarming testimony about the Rangers' investigative techniques.

Carolyn Sue Huebner, the missing-children's advocate, described witnessing Prince's questioning of Lucas on a typical case from out of state: "Bobby would proceed to open up the envelopes . . . which would be the whole contents of the crime, and he would take a live picture, a picture of the person in the live state and show Henry." Prince would ask Lucas if he knew her. "And Henry with coffee and cigarette in hand [would] scratch his head and say, 'Yes, I think so.'" Then Prince would say, "Is she one of your murders?" Lucas typically answered, "I think so." Next, Huebner said, Prince would show Lucas crime scene photos. "And he [Prince] would sit them in front of him and say, "Is this how you left her? Now take a good look at it, and make sure, now. We don't want to make any mistakes.'" The answer from Lucas: "Yeah, that's how I did it."

Lucas, turning contrite, told the same story to the grand jury. "They show me a photograph, and I say, 'Yeah, that is her.' So they want to know how she died. So I look at them, and I say, 'Well, that looks like one of them I have strangled.' They say, 'Now, you think on that.' So I think a little bit, and I say, 'No, maybe she is one I shot.'"

All he had to do was play along and keep guessing. "Eventually," he said, "I will work everything out of them."

That was bad enough, but the Rangers' tactics allegedly went beyond suggestive questioning. They sometimes left Lucas alone for long periods in the task force office, Huebner testified, "so Henry had plenty enough time to have access to those files and read whatever he wanted to." Exactly, Lucas said: "I go through them. I read this one. I read that one. I read the other one, and I just skip through there reading."

Many years later, Ranger Prince denied this account. "That is absolutely untrue," he said. "At no time was he left alone in the office."

If he was armed with ample foreknowledge, Lucas could direct police to the scenes of murders by simply picking up cues. It wasn't all that difficult when detectives drove him past a house several times, slowed the car, and asked, "Henry, does anything look familiar?" On one case, he said, police flew him over the crime locale in a helicopter. "So I said, 'Yeah, down there is the scene where the . . . case was,' and so I could be pointing a mile away, and it wouldn't make no difference."

District Attorney Feazell arranged a meeting with Colonel Adams, the head of DPS, in Austin. His purpose, as he described it, was to warn the Rangers that they were fomenting "the biggest botched mess in the history of law enforcement." If they would agree to reopen these murder cases, Feazell said, he could scale back and perhaps shut down the grand jury's Lucas truth-quest.

"I said, 'We'd rather not go forward with this,'" Feazell recalled telling Adams. "That's when Adams leaned over his desk and said, 'We're not going to re-open any of the Lucas cases.' But he said, 'We're going to open an investigation of you.' His eyes were just as cold as a snake's."

As punctuation, Feazell said, Adams added this advisory: "If you are attacking the Rangers, you are attacking America."

The Waco grand jury declined to indict Lucas for murder and adjourned. If its term could have been extended, Feazell said then, "there would have been indictments handed down against two Texas Rangers." Feazell's taunting—he was referring to the task force—hardly quieted the Rangers. Prince made no secret of his anger and disgust. "Do you believe the word of a convicted murderer and habitual liar, or do you believe the word of law enforcement officers across the United States?" he asked. "Were they all duped?"

Yes, answered Texas attorney general Jim Mattox, in many instances they were. Mattox, who had been working with Feazell and the grand jury, directed his staff to investigate Lucas's movements between the time of his 1975 Michigan prison release and his 1983 arrest in Montague County. Their conclusion: "numerous discrepancies between Lucas's confessions and obtainable evidence regarding his whereabouts," and substantial evidence that officials had cleared cases simply to take them off the books.

While not specifically naming the Rangers, Mattox wrote that "those with custody of Lucas did nothing to bring an end to his hoax." It had been an elaborate scam, and as with many cons, the mark was complicit. "Henry was taking a lot of people on a ride," Mattox said. "And it appeared that some of them wanted to be taken on a ride."

Now the ride was over. The Rangers quietly folded their task force and shipped the famous killer to Death Row, where he could await execution for the murder of Orange Socks. He would enjoy no more home-cooked meals, no cable TV, no Sister Clemmie.

Before departing, Lucas offered explanations for his criminal medicine show. He sought revenge on police for earlier abuses, he said. "They think I'm stupid. But before all this is over, everyone will know who's really stupid. And we'll see who the real criminals are." On top of that, he said, he had pursued a death wish. "I made up my mind to commit legal suicide, and that is, in other words, have people kill me."

A simpler reason might have edged closer to the truth: Lucas enjoyed the attention and the special treatment. "What you had is a person who . . . popped off his mouth and said, 'I killed 150 people,'" said Parker McCullough, one of his lawyers, "and then all of a sudden this dumb schizophrenic is somebody."

This principle of the ascendant sad sack may have explained Lucas's behavior. But why would the Rangers hitch their institutional prestige to such a figure? Their motive, it turned out, might not have been all that different from Lucas's. "They were living a celebrity life," Bob Lemons said, "flying in a private jet all over the country, living well, eating well, something that I'm sure you couldn't do on a Texas Ranger salary."

The Rangers had their vaunted public image, and that image needed feeding. "They got to thinking they were heroes," Aynesworth said, "and they played it to the hilt. They wanted to be part of the biggest, baddest guy who ever got caught."

As District Attorney Feazell noted, he had been warned not to mess with the

Lucas investigation. One morning in 1986, he drove to work as usual and found FBI agents waiting for him in the courthouse parking lot. A television news crew caught it all as he was led away in handcuffs. Charged in federal court with racketeering, Feazell was accused of accepting $19,000 in bribes from Waco lawyers to drop or reduce drunk driving and drug charges against their clients.

After a five-week trial, a jury found Feazell not guilty. Several jurors said publicly they believed he had been framed. "I made some very powerful people mad at me," Feazell said. The Rangers denied they had played any role in the matter, as did the prosecutor who had brought the case, but Feazell never harbored any doubts. "If I had not stepped on the toes of the Texas Rangers," he said, "this would never have happened."

The appellate process for the Orange Socks case, as with all capital murders, ground on for years. When all appeals were finally exhausted, Lucas's execution was set for June 30, 1998. Less than a week before the death date, reporter Aynesworth persuaded Texas governor George W. Bush to meet with him during a brief stopover in Dallas. "Governor Bush, I know you're a fair man," Aynesworth told him. "I can prove Lucas wasn't in Texas when this crime was done." Bush asked for the proof, and Aynesworth sent it to him in Austin.

Four days before Lucas was to die by lethal injection, Bush commuted the sentence to life in prison. "I believe there is enough doubt about this particular crime," Bush said, "that the State of Texas should not impose its ultimate penalty." Bush spent six years in the Governor's Mansion. During that time 152 inmates were executed in Texas. This was the only death sentence he commuted.

Lucas was removed from death row and placed with the general prison population. He gained weight and his hair turned gray. Occasionally, in an interview or a letter, he expressed regret about his role in the great charade. Meanwhile, he settled into his life as just another inmate at the Texas prison system's Ellis Unit. Reporters had stopped accepting his collect calls, and the serial-murderer film and book industry moved on to other macabre attractions. On March 12, 2001, he complained of chest pains. Lucas was unconscious by the time they got him to the infirmary, and he died not long after at age sixty-four.

No family members claimed the body, so his white coffin was borne by six inmate pallbearers to Peckerwood Hill, the cemetery for indigent prisoners. Only four mourners showed for the brief graveside service, Sister Clemmie among them. She read from a letter that Lucas had written to her years before: "My life," he said, "had been truly on the wrong side of reality."

He might have been much more than a nobody buried in a state potter's field, if only the facts had not intervened. "Henry once said, 'I was as famous as Elvis,'" Vic Feazell remembered. "He said, 'If they had just let me keep confessing, I would've had more murders than Hitler.'"

A number of pending court cases against Lucas were dropped in the ensuing years. Police quietly reopened some of the investigations, including the murder of the daughter of Bob and Joyce Lemons. It has remained unsolved. The murder of the twelve-year-old Wisconsin girl who had been kidnapped and beaten was closed in 1991 with the guilty plea of a local homeless man. Since the advent of DNA technology, other men have been charged with many of the murders once attributed to Lucas. In 2016, for example, DNA helped convict a methamphetamine addict in the death of sixteen-year-old Hollie Marie Andrews. She had been raped and stabbed, and her body abandoned, on a Colorado roadside in 1976. Lucas had confessed to killing her.

For the Rangers, the great triumph turned to dust. As the years wore on, the agency's hagiographers tended to ignore the matter or, at most, gloss over it. "No credible evidence survives," one friendly historian wrote in 2007 of the Lucas affair, "to convict [the Rangers] of slipping from the most rigid professionalism in the handling of an impossible mission." After the Lucas task force was shut down, Prince was promoted to captain. "I don't regret it at all," he said of the Rangers' role. "We served a very necessary function."

Initially, when the Lucas extravaganza had begun to fracture, the Rangers responded with a combination of defiance and a shrug. They dismissed the critical newspaper stories as "ludicrous" and unfair. At the same time, they downplayed their role in confirming—or potentially disproving—that Lucas committed more than two hundred murders. The Rangers felt no need to document Lucas's actual whereabouts when the crimes in question occurred. "It wasn't practical for us to go and try to determine where Lucas was," Prince said. "We didn't feel like that was our responsibility."

Colonel Adams, head of DPS, supported that in 1985: "We are not going to assign personnel to go all over the country and try to establish his itinerary, when we would be doing that for the next 100 years." They had served as a mere conduit of information, a clearinghouse, the Rangers said, not an investigative agency. And though they conducted hundreds of hours of interviews with Lucas, Adams said, they never asked him where he really was when the murders were committed. "We never had access to him, for that alibi information."

That was, and continued to be, the Rangers' primary excuse: *We didn't know.* But to accept that, one must ignore the hidden files. Those files prove the Rangers lied.

In 2008, DPS shipped some of its inactive internal records to the state archives. Among them were the Lucas case papers. At the Texas State Library, a massive pink granite structure next to the capitol, no one but archivists touched these Lucas documents. For most of a decade, they sat on a shelf in seven cardboard boxes. Within those boxes are thousands of pages that tell the real story.

Contrary to what the Rangers had said, they did track Lucas's movements. Four black binders contain an eight-year, day-by-day log of Lucas's whereabouts, and the murders to which he confessed. It is a catalog of wild improbabilities, if not impossibilities, and it shows the Rangers were aware—even before press accounts and grand jury investigations—that there were serious questions about more than 125 of the murders attributed to Lucas. An internal memo, produced by a DPS crime analyst in 1985, listed cases one by one. These are just a few:

On September 8, 1975, a time sheet indicates he either worked or was paid in Avondale, Pennsylvania. One day later, the Rangers say, he was fourteen hundred miles away in East Texas, where he supposedly killed a man by shooting him in the head. Two days after that he was back in Pennsylvania.

The Rangers' log shows that in the space of eight days in 1978, Lucas—in this order—supposedly strangled a woman in Louisiana, decapitated a woman in Washington state, stabbed a woman in Missouri, and shot two people in separate cities in Texas. As always, he left not a clue. During this period records state that he also cashed a payroll check in Jacksonville, Florida.

On March 25, 1979, the log said that Lucas was "being cared for at the Union Mission in Bluefield, Virginia." Yet the Rangers list him as having killed a man that same day in Jackson, Mississippi.

On April 18, 1979, the Rangers said, he abducted and killed a woman in Uvalde, Texas. But on April 19, according to their own log, Lucas endorsed a paycheck in Florida. And that same day, the Rangers said, he killed and dismembered a woman in Oklahoma City.

In other instances, the archived files present indisputable evidence not only of botched cases but of professional misconduct. Here is one of them:

On June 23, 1981, around three a.m., someone walked into a 7-Eleven store in Baytown, Texas, southeast of Houston, and killed the clerk. Diana Lynn Underwood, twenty-three, was shot in the head and neck three times at close range. Nothing was taken from the store, including cash, and police found no clues.

The killing remained unsolved for nearly three years, until Lucas confessed to it. He never stood trial, but police closed the case and the investigation. And another pin went in the Ranger task force map.

In the old Ranger files, however, are records from a company called Commercial Metals in Jacksonville, Florida. They show that Lucas sold the company scrap metal, and was paid $19.80 cash, on the same day that he was said to be in Baytown, murdering the clerk. Baytown is 850 miles west of Jacksonville.

The Rangers had an explanation. They believed Lucas's signature on the Commercial Metals receipt was a forgery. To prove this, a DPS handwriting analyst examined the document. But the analyst determined the signature from June 23, 1981, was indeed Lucas's, as was the signature on a receipt from the next day. He could not possibly have been in Baytown when the woman was killed. Yet decades later, the Baytown Police Department still listed the murder as a closed case, with Lucas the confirmed suspect.

The Baytown police say the Rangers never informed them of the handwriting analysis. In response to this new information, provided to them by the author, Baytown investigators reopened the Underwood case in late 2019.

The Rangers could have acknowledged that Lucas did not murder all those people. But that would have exposed them as dupes and fools. No longer would they have been the captors of the most dangerous man in America. The lights would dim on the celebration, so the Rangers buried the evidence deep in their files.

Their attempt at damage control may have helped to protect the agency's reputation, but there were serious, tragic ramifications. When Lucas's bogus confessions were allowed to stand, when those cases were cleared and packed away, any investigations into them stopped. That meant the real killer of twenty-three-year-old Diana Underwood, and the killers of dozens—perhaps hundreds—of other purported victims of Henry Lee Lucas, walked free. This the Rangers knew.

Ranger Stan Guffey died in a gunfight that erupted when he and another Ranger halted the kidnapping of a two-year-old girl.

Chapter 23

TODAY'S RANGER

Bible on the Dashboard, Bushmaster in the Back

The worst Ranger was a good Ranger.

—FORMER SENIOR CAPTAIN MAURICE COOK, 2016

The National Football League played its 2017 Super Bowl in Houston, and the New England Patriots won. Quarterback Tom Brady, the game's MVP, led his team to a comeback for the record books. Only the theft of his jersey afterward marred this triumph.

As offenses against humanity go, it wasn't the Lindbergh baby kidnapping, but it happened in Texas with the world watching. Lieutenant Governor Dan Patrick called upon the Rangers to investigate. "In Texas we place a very high value on hospitality and football," Patrick said. "Whoever took this jersey should turn it in. The Texas Rangers are on the trail."

This was a comical and telling display of hubris. The Houston Police Department, the FBI, and NFL security teams already were on the case. Yet Patrick's announcement—with its "on the trail" cowboy allusion—offered a Texas-sized reassurance: Brady and the Patriots Nation now could rest easy, for one of the planet's greatest law enforcement organizations had stepped in.

As it turned out, the Rangers played little to no role in solving the theft. A memorabilia collector's tip led investigators to a Mexican journalist who had lifted the jersey from Brady's bag, after which he made his way back across the border. One could imagine that if Captain Leander McNelly were still around, he would have charged over the Rio Grande with guns blazing to seize the stolen treasure, as he once repatriated King Ranch cows. This time, however, the arrest of the suspect and repossession of the merchandise were left to Mexican authorities.

The Rangers may have come up empty-handed in the great jersey heist, but the incident served to remind of their endurance, and of their folklore. Their name alone still paints a picture. Nearly two hundred years after their misty birth in 1823—which occurred, as they like to say, before Texas was Texas—the Rangers are still here. All the attempts to abolish them have failed, the eulogies wasted. They're still answering the call, still ready to ride to the rescue. Ready to chase robbers, lasso rustlers, punish killers, and nab locker-room pickpockets. And to do it with the swagger—if not the abandon—of old.

Today's Texas Rangers must evoke and honor the past, which creates a challenge: to perpetuate the image yet supersede some unflattering events. Even the current dress code harks back to the cowboy days. Modern Rangers have no uniform, but they are required to wear a western hat, a western belt, and a pair of western boots. Regulations stipulate that this apparel be clean and sharp. Those famed Rangers of the Mexican War, with their soiled floppy hats, greasy shirts, and bloodstained pants, wouldn't pass muster.

It may be easier to assess the first 170 years of the Rangers than the last thirty. The agency's current duties are more complex, its personalities less colorful, its actions more muted, its image scrubbed. Tamed by scrutiny and bureaucracy, the relentless attention-grubbing of a Captain Bill McDonald has given way to a calm sea of anonymous faces. Well-read devotees who invoke the sacred names of McNelly and Hamer might be hard-pressed to name a single current member of the force.

The Rangers now present themselves as a new model that retains its classic lines, but only the good ones. Contemporary Rangers do not stand accused of widespread, officially sanctioned racial oppression. They do not steal land from poor folks en masse anymore, or serve as a private police force for union busters. It's been a long time since they galloped across the prairie at dawn to attack a sleeping village. Yet many decades after Jack Hays shot his last Indian and Sam Walker killed his final Mexican, the sense of history hangs like heavy smoke.

Their two hundredth anniversary celebrations will give the Rangers ample chances to trumpet exceptionalism long and loud. The lions of the past will be summoned again and again, while the sins of the past may be granted a nod or two as well, but then will be pushed to the side. The Rangers have changed, but not that much. Though the flesh-and-blood Rangers have evolved, the frontier archetypes hover. The old ways vanished, but the image never died. Many of the venerable tales have suffered fact-based bullets to the heart, but the aura they created has gained immortality. With the Rangers, history often proves to be the weaker foe of romance.

It has been said and will be said many times: as long as there is a Texas, there will be Rangers. This yoking of the state's soul and essence to the force can sometimes sound like yet another tiresome Lone Star boast, but the proof is in the statutes.

In 1957 state legislation reorganized the DPS. Only two years earlier, a San Antonio legislator had introduced a bill that would eliminate the Rangers. "We don't need a state Gestapo any more," Representative Charles Lieck said. The Rangers, he added, were a relic of "the horse and buggy, pistol-whipping days." To that the Dallas Morning News harrumphed, "He might almost as well propose that the Alamo be razed and the ground used for a parking lot."

Lieck's bill failed. Nonetheless, legislators felt the storied agency needed some legal protection, so as part of DPS reforms they added subsection 411.015 (b) to the state Government Code. It is still on the books. Only one sentence long, its meaning is absolutely clear: Abolishing the Rangers is against the law.

Many Rangers acknowledge that some of their predecessors engaged in excesses and committed atrocities, but they insist today's force exemplifies rigorous professionalism. The Rangers now have access to sophisticated technology and state-of-the-art crime labs. They receive specialized training. They adhere to accepted police procedures. And they must navigate governmental systems like any other cops.

Rigid members of the old guard—those accustomed to near-absolute self-rule—did not pass happily into the age of Miranda warnings, civil rights suits, and deadly force regulations. Courts came to frown on pistol-whippings as an interrogation technique. No longer could Rangers use the "East Texas Merry-Go-Round" to keep suspects from legal counsel. "They [would] get an old boy arrested in one place and they'd just haul him around all over the country . . . maybe evading the lawyers or evading somebody trying to get him out of jail," former Ranger Max Womack explained. Such tactics, and the Rangers who employed them, are long gone.

The all-Anglo, all-male Rangers force also disappeared years ago, but the transition was tardy and tortured. As late as 1979, a top Ranger responded to a question about black candidates with benighted puzzlement, if not blatant racism. "We've never had a colored to pass the exam," senior captain Bill Wilson told a reporter. "They just don't, well, there's no interest. It's not that big a deal, you know."

The first Hispanic Ranger of the modern era joined in 1969, two years after the Starr County farmworkers' strike called attention to the lack of same. The first black Rangers were hired in 1988, but only after the NAACP filed a federal complaint. In 1993, under pressure from the legislature and Governor Ann Richards, two women became Rangers. With that, some disgusted Rangers resigned or retired. "It was rough," said Maurice Cook, who was senior captain then. "One of the captains told one of the females, he told her that when a female comes into the Rangers, that will be the blackest day in Ranger history. That was the mindset of the old-time Rangers."

The first two women appointed came from clerical positions within DPS, and neither had worked a criminal case before. One of them, Cheryl Steadman, resigned after a year on the job. "It was, 'Welcome aboard, get to the back of the bus and just sit there and smile and be grateful,'" she said of her time as a Ranger. She filed a federal suit alleging harassment and discrimination and settled out of court.

In mid-2019, Texas employed 159 commissioned Rangers, four of whom were women. Eight of the Rangers were African American and thirty-four were Hispanic.

Antonio "Tony" Leal was named senior Ranger captain in 2008, the first Hispanic to hold that post. Leal said he never faced hostility or discrimination within the agency, and that an Anglo Ranger captain encouraged him to apply in the first place. Certainly there were serious racial problems in the past, he said, especially along the border. "But the United States Army has the same types of things in their history," he said. "Police departments have the same things in their history. I don't think of that so much as the history of the Texas Rangers. I think it's part of the history of our country and our state."

Leal, who retired from the agency in 2011, finds the current Rangers to be an ever-improving elite force. "There's just a different cut to a Ranger. . . . There's just something about the way Rangers carry themselves," he said. "It's a calling to do that profession, to serve and protect the public. After you have that calling, the rest is talent. Are you the best in your field?"

The early days of Indian fighting and border wars saw Rangers rushing into danger with an almost gleeful zeal. The perils have dwindled in the modern era—no one is pulling Comanche arrows from their foreheads anymore—but the job still carries risks and, on occasion, calls for astounding courage.

In 1987 an ex-con named Brent Albert Beeler, twenty-three, abducted, tortured, and killed twenty-two-year-old Denise Johnson. She worked as a housekeeper and nanny for William and Leigh Whitehead of Horseshoe Bay, an affluent Central Texas lakeside community. The Whiteheads had two children. One of them was two-year-old Kara-Leigh Whitehead.

About a week after he kidnapped Johnson, Beeler broke into the Whitehead home before dawn. He crept upstairs as the family slept and snatched Kara-Leigh from her bed. Beeler carried her to his hideout—a house across the street whose owners were out of town. At four a.m. he phoned the Whiteheads, waking them, and told them he had their daughter. Beeler said: "Listen to me. Here are the rules. Number one, no cops. Number two, I want thirty thousand dollars in twenty-dollar bills." He also demanded a car with a full tank of gas. "I made hamburger out of your maid," he said, "and I'll make hamburger out of your little girl." The Whiteheads had twenty-four hours.

Local police, the FBI, and the Rangers responded but stayed out of sight. They secured the $30,000 and borrowed a new Lincoln Town Car from the local district attorney. As instructed, William Whitehead parked the Lincoln in the driveway of the vacant house, with the motor running, and returned home. The ransom money was in a briefcase on the car's front seat. On the backseat floorboard, Rangers Stan Guffey and Johnnie Aycock had hidden themselves under a bedspread. Both men, who had volunteered for the mission, held handguns.

It was 9:30 p.m. Less than a minute after the car was parked, the Rangers heard footsteps. Beeler leaned into the car, placed Kara-Leigh on the front seat, and covered her with a silk scarf. Then he moved the briefcase from the front to the back, placing it on top of Aycock.

Guffey and Aycock rose up and identified themselves as state police. Beeler exclaimed, "Oh, goddamn!" He backed out of the car and fired his handgun, a stolen .44 Magnum loaded with hollow-point ammunition. The Rangers fired back. One of Beeler's shots struck Guffey in the head. Aycock pulled the child behind him, shielding her, and shot Beeler as he backed toward the house. Beeler crumpled and fell next to a flower bed. In all, fourteen shots had been fired.

Kara-Leigh was unharmed. Beeler was dead at the scene. Guffey was loaded into a car driven by an FBI agent and rushed to a local hospital, where a doctor pronounced him dead.

A Ranger since 1979, Guffey was forty, married, and the father of four sons. He and Aycock received state medals of valor. More than twelve hundred people attended Guffey's funeral, where DPS head Jim Adams delivered a eulogy. "His courage in doing what was right," Adams said, "cost him his life." Among the mourners were the Whiteheads. "The Rangers are the finest bunch of people I've met," Bill Whitehead said. Guffey's widow, Josie, kissed Kara-Leigh on the cheek.

It would be wonderful to say that Guffey's sacrifice allowed Kara-Leigh to blossom into a lovely and accomplished young woman. But a little more than five years after the kidnapping, she—now eight years old—and her parents were aboard a private twin-engine turbo-prop operated by William Whitehead's company. The Mitsubishi MU-2B-30 departed Alamogordo, New Mexico, en route to Texas, before midnight on June 24, 1992.

The pilot was unfamiliar with the area and its rugged terrain. A few minutes after takeoff, at an altitude of about six thousand feet, the plane flew into a mountainside. The pilot, the Whiteheads, and two other passengers were killed. A headline in the Carlsbad, New Mexico, newspaper delivered this succinct summation: "PLANE CRASH VICTIMS NO STRANGERS TO TRAGEDY."

To become a Ranger now, an applicant must have eight years of law enforcement experience and be a trooper with the state highway patrol. Critics have long questioned whether catching speeders on Texas interstates provides the proper training for the demands of Ranger work.

"I'm not going to say that most of the Rangers they hire today don't know one thing about criminal investigation when they come into the Ranger service," retired Ranger Womack said in 1995. "Most of them have been highway patrolmen . . . [and] the highway patrolman deals primarily with traffic. You do get involved in some criminal investigations, but very little." When a patrolman becomes a Ranger, Womack said, "[they] kind of throw you to the wolves and let you kind of learn by experience, and that's the best way to learn."

The Rangers' involvement in sophisticated investigations over the past few decades has produced some notable successes and some embarrassing failures. A sampling:

In 1960 a twenty-five-year-old beauty-pageant queen, Irene Garza, was pulled dead from a South Texas irrigation canal. She had been raped, beaten, and suffocated before her body was thrown into the brown water. Initial suspicion fell on a priest, John Feit, who was the last person known to have seen Garza alive. He had heard her confession in a McAllen church rectory before she disappeared. Significant circumstantial evidence—including strange scratches on his hands and his prior attack of a female parishioner—implicated Feit. He also failed a polygraph. He escaped prosecution, however. Authorities in deeply Catholic Hidalgo County would not pursue a murder case against a priest, and the church spirited him out of town. "Father Feit, they put him out of here real quick," former McAllen police chief Clint Mussey said. "By the time we got the girl out of the water, he was gone."

More than forty years after Garza's death, Feit had left the priesthood. Married and living in Arizona, he told a journalist in 2002, "I'm just hanging out and having fun." While the ex-priest issued such cavalier pronouncements, Ranger Rudy Jaramillo was pursuing the murder as a cold-case investigation. Jaramillo kept a framed photograph of Garza on his desk as he pored over old files. The break came when Jaramillo, working with local police, interviewed a Trappist monk and a retired priest, both of whom said Feit told them decades ago that he killed Garza.

The Rangers submitted their case to the Hidalgo County district attorney, who refused to take the new evidence before a grand jury. But after a different DA was elected, Feit stood trial for murder. He was convicted in 2017 and, at age eighty-five, sentenced to life in prison.

Rangers have complained about reluctant prosecutors since the days of McNelly. In 2005 a teacher at the West Texas State School, a secure facility for juvenile offenders, phoned Ranger sergeant Brian Burzynski. The teacher claimed that the school's assistant superintendent was sexually assaulting teenaged boys incarcerated there. Burzynski conducted a year-long investigation and produced a 229-page report detailing the sexual assaults. For reasons he never quite made clear, the local district attorney refused to prosecute. Only after multiple press reports and legislative hearings did the assistant superintendent stand trial. He was convicted and sentenced to ten years in prison. The Texas Legislature honored Burzynski with a special resolution.

The Rangers also played an important role in the 1999 arrest of Ángel Maturino Reséndiz, the so-called Railroad Killer. Reséndiz, who sometimes hopped freight trains for transport, was suspected of killing perhaps a dozen people in brutal fashion. For a short time he held the top spot on the FBI's most-wanted list. Ranger Drew Carter was credited with persuading Reséndiz's half sister to coax him to surrender.

Other cases, however, have shown the Rangers to be overmatched or far too quick to accuse.

In 1994 a black man was convicted and sentenced to death for the murder of a family in Somerville, northwest of Houston. A jury found that Anthony Graves stabbed a woman, her teenage daughter, and four grandchildren, then set their house on fire. The case's lead investigator was a Ranger.

After eighteen years behind bars Graves was freed from prison. "There's not a single thing that says Anthony Graves was involved in this case," said the current district attorney, who did not prosecute the original case. "There is nothing." The U.S. Fifth Circuit Court of Appeals found that Graves was convicted in part by false trial testimony from the Ranger. The court overturned the verdict.

Another: On a summer night in 2008 someone tossed a Molotov cocktail into the unoccupied Texas Governor's Mansion, which was undergoing renovations. The fire caused severe damage to the residence, a white-columned Greek Revival structure built in 1856.

Suspicion for the arson soon fell on a coterie of Austin anarchists, and the Rangers waded into strange waters. "Rangers in their trademark cowboy hats have fanned out across Austin and penetrated the city's counterculture hangouts, where the fashion accessories tend toward piercings and tattoos, the music is alternative rock and globalization is a dirty word," the *New York Times* reported at the time. "Not surprisingly the investigation has been met with some suspicion." Despite a $50,000 reward, the arson remained unsolved after more than a decade.

Since 2015 the Rangers have been responsible for investigating any alleged crimes committed by state officers and state employees, as well as suspected cases of public corruption. The results have been mixed. The Rangers looked, for example, into the state agriculture commissioner's use of public funds to pay for two out-of-state trips in 2015. One of the trips was to Mississippi for a rodeo. The other, to Oklahoma, enabled Commissioner Sid Miller to receive a "Jesus shot" of painkilling medication. Miller was not indicted, but the Texas Ethics Commission fined him $500.

Though the Rangers are not considered experts in financial crimes, in 2016 they investigated allegations that Texas attorney general Ken Paxton had committed securities fraud. Paxton was indicted.

The Rangers also were asked to probe malfeasance by city officials in Crystal City. They conducted what the local district attorney called "a very diligent investigation." But their efforts in the famously corrupt "Spinach Capital of the World" yielded not a single prosecutable case. When the Rangers were done, the FBI came in. Its agents seized a "truckload of documents" and other evidence, according to a San Antonio newspaper. The bureau's work resulted in the felony convictions of the mayor, the city manager, and three council members in 2017.

Some Rangers complain that the number of public integrity cases has left the force stretched too thin, in part because not all alleged offenses rise to the level of major crimes. In 2017, for example, Lampasas County district clerk Cody Reed spotted a used mini-refrigerator in a courthouse hallway. It was worth, in the estimation of Reed's lawyer, "somewhere between zero and $50." Reed said he thought the appliance had been abandoned, because it sat empty and unplugged for more than a month. He hauled it away, he said, and threw it in a dumpster. When the refrigerator's owner filed a criminal complaint against Reed, the Texas attorney general's office requested that the Rangers investigate.

Ranger Jason Bobo conducted a probe that spanned more than three months and included an examination of surveillance video, courthouse electronic entry logs, and county deed records. The Ranger's account of his interview with the suspect read like a *Dragnet* script by way of *Greater Tuna*. "District Clerk Reed confirmed he had removed the refrigerator on a Saturday because he did not want to get his dress clothes dirty," Bobo wrote in an affidavit. "He stated it was a dirty little nasty refrigerator leaking stinky, smelly water. (Note: the information regarding cleanliness was not supported by information obtained from several other county employees)." The interview continued: "I advised District Clerk Reed the thing I did not like about this matter was that the refrigerator was not his property to dispose of. . . . District Clerk Reed stated [he] 'should have left the fucking thing where it was at.' I agreed with District Clerk Reed. . . . I told District Clerk Reed to get the refrigerator back. District Clerk Reed responded, 'It's gone, Jason.'"

Reed was charged with class B misdemeanor theft by a public servant, arrested, and freed on bond, but the attorney general's office dismissed the case.

With the two hundredth anniversary close upon them, the Rangers are showcasing the many special units they operate now. Programs such as a SWAT team, a bomb squad, and crisis negotiators take the agency far beyond its roots. There's also the Ranger Reconnaissance Team, which engages in undisclosed "extended covert operations in remote areas," especially along the Mexican border. And the Rangers run the Border Security Operations Center, headquartered in Austin, which analyzes and disseminates intelligence.

It could be argued that this striving for relevance, an embrace of missions already assumed by other police forces, diminishes the Rangers. They have abandoned their uniqueness, have drifted from what made a Ranger a Ranger.

But through all the upheaval and evolutions, the traditional Ranger continues to exist, if in modified form. Not all of them are forming SWAT teams or gathering secret intelligence on the border. Some still range. For example, there's Brandon Bess, a member of Company A who operates in boggy southeast Texas. Handsome and expansive, Bess walks and talks like someone from a Rangers recruitment catalog. "A friend of mine said, 'Man, you're playing in the Super Bowl,'" he said of being a Ranger. "You get to do things that nobody in law enforcement gets to do. . . . The Ranger job is a dream job."

Bess works from a small one-man office on the third floor of the county courthouse, on Sam Houston Street in downtown Liberty, a town of ten thousand. His cowboy hat, a $500 Atwood silverbelly, hangs on a rack of deer antlers attached to the wall. He wears black Justin ostrich-leather boots, each with a Ranger insignia, and carries a Colt .38 Super on his hip. The gun's grip handle, made by state prisoners, is engraved with his and his wife's initials, along with *Texas Rangers Co A*. Bess pins his Ranger badge on his blue shirt, over his heart.

Born in East Texas, he earned an associate degree from Kilgore College, became a deputy sheriff, and joined the highway patrol in 1995—a position he had long wanted because "he's a guy who gets to drive fast for a living." He spent ten years with the highway patrol and eight with the DPS special crimes division, and joined the Rangers in 2013. This warm winter morning Bess, forty-seven, sat at his desk, on the phone with a man who claimed to have information about a 2003 murder, and who said a hit man named Chainbreaker was stalking him because of that. The informant talked for ten minutes or so, going at top speed but making little sense. Bess wrote on a notepad, *Meth kills your brain*. Meth and hit men have become a specialty of Bess's. He has worked a number of cases against the Aryan Brotherhood, a murdering and drug-dealing fixture of East Texas.

Bess spends much of his time assisting rural sheriffs and small-town police in his three-county territory. That is a primary function of Rangers across Texas. The Houston Police Department, forty miles down the highway from Liberty and a world away, employs a fleet of experienced homicide detectives. But a backwoods town may have next to none, which means a Ranger's help is usually welcome. Bess opened a cabinet and thumbed through his case files one by one. "Murder," he said. "Murder. Aggravated sexual assault. Sexual assault of a child. Murder. Murder. Missing person. This gal's been missing since 1989. Solicitation of capital murder . . . Search warrant. Murder, cold case. Fugitive. Questionable death . . . Murder. Murder. That's a murder. Murder. Officer-involved shooting . . . Threat to a district judge . . . The city councilman in one of the counties I cover was a tombstone salesman. He cheated a widow out of fifteen grand."

In 2019 he worked with Port Arthur police on a thirty-one-year-old murder. Patricia Ann Jacobs, thirty-six, disappeared from an East Texas tavern in 1988. She was found the next day, dead, in the Neches River. The case remained unsolved, but in 2018 the woman's daughter called Bess and asked him to take a fresh look. He and a Port Arthur detective located evidence—a man's semen on the woman's underwear—that had been stored in a police department file cabinet. DNA analysis led them to arrest and charge a sixty-year-old convicted sex offender with the murder. "It's the most rewarding case in my twenty-six years," Bess said.

Bess roams with an independence that traces its lineage to centuries past, when Rangers traversed Texas unbound by county lines or jurisdictional concerns. They went where they were needed or thought they needed to be. "You rarely get assigned to anything," he said. "You're not given a schedule. . . . Rangers don't need supervising."

Now he sat behind the wheel of his black Ford F-150, headed to the all-you-can-eat buffet lunch at the Texas Kountry Kitchen. In the truck's covered bed he had stored his other guns: a Smith & Wesson .357 Magnum handgun, a LaRue Optimized Battle Rifle, and a Bushmaster semiautomatic. On the dashboard he kept his Bible.

Bess drove his truck across a long low bridge, over the Trinity River. Here, about twenty-five miles upstream from its discharge into Galveston Bay, the river runs wide, dark, and slow through marshland and hardwood thickets. This had been, two centuries back, the hunting grounds of the Karankawas. They were the towering Indians—man-eaters it was claimed—who had so alarmed Stephen F. Austin on his first visit to Texas, and whose fight for survival brought forth the very first Rangers.

The truck flew over the river, the same murky stream where the Native Americans had paddled their dugout canoes. For a few miles the trees, water, and sky dominated the view—not too different from what the Rangers of 1823 might have seen. Then the vista yielded to the ragged edges of a small town: a farm and ranch store, Family Dollar, Chicken Express.

Bess stopped his truck at a red light. He pulled the brim of his hat low. It was a small gesture that seemed to span the centuries. The Karankawas are extinct, but murderers, meth dealers, and tombstone scammers are still out there. "The best part of the job," he said, "is you're working every day as a part of history."

Colonel Homer Garrison, head of the Texas Department of Public Safety from 1938 to 1968, was an ardent promoter of the Rangers and their image.

Acknowledgments

Over the past five years I have spent countless days in many libraries, and I have enjoyed every minute of it. Librarians are, as many writers have noted, the unsung and underfunded heroes of our pursuits. I want to thank the staffs of these libraries, museums, and archives for their great assistance: the Dallas Public Library's Dallas History and Archives Division, the Dolph Briscoe Center for American History at the University of Texas at Austin, the Hutchinson County Historical Museum, the Archives of the Big Bend at Sul Ross State University, the Hillman Library at the University of Pittsburgh, and the National Archives at College Park, Maryland. I'm also grateful to the Texas Ranger Hall of Fame and Museum and its executive director, Byron Johnson. The online archives of the Texas State Historical Association were crucial to my research. And I extend special thanks to archivist Tony Black and the staff at the Texas State Library and Archives, who endured my many questions and requests with patience and professionalism. The TSLA is a state treasure.

Beginning in 2016, I submitted multiple requests—via telephone, email and U.S. mail—to interview senior Rangers. All were rebuffed or ignored. I also asked repeatedly to tour the Rangers' Border Security Operations Center in Austin. Those queries received no response. There were a couple of notable exceptions to this resolute inaction. Brandon Bess allowed me to tag along with him for a day to see how a Ranger works. He's a dedicated professional and a fine lunch companion. Also, retired Ranger captain Bob Prince took time to speak with me about the Henry Lee Lucas affair. Though this book is highly critical of the Rangers' handling of Lucas, Prince answered every question I asked.

Several fellow writers—Glenn Justice, Jim Donovan, Scott Farwell, and Skip Hollandsworth—shared important research material with me. Phil Oakley assisted greatly with contacts. Doug Caddy helped explain one of those singular Texas characters, Billie Sol Estes. And Vic Feazell and Hugh Aynesworth, two prime actors in the Lucas saga, spent hours walking me through that strange episode.

I'm also grateful to friends and colleagues who provided valuable counsel. They include Sam Gwynne, Scott Parks, Jeff Guinn, Carlton Stowers, and the late, great Bob Compton. As he has done before, George Getschow—a man who survived both the toxins of academia and the venom of a copperhead snake—went above and beyond the norms of friendship. George's considerable wisdom and keen editing eye rescued me many times. I can't thank him enough.

David Patterson at Stuart Krichevsky Literary Agency has been a steadfast champion and adviser for years now, and was doubly so with this book. Every writer should have an agent like David. At Viking, executive editor Paul Slovak took over this project at midstream with a steady, calming hand. I'm deeply appreciative of his astute guidance and expansive vision.

Notes

PROLOGUE: THE REAL RANGER

1 **A newspaper headline of the era:** *Ogden (Utah) Standard*, April 11, 1914.

2 **"Nowhere," historian T. R. Fehrenbach wrote:** Fehrenbach, *Lone Star*, 447.

2 **"There are still the Texas Rangers":** Davis, *The West from a Car-Window*, 11–14.

2 **No law enforcement agency has been celebrated:** The Texas Ranger Hall of Fame and Museum maintains an exhaustive list of movies, TV shows, and books about Rangers. Its approximate total of movies, cited in the text, may be an undercount. Don Graham in *Cowboys and Cadillacs* identifies a number of other Ranger-related films not included in the museum's list. See also Pitts, *Western Movies*.

3 **Larry McMurtry's 1985 novel *Lonesome Dove*:** Not all of McMurtry's fictional Rangers were heroic. In *All My Friends Are Going to Be Strangers*, a contemporary novel published in 1972, two Rangers named E. Paul and Luther beat the long-haired protagonist and toss him into a cactus patch because he looks like "a little old fairy."

3 ***To Love a Texas Ranger,* published in 2016:** Broday, *To Love a Texas Ranger*, 2.

3 **"For courage, patriotic devotion, instant obedience":** Gillett, *Six Years with the Texas Rangers*, 21–22.

3 **"The Texan has no equal anywhere":** Paredes, *"With His Pistol in His Hand,"* 16.

3 **"The real Ranger," he wrote in 1935:** Webb, *The Texas Rangers*, xv.

3 **"There is no question but that a definite potency":** Sterling, *Trails and Trials of a Texas Ranger*, 524.

4 **Joe Davis was a real Ranger:** Author interview with Joe Davis.

CHAPTER 1. THE GUNS OF EDEN

Records of the activities of Texas's early settlers can be scarce, and some of the records that do exist are not consistent. History from this period depends in many instances on the reminiscences of the pioneers, and these were often dictated orally, decades after the fact. Therefore, the stated dates and locations of some important events may vary by source. Likewise, the correct spelling of some settlers' names can be impossible to pin down with certainty. Significant discrepancies are noted herein.

Though I am aware that not all white immigrants to Texas were of Anglo-Saxon ancestry, I have used the word "Anglo" as a general term for those of European non-Hispanic origin. I also employ the term "Indians" for Native Americans. These are stylistic and not political decisions.

9 **"I entered this country in 1821":** Letter extracted in the *Missouri Intelligencer*, July 18, 1828.

9 **The land lay before him:** "Journal of Stephen F. Austin on His First Trip to Texas, 1821," *The Quarterly of the Texas State Historical Association*, April 1904.

11 **"The country," he wrote, "should be given back to Nature":** Fehrenbach, *Lone Star*, 65.

11 **However, the Native American population in the early 1800s:** Calvert et al., *The History of Texas*, 38.

11 **Texas "presents almost literally a vast and noiseless desert":** *Natchez Press*, reprinted in the *Pittsfield (Mass.) Sun*, Aug. 18, 1819.

11 **A sum that would buy eighty acres of arable land:** Fehrenbach, *Lone Star*, 142.

12 **Most hailed from Alabama, Arkansas, Missouri, Louisiana, or Tennessee:** Christopher Long, "Old Three Hundred," *Handbook of Texas Online*.

12 **"The primary product that will elevate us from poverty is Cotton":** Torget, *Seeds of Empire*, 55.

12 **Lafitte operated such a thriving practice in selling slaves:** Davis, *Three Roads to the Alamo*, 55.

12 **Jim Bowie, destined to become a Texas martyr at the Alamo, made a handsome living:** Eugene C. Barker, "The African Slave Trade in Texas," *The Quarterly of the Texas State Historical Association*, October 1902.

12 **Of those, 443 were slaves:** Long, "Old Three Hundred."

13 **"He begged us to cut it off":** "Reminiscences of Capt. Jesse Burnam," *The Quarterly of the Texas State Historical Association*, July 1901.

13 **A "new country," one early settler wrote:** Sowell, *Rangers and Pioneers of Texas*, n.p.

13 **Pioneers told and retold campfire tales of alligators on the prowl:** Smithwick, *The Evolution of a State*, 5.

13 **According to official state history, the Caddos even gave:** Alvarez, *Texas Almanac*, 31, and Phillip L. Fry, "Texas, Origin of Name," *Handbook of Texas Online*.

14 **approaching a Colorado River settlement in 1826 "professing friendship":** J. H. Kuykendall, "Reminiscenses of Early Texans: A Collection from the Austin Papers," *The Quarterly of the Texas State Historical Association*, July 1903.

14 **"Our people were troubled by a continual sense of insecurity":** Ford, *Rip Ford's Texas*, 28.

15 **The Indians attacked it around 1687 and killed everyone except five children:** Brands, *Lone Star Nation*, 33.

15 **They stood larger than most—"magnificently formed," one nineteenth-century ethnologist recorded:** Quoted in Davis, *The Gulf*, 64.

15 **"Their words, or rather grunts, seemed to issue from some region low down":** Wilbarger, *Indian Depredations in Texas*, 199.

15 **"After proceeding some distance":** Sowell, *History of Fort Bend County*, 91.

16 **One Texian immigrant circulated poetry critical of Stephen F. Austin:** Kuykendall, "Reminiscenses of Early Texans."

16 **"The 'border ruffians' ceased their depredations":** Kuykendall, "Reminiscenses of Early Texans."

16 **"It was a comical sight":** Mark E. Nackman, "The Making of the Texan Citizen Soldier, 1835–1860," *Southwestern Historical Quarterly* (hereafter *SWHQ*), January 1975.

16 **In 1822 two white men were ambushed and killed:** Some accounts say this incident occurred in 1823.

17 **Young volunteer John H. Moore crept close to the camp:** "Reminiscences of Capt. Jesse Burnam."

17 **"a young man of worth and bravery," Tumlinson wrote:** Winkler, *Manuscript Letters and Documents of Early Texans*, 23. Some sources spell his surname Morrison.

17 **They were by no means aristocrats:** Biographical information on these earliest of Rangers comes from their individual entries in the *Handbook of Texas Online* and entries in Winkler, *Manuscript Letters and Documents of Early Texans*.

18 **"We are obliged continually to keep a party out Hunting":** Winkler, *Manuscript Letters and Documents of Early Texans*, 27.

18 **there is no record that they were ever paid for their service:** Barbara L. Young, "John Smith," *Handbook of Texas Online*.

18 **Kuykendall, whom some consider the captain of these first Rangers:** Kuykendall, *They Slept Upon Their Rifles*, 55.

18 **"I have been compelled in view of the security of our people":** Himmel, *The Conquest of the Karankawas and the Tonkawas*, 50.

19 **Morrisson "clung to his gun":** Wilbarger, *Indian Depredations in Texas*, 210.

19 **About thirty-five or forty who weren't slain were forced to work:** Himmel, *The Conquest of the Karankawas and the Tonkawas*, 54.

19 **Some colonists, it was said, took women home as sex prisoners:** Himmel, *The Conquest of the Karankawas and the Tonkawas*, 51.

19 **a few surviving warriors murdered their women and children:** This tale is mentioned in Reid, *The Scouting Expeditions of McCulloch's Texas Rangers*, 40.

CHAPTER 2. THE LONG WAR

21 **"Texas Indians were of a different mold"**: Smithwick, *The Evolution of a State*, 73.

21 **Sometime in 1829, probably in the bounteous warm spring:** The arrival of the Jenkins family in Texas has been reckoned in various accounts from 1828 to 1830. Jenkins's great-great-grandson, who edited his memoirs, wrote that close examinations of records likely puts their emigration from Alabama in early 1829.

21 **They lay, as he remembered, "grim and ghastly in the green grass"**: Jenkins, *Recollections of Early Texas*, 5.

22 **"The conquest of Texas"**: Hagedorn, *The Works of Theodore Roosevelt*, vol. 7, 115.

22 **"a singular, if not barbarous, method of sending destruction"**: Jenkins, *Recollections of Early Texas*, 25, 26.

22 **"Unencumbered by baggage, wagons or pack trains"**: John Caperton, "Sketch of Colonel John C. Hays, Texas Ranger," 8ff, Dolph Briscoe Center for American History, University of Texas at Austin (hereafter CAH).

23 **He traveled in regal splendor:** Henderson, *A Glorious Defeat*, 52.

23 **"If it is bad for a nation to have vacant lands"**: Jackson, *Texas by Teran*, 33, 101.

24 **"He impressed one with the idea that he possessed force of character"**: Ford, *Rip Ford's Texas*, 36.

25 **"He said he had led his people a long time"**: John H. Reagan, "Expulsion of the Cherokees from East Texas," *The Quarterly of the Texas State Historical Association*, July 1897.

25 **"Many of the Indian tribes have acquired only the vices"**: Clarke, *Chief Bowles and the Texas Cherokees*, 16.

25 **"What is to be done with us poor Indians?"**: Everett, *The Texas Cherokees*, 27.

26 **With the stated goal of "a firm and lasting peace forever"**: Winfrey and Day, *The Indian Papers of Texas and the Southwest, 1825–1916*, 14–17.

26 **presented the chief with a sword, a silk vest, a sash, and a military hat:** Clarke, *Chief Bowles and the Texas Cherokees*, 65.

26 **"Your land is secured to you"**: Clarke, *Chief Bowles and the Texas Cherokees*, 62.

26 **"the *Promises* expressed in that declaration are *false*"**: Winfrey and Day, *The Indian Papers of Texas and the Southwest, 1825–1916*, 22–28.

26 **The republic's land office issued white settlers several hundred titles:** Everett, *The Texas Cherokees*, 87, 88.

26 **He enjoyed an easy path to the presidency:** Herbert Gambrell, "Mirabeau Buonaparte Lamar," *Handbook of Texas Online*.

27 **"The white man and the red man cannot dwell in harmony"**: Fehrenbach, *Comanches*, 305.

27 **"You and your people have been deceived by evil counselors"**: Winfrey and Day, *The Indian Papers of Texas and the Southwest, 1825–1916*, 61–66.

27 **Lamar had nine hundred soldiers and several companies:** Moore, *Savage Frontier*, vol. 2, 246–59.

28 **"His horse had been wounded many times"**: Reagan, "Expulsion of the Cherokees from East Texas."

28 **A former Ranger captain, William Sadler, fired as well:** Stephen L. Moore, "Rangers of the Cherokee War," Texas Ranger Hall of Fame.

28 **He "rose to a sitting position facing us"**: Reagan, "Expulsion of the Cherokees from East Texas."

28 **Someone took Houston's sword from the chief's dead hand:** Clarke, *Chief Bowles and the Texas Cherokees*, 109.

28 **When they were gone, white families:** In 1846 the area was officially named for the dispossessed: Cherokee County. By 1860 the population of the county had grown to about nine thousand whites and more than three thousand slaves, and cotton had become a major crop, according to the *Handbook of Texas Online*.

28 **As for Chief Bowles, his body was left to rot:** "Mr. Tom Ingram who, as a boy, lived near the vicinity of this fight, stated that he has often seen Bowles's skeleton near the Neches River," a local historian wrote in 1924. "The skull remained for many years, but finally disappeared in 1857, after a barbecue was held on the river." Mildred Stanley, "The Cherokee Indians in Smith County," *Texas History Teachers Bulletin*, Oct. 22, 1924.

29 **They picked wild berries, killed rodents and small game:** Fehrenbach, *Comanches*, 34.

29 **And if a mustang could not find grass to eat:** Wallace and Hoebel, *The Comanches*, 41.

29 **the use of horses altered life as profoundly as the Industrial Revolution:** Wallace and Hoebel, *The Comanches*, 35, quoting Walter Prescott Webb, *The Great Plains*: "Steam, electricity, and gasoline have wrought no greater changes in our culture than did horses in the culture of the Plains Indians."

30 **For the next hundred years they were the dominant power:** Hämäläinen, *The Comanche Empire*, 2.

30 **"half horse, half man"**: Homer Thrall, quoted in Wallace and Hoebel, *The Comanches*, 49.

30 **"on their feet the most unattractive and slovenly looking"**: Catlin, *North American Indians*, vol. 2, 66.

30 **wheeling buzzards marked the Comanches' receding presence:** Dobie, *The Mustangs*, 64–68.

30 **Among Comanches, the killing of one's favorite horse:** Wallace and Hoebel, *The Comanches*, 37.

30 **Hanging by a loop of rope:** Wallace and Hoebel, *The Comanches*, 48.

31 **"The bow is placed horizontally in shooting":** Ford, *Rip Ford's Texas*, 135.

31 **"They are a warlike and brave race":** Thomas J. Farnham, quoted in Thwaites, *Early Western Travels*, 151.

31 **"They have been so long accustomed to give a loose rein":** *Telegraph and Texas Register*, April 26, 1843.

31 **"There was never a more splendidly barbaric sight":** Dixon, *Life of "Billy Dixon,"* 158, 159.

31 **the Comanches would steal more horses and kill more whites:** DeVoto, *The Year of Decision, 1846,* 265.

32 **"I was but a boy":** Smithwick, *The Evolution of a State*, 1.

32 **"I was working at the anvil":** Smithwick, *The Evolution of a State*, 57.

32 **The Ranger captain showed himself as one quick to vengeance:** Moore, *Savage Frontier*, vol. 2, 10.

32 **"Just as we were preparing for our supper":** Smithwick, *The Evolution of a State*, 82–87. Smithwick's account is one of two versions by participants in the unfolding battle with Comanches. The other is that of Captain John J. Tumlinson, which was published in John Henry Brown's *Indian Wars and Pioneers of Texas.* The two men disagree on several facts, including the death of the brave first shot by Smithwick. Tumlinson said he shot the Indian dead, while Smithwick said Rohrer clubbed him to death with a gun. The versions also differed on the number of Rangers involved. Tumlinson said he had eighteen men. Smithwick counted sixty mounted Rangers. Both versions were printed decades after the actual encounter.

34 **the Rangers' first battle with the Comanches:** Wilkins, *The Legend Begins*, 18.

CHAPTER 3. BUTCHERIES

37 **"Oh, pray for the Ranger, you kind-hearted stranger":** Dobie, *The Mustangs*, 67.

37 **By one reckoning, about half of the early Rangers were killed every year:** Caperton, "Sketch of Colonel John C. Hays, Texas Ranger," CAH.

38 **And they did so with unbounded gusto:** For more on this, see Fehrenbach, *Comanches*, 473, and S. C. Gwynne's great history of the Comanche wars, *Empire of the Summer Moon*, 82.

38 **Perry produced a brief memoir that conveyed:** Kesselus, *Memoir of Capt'n C. R. Perry*, 3–33.

40 **"I would, if possible, place before your eye":** Jenkins, *Recollections of Early Texas*, 192–93.

40 **"Huzza for McCulloch, the brave rifle Ranger":** Cutrer, *Ben McCulloch and the Frontier Military Tradition*, 2.

41 **"a slow country and slow people live in it":** Cutrer, *Ben McCulloch and the Frontier Military Tradition*, 15.

41 **he was a "black-hearted cowardly villain":** Cutrer, *Ben McCulloch and the Frontier Military Tradition*, 37.

41 **A Galveston newspaper described him as a "gallant but rash man":** *Galveston Daily News*, April 21, 1874.

41 **Sweitzer was killed two years later:** His killer was Robert S. Neighbors, later a noteworthy Indian agent. See Chapter 9.

42 **"We have set up our lodges in these groves":** Smithwick, *The Evolution of a State*, 134.

42 **"Both nostrils were wide open and denuded of flesh":** Green, *Memoirs of Mary A. Maverick*, 44.

43 **"When the fight began he wrenched a gun from an Indian":** Green, *Memoirs of Mary A. Maverick,* 34.

43 **"What a day of horrors!":** Green, *Memoirs of Mary A. Maverick*, 36.

44 **The Comanches roped him and dragged him from the water:** Jenkins, *Recollections of Early Texas*, 61, 62.

44 **set out with twenty-four Rangers and volunteers:** *Telegraph and Texas Register*, Sept. 9, 1840.

45 **The same warrior ran his lance through him:** McDowell, *Now You Hear My Horn*, 57. Some accounts report that only one child was killed.

45 **a massive crescent across the prairie:** "Brazos," *Life of Robert Hall*, 54.

45 **every building in town but one had been burned:** Brown, *Indian Wars and Pioneers of Texas*, 80.

46 **"hideously bedaubed after their own savage taste":** *Telegraph and Texas Register*, Sept. 9, 1840.

46 **"They seemed to have a talent for finding and blending":** Jenkins, *Recollections of Early Texas*, 64–65.

46 **It was "intensely hot":** Brown, *Indian Wars and Pioneers of Texas*, 81.

47 **This was his best chance to "kill and take Indians":** Cutrer, *Ben McCulloch and the Frontier Military Tradition*, 42.

47 **"In the name of God, General Huston":** Cutrer, *Ben McCulloch and the Frontier Military Tradition*, 43. As with many such quotations, these are of uncertain veracity.

47 **One Comanche warrior's head was "nearly blown off":** "Brazos," Life of Robert Hall, 56–57.
48 **An "old Indian squaw" had shot the woman:** McDowell, Now You Hear My Horn, 63.
48 **Mrs. Watts "possessed great fortitude":** "Brazos," Life of Robert Hall, 55.
48 **The Tonkawas "retired with the prisnrs":** McDowell, Now You Hear My Horn, 72.
48 **"Our allies were cooking [a] Comanche warrior":** "Brazos," Life of Robert Hall, 57.
48 **"He drew his long hack knife":** McDowell, Now You Hear My Horn, 65, 66.
48 **"We captured the Indian pack train":** "Brazos," Life of Robert Hall, 58.
49 **For the first time in a major battle, they had used Indian tactics:** Gwynne, Empire of the Summer Moon, 99.
49 **"But for our early interventions":** Telegraph and Texas Register, Sept. 9, 1840.
49 **Most of the Indians, along with hundreds of their stolen horses:** Moore, Savage Frontier, vol. 3, 128.
49 **"Thay got a way with evry thing wee had":** Kesselus, Memoir of Capt'n C. R. Perry, 12.
50 **"The first who go will surely get a fight":** Moore, Savage Frontier, vol. 3, 146.
50 **"Every countenance beamed with feelings of pride":** Telegraph and Texas Register, Nov. 18, 1840.
51 **where they were sold into slavery:** Smithwick, The Evolution of a State, 184.
51 **"gave a splendid ball in honor":** Jenkins, Recollections of Early Texas, 174.
51 **"Little did these blood thirsty monsters think":** Wilbarger, Indian Depredations in Texas, 185.

CHAPTER 4. ARMS AND THE MAN

53 **"The Pocket and Short Barrel Belt Pistol":** New York Daily Herald, Dec. 5, 1844.
53 **He called himself "The Celebrated Dr. Coult":** New York Evening Post, July 7, 1832; Fayetteville (N.C.) Weekly Observer, Oct. 8, 1833. Much of Colt's early background is taken from Edwards, The Story of Colt's Revolver, 21–28.
54 **"a handsome baby, not red like most newcomers to this planet":** Greer, Texas Ranger, 15.
54 **"With a movement as quick as lightning":** I. D. Affleck, "History of John C. Hays," CAH.
55 **"He jumped up and hallooed, 'I've killed an Indian!'":** Caperton, "Sketch of Colonel John C. Hays, Texas Ranger," CAH.
55 **"His figure, though scarce the average height":** Webber, Tales of the Southern Border, 54–55.
55 **"When Jack Hays's eyes begin to darken":** Greer, Texas Ranger, 76.
56 **"a large quantity of goods":** Telegraph and Texas Register, May 31, 1843.
56 **"We made a charge," Hays wrote, "and the enemy gave way":** Moore, Savage Frontier, vol. 3, 215.
56 **"Capt. Hays arrested three of these spies . . . and shot them":** Telegraph and Texas Register, July 12, 1843.
56 **The chief justice of the district was reputed to be dead drunk:** Solms-Braunfels, Texas 1844–45, 59.
56 **"That man eminently deserves the gratitude of his country":** Telegraph and Texas Register, Oct. 23, 1844.
57 **a "moral monstrosity," as well as a "cold-blooded assassin":** Linn, Reminiscences of Fifty Years in Texas, 323–24.
57 **"Though a lamb in peace":** Lee, Three Years among the Comanches, 15–16. In this description, Lee echoes that of many others who met and rode with Hays. But Lee made a number of dubious claims in this book, which was originally published in 1859. Among them: he fought in numerous Indian battles with the Rangers and was held captive by Comanches. No official records have been found that substantiate any of this. Like many Ranger tales, Lee's can be placed somewhere between exaggeration and outright fiction. Nonetheless, some historians have given him credit for accurate descriptions of Rangers and the conditions they faced.
57 **"Yonder are the Indians, boys, and yonder are our horses":** Wilbarger, Indian Depredations in Texas, 73. Like Nelson Lee, Wilbarger has been accused by historians of propagating inaccuracies and fable. At the least, his book provides an insight into the thinking of white Texans of this era.
58 **"to sell his life dearly, for he had scarcely a gleam of hope":** Reid, The Scouting Expeditions of McCulloch's Texas Rangers, 111–12.
58 **"He would come out of his retreat, fire on them, and drive them back":** Caperton, "Sketch of Colonel John C. Hays, Texas Ranger," CAH, 31.
59 **"The Indians who had believed for a long time that he bore a charmed life":** Reid, The Scouting Expeditions of McCulloch's Texas Rangers, 112.
59 **"Hays, while surrounded by Comanche Indians":** Texas Historical Commission, Marker Number 10035, Atlas Number 5171010035.
59 **However, no actual evidence, from agency records to contemporary diaries:** For more on questions about Hays and Enchanted Rock, see Wilkins, The Legend Begins, 201–5, and Moore, Savage Frontier, vol. 3, 341–48.
60 **Americans in Texas loved money more than anything, the prince said:** Solms-Braunfels, Texas 1844–45, 49, 87.

60 **"After practisng for three or four months we became so purfect":** McDowell, *Now You Hear My Horn*, 123.

61 **"The men are all well-armed, and are probably the most happy":** *Telegraph and Texas Register*, April 17, 1844.

61 **it was "in the most secluded situation we could discover":** Lee, *Three Years among the Comanches*, 21.

61 **Should a snake bite one of them:** The list of trail remedies comes from Haley, *Charles Goodnight*, 85.

61 **"I have frequently seen him sitting by his camp fire at night":** Wilbarger, *Indian Depredations in Texas*, 72.

62 **One historian described him as "unassuming to the point of girlish modesty":** Edwards, *The Story of Colt's Revolver*, 215.

62 **"Several shots at close quarters were interchanged":** Edmund L. Dana, "Incidents in the Life of Capt. Samuel H. Walker, Texan Ranger," *Proceedings of the Wyoming Historical and Geological Society*, 1882.

62 **"I could have no doubt but their intentions were hostile":** Wilkins, *The Legend Begins*, 181.

63 **Problems plagued the early versions:** The story of Colt and the development of his revolver is taken from Hosley, *Colt*, 18ff.

63 **"I hardly knew where the dinner of tomorrow would come from":** "10 Things You May Not Know about Samuel Colt," History.com.

63 **the ill-fated Texas Navy had ordered 180 of the new Colts:** Jordan, *Lone Star Navy*, 180.

64 **Three of the rebellious sailors:** "The Texas Navy," U.S. Naval History Division, Washington, D.C., 1968, 14–16. Archived at the University of North Texas Portal to Texas History, https://texashistory .unt.edu.

64 **the ship's hull was, according to one report, "considerably worm-eaten":** *Telegraph and Texas Register*, July 6, 1842.

64 **a "bloated maggot," in Houston's description:** Jordan, *Lone Star Navy*, 273.

65 **the Comanches gathered on horseback on the crest of a rocky hill:** Moore, *Savage Frontier*, vol. 4, 146.

65 **"Aboute Sixty of the read devels come oute of the brush":** Kesselus, *Memoir of Capt'n C. R. Perry*, 21.

65 **"At a distance of 30 steps the ball did its office":** *Telegraph and Texas Register*, July 3, 1844.

65 **"We were right glad they fled":** Green, *Memoirs of Mary A. Maverick*, 83.

65 **"I cannot recommend these arms too highly":** Wilkins, *The Legend Begins*, 180–81.

66 **Hays named the stream along which the engagement occurred:** James Donovan, "Two Sams and Their Six-Shooter," *Texas Monthly*, April 2016.

66 **"Up to this time these daring Indians had always supposed themselves":** Parsons, *Samuel Colt's Own Record of Transactions with Captain Walker and Eli Whitney, Jr., in 1847*, 10, 75.

CHAPTER 5. "AN INSOLENT AND SAVAGE RACE"

69 **"Half the Nation are thieves in Prison":** McCutchan, *Mier Expedition Diary*, 113.

69 **They belonged to a class, a white Methodist minister wrote:** De Leon, *They Called Them Greasers*, 17.

69 **A Mexican "will feed you on his best, 'senor' you and 'muchas gracias' you":** Duval, *The Adventures of Big-Foot Wallace*, 163. Duval insisted that his 1871 book was not "a compilation of imaginary scenes and incidents" but was "written out from notes furnished by [Wallace] and told, as well as my memory serves me, in his own language."

70 **Without them, it could be argued, America would look nothing:** For an extended and cogent discussion of this, see Haynes, *Soldiers of Misfortune*.

71 **"They went down close to the Alamo":** Morrell, *Flowers and Fruits from the Wilderness*, 168.

71 **The "motley mongrels" . . . mounted a full charge:** *Telegraph and Texas Register*, Nov. 2, 1842.

71 **"Here, there and everywhere we see the wretches tumble down like beeves":** *Telegraph and Texas Register*, Nov. 2, 1842.

71 **"Thare was so many of them kild":** McDowell, *Now You Hear My Horn*, 102–7.

72 **They had confidence . . . that "they could whip 200 Mexicans":** *Telegraph and Texas Register*, Nov. 16, 1842.

72 **"That is the way I used to do":** *Telegraph and Texas Register*, Nov. 16, 1842.

72 **This "made an awful havoc among our men":** *Telegraph and Texas Register*, Nov. 16, 1842.

72 **"The enemy showed no respect":** *Telegraph and Texas Register*, Nov. 16, 1842.

72 **"That was the moast horrowble Sight I ever saw":** Kesselus, *Memoir of Capt'n C. R. Perry*, 15.

72 **"Thirty-five dead":** Morrell, *Flowers and Fruits from the Wilderness*, 172.

73 **"one of the most cruel and murderous massacres":** Jenkins, *Recollections of Early Texas*, 97.

73 **The Lone Star republic, he wrote, was "a young nation just emerging":** "A Letter Book of Joseph Eve, United States Chargé d'Affaires to Texas," ed. Joseph Milton Nance, *SWHQ*, April 1940.

73 **The president's office was a one-room cabin on Ferry Street:** Haynes, *Soldiers of Misfortune*, 25.

74 **"no more fit to command an army of men," one soldier wrote:** Harvey Adams, "Somervill's [sic] Expedition against the Southwest," typescript, CAH, 70.

74 **Another said his particular company "loathed General Somervell":** Sterling Brown Hendricks, "The Somervell Expedition to the Rio Grande, 1842," *SWHQ*, October 1919.

74 **Still another claimed the general had a "weak heart, and old woman's Soul":** Nance, *Attack and Counterattack*, 563.

74 **"a man designed by Houston to ruin the expedition":** McCutchan, *Mier Expedition Diary*, 111.

74 **"[His] delight has been to rob, murder, and spread devastation among the Saints":** Alexander L. Baugh, "Guilty of High Misdemeanors, Villainy, Conspiracy and Treason: Samuel Bogart's 1839 Letter about the Mormons to the Quincy, Illinois Postmaster," *Mormon Historical Studies*. Additional information comes from Nicholas A. Ballesteros, "Samuel Bogart," *Handbook of Texas Online*.

75 **"A motley mixed-up crowd we were":** Duval, *The Adventures of Big-Foot Wallace*, 159–60.

75 **"ashes, charcoal and remnants of bones":** Adams, "Somervill's [sic] Expedition against the Southwest," 18–19.

75 **Most of the Anglos had evacuated San Antonio:** Haynes, *Soldiers of Misfortune*, 27.

75 **"I stood by the fire all night":** Adams, "Somervill's [sic] Expedition against the Southwest," 30.

75 **"in order to gratify their beastly lusts":** Adams, "Somervill's [sic] Expedition against the Southwest," 32.

75 **Southwest Army of Operations . . . "There":** Sowell, *The Mier Expedition*, 1.

76 **"been made subject to every rude assault that a ruffian set could offer":** Hendricks, "The Somervell Expedition to the Rio Grande, 1842."

76 **"left . . . their bones to bleach in that desolate country":** Adams, "Somervill's [sic] Expedition against the Southwest," 40.

76 **"punished by a few hours of torturing sickness":** McCutchan, *Mier Expedition Diary*, 19.

77 **"all care-free people who are fond of dancing":** José María Sánchez, "A Trip to Texas in 1828," trans. Carlos E. Castañeda, *SWHQ*, April 1926.

77 **the inmates "did with high glee":** *Telegraph and Texas Register*, Jan. 4, 1843.

77 **"The plunder when deposited":** Hendricks, "The Somervell Expedition to the Rio Grande, 1842."

77 **"It was a mountain of no inconsiderable size":** Adams, "Somervill's [sic] Expedition against the Southwest," 52.

78 **the men of the village "looked daggers at us":** Adams, "Somervill's [sic] Expedition against the Southwest," 68.

78 **"The men became perfectly wild":** Adams, "Somervill's [sic] Expedition against the Southwest," 69–70. After this invasion fiasco, Somervell was appointed a collector of customs on the Texas coast. He drowned in 1854; his body was discovered lashed to a capsized boat carrying a substantial amount of money. Nonetheless, Somervell County in north-central Texas is named for him.

78 **"one of the tallest men in the country":** McCutchan, *Mier Expedition Diary*, 33n.

79 **"You have had a trap laid for you":** Cutrer, *Ben McCulloch and the Frontier Military Tradition*, 61.

79 **"They are good for nothing":** Duval, *The Adventures of Big-Foot Wallace*, 165.

79 **A Mexican attack from the rear:** Haynes, *Soldiers of Misfortune*, 72.

79 **The Texans were "bound hand and foot":** Duval, *The Adventures of Big-Foot Wallace*, 170–71.

79 **insisting his men be held under the "principles of civilized warfare":** *New Orleans Daily Picayune*, April 23, 1843.

79 **The men of these villages were "cursing and stoning them":** Reid, *The Scouting Expeditions of McCulloch's Texas Rangers*, 53.

80 **"the weak began to perish of hunger and thirst":** "Brazos," Life of Robert Hall, 113.

80 **"Boys, this is the largest stake I ever played for":** Sowell, *The Mier Expedition*, 11.

80 **"Well, they just took them out and shot them":** A. Russell Buchanan, "George Washington Trahern: Texan Cowboy Soldier from Mier to Buena Vista," *SWHQ*, July 1954.

80 **"When the Mexican Government saw that he did not draw":** McCutchan, *Mier Expedition Diary*, 92.

80 **"I am now . . . in the confines of the most miserable prison":** *Austin Statesman*, March 5, 1874.

81 **rice "spoiled by a rat being cooked in it":** McCutchan, *Mier Expedition Diary*, 126–27.

81 **Cameron, a barely literate Scottish stonemason, had been one of Mustang Gray's:** McCutchan, *Mier Expedition Diary*, 37n, and Haynes, *Soldiers of Misfortune*, 44.

82 **"running about town as gay as a lark":** *The Radical* (Bowling Green, MO), Feb. 18, 1843.

82 **Santa Anna ordered that he be released and given a room:** Thompson, *Recollections of Mexico*, 75–76.

82 **"*My blood boils* within me as if *heated by the demons*":** McCutchan, *Mier Expedition Diary*, 164.

82 **"*We would soon be on the soil of that country*":** McCutchan, *Mier Expedition Diary*, 186.

82 **On that same day, James K. Polk was well on his way:** Polk's vice president was George Mifflin Dallas, a former mayor of Philadelphia for whom Dallas County in Texas was named. The city of Dallas, which is in Dallas County, may have been named for someone else, though that is unclear. "In truth, we will probably never know for whom [founder] John Neely Bryan intended to name the city," says the City of Dallas website. "Bryan never managed to write down memoirs or reminiscences; he died in the State Lunatic Asylum in Austin in 1877."

83 **An excruciating surgical procedure to remove urinary stones:** Seigenthaler, *James K. Polk*, 19.

83 **"smaller-than-life figure with larger-than-life ambitions":** Robert W. Merry author's biography, amazon.com.

83 **To get California, he probably would have to go to war:** DeVoto, *The Year of Decision, 1846*, 7, and Greenberg, *A Wicked War*, 25–37.

83 **"Annexation and war with Mexico are identical":** Merry, *A Country of Vast Designs*, 75.

84 **"Mexico has passed the boundary of the United States":** Merry, *A Country of Vast Designs*, 241–45.

CHAPTER 6. CRY VENGEANCE

87 **"Then mount and away!":** Reid, *The Scouting Expeditions of McCulloch's Texas Rangers*, 37.

87 **"Instantly [Walker] dropped the burden he was carrying":** Dana, "Incidents in the Life of Capt. Samuel H. Walker, Texan Ranger."

88 **his friends took to calling him "Mad" Walker:** Robert Nieman, "Sam Walker," *Texas Ranger Dispatch*, Winter 2002.

88 **"My experience thus far has only increased my anxiety and ambition":** Samuel Walker file, Texas State Library and Archives (hereafter TSLA).

88 **Taylor wore civilian clothes and a large straw hat:** Greenberg, *A Wicked War*, 98. Greenberg's 2012 book is an excellent history of the events leading up to the war and the invasion itself.

88 **"a plain old farmer-looking man":** James K. Holland, "Diary of a Texan Volunteer in the Mexican War," *SWHQ*, July 1926.

88 **"This is the dirtiest place":** Ferrell, *Monterrey Is Ours!*, 7.

88 **"not fit for a hog to live in":** Holland, "Diary of a Texan Volunteer in the Mexican War."

89 **"The sun streamed upon us like living fire":** Blackwood, *To Mexico with Scott*, 25, 28.

89 **So thick were the snakes in places:** Spurlin, *Texas Volunteers in the Mexican War*, 5.

89 **"We are completely overrun with wood ticks":** Blackwood, *To Mexico with Scott*, 37.

89 **Taylor settled his men across the river from the Mexican town of Matamoros:** That is the modern spelling of the city's name. It was then known as Matamoras.

89 **An army band played "The Star-Spangled Banner" and "Yankee Doodle":** Merry, *A Country of Vast Designs*, 240.

89 **"that two or three of the deserters were reached by musket-balls":** Greenberg, *A Wicked War*, 101, and *Baltimore Daily Commercial*, May 11, 1846.

89 **he relented and put Walker in charge of a company of "Texas Mounted Rangers":** Wilkins, *The Highly Irregular Irregulars*, 25.

90 **He "was probably choked to death":** Henry, *Campaign Sketches of the War with Mexico*, 85.

90 **"They were so heavy and strong against us":** A. Russell Buchanan, "George Washington Trahern: Texan Cowboy Soldier from Mier to Buena Vista," *SWHQ*, July 1954.

90 **"Had the men who were left obeyed the injunctions of the captain":** Taylor to adjutant general, May 3, 1846, Walter Prescott Webb Collection, CAH.

90 **"The four gun battery in our camp was immediately opened":** *Richmond (Va.) Enquirer*, May 19, 1846.

90 **"six miles of the worst thicket":** Oury's recollections appear in Dana, "Incidents in the Life of Capt. Samuel H. Walker, Texan Ranger." Oury, who had been a member of Jack Hays's Ranger company, survived his service in the Mexican War and went on to become the mayor of Tucson, Arizona.

91 **"Walker ran a great many risks making his way to the fort":** Henry, *Campaign Sketches of the War with Mexico*, 89.

91 **These weapons launched a deadly array of projectiles:** National Park Service, "Palo Alto Battlefield: A Thunder of Cannon," www.nps.gov.

91 **"They rode upon us eight hundred strong":** Blackwood, *To Mexico with Scott*, 48. Captain Smith's observations and reflections were delivered in a series of vivid letters to his wife. He died in 1847 after being shot during a battle near Molino del Rey. His last written words, penned to his wife a few hours beforehand, were: "I am thankful that you do not know the peril we are in. Good night!"

92 **"Repeatedly were bayonets crossed":** Henry, *Campaign Sketches of the War with Mexico*, 96.

92 **"The enemy here fought like devils":** Blackwood, *To Mexico with Scott*, 51.

92 **The American victory, he said, "showed most plainly and beautifully":** Greenberg, *A Wicked War*, 120.

93 **"POOR CAPTAIN PAGE!!!" read a headline:** Historical Society of Pennsylvania, "A Forgotten American Hero: Capt. John B. Page," *History Hits*, Aug. 10, 2010.

93 **"Her spirit was disturbed by the reflection":** *New Orleans Picayune*, June 24, 1846.

93 **"a gallant soldier in whose bosom dwelt the soul of honor":** *Vicksburg (Miss.) Daily Whig*, July 25, 1846.

93 **"Capt. Walker's company of volunteers effectively repulsed the enemy":** *New York Daily Tribune*, June 15, 1846.

93 **Walker's "services upon the Rio Grande have endeared his name":** *New Orleans Daily Picayune*, June 5, 1846.

93 **"As a scout, or skirmisher, he has not a superior":** *Spirit of Jefferson (W.V.)*, July 3, 1846.

93 **"so desperate as to be thought fool hardy":** *Richmond (Va.) Enquirer*, May 19, 1846.

94 **"We nominate Walker, the brave Texan soldier":** *New York Herald*, May 20, 1846.

94 **"A thief calling himself Capt. Walker of the Texan [sic] Rangers":** *Mississippi Free Trader*, Aug. 18, 1846.

94 **"He came in ahead of the remnant of his flying corps":** *New York Daily Tribune*, May 18, 1846.

94 **Walker and only twelve Rangers had battled and subdued a force:** *Palmyra (Mo.) Weekly Whig*, May 21, 1846.

94 **"The moment the Mexican's horse was within his reach":** *Joliet (Ill.) Signal*, Nov. 17, 1846.

94 **"The gallant Captain, when mounted on Tornado":** *New York Herald*, May 24, 1846.

95 **Walker called on none other than President Polk:** Wilkins, *The Highly Irregular Irregulars*, 115.

95 **"At the instance of Capt Walker, the Secretary of War desires":** Edwards, *The Story of Colt's Revolver*, 218.

96 **"We are now on our way to the seat of War":** Parsons, *Samuel Colt's Own Record*, 64.

96 **"They are all fine, strong, healthy and good looking men":** Oswandel, *Notes of the Mexican War*, 89ff.

96 **"I of course took summary measures with them":** Letter of June 6, 1847, Samuel Walker file, TSLA.

96 **"Who, I ask, has not seen or heard of the gallant Walker's bravery?":** *Baltimore Sun*, Nov. 16, 1847.

97 **A "beautiful town," said Lieutenant William D. Wilkins:** Smith and Judah, *Chronicles of the Gringos*, 270.

97 **"Here rose a wild yell":** *Brooklyn Daily Eagle*, Dec. 3, 1850.

98 **Now "maddened with liquor," Lieutenant Wilkins said, they committed:** Smith and Judah, *Chronicles of the Gringos*, 271.

99 **"I could do nothing with them":** Thompson, *Fifty Miles and a Fight*, 8.

99 **"Walker's splendid record attracted to him public attention":** Dana, "Incidents in the Life of Capt. Samuel H. Walker, Texan Ranger."

99 **"There is, perhaps, no man whose history . . . is so deeply fraught":** *Baltimore Sun*, Nov. 17, 1847.

99 **"For a braver, or a better, or a more chivalrous knight":** Henry Kirby Benner, "Ballads of the Campaign in Mexico," *Graham's Magazine*, Feb. 1850.

99 **"the terrible Texan Walker":** Alcaraz et al., *The Other Side*, 402, 442.

100 **"Endowed with great activity and skill":** *Baltimore Sun*, Nov. 16, 1847. Walker was initially buried in Mexico. His body was exhumed and reburied in San Antonio near the Alamo. Walker County in southeast Texas is named for him.

100 **"The rangers are all well mounted":** *Telegraph and Texas Register*, May 6, 1846.

100 **"Some of us . . . had traveled six hundred miles":** Greer, *Buck Barry*, 40.

100 **"A Mexican was shot by a Texan Ranger":** *New Orleans Picayune*, July 7, 1846.

101 **"About all of the Texans seem to think it perfectly right":** Greenberg, *A Wicked War*, 131.

CHAPTER 7. *LOS DIABLOS*

103 **"The Rangers were the Scouts of our Army":** Chamberlain, *My Confession*, 39.

103 **"Strictly speaking, the army does not exist":** Ramírez, *Mexico during the War with the United States*, 124. See also Henderson, *A Glorious Defeat*, 148.

104 **Desertion among the ranks was epidemic:** Henderson, *A Glorious Defeat*, 148–49.

104 **Their uniform . . . was "a dirty shirt and a five-shooter":** Giddings, *Sketches of the Campaign in Northern Mexico*, 97n.

104 **"The best of them . . . looked as if they could steal sheep":** Ferrell, *Monterrey Is Ours!*, 14.

104 **"Some wore buckskin shirts, black with grease and blood":** Chamberlain, *My Confession*, 39.

104 **The "untutored greaser," Ranger Ephraim Daggett said:** George, *Heroes and Incidents of the Mexican War*, 213.

105 **"Such yells exploded on the air":** Evans, *Confederate Military History*, vol. 11, 146, and Oates, *Visions of Glory*, 43.

105 **"As a mounted soldier [the Ranger] has had no counterpart:** Giddings, *Sketches of the Campaign in Northern Mexico*, 97.

105 **The Rangers, he said, "love to fight better":** *The Tennessean*, Oct. 30, 1846.

105 **they would "not easily submit to discipline":** Ripley, *The War with Mexico*, 98.

105 **"too hot for a lizard to live":** James K. Holland, "Diary of a Texan Volunteer in the Mexican War," *SWHQ*, July 1926.

105 **soldiers felt "the sun pouring its hottest rays":** Kendall, *Dispatches from the Mexican War*, 69.

105 **"We used the river water":** "Reminiscences of Jno. Duff Brown," *SWHQ*, April 1909.

105 **"Sometimes we traveled for miles, without a single sign":** Reid, *The Scouting Expeditions of McCulloch's Texas Rangers*, 47.

105 **"In all my life I was never as hot":** Holland, "Diary of a Texan Volunteer in the Mexican War."

106 **"Never were a set of men or horses more heartily tired":** Reid, *The Scouting Expeditions of McCulloch's Texas Rangers*, 39–43.

107 **assault on Monterrey:** This is the modern spelling. At the time it was spelled Monterey.

107 **"There was not a minute at any time":** Kendall, *Dispatches from the Mexican War*, 57.

107 **"A river, clear as crystal, flows on one side of the city":** Giddings, *Sketches of the Campaign in Northern Mexico*, 141.

107 **"Every fire was met with a hearty response":** Holland, "Diary of a Texan Volunteer in the Mexican War."

107 **"Like boys at play . . . those fearless":** Giddings, *Sketches of the Campaign in Northern Mexico*, 143, 144.

108 **for whom the city of Fort Worth later was named:** After the war, Worth was named commander of the newly created Department of Texas. But he contracted cholera in 1849 and died in San Antonio.

108 **"Now that danger is expected":** Holland, "Diary of a Texan Volunteer in the Mexican War."

108 **"Within a few feet of the Mexican":** Greer, *Buck Barry*, 34. Also Greer, *Texas Ranger*, 139–40.

108 **Wilcox and others say Najera was mortally wounded:** Kendall, *Dispatches from the Mexican War*, 123–26, and Reid, *The Scouting Expeditions of McCulloch's Texas Rangers*, 156–60. See also Wilcox, *History of the Mexican War*, 92–93.

108 **"He was a tall, splendid-looking fellow":** Reid, *The Scouting Expeditions of McCulloch's Texas Rangers*, 157.

109 **"The dreaded Texans, who had unnumbered wrongs to avenge":** Kendall, *Dispatches from the Mexican War*, 131.

109 **the Rangers "brave as lions":** Ferrell, *Monterrey Is Ours!*, 135.

109 **"[It] was done in quick time under the heaviest firing":** Holland, "Diary of a Texan Volunteer in the Mexican War."

109 **"Which made every house a fortress":** Greer, *Buck Barry*, 38, 39.

109 **they "were maddened with disappointment":** Reid, *The Scouting Expeditions of McCulloch's Texas Rangers*, 204.

109 **"Their tiger-like ferocity at Monterrey":** Reprinted in *Detroit Daily Free Press*, Oct. 31, 1846.

110 **"They were warmly greeted by thousands":** *New Orleans Picayune*, Nov. 13, 1846.

110 **"The services rendered by Major McCulloch and his men":** 30th U.S. Congress, 1st Session, Executive Document No. 60, letter of June 8, 1847.

110 **"This is one of the seven wonders":** Oswandel, *Notes of the Mexican War*, 225.

111 **"the last man to quit the field" when the battle was done:** *Washington Union*, Jan. 13, 1848.

111 **"He was almost idolized by many":** Ford, *Rip Ford's Texas*, 107–8.

111 **"We come to make no war upon the people of Mexico":** Johannsen, *To the Halls of the Montezumas*, 32.

111 **"I do not think there was ever a more wicked war":** Greenberg, *A Wicked War*, vii.

111 **"They make a wasteland and call it peace":** Greenberg, *A Wicked War*, 247.

112 **"A rough crucifix was fastened to a rock":** Chamberlain, *My Confession*, 86–88. Some accounts dispute Chamberlain's estimate of the number of dead, placing it closer to four.

112 **"On the day of battle I am glad to have Texas soldiers":** Mark E. Nackman, "The Making of the Texan Citizen Soldier, 1835–1860," *SWHQ*, Jan. 1975.

112 **"The constant recurrence of such atrocities":** House Executive Document No. 60, letter of June 16, 1847.

112 **"They were excellent light troops":** Giddings, *Sketches of the Campaign in Northern Mexico*, 221–22.

113 **"They . . . spare none, but shoot down every one they meet":** Edwards, *A Campaign in New Mexico*, 156.

113 **"The loveliest of the mingled blood of the Spaniard and the Aztec":** Clemens, *Mustang Gray: A Romance*, 291.

113 **"There was a noble Ranger":** Frank Wagner, "Mabry B. (Mustang) Gray," *Handbook of Texas Online*.

114 "This party, in cold blood, murdered almost the entire male population": Smith, *Chile con Carne*, 294–95.

114 "After being smeared with tar": Giddings, *Sketches of the Campaign in Northern Mexico*, 304–5.

115 "The grim old Ranger would coolly fire his rifle": Chamberlain, *My Confession*, 176–77. Some historians accuse Chamberlain of exaggerations and fabrications in his book, but contemporary news accounts also mention Gray's retaliatory strike.

115 General Taylor wrote that he believed Rangers and others had committed an "atrocious massacre": Walter Prescott Webb collection, CAH.

115 Gray returned to the Nueces Strip and died the next year of cholera: Collins, *Texas Devils*, 245.

115 "Here they came, rag-tag and bob-tail": *Washington Union*, March 6, 1848.

115 "Women, affrighted, rushed from the balconies": *Abbeville (S.C.) Banner*, Jan. 5, 1848.

116 "In a very few minutes there were ten dead Mexicans": *Abbeville (S.C.) Banner*, Jan. 5, 1848.

116 the Rangers were "not in the habit of being insulted": *Washington Union*, March 6, 1848.

116 "The two men talked pleasantly over coffee": Ford, *Rip Ford's Texas*, 85n.

116 "He was assailed by a murderous crowd": Ford, *Rip Ford's Texas*, 83–84.

116 newspaper correspondent wrote: *Detroit Free Press*, Oct. 31, 1846.

117 "Suppose you let me present you to General Santa Anna": Kenly, *Memoirs of a Maryland Volunteer*, 395.

117 "We discovered everything at a white heat": Ford, *Rip Ford's Texas*, 103–4.

118 "Some seventy-five or eighty of the Texas Rangers": *The (Boston) Liberator*, Oct. 27, 1848.

118 "The Rangers . . . are the very dregs of society": Domenech, *Missionary Adventures in Texas and Mexico*, 176.

119 "Nothing born south of the Rio Grande can withstand Walker": Ingraham, *The Texan Ranger*, 41, 42.

119 "Was it a wonder that it was sometimes difficult": Ford, *Rip Ford's Texas*, 72.

119 "Yes! some of the incarnate fiends . . . boldly walked the streets": Reid, *The Scouting Expeditions of McCulloch's Texas Rangers*, 53.

120 "Is it any wonder . . . with the recollection": Duval, *The Adventures of Big-Foot Wallace*, 11, 175.

120 "A nobler set of fellows than these . . . never unsheathed a sword": *Washington Union*, March 6, 1848.

CHAPTER 8. CROSSING THE RIVER

123 "It is hard to convince the Texans": House Executive Document No. 277, 42nd Congress, 2nd Session, "Claims of the State of Texas," 103–4.

123 "Some of the fiercest and most insolent of the tribes": *New York Times*, Dec. 3, 1851.

123 "At this moment there is not a father of a family": *New Orleans Daily Picayune*, Oct. 23, 1855.

124 "His whole attire had the rather un-Indian merit of neatness": Montgomery, *Eagle Pass*, 75.

124 "Seminole Indians are committing depredations on the frontier": *New York Times*, March 28, 1854.

124 "Many suffer from the scurvy, for want of lime-juice": House Executive Document No. 277, 71, 77.

125 "one of the most horrible and cold-blooded massacres": Texas Adjutant General Records, CAH.

125 but the Rangers still lacked permanent financing and institutional structure: As Walter Prescott Webb wrote in his 1935 history of the Rangers: "For ten years after the Mexican War the Texas Rangers were little more than a historical expression." Webb, *The Texas Rangers*, 130.

125 "Rangers are rowdies," wrote General Albert J. Myer: "General Albert J. Myer: The Father of the Signal Corps," *West Texas Historical Association Yearbook*, 1953.

126 Pease authorized Ranger captain James H. Callahan to "raise a company of mounted men": Texas Adjutant General Records, CAH.

126 The man, who had been shot in the leg, signaled that he wished to surrender: Sowell, *Rangers and Pioneers of Texas*, n.p.

126 Historical evidence strongly points to a secret plan by Callahan: Though the general historical consensus is that Callahan was pursuing runaway slaves—and in this writer's opinion there should be little doubt—the debate continues. The April 2018 edition of the *Southwestern Historical Quarterly* contains an essay in which author Curtis Chubb argues that the "goal of the expedition was exactly what Captain Callahan stated: to punish the Lipans for what they had done to Texans."

127 In Fort Worth a vigilante mob seized abolitionist Methodist minister: Donald E. Reynolds, "Anthony Bewley," *Handbook of Texas Online*.

127 the Mosquito Coast could be used as a way station: This account of the Nicaraguan misadventure is taken from Earl W. Fornell, "Texans and Filibusters in the 1850's," *SWHQ*, April 1956.

128 "It appears that the company reported as having deserted in a body": *Daily News* (London), Sept. 15, 1856.

128 **"There wasn't no reason to run up North":** National Humanities Center, "Runaways: Selections from the WPA Interviews of Formerly Enslaved African Americans, 1936–1938." 2007.

128 **a "celebrated pack of negro dogs" for $5 a day:** Texas Runaway Slave Project, East Texas Research Center, Stephen F. Austin State University.

128 **"One Hundred Dollars' Reward!":** Texas Runaway Slave Project.

129 **In 1850, army captain Randolph B. Marcy came upon two slave girls:** Marcy, *Thirty Years of Army Life on the Border*, 55–56.

129 **"Brave negro! say I":** Olmsted, *A Journey through Texas*, 327.

129 **one fugitive floated across the Rio Grande on a bale of cotton:** Martin Kohn, "South to Freedom," *Humanities*, March/April 2013.

129 **"The average value of each negro":** *Texas State Times*, June 2, 1855.

129 **"vie in grandeur with the old Roman Empire":** Roy Sylvan Dunn, "The KGC in Texas, 1860–61," *SWHQ*, April 1967.

129 **"The evil is augmenting daily":** *Texas State Times*, June 2, 1855.

130 **"Heaven," he wrote, "would bless this enterprise with success":** Ronnie C. Tyler, "Fugitive Slaves in Mexico," *Journal of Negro History*, January 1972.

130 **"he was arrested by the vigilant Rangers [and] thrown into chains":** C. W. Webber, "My First Day with the Rangers," *American Whig Review*, March 1845.

130 **"But seeing that his shot did not kill him, [a] ranger dismounted":** Sowell, *Rangers and Pioneers of Texas*, n.p.

130 **"He told me that there would be no difficulty to my crossing":** *Texas State Gazette*, Oct. 20, 1855.

131 **"If any property is taken," he wrote:** Edward J. Burleson Papers, CAH.

131 **Major General Smith, the army commander, had heard reports:** House Executive Document No. 277, 100.

131 **Callahan's company of eighty-eight men ranged in age:** Ernest C. Shearer, "The Callahan Expedition, 1855," *SWHQ*, April 1951.

131 **"I have now charges on hand against the captain":** House Executive Document No. 277, 83.

131 **The commander of the fort, an army captain and West Point graduate:** Ronnie C. Tyler, "The Callahan Expedition of 1855: Indians or Negroes?," *SWHQ*, April 1967.

132 **they seized some private ferry boats at gunpoint:** Sowell, *Early Settlers and Indian Fighters of Southwest Texas*, 531.

132 **"We met a Mexican":** *Galveston Daily News*, Jan. 8, 1893.

132 **"Then," McDowell said, "the movement of men and the glistening of arms":** *Galveston Daily News*, Jan. 8, 1893.

132 **"Callahan now rode down his line and gave the men a short talk":** Sowell, *Early Settlers and Indian Fighters of Southwest Texas*, 532.

133 **Their real plan, he concluded, was to "induce me to march":** *Texas State Gazette*, Oct. 20, 1855.

133 **"Their houses were chiefly *jacales*":** House Executive Document No. 277, 151.

133 **"they seemed to take delight in displaying":** Jesse Sumpter Papers, CAH.

133 **Burbank had ordered the turning of several cannons toward Piedras Negras:** House Executive Document No. 277, 95.

133 **"We are in hourly expectation of an attack from a thousand Mexicans and Indians":** *Richmond Dispatch*, Oct. 26, 1855.

134 **"was originally intended as an inroad into Mexico in search of negroes":** House Executive Document No. 277, 100.

134 **"To my astonishment, the Texans commenced firing the town":** House Executive Document No. 277, 98.

134 **"a wall of fire now preventing any attack upon us":** *Texas State Gazette*, Oct. 20, 1855.

134 **"about thirty pistols, guns, or rifles":** House Executive Document No. 277, 99.

134 **"A multitude of innocent families are without shelter":** Shearer, "The Callahan Expedition, 1855."

134 **"The Mexicans have themselves alone to blame":** Olmsted, *A Journey through Texas*, 506.

135 **insisting that the border crossing was "justifiable by the law of nations":** Collins, *Texas Devils*, 87.

135 **"The Indians will be led to retaliate":** House Executive Document No. 277, 102–3.

135 **"Your encounter with and defeat of such a large body of Indians":** Texas Adjutant General Records, CAH.

135 **"He plumped him in the back with his six-shooter":** Olmsted, *A Journey through Texas*, 501.

135 **"Capt. Callahan, the gallant ranger, the quiet but fearless gentleman":** *New Orleans Daily Picayune*, April 23, 1856.

136 **a "free negro population is a curse to any people":** Phillips, *White Metropolis*, 25–31.

136 **Callahan "displayed such admirable tact and courage":** Brown, *Indian Wars and Pioneers of Texas*, 601–602.

136 The "brave and daring Callahan," this version said, had a singular purpose": *Galveston Daily News*, Jan. 8, 1893.

137 "Texas was awake to their crimes and did not propose": Cox, *The Texas Rangers*, 138–39.

137 "May those who pass this way or read the romantic pages": *Abilene Reporter-News*, Jan. 25, 1931.

137 "Fiery Callahan's Forgotten Feats," the headline trumpeted: *Dallas Morning News*, Aug. 30, 1931.

138 "Historical and cultural icons are recognized and honored": Texas State Cemetery Visitors' Guide.

CHAPTER 9. HEATHEN LAND

141 "The sight of an American makes me feel like eating little kids": Ford, *Rip Ford's Texas*, 204.

141 "Ours has been a wild life": Ford, *Rip Ford's Texas*, 188.

141 A frontier polymath in buckskin: Historian Michael Collins, in *Texas Devils*, has perceptively written that Ford "arguably stood closer than any person then living to being the Texan everyman."

141 "If savagery is right": Ford, *Rip Ford's Texas*, 118.

142 These were by some reckonings the bloodiest: Webb, *The Texas Rangers*, 151.

142 and hung his shingle: John Salmon Ford, Doctor: Stephen B. Oates, preface to Ford, *Rip Ford's Texas*, xvii.

142 "There is a devil-may-care, confident, contented look": Walter Prescott Webb Collection, CAH.

142 as he signed each one with the valediction *RIP*: Oates, preface to Ford, *Rip Ford's Texas*, xxiii.

143 "the greatest whore in the west": J. F. Elliott, "The Great Western: Sarah Bowman, Mother and Mistress to the U.S. Army," *Journal of Arizona History*, Spring 1989.

143 "Who wants a wife with fifteen thousand dollars": Regina Bennett McNeely, "Sarah Bowman," *Handbook of Texas Online*.

143 "She had the reputation of being something of the roughest fighter": Ford, *Rip Ford's Texas*, 126.

144 "caused Texians to sympathize with a people struggling for liberty": Ford, *Rip Ford's Texas*, 196.

144 "a temporary forgetfulness of words": Hughes, *Rebellious Ranger*, 103, and Ford, *Rip Ford's Texas*, 200.

144 Some of the remaining Americans set fire to the town: Domenech, *Missionary Adventures in Texas and Mexico*, 334.

144 The Texans had fought with "indomitable courage": Ford, *Rip Ford's Texas*, 202, 204.

144 "If there is any one institution by the Word of God": Ford, *Rip Ford's Texas*, 314n.

144 "If slavery is wrong," he thundered, "the Bible is wrong": Hughes, *Rebellious Ranger*, 125.

145 "The risk of landing in Cuba": Ford, *Rip Ford's Texas*, 217.

145 "Within a few months after the [cavalry] patrolling ceased": Fehrenbach, *Comanches*, 428.

145 In 1857, "the fall and winter saw them entering": Greer, *Buck Barry*, 96.

145 "I ask you to give us one regiment of a thousand men of Rangers": *Congressional Globe*, 35th Congress, 1st Session, 672.

145 crossing the Rio Grande to conquer "our poor, distracted, adjoining neighbor": Collins, *Texas Devils*, 103–5.

145 "Thus Texas . . . is left by the Federal Government": Ford, *Rip Ford's Texas*, 223.

146 "I impress upon you the necessity of action": Ford, *Rip Ford's Texas*, 224, 225. See also Fehrenbach, *Comanches*, 428ff.

146 "Some sounded the fear-inspiring warwhoop": Ford, *Rip Ford's Texas*, 228.

146 They came from at least half a dozen tribes: Hughes, *Rebellious Ranger*, 138.

147 "He was a great medicine man": Ford, *Rip Ford's Texas*, 233.

147 "About six rifle shots rang": Ford, *Rip Ford's Texas*, 233. See also Fehrenbach, *Comanches*, 431.

147 "It reminded me of the rude and chivalrous days": *Public Ledger* (Philadelphia, Pa.), June 17, 1858.

147 "The din of the battle had rolled back from the river": Ford, *Rip Ford's Texas*, 234.

148 "one of the greatest scenic and dramatic incidents": *Dallas Morning News*, Dec. 29, 1907.

148 Ford's incursion into Indian Territory violated federal laws: Bob Rea, "Battle of the Antelope Hills," *The Encyclopedia of Oklahoma History and Culture*, www.okhistory.org.

148 "There, on their beds, lay the bodies": George Klos, "'Our People Could Not Distinguish One Tribe from Another': The 1859 Expulsion of the Reserve Indians from Texas," *SWHQ*, April 1994.

148 "the annals of Texas furnish no darker record of blood": *Dallas Daily Herald*, Feb. 9, 1859.

148 "We have no apology to offer": Klos, "'Our People Could Not Distinguish One Tribe from Another.'"

149 "There is probably no set of men on earth readier for a fight": *Texas Democrat*, Sept. 9, 1846. Reprint in Walter Prescott Webb Collection, CAH.

149 "Now, how did [the judge] expect an organized body of men": Ford, *Rip Ford's Texas*, 252–53, 259.

149 Three white men in Indiana were hanged in 1825: Indiana Historical Bureau marker, Madison County, Indiana.

149 "when we saw an Indian we knew how to treat him": Greer, *Buck Barry*, 117.

149 "I have this day crossed all the Indians out of the heathen land": Fehrenbach, *Comanches*, 437.

149 they wept and keened for days: Ford, *Rip Ford's Texas*, 455n.

150 These robbers were known for "seizing any property": Olmsted, *A Journey through Texas*, 443.

150 "The city is infected with lewd and abandoned women": Coker, *The News from Brownsville*, 376.

150 a cholera epidemic that spring killed nearly half its people: Alicia A. Garza and Christopher Long, "Brownsville, TX," *Handbook of Texas Online*.

150 "The Destroying Angel is among us": Coker, *The News from Brownsville*, 116–17.

150 Only one medical doctor practiced in the region: Horgan, *Great River*, 785.

150 This was a "land of pestilence and cutthroats": *Brooklyn Daily Eagle*, June 4, 1859.

151 a society that was "eminently impulsive, unsettled and lawless": Marcy, *Thirty Years of Army Life on the Border*, 389–90.

151 "One of our officers remarked to me one day": Chance, *My Life in the Old Army*, 49.

151 "I saw at Brownsville Mexicans whom the sheriff was flogging": Domenech, *Missionary Adventures in Texas and Mexico*, 238.

151 a man "with eyes deeply sunken and bloodshot": Chamberlain, *My Confession*, 40.

152 In 1755, the lieutenant governor of the province: Spencer Phips Proclamation, Maine Historical Society.

152 they said the scalps came from Indians: Ralph A. Smith, rev. by Sloan Rodgers, "John Joel Glanton," *Handbook of Texas Online*.

152 "In the carnival of blood," a contemporary wrote: Bell, *Reminiscences of a Ranger*, 274. Glanton was killed in 1850 by Yuma Indians in Arizona, who slit his throat and burned his corpse. Some sources claim he was scalped. Glanton and his crew are given an extended fictional treatment in Cormac McCarthy's justly acclaimed and luridly violent 1985 novel, *Blood Meridian*. "The old man raised the axe," McCarthy writes in describing Glanton's death, "and split the head of John Joel Glanton to the thrapple."

152 "Whatever the morality of this contract": *New York Herald*, Aug. 19, 1849.

152 "By the latest accounts he had with him": *New Orleans Picayune*, Aug. 19, 1849.

152 "The Mexicans were treated for a while after annexation": Olmsted, *A Journey through Texas*, 163. See also Alonzo, *Tejano Legacy*.

153 "I saw myself compelled in Texas to defend the Mexican name": Thompson, *Cortina*, v. For anyone wishing to learn the full story of Cortina, Thompson's work is essential.

153 "He was the enemy of the United States": Ford, *Rip Ford's Texas*, 262.

153 which made him an American citizen: José T. Canales, "Juan N. Cortina Presents His Motion for a New Trial," Bernal file, Benson Latin American Collection, University of Texas at Austin.

153 he also fought to defend Matamoros against the so-called liberating army: Thompson, *Cortina*, 23.

153 Shears said later he possessed a warrant "to arrest a disorderly Mexican": Texas Adjutant General Records, CAH.

154 "Fortunately I had absented myself": Texas Adjutant General Records, CAH.

154 someone identified only as Mrs. Woodhouse also died—"of nervous excitement": *Dallas Daily Herald*, Dec. 7, 1859.

154 He and his followers only wished to punish the "criminal, wicked men": Collins, *Texas Devils*, 116.

154 "He was fearless, self-possessed and cunning": Ford, *Rip Ford's Texas*, 261, 262, 298; Collins, *Texas Devils*, 115.

155 With cries of "Death to all Americans": *New Orleans Delta*, Nov. 13, 1859. Some accounts identify him as W. A. Miller.

155 Some envisioned this legion of marauders galloping 350 miles north: Collins, *Texas Devils*, 122.

155 Powers asked that one hundred "well-armed men" board a steamship: *New Orleans Crescent*, Nov. 7, 1859.

155 a letter from "a highly respectable gentleman in Brownsville": *New Orleans Crescent*, Nov. 7, 1859.

155 "Mexicans are against us": *New Orleans Delta*, Dec. 10, 1859.

156 New England abolitionists secretly funded his rebellion: Thompson, *Cortina*, 62.

156 A report by a Brownsville grand jury framed the matter: Texas Adjutant General Records, CAH.

156 "Many of you have been robbed of your property": Archives of *The West*, "Documents on the Brownsville Uprising of Juan Cortina," www.pbs.org.

156 "They insisted that I should give this amount": Texas Adjutant General Records, CAH.

157 The Knights of the Golden Circle resurfaced: Thompson, *Cortina*, 61.

157 residents mistook them for Cortinistas and began firing at them: Thompson, *Fifty Miles and a Fight*, 32.

157 "We had looked to [Tobin's] arrival here as the end of our immediate troubles": *New Orleans Delta*, Dec. 11, 1859.

157 **The mob of Rangers and others hauled Cabrera out of the jail:** House Executive Document No. 81, 36th Congress, 1st Session, "Troubles on the Texas Frontier"; Thompson, Cortina, 63; and Collins, *Texas Devils*, 125.

157 **"We are now at a great loss in regard to having a good officer":** Texas Adjutant General Records, CAH

157 **The Texans found the bodies the next day, stripped and mutilated:** House Executive Document No. 81.

158 **"This is quite a good sized town":** Thompson, *Fifty Miles and a Fight*, 132ff.

158 **"The Rangers are shooting all the dogs & killing all the chickens":** Thompson, *Fifty Miles and a Fight*, 138, 143, 147, 148, 161, 162.

158 **"The fight will commence tonight or in the morning":** *New Orleans Picayune*, Nov. 26, 1859.

158 **"It is not his policy to stand and receive an open attack":** Texas Adjutant General Records, CAH.

159 **"In their disorganized condition an attack":** House Executive Document No. 81.

159 **"Here the Rangers had an admirable opportunity":** Thompson, *Fifty Miles and a Fight*, 140–41.

159 **"It is reported that Col. Ford and 120 picked men are within three days' march":** *New Orleans Sunday Delta*, Dec. 11, 1859.

159 **Now his eyes "danced wildly in their sockets":** Ford, *Rip Ford's Texas*, 265–66.

159 **"I arrived here yesterday":** Texas Adjutant General Records, CAH.

160 **"He is by all odds the better man":** Thompson, *Fifty Miles and a Fight*, 142.

160 **"He burnt the ranches of the brothers Turner":** Statement to the General Claims Commission, United States and Mexico, *Richard King v. United Mexican States*, 80–89. Statement taken on Aug. 6, 1872.

160 **"The fire of the enemy was terrific for a while":** Ford, *Rip Ford's Texas*, 272–74.

161 **Cortina "has been beaten well":** Ford letter to Kenedy, private collection. When the Civil War began in 1861, Ford signed on with the Confederacy. Cortina, however, worked from Mexico on behalf of U.S. forces. "He showed his sympathy for the union cause," wrote J. T. Canales, "because of his conviction that human slavery was wrong."

161 **"Cortina is simply a creation":** Michael G. Webster, "Intrigue on the Rio Grande: The *Rio Bravo* Affair, 1875," *SWHQ*, October 1970.

CHAPTER 10. ON THE BLEEDING FRONTIER

163 **"The Indians are again amongst us":** Winfrey and Day, *The Indian Papers of Texas and the Southwest, 1825–1916*, 44.

164 **"They had to fight the red man at every step":** Sowell, *Rangers and Pioneers of Texas*, n.p.

164 **Drought, overhunting, and Anglo incursions had depleted the buffalo herds:** Hämäläinen, *The Comanche Empire*, 296.

164 **They threw Katherine, fifteen, across a horse:** Michno, *A Fate Worse Than Death*, 184–85.

165 **"The agonizing screams of the victim seemed to delight":** Wilbarger, *Indian Depredations in Texas*, 516.

165 **Comanches often took books from settlers:** Haley, *Charles Goodnight*, 54.

165 **the Comanche raiders killed twenty-three people over the span of two days:** Gwynne, *Empire of the Summer Moon*, 156.

165 **Martha Sherman's mutilated body was displayed in an open-casket funeral:** Michno, *A Fate Worse Than Death*, 186.

166 **"As he turned it carefully over the fire":** Haley, *Charles Goodnight*, 50.

166 **"A norther last night, little rain":** Willis Lang Diary, CAH, 26.

166 **The story is told of a Ranger named Jim Tackitt:** Haley, *Charles Goodnight*, 84–85; *Canyon News*, March 8, 1928; W. K. Baylor, "The Old Frontier, Events of Long Ago," *Frontier Times*, June 1925. Tackitt's name does not appear in the Texas Adjutant General Service Records, but that is not unusual for a Ranger of this period. Haley refers to him as a Ranger, as do the writings of some contemporaries. A 1938 oral history account by his daughter-in-law, Lillie Virginia Tackitt, says he was a Ranger captain. A transcript is in the University of Oklahoma Western History Collections, digital.libraries.ou.edu: "Tackitt, Lillie Virginia, Second Interview."

167 **"True, the Indian mode of indiscriminate warfare was barbarous":** Smithwick, *The Evolution of a State*, 151.

167 **"Some of the boys got drunk":** Willis Lang Diary, CAH, 7.

167 **"Most of the men [were] compelled to reach the settlements on foot":** Wilbarger, *Indian Depredations in Texas*, 335.

167 **a blaze that scorched hundreds of thousands of acres:** Benner, *Sul Ross*, 43.

167 **"They were under the control of the Col., and upon him rests the responsibility":** *White Man*, Sept. 13, 1860.

168 **A "large piece of his scalp" had been ripped away:** *El Paso Herald*, Aug. 3, 1901.

168 **It was a joyous "war dance among the white folks":** *Fort Worth Daily Gazette*, June 9, 1884.

168 **"I determined to attempt to curb the insolence":** White, *Experiences of a Special Indian Agent*, 267.

168 **"We took our time":** J. Marvin Hunter, "'Uncle' Ben Dragoo, A Texas Ranger," *Frontier Times*, April 1929.

169 **"We could see the Indian children playing about the tepees":** J. Marvin Hunter, "The Capture of Cynthia Ann Parker," *Frontier Times*, May 1939.

169 **There were "eight or nine grass huts," Ross said:** Undated and unidentified newspaper reprint of Ross's report, Texas Ranger Papers, CAH.

170 **"As the years rolled by Cynthia Ann developed the charms":** *Phillipsburg (Kan.) Herald*, Sept. 18, 1890.

170 **"She has adopted all the manners and customs of the Indians":** *New Orleans Crescent*, Feb. 12, 1861.

170 **Ross mentioned a "woman prisoner" but said little else:** *Dallas Daily Herald*, Jan. 2, 1861.

170 **He did not identify her as Cynthia Ann Parker:** Texas Ranger Papers, CAH.

170 **the woman captured during the battle was "one of the Parker children":** *Galveston Daily News*, June 3, 1875.

171 **Ross "in a single hand-to-hand combat" killed a Comanche chief:** *Fort Worth Daily Gazette*, Aug.14, 1886.

171 **Cynthia Ann Parker and a child also were "mounted on a fleet pony":** White, *Experiences of a Special Indian Agent*, 270–71.

171 **the capture of Parker "made Sul Ross the governor of Texas":** Benner, *Sul Ross*, 58.

171 **"DARING SUL ROSS, BRAVE TEXAS RANGER":** *Austin American*, March 17, 1918.

172 **"She stood on a large wooden box":** Exley, *Frontier Blood*, 170–71, quoting Medora Robinson Turner.

172 **her "little barbarian" in one Texas congressman's phrasing:** *El Paso Herald*, Feb. 26, 1908.

172 **Cynthia Ann died of influenza, possibly complicated by starvation:** Gwynne, *Empire of the Summer Moon*, 192; Hacker, *Cynthia Ann Parker*, 35.

172 **"He no kill my father," Parker said:** *El Paso Times*, Oct. 30, 1910.

173 **"I was in the Pease River fight, but I am not very proud of it":** Carlson and Crum, *Myth, Memory, and Massacre*, 37. Paul Carlson and Tom Crum have written an exhaustive examination of the Battle of Pease River, Ross's role, the changes in the narrative, and the making of the myth. The kidnapping of, and quest for, Cynthia Ann Parker provided the basic storyline for the classic John Ford film *The Searchers*.

173 **Unfounded rumors spread through the North:** Cutrer, *Ben McCulloch and the Frontier Military Tradition*, 189.

173 **"When the ruthless savage threatens their homes":** *Dallas Daily Herald*, July 8, 1863.

173 **They became the home-front manifestation of the Rangers:** Robert Dunham, "Frontier Regiment," and David Paul Smith, "Frontier Organization," *Handbook of Texas Online*.

173 **In early December 1864, Ranger captain N. M. Gillentine:** Some accounts refer to him as N. W. Gillintine.

174 **"I sopose them to be 500 . . . or more Indians":** William C. Pool, "The Battle of Dove Creek," *SWHQ*, April 1950.

174 **He was "unpopular with certain classes":** Pool, "The Battle of Dove Creek."

174 **"It was a wild and uninhabited country without roads":** J. Marvin Hunter, "The Battle of Dove Creek," *West Texas Historical Association Year Book*, vol. 10, 1934, 74–87.

175 **Reinforcements arrived in the form of Totten's militia:** Smith, *Frontier Defense in the Civil War*, 153.

175 **"Without any distribution of orders, without any formation of a line of battle":** Pool, "The Battle of Dove Creek."

175 **An Indian waved a white flag:** "The Tankersley Family," in Hunter, ed., *The Trail Drivers of Texas*.

176 **"Aski tried to shake hands and make peace":** "No-ko-aht's Talk," Kansas Historical Society, February 1932.

176 **"Shoot them all, boys, big, little, old and young":** Franks, *Seventy Years in Texas*, p 32.

176 **"To get at the Indians, it was necessary to wade Dove Creek":** Greer, *Buck Barry*, 190.

176 **"Nobody being in command," Strong said:** Gunter and Calvert, *W. R. Strong*, 35.

177 **The final casualty count for the Texans:** Smith, *Frontier Defense in the Civil War*, 154.

177 **"Made the attack. Got whipped":** Greer, *Buck Barry*, 194.

177 **"All the officers in the fight acquitted themselves honorably":** *Galveston Daily News*, March 14, 1865.

178 **"It was not a victory for the whites":** Greer, *Buck Barry*, 184, 186, 196.

178 **"unmatched for calculated viciousness, vindictiveness":** Latorre and Latorre, *The Mexican Kickapoo Indians*, 20.

178 "In the last raid of the Mexican Kickapoos into Texas": *Independent Record* (Helena, Mont.), July 29, 1874.

178 "It has been a long time ago": Hunter, "The Battle of Dove Creek," *West Texas Historical Association Year Book, 1934.*

178 "Fifty [*sic*] brave frontiersmen lost their lives": Austin Callan, "Battle of Dove Creek," *Frontier Times*, September 1947.

CHAPTER 11. THE STRANGE CAREER OF LEANDER McNELLY

183 "The Texas Rangers, so called, have been a source of danger": Senate Executive Document No. 19, 45th Congress.

183 he appeared as "the very reverse of robust": Parsons and Hall Little, *Captain L. H. McNelly, Texas Ranger*, 1.

183 "sick and puny . . . a little runt of a feller": Durham, *Taming the Nueces Strip*, 5, 75.

184 He "didn't have a man in his company": Callicott, *Bill Callicott Reminiscences*, 78.

184 "McNelly is an appealing composite of warlord and Christ figure": Robert Draper, "The Twilight of the Texas Rangers," *Texas Monthly*, February 1994.

184 Leander McNelly arrived in Texas as a child: Parsons and Hall Little, *Captain L. H. McNelly, Texas Ranger*, 5, 9, 47.

185 "the worst mixed lot of men that ever came together": Dunn, *Perilous Trails of Texas*, 47–96.

185 At the end of the Civil War, Jones went to Mexico: Thomas W. Cutrer, "John B. Jones," *Handbook of Texas Online.*

185 "By birth and education a gentleman": Reprinted in the *Dallas Daily Herald*, Dec. 22, 1877.

186 "I find much dissatisfaction," Jones wrote: Walter Prescott Webb Collection, CAH.

186 "Though we have not exterminated the Comanches": *Galveston Daily News*, June 5, 1875.

186 "There is a considerable element in the country": Report of the Adjutant General, August 1875, TSLA.

186 Wallace compiled a "registration": Walter Prescott Webb Collection, CAH.

186 "Captain Wallace appears to have exercised no control": Taylor, *An American-Mexican Frontier*, 58.

186 "We had been indicted": Dunn, *Perilous Trails of Texas*, 121.

187 "Men have been murdered in cold blood": Walter Prescott Webb Collection, CAH.

187 "These thieves have, with astonishing boldness": House Executive Document No. 39, 42nd Congress, 3rd Session, "Depredations on the Frontiers of Texas," 6.

187 "They are quite capable of any crime": *Reports of the Committee of Investigation Sent in 1873 by the Mexican Government to the Frontier of Texas*, 393.

187 "Most of the depredations were incited by renegade white men": Dunn, *Perilous Trails of Texas*, 80.

187 "Somehow you wouldn't pick a one of them": Durham, *Taming the Nueces Strip*, 13, 16, 46.

188 "Billy McMahan, a very popular inoffensive American school teacher": Pierce, *A Brief History of the Lower Rio Grande Valley*, 108.

189 "The acts committed by Americans in this section are horrible": Texas Adjutant General Records, CAH.

189 "I do not know of any Mexican who owns a ranch": Graham, *Kings of Texas*, 142.

189 Farther on, they came upon two dead Mexicans: Durham, *Taming the Nueces Strip*, 23.

189 by common reckoning the richest man in the state: Graham, *Kings of Texas*, 163.

189 "Those old smoke poles": Sterling, *Trails and Trials of a Texas Ranger*, 467.

190 "It was only about ten miles back from the Rio Grande": Durham, *Taming the Nueces Strip*, 46.

190 "I think you will hear from us soon": Chuck Parsons, "McNelly's Rangers," *True West*, February 1962.

190 "I am *well* posted in all that the thieves are doing": McNelly letter to Kenedy, Nov. 5, 1875, private collection.

190 blue eyes that, to Durham, "seemed to throw off sparks": Durham, *Taming the Nueces Strip*, 44.

190 and he claimed that Mexican raiders had raped his wife and killed his daughter: In an 1875 affidavit, Sandoval said desperados had threatened to kill him and his wife and "attempted to assassinate me." He made no mention of rape and actual murder.

190 "but he could say, 'Son-of-a-bitch, kill 'em'": Callicott, *Bill Callicott Reminiscences*, 61, 63.

190 "As far as we knew," Callicott said: Parsons, "McNelly's Rangers."

191 "Their own mothers could not be more tender": Chuck Parsons, "Jesús Sandoval, McNelly's Enforcer," *Texas Ranger Dispatch*, no. 32, 2011.

191 "Dear Madam, he is gone": Texas Adjutant General Correspondence, TSLA.

191 "I have never seen men fight with such desperation": Texas Adjutant General Records, CAH.

191 "Captain McNelly and His Rangers Heard From": *Galveston Daily News*, June 13, 1875.

191 **"The skill and gallantry displayed by all":** McNelly file, Albert and Ethel Herzstein Library, San Jacinto Museum of History.

192 **"The Mexican residents of Brownsville . . . are public and violent":** Texas Adjutant General Records, CAH.

192 **"They claimed that Palo Alto was a butcher job":** Durham, *Taming the Nueces Strip*, 96.

192 **"that will forever stop our border troubles":** McNelly letter to Kenedy.

192 **"You may feel sure that I am going to have the U.S. authorities onto it":** McNelly letter to Kenedy.

192 **"The meeting was held by the order of Gen. [E. O. C.] Ord":** McNelly letter to Kenedy.

193 **Thomas Wilson, the American consul in Matamoros, learned of the plan:** Michael G. Webster, "Intrigue on the Rio Grande: The *Rio Bravo* Affair, 1875," *SWHQ*, October 1970.

193 **"He said, 'It is like going into the jaws of death'":** Callicott, *Bill Callicott Reminiscences*, 58–61, 68.

193 **"I heard later it was twelve":** Durham, *Taming the Nueces Strip*, 108.

194 **"Instead of being surrounded by Mexicans and treating for surrender":** *Galveston Daily News*, Nov. 26, 1875.

195 **"It is useless to bring prisoners here":** Walter Prescott Webb Collection, CAH.

195 **"He can lift two bales of cotton at a time":** *New York Herald*, Dec. 20, 1875.

195 **Another doctor found that he had "fever, tape-worm":** Texas Adjutant General Correspondence, TSLA.

195 **He was not, a medical report said, "fit for active service":** *Galveston Daily News*, Feb. 6, 1877.

195 **Steele said he took the action because the captain's medical bills were mounting:** *Galveston Daily News*, Feb. 6, 1877.

195 **McNelly had been "extremely negligent in making his reports":** Parsons and Hall Little, *Captain L. H. McNelly, Texas Ranger*, 295.

195 **"The dashing frontier soldier is gradually sinking":** Reprinted in *Dallas Daily Herald*, Aug. 19, 1877.

196 **"I made up my mind that life would not be worth living":** Jennings, *A Texas Ranger*, 2.

196 **Jennings spent about eight months with the Rangers:** Stephen L. Hardin, introduction to Jennings, *A Texas Ranger*, xi. Hardin details many errors in Jennings's text. "The factual errors ought not to astonish new readers," Hardin writes. "Considering the time separating events from publication, the wonder is that Jennings got anything right. Did Jennings seek to elaborate his role in the famed events of Texas Rangers history? Undoubtedly, but probably no more than many other older rangers. Seasoned students of western history understand that artistic aggrandizement is just part of the terrain."

196 **"General Jupiter Pluvius Dyrenforth," a man of science:** *New York Sun*, Sept. 6, 1891.

197 **"Great is the name of Dyrenforth" in West Texas:** *New York Sun*, Sept. 6, 1891.

197 **The Texas experiments, he wrote, were in truth a ridiculous failure:** *Chicago Tribune*, Oct. 7, 1891.

197 **"This article," the *Times* found, "is a tissue of falsehoods":** *New York Times*, Nov. 16, 1891.

197 **"There is, I will venture to say, not a member of the Texas Rangers today":** *Salt Lake Herald*, Oct. 14, 1895.

197 **Among the talents he perfected with the Rangers:** *Wichita (Kan.) Eagle*, May 29, 1910.

197 **"I needed money. I had a story to tell":** J. Frank Dobie, foreword to Jennings, *A Texas Ranger*, vii.

198 **"Their broad-brimmed, picturesque cowboy hats, flannel shirts":** Jennings, *A Texas Ranger*, 59–64.

198 **"I must have succeeded, if I may judge by the hundreds of splendid notices":** Letter from Jennings to Mrs. L. H. McNelly, July 7, 1899, Albert and Ethel Herzstein Library, San Jacinto Museum of History.

198 **The *Detroit Free Press* cited the book's accuracy and liveliness:** *Detroit Free Press*, June 11, 1899.

198 **"The boy took it mostly out of his head":** Durham, *Taming the Nueces Strip*, 136.

198 **"Captain put spurs to his horse":** Jennings, *A Texas Ranger*, 68.

199 **finds the captain to be "shrewd, stern, strong, yet not wanting in kindness":** Grey, *The Lone Star Ranger*, 175, 314.

199 **"I defy anyone to read it without being engaged":** Dobie, foreword to Jennings, *A Texas Ranger*, x. Walter Prescott Webb, whose landmark book *The Texas Rangers* was published in 1935, devotes several chapters to McNelly and his company. But Webb does not quite anoint him to sainthood, saying this of the Las Cuevas raid: "Had the action of McNelly there been in the cause of freedom, or under some banner of patriotism, it would have conferred glory on him and this thirty men. But that battle was fought for a herd of cattle, for the purpose of crushing banditry and making life safe for the cows on the Rio Grande." It was Webb who first encouraged Bill Callicott to write about his experiences with McNelly. Callicott's letters to Webb were later compiled and published by the Texas Ranger Hall of Fame. Webb also said that Jennings's book "abounds in errors and misrepresentations." J. Frank Dobie's praise of the Jennings tome caused some friction with Webb, who was a colleague and a friend of Dobie's. A statue of the two writers and naturalist Roy Bedichek stands outside Barton Springs Pool in Austin, where the men would often gather to talk.

199 **"one of the greatest of the bold captains who rode the wild border":** Douglas, *The Gentlemen in the White Hats*, 133.

200 **"The farther the years moved us away from the man":** Durham, *Taming the Nueces Strip*, 17.

200 **"perhaps the best account of the Ranger chieftain's exploits":** *Bryan (Tex.) Eagle*, Nov. 9, 1943. According to www.wrecksite.eu, the ship was sold after the war. It was lost in a storm in 1967 while transporting iron ore off the coast of Chile with a crew of thirty-seven.

200 **"One of the stories . . . I have repeated most often":** Lyndon Johnson, foreword to Webb, *The Texas Rangers*, x.

200 **"As if, literally, such men were bulletproof":** Larry L. King, "Bringing Up Lyndon," *Texas Monthly*, January 1976.

200 **it was presented at the White House in 1972 to celebrate:** Richard Nixon Presidential Library and Museum.

200 **the original screenplay was based on N. A. Jennings's book:** Author interview with screenwriter Scott Busby.

CHAPTER 12. SALT WAR

203 **"I have been attacked by the mob":** Texas Adjutant General Records, CAH.

204 **"In any other country than this":** House Executive Document No. 93, 45th Congress, 2nd Session, "El Paso Troubles in Texas," 156.

204 **The state's laws, a U.S. Army colonel observed, were "very loosely administered":** House Executive Document No. 93, 17.

204 **"These lakes are very valuable":** *Memphis Daily Appeal*, reprinting the *Mesilla Valley (N.M.) Independent*, Oct. 27, 1877.

205 **"If it was in any other county but this":** House Executive Document No. 93, 156.

205 **"There is neither law nor order in the county":** House Executive Document No. 93, 143.

205 **"not a company of the Frontier Battalion was within five hundred miles":** Gillett, *Six Years with the Texas Rangers*, 137.

205 **"It is some 700 miles from the settlement of Texas:** *Topeka Weekly Times*, Jan. 4, 1878.

206 **"Serious trouble here":** Walter Prescott Webb Collection, CAH.

206 **"Be on the lookout, Major":** Texas Adjutant General Records, CAH.

206 **Tays had done some farming, smuggled cattle from Mexico:** Cool, *Salt Warriors*, 143.

206 **Jones said he selected Tays "for his courage and coolness":** *Topeka Weekly Times*, Jan. 4, 1878.

206 **"John Tays is a good man":** Walter Prescott Webb Collection, CAH.

206 **Tejanos served in earlier versions of an El Paso Ranger company:** Paul Cool, "J. A. Tays: The Frontier Battalion's Forgotten Officer," *Texas Ranger Dispatch*, Summer 2004, www.texasranger.org.

206 **"I determined not to enlist Mexicans":** *Galveston Daily News*, Dec. 20, 1877.

206 **Ranging in age from nineteen to over sixty, the new company:** Cool, *Salt Warriors*, 144–46.

206 **He also "incensed the Mexicans by calling them 'greasers'":** *Sioux City (Iowa) Journal*, Jan. 5, 1878.

207 **"We could hear them yelling and giving orders":** House Executive Document No. 93, 81.

207 **"His body was found in the sand hills":** House Executive Document No. 93, 81.

207 **"We were surrounded by not less than from 120 to 150 men":** House Executive Document No. 93, 56. Blair later was court-martialed for bigamy, was discharged from the army, and moved to Arizona. See Cool, *Salt Warriors*, 285, 289. "After a brief stint as a postmaster in Tombstone," Cool writes, Blair "lived out his days in Chihuahua. He ran a small store until one day in 1896, when he turned his back on the wrong customer, who picked up an axe and drove it through his head."

207 **"He cried out, 'I am shot'":** Cool, *Salt Warriors*, 81.

208 **The United States, Hubbard said, had suffered an "invasion":** *Austin Statesman*, Dec. 15, 1877.

208 **"Hubbard is an imbecile":** *New York Herald*, Dec. 17, 1877.

208 **"Your telegram received":** House Executive Document No. 93, 147.

208 **"He said, 'I will go'":** House Executive Document No. 93, 81.

208 **Chico Barela, their leader, "swore by the holy cross":** House Executive Document No. 93, 98.

208 **"He . . . told the boys that I had ordered them to come down":** House Executive Document No. 93, 82.

209 **"Howard instantly stopped and . . . faced the mob":** House Executive Document No. 93, 98. García's eyewitness account was initially printed in a New Mexico newspaper. He later acknowledged that he did not personally witness all the events, and based some of his facts on information given to him by others who were there.

209 **The insurgents now called for the blood of the remaining Rangers:** House Executive Document No. 93, 82.

209 **The insurgents took from them thirteen rifles:** Texas Adjutant General Records, CAH.

210 **"He is a braggart":** *Boston Globe*, reprinting *Santa Fe New Mexican*, April 30, 1883.

210 "I heard sharp, desultory firing": House Executive Document No. 93, 87.

210 "They reported that Telles had resisted arrest": House Executive Document No. 93, 87.

211 "I then denounced this inhumanity in no measured terms": House Executive Document No. 93, 87.

211 "The Rangers then commenced firing through the door": House Executive Document No. 93, 84.

211 When he refused, Chavez said, a Ranger shot him in the chest: House Executive Document No. 93, 85.

211 Noverto Pais claimed that Rangers pistol-whipped him: House Executive Document No. 93, 94.

211 "pointed the pistol at my breast and forced me to give up": House Executive Document No. 93, 90.

211 "All people . . . came out to meet us": House Executive Document No. 93, 88.

211 Frazer had bragged of working as a hired killer: Cool, Salt Warriors, 247.

211 Ford leveled a double-barreled shotgun at Frazer: House Executive Document No. 93, 86.

212 "The force of rangers thus suddenly called together": House Executive Document No. 93, 17.

212 "I know Lieutenant Tays by sight": House Executive Document No. 93, 93.

212 When Howard killed Cardis, the report said: House Executive Document No. 93, 15.

213 Those who revere the force have over the years dismissed Tays: Webb, The Texas Rangers, 367.

213 In 1883, he moved to Southern California: Cool, Salt Warriors, 259, 290.

213 "The steamer, as soon as she got in the rapids": Philadelphia Inquirer, June 22, 1900.

CHAPTER 13. THE FADING FRONTIER

215 "Soon the name of Texas Rangers will be an echo": Baylor, Into the Far, Wild Country, 318.

215 and more than 93 percent of Texans made their homes in rural areas: Calvert et al., The History of Texas, 182.

216 "Whole districts of country have been terrorized": Dallas Weekly Herald, Sept. 8, 1877.

216 The era produced a "frightful story of blood": Crouch, The Dance of Freedom, 95–99.

216 "I have arrested two citizens of Bosque and McLennan counties": Texas Adjutant General Records, CAH.

217 It was a "slaughter of the innocents": Panola (Tex.) Watchman, Feb 24, 1875.

217 "Dear Sir," it said in an even hand on lined paper: Texas Adjutant General Correspondence, TSLA.

217 The 10th Cavalry had fought well in campaigns: William H. Leckie, "Tenth United States Cavalry," Handbook of Texas Online.

217 "In the place of keeping the peace": Texas Adjutant General Records, CAH.

217 "These blacks had associated with white gamblers and lewd women": Gillett, Six Years with the Texas Rangers, 89–92.

218 "The negroes refused to deliver the pistol": Austin Statesman, Jan. 12, 1878.

218 "It was right lively for a little while": Parsons and Brice, Texas Ranger N. O. Reynolds, 148–52.

218 "The Citizens are Jubilent over the Killing of the Negroes": Parsons and Brice, Texas Ranger N. O. Reynolds, 145–54.

219 The jury ruled that the ex-soldiers "came to their death": Austin Statesman, Jan. 12, 1878.

219 The diminutive son of a Methodist minister, Hardin committed: Much of the information on Hardin's life is taken from Metz, John Wesley Hardin, 12–13; O'Neal, Encyclopedia of Western Gunfighters, 126–31; and Parsons and Brown, A Lawless Breed.

219 a member of a traveling circus troupe: Though Hardin claimed he shot the circus man "between the eyes," some have speculated that the victim may have survived the attack. See Parsons and Brown, A Lawless Breed, 38.

219 "He did not like to be disturbed in his sleep": New Orleans Picayune, Sept. 15, 1877.

219 "a big black negro with his pistol cocked": Hardin, The Life of John Wesley Hardin, 62.

220 "I met them prepared and killed three of them": Hardin, The Life of John Wesley Hardin, 63.

220 "He kills men just to see them kick": Austin Statesman, Sept. 24, 1874.

220 "4 men grabed me one by each arm": Parsons and Brown, A Lawless Breed, 225.

220 "Everybody in the car stampeded": Dallas Morning News, Aug. 22, 1895.

220 "Arrested John Wesley Hardin, Pensacola, Florida this afternoon": Texas Ranger Papers, CAH; Austin Statesman, Aug. 25, 1877.

220 "The officers treated me kindly": Austin Statesman, Aug. 30, 1877.

220 Hardin stood trial for the murder of the deputy sheriff: In prison Hardin studied law. He was pardoned in 1894 and admitted to the bar. The next year, Hardin was shot dead in El Paso's Acme Saloon, possibly the consequence of his affair with a client's wife. He was buried in the Concordia Cemetery in El Paso, where an iron-fence enclosure covers his grave site. "The concrete and cage of course are there not to keep Hardin in," wrote his biographer Leon C. Metz, "but to prevent screwballs, idiots and lunatics from digging Hardin up."

220 "The arrest of this notorious character with two of his men": Austin Statesman, Aug. 25, 1877.

221 **"No police organization has ever rendered better service"**: *Dallas Daily Herald*, Aug. 26, 1877.

221 **Bass was an illiterate, orphaned Indiana farm boy**: Much of the information on Bass is drawn from Gard, *Sam Bass*.

221 **"Bass and his gang ... played with it as a child plays with toys"**: Gillett, *Six Years with the Texas Rangers*, 116.

221 **"His friends watch and even question every stranger"**: *Galveston Daily News*, April 25, 1878.

222 **"I am Sam Bass, shot to pieces, and no use to deny"**: *Galveston Daily News*, July 21, 1878.

222 **"The name of Sam Bass, the dead robber chieftain"**: Reprinted in the *Great Bend (Kan.) Weekly Tribune*, Aug. 10, 1878.

222 **he required a new commander there "of some established character"**: Cool, *Salt Warriors*, 281.

222 **"I want you to remember"**: Baylor, *Into the Far, Wild Country*, 1. Much of the background on Baylor comes from Jerry Thompson's excellent introduction to this collection of Baylor's writings.

222 **"It did not take them long," he wrote**: Baylor, *Into the Far, Wild Country*, 117.

222 **"killed and scalped six Indians one morning before breakfast"**: *El Paso Herald*, Aug. 10, 1901.

222 **he listed his occupation as "Indian Killer"**: Baylor, *Into the Far, Wild Country*, 9.

223 **Baylor said the incident lingered for years**: Baylor, *Into the Far, Wild Country*, 239, 240.

223 **"Not a drop of rain fell," Gillett recalled**: Gillett, *Six Years with the Texas Rangers*, 141–50. Gillett's book was originally published in 1921. Baylor's writings appeared in the *El Paso Herald* beginning in 1901. In his introduction to Baylor's collection, Jerry Thompson notes that Gillett, who was for a time Baylor's son-in-law, plagiarized much of Baylor's work.

223 **"His open, friendly personality endeared him"**: Gillett, *Six Years with the Texas Rangers*, 199.

223 **The marshal of El Paso, Dallas Stoudenmire, complained**: Texas Ranger Papers, CAH.

223 **"Sometimes we would have as many as six or eight criminals"**: Gillett, *Six Years with the Texas Rangers*, 199.

224 **In the 1850s Victorio had ridden with Geronimo**: Joseph A. Stout, Jr., "Victorio," *Handbook of Texas Online*.

224 **"Victorio knew every foot of the country"**: Baylor, *Into the Far, Wild Country*, 284–89.

224 **"At once this band began a series of pillages and murders"**: Gillett, *Six Years with the Texas Rangers*, 200.

225 **"I deemed it best to go down & see for myself"**: Texas Adjutant General Records, CAH. Except where noted, Baylor's account of the pursuit and ensuing battle comes from this report to the adjutant general.

225 **The Apaches "were huddled up around their fires"**: Baylor, *Into the Far, Wild Country*, 312.

226 **"My little girl had always asked me to bring her ferns"**: Baylor, *Into the Far, Wild Country*, 314.

227 **By the end of the day Gates had sold hundreds of miles of the wire**: McCallum and McCallum, *The Wire That Fenced the West*, 68–72.

227 **"Wire, wire, wire! Everywhere!"**: Haley, *Charles Goodnight*, 323.

227 **Landowners fenced their property with it**: Wayne Gard, "The Fence-Cutters," *SWHQ*, July 1947.

228 **"who whipped the Indians out of the country"**: McCallum and McCallum, *The Wire That Fenced the West*, 159.

228 **which ultimately stretched for six thousand miles**: Duke and Frantz, *6,000 Miles of Fence*, 6.

228 **"Down with monopolies"**: *Fort Worth Daily Gazette*, Nov. 7, 1883.

228 **"I do not believe," he wrote, "that eternal Providence"**: *Galveston Daily News*, Oct. 4, 1883.

228 **Shots were fired into homes at night**: *Galveston Daily News*, Jan. 11, 1884.

228 **"Yesterday was a very awful day in Brownwood"**: *Austin Statesman*, Dec. 13, 1883.

229 **"I believe the man who can educate himself to think"**: *Austin Statesman*, Jan. 17, 1884.

229 **"provide a remedy for wanton destruction of fences"**: *Galveston Daily News*, Oct. 17, 1883.

229 **"fence cutting was not discussed with much feeling"**: Texas Adjutant General Correspondence, TSLA.

229 **"Detectives has been sent into that country many times"**: "Six and One-Half Years in the Ranger Service: Memoirs of Ira Aten, Sergeant Co. D, Texas Rangers," *Frontier Times*, February 1945.

229 **a few of them "may have been drawn into fence cutting"**: Texas Adjutant General Correspondence, TSLA.

229 **"They are the best organized band that I ever worked after"**: Texas Adjutant General Records, CAH.

230 **And the Erath County sheriff ... enjoyed "strong support among the fence-cutters"**: Texas Adjutant General Correspondence, TSLA.

230 **"The fence cutting element in the interior"**: *Austin Statesman*, Feb. 14, 1885, and March 26, 1885.

230 **"I posed as a poor orphan boy with no home"**: "Six and One-Half Years in the Ranger Service."

231 **"They sent me here to stop fence-cutting any way I could"**: Texas Adjutant General Records, CAH.

231 **"Keep your ears pricked, you may hear my boom"**: Walter Prescott Webb Collection, CAH.

231 **"That bald head of his got redder and redder":** "Six and One-Half Years in the Ranger Service."

231 **"The pride of the Lone Star State, the Texas Ranger":** *Philadelphia Times*, Feb. 5, 1899.

232 **The new statute empowered the governor:** "Organization of the Ranger Force in 1901, House Bill No. 52," Texas Ranger Hall of Fame.

CHAPTER 14. CAPTAIN BILL TO THE RESCUE

235 **"Indeed, they have been from the beginning":** Paine, *Captain Bill McDonald*, 132.

235 **News out of Brownsville, Texas:** *Shreveport (La.) Times*, Aug. 15, 1906; *Jackson (Miss.) Daily Clarion-Ledger*, Aug. 17, 1906.

235 **"makes the pulse of a good citizen":** Paine, *Captain Bill McDonald*, 13.

236 **"go down and settle that Brownsville business":** Paine, *Captain Bill McDonald*, 324.

236 **The man in charge of the Rangers:** Weaver, *The Brownsville Raid*, 80.

236 **"Why, them hellions have violated the laws":** Paine, *Captain Bill McDonald*, 324.

237 **"If he did not help pull a rope that night":** Paine, *Captain Bill McDonald*, 27–30. Paine did not note his source material for most of the biography, but a great deal of the information apparently came from McDonald himself.

237 **He graduated from Soule's Commercial College:** McDonald's life story is presented in great detail in Weiss, *Yours to Command*.

237 **a "manly looking set of men":** Weiss, *Yours to Command*, 110.

237 **The lion caused a stir one morning:** *Indianapolis Journal*, Feb. 11, 1896.

238 **"I think I'm a dead rabbit":** Paine, *Captain Bill McDonald*, 173.

238 **had accused the Rangers of rustling:** Weiss, *Yours to Command*, 94.

238 **"one of the bravest officers of Texas":** *Los Angeles Times*, Dec. 11, 1893.

238 **"To hell with the colored soldiers":** Blocksom, *Affray at Brownsville, Tex.*, 94.

238 **a black man in uniform had grabbed a white woman:** *Brownsville Herald*, Aug. 13, 1906.

239 **"Citizens of Brownsville entertain race hatred":** Morris, *Theodore Rex*, 454.

239 **"I told them he could do it in ten minutes":** McDonald report to Lanham and Hulen, Texas Adjutant General Correspondence, TSLA.

239 **"The guns he carried were almost half his size":** Weaver, *The Brownsville Raid*, 80.

239 **"You niggers, hold up there!":** Paine, *Captain Bill McDonald*, 328.

239 **"If McDonald started hellwards":** *Wichita Eagle*, Feb. 3, 1907.

239 **"A white man who has committed a crime":** Paine, *Captain Bill McDonald*, 329.

239 **"There was a ring in the captain's voice":** *Houston Post*, Dec. 24, 1906.

240 **"We didn't say anything":** *Arizona Daily Star*, Dec. 26, 1972.

240 **"people who tried to shield criminals were accessories":** McDonald report to Lanham and Hulen, Texas Adjutant General Correspondence, TSLA.

240 **"I hereby demand the delivery":** McDonald report to Lanham and Hulen.

240 **"The [army] officers are trying to cover up":** *Dallas Morning News*, Aug. 30, 1906.

240 **"He said, 'McDonald, I am a friend of yours'":** Hearings Before the Committee on Military Affairs of the United States Senate, 60th Congress, First Session, Document No. 402, "Affray at Brownsville, Tex.," 2397.

241 **"You all look like 15 cents":** McDonald report to Lanham and Hulen.

241 **"Of course I could do no more":** McDonald report to Lanham and Hulen.

241 **The *Brownsville Herald* was glad to see them go:** *Brownsville Herald*, Oct. 3, 1906.

241 **"trying to cover this outrageous murder up":** McDonald letter to Senator Culberson, Texas Adjutant General Correspondence, TSLA.

241 **"The townspeople were completely surprised":** "Message Regarding Disturbances in Texas," December 19, 1906, Presidential Speeches, Miller Center, University of Virginia.

242 **The *Brownsville Herald* accused him:** *Brownsville Herald*, Oct. 3, 1906.

242 **But he asked for captains other than McDonald:** Weaver, *The Brownsville Raid*, 87.

242 **urged local authorities to throw McDonald in the Brownsville jail:** *Houston Post*, May 26, 1907.

242 **"He is a thorough coward":** *Brownsville Herald*, March 11, 1907.

242 **"To be accurate, the old-timers":** Walter Prescott Webb Collection, CAH.

242 **The publication was arranged by Edward M. House:** Weiss, *Yours to Command*, 296.

243 **"He walked into the very muzzles":** *Brooklyn Daily Eagle*, March 15, 1914.

243 **McDonald conducted a "courageous investigation":** Webb, *The Texas Rangers*, 466.

243 **"Here's Captain Bill!":** House, as told to Mason, *Riding for Texas*, 209.

243 **"the most spectacular Ranger commander of his era":** Sterling, *Trails and Trials of a Texas Ranger*, 334, 348.

244 **"so brave he would charge hell":** Blocksom, *Affray at Brownsville, Tex.*, 9.

244 **"the coons who were committing murder":** McDonald report to Lanham and Hulen.

CHAPTER 15. THE POLITICS OF MASSACRE

247 **"I knew what that meant"**: "Proceedings of the Joint Committee of the Senate and the House in the Investigation of the Texas State Ranger Force" (hereafter CIR), TSLA, 676ff. Some accounts refer to the locale mentioned here as Ebenoza.

248 **"Twenty-five or thirty years ago"**: George Marvin, "Bandits and the Borderland," *The World's Work: A History of Our Time*, Oct. 1916.

249 **At one point it shrank to only thirteen men**: Harris and Sadler, *The Texas Rangers and the Mexican Revolution*, 67.

249 **"It was not intended when the Rangers were created"**: *Houston Post*, May 4, 1910.

249 **"We look upon the Rangers"**: CIR, 21.

250 **"They are courageous"**: CIR, 64.

250 The *Waco Morning News* **summarized it**: *Waco Morning News*, Aug. 14, 1915. For an extensive and groundbreaking study of the plan, see Johnson, *Revolution in Texas*.

250 **District Attorney John A. Valls**: Texas Adjutant General Correspondence, Aug. 28, 1915, TSLA.

250 **"The San Diego Revolutionists still continue"**: Texas Adjutant General Correspondence, March 1, 1915, TSLA.

250 **"For God's sake"**: *Austin American*, Aug. 7, 1915.

250 **Suspected** *sediciocos* **burned railroad trestles**: *Houston Post*, Oct. 29, 1915; Harris and Sadler, *The Texas Rangers and the Mexican Revolution*, 262–63.

251 **"the hatred for gringos that burns"**: *Chicago Tribune*, May 14, 1916.

251 **Those who remained were to be killed**: Harben Davenport letter, Walter Prescott Webb Collection, CAH.

251 **The cards were sold in drugstores**: Richard Ribb, "José Tomás Canales and the Texas Rangers: Myth, Identity, and Power in South Texas, 1900–1920" (PhD diss., University of Texas at Austin, 2001), 316.

251 **Kleberg, manager of the Norias section, supplied the Rangers**: Texas Adjutant General Correspondence, Sept. 20, 1915, TSLA.

251 **"Immediately following the Las Norias Raid"**: Pierce, *A Brief History of the Lower Rio Grande Valley*, 114.

252 **"the most spectacular and bloodiest train robbery"**: *Daily Advocate* (Victoria, Tex.), Oct. 20, 1915.

252 **"The tales [he and others] told about executing Filipinos"**: Sterling, *Trails and Trials of a Texas Ranger*, 47.

252 **"Captain Ransom . . . walked over to me"**: CIR, 574.

252 **"Three of them entered our home"**: Ribb, "José Tomás Canales and the Texas Rangers," 114.

253 **the Rangers compiled a "black list"**: CIR, 355, 372.

253 **"Yesterday we caught a Mexican"**: Texas Adjutant General Correspondence, Aug. 21, 1915, TSLA.

253 **Roland Warnock, a South Texas cowboy**: Warnock, *Texas Cowboy*, 49–51. Warnock's grandson Kirby Warnock tells a compelling story of the border war in his 2004 documentary film, *Border Bandits*.

253 **"I want to say this for the Rangers"**: Texas Adjutant General Correspondence, TSLA.

254 **C. B. Hudspeth, a congressman from West Texas**: CIR, 992.

254 **cease the "summary execution of Mexicans"**: Texas Adjutant General Correspondence, TSLA.

254 **"Considerable adverse criticism of the Ranger Force"**: Walter Prescott Webb Collection, Sept. 28, 1916, CAH.

254 **They captured Johnson**: *New York Times*, Sept. 29, 1915.

255 **"They started to run"**: *Boston Globe*, May 27, 1916. For accounts of the incident, see Special Claims Commission, United States and Mexico, Opinions of Commissioners, April 26, 1926, to April 24, 1931, 18–24; and Senate Committee on Foreign Relations, 66th Congress, 2nd Session, Document 285, "Investigation of Mexican Affairs," 2757–60.

255 **The editor "then seemed to be very sorry"**: Texas Adjutant General Correspondence, TSLA.

255 **The small Laredo newspaper** *El Progreso*: Elizabeth Garner Masarik, "Por la Raza, Para la Raza: Jovita Idar and Progressive-Era Mexican Maternalism along the Texas–Mexico Border," *SWHQ*, January 2019."

255 **"Are you the son of a bitch that wrote that petition?"**: CIR, 244.

256 **"I struck at him with my six-shooter"**: CIR, 1397–1404.

256 **Mexico had never really recovered**: Meyer et al., *The Course of Mexican History*, 442–46.

256 **"Those caught swimming"**: Texas Adjutant General Correspondence, TSLA.

256 **"The taxable property in Cameron County alone"**: Hardy and Roberts, *Historical Review of South-East Texas*, 369–71.

256 **"Lands which fifteen years ago were selling"**: Pierce, *A Brief History of the Lower Rio Grande Valley*, 128.

256 "The home suckers succumb": Marvin, "Bandits and the Borderland."

257 The typical "border Mexican": Texas Adjutant General Correspondence, Feb. 12, 1918, TSLA.

257 "There are only a few men around Brownsville": Texas Adjutant General Correspondence, June 21, 1916, TSLA.

257 "The Rangers make more trouble than peace": Texas Adjutant General Correspondence, Jan. 14, 1919, TSLA.

257 Brownsville lawyer Creager said the Rangers' tactics: CIR, 380–82.

258 "Each plant in this land": Quoted in Tyler, *The Big Bend*, 10.

258 "The land is dry and barren": Keil, *Bosque Bonito*, 4.

258 some called it the "Bloody Bend": Tyler, *The Big Bend*, 159.

259 "O bury me not": Montejano, *Anglos and Mexicans in the Making of Texas*, 102.

259 "They are killing and plundering": *El Paso Herald*, April 8, 1918.

259 Sanders cited the "lack of discipline": Texas Adjutant General Correspondence, July 15, 1915, TSLA.

259 "These men are stationed at Marfa": Harris and Sadler, *The Texas Rangers and the Mexican Revolution*, 195.

260 "Everything quite": Texas Adjutant General Correspondence, April 26, 1915, TSLA.

260 Three dozen citizens asked for a detachment: Texas Adjutant General Correspondence, Jan. 3, 1916, TSLA.

260 "I have been here all day": Walter Prescott Webb Collection, CAH.

260 "with which Cano and his gang seem to be": Bureau of Investigation, "In Re Chico Cano Villista Activities," Sept. 8, 1917. In 1935 the agency became formally known as the Federal Bureau of Investigation—the FBI.

260 Joe Sitter, a customs inspector: Some sources spell his name Sitters or Sittre.

261 Sitter "had been shot about ten times": Texas Adjutant General Correspondence, May 27, 1915, TSLA.

261 "We knew what we were up against": Senate Committee on Foreign Relations, 66th Congress, 2nd Session, Document 285, "Investigation of Mexican Affairs," 1550ff.

261 The body fell to the floor: Justice, *Little Known History of the Texas Big Bend*, 133.

262 "I have never seen such whipping and spurring": Keil, *Bosque Bonito*, 18.

262 "They were only the words of a bandit": Keil, *Bosque Bonito*, 19, 25.

262 "come out and see the circus show": Ribb, "José Tomás Canales and the Texas Rangers," 333.

262 One was Bud Weaver: Information on these Rangers is taken from Harris, Harris, and Sadler, *Texas Ranger Biographies*, and Ranger enlistment records in TSLA.

263 a fine of $20, which the Rangers would pocket: Justice, *Revolution on the Rio Grande*, 37.

263 "Not once had any of them caused us any trouble whatever": Keil, *Bosque Bonito*, 29–34.

263 "was shining nearly as bright as day": Henry Warren Papers, Archives of the Big Bend, Sul Ross State University.

263 The nearest store: Justice, *Revolution on the Rio Grande*, 36.

264 All told, forty-two children: Henry Warren Papers, Archives of the Big Bend.

264 When the bodies were gone: Justice, *Revolution on the Rio Grande*, 41.

264 "I beg to make a report": Texas Adjutant General Correspondence, Jan. 30, 1918, TSLA.

264 seeking additional Winchester cartridges: Texas Adjutant General Correspondence, Jan. 31, 1918, TSLA.

265 "bandits and generally bad characters": Walter Prescott Webb Collection, CAH.

265 "It is a well known fact they act as spies": Walter Prescott Webb Collection, CAH.

265 "There was not a single bandit": CIR, 850.

265 "He married a Mexican woman": Walter Prescott Webb Collection, CAH.

266 "Every effort apparently was made": *Arizona Daily Star*, Feb. 8, 1918.

266 the Rangers at Porvenir "were fired upon": *El Paso Herald*, Feb. 23, 1918.

266 He was forced from the country: Ribb, "José Tomás Canales and the Texas Rangers," 145.

267 "I suggested to him that the saloons": Texas Adjutant General Correspondence, June 18, 1918, TSLA.

267 "I will further suggest that each one": Texas Adjutant General Correspondence, June 27, 1918, TSLA.

267 "Every time a bunch of these same bandits": Texas Adjutant General Correspondence, Feb. 8, 1918, TSLA.

267 "This unlawful deed": CIR, 850.

268 With his son, Glenn, he ate supper: Senate Committee on Foreign Relations, 66th Congress, 2nd Session, Document 285, "Investigation of Mexican Affairs," 1511.

268 The maid had been raped: Keil, *Bosque Bonito*, 41.

269 **The cavalrymen burned Pilares:** Justice, *Revolution on the Rio Grande*, 53.

269 **had family who had been executed there:** Justice, *Revolution on the Rio Grande*, 53.

269 **"We learned later," he wrote:** Keil, *Bosque Bonito*, 38.

269 **"I think some action must be taken":** Walter Prescott Webb Collection, CAH.

269 **Captain Fox "was a snake in the grass":** Texas Adjutant General Correspondence, June 15, 1918, TSLA.

269 **"I don't feel that I am getting a fair deal":** Texas Adjutant General Correspondence, May 31, 1918, TSLA.

269 **Fox penned an angry letter of resignation:** CIR, 839, 840.

269 **Harley drafted a heated response:** CIR, 840, 841.

270 **"For those sort of greasers":** Walter Prescott Webb Collection, CAH.

270 **Harley's reply to the sheriff dispelled it:** Walter Prescott Webb Collection, CAH.

270 **Hobby outpolled his opponent by a 3–1 margin:** *Houston Post*, July 30, 1918.

270 **"There are now, and there have been for some time":** CIR, 148.

270 **"I charge on or about January 28, 1918":** Walter Prescott Webb Collection, CAH.

271 **Front-page headlines told the story:** *Washington Herald*, Feb. 1, 1919; *Bisbee (Ariz.) Daily Review*, Jan. 24, 1919.

271 **A United Press report cast a hard eye:** *Salina (Kan.) Daily Union*, Jan. 31, 1919.

271 **The committee report faulted some "unnecessary taking of life":** Ribb, "José Tomás Canales and the Texas Rangers," 358.

271 **"Committee report all we could ask for":** Texas Adjutant General Correspondence, Feb. 19, 1919, TSLA.

271 **"I do not recognize my own child":** Ribb, "José Tomás Canales and the Texas Rangers," 366.

272 **"We had to abandon it":** Senate Committee on Foreign Relations, 66th Congress, 2nd Session, Document 285, "Investigation of Mexican Affairs," 1515.

272 **As his daughter, Kelley, told it:** Clifford Casey Papers, Archives of the Big Bend, Sul Ross State University.

272 **In his seventies, retired from Big Bend duties:** Author interview with J. D. McCollum.

272 **Wearing a Stetson and drinking beer:** Douglas, *The Gentlemen in the White Hats*, 165–74.

273 **Night after night in his Tucson home:** Author interview with Linda Davis.

273 **But in 2015 a group led by historian Glenn Justice:** Author interview with Glenn Justice. For more, see Justice's website, www.rimrockpress.com.

274 **"The waters of the Rio Grande":** J. J. Kilpatrick Sr. Papers, CAH. In 2018, a full one hundred years after Porvenir, the Texas Historical Commission posted a marker in Presidio County describing the massacre and the Rangers' role.

CHAPTER 16. BOOGER TOWN

277 **"There is the mighty Frank Hamer":** *Waco News-Tribune*, Feb. 3, 1929.

278 **"one of the greatest oil and natural gas fields":** Wolters, *Martial Law and Its Administration*, 174.

278 **"Your Opportunity Lies in Borger":** Sinise, *Black Gold and Red Lights*, 19.

278 **"Thousands of human parasites":** Wolters, *Martial Law and Its Administration*, 174.

278 **"It is not a community":** *Dallas Morning News*, Oct. 14, 1926.

278 **"Oil seems to have corroded this little settlement":** *Los Angeles Times*, Sept. 29, 1929.

278 **"It was a town then of rough shacks":** Benton, *An Artist in America*, 201–6.

279 **"He was symbolical of the gang in action":** Wolters, *Martial Law and Its Administration*, 175.

279 **"On Dixon Street over a thousand of these women lived":** From *Borger*, monograph, Hutchinson County Historical Museum.

279 **faces "decorated with livid rouge":** Sinise, *Black Gold and Red Lights*, 26.

280 **the district attorney got so drunk during business hours:** Letter from H. M. Hood to Gov. Dan Moody, Hutchinson County Historical Museum.

280 **Crooked undertakers . . . were believed to kill intoxicated vagrants:** Sterling, *Trails and Trials of a Texas Ranger*, 99.

280 **those "picturesque detectives of the plains":** *Lincoln (Neb.) Evening Journal*, Sept. 19, 1929.

280 **"The gentlemen of the press asked me":** Sterling, *Trails and Trials of a Texas Ranger*, 100.

280 **A "giant of a man":** *Dallas Morning News*, July 12, 1955.

280 **"Several of those bullets are in me yet":** Jenkins and Frost, *"I'm Frank Hamer,"* 226.

281 **A "fearless man-hunter":** *Valley (Harlingen, Tex.) Morning Star*, May 24, 1934.

281 **"Bullets of bandits":** *Dallas Morning News*, Nov. 7, 1929.

281 **"This big man who has worn a six-shooter":** *Vernon (Tex.) Daily Record*, Nov. 8, 1929.

281 **"If all the criminals in Texas were asked to name":** Webb, *The Texas Rangers*, 519.

281 **"nothing was as effective as a .45 slug in the gut":** Procter, *Just One Riot*, 9.

281 **by age sixteen young Frank had already killed a man:** Jenkins and Frost, *"I'm Frank Hamer,"* 7.

281 **The man he was said to have killed died years later:** Boessenecker, *Texas Ranger*, 17. This deeply researched biography, published in 2016, paints a largely favorable portrait of Hamer, who the author says "might be remembered as the greatest lawman of the twentieth century."

281 **Gladys Sims . . . had, while still a young woman, shot at least three men:** O'Neal, *The Johnson-Sims Feud*, 119.

281 **"These extra guards and gun displays are only agitating trouble":** Walter Prescott Webb collection, CAH.

282 **"The shooting began immediately":** *Dallas Morning News*, Oct. 2, 1917.

282 **"I couldn't shoot the damned coward in the back":** Boessenecker, *Texas Ranger*, 158.

282 **They opened fire on Hamer's orders:** Boessenecker, *Texas Ranger*, 227.

282 **"Driving through the woods in the daytime":** Sterling, *Trails and Trials of a Texas Ranger*, 418.

283 **"Captain Hamer's open palm always took the fight out of the hardiest ruffian":** Sterling, *Trails and Trials of a Texas Ranger*, 421.

283 **In 1918, Hamer confronted Texas state representative J. T. Canales:** CIR, 886.

283 **"Under Governor's orders," the adjutant general told Hamer:** CIR, 895.

283 **Hamer pleaded guilty to aggravated assault:** *Houston Post*, June 12, 1913.

284 **"'I'm Frank Hamer, Texas Ranger,'" he said:** Jenkins and Frost, *"I'm Frank Hamer,"* 69–70.

284 **Hamer merely "ordered them placed within cells in the jail":** *Austin Statesman*, Oct. 16, 1922.

284 **The police chief "hasn't been of the slightest assistance to us":** Boessenecker, *Texas Ranger*, 273.

285 **Less than two years later, twenty-two wells were producing:** Noel Wiggins, "Ranger, Texas," *Handbook of Texas Online*.

285 **"The boys had to kill a fellow":** Texas Adjutant General Correspondence, Dec. 20, 1918, CAH.

285 **Though some were "excellent officers," Burkett said:** *Austin Statesman*, Feb. 25, 1921.

285 **Officials there said the Rangers:** *El Paso Herald*, Jan. 3, 1920.

286 **Citing his own "moral, political and physical courage":** *El Paso Herald*, Feb. 28, 1921.

286 **The governor sent the Rangers to Borger in early April 1927:** *Dallas Morning News*, April 2, 1927.

286 **She exited the scene in her yellow Cadillac:** Agee, *Images of America*, 16.

286 **"Practically all women [were] ordered to leave Borger":** *Dallas Morning News*, April 10, 1927.

286 **One newspaper story told of "more than a dozen girls":** *Shreveport Times*, April 9, 1927.

286 **"If an examination . . . showed callouses or other evidence":** Sterling, *Trails and Trials of a Texas Ranger*, 110.

287 **Herwig protested, "I'm deputy sheriff here":** *El Paso Herald*, March 28, 1928.

287 **"We have broken the backbone of the lawlessness":** *Dallas Morning News*, April 23, 1927.

287 **"BORGER IS NO LONGER LAWLESS":** *Dallas Morning News*, April 23, 1927.

287 **"RANGERS TAME BORGER":** *Austin Statesman*, April 3, 1927.

287 **Borger's former city secretary wrote a letter to the governor:** General collection, Hutchinson County Historical Museum.

288 **"They claim that the rangers are dishonest":** General collection, Hutchinson County Historical Museum.

288 **Borger merchants conducted a "rat war":** *Dallas Morning News*, Sept. 9, 1927.

289 **"I can clean up conditions in this county":** General collection, Hutchinson County Historical Museum.

289 **A federal grand jury was scheduled to convene:** Wolters, *Martial Law and Its Administration*, 180.

289 **"The hand that fired the gun":** *Austin Statesman*, Sept. 21, 1929.

289 **"They sent one of those clear-eyed, calm-spoken, straight-shooting westerners":** *Pittsburgh Press*, Oct. 1, 1929.

289 **The slaying grew from the illegal liquor trade, Hamer said:** *Amarillo Globe*, Oct. 4, 1929.

290 **In Borger, the general said, the Rangers were badly overmatched:** Wolters, *Martial Law and Its Administration*, 182.

290 **"Occupation of the town was accomplished quietly and quickly":** Wolters, *Martial Law and Its Administration*, 190.

291 **"Some of them tried to get smart with us":** Malsch, *"Lone Wolf" Gonzaullas*, 78.

291 **"The entrenched criminal ring . . . had been destroyed":** Wolters, *Martial Law and Its Administration*, 208.

CHAPTER 17. ONE RIOT

293 **"Get this, boy":** *Albany (Tex.) News*, May 16, 1930.

294 **There were more than 450 lynchings in Texas:** John R. Ross, "Lynching," *Handbook of Texas Online*.

295 **"the most horrible death ever inflicted":** Walter L. Buenger, "Making Sense of Texas and Its History," *SWHQ*, July 2017.

295 **In 1908, Hamer was sent to Beaumont:** Walter Prescott Webb Collection, CAH.

295 **Hamer stood on the courthouse steps:** *Austin American*, May 27, 1922; and Boessenecker, *Texas Ranger*, 168–69.

296 **"These negroes have done no wrong":** *Buffalo (N.Y.) Commercial*, Aug. 1, 1910. Eight deaths is the official tally. As E. R. Bills notes in his groundbreaking book *The 1910 Slocum Massacre*, the "consensus among descendants of the . . . victims is that hundreds died in the bloodshed."

296 **Dozens of women and children:** *Dallas Express*, July 19, 1919.

296 **That year, 1919, is generally considered the worst year:** See Cameron McWhirter's excellent *Red Summer: The Summer of 1919 and the Awakening of Black America.*

296 **One of those riots took place:** For a detailed retelling of the Longview affair, see Kenneth R. Durham, "The Longview Race Riot of 1919," *East Texas Historical Journal*, Fall 1980. It has been reprinted as an ebook by the Texas Ranger Hall of Fame.

297 **And the Rangers, he said, had a duty:** *Houston Post*, Aug. 23, 1919.

297 **A 1919 memo . . . was titled "Investigating Negroes' Organizing":** Walter Prescott Webb Collection, CAH.

297 **In August 1919, two high-ranking Rangers:** Roy Wilkinson Aldrich Papers, Archives of the Big Bend, Sul Ross State University.

297 **The minutes of the meeting stated:** Roy Wilkinson Aldrich Papers, Archives of the Big Bend, Sul Ross State University.

298 **"If you're such a nigger lover":** *New York Age*, Sept. 6, 1919.

298 **"Judge Pickle's right hand was badly sprained":** *Corsicana (Tex.) Daily Sun*, Aug. 23, 1919.

298 **"I believe in Texas for Texans only":** *Salisbury (N.C.) Evening Post*, Sept. 2, 1919.

298 **called his language "plug-ugly":** *Bryan (Tex.) Eagle*, Sept. 10, 1919.

298 **As many as three hundred people, almost all of them black:** Tulsa Historical Society and Museum, "1921 Tulsa Race Massacre."

299 **"I will positively handle the situation":** *Galveston Daily News*, Nov. 18, 1922.

299 **"NEGRO HELD FOR ASSAULT":** *Sherman Democrat*, March 17, 1996. The newspaper reprinted its 1930 headline in a 1996 retrospective.

299 **the earliest possible date under Texas law:** Edward H. Phillips, "The Sherman Courthouse Riot of 1930," *East Texas Historical Journal*, October 1987.

300 **Trial day, Friday, brought the big crowds:** Phillips, "The Sherman Courthouse Riot of 1930."

300 **"the negro was guarded":** *Dunkirk (N.Y.) Evening Observer*, May 10, 1930.

301 **"It was while the first State witness was on the stand testifying":** Hamer letter to Moody, May 13, 1930, Records of Dan Moody, Texas Office of the Governor, TSLA.

301 **"was clamoring for the negro":** *Dallas Morning News*, May 10, 1930.

301 **"In a few minutes the mob attempted to rush":** Hamer letter to Moody, TSLA.

301 **"Any time you feel lucky":** Hamer letter to Moody, TSLA.

301 **Someone tossed in a lighted match:** *Dallas Morning News*, May 10, 1930.

301 **"One large man," a reporter observed:** *Dallas Morning News*, May 10, 1930.

301 **"Then all at once":** Hamer letter to Moody, TSLA.

302 **"Bidding good-bye to the mob":** *Dallas Morning News*, May 10, 1930.

302 **"I thought it necessary for me to communicate with you":** Hamer letter to Moody, TSLA.

302 **By Gonzaullas's account, he set up a one-man guard post:** Phillips, "The Sherman Courthouse Riot of 1930."

303 **"Here he is":** Phillips, "The Sherman Courthouse Riot of 1930."

303 **"Women screamed and clapped":** *Galveston Daily News*, May 10, 1930.

303 **"There were two pregnant ladies":** *Sherman Democrat*, March 17, 1996.

303 **One man with a knife severed Hughes's penis:** *Sherman Democrat*, March 17, 1996.

303 **"A brilliant Texas moon":** *Jefferson City (Mo.) Post-Tribune*, May 10, 1930.

304 **"There was not a Negro in sight":** *Dallas Morning News*, May 11, 1930.

304 **"I asked Adjutant General Robertson":** Sterling, *Trails and Trials of a Texas Ranger*, 243.

304 **"We never dreamed of the gang doing that":** Hamer letter to Moody, TSLA.

304 **But only one of them:** *Dallas Morning News*, Oct. 14, 1931.

304 **"He doubly deserved every pain he endured":** *Saint Jo (Tex.) Tribune*, May 16, 1930.

305 **"A brute in human form":** *Albany (Tex.) News*, May 16, 1930.

305 **"Not just one ranger, but several":** *Wichita Falls (Tex.) Times*, May 20, 1930.

305 **"Waal, it's our law here in Texas":** Reprinted in the *El Paso Evening Post*, June 6, 1930.

305 **"Capt. Hickman will assure London":** *Brownsville Herald*, June 11, 1930.

305 **"In Texas we respect the law":** *El Paso Evening Post*, Nov. 26, 1930.

306 **"You learn every time you get kicked":** Phillips, "The Sherman Courthouse Riot of 1930."

306 **"The Rangers brought with them":** *Pampa (Tex.) Daily News*, Aug. 16, 1930.

306 **The state did not record another one:** *Corsicana (Tex.) Semi-Weekly Light,* April 5, 1932.

306 **He confiscated the signs on the spot:** *Dallas Morning News,* Feb. 11, 1931.

306 **"I have been receiving information":** *Corsicana Semi-Weekly Light,* April 28, 1931.

306 **"I slapped that guy clear across the room":** *Dallas Morning News,* March 3, 1935.

306 **"Hamer strode up to the largest man":** Jenkins and Frost, *"I'm Frank Hamer,"* 223.

307 **The strike lasted two months:** *Corsicana Semi-Weekly Light,* Oct. 15, 1935.

307 **"There is not a man in Texas":** *Dallas Morning News,* May 10, 1939.

307 **They said they would defend the country:** *Southern (Carbondale, Ill.) Illinoisan,* Nov. 10, 2002.

307 **Walter Prescott Webb's massive 1935 history:** Webb, *The Texas Rangers,* 517–46. Webb's research files for the book, however, contain significant material about the riot, as well as the Rangers' effort to undermine the NAACP. That too was omitted from the book. Walter Prescott Webb Collection, CAH.

307 **Hamer and his Rangers "held a mob of 5,000 at bay":** Reprinted in the *Kerrville (Tex.) Mountain Sun,* Aug. 29, 1935.

307 **"He stood on the steps of the courthouse":** Douglas, *The Gentlemen in the White Hats,* 192.

307 **More than two decades later:** *Lubbock Avalanche-Journal,* Sept. 9, 1956.

CHAPTER 18. THE SINGING RANGER

311 **"And so it is with the Ranger":** Webb, *The Texas Rangers,* xv.

311 **"The Earl Carroll Theater was the scene":** *Brooklyn Daily Eagle,* Oct. 7, 1929.

312 **A number of other fictional Rangers:** "Texas Rangers on the Silver Screen," Texas Ranger Hall of Fame, texasranger.org; Pitts, *Western Movies.*

312 **"Other Texas Rangers all dead":** Rothel, *Who Was That Masked Man?,* 26.

313 **"the thief, the gambler, the bootlegger":** New York *Daily News,* Jan. 19, 1925.

313 **"unoffending communities to establish":** Austin *Statesman,* Feb. 25, 1925.

313 **The chairman of the bar exam committee:** Anne Dingus, "Pa Ferguson," *Texas Monthly,* June 1998.

313 **"His leaning was always toward the criminal element":** Sterling, *Trails and Trials of a Texas Ranger,* 255.

314 **In truth, it had only fifteen:** John Nova Lomax, "Inside Texas's White House," June 13, 2016, texasmonthly.com.

314 **She dismissed the entire force of forty-four Rangers:** Wilson, *In the Governor's Shadow,* 181.

314 **The state legislature piled on:** Stephen W. Schuster IV, "The Modernization of the Texas Rangers: 1933–1936," in Glasrud and Weiss, *Tracking the Texas Rangers: The Twentieth Century,* 135.

314 **name-brand criminals landed starring roles:** The definitive book on the major crime figures of this era is Bryan Burrough's excellent *Public Enemies.*

314 **Rangers now drove their personal cars:** Schuster, "The Modernization of the Texas Rangers," 134.

314 **"They emptied their pistols":** *Waco News-Tribune,* Feb. 3, 1934.

315 **The additional arrest of a suspicious-looking woman:** *Waco News-Tribune,* Feb. 3, 1934.

315 **Soon their syndicate controlled the town:** Cartwright, *Galveston,* 212ff.

315 **A squad of Maceo vigilantes:** Gary Cartwright, "One Last Shot," *Texas Monthly,* June 1993.

315 **"There has existed for some time in Texas":** "Report and Recommendations of the Senate Committee Investigating Crime," 43rd Legislature, 1933–1934 (hereafter SCIC).

315 **"We have in this state too many killings":** SCIC, 23–24.

316 **"Our Rangers are selling liquor personally and openly":** SCIC, 52.

316 **a state senator to whom Robbins paid a $3,200 bribe:** *Austin American,* April 28, 1934.

316 **At one point Robbins and his Rangers:** SCIC, 63, 64. Sterling, *Trails and Trials of a Texas Ranger,* 519; Schuster, "The Modernization of the Texas Rangers," 136.

316 **Tom Mix got a badge too:** *El Paso Times,* Dec. 9, 1934.

316 **"For what purpose all these commissions were issued":** SCIC, 58, 59.

317 **"Work of the Rangers is not what it was":** *Abilene (Tex.) Reporter-News,* Dec. 16, 1937.

317 **"Every patrolman and Ranger I knew":** Jackson with Haley, *One Ranger Returns,* 35.

317 **Webb had labored over the book for seventeen years:** Llerena Friend, "W. P. Webb's Texas Rangers," *SWHQ,* January 1971.

318 **It was "a bit on the patriotic side, perhaps":** Friend, "W. P. Webb's Texas Rangers."

318 **Webb did write about Rangers' misdeeds:** Webb, *The Texas Rangers,* 14, 486. Webb told friends in later years that he planned a new edition of *Texas Rangers,* one that would include Mexican and Tejano points of view. But he died in a 1963 car wreck before completing the revisions.

318 **Webb sold the film rights:** Walter Prescott Webb Collection, CAH.

318 **"Their record has brought glory":** Quoted in "Science against the Criminal: Captain M. T. Gonzaullas," in Glasrud and Weiss, *Tracking the Texas Rangers: The Twentieth Century,* 155, 156.

318 **"It stopped just short":** Graham, *Cowboys and Cadillacs,* 27.

318 **one of the most "thoroughly spine-chilling adventure films"**: *Boston Globe*, Sept. 4, 1936.

319 **from "hostile Indians, cattle rustlers and civic corruption"**: New York *Daily News*, Sept. 24, 1936.

319 **"historically accurate" production that "outlines the work of the band of fearless men"**: *Appleton (Wis.) Post-Crescent*, Sept. 5, 1936.

319 **Their role, he lamented, would "gradually slip away"**: Webb, *The Texas Rangers*, 567.

319 **"The Texas Rangers, perhaps the best known peace officers"**: *Dallas Morning News*, Sept. 10, 1941.

CHAPTER 19. "WHAT GOD HAS MADE"

321 **"I don't think it would be safe"**: *Dallas Morning News*, Sept. 2, 1956.

322 **"Then you go to work on him"**: Procter, *Just One Riot*, 94.

322 **"I wouldn't swap the job"**: *Dallas Morning News*, Sept. 30, 1956.

322 **he grabbed his .22-caliber . . . and told**: John Earl Reese file, Texas Department of Public Safety, TSLA.

323 **"We were children"**: Kaylie Simon, *Lost Life, a Miscarriage of Justice: The Death of John Earl Reese*, 5, Northeastern University School of Law, Civil Rights and Restorative Justice Project, John Earl Reese Collection.

323 **"I held the steering wheel"**: John Earl Reese file, TSLA.

323 **"It could be whites"**: Ronnie Dugger, "Negro Boy Murdered in East Texas," *Texas Observer*, Nov. 2, 1955. Dugger's coverage of the case over the course of eighteen months offered a display of journalistic dedication and mastery.

323 **"A feeling of security has been re-established"**: John Earl Reese file, TSLA.

324 **"They told me that"**: Dugger, "East Texas Justice," *Texas Observer*, April 30, 1957.

324 **"Call it a bad day"**: Dugger, "East Texas Justice."

324 **The miserly budget allowed for little**: Rusk State Hospital Annual Report, Medical Division, 1955–1956.

324 **They would "just sit"**: Procter, *Just One Riot*, 96.

324 **Trustees known as floor bouncers**: Procter, *Just One Riot*, 96.

325 **"crazed Negroes"**: *News-Review* (Roseburg, Ore.), April 18, 1955.

325 **"His head was beaten to a pulp"**: *Dallas Morning News*, April 19, 1955.

325 **"I don't want no foolishness"**: Procter, *Just One Riot*, 100.

325 **"Captain Crowder, a big, impressive man"**: *Dallas Morning News*, April 17, 1955.

325 **"I had a sniper rifle trained on this person"**: "Interview with Captain Jim Ray," Texas Ranger Hall of Fame, ebook, 2006.

325 **If the rioters surrendered**: *Dallas Morning News*, April 17, 1955.

326 **With "perspiration gleaming"**: *Dallas Morning News*, April 17, 1955.

326 **Riley was thrown into twenty-four-hour solitary confinement**: *Waco Tribune*, April 18, 1955.

326 **"We are not against the Negro"**: Ladino, *Desegregating Texas Schools*, 5.

327 **"No court can hand down an edict"**: *Lubbock Avalanche-Journal*, July 18, 1954.

327 **This was the first time a federal court**: George N. Green, "Mansfield School Desegregation Incident," *Handbook of Texas Online*.

327 **THIS IS A WHITE SCHOOL**: Ladino, *Desegregating Texas Schools*, 97.

327 **"Anyone with a silk shirt"**: Ladino, *Desegregating Texas Schools*, 101.

328 **"There ain't nobody leading this"**: Denton (Tex.) *Record-Chronicle*, Aug. 31, 1956.

328 **THIS WOULD BE A HORRIBLE WAY TO DIE**: *Dallas Morning News*, Aug. 30, 1956.

328 **The school principal, a man named Willie Pigg**: *Dallas Morning News*, Sept. 1, 1956.

328 **Davis warned in a telegram**: Ladino, *Desegregating Texas Schools*, 98, 99.

328 **"If anybody shows up"**: *Pharos-Tribune* (Logansport, Ind.), Sept. 6, 1956.

328 **"He was always on the cover"**: Utley, *Lone Star Lawmen*, 209.

328 **"I was part of all these festivities"**: Puckett, *Cast a Long Shadow*, 86, 87.

329 **Banks wrote in his official report**: Bureau of Intelligence Case No. 64921, Texas Department of Public Safety, Oct. 5, 1956.

329 **"The people gathered did not have the appearance"**: Puckett, *Cast a Long Shadow*, 93.

329 **"It is not my intention"**: *Lubbock Morning Avalanche*, Sept. 1, 1956.

329 **"He was somewhat reluctant"**: Puckett, *Cast a Long Shadow*, 93.

330 **"Negroes aren't our neighbors"**: *Dallas Morning News*, Sept. 5, 1956.

330 **"The swarm of angry faces grew tighter"**: *Lubbock Avalanche-Journal*, Sept. 9, 1956.

330 **"I suggested he go home"**: Puckett, *Cast a Long Shadow*, 94.

330 **"The tall Ranger captain went about his work"**: *Dallas Morning News*, Sept. 30, 1956.

330 **"When he puts his booted foot up"**: Lasswell, *I'll Take Texas*, 315.

330 **"no Negro students showed up" to enroll**: Bureau of Intelligence Case No. 64921, Texas Department of Public Safety.

330 **"We could not take them in there"**: *Dallas Morning News*, Sept. 5, 1956.

331 **as an NAACP lawyer complained:** Ladino, *Desegregating Texas Schools*, 124.

331 **In 1942 a black man accused of assaulting a white woman:** *Louisville Courier-Journal*, July 14, 1942.

331 **In a public speech on integration:** *Dallas Morning News*, Sept. 8, 1956.

331 **Without it, the lawyer said in a telegram:** *Denton Record-Chronicle*, Sept. 11, 1956.

331 **Upon his arrival in Texarkana, Banks surveyed the protesters:** Puckett, *Cast a Long Shadow*, 97.

331 **"The nigger who crosses this line will die":** *Baytown (Tex.) Sun*, Sept. 10, 1956.

332 **"I told him exactly what his group could do without crossing us":** Puckett, *Cast a Long Shadow*, 97.

332 **"We were expecting to start school":** Author interview with Jessalyn Gray Johnson.

332 **"They were obviously out of town reporters":** Puckett, *Cast a Long Shadow*, 97, 98.

332 **One man shouted:** *Baytown (Tex.) Sun*, Sept. 10, 1956.

332 **They surrounded Posten:** *Dallas Morning News*, Sept. 11, 1956.

332 **"The two black students found":** Puckett, *Cast a Long Shadow*, 98.

333 **"We were under no obligation":** Puckett, Cast a Long Shadow.

333 **"I've never seen a meaner mob":** Ben Cosgrove, "How to Fool a Racist Mob: Lesson One," www .time.com, Sept. 8, 2014.

333 **She enrolled instead at North Texas State College:** Author interview with Jessalyn Gray Johnson. The institution is now known as the University of North Texas.

333 **Council president Williamson sent a telegram:** Puckett, *Cast a Long Shadow*, 99.

333 **"who forever looks like an angry toad":** *Texas Observer*, Sept. 2, 1966.

333 **While he was at it, Pool promised:** "The Crisis at Mansfield," University of North Texas, mansfield crisis.omeka.net.

334 **Marshall said unnamed Rangers went to the homes:** Thurgood Marshall file, Federal Bureau of Investigation.

334 **"We have done nothing worse":** Ladino, *Desegregating Texas Schools*, 136.

334 **The judge declared, "I ain't got nothing":** Ladino, *Desegregating Texas Schools*, 137.

334 **"Times have changed":** Ladino, *Desegregating Texas Schools*, 142.

335 **"This was probably the first time":** *San Antonio Light*, Jan. 9, 1962.

335 **Some years later, Garland Smith:** Clint Peoples file, Dallas Public Library.

335 **"represented all the respect—and almost reverence":** *Corpus Christi Caller*, Sept. 9, 1956.

335 **Banks's "latest exploits":** *Logansport (Ind.) Press*, Nov. 1, 1957.

335 **"The big Ranger—six-shooters strapped to his side":** *Dallas Morning News*, March 3, 1960.

336 **The governor who had ordered the Rangers to block:** Puckett, *Cast a Long Shadow*, 152.

336 **"Sergeant Banks and his fellow Rangers kept things quiet":** "21st Century Shining Star: Capt. Jay Banks," *Texas Ranger Dispatch*, Spring 2004.

336 **"walked unarmed into the midst of a violent riot":** *Lubbock Avalanche-Journal*, Sept. 9, 1956.

336 **The "surly and belligerent rioters":** *Dallas Morning News*, March 5, 1960.

336 **"That's the Rangers," the *Paris News* proclaimed:** *Paris (Tex.) News*, Nov. 29, 1960.

CHAPTER 20. "BILLIE SOL WHO?"

339 **"Remember, even liars sometimes tell the truth":** *Texas Observer*, Nov. 7, 1986.

340 **It would be, Peoples vowed:** Clint Peoples file, Dallas Public Library. Peoples left many of his papers to the library and gave an extensive oral history.

340 **"Well, you better get your teeth in it":** Clint Peoples file, Dallas Public Library.

340 **The "Billie Sol Estes Scandal":** *Time*, May 25, 1962.

340 **The son of an itinerant East Texas farmer:** Much of the information on Peoples's background is taken from Day, *Captain Clint Peoples, Texas Ranger*.

341 **"I stuck my sawed-off .12-gauge":** *Longview (Tex.) News-Journal*, March 16, 1987.

341 **But an inquest showed:** *Waco Citizen*, May 8, 1958.

341 **The bullet knocked off the Ranger's hat:** Day, *Captain Clint Peoples, Texas Ranger*, 109.

341 **With regal aplomb, he posed:** *Waco News-Tribune*, May 16, 1955.

341 **After washing off blood and tear gas:** Day, *Captain Clint Peoples, Texas Ranger*, 110.

342 **"If he can kill himself with this gun":** *Lubbock Evening Journal*, March 21, 1984.

342 **Henry Marshall also grew up on a farm:** Much of the information on Marshall and his case comes from Bill Adler, "The Killing of Henry Marshall," *Texas Observer*, Nov. 7, 1986,

342 **"The son of a bitch shot himself":** "The Killing of Henry Marshall."

343 **"There is nowhere to go but up":** Pam Estes, *Billie Sol*, 26.

343 **when he was twelve he traded a barn full of oats:** *Time*, May 25, 1962.

343 **"Making a deal":** Billie Sol Estes, *Billie Sol Estes*, 98.

343 **"Let those big shots from Dallas":** Billie Sol Estes, *Billie Sol Estes*, 98. Details about Estes's home life are drawn from his and his daughter's books.

344 **parakeets would not take to the air in unison:** *Time*, May 25, 1962.

344 **"He'd lie about anything":** Author interview with Hugh Aynesworth.

344 **"The government is staying right on Mr. Estes's tail":** *New York Times*, May 14, 2013.

344 **"The President would like to know":** Billie Sol Estes file, Federal Bureau of Investigation (hereafter FBI).

345 **"The Ballad of Billie Sol":** *New York Times*, May 14, 2013.

345 **"The sad part of it":** *Time*, May 25, 1962.

345 **He vowed to crack down:** "The Killing of Henry Marshall."

345 **"I couldn't get any cooperation":** Clint Peoples file, Dallas Public Library.

346 **Marshall's aorta was severed:** Henry Marshall file, FBI.

346 **Suicide was "most improbable":** Haile, *Murder Most Texan*, 91.

346 **"If, in fact, this is a suicide":** Clint Peoples file, Dallas Public Library.

346 **Vice President Johnson's office called as well:** "The Killing of Henry Marshall."

346 **"I just can't understand":** Henry Marshall file, FBI.

346 **"Peoples has stimulated publicity":** Henry Marshall file, FBI.

346 **This caused, a local state senator said:** "The Killing of Henry Marshall."

346 **"That was the end of the day with him":** Clint Peoples file, Dallas Public Library.

346 **"He was sent down there by Bobby Kennedy":** Clint Peoples file, Dallas Public Library.

347 **Despite Director Hoover's initial skepticism:** Henry Marshall file, FBI.

347 **His findings of murder:** Henry Marshall file, FBI.

347 **"I wish this 'blabber-mouth' would stop speaking":** Billie Sol Estes file, FBI.

347 **"That little FBI agent down there":** Clint Peoples file, Dallas Public Library.

347 **"I feel like one of these days":** United Press International, July 24, 1962, referenced in Henry Marshall file, FBI.

347 **men under his command could not divorce:** Clint Peoples file, Dallas Public Library.

348 **"an authentic series about a great police force":** *Trackdown* Television Series Archives, CAH.

348 **"Gonzaullas's gray-green eyes disconcerted men":** Malsch, *"Lone Wolf" Gonzaullas*, 5–6.

348 **"The most dangerous place in Texas":** "The Lone Wolf Was Camera Shy," *Texas Ranger Dispatch*, Summer 2001.

348 **"Neat," said Ranger Glenn Elliott:** Interview with Glenn Elliott, February 14, 1994, Texas Ranger Hall of Fame.

348 **"Just write that I found it necessary":** *Dallas Morning News*, Feb. 15, 1977.

348 **"He said he served with the Mexican army":** Interview with Glenn Elliott.

349 **The *Dallas Morning News* christened Gonzaullas:** *Dallas Morning News*, June 21 and July 11, 1951.

349 **When he shaved in the morning:** *Denton (Tex.) Record-Chronicle*, July 7, 1967.

349 **"I remember the day they brought the crew":** "The Lone Wolf Was Camera Shy."

349 **In 1972 he flew to New York:** Day, *Captain Clint Peoples, Texas Ranger*, 171.

349 **"He had access to the [case] files":** Clint Peoples file, TSLA.

350 **"Peoples had reached the top of his profession":** Day, *Captain Clint Peoples, Texas Ranger*, 164.

350 **"Regretfully," he testified in court:** Pam Estes, *Billie Sol*, 173.

350 **"I asked him, 'Billie Sol'":** Clint Peoples file, Dallas Public Library.

350 **"There's one thing I want you to tell me":** Clint Peoples file, Dallas Public Library.

351 **Kinser also hoped to lure LBJ:** Mellen, *Faustian Bargains*, 82.

351 **"All investigations showed that Doug Kinser":** Clint Peoples file, Dallas Public Library.

351 **"Five years suspended for murder with malice!":** Clint Peoples file, Dallas Public Library.

352 **"The smell of politics was all around there":** Day, *Captain Clint Peoples, Texas Ranger*, 82.

352 **"I was just a broken down old farmer":** Billie Sol Estes, *Billie Sol Estes*, 98.

352 **For the next four and a half hours:** Clint Peoples file, Dallas Public Library.

352 **Then, Estes claimed, Johnson said:** *Texas Observer*, op. cit.

353 **"Billie Sol Estes is a con man":** *Odessa (Tex.) American*, March 24, 1984.

353 **He directed his lawyer, Douglas Caddy:** Author interview with Douglas Caddy.

353 **some "Italian friends" warned him:** Mellen, *Faustian Bargains*, 240.

353 **Peoples put forth his own theory:** Author interview with Douglas Caddy.

353 **"A lot of people take the position":** Clint Peoples file, Dallas Public Library.

354 **Peoples still yearned for Hollywood:** All information on scripts and proposals is drawn from the Clint Peoples file, Dallas Public Library.

355 **LBJ wanted to be sure that Marshall "would never disclose":** Billie Sol Estes, *Billie Sol Estes*, 98.

356 **"The greatest actor in the world":** *Longview News-Journal*, May 13, 1984.

CHAPTER 21. THE MELON HARVEST

359 **"This civil rights":** *New York Times*, March 23, 1970.

359 **"like a sunburned potato":** *San Antonio Express*, Sept. 13, 1970.

359 **"There has never been a greater Ranger Commander"**: Clint Peoples file, Dallas Public Library.

360 **"He was always trying to be meaner"**: Author interview with José Ángel Gutiérrez.

360 **"Sometimes we had to get a little rough"**: James Randolph Ward, "The Texas Rangers, 1919–1935: A Study in Law Enforcement" (PhD thesis, Texas Christian University, May 1972), 200.

360 **"He could be meaner than a barrel of rattlesnakes"**: Jackson with Haley, *One Ranger Returns*, 259.

360 **"And he counted to three"**: Interview with Joaquin Jackson, 2008, Texas Ranger Hall of Fame.

361 **Average per capita income**: *McAllen (Tex.) Monitor*, May 31, 2016.

361 **"There is nothing but stoop labor"**: *Texas Observer*, June 9, 1967.

361 **"We would drink from puddles"**: Joy Diaz, "Texas Farmworker: 1966 Strike 'Was Like Heading into War,'" NPR, Aug. 12, 2016.

361 **One bureau memo reported that a "sullen looking"**: File 100-EP-6013, FBI.

362 **informants "did not observe any subversives"**: Cesar Chavez file, FBI.

362 **As a Starr County grand jury declared**: Robert Hall, "Farmworkers Strike in South Texas," bobsremonstrance.com.

362 **"The march did not win any contracts"**: *McAllen Monitor*, May 31, 2016.

362 **The ranchers brought the Rangers in**: *Chicago Tribune*, April 19, 1883.

362 **supplemented the Rangers' pay and treated them**: Andrew Graybill, "Texas Rangers, Canadian Mounties, and the Policing of the Transnational Industrial Frontier, 1885–1910," *Western Historical Quarterly*, Summer 2004.

363 **The workers' union claimed in a lawsuit**: *Corpus Christi Caller*, Sept.. 28, 1947; *Paris (Tex.) News*, Aug. 12, 1948.

363 **But Lone Star Steel was secretly picking up the tab**: Clint Peoples file, Dallas Public Library.

363 **"Whether it was last year or one hundred years ago"**: Author interview with José Ángel Gutiérrez.

363 **The Rangers "are the Mexican Americans' Ku Klux Klan"**: *Texas Observer*, June 9, 1967.

363 **"All Rangers have Mexican blood"**: Ignacio M. García, "'The Best Bargain . . . Ever Received': The 1968 Commission on Civil Rights Hearing in San Antonio, Texas," *SWHQ*, Jan. 2019.

363 **"No one fears the Rangers"**: Interview with Captain A. Y. Allee, Feb. 21, 1969, North Texas State University Oral History Collection.

363 **"We're not damn strike breakers"**: *Texas Observer*, June 9, 1967.

363 **"It is not necessary to have a doctor's degree"**: *Corpus Christi Caller*, Dec. 15, 1968.

364 **"We rode horseback and we had pack mules"**: *New York Times*, March 23, 1970.

364 **"There are many times"**: "A Ranger's Horse," *The Cattleman*, Sept. 1967.

364 **"My family's fought for Texas"**: *New York Times*, March 23, 1970.

364 **The grandfather was convicted in none of these shootings**: De la Garza, *A Law for the Lion*, 33–39, 123.

364 **"A mild reprimand"**: *Brownsville Herald*, Aug. 24, 1948.

364 **Allee met the attorney in the courthouse hallway**: *Corpus Christi Caller*, March 19, 1953.

364 **Allee took him aside afterward**: *Longview News-Journal*, May 21, 1961.

364 **"When they got to talking about the traffic stop"**: Interview with Joaquin Jackson, Texas Ranger Hall of Fame.

365 **"I personally don't like nothing about him"**: *Abilene Reporter-News*, Feb. 24, 1954.

365 **"I mean he guarded over us men"**: Interview with Joaquin Jackson, Texas Ranger Hall of Fame.

365 **"Y'all hungry?"**: Jackson with Haley, *One Ranger Returns*, 154.

365 **"[Allee] tells him, 'You goddamn Mexican'"**: Oral History Interview with Joaquin Jackson and José Ángel Gutiérrez, 1996, University of Texas at Arlington.

365 **"I spoke the Mexican language as much as my own"**: "A Ranger's Horse."

365 **"I don't see any Japanese here"**: Robert Draper, "The Twilight of the Texas Rangers," *Texas Monthly*, Feb. 1994.

365 **a "two-story hostelry"**: *Texas Observer*, June 9, 1967.

366 **By sunrise, he said, he had killed 212 cockroaches**: *Texas Observer*, June 9, 1967.

366 **"Union pickets followed a train of melons"**: Clint Peoples file, Dallas Public Library.

366 **Some were cited for "using abusive language"**: Clint Peoples file, Dallas Public Library.

366 **"It must be an unsavory duty"**: *Texas Observer*, June 9, 1967.

367 **"If you want that camera busted"**: *Wall Street Journal*, Sept. 13, 1967.

367 **"They were pushing people"**: *Texas Observer*, June 9, 1967.

367 **Then, he said, the Rangers beat the men**: *Denton Record-Chronicle*, Jan. 3, 1968.

367 **"He said, 'Krueger, you ain't a preacher'"**: Author interview with Ed Krueger.

368 **A Ranger opened the camera**: *Dallas Morning News*, June 10, 1967.

368 **Mrs. Krueger was arrested, Allee said**: *Corpus Christi Caller*, Dec. 15, 1968.

368 **"Magdaleno had gone rabbit hunting"**: Author interview with Alejandro Moreno.

368 **"He was an enforcer for the union":** Interview with Joaquin Jackson, Texas Ranger Hall of Fame.

368 **they leveled shotguns at union organizers:** Undated farmworkers' newsletter, Clint Peoples file, Dallas Public Library.

368 **"that son-of-a-bitch Dimas":** Letter from State Senator Joe Bernal to Governor John Connally, June 3, 1967.

368 **"He was beaten out of his wits":** *Texas Observer*, June 9, 1967.

368 **"I could have killed him":** *Dallas Morning News*, June 14, 1968.

369 **"I honestly believe," Allee said:** Clint Peoples file, Dallas Public Library.

369 **"This damn era we live in now":** *Wall Street Journal*, Sept. 13, 1967.

369 **"This has severely tarnished the image":** Clint Peoples file, Dallas Public Library.

369 **"I feel that the people of Rio Grande City":** *San Antonio Express*, June 3, 1967.

369 **Its field representative, William B. Oliver III:** Clint Peoples file, Dallas Public Library.

369 **The file noted that Oliver subscribed:** Clint Peoples file, Dallas Public Library.

370 **see the Rangers as "a symbol of oppression":** *Mexican Americans and the Administration of Justice in the Southwest*, A Report of the United States Commission on Civil Rights, March 1970.

370 **"Those who know him best":** *Dallas Morning News*, July 9, 1967.

370 **"the high regard we have for him as a man":** *Carrizo Springs (Tex.) Javelin*, Aug. 24, 1967.

370 **"Most of these smart punks":** Clint Peoples file, Dallas Public Library.

371 **"You have no doubt noticed that some of the enemies of the Rangers":** Clint Peoples file, Dallas Public Library.

371 **"Texas' finest stood accused":** *Newsweek*, June 19, 1967.

371 **Next came the courts:** *Medrano v. Allee*, 347 F. Supp. 605 (S.D. Texas, 1972), Civ. A. No. 67 B 36.

372 **"Political insurgency was sparked":** Hall, "Farmworkers Strike in South Texas."

372 **"Was he a racist?":** Jackson and Wilkinson, *One Ranger*, 152.

373 **"The actual events have become shrink-wrapped":** Jackson with Haley, *One Ranger Returns*, 1–18.

373 **"Captain Allee was a great law enforcement officer":** *El Paso Herald Post*, May 20, 1972.

373 **"Widespread recognition from the world at large":** *McAllen Monitor*, Sept. 22, 1969.

373 **"I'm not quite the bad character":** Interview with Captain A. Y. Allee, North Texas State University.

373 **"As long as my folks and my friends remember me":** *El Paso Herald Post*, May 20, 1972.

373 **"I don't regret anything":** *San Antonio Express*, Sept. 13, 1970.

374 **He slapped the clerk:** *San Antonio Express*, June 19, 1971.

CHAPTER 22. CELEBRITY

377 **"It all seemed fun to start with":** *Los Angeles Times*, Sept. 12, 1993.

378 **His childhood had unspooled:** Evaluation, Beaumont Training School for Boys, Beaumont, Virginia, 1952.

378 **"They was all the time pounding on me":** Psychiatric evaluation, Michigan Bureau of Pardons and Paroles, March 22, 1961.

378 **"I've done some bad things":** Transcript, *State v. Lucas*, No. 43314-120, District Court, El Paso County, Texas. The quotations are taken from sworn testimony.

379 **"it was no secret that Henry was lying":** Transcript, *State v. Lucas*.

379 **"a terrible new phenomenon":** *New York Times*, April 24, 1984.

380 **"Things really skyrocketed in Georgetown":** Rosenbaum, *The Secret Parts of Fortune*, 408.

380 **"enough to jog his memory":** Transcript, McLennan County grand jury, March Term, 1985.

380 **"and he would get plumb weird looking":** Transcript, McLennan County grand jury.

380 **In 1982 alone, he said, he murdered thirty-five people:** Texas Department of Public Safety file, TSLA.

381 **"He may have had a low IQ":** Author interview with Bob Prince.

381 **"We cut 'em up":** *Houston Chronicle*, March 14, 2001.

381 **"I don't like barbecue sauce":** Rosenbaum, *The Secret Parts of Fortune*, 400.

381 **"Whatever Henry wanted":** Transcript, McLennan County grand jury.

382 **"I never had a house this nice before":** Author interview with Vic Feazell.

382 **Some of them would give him $20:** Transcript, McLennan County grand jury.

382 **"Henry was made to feel really good":** Transcript, McLennan County grand jury.

382 **As many as forty Rangers:** Testimony of Captain Bob Prince, *State v. Lucas*, No. 43314-120.

382 **"Like a teacher's pet":** *Chicago Tribune*, March 24, 1985.

383 **"If he was going to do a couple of murders":** *Paris (Tex.) News*, June 28, 1984.

383 **police agencies in twenty-six states closed the books:** *Houston Chronicle*, March 14, 2001.

383 **"He has all these diamond rings":** Transcript, McLennan County grand jury.

383 **The *Waco Citizen* made it front-page news:** *Waco Citizen*, May 29, 1984.

384 **"I thought, I gotta talk to this guy"**: Author interview with Hugh Aynesworth.

384 **"To accept that Lucas could kill 210 people"**: *Dallas Times Herald*, April 14, 1985.

385 **"I don't recall him being right on anything"**: Transcript, *State v. Lucas*.

385 **"Seems like I chased her"**: *Lubbock Avalanche-Journal*, May 28, 2006.

386 **"We both realized," Bob Lemons said**: Information on and quotations from Lemons are from *State v. Lucas* and the McLennan County grand jury transcripts.

386 **Prince said many years later that he asked Lemons**: Author interview with Bob Prince.

387 **"It will be a good photo op"**: Information and quotations are drawn from an author interview with Vic Feazell and an autobiographical sketch provided by Feazell.

387 **"Bobby would proceed to open up the envelopes"**: Transcript, McLennan County grand jury.

387 **"They show me a photograph"**: Transcript, McLennan County grand jury.

388 **Ranger Prince denied this account**: Author interview with Prince.

388 **"So I said, 'Yeah, down there is the scene'"**: Transcript, McLennan County grand jury.

388 **District Attorney Feazell arranged a meeting with Colonel Adams**: Author interview with Vic Feazell. Adams did not respond to several requests from the author for comment.

388 **"Do you believe the word of a convicted murderer"**: *Los Angeles Times*, April 24, 1985.

389 **Yes, answered Texas attorney general Jim Mattox**: Lucas Report, Office of the Attorney General of Texas, April 1986.

389 **"Henry was taking a lot of people on a ride"**: Associated Press, Nov. 29, 1985.

389 **"They think I'm stupid"**: *Dallas Times Herald*, April 14, 1985.

389 **"I made up my mind to commit legal suicide"**: Transcript, McLennan County grand jury.

389 **"What you had is a person who"**: Transcript, McLennan County grand jury.

389 **"They were living a celebrity life"**: Transcript, *State v. Lucas*.

389 **"They got to thinking they were heroes"**: Author interview with Hugh Aynesworth.

390 **"I made some very powerful people mad at me"**: *Dallas Morning News*, June 24 and June 30, 1987.

390 **"I believe there is enough doubt"**: *Austin American-Statesman*, June 25, 1998.

390 **This was the only death sentence he commuted**: *Amarillo Globe-News*, March 16, 2001.

391 **"My life," he said, "had been truly on the wrong side"**: *Amarillo Globe-News*, March 16, 2001.

391 **"I was as famous as Elvis'"**: Author interview with Vic Feazell.

391 **In 2016, for example, DNA helped convict**: New York *Daily News*, Dec. 4, 2016. In addition, the case of the young woman originally known only as Orange Socks has yielded something new. In 2019 she was identified through DNA testing as Debra Jackson from Abilene, Texas.

391 **"No credible evidence survives"**: Utley, *Lone Star Lawmen*, 301.

391 **"I don't regret it at all"**: Author interview with Prince.

391 **"It wasn't practical for us to go"**: Transcript, McLennan County grand jury.

391 **"We are not going to assign personnel"**: Transcript, McLennan County grand jury.

392 **Contrary to what the Rangers had said**: Texas Department of Public Safety file, TSLA. According to TSLA, the files had remained unexamined by outsiders until the author's inspections of them in 2015.

393 **Yet decades later, the Baytown Police Department**: Author correspondence with Baytown Police Department.

CHAPTER 23. TODAY'S RANGER

395 **"The worst Ranger was a good Ranger"**: Author interview with Maurice Cook.

395 **"Whoever took this jersey"**: Leif Reigstad, "Dan Patrick Unleashes the Texas Rangers to Find Tom Brady's Stolen Jersey," texasmonthly.com, Feb. 6, 2017.

396 **memorabilia collector's tip**: ESPN.com, March 21, 2017.

397 **"We don't need a state Gestapo any more"**: *Taylor (Tex.) Daily Press*, March 3, 1955.

397 **"He might almost as well propose that the Alamo be razed"**: *Dallas Morning News*, March 6, 1955.

397 **they added subsection 411.015 (b)**: Texas Legislative Reference Library.

397 **"They [would] get an old boy arrested"**: "Interview with Max Womack, Texas Ranger, Retired," Texas Ranger Hall of Fame, 1995.

398 **"We've never had a colored to pass"**: *Austin American-Statesman*, May 13, 1979.

398 **"It was rough"**: Author interview with Maurice Cook.

398 **"It was, 'Welcome aboard'"**: *Dallas Morning News*, June 19, 1995.

398 **Leal said he never faced hostility**: Author interview with Antonio Leal.

399 **In 1987 an ex-con named Brent Albert Beeler**: Department of Public Safety file, TSLA.

400 **"PLANE CRASH VICTIMS NO STRANGERS TO TRAGEDY"**: *Carlsbad (N.M.) Current-Argus*, June 26, 1992.

400 **"I'm not going to say"**: "Interview with Max Womack, Texas Ranger, Retired."

401 **"Father Feit, they put him out of here"**: Author interview with Clint Mussey, 2002.

401 **"I'm just hanging out"**: Author interview with John Feit, 2002.

401 **Jaramillo kept a framed photograph:** Pamela Colloff, "Unholy Act," *Texas Monthly*, April 2005.

401 **Burzynski conducted a year-long investigation:** Report of Investigation, Texas Ranger Division, Feb. 23, 2005.

402 **Ranger Drew Carter was credited with persuading:** *Houston Chronicle*, June 25, 2006.

402 **"There's not a single thing":** Pamela Colloff, "Free at Last," *Texas Monthly*, November 2010.

402 **false trial testimony from the Ranger:** *Graves v. Dretke*, U.S. Circuit Court of Appeals for the Fifth Circuit.

402 **"Rangers in their trademark cowboy hats":** *New York Times*, Feb. 23, 2011. No one had been charged in the case as of mid-2019.

403 **Miller was not indicted:** *Texas Tribune*, Dec. 21, 2018.

403 **Paxton was indicted:** As of late 2019, he had yet to stand trial.

403 **Its agents seized a "truckload of documents":** *San Antonio Express-News*, Oct. 29, 2018.

403 **"District Clerk Reed confirmed":** Arrest warrant affidavit, Lampasas County, Jan. 5, 2018.

404 **undisclosed "extended covert operations in remote areas":** dps.texas.gov/TexasRangers/special Units.htm.

404 **"A friend of mine said":** Author interview with Brandon Bess.

Selected Bibliography

Agee, Jane Snyder. *Images of America: Borger*. Charleston, SC: Arcadia, 2012.

Alcaraz, Ramón, et al. *The Other Side: or Notes for the History of the War between Mexico and the United States*. Translated from the Spanish by Albert C. Ramsey. New York: Wiley, 1850.

Alexander, Bob. *Riding Lucifer's Line: Ranger Deaths along the Texas-Mexico Border*. Denton: University of North Texas Press, 2013.

———. *Winchester Warriors: Texas Rangers of Company D, 1874–1901*. Denton: University of North Texas Press, 2009.

Alexander, Bob, and Donaly E. Brice. *Texas Rangers: Lives, Legend, and Legacy*. Denton: University of North Texas Press, 2017.

Alonzo, Armando C. *Tejano Legacy: Rancheros and Settlers in South Texas, 1734–1900*. Albuquerque: University of New Mexico Press, 1998.

Alvarez, Elizabeth Cruce, ed. *Texas Almanac, 2018–2019*. Austin: Texas State Historical Association, 2018.

Anderson, Gary Clayton. *The Conquest of Texas: Ethnic Cleansing in the Promised Land, 1820–1875*. Norman: University of Oklahoma Press, 2005.

Bainbridge, John. *The Super-Americans*. New York: Doubleday, 1961.

Bannon, John Francis. *The Spanish Borderlands Frontier, 1513–1821*. Albuquerque: University of New Mexico Press, 1976.

Baylor, George Wythe. *Into the Far, Wild Country: True Tales of the Old Southwest*. El Paso: Texas Western Press, 1996.

Bell, Horace. *Reminiscences of a Ranger: Early Times in Southern California*. Norman: University of Oklahoma Press, 1999.

Benner, Judith Ann. *Sul Ross: Soldier, Statesman, Educator*. College Station: Texas A&M University Press, 1983.

Benton, Thomas Hart. *An Artist in America*. Columbia: University of Missouri Press, 1983.

Bills, E. R. *The 1919 Slocum Massacre: An Act of Genocide in East Texas*. Charleston, SC: History Press, 2014.

Blackwood, Emma Jerome, ed. *To Mexico with Scott: Letters of Captain E. Kirby Smith to His Wife*. Cambridge, MA: Harvard University Press, 1917.

Blocksom, Augustus. *Affray at Brownsville, Tex., August 13 and 14, 1906*. London: Forgotten Books, 2015. Reprint.

Boatman, T. Nicole, Scott H. Belshaw, and Richard B. McCaslin. *Galveston's Maceo Family Empire: Bootlegging and the Balinese Room*. Charleston, SC: History Press, 2014.

Boessenecker, John. *Texas Ranger: The Epic Life of Frank Hamer, the Man Who Killed Bonnie and Clyde.* New York: Thomas Dunne Books, 2016.

Brammer, Billy Lee. *The Gay Place.* Austin: University of Texas Press, 1995.

Brands, H. W. *Lone Star Nation: The Epic Story of the Battle for Texas Independence.* New York: Anchor Books, 2005.

"Brazos" (pseudonym). *Life of Robert Hall, Indian Fighter and Veteran of Three Great Wars.* Austin: State House Press, 1992.

Broday, Linda. *To Love a Texas Ranger.* Naperville, IL: Sourcebooks Casablanca, 2016.

Brown, John Henry. *Indian Wars and Pioneers of Texas.* Austin: L. E. Daniell, 189[?].

Bryan, Jimmy L., Jr., ed. *The Martial Imagination: Cultural Aspects of American Warfare.* College Station: Texas A&M Press, 2013.

Burrough, Bryan. *Public Enemies: America's Greatest Crime Wave and the Birth of the FBI, 1933–34.* New York: Penguin Press, 2004.

Callicott, Bill. *Bill Callicott Reminiscences.* Waco: Texas Ranger Hall of Fame E-Book, 2006.

Calvert, Robert A., Arnoldo De Leon, and Gregg Cantrell. *The History of Texas.* Malden, MA: John Wiley & Sons, 2014.

Carlson, Paul H., and Tom Crum. *Myth, Memory, and Massacre: The Pease River Capture of Cynthia Ann Parker.* Lubbock: Texas Tech University Press, 2010.

Carrigan, William D. *The Making of a Lynching Culture: Violence and Vigilantism in Central Texas, 1836–1916.* Urbana: University of Illinois Press, 2006.

Carrigan, William D., and Clive Webb. *Forgotten Dead: Mob Violence against Mexicans in the United States, 1848–1928.* New York: Oxford University Press, 2013.

Cartwright, Gary. *Galveston: A History of the Island.* Fort Worth: TCU Press, 1998.

Catlin, George. *Illustrations of the Manners, Customs, and Condition of the North American Indians.* Vol. 2. London: Henry G. Bohn, 1848.

———. *North American Indians.* Vol. 2. London: Henry G. Bohn, 1848.

Chamberlain, Samuel E. *My Confession.* New York: Harper & Brothers, 1956.

Chance, Joseph E., ed. *My Life in the Old Army: The Reminiscences of Abner Doubleday.* Fort Worth: TCU Press, 1998.

Clarke, Mary Whatley. *Chief Bowles and the Texas Cherokees.* Norman: University of Oklahoma Press, 1971.

Clemens, Jeremiah. *Mustang Gray; A Romance.* Philadelphia: J. B. Lippincott, 1858.

Coker, Caleb, ed. *The News from Brownsville: Helen Chapman's Letters from the Texas Military Frontier, 1848–1852.* Austin: Texas State Historical Association, 1992.

Collins, Michael L. *Texas Devils: Rangers and Regulars on the Lower Rio Grande, 1846–1861.* Norman: University of Oklahoma Press, 2010.

Cool, Paul. *Salt Warriors: Insurgency on the Rio Grande.* College Station: Texas A&M University Press, 2008.

Cox, Mike. *Texas Ranger Tales II.* Lanham, MD: Republic of Texas Press, 1999.

———. *The Texas Rangers.* Vol. 1, *Wearing the Cinco Peso, 1821–1900.* New York: Tom Doherty Associates, 2008.

———. *Time of the Rangers.* Vol. 2, *From 1900 to the Present.* New York: Tom Doherty Associates, 2009.

Cozzens, Peter. *The Earth Is Weeping: The Epic Story of the Indian Wars for the American West.* New York: Vintage Books, 2016.

Crouch, Barry A. *The Dance of Freedom: Texas African Americans during Reconstruction.* Austin: University of Texas Press, 2007.

Cutrer, Thomas W. *Ben McCulloch and the Frontier Military Tradition.* Chapel Hill: The University of North Carolina Press, 1993.

Davidson, Homer K. *Black Jack Davidson: A Cavalry Commander on the Western Frontier.* Glendale, CA: Arthur H. Clark, 1974.

Davies, Nick. *White Lies: Rape, Murder and Justice Texas Style.* New York: Avon Books, 1993.

Davis, Jack E. *The Gulf: The Making of an American Sea.* New York: Liveright, 2017.

Davis, John L. *The Texas Rangers: Images and Incidents.* San Antonio: University of Texas Institute of Texan Cultures at San Antonio, 2000.

Davis, Richard Harding. *The West from a Car-Window.* New York: Harper & Brothers, 1892.

Davis, William C. *Three Roads to the Alamo: The Lives and Fortunes of David Crockett, James Bowie, and William Barret Travis.* New York: HarperPerennial, 1999.

Day, James M. *Captain Clint Peoples, Texas Ranger: Fifty Years a Lawman.* Waco, TX: Texian Press, 1980.

De la Garza, Beatriz. *A Law for the Lion: A Tale of Crime and Injustice in the Borderlands.* Austin: University of Texas Press, 2003.

De Leon, Arnoldo. *They Called Them Greasers: Anglo Attitudes toward Mexicans in Texas, 1821–1900.* Austin: University of Texas Press, 1983.

DeVoto, Bernard. *The Year of Decision: 1846.* New York: Book-of-the-Month Club, 1984.

Dixon, Olive K. *Life of "Billy" Dixon, Plainsman, Scout and Pioneer*. Dallas: P. L. Turner, 1927.

Dobie, J. Frank. *The Mustangs*. Boston: Little, Brown, 1952.

Domenech, The Abbe. *Missionary Adventures in Texas and Mexico*. London: Longman, Brown, Green, Longmans, and Roberts, 1858.

Douglas, C. L. *The Gentlemen in the White Hats: Dramatic Episodes in the History of the Texas Rangers*. Austin: State House Press, 1992.

Duke, Cordia Sloan, and Joe B. Frantz. *6,000 Miles of Fence: Life on the XIT Ranch of Texas*. Austin: University of Texas Press, 1961.

Dunn, J. B. (Red). *Perilous Trails of Texas*. Corpus Christi, TX: Nueces Press, 2015.

Durham, George, as told to Clyde Wantland. *Taming the Nueces Strip: The Story of McNelly's Rangers*. Austin: University of Texas Press, 2012.

Duval, John C. *The Adventures of Big-Foot Wallace, the Texas Ranger and Hunter*. New York: Skyhorse, 2015.

Edwards, Frank S. *A Campaign in New Mexico with Colonel Doniphan*. Philadelphia: Carey and Hart, 1847.

Edwards, William B. *The Story of Colt's Revolver: The Biography of Col. Samuel Colt*. Harrisburg, PA: Stackpole, 1957.

Estes, Billie Sol. *Billie Sol Estes: A Texas Legend*. Granbury, TX: BS Productions, 2005.

Estes, Pam. *Billie Sol: King of Texas Wheeler-Dealers*. Abilene, TX: Noble Craft Books, 1983.

Evans, Clement A., ed. *Confederate Military History*. Vol. 11. New York: Thomas Yoseloff, c. 1962.

Everett, Dianna. *The Texas Cherokees: A People Between Two Fires, 1819–1840*. Norman: University of Oklahoma Press, 1990.

Exley, Jo Ella Powell. *Frontier Blood: The Saga of the Parker Family*. College Station: Texas A&M University Press, 2001.

Fehrenbach, T. R. *Comanches: The Destruction of a People*. New York: Alfred A. Knopf, 1974.

———. *Lone Star: A History of Texas and the Texans*. New York: Collier, 1980.

Ferrell, Robert H., ed. *Monterrey Is Ours! The Mexican War Letters of Lieutenant Dana, 1845–1847*. Lexington: University Press of Kentucky, 1990.

Foos, Paul. *A Short, Offhand, Killing Affair: Soldiers and Social Conflict during the Mexican-American War*. Chapel Hill: University of North Carolina Press, 2002.

Ford, John Salmon. *Rip Ford's Texas*. Austin: University of Texas Press, 2002.

Frankel, Glenn. *The Searchers: The Making of an American Legend*. New York: Bloomsbury, 2013.

Franks, J. M. *Seventy Years in Texas*. Originally published Gatesville, TX: J. M. Franks, 1924. Reprint.

Gard, Wayne. *Sam Bass*. Boston: Houghton Mifflin, 1936.

George, Isaac. *Heroes and Incidents of the Mexican War*. Greensburg, PA: Review Publishing, 1903.

Giddings, Luther. *Sketches of the Campaign in Northern Mexico in Eighteen Hundred Forty-Six and Seven*. New York: George P. Putnam, 1853.

Gillett, James B. *Six Years with the Texas Rangers: 1875–1881*. New York: Cosimo, 2007.

Glasrud, Bruce A., and Harold J. Weiss, Jr., eds. *Tracking the Texas Rangers: The Nineteenth Century*. Denton: University of North Texas Press, 2012.

———. *Tracking the Texas Rangers: The Twentieth Century*. Denton: University of North Texas Press, 2013.

Graham, Don. *Cowboys and Cadillacs: How Hollywood Looks at Texas*. Austin: Texas Monthly Press, 1983.

———. *Kings of Texas: The 150-Year Saga of an American Ranching Empire*. Hoboken, NJ: John Wiley & Sons, 2003.

Graybill, Andrew R. *Policing the Great Plains: Rangers, Mounties, and the North American Frontier, 1875–1910*. Lincoln: University of Nebraska Press, 2007.

Green, Rena Maverick, ed. *Memoirs of Mary A. Maverick Arranged by Mary A. Maverick and Her Son Geo. Madison Maverick*. San Antonio, TX: Alamo Printing, 1921.

Greenberg, Amy S. *A Wicked War: Polk, Clay, Lincoln, and the 1846 U.S. Invasion of Mexico*. New York: Alfred A. Knopf, 2012.

Greer, James Kimmins. *Texas Ranger: Jack Hays in the Frontier Southwest*. College Station: Texas A&M Press, 1998.

———, ed. *Buck Barry: Texas Ranger and Frontiersman*. Lincoln: University of Nebraska Press, 1984.

Grey, Zane. *The Lone Star Ranger*. New York: Kensington, 2013.

Guinn, Jeff. *Go Down Together: The True, Untold Story of Bonnie and Clyde*. New York: Simon & Schuster, 2010.

Gunter, Pete A. Y., and Robert A. Calvert, eds. *W. R. Strong, His Memoirs*. Denton, TX: Denton County Historical Commission, 1982.

Gwynne, S. C. *Empire of the Summer Moon: Quanah Parker and the Rise and Fall of the Comanches, the Most Powerful Indian Tribe in American History*. New York: Scribner, 2010.

Hacker, Margaret Schmidt. *Cynthia Ann Parker: The Life and The Legend*. El Paso: Texas Western Press, 2000.

Hagedorn, Hermann, ed. *The Works of Theodore Roosevelt*. Vol. 7. New York: Scribner, 1926–27.

Haile, Bartee. *Murder Most Texan*. Charleston, SC: History Press, 2014.

———. *Texas Boomtowns: A History of Blood and Oil*. Charleston, SC: History Press, 2015.

Haley, J. Evetts. *Charles Goodnight: Cowman and Plainsman*. Norman: University of Oklahoma Press, 1949.

Hämäläinen, Pekka. *The Comanche Empire*. New Haven, CT: Yale University Press, 2008.

Hardin, John Wesley. *The Life of John Wesley Hardin, from the Original Manuscript, as Written by Himself*. Seguin, TX: Smith & Moore, 1896.

Hardy, Dermot H., and Ingham S. Roberts. *Historical Review of South-East Texas and the Founders, Leaders and Representative Men of Its Commerce, Industry and Civic Affairs, Vol I*. Chicago: Lewis, 1910.

Harper, William T. *Eleven Days in Hell: The 1974 Carrasco Prison Siege at Huntsville, Texas*. Denton: University of North Texas Press, 2004.

Harris, Charles H., III, Frances E. Harris, and Louis R. Sadler. *Texas Ranger Biographies: Those Who Served, 1910–1921*. Albuquerque: University of New Mexico Press, 2009.

Harris, Charles H., III, and Louis R. Sadler. *The Texas Rangers and the Mexican Revolution: The Bloodiest Decade, 1910–1920*. Albuquerque: University of New Mexico Press, 2004.

———. *The Texas Rangers in Transition: From Gunfighters to Criminal Investigators, 1921–1935*. Norman: University of Oklahoma Press, 2019.

Haynes, Sam W. *Soldiers of Misfortune: The Somervell and Mier Expeditions*. Austin: University of Texas Press, 1990.

Henderson, Timothy J. *A Glorious Defeat: Mexico and Its War with the United States*. New York: Hill and Wang, 2007.

Henry, Capt. W. S. *Campaign Sketches of the War with Mexico*. New York: Harper & Brothers, 1847.

Himmel, Kelly F. *The Conquest of the Karankawas and the Tonkawas, 1821–1859*. College Station: Texas A&M University Press, 1999.

Hodge, Roger D. *Texas Blood: Seven Generations among the Outlaws, Ranchers, Indians, Missionaries, Soldiers, and Smugglers of the Borderlands*. New York: Alfred A. Knopf, 2017.

Horgan, Paul. *Great River: The Rio Grande in North American History, Volume Two, Mexico and the United States*. New York: Rinehart., 1954.

Hosley, William. *Colt: The Making of an American Legend*. Amherst: University of Massachusetts Press, 1996.

House, Edward M., as told to Tyler Mason. *Riding for Texas: The True Adventures of Captain Bill McDonald of the Texas Rangers*. New York: Reynal & Hitchcock, 1936.

Hughes, W. J. *Rebellious Ranger: Rip Ford and the Old Southwest*. Norman: University of Oklahoma Press, 1964.

Hunter, J. Marvin, ed. *The Trail Drivers of Texas*. Austin: University of Texas Press, 2000.

Ingraham, J. H. *The Texan Ranger; or, The Maid of Matamoras, a Tale of the Mexican War*. New York: Williams Brothers, 1847.

Ivey, Darren L. *The Texas Rangers: A Registry and History*. Jefferson, NC: McFarland, 2010.

Jackson, H. Joaquin, with James L. Haley. *One Ranger Returns*. Austin: University of Texas Press, 2008.

Jackson, H. Joaquin, and David Marion Wilkinson. *One Ranger: A Memoir*. Austin: University of Texas Press, 2005.

Jackson, Jack, ed. *Texas by Teran*. Austin: University of Texas Press, 2000.

Jenkins, John H., and Gordon Frost. *"I'm Frank Hamer": The Life of a Texas Peace Officer*. Buffalo Gap, TX: State House Press, 2015.

Jenkins, John Holmes, III, ed. *Recollections of Early Texas: The Memoirs of John Holland Jenkins*. Austin: University of Texas Press, 2003.

Jennings, N. A. *A Texas Ranger*. Norman: University of Oklahoma Press, 1997.

Johannsen, Robert. W. *To the Halls of the Montezumas: The Mexican War in the American Imagination*. New York: Oxford University Press, 1987.

Johnson, Benjamin Heber. *Revolution in Texas: How a Forgotten Rebellion and Its Bloody Suppression Turned Mexicans into Americans*. New Haven, CT: Yale University Press, 2003.

Jordan, Jonathan W. *Lone Star Navy: Texas, The Fight for the Gulf of Mexico, and the Shaping of the American West*. Lincoln, NE: Potomac Books, 2007.

Justice, Glenn. *Little Known History of the Texas Big Bend: Documented Chronicles From Cabeza de Vaca to the Era of Pancho Villa*. Odessa, TX: Rimrock Press, 2001.

———. *Revolution on the Rio Grande: Mexican Raids and Army Pursuits, 1916–1919*. El Paso: Texas Western Press, 1992.

Keil, Robert. *Bosque Bonito: Violent Times along the Borderland during the Mexican Revolution*. Alpine, TX: Center for Big Bend Studies, 2002.

Kendall, George Wilkins. *Dispatches from the Mexican War*. Norman: University of Oklahoma Press, 1999.

Kenly, John R. *Memoirs of a Maryland Volunteer. War with Mexico, in the Years 1846–7–8*. Philadelphia: J. B. Lippincott, 1873.

Kesselus, Kenneth, ed. *Memoir of Capt'n C.R. Perry of Johnson City, Texas*. Austin: Jenkins, 1990.

King, Duane H., ed. *The Cherokee Indian Nation: A Troubled History*. Knoxville: University of Tennessee Press, 1979.

Knowlton, Christopher. *Cattle Kingdom: The Hidden History of the Cowboy West*. New York: Houghton Mifflin Harcourt, 2017.

Kuykendall, Marshall E. *They Slept Upon Their Rifles*. Fort Worth, TX: Nortex Press, 2005.

Ladino, Robyn Duff. *Desegregating Texas Schools: Eisenhower, Shivers, and the Crisis at Mansfield High*. Austin: University of Texas Press, 1996.

Lasswell, Mary. *I'll Take Texas*. Boston: Houghton Mifflin, 1958.

Latorre, Felipe A., and Dolores L. Latorre. *The Mexican Kickapoo Indians*. New York: Dover, 1991.

Lea, Tom. *The King Ranch*. Boston: Little, Brown, 1957.

Lee, Nelson. *Three Years among the Comanches: The Narrative of Nelson Lee, Texas Ranger*. Guilford, CT: TwoDot, 2016.

Linn, John J. *Reminiscences of Fifty Years in Texas*. New York: D. & J. Sadlier, 1883.

Litwack, Leon F. *Been in the Storm So Long: The Aftermath of Slavery*. New York: Vintage Books, 1980.

Luther, Joseph. *The Odyssey of Texas Ranger James Callahan*. Charleston, SC: History Press, 2017.

Malsch, Brownson. *"Lone Wolf" Gonzaullas, Texas Ranger*. Norman: University of Oklahoma Press, 1998.

Marcy, Randolph B. *Thirty Years of Army Life on the Border*. New York: Harper & Brothers, 1866.

Martinez, Monica Muñoz. *The Injustice Never Leaves You: Anti-Mexican Violence in Texas*. Cambridge, MA: Harvard University Press, 2018.

Massey, Cynthia Leal. *Death of a Texas Ranger: A True Story of Murder and Vengeance on the Texas Frontier*. Guilford, CT: TwoDot, 2014.

Maverick, Mary A. *Memoirs of Mary A. Maverick*. San Antonio, TX: Alamo Printing, 1921.

May, Robert E. *Manifest Destiny's Underworld: Filibustering in Antebellum America*. Chapel Hill: University of North Carolina Press, 2002.

McCallum, Henry D., and Frances T. McCallum. *The Wire That Fenced the West*. Norman: University of Oklahoma Press, 1966.

McCutchan, Joseph D. *Mier Expedition Diary: A Texas Prisoner's Account*. Austin: University of Texas Press, 1978.

McDowell, Catherine W., ed. *Now You Hear My Horn: The Journal of James Wilson Nichols, 1820–1887*. Austin: University of Texas Press, 1967.

McEvoy, John. *Great Horse Racing Mysteries: True Tales from the Track*. Lexington, KY: Blood-Horse, 2003.

McMurtry, Larry. *All My Friends Are Going to Be Strangers*. New York: Simon & Schuster, 1972.

McWhirter, Cameron. *Red Summer: The Summer of 1919 and the Awakening of Black America*. New York: St. Martin's Griffin, 2012.

Mellen, Joan. *Faustian Bargains: Lyndon Johnson and Mac Wallace in the Robber Baron Culture of Texas*. New York: Bloomsbury, 2016.

Merry, Robert W. *A Country of Vast Designs: James K. Polk, the Mexican War, and the Conquest of the American Continent*. New York: Simon & Schuster, 2009.

Metz, Leon. *John Wesley Hardin: Dark Angel of Texas*. Norman: University of Oklahoma Press, 1996.

Meyer, Michael C., William L. Sherman, and Susan M. Deeds. *The Course of Mexican History*. New York: Oxford University Press, 2003.

Michno, Gregory, and Susan Michno. *A Fate Worse Than Death: Indian Captivities in the West, 1830–1885*. Caldwell, ID: Caxton Press, 2007.

Montejano, David. *Anglos and Mexicans in the Making of Texas, 1836–1986*. Austin: University of Texas Press, 1989.

Montgomery, Cora. *Eagle Pass; or, Life on the Border*. New York: George P. Putnam, 1923.

Moore, Stephen L. *Savage Frontier*. Vol. 1, *1835–1837: Rangers, Riflemen, and Indian Wars in Texas*. Denton: University of North Texas Press, 2002.

———. *Savage Frontie*. Vol. 2, *1838–1839: Rangers, Riflemen, and Indian Wars in Texas*. Denton: University of North Texas Press, 2006.

———. *Savage Frontier*. Vol. 3, *1840–1841: Rangers, Riflemen, and Indian Wars in Texas*. Denton: University of North Texas Press, 2007.

———. *Savage Frontier*. Vol. 4, *1842–1845: Rangers, Riflemen, and Indian Wars in Texas*. Denton: University of North Texas Press, 2010.

Morrell, Z. N. *Flowers and Fruits from the Wilderness; Or, Thirty-six Years in Texas and Two Winters in Honduras*. Boston: Gould and Lincoln, 1872.

Morris, Edmund. *Theodore Rex*. New York: Random House, 2001.

Mulroy, Kevin. *Freedom on the Border: The Seminole Maroons in Florida, the Indian Territory, Coahuila, and Texas.* Lubbock: Texas Tech University Press, 1993.

Nance, Joseph Milton. *Attack and Counterattack: The Texas-Mexican Frontier, 1842.* Austin: University of Texas Press, 1964.

Oates, Stephen B. *Visions of Glory: Texans on the Southwestern Frontier.* Norman: University of Oklahoma Press, 1970.

Olmsted, Frederick Law. *A Journey through Texas, or a Saddle-Trip on the Southwestern Frontier.* Lincoln: University of Nebraska Press, 2004.

O'Neal, Bill. *Encyclopedia of Western Gunfighters.* Norman: University of Oklahoma Press, 1979.

———. *The Johnson-Sims Feud: Romeo and Juliet, West-Texas Style.* Denton: University of North Texas Press, 2010.

Oswandel, J. Jacob. *Notes of the Mexican War, 1846–1848.* Knoxville: University of Tennessee Press, 2010.

Paine, Albert Bigelow. *Captain Bill McDonald, Texas Ranger: A Story of Frontier Reform.* New York: J. J. Little & Ives, 1909.

Paredes, Américo. *"With His Pistol in His Hand": A Border Ballad and Its Hero.* Austin: University of Texas Press, 1958.

Parsons, Chuck. *Images of America: The Texas Rangers.* Charleston, SC: Arcadia, 2011.

Parsons, Chuck, and Donaly E. Brice. *Texas Ranger N. O. Reynolds, the Intrepid.* Denton: University of North Texas Press, 2014.

Parsons, Chuck, and Norman Wayne Brown. *A Lawless Breed: John Wesley Hardin, Texas Reconstruction, and Violence in the Wild West.* Denton: University of North Texas Press, 2013.

Parsons, Chuck, and Marianne E. Hall Little. *Captain L. H. McNelly, Texas Ranger: The Life and Times of a Fighting Man.* Austin: State House Press, 2001.

Parsons, John E., ed. *Samuel Colt's Own Record of Transactions with Captain Walker and Eli Whitney, Jr., in 1847.* Prescott, AZ: Wolfe, 1992. Reprint.

Phillips, Michael. *White Metropolis: Race, Ethnicity, and Religion in Dallas, 1841–2001.* Austin: University of Texas Press, 2006.

Pierce, Frank C. *A Brief History of the Lower Rio Grande Valley.* Menasha, WI: George Banta, 1917.

Pitts, Michael R. *Western Movies: A Guide to 5,105 Feature Films.* Jefferson, NC: McFarland, 2013.

Presley, James. *The Phantom Killer: Unlocking the Mystery of the Texarkana Serial Murders: The Story of a Town in Terror.* New York: Pegasus Books, 2014.

Procter, Ben. *Just One Riot: Episodes of Texas Rangers in the 20th Century.* Austin: Eakin Press, 2000.

Puckett, Linda Jay. *Cast a Long Shadow: Biographical Sketch and Career Casebook of Legendary Ranger Captain E. J. (Jay) Banks.* Dallas, TX: Ussery Printing, 1984.

Ramírez, José Fernando. *Mexico during the War with the United States.* Columbia: University of Missouri Press, 1950.

Reid, Samuel C. *The Scouting Expeditions of McCulloch's Texas Rangers.* Philadelphia: J. W. Bradley, 1860.

Remington, Frederic. *Crooked Trails*, 1898. Reprint by Perfect Library.

Rieff, David. *In Praise of Forgetting: Historical Memory and Its Ironies.* New Haven, CT: Yale University Press, 2016.

Ripley, R. S. *The War with Mexico.* Vol. 1. New York: Harper & Brothers, 1849.

Roberts, Lou Conway. *A Woman's Reminiscences of Six Years in Camp with the Texas Rangers.* Middletown, DE: Word Bird Press. Reprint.

Robinson, Charles M., III. *The Men Who Wear the Star: The Story of the Texas Rangers.* New York: Random House, 2000.

Rosales, F. Arturo. *Pobre Raza: Violence, Justice, and Mobilization among Mexico Lindo Immigrants, 1900–1936.* Austin: University of Texas Press, 1999.

Rosenbaum, Ron. *The Secret Parts of Fortune: Three Decades of Intense Investigations and Edgy Enthusiasms.* New York: Random House, 2000.

Rothel, David. *Who Was That Masked Man? The Story of the Lone Ranger.* Nashville: Riverwood Press, 2013.

Samora, Julian, Joe Bernal, and Albert Pena. *Gunpowder Justice: A Reassessment of the Texas Rangers.* Notre Dame, IN: University of Notre Dame Press, 1979.

Scroggs, William O. *Filibusters and Financiers: The Story of William Walker and His Associates.* New York: Macmillan, 1916.

Seigenthaler, John. *James K. Polk.* New York: Times Books/Henry Holt, 2003.

Serven, James E. *Conquering the Frontiers: Stories of American Pioneers and the Guns Which Helped Them Establish a New Life.* La Habra, CA: Foundation Press, 1974.

Shipman, Mrs. O. L. *Taming the Big Bend: A History of the Extreme Western Portion of Texas from Fort Clark to El Paso.* Marfa, TX, 1926.

Shockley, John Staples. *Chicano Revolt in a Texas Town.* Notre Dame, IN: University of Notre Dame Press, 1974.

Sinise, Jerry. *Black Gold and Red Lights*. Austin: Eakin Press, 1982.

Smith, David Paul. *Frontier Defense in the Civil War: Texas' Rangers and Rebels*. College Station: Texas A&M University Press, 1994.

Smith, George Winston, and Charles Judah, eds. *Chronicles of the Gringos: The U.S. Army in the Mexican War, 1846–1848, Accounts of Eyewitnesses and Combatants*. Albuquerque: University of New Mexico Press, 1968.

Smith, S. Compton. *Chile con Carne; or, The Camp and the Field*. New York: Miller & Curtis, 1857.

Smithwick, Noah. *The Evolution of a State or Recollections of Old Texas Days*. Austin: University of Texas Press, 1984.

Solms-Braunfels, Carl, Prince of. *Texas 1844–45*. Houston: Anson Jones Press, 1936.

Sowell, A. J. *Early Settlers and Indian Fighters of Southwest Texas*. Austin: Ben C. Jones, 1900.

———. *History of Fort Bend County*. Houston: W. H. Coyle, 1904.

———. *The Mier Expedition*. Houston: Union National Bank, 1929.

———. *Rangers and Pioneers of Texas*. Lexington, KY: First Rate, 2015.

Spurlin, Charles D. *Texas Volunteers in the Mexican War*. Austin: Eakin Press, 1998.

Stephens, A. Ray. *Texas: A Historical Atlas*. Norman: University of Oklahoma Press, 2012.

Sterling, William Warren. *Trails and Trials of a Texas Ranger*. 1959.

Taylor, Paul Schuster. *An American-Mexican Frontier: Nueces County, Texas*. Chapel Hill: University of North Carolina Press, 1934.

Thompson, Jerry. *Cortina: Defending the Mexican Name in Texas*. College Station: Texas A&M University Press, 2007.

Thompson, Jerry, ed. *Fifty Miles and a Fight: Major Samuel Peter Heintzelman's Journal of Texas and the Cortina War*. Austin: Texas State Historical Association, 1998.

Thompson, Waddy. *Recollections of Mexico*. New York: Wiley and Putnam, 1846.

Thwaites, Ruben Gold, ed. *Early Western Travels, 1748–1846*. Vol. 28. Cleveland: Arthur H. Clark, 1906.

Torget, Andrew J. *Seeds of Empire: Cotton, Slavery, and the Transformation of the Texas Borderlands, 1800–1850*. Chapel Hill: University of North Carolina Press, 2015.

Treuer, David. *The Heartbeat of Wounded Knee: Native America from 1890 to the Present*. New York: Riverhead Books, 2019.

Tyler, Ron C. *The Big Bend: A History of the Last Texas Frontier*. College Station: Texas A&M University Press, 1996.

Utley, Robert M. *Lone Star Justice: The First Century of the Texas Rangers*. New York: Berkley, 2003.

———. *Lone Star Lawmen: The Second Century of the Texas Rangers*. New York: Berkley, 2008.

Wallace, Ernest, and E. Adamson Hoebel. *The Comanches: Lords of the South Plains*. Norman: University of Oklahoma Press, 1952.

Warnock, Kirby F. *Texas Cowboy: The Oral Memoirs of Roland A. Warnock and His Life on the Texas Frontier*. Dallas: Trans Pecos Productions, 1992.

Weaver, John D. *The Brownsville Raid*. College Station: Texas A&M University Press, 1992.

———. *The Senator and the Sharecropper's Son: Exoneration of the Brownsville Soldiers*. College Station: Texas A&M University Press, 1997.

Webb, Walter Prescott. *The Texas Rangers: A Century of Frontier Defense*. Austin: University of Texas Press, 1980.

Webber, C. W. *Tales of the Southern Border*. Philadelphia: J. B. Lippincott, 1887.

Weiss, Harold J., Jr. *Yours to Command: The Life and Legend of Texas Ranger Captain Bill McDonald*. Denton: University of North Texas Press, 2009.

White, E. E. *Experiences of a Special Indian Agent*. Norman: University of Oklahoma Press, 1965.

Wilbarger, J. W. *Indian Depredations in Texas*. Austin: Steck, 1935.

Wilcox, Cadmus M. *History of the Mexican War*. Washington, DC: Church News, 1892.

Wilkins, Frederick. *The Highly Irregular Irregulars: Texas Rangers in the Mexican War*. Austin: Eakin Press, 1990.

———. *The Law Comes to Texas: The Texas Rangers, 1870–1901*. Austin: State House Press, 1999.

———. *The Legend Begins: The Texas Rangers, 1823–1845*. Austin: State House Press, 1996.

Wilson, Carol O'Keefe. *In the Governor's Shadow: The True Story of Ma and Pa Ferguson*. Denton: University of North Texas Press, 2014.

Winfrey, Dorman H., and James M. Day, eds. *The Indian Papers of Texas and the Southwest, 1825–1916*. Austin: Texas State Historical Association, 1995.

Winkler, E. W., ed. *Manuscript Letters and Documents of Early Texans, 1821–1845*. Austin: Steck, 1937.

Wolters, Jacob F. *Martial Law and Its Administration*. Originally published 1930. Reprint, Texas Ranger Hall of Fame E-Book.

Image Credits

Index

Blood Aces

The Wild Ride of Benny Binion, the Texas Gangster Who Created Vegas Poker

They say in Vegas you can't understand the town unless you understand Benny Binion—mob boss, casino owner, and creator of the World Series of Poker. Beginning as a horse trader, Binion built a gambling empire in Depression-era Dallas. When the law chased him out of town, he loaded up suitcases with cash and headed for Vegas. The place would never be the same.

Doug J. Swanson provides the definitive account of a great American antihero, a man whose rise to prominence and power is unmatched in the history of American criminal justice.

"Technically, a biography, but it reads like the best kind of crime drama—where you find yourself rooting for the bad guy." —*The Daily Beast*

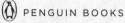

PENGUIN BOOKS